# Living at the Edge

# Living at the Edge

*A Biography of D. H. Lawrence
and Frieda von Richthofen*

## Michael Squires
### and
## Lynn K. Talbot

THE UNIVERSITY OF WISCONSIN PRESS

The University of Wisconsin Press
1930 Monroe Street
Madison, Wisconsin 53711

www.wisc.edu/wisconsinpress/

3 Henrietta Street
London WC2E 8LU, England

Library of Congress Cataloging-in-Publication Data
Squires, Michael.
Living at the edge : a biography of D.H. Lawrence and Frieda von Richthofen /
Michael Squires and Lynn K. Talbot.
    pp.      cm.
    Includes bibliographical references and index.
    ISBN 0-299-17750-5 (Cloth : alk. paper)
    1. Lawrence, D. H. (David Herbert), 1885–1930—Marriage. 2. Lawrence, Frieda von
Richthofen, 1879–1956—Marriage. 3. Authors, English—20th century—Biography.
4. Authors' spouses—Great Britain—Biography. 5. Married people—Great Britain—
Biography.
I. Talbot, Lynn K. II. Title.
PR6023.A93 Z92386       2002
823'.912—dc21       2001005419

Publication of this book has been made possible in part by the generous support of the
Anonymous Fund of the University of Wisconsin–Madison

For our Mothers

Arvilla Windell Squires
Elizabeth Ferguson Talbot

*"I feel as if we were all living on the edge of a precipice."*

D. H. Lawrence to Bertrand Russell,
19 February 1916

# Contents

## Contents

# Illustrations

# Illustrations

# Preface

For years we collected Frieda Lawrence's letters—hundreds and hundreds of them. Some were laid inside books we found for sale; others were kept in drawers or hidden in libraries around the world. Few had been published. One day we realized that in many ways Frieda's letters altered the life story of D. H. Lawrence. How, we asked, can readers understand a novelist of towering genius, like Lawrence, without knowing about his wife's personality and influence? How could his novels and stories and poems—many of them strongly autobiographical—be fully fathomed without drawing insight from her character? On that day we began this biography—focused naturally on Lawrence as the major figure but taking its direction from the rich material in Frieda's letters, which at last count numbered sixteen hundred.

The Lawrences were a contentious couple. What surprised us is that they did not trample down in each other their essential differences. They were always strong, even at times truculent, insisting fiercely on truth; but they were also painfully sensitive and vulnerable. Despite their powerful convictions, they were often insecure: Lawrence was caught in contradictory emotions that baffled him, and Frieda, though she prized freedom, was astonishingly dependent on men to confirm her sense of self. This volatile blend of temperaments, newly calibrated by Frieda's letters, seemed ripe for reinterpretation.

Why did we write this book? We wanted to present the Lawrences whole. In truth, our book differs from other biographies of the Lawrences. Although we were zealous about scholarly accuracy, we had no interest in providing an exhaustive, multivolume life. Nor did we aim for a flashy account that reshuffled a familiar deck of anecdotes. We aimed to go beyond the standard biographical poses, beyond easy appreciation or smug antipathy, beyond a shimmering surface or a catty exposé. We intended to write a biography that valued understanding above all.

We set out to share the inside story of an extraordinary couple. All over the world Lawrence is still read with pleasure—partly because his genius has lighted so many areas of human experience, partly because his characters struggle so hard to penetrate the mysteries around them, partly because he writes with such delicious vitality. The contradictions and ambivalences of his short life—he died at forty-four—make him the most interesting literary figure of his time. He was a man of ferocious integrity. Alive to radical cultural shifts, eager to explore subterranean motives, unafraid to champion the splendor of sexual experience, always a friend to controversy, Lawrence is like a crux of our whole troubled century. He often told Frieda that it was more important to "[b]e yourself" than it was to "know yourself." He wanted others to do the same—to seek not success or social recognition but to live intensely the life around them, absorbing every fresh nuance, rediscovering connections between themselves and their world.

We aimed to clarify and even celebrate Frieda's life—to make her more than a pale moon to Lawrence's bright sun. Also an iconoclast, she broke with her upbringing as forcefully as Lawrence did. "I take myself, my ideals and [my] life quite as seriously as he does his," she once said. In fresh ways we tried to hear her voice, probe her motives, recognize her power, assess her influence. Even though she outlived Lawrence by twenty-six years, our interviews with people she knew document the way her love for Lawrence sustained her interest and energy—and that of her third husband, Angelo Ravagli, who lived with her from 1931 until her death in 1956.

As we considered Lawrence and Frieda together, our priorities were clear. We wanted to capture the give-and-take of a marriage in which two people spent most of their time together—talking endlessly, traveling, often writing joint letters to their friends, discussing the same books, even jointly translating his works. For Lawrence, Frieda was a crucial link: she was the means by which he could reconnect himself to the unknown forces that he believed would liberate his soul. From that premise we wished to illuminate the passion and the conflict, the silences and the sharing, the intensity and the disenchantment that made their marriage so potent and human. Still, they preserved their sharply distinct identities with fewer zones of overlap than most couples could tolerate. "We quarrelled a lot," Frieda wrote in 1949, "but that was because the connection was so deep." We had to acknowledge their sharp, cutting edges.

To the book we also brought—inevitably—the lens of our own marriage. We firmly believed that the Lawrences could best be understood not by a single person but by a couple who could probe, from inside a marriage, the emotional dynamics they constructed. What were their expectations? demands? disappointments? fulfillments? Although we have been careful to keep our personal experiences out of the book, they inform our understanding in every chapter. For instance, following the Lawrences' trail, we wandered through the majesty and misery of Mexico—first in 1987, then again in 1995, only one of us fluent in Spanish—and discovered firsthand the ways in which dependency would have strengthened, but also strained, the Lawrences' relationship. Later, when we came to revise the manuscript, we faced a dilemma resembling that which the Lawrences sometimes faced: how to improve our text without yielding what each of us valued as strengths.

We tried to write a compact, lively book. In Lytton Strachey's words, we aimed for "a brevity which excludes everything that is redundant and nothing that is significant." We assumed that the letters written by Lawrence and Frieda—about eight thousand in all—provided documents whose immediacy and veracity no one could challenge. We made them our main source of evidence. They reflect the Lawrences' directness, spontaneity, even combativeness, and often have the emotional gristle more typical of journal entries. By contrast, the many memoirs written by their friends we used with caution. Not only does distance taint memory with inaccuracy, but memoirs are more likely than letters to construct a personality that justifies the writer—"it's always their own glory they are grinding," Frieda once quipped.

That leaves Lawrence's work—of which little is dull, much profound. Throughout, we assumed that Lawrence's art always stands at an angle to his life—and that the angle linking a novelist and his characters reveals a great deal about him. Since the angle changes as Lawrence matures and as his energizing tensions rearrange themselves, we wanted to trace the design we uncovered—from the disguises of gender in the early work, to revelations of startling intimacy in the later work. Often modifying what has been said before, our book reshapes the space between Lawrence's life and art. In the chapter on *Women in Love,* for instance, we offer a fresh account of the way he employed the lives of those close to him as material for his greatest novel. In the chapters on *Lady Chatterley's Lover,* to cite another example, we show how his most famous novel arose directly out of the pathos of his life, after 1926, when Frieda found herself enamored of another man.

In 1915 Lawrence wrote to a friend, "We are all like tortoises who have to smash their shells and creep forth tender and overvulnerable, but alive." The Lawrences were like that, always asking troubling questions about sexuality and fidelity, about the cosmos and the human spirit, about the dark depths of passion—always exploring their potential for fulfillment. We think they reached their potential more fully than most of us ever do.

# PART ONE

# I

# Lawrence in the English Midlands

## 1885–1902

*Near the end of his third year of teaching, he grew restless, with a fierce longing for change. He had come to feel shackled by fifty boys whose poverty of character appalled him. He could not last. Nevertheless, bred to stern duty, he could not bring himself to quit his teaching job in the London suburb of Croydon. He had worked too hard to get there. But his body, with its own secret knowledge, could quit. In November 1911 it did. A grave illness shattered him. For two and a half months he slowly mended. But he was never the same again. He had turned his face against the humming town, against the harness that its lights and streets and red brick buildings had laid on him. He would not go back. He had broken from all that held him—respectability, duty, upward mobility. His momentous decision, so riveting and final, grew directly out of his unsettled childhood. It was a childhood of tempest and opposition.*

David Herbert Lawrence, nicknamed "Bert," was born in England on 11 September 1885, in the small mining town of Eastwood. It lay about 8 miles from the industrial center of Nottingham and 126 miles from London. The town, crowded with dozens of small shops, was grimy and dark. Every day its nearby mines, at Moorgreen and Brinsley, spewed coal dust.

Lawrence's good friend Enid Hopkin, who also grew up in Eastwood, remembered the mines as oily and ugly, "grow[ing] in the fields like dirty mushrooms, always there, the town's livelihood yet an unspoken threat." While the ventilating fans sang monotonously, the winding engines unleashed a metallic racket, bruising the stillness. True, the town of nearly five thousand people provided jobs and, for miners' families, some company housing; but in 1927 Lawrence, who had come to hate it, described Eastwood's grimy little brick houses, topped with slate roofs, as the fruit of a "fathomless ugliness."

Lawrence's father, Arthur John (1846–1924), was a miner who sweated underground at Brinsley for twelve hours a day, hacking seams of coal with his pick. He had started when he was only seven. Not until 1893—after he was grown—was the minimum age for leaving school set at eleven in England (in 1899 it was raised to twelve). Arthur's father and mother lived in a cottage in Brinsley, a mile from Eastwood. As a boy his father had been apprenticed to a tailor and grew to be a tall, strong, shambling man whose ready snuffbox was a sure sign of friendship; Arthur's mother, ill tempered and rife with complaints, sold aprons and shawls and handkerchiefs from her husband's tailor shop. From her Arthur learned to tolerate scolding as a staple of female behavior.

Some years later, Arthur became a "butty," or foreman, charged with getting the coal, section by section, out of the mines. He had hardened himself to endure the kneeling and stooping and perpetual dust. Impressed, his friend Arthur Coleman remembered him as a first-rate workman. On Friday and Saturday nights Arthur eased his physical exhaustion by joining his drinking pals at the local pub, the Three Tuns. He loved the camaraderie and sometimes stayed till closing. Dark eyed and dark bearded, he was rough, fun loving, and uneducated. Unlike his wife, he spoke an English Midlands dialect, using "thee" for "you," "coom" for "come," "s'll" for "shall," and "nowt" for "nothing."

Lawrence's mother, Lydia Beardsall (1851–1910), was a small, prim, slightly cultured, self-righteous woman. Five years younger than her husband—and born a rung higher—she instilled in her children a strong pride, a fervent religiosity, and an intense need to achieve. Her own mother, also named Lydia, was, by contrast, a pitiable drudge—was always "worse and fading fast," Lawrence remembered. George Beardsall, her puritanical father, had assembled engines until 1870 when he suffered an injury and could no longer work. Lydia (still at home with her two younger sisters) labored in the Nottingham lace industry until she met Arthur in 1874. Impressed by his muscular physique and his good wages of about one hundred pounds a year, she married him in 1875.

The couple's pleasure in each other was brief. Lydia's wonderfully comic phrases were soon edged with disappointment or tart disapproval. Her dream of a better life had been crippled. While she kept house in a gloomy, cramped, company row house called the Breach, she proved herself to be thrifty, tidy, intelligent, proud, and reserved. She was a woman whose aversion to liquor almost matched her growing aversion to her husband.

Their mutual dislike had remarkable consequences. It forged a powerful bond between Lydia Lawrence and her five children, allowing her to measure the value of her life by her children's successes, and it made Lawrence distrust his father and emulate his mother's strength, control, and certainty—qualities he might, under other circumstances, have emulated in his father. Most important, his parents' brutal disrespect for each other left him with a peculiar legacy: early, he understood active relationships as bonds of strife, as mechanisms of manipulation, as vehicles of emotional violence and abuse. Love and affection flourished in moments of peace. As a writer, Lawrence never forgot this initial conception of human interaction, even as his penetrating intelligence allowed him to transcend the abusive model his parents offered.

Like the place where one is born, birth order also affects one's nature— responsible, ambitious, spoiled, rebellious, or affectionate. Lawrence, the fourth of five children, was the youngest son, and a youngest son, especially one who is ill, merits special treatment. The oldest son, George, born in 1876, was a handsome, common lad who left school at fourteen and went to work as an apprentice. "He always spoke dialect," his niece Margaret recalled. A wild youth, fond of drinking, a lad forced to get married, he provided a poor role model for a young boy like Bert. Years later, Frieda Lawrence remembered a story about his dishonesty: "when he was young George took some money once and his poor mother had to replace it."

Within ten years, the Lawrences had four more children. Ernest, the second son, born in 1878, fared better than George. Combining his mother's hunger for success with his father's robust physical vitality, Ernest was the prize. The first daughter, Emily, was born in 1882. She was less gifted but dependable, kind, and the most conventional of the children. Lawrence himself, the next to arrive, was a frail child, never robust or strong. He and his younger sister, Ada—born less than two years apart—bonded tightly. Clever and upright, lively and pretty, Ada, the baby, assumed the role of her brother's confidante. The five children, surprisingly different in temperament and achievement, had one thing in common: all of them escaped direct contact with the mines.

Lawrence's childhood, though far from ordinary, left him time to pursue whatever interested him. Roy Spencer, whose grandfather was Lawrence's schoolmate, remembered that many Eastwood residents "were struck by Lawrence's *unusualness.*" Growing up in Eastwood at the turn of the century, Lawrence endured a gritty poverty and a puritanical code of behavior reinforced by the Victorian code of self-help that inspired the

D. H. Lawrence's family, c. 1897 (left to right): Ada, Emily, Lydia, George, Bert, Ernest, Arthur (Courtesy of Nottingham City Council Leisure and Community Services, Local Studies Library)

British working class. Frail and sensitive as a young boy—rough lads called him a sissy—he was, said his brother George, "petted and spoiled" from birth. William Hopkin, a longtime friend (and Enid's father), remembered that Lawrence in his early days "did not get on with other boys." He was not strong enough for combat sports. Like another gifted writer, Marcel Proust, Lawrence preferred indoor pursuits—copying pictures in watercolor and oil, performing charades, telling stories, baking bread. But he also relished long rambles into the splendid, rolling countryside of England, which he embroidered with bright, informed commentary for his friends. His long walks were a *verbal* excursion, a journey into the mysteries of nature.

Like most novelists, Lawrence had an early sense of himself as different, an observer set apart, marginalized, defined as a critical onlooker. Whereas the Eastwood bullies were street tough, Lawrence became a different kind of fighter. He learned to internalize the violence and brutality that he saw at home, at school, in his neighborhood. Words became a medium for negotiating what he witnessed. They became instruments of power. When just a boy, he used to extract comfort (he said) from "round little white pebbles we called 'milk stones', and sucked in the firm faith that one sucked milk out of them." From early childhood, he used the power of his imagination to transform what was ordinary, to reshape what was difficult or painful.

During Lawrence's boyhood the family moved several times within Eastwood—to the tenementlike Breach in 1887, to Walker Street in 1891, to Lynn Croft Road at the top of a hill in 1902, when Lawrence was sixteen. At Walker Street the family could boast a bay window and a good view of the hedgerows and fields; at Lynn Croft Road they proudly added a small entrance hall and could tend a fine garden set against an open field. Each new home announced the Lawrences' rising status, partly because George and Ernest—the older boys—had gone out to work. Emily, who sewed dresses to boost the family's income, lived at home until she married in 1904 at age twenty-two.

The Beauvale School, which young Lawrence attended from 1892 to 1898, was typical of provincial public education: very large classes, rote learning, strict discipline, occasional thrashings. The headmaster, William Whitehead, was responsible and efficient. Besides writing and reading and math, he taught poems such as *The Lady of the Lake,* history, geography, Bible readings, science, and songs such as "The Flag of England." On his own Lawrence read prodigiously and, much later, recommended to a friend books of adventure "like *Treasure Island,* or books by Henty, or Kingston, or Collingwood. I used to *love* them." Typical is G. A. Henty's *Wulf the Saxon* (1895), which young Bert might have read. As it follows Wulf from ages fourteen to eighteen, this engrossing story, full of sweeping action and historical pageantry, would have immersed Lawrence in the conflict between the eleventh-century Saxons and their Norman foes. Extended battles, male bonding, and political intrigue climax when William claims victory at the Battle of Hastings.

Outside of school Lawrence learned a great deal too. From his mother, a thrifty housekeeper, he learned to cook, sew, bake, and scrub. Writing much later, Frieda Lawrence thought that from his mother "he got the almost puritan sense of responsibility." That puritan sense included honesty and courage. From his mother he also drew his conviction of absolute self-worth. One careful observer was surprised to find Lawrence's mother "so certain of herself and of her own rightness." Unlike George Eliot or Virginia Woolf, Lawrence was rarely plagued by self-doubt. Once he started writing, he recognized—and submitted to—his own genius. It was his mother's gift.

His religious life grew also. On Sundays Lydia made sure her children attended the Congregational chapel in Eastwood. There, lessons from the Bible grounded them in Christian thought, swaddled them in hymns of salvation, and trained their young minds to believe that every choice is a moral challenge. The Congregationalists had inherited the Puritan belief in the inviolable bond between God and the individual. Lawrence learned to guard that bond with scrupulous intensity.

What Lawrence drew from his father in these early years is more complex to assess. Given his dislike of the man (often expressed), Lawrence drew more than he ever acknowledged. "Adolf," a vivid biographical sketch that Lawrence wrote in middle age, offers an affectionate but rare portrait of Arthur, who, walking home from the last shift at Brinsley Colliery, "loved the open morning" as he observed every bird and "tweeted to the wrens," who never scolded in reply. Says the narrator: "He liked non-human things best." His sudden arrival home, though it sent shivers through the children, brought a silent, crouching present from his pocket—a tiny brown rabbit, an orphan whose wild insouciance, though it distressed Lydia, filled both Arthur and the sympathetic narrator with joy. The rabbit, like the solitary man who filched him, stands for what the narrator calls "the inconquerable fugitive." Arthur, like his son Bert, always insisted on being himself, on staking out a separate path to follow. Much later Frieda laughingly recalled one of Arthur's colorful phrases: "'May all their rabbits die' as Lawrence's old miner father would have said." It was a curse on whatever invaded one's territory. Frieda thought that Lawrence got from his father "the fun of the immediate living, quick and often violent in reaction." Emotions, quivering under the surface, lay ready to leap. They might strike anywhere.

But from this unpredictable man Lawrence also imbibed a silent affirmation of himself as *male*, empowered by his gender, endowed with expectations of success, and accepting the patriarchal claim to dominance. Despite his uneasy dislike of his father, Lawrence was silently aware of rough miners bonding together in their work, drinking and laughing on Friday and Saturday nights, tramping across the fields on weekends, and instilling in their sons a fierce resistance to middle-class modes of thought. Covered with pit dust at the end of each day, these men required their wives to wash them but otherwise, as the boy would have observed, remained aloof, aglow in their manly independence and indifference. "When I was a boy," Lawrence remembered near the end of his life, "a [miner] who was a good husband was an exception to the rule." As Lawrence daily witnessed his parents' codes in conflict, he drew confidence and ambition from his mother's code but always longed for the easy male solidarity of his father's. Struggling to shed his hurtful childhood conditioning, he challenged himself, scaled his privations, even reveled in provincial life and its small joys, but propelled himself *away* from a painful past.

ᴏᴥᴓ

As Lawrence matured, schoolwork came more easily. Had he been his father's son, he might have left school and, at a tender age, followed the paternal footsteps into the mines. He did not. Yielding both to his mother, who caustically maligned the coarse work of the "pits," and to Whitehead, his fierce old headmaster, Lawrence on 23 July 1898 sat for (and surprised his family by winnng) a County Council scholarship worth fourteen pounds to attend Nottingham High School, whose faculty offered strong academic training. Having completed what the Beauvale School could offer, Lawrence on 14 September began commuting daily to Nottingham, wearing an Eton coat and collar, and taking the train in the company of a few friends. He had just turned thirteen. To his better-off contemporaries he seemed withdrawn. As biographer John Worthen remarks, "He was mixing with the middle classes without actually rising into them." At the end of his first year he had excelled in English and drawing, earning third place in both. He also studied French, German, writing, and Scripture; in 1900 he even won a mathematics prize.

His days were long. He awakened each morning about six, walked to the station at seven to catch the train (his mother having packed his lunch), reached class by nine, caught a train again at five, arrived home by seven, and after supper faced two hours of lessons which had to be done amid the noise of a discordant family living together in four rooms. Lawrence learned early to concentrate on a task against the grain of interruption. He was diligent. Yet after 1900 the rigid pace and strict preparation wearied him, and since high school fees took most of his scholarship money, the expense of his schooling drained the family too.

9

Every shilling of extra money had to be husbanded for his books, supplies, clothes, boots, lunches, and train fare. Like Charles Dickens before him, he never forgot his family's penury. "Usually," he told a friend in 1926, "we had only one shilling extra every week—only one. . . . Every little thing we needed extra, meant saving and scraping for, and not having enough to eat." Waste was ignoble. To escape these conditions meant effort and discipline. It is not hard to imagine a spirited, highly strung boy pushing himself toward accomplishment, happily immersing himself in his school subjects while teaching himself to observe the behavior and speech of those he saw as superior. Ripe with expectation, he devoured the experiences that lay around him. He was hungry for enlargement, opportunity, expansion. But some opportunities for growth did not lead as far as Lawrence might have hoped. His lack of experience provided little notion of what kind of girl—or job—might suit him.

Once Lawrence became a teenager, his circle widened. Among his new acquaintances was an intriguing girl named Jessie Chambers (1887–1944), about a year younger than he, whose parents, Edmund and Sarah, had met Lydia Lawrence at the Congregational chapel in Eastwood. Jessie was distant, shy, and highly intelligent. Having been invited out one summer's day in 1901, Lawrence and his mother walked the two miles to the Chamberses' farm—past Felley Mill and Moorgreen Reservoir, through High Park Wood, across the warren and the fragrant meadows which shed their potent scent of new-mown hay. The small farm, called the Haggs, was home to cows and dogs, horses and birds and cats, as well as Jessie's sister and three brothers (her older sister, May, had married). For young Lawrence the farm was a marvel. It illustrated an ecosystem based not on exploitation (as in the mines) but on connectedness, where humans and nature coexisted, grounded in cycles of planting and harvest, birth and death. Much later, in 1929, he wrote to Jessie's youngest brother, David Chambers: "Whatever I forget, I shall never forget the Haggs—I loved it so. I loved to come to you all, it really was a new life began in me there." It was the farm, he said later, that first inspired him to write.

As soon as his visits became regular, he and Jessie drew together. They inspired each other—he unfolding the ideas in serious books, she unfolding to him a manifold world of nature that powerfully enriched his store of perceptions. She had a firm chin, straight nose, and piles of soft dark curls. She was plain rather than beautiful, sturdy rather than petite. To her friends she seemed principled and pious rather than delightful, earnest and reflective rather than spontaneous. Like many late-Victorian girls, she was repelled by vulgarity. Initially, she found Lawrence diffident and withdrawn as he closely inspected her and then her surroundings. According to the autobiographical *Sons and Lovers*, Lawrence found Jessie at age fifteen pining to imagine herself as a princess turned swine girl. She ennobled herself with romantic notions of Christ and Rob Roy, which helped her endure the drudgery of peeling potatoes and scrubbing floors. "A shy, wild, quivering sensitive thing" whose soul rose toward rhapsody, she seemed unaware of her astonishing inner beauty. Their outings together, with family members in tow, were intensive explorations of the hedgerows and pastures, the forests and abandoned cottages. Jessie remembered that Lawrence "would walk briskly along with his lithe, light step, tirelessly observant, his eager eyes taking everything in, his pale skin whipped into colour." Their meandering talk would often turn to religion, for Lawrence was fascinated by the Infinite. Although he never ridiculed his mother's convictions, he resented the church's presumed monopoly on defining a moral life and scoffed at its many "thou shalt not" commandments. Eager to learn from him, Jessie stimulated his mind and his feelings while—regrettably—her natural timidity annoyed him. Her deep feelings lay mostly hidden. She could not assert herself.

"It is a great error," Jessie recalled in 1933, three years after Lawrence's death, "to suppose that his early life was unhappy. In our home his name was a synonym for joy—a radiant joy in simply being alive. He communicated that joy to all of us." What Jessie omits is the stressful family life that his "radiant joy" helped to camouflage. Still, for eleven years she prized that joy, offering him her devotion and her steady encouragement. She also taught herself to tolerate a high level of personal frustration. Like Lawrence's mother, Jessie was a woman who shouldered many crosses.

In July 1901 Lawrence completed the three-year course at Nottingham High School. At the end he had not distinguished himself, placing in the bottom quarter of a competitive and capable group of boys. Given that neither of his parents could help him master difficult academic work and that he felt socially inadequate, his placement is not a great surprise. Because he never wrote about his high school experience, he may have felt both enabled and demeaned by it, both empowered and abused. Having just turned sixteen, he agreed to work for a time. Money was still scarce.

The first of Lawrence's preserved letters replies to an advertisement for a junior clerk at Haywood's Surgical Appliances in Nottingham, which today houses a W. H. Smith bookstore. Lawrence worked in the office for three months, as a copyist and errand boy, observing a slice of working-class life in a factory that employed mostly women. A surviving photograph of Haywood's factory girls shows long narrow tables at which about twenty young women, astride wooden stools, tend their sewing machines. Again, Lawrence commuted daily, but the hours were longer, and he may have been away from home almost fourteen hours a day. Each week yielded a few more welcome shillings. But Lawrence may also have emanated, like an aroma, some of his mother's icy disdain for inferiors. George Neville, a neighbor and close friend one year younger, believes that the factory girls, who were devilish and coarse, may once have trapped Lawrence in a basement storeroom and—to topple his pride—attempted to expose his penis before he escaped, shocked and disgusted. Years later Lawrence wrote an alarming story called "Tickets Please," in which six vengeful girls, "strange, wild creatures" living in "lawless" times, similarly attack a conceited man.

Finally, the strain of long hours, little rest, and perpetual economizing was too great. Lawrence's health, never robust, collapsed. Its collapse may have been precipitated by the unexpected death of his older brother Ernest, on 11 October 1901 at age twenty-three, and by his mother's stunned grief. She was utterly devastated. Ernest had fulfilled his mother's dream of a desk job in London but had then contracted erysipelas, a strep infection marked by red, shiny skin and treated at that time with tincture of iodine. When Lydia arrived at his bedside, he was already delirious. As if in delayed reaction two months later, Lawrence himself suffered an infection that turned into pneumonia. Without antibiotics, his recovery was agonizingly slow. His mother, whom Jessie Chambers once described as brimming with "vigour and determination," grew alarmed. Determined not to lose another son, she concentrated all her energy into helping him recover. Gradually her devotion intensified, narrowing to adoration. Their relationship, saturated now with intimate understanding and tinged even with passion, altered Lydia. It licensed her to feel a brooding jealousy of Lawrence's friendship with Jessie. *That* tender friendship had ripened not into loving affection but into an unsettling closeness that satisfied neither Lawrence nor Jessie. Both felt somehow betrayed. She probably counted on marriage; he, confused by his feelings, was unsure what he wanted. To break free of his mother's loving grasp would demand a powerful effort on his part—and the love of a wholly different kind of woman, one who was freer, more vital, more emancipated than Jessie.

# 2

# The Apprentice Schoolteacher

## 1902–11

As Lawrence's health improved, he knew he must earn a better living. Teaching seemed appropriate because he prized knowledge, he liked sharing it with others, and his mother preferred that he teach. Yet teaching was not a good choice. Lawrence invested immense effort preparing for a career as a teacher. After only three and a half years—and without a single regret—he left teaching forever. Why? His confused emotions explain it best.

In Great Britain, as in America, the goal of a broadly educated public became more and more important as industrialization created new occupations, such as factory manager, bank teller, accountant, and stenographer. In 1851 only a quarter of a million children attended inspected primary day schools; half a century later, in 1900, that figure shot up almost twentyfold, to 4.7 million children. By educating their children, working-class families could nudge higher their social and economic status and open doors that had long been closed. The consequent demand for teachers spawned opportunities in every provincial town. When the Education Act of 1902 created a public system of secondary education in England, prospective elementary school teachers typically attended secondary schools as scholarship students, then transferred to a training college to finish their professional education. Yet the numbers were smaller than one might expect. In 1900–1901 only five thousand students in Great Britain were engaged in teacher training, and only 2 percent of seventeen-year-olds were attending *any* school full time.

In October 1902 the seventeen-year-old Lawrence, urged on by his mother, began a six-year teaching apprenticeship at the British School in Eastwood, under George Holderness, who was strict and quick to cane the most insolent lads, yet supportive of his apprentices. Lawrence was bright and imaginative but also willful. Never one to find compromise easy, he chafed against restrictions. Jessie's brother David Chambers remembered always "something incalculable or uncontrollable about him." Yet Lawrence was disciplined and smart, exact as well as exacting. The course of study was organized as a practicum so that apprentices could soon assist with teaching duties. Because classes were large at the British School, rote work was the norm: multiplication tables, spelling, geography, grammar. A former student remembers Lawrence as knowledgeable, entertaining—and quick tempered.

Lawrence spent many hours with his fellow apprentice teachers, especially Jessie and her brother Alan, his sister Ada, and Gertrude and Frances Cooper. They often organized expeditions into the countryside, exploring Annesley or (as they did in 1905) taking the train to Pye Bridge, then wandering through Alfreton Park and on to Wingfield Manor, Crich, and Matlock. Sometimes they picnicked at Beauvale Abbey or walked to Codnor Castle. Outdoors all day, they reveled in nature.

Lawrence's involvement with Jessie had deepened emotionally but also darkened as Lydia Lawrence's disapproval became more insistent. He loved Jessie as a friend but felt ambivalent about a permanent commitment. Ada recalled that although their mother "accused him of being in love he would not admit it." Lawrence told his version of the relationship in chapters 7–9 of *Sons and Lovers,* his third novel; Jessie told her version in a manuscript entitled "Eunice Temple," which she destroyed. Lawrence's family believed that the couple ought either to be engaged or to see each other only publicly, so that Jessie would be free to meet other boys. Looking into his heart, Lawrence worried that he could not love her "as a husband should love his wife." In short, their relationship was gradually clouded by the issue of sex. How close could he and Jessie come without becoming lovers? She maintained that companionship and intimacy that developed in books jointly read surpassed anything that spoke of lust. Inexperienced, Lawrence wanted the sexual act but not its implications. He wanted openness and bravery, she preferred prudence and caution. In *Sons and Lovers* he chided Jessie (in the guise of Miriam Leivers) for her discouraging purity, her horror of passion, her view of sex as a female sacrifice. In time Lawrence grew to resent women who weren't free and generous *at the same time* that he subscribed wholly to his mother's puritan code of restraint in all matters. This key contradiction lasted a lifetime.

The years of Lawrence's apprenticeship passed quickly, filled with sample lessons on algebra, Napoleon's wars, or *As You Like It*. From March 1904 Lawrence attended the Pupil-Teacher Centre in nearby Ilkeston, where the headmaster admired his unusual gifts. For about a year (August 1905 to September 1906) he served full time as an uncertified assistant teacher, again at the British School, earning fifty-five pounds a year. George Holderness, still his supervisor, praised him as "an exceptionally efficient teacher." Then he advanced. From 1906 to 1908 he attended Nottingham University College—not to study for a prestigious three-year degree but to earn a two-year teaching certificate. He was changing. "His real interest," concluded Jessie, "centred on his writing and not on his studies." Years later, he told a friend that from the outset his writing had been misunderstood. When he had used the word *stallion* in one of his papers, his English professor had said to him privately, "My boy, that is a word we do not use." Already the interference of editors had begun.

In these early years his first significant letter went to an attractive girl named Louisa "Louie" Burrows (1888–1962), a fellow teacher from Cossall, a village near Eastwood. Three years younger than Lawrence, Louie was tall, winsome, more assertive than Jessie, but equally conventional. He soon described Louie as "a girl I am very fond of." In some curious way she aroused him. He liked her enthusiasm. Spirited and direct, tactful yet judgmental, Lawrence's letter (from 1906) captures his youthful presence. Commenting on the style of one of Louie's essays, he wrote, "Like most girl writers you are wordy. I have read nearly all your letters to J[essie], so I do not judge only from this composition. Again and again you put in interesting adjectives and little phrases which make the whole piece loose, and sap its vigour. Do . . . try and be terse, there is so much more force in a rapid style that will not be hampered by superfluous details." His concern for economy, speed, telling detail, and freshness marks his own mature prose. Solemnly he advised Louie to write about what others "have not seen, or have not thought" in order to find the "living soul" of others. But of course he was working out his own artistic credo, letting it develop from the educational pieties of the times. In just a year Lawrence, still at home, would be writing his first three stories, for a literary competition announced on 8 October 1907 by the *Nottinghamshire Guardian,* which offered a prize of three pounds in each of three categories: Amusing, Legend, and Enjoyable Christmas.

Composing narratives proved highly stimulating. Lawrence wrote three stories, but because contestants could submit only one he asked Louie to submit his story "The White Stocking" (Amusing) in her name and Jessie to submit his "Prelude" (Enjoyable Christmas). He submitted "A Fragment of Stained Glass" (Legend). Auspiciously "A Prelude" won. Although it was published on 7 December as if by Jessie Chambers, Lawrence had

D. H. Lawrence, 1908 (Courtesy of Nottingham City Council Leisure and Community Services, Local Studies Library)

launched, however inconspicuously, his writing career. This first small step was soon followed by others. Lawrence was busily composing a novel he called "Laetitia." By April 1908, now age twenty-two, he was asking an acquaintance named Blanche Jennings, who lived in Liverpool, to criticize his "erotic" novel and to tell him if "it is bright, entertaining, convincing."

He reminded her that he had "never left my mother, you see." But with his first novel he was already leaving behind Eastwood's diminished expectations and narrow provincialism.

On Saturdays Lawrence still walked out to the Haggs Farm to see the Chambers family. There he discussed radical books like Charles Darwin's *Origin of Species,* sang entertaining songs like "There Is a Tavern in the Town" or "Larboard Watch," peeled vegetables, and helped with the milking. On Sundays he still went to chapel. Jessie's sister May remembered Lawrence sitting erect in his pew, presenting a "well-shaped head with thick, fine, light hair, the chin firm and uplifted, the closed lips, and eyes set under a forehead that overhung them and was very full above the temples, with the ears delicate and flat to the head." Standing five feet nine inches, he looked handsome—refined rather than virile. But May also remembered his keen unhappiness with college, except for botany, which he loved. "College gave me nothing," he wrote Jennings in May. Angry and bored, he was "bitten so deep with disappointment that I have lost forever my sincere boyish reverence for men in position." His sentiment echoes his father's stubborn resistance to authority.

Once his final examinations ended in June 1908, he found that he had earned four distinctions (including one in math, though none in English— "is it not a joke?" he snapped). Unfortunately the market for assistant masters was saturated. While he waited anxiously for an opening, he loafed. He spent part of his summer working at Haggs Farm, he painted *Nasturtiums* in oil, and he wrote long, whimsical letters to his women friends. Anticipation ran high. He was like a kite, whipped aloft, whose string stretched to breaking.

## To Croydon

Lawrence's first job promised challenge, independence, security. As he waited to hear from the numerous applications he had mailed (he even wrote to a school in Egypt), he spent July in the Chambers' hayfields, from morning till night, operating the horse rake or, by hand, turning the hay, singing songs, even spending one night under a haystack, which gave rise to his story "Love among the Haystacks." It follows two oddly matched couples into darkness as each couple discovers the healing power of touch, and it improvises on an idea that Lawrence had espoused in his essay "Art and the Individual," in which (he says) the writer should lead readers "to the edge of the great darkness."

After a mid-August holiday with his family in Yorkshire, Lawrence returned home, still (he said) a poor, hungry, unemployed man. But in September he had an interview (though unsuccessful) at a dirty, ugly place called Stockton, then another interview a few days later in Croydon, a

Jessie Chambers, c. 1908 (Courtesy of the University of Nottingham Library)

suburb nine miles south of London. It seemed decent and clean. In early October 1908 he was offered a position as assistant master to teach fourth grade, or Standard IV, boys at the Davidson Road School. His salary was ninety-five pounds per year, less than a miner would have earned in Eastwood. He was thrilled: "Soon I shall be far away in Croydon."

While he waited to be hired, his twenty-third birthday passed. He had had many unfettered weeks to think, to sort out for himself differences between men and women, and to clarify their natures. His gospel of sexual love was already shaping itself. In a letter to Blanche Jennings, he "held forth," arguing that a woman's emotional soul is organized to respond wholly but weakly to another, whereas a man's emotional soul responds more fully: yet a man offers only "a part, not the whole, of his soul," which makes him, Lawrence concluded, "much more satisfactory." And he observed that most people marry with their souls vibrating not with the finer harmonies of friendship or religious feeling but with sexual love. Then an insight: "I am not sure whether the chords of sex, and the fine chords of noble feeling do not inevitably produce a discord; in other words, whether one could possibly marry and hold as a wife a woman before whom one's soul sounded its deepest notes. I am half inclined to think that a man must marry on the strength of sex sympathy."

It is worth pausing over this letter's *ambivalence* between the spiritual and the erotic. His comments describe a contest between male and female attractions, yet modulate toward marriage. No doubt that was Lawrence's own situation. He was physically drawn to quiet, simple, strong men who would help him complete his manhood, as his father had not; yet he recognized early the difficulty—perhaps the impossibility—of combining sex and friendship in his relations with women. His male friends treated him as if something in his makeup were ambiguous. "I wish I were just like ordinary men," he wrote on 20 December 1910. "I *am* a bit different—and god knows, I regret it." The meaning of his confession will need to be teased out over the course of this book. To be different, and to be keenly aware of his difference, posed a special burden.

But he also enjoyed women, sought them out, excited them, caused their souls to tremble and vibrate. One might say he was a flirt who lacked the strong sexual inclination to seduce; he was interested in experimenting sexually, but the physical consummation was also, in a measure, unsatisfactory. Marriage, as he envisioned it now, signified compromise; it excluded something. Precisely what, he could not have said, though certainly marriage excluded his mother, unless he could find a girl who would expect little—and demand less. Perhaps Louie Burrows, spirited and enthusiastic, would do.

But first he must establish himself. The big city of London inspired wonder; the teaching, surprise. He found room and board, at eighteen shillings a week (about half his salary), with the Jones family: the moustached husband, John, who coordinated school attendance officers in Croydon; his plain wife, Marie, once a teacher, who kept house; and two beguiling young daughters, Winifred and Hilda Mary. They lived at 12 Colworth Road, on a quiet street of identical homes at the edge of town. Lawrence thought the Jones family exceptionally nice, and they made him feel at home. He remained with them as one of their family from 1908 until December 1911, when he was forced to leave.

What was most striking about Davidson Road School, to which Lawrence could walk each day, was not its imposing red-brick handsomeness or its spacious, well-lighted rooms, but the size of its classes. Every day Lawrence was expected to discipline and teach up to fifty Standard IV boys, a mix of both able and impoverished students, of both the quick and the broken. He found the job wearisome: some boys were insolent, and discipline was slack, partly because the headmaster, Philip Smith, was unwilling to punish. Smith, a moustached, square-faced man, "nice, but very flabby," avoided conflict. Writing in 1951, when he was eighty-five, Smith remembered that, at work, Lawrence was conscientious and untiring, attentive to detail, confident, adept at nature study and drawing, but also intolerant of authority: "Lawrence hated the slightest interference with his class work." But the headmaster was also enlightened and kindly and gave Lawrence very free rein, according to Arthur McLeod, a fellow teacher at the school. McLeod, a thin, lanky youth who loved Shakespeare and lived with his mother, would become Lawrence's closest school friend.

Lawrence did not, however, seem fully engaged in teaching. On 26 October he wrote to Blanche Jennings: "Think of a quivering grey hound set to mind a herd of pigs and you see me teaching." Although he found the ensuing struggle petty and debasing, and came to hate it, he must also have been proud, at last, to be earning his own modest living. Years later he recalled how he had relished teaching drawing and botany but ruefully told a friend, "I always felt there was something so mean in tormenting one's teacher." His disappointment lingered long.

Yet he was also driven to write—to capture what he called "the zest of Life." He worked on numerous poems and persevered on the draft of his novel "Laetitia." Its protagonist, Lettie Beardsall, a finely wrought version of his own sensibility, negotiates her dual attraction, split between a refined man and a simple farmer. Lawrence worked steadily, in the evenings after school. He never minded rewriting: "I have a wicked delight in smashing things which I think I can make better," he said on the last day of 1908.

During the next two years, 1909 and 1910, Lawrence moved in contrary directions—toward Louie Burrows as he gained distance from his mother, but also toward Jessie Chambers, the anvil on whom he hammered out his writing, then again toward his mother when she became ill. No one completed him; no one made him whole. Lawrence complicated this struggle by involving himself with a Croydon teacher, Helen Corke, three years older than he, who was independent and intelligent, with dark hair, thick eyebrows, and a ready smile. She was prettier than Jessie. At this time Lawrence was fascinated by women, and they by him. His letters, written mainly to Louie Burrows and Blanche Jennings, provide most of what we know about him until he met Helen Corke, who had taught under Philip Smith before Smith moved to Davidson Road in 1907. Lawrence, always sensitive to the strict binaries of his religious heritage, gradually created roles into which he could position the many women (and occasionally men) to whom he was drawn.

In his highly personal script, he created two major roles. Jessie was the prototype of the intelligent, adoring, neurotic woman who encouraged but did not excite Lawrence. Such women were sister figures, best friends, intimate companions, confidantes. They copied his poems, typed his manuscripts, responded to his writing, gossiped, traded secrets, and occasionally disagreed with him. Across the years, Jessie's role would be assumed by Blanche Jennings, Lady Ottoline Morrell, Catherine Carswell, Dorothy Brett, Mollie Skinner, Maria Cristina Chambers, and Maria Huxley.

By contrast, Louie Burrows was the prototype of the woman whose sensuality excited Lawrence, whose power threatened, who offered risk, danger, temptation. Once, in Eastwood, Lawrence had apparently engaged in a flirtation with such a woman. Alice Dax, a married suffragette, older than he, gaunt rather than pretty, claimed—many years later—that she had had intercourse with him in 1912. His predilection for this type of woman showed itself early. Lawrence wrote to a friend, "I prefer a little devil—a Carmen—I like not things passive. The girls I have known are mostly so." What Lawrence admired in Louie was not her critical acumen, nor her culture or sensitivity, nor even her femininity, but her "lusty Atalantan strength," her "good health" and "fresh savage blood." He thought she would make "a good Bacchante." "[Y]ou are the . . . wild barbarian—do not ever pretend to be cultivated," he wrote in mock admonishment. Later he confessed: "As for your flinging yourself at me—I like you for this frankness." These are the qualities he would look for—and find—not only in his future wife, Frieda, but also in Katherine Mansfield, Rosalind Baynes, and Mabel Dodge Luhan. And certainly in the insouciant Helen Corke, who proved a stimulating and tempting companion until a great sadness spoiled her life.

While Helen sometimes spent whole days with Lawrence, wandering

Louisa Burrows, c. 1910 (Courtesy of James T. Boulton and the University of Nottingham Library)

over the downs in the spring of 1909, occasionally arousing his sexual appetite, Jessie Chambers, who would not start teaching for another year, offered again to be useful. She had often commented on Lawrence's stories and had grown to love him deeply, while simultaneously recognizing the painful truth that Lawrence—although he cherished her friendship and even depended on her—would never marry her. (Finally, despite her impressive gifts, she was too limited: she failed to stir his physical manhood.) Yet Jessie believed in his genius and struggled to promote it until the emotional cost became unendurable. With horror she heard him say, probably at Easter 1909, and probably with Louie Burrows in mind, "that he had definitely come to the conclusion he must marry." She stifled her pain.

Still, if Jessie could not marry him, she could help launch his career. In December 1908 she first saw the *English Review* when Lawrence brought it out to Haggs Farm, where it became an "event" in their lives. The *Review* published writers of the new school of realism. When Jessie urged Lawrence to submit some of his work, he refused, afraid of the sting of possible rejection. "'*You* send something,'" he countered; "I looked through the poems Lawrence had sent in letters to me since he left home, picked out what I thought were the best, and copied them out one beautiful June morning. I was careful to put the poem 'Discipline' first . . . hoping that an unusual title might attract the editor's attention." It did. Jessie's was one of those pivotal, providential acts of kindness, like freeing a trapped bird. When the editor, Ford Madox Hueffer, replied with enthusiasm in August, Lawrence said to Jessie with barely controlled excitement, "Let me take [the letter] to show Mother." In September he was busy, he told Louie, revising the four poems Jessie had submitted. He had never considered himself a poet but had always put his faith in his prose.

In a patronizing account, Hueffer, a middle-aged writer who lived with novelist Violet Hunt, recalled that around 1910, "we enormously wanted authentic projections of that [working-class] type of life which hitherto had gone quite unvoiced." He saw at once, he said, Lawrence's authoritative mind. With trepidation he met the younger man, found him ambitious, urged him to "get out" of teaching in order to write, took him to lunch, and treated him kindly. Impressed by Lawrence's natural sense of form, Hueffer eventually published several of his poems and short stories, such as (in June) "Odour of Chrysanthemums." Although the *Review* changed editors in December 1909, it, exposed Lawrence to the publishers of London. On 2 June 1911, for instance, Martin Secker nibbled: "[T]he excellent story in this month's *English Review* which I have just read prompts me to ask if you would care to offer me a volume of short stories, when you have sufficient material." Buoyed by such interest, Lawrence began to consider "getting out" of teaching.

## Two Novels Launched

Meanwhile, Hueffer—"a gentleman indeed"—did more than publish Lawrence's poems and stories. He also read the novel "Laetitia" (soon to become *The White Peacock*): "He says it's good, and is going to get it published for me," Lawrence proudly told Louie Burrows. Accordingly, on 15 December Lawrence offered the complete handwritten manuscript to William Heinemann, a major London publisher.

While his first novel was being scrutinized, he dabbled furiously with his women friends. He had added a new one—Agnes Holt, a striking woman with auburn hair and a peppery tongue. Like the others, she was a teacher. She didn't last long, for she was only useful as a means for Lawrence to break his mother's grip. Although the many letters he sent home have been lost, the accounts that survive suggest his continued dependence. Shortly after the Lawrence family vacationed at Shanklin on the Isle of Wight (paid for with his earnings), Lawrence got so drenched with rain, and his mother "so upset about my state yesterday," that she discouraged him from cycling over to see Louie. Later, he hoped to see Louie at Christmas, then hesitated: "I will see what mother says." Hueffer, too, recalled that Lawrence often cited his mother's opinions. Lawrence still spent his vacations in Eastwood, visited friends, wrote, cycled, read. A verbal snapshot, written to an acquaintance on 4 August 1910, when he was almost twenty-five, reveals his dreary domestic life:

My father is a coal miner: the house has eight rooms: I am writing in the kitchen, or the middle parlour as it would be called if my mother were magniloquent—but she's not, she's rather scornful. It is cosy enough. There's a big fire—miners keep fires in their living rooms though the world reels with sun-heat—a large oval mahogany table, three shelves of study-books, a book-case of reading-books, a dresser, a sofa, and four wooden chairs. Just like all other small homes in England.

My mother, who is short and grey haired, and shuts her mouth very tight, is reading a translation of Flaubert's *Sentimental Education,* and wears a severe look of disapproval. My father is out—drinking a little beer with a little money he begged of me. My sister [Ada], who is tall and slender and twenty three years old, has cycled to the theatre in Nottingham with her sweetheart. I have a married brother [George] and a married sister [Emily]—they do not count.

One image stands out: Lawrence's mother, scornful, disapproving, yet sensitive to his sulking dissatisfaction. As he once said to Jessie, with bottomless chagrin, "I've never really had a father."

Then a horrible revelation. In August, while Lawrence's mother visited her sister Ada Krenkow in Leicester, a malignant tumor flared in her abdomen, causing the doctor to express grave concern. By the time Lawrence returned to Croydon, to begin his third year of teaching, she was worse, barely able to write, unable to read, suffering great pain. No doubt she had been ill for months. By October, his mother fearfully ill and failing rapidly, Lawrence felt wretched. He visited her every other weekend. Jessie remembered "how terribly alone he was in his grief." "It behoves me to be gay, I am so sick inside," he wrote to Rachel Annand Taylor, a London author whose poetry he admired. In November the doctor warned Lawrence that his mother might last only two weeks longer. The great love of his life was waning so fast that he could make no sense of his impending loss. The days "crawl over me like horrid tortoises," he lamented.

While her cancer advanced, Lawrence heard from William Heinemann. In January 1910 he had gone to Heinemann's office to hear the criticisms of the publisher's reader, Frederick Atkinson. He learned that if he altered a few bits, *The White Peacock* would be accepted, he would earn royalties, and he would be established as a writer. With his apprenticeship behind him, Lawrence was intensely pleased. He had managed a kind of victory over his humble circumstances—and been handed a vindication of his mother's iron faith in his talent. Working diligently, he finished his revisions by April, eliminated the "offensive morsels," compressed the prose where he could, and proved himself "the most docile" of pens. Tamed and tidied, the novel had become, he declared, "a kind of exquisite scented soap."

Full of youthful spontaneity, *The White Peacock* (1911) is less a coherent whole than a rich amalgam of lyrical, elegiac, and realistic elements. As the ancient farming life collapses, Lettie Beardsall and George Saxton turn frustrated and disillusioned. Yet in the pastoral landscape that Lawrence evokes, lush metaphor holds frustration at bay. Birds "fluttered in and out of the foamy meadow-sea, plunging under the surf of flowers washed high in one corner, swinging out again, dashing past the crimson sorrel cresset." Lawrence's favorite fictional device is the sprightly walk into the countryside taken by characters who converse volubly—not to disclose crucial elements of the plot but to strip off their reserve and reveal new dimensions of themselves. In the chapter called "The Fascination of the Forbidden Apple," Lettie tells George, whom she desires, "'Don't you wish we were wild . . . like peewits! Shouldn't you love flying and wheeling and sparkling and—courting in the wind!'" The dash before "courting" shows that even as Lettie remains safe within the mobilized group, she taunts her friend with risqué insinuation. Lawrence had settled on two conflicts that would permeate his fiction. First, he would pit characters who have culture and power against those who are rooted in nature and attuned to its music; second, he would pit characters who can create the conditions of their fulfillment against those who cannot, amid the torture of "complex modern life."

Lawrence struggled personally with these conflicts. A nagging sense of inferiority perplexed him. For the narrator of *The White Peacock,* who flaunts his favorite quotations, Lawrence envisioned an identity that is whimsically literate and a little pompous. He fashioned a *cultured* self to claim the attention of serious readers without sacrificing his own rootedness in nature. This separation from self extends also to love. The passive, androgynous narrator, Cyril Beardsall, seems to show Lawrence's timidity. But Lawrence was only marking time with pastoral themes until he could gain sexual confidence. That confidence would free him to depict erotic themes and to charge landscape description with a new significance.

⧼⧽

Meanwhile, Lawrence had suddenly begun a second novel, as if the thrill of Heinemann's acceptance had inspired a strong creative surge. One of his Croydon friends had taken him to visit a bereaved woman. It was none other than Helen Corke. Her middle-aged lover, Herbert Macartney—after their brief summer tryst on the Isle of Wight—had killed himself. Lawrence, deeply moved by her pain, thought he could turn her story into a novel (a "saga" he called it). He began it just after the Easter holidays of 1910. In 1974 Corke recalled: "Lawrence wrote at high pressure, and the first draft was finished in three months." It retained the sequence and detail of the manuscript that Corke had already drafted but it invented a great deal. Lawrence sought to interpret the forces that bedeviled Macartney, who had played the violin in the Covent Garden Opera orchestra, taught Corke music—and was married with four children. To ruminate over the story, Lawrence and Corke often roamed over the North Downs and the Kentish Weald, pacing the green hills, savoring the drama of the low-lying clouds, absorbing the sea winds. All of it fired Lawrence's imagination. He seemed mesmerized by the story and on 24 June told Frederick Atkinson: "It is horribly poetic." He finished a draft in July, then paused before he attempted to chisel and shape the manuscript.

*The Trespasser* probes, at a useful distance, Lawrence's own condition. It allowed him to test the range and limits—as well as the dangers—of passion. The protagonist, Siegmund, struggles to express his intensely sensual and sensitive nature while being crushed by the grinding need to support his large family. "For years, he had suppressed his soul, in a kind of mechanical despair doing his duty and enduring the rest." With lush intensity Lawrence explores the response of a disappointed woman (his own Jessie Chambers will soon play Helena's role of the cruelly hurt woman), the beauty and the immense cost of passion, nature's vital role in the human drama, and the unfathomable barriers that block Siegmund's escape from his neurotic construction of identity. Technically Lawrence experimented with the way he could alternate the symbols of Wagnerian opera with those of guilt-ridden Christianity. Despite the strange artificiality of the narrative design, the motif of insecurity broods plangently over the novel.

26

"'Now I am no more sure of myself, have no more confidence than a boy of twenty,'" Siegmund thinks to himself. "'What can I do? It seems to me a man needs a mother all his life.'" Yet Lawrence was not anxious to publish the novel, judging it incoherent, and he knew that the powerful circulating libraries, which posted books to its many subscribers, might object to its content. Anyway, he needed to wait for Corke's consent.

Both now and later, Lawrence marshals his life forces at the very edge of fulfillment. All who knew him comment on the quality of his insight, his quick intuition, his piercing critical acumen. Yet, as in the case of most writers, that penetration rarely extended to his personal life, so that he often remained stalled just shy of personal insight. At this time he did not understand the connection between having a weak father and fearing the castrating power of a strong female. He sought male strength in female bodies, and came to resist those who were unable to combine sensitivity and strength—as he had done. Yet how was he to fulfill this "self" he had finally constructed? Siegmund offered a warning: marriage could mean imprisonment.

The cluster of relationships that Lawrence developed between 1910 and 1912 set a defining pattern: he required a central relationship around which he could arrange a small number of intimate female friends (and occasional male friends like George Neville or Arthur McLeod). At this time the enigma he confronted was not unusual: he believed he must marry, yet he could not identify an appropriate marriage partner. Jessie Chambers, Louie Burrows, Helen Corke—all met him halfway. Hence Helen Corke judged him "miserably uncertain which course to follow." To others he seemed simply disagreeable. His family believed he must choose Jessie, rewarding her for her unwavering loyalty, or break with her. Finally, he chose to break, abetted by his mother's fierce antagonism—but not before he and Jessie yielded briefly to their natural, though deeply thwarted, attraction. "She will do me great, infinite good—for a time," Lawrence, now passive and weary, admitted to Corke on 11 May 1910. "Whatever happens, in the near present, I can't help it—I cannot."

That left Helen and Louie. Helen Corke's mother had hoped that Lawrence would marry Helen, but Corke, who had discovered she was bisexual, could not readily respond to Lawrence's physical needs. "My desire [was] not towards him," she wrote later. She could offer affection and great admiration for the power and subtlety of his mind. Lawrence accepted, even if he resented, her preference for friendship. On 21 June he wrote to assure her: "Gradually we shall exterminate the sexual part." Anyway, she remained "betrothed" to the dead Macartney, enjoined by his final words to her: "to persist, to continue in action."

Louie Burrows fluttered in the wings after the others had left the stage. She enjoyed Mrs. Lawrence's restrained approbation, and she genuinely appealed to Lawrence, although she was as limited intellectually as Jessie

was physically. On 3 December 1910 he met Louie on the train and suddenly—agitated by his mounting indecision, and diverted by her vitality
and charm—proposed marriage. She accepted at once. "I am 25—you 23:
very good ages," he wrote gaily. The dozens of long, intimate letters he subsequently wrote to Louie are only a preparation, an exordium, an extended runway to his embrace of Frieda von Richthofen. In "The Hands
of the Betrothed," an autobiographical poem composed at this time, the
narrator uses a strangely mercantile simile when he says:

> I know from her hardened lips that still her heart is
> Hungry for love, yet if I lay my hand in her breast
> She puts me away, like a saleswoman whose mart is
> Endangered by the pilferer on his quest.

This intriguing combination of desire and resistance echoes a similar conflict in Lawrence's early novels, where a woman's struggle to resist matches
the man's predatory hunt.

కురా

Louie's sturdiness and warmth—she was "big and dark and handsome,"
with black hair and tawny eyes—provided a vital antidote to the crushing
misery of his mother's rapidly approaching death. Now fifty-nine, his
mother had turned into "a hieroglyph of woe." In the character of Siegmund, Lawrence had recently imagined the horror of death; now, as his
mother's chief nurse, he saw its pain clenched into a fist of furious agony,
bearing down with slow torture as he and Ada took turns at the upstairs
bedside, his lonely vigil prodding a major realization: the intense bond he
and his mother had shared—so sensitive to each other they never needed
words to communicate—had made him "abnormal." He felt, he told a
friend, as if "[n]obody can come into my very self again, and breathe me
like an atmosphere." It is likely he did not *wish* again so claustrophobic a
bond. From this juncture we can mark Lawrence's unusual need for distance in personal relationships. Henceforth he will avoid relationships that
press him for affection, preferring individuals who can offer closeness
without possessiveness, intimacy without entanglement, stimulation without smothering. "I *cannot* marry," he told Helen Corke some months later,
"save where I am not held."

His mother had been, he told Louie on 6 December 1910, three days
before Mrs. Lawrence died of stomach cancer, "a wonderful, rare woman
. . . as strong, and steadfast, and generous as the sun." He identifies the
qualities that he himself would emulate. A poem entitled "Death-Paean of
a Mother"—not found until 1990 in the London safe of Frieda's attorney,
C. D. Medley—appears to have been written soon after Lawrence's mother

died. It radiates a discomfiting immediacy. What will strike most readers is the way Lawrence converts his mother into a masculine figure, a father in mother's clothes, a strong and powerful Viking whose fierce integrity death cannot eclipse. Here are the first and last parts:

> I hail you, Mother magnificent.
> Maiden in dream.
> This sleep in you
> Is perfect you.
>
> Straight and splendid
> A thing to fear!
> Straight, and laid in line,
> Severe, cast in the mould
> Of accomplished death!
>
> Oh mother, inflexible,
> Lonely and stern;
> I see you at last, then,
> You stern spear!
> You shaft of destiny!
> Distaff
> That spun my life.
> . . . . . . .
> I hover near
> I beat at your silence
> Like a bird at the window of a darkened room,
> When it wants to come in.
>
> If I could but kiss from your mouth
> The open-lipped, wondering agony!
> If I could but kiss it away, now, at last,
> Now, at the very last.
> If only I could kiss it away from your dead face
> I would bury you with pride.
>
> Warrior, warrior,
> If I had my way
> I would lay you to sleep in a ring of fire
> Within a ring of best fire.
> Viking, fallen in battle,
> Woman, invincible spear.
>
> But oh, I hover round you
> Like a spirit in woe about its body.
> Unable to close your eyes in the perfect sleep,
> Unable to kiss the wound-cry off your mouth.

Despite its lack of finish, the poem has great intensity. In contrast to the mother as "invincible spear," the narrator is pale, weak, ineffectual, his strength buried in wishful "if" clauses as he compares himself first to a bird and then to a spirit, fluttering, hovering, mute with frustration, immobilized by grief. Even in death the mother grips her strength, holds it intact, conferring none of it on her stricken son, whose anguish at their separation finds no relief.

## Taking a Risk

Reluctant to write directly about his mother, Lawrence had begun his third novel two months earlier, in October. Now, chastened by grief and by the first bewildering explosion of maturity, he imagined himself composing "a restrained, somewhat impersonal novel." He called it "Paul Morel." But he made little progress and may well have scrapped his early efforts. Spiritually he collapsed, "a spirit in woe." He had strength to keep intact only the scaffolding of his life. Inside, the crumbling went on, like Mrs. Clennam's house in Dickens's *Little Dorrit*. Rejecting self-pity, he could affect gaiety, could force effervescence into his letters, could be "bright and strong" at Christmas. "I take care," he wrote, "not to allow any blank spaces in these days." He wanted desperately to hurl himself toward Louie's solicitous care, to drown his dark despair in her abundant love.

Inwardly some vital part of him had yielded to death. Using an image that will often remind him of his early life, he wrote archly in January 1911: "We crawl, like blinking sea-creatures, out of the Ocean onto a spur of rock, . . . then we drop in the ocean on the other side: and the little transit doesn't matter so much." His health declined. Helen Corke remembered that in 1911 he was "ironic and bitter." His "home" having vanished with his mother's death, he had finished with Eastwood. "Let us go away again [at Easter], shall we?" he begged his sister Ada, surely aware that the cost was unaffordable. "I *don't* want to come to Eastwood." Punctuating his letters of 1911 are worrisome statements—like this one to Ada on 17 February—that show something festering in his subconscious life: "[T]here is more *real* strength in my regard for you than there is for Louie." It is as if Lawrence had temporarily transferred to Ada some of his reverence for his mother. But why not to Louie?

To Helen Corke went this blunt volley on 14 March: "The common everyday—rather superficial man of me really loves Louie. Do you believe that? But do you not think the open-eyed, sad critical, deep seeing man of me has not had to humble itself pretty sorely to accept the imposition of the masculine, stupid decree." This was a moment of revelation. Lawrence unerringly labeled the warring selves within, but could not locate or even identify the ground on which they might meet. He believed he must *choose*.

To choose Louie would, he thought, require him to suppress his personal depths, for she would offer no refuge from the emotional illness he endured. Believing her way healthy even if shallow, he considered his way not an alternative but "a form of abnormality." Later, in July, he shot back at Corke: "Even set me down that disgraceful thing, abnormality, so long as you believe me. I love Louie in a certain way that doesn't encroach on my liberty, and I can marry her, and still be alone." That poignant sentence indexes his plight. It is a tribute to the force and richness of his character that he wrestled at length with such troubling, painful, unsettling conundrums. For months he sought a solution to his perplexed personal state.

His conflict expressed itself in the opposition he now felt between teaching and writing. He wanted to write. While on holiday in August he wrote to May Chambers Holbrook, Jessie's older sister: "I'm dreading the return to school." After two days of struggling with fifty new boys, he concluded that teaching "wearies me to death." He wanted fulfillment from something else. A letter from Edward Garnett, a reader for the London publishing firm of Duckworth, requesting some stories, may have inspired Lawrence to think that he could follow Ford Madox Hueffer's advice and quit teaching, despite the money anxieties that often distressed him. In order to marry he needed, he said, £150 a year and £100 in savings. Could he attain these heights?

Finally, on 15 September 1911, he tested the frigid waters of change. He admitted to Louie his distaste for schoolmastering when he wanted to write and gingerly asked her: "Should you be cross if I were to—and I don't say I shall—try to get hold of enough literary work, journalism or what not, to keep me going without school. Of course, it's a bit risky, but for myself I don't mind risk—like it. And then, if I get on with literature, I can increase my income." This is the first clear sign of an intended break with the exterior world of convention and success. Had her mind been more penetrating, Louie might have read it as a danger signal: Lawrence had fulfilled his *mother's* ambition, but not his own. His remarkable creative powers demanded more and more space for expression.

Two months earlier, on 15 July, he had spent all day pouring out of his inner self thirty-eight pages of a long story entitled "Two Marriages" (later retitled "Daughters of the Vicar"). In its final form, it is a remarkably good story that uses a pair of sisters, Louisa and Mary Lindley, to explore the emotional tension that pulled Lawrence so violently in contrary directions. As he said of himself in April, writing to Louie: "I am just as emotional and impulsive as [the Italians], by nature. It's the damned [English] climate and upbringing and so on that make me cold-headed as mathematics." These warring elements, stretched across the polarities of his personality, were working themselves out in fictional form.

Louisa Lindley represents the part of Lawrence that quietly but firmly rejects conventional solutions. As she seeks out a sensitive but unappreciated young miner, Alfred Durant, distinctly beneath her in origin, his social *difference* releases in her some pent-up and repressed feeling. "She was going on her own way," the narrator reports. Louisa is also, of course, Louisa Burrows, who has chosen to marry a man perceived as "different" by her friends and family. By contrast, Mary Lindley, beautiful and proud, is a model of control, repression, and violated instincts who can embrace, as a suitor, a man more cold hearted than mathematics. Mr. Massey, timid and small and bespectacled, lacks the full range of human feelings. He lives from his intellect, his behavior having its axis in a "mathematical working out" of human situations. To choose a man like Mr. Massey is (in Lawrence's imagination) to choose a woman like Jessie Chambers—worthy but wrong; to choose a man like Alfred is to imagine choosing Louie—limited but worthy. Of perhaps greatest interest, Alfred cannot be emotionally available to Louisa until after his mother dies of a malignant tumor in her abdomen. Although Alfred feels that he is a failure, gnawed by incompleteness, "not [yet] a man," Louisa succeeds in vaulting his self-esteem— much as Lawrence's mother (and perhaps Louie) had done for him. At the close, Louisa and Alfred turn their backs on their English village and prepare to emigrate to Canada. Lawrence's soul had spoken.

In the autumn of 1911 Lawrence, though busier than usual, eagerly sought new friends to help release him from the forms of entrapment he had begun to feel. Invited to lunch, he met Edward Garnett on 4 October 1911. The following weekend he visited the Cearne, Garnett's quasi-medieval stone cottage in Kent. Set at the far edge of the beautiful north downs, overlooking the Weald of Kent, the house impressed Lawrence immensely, with its "brick floored hall, bare wood staircase, deep ingle nook with a great log fire, and two tiny windows one on either side of the chimney: and beautiful old furniture—all in perfect taste." Garnett, forty-two, his long pale face showing tired eyes, was a skilled editor and a genial and approving host who lived in the cottage alone. His wife, Constance, and their teenage son, David, commuted from London for occasional weekends; unknown to Lawrence, Garnett's mistress, a painter named Nellie Heath, lived nearby. The two men had a splendid time, drinking wine in the ingle nook and furiously discussing books. "Garnett rather flatters me. He praises me for [the] sensuous feeling in my writing," Lawrence allowed when he wrote to Louie on 16 October.

Responding to Garnett's encouragement, Lawrence drove himself to write. "Garnett is going to get my verses published, and perhaps a vol[ume] of plays, in Spring," he told Ada. "I am terribly busy." Then, at a business luncheon on 20 October, he promised publisher William Heinemann a manuscript—probably, he said, "Paul Morel," the novel he had been writing. Lawrence was stretching the string of his life thinner and thinner. By

3 November he wrote to Louie: "Tonight I am going to begin Paul Morel again, for the third and last time." Driven and weary, he was at the edge of collapse.

After a fine weekend spent with Louie, basking in her lively warmth and high spirits, he found the long, slow drag at Davidson Road School exhausting. He and Louie—his betrothed—may have aroused each other to a feverish pitch of erotic excitement, for on 30 October he wrote to her: "I've now got to digest a great lot of dissatisfied love in my veins. It's very damnable, to have slowly to drink back again into oneself all the lava and fire of a passionate eruption. . . . The most of the things, that just heave red hot to be said, I shove back. And that leaves nothing to be said." In anguish Lawrence struggled to control himself. He felt constrained rather than contented, entrapped rather than enthralled. On 7 November he confessed to Garnett: "This last fortnight I have felt really rotten—it is the dry heat of the pipes in school, and the strain—and a cold. I must leave school, really." Though feeling sick, Lawrence went on to the Cearne on Saturday, 18 November, taking the train to Oxted, then walking several miles to Garnett's cottage. The biting wind chilled him.

By Sunday, 19 November, Lawrence's cough had developed rapidly into pneumonia. One might say that his body had come to the rescue of his soul. He plunged into an illness so frightening that his landlady, Mrs. Jones, wrote to Ada to hurry to Croydon. Ada arrived on 25 November, surely remembering that her own mother had rushed to London in 1901, in order to nurse twenty-three-year-old Ernest, only to find him within an hour of his death. Lawrence's crisis came three or four days later. Although he survived it, he was compelled for weeks to lie flat on his back. All exterior claims shriveled during this siege of illness. Day after day, as he lay prone, he must have realized that fulfilling his destiny as an artist would require that he reconsider the demands of a job, of a long engagement, of service as a dutiful brother. How could he flourish if he were bound? A new creature, shedding its thick skin, was being born. No longer could he feel trammeled or subservient.

Within a few months Lawrence, slowly recuperating, would meet Mrs. Frieda Weekley, who lived with her husband and three children in a fine house in Nottingham. The city was just a brief train ride from Croydon.

# 3

# Frieda Finds Her Destiny

## 1879–1912

Across her lifetime Frieda Lawrence reinvented herself more than once. That is no surprise, given her talent for shaping a distinctive identity as a woman. What will surprise most readers is not her need for liberation but the sequence of romantic choices that she made. The four men with whom she had serious, sustained relationships form a neat (if simplified) pattern: restrained, free, restrained, free. Each is a reaction to the other. Frieda's choices respond to the changing circumstances in which she found herself. Like many women, she first chose a man not greatly different from her father.

Born 11 August 1879, six years before D. H. Lawrence, Frieda came into the world just as the patriarchal German matrix of military might and imperialist fervor began to labor toward its ugly climax in Nazi Germany. Otto von Bismarck—the autocratic German chancellor and a crucible of male power—unified the German states and, before he resigned in 1890, fostered a highly potent sense of national identity. Imitating Bismarck's wife, Johanna, German women subordinated themselves to male dominance, yielded to masculine privilege, sought subservience. Adolf Lasson, who taught at the University of Berlin, judged men the "natural lords" of women. Yet only on the surface did Frieda's parents reflect this neat gender split.

Frieda's mother, Anna Marquier (1851–1930), was solid bourgeois French, but her Catholic ancestors had fled the French Revolution to settle in Donaueschingen, a small German town in the Black Forest. Though not a beauty, Anna was sedately pretty, with a rich complexion, a firm mouth, and dark hair. Her temperament, though phlegmatic and sentimental, was warm, her disposition rarely interrupted by bursts of irritation. In 1912 Lawrence described her as "utterly non-moral, [and] very kind." Janet Byrne's investigations have revealed that at age fourteen Anna entered a convent school in Villingen and at age sixteen attended the Institute Blas in Freiburg, a progressive school operated by two young sisters who would eventually become favorites of Anna's three daughters. In 1871, at the age of twenty, Anna met her future husband at a celebration for Kaiser Wilhelm I; they married the following year.

Frieda's father, Friedrich von Richthofen (1845–1915), had faced a far less settled childhood in Upper Silesia, a farming region that is now part of Poland. The von Richthofens had lived there since the middle of the sixteenth century. Unfortunately, Friedrich's father, an aristocrat but also a daring speculator, had lost his family's ancestral lands; Friedrich's mother had died. It is no surprise that Friedrich did what young, unsettled men often do. When he was only sixteen, he joined the army, hoping for a military career. The renowned Bismarck, appointed foreign minister in 1862 and enamored of military might, demanded that the German army aspire to a high level of efficiency. A diary that Friedrich kept during the Franco-Prussian War of 1870–71 reveals his fortitude in battle and his enviable stamina (which later facilitated his long hunting expeditions and long nights of gambling). The diary describes the roads, fortifications, enemy grenades—and the beer and card games that consumed his evenings. Rare is the kind of emotion found in a laconic 1870 entry about his comrade: "On my return heard that Nehmitz fell with his horse and lies hopelessly wounded, skull fracture. That touches me very closely, he was a dear fellow and splendid soldier." But when he was twenty-five, fighting in the Franco-Prussian War, Friedrich too was wounded, then briefly taken prisoner. His right hand badly crippled, he was given an honorable discharge, made a lieutenant, and awarded an Iron Cross. Robert Lucas aptly remarks: "The injury to his hand soon healed, the wound in his heart never."

Where now was the penniless young baron to go? Friedrich believed that the border provinces of Alsace and Lorraine to the west, which France had been forced to relinquish during the war, might enhance his position. He gravitated from Château-Salins to Saarburg, then to Metz, a small city not far from Strasbourg, which lay on the fertile banks of the Moselle River. There, in 1877, he joined the civil administration set up to govern the newly acquired German district of Lothringen; Frieda says he was appointed "a maître-des eaux et forêts" to oversee the area's land. A photograph taken a year later shows a slender, attractive man with brown hair parted in the middle, small dark eyes, a full bush of a beard, and small hands. Soon he had earned the title of *Kulturingenieur,* or cultural engineer. In 1912 Lawrence described him as "a fierce old aristocrat," and Frieda remembered him as being "alert, interested in doing things, impatient." She admired his strength.

## A WILD CHILD

Like Lawrence, Frieda was a middle child. Her sister Else (1874–1973) was five years older, her sister Johanna (1882–1971) three years younger. Else, a reformist with wide gray eyes and a soft mouth, had (Frieda remembered) "a delicate cameo face" much at odds with her zeal for the underdog. Frieda decided early that she would not try to compete with Else's intellectual brilliance. Nor could she rival Johanna's charm, svelte beauty, and impeccable sense of style. She would make her mark elsewhere—how or where she did not know. Recognizing their salient differences, Else prized Frieda's "noble generosity and fascinating originality, her belief in life." Johanna, who shared a bedroom with Frieda, admired her sister's bold gusto.

"Mine had been a happy childhood," Frieda remembered. "We had a lovely house and gardens outside Metz." Their home resembled a Swiss chalet, and the garden became the masterwork of her father, who sometimes rose at four in the morning to tend the flowers and vegetables. Like Lawrence, Frieda savored flowers—snowdrops, scyllae, crocuses, delicate irises, and vivid oriental poppies. She was fascinated by textures, colors, flavors. When her father cut the first asparagus and picked the first strawberries, she trotted behind. In the summer she lived on the fruit from apple, cherry, pear, plum, and peach trees. Everything grew abundantly.

Active and fearless, Frieda described herself as "a wild, sunburnt child with straw-coloured hair." She climbed trees, scratched her knees, and hated brushes and combs.

Once, to escape the heat, her father took her to the river, positioned her on his shoulders, and fearlessly dived from a board: "I remember the surprise of being under water, but I emerged and swam around like a tadpole." This is the kind of initiation a father usually reserves for his son. He and Frieda had bonded. In 1914 she reminisced: "I used to think war so glorious, my father such a hero with his iron cross and his hand that a bullet had torn."

Frieda loved festivities. At Christmastime, she and her sisters relished the warm kitchen scents of honey and spices; made marzipan figures from sugar and ground almonds; refurbished toys for their scrubwoman's children; lay in the soft snow to make imprints of their bodies; sallied forth to the larder, festooned with a flock of sausages; and prized the wild game—partridges, rabbits, even a boar—which hung from the smokehouse ceiling. Their father, a crack shot, enjoyed frequent hunting expeditions with the French aristocrats in Lorraine. The season's finale arrived with a gala Christmas Eve feast of many courses, prepared by Emma the cook and served by Wilhelm the manservant.

Details of Frieda's early life come mostly from a few adolescent letters and some fragments often thinly disguised by assumed names. A moment of her preadolescence emerges in a letter she wrote to Else when she was ten: "I can now crochet very nicely, and I have made a dress for your poor doll and put it carefully away." That Frieda had made a dress for Else's doll, not her own, reveals (early) her generosity.

Although Frieda had learned to sew, at heart she was a tomboy. She liked to be dominant. "I was happiest with the soldiers, who had temporary barracks outside our house for years." Apart from her family, girls and women—who delighted Lawrence—frightened Frieda. "I always liked being with boys and men," she recalled. "Only they gave me the kind of interest I wanted." In a sense Lawrence and Frieda *as adolescents* had reversed their roles. Whereas men sometimes intimidated Lawrence, they challenged Frieda; they were bold, absorbed her energy, whetted her spunk, gave her strength. "What I loved most of all was playing with my boy friends in the fortifications around Metz, among the huts and trenches the soldiers had built." Nothing frightened her. She was also a brash tease, engaging in pranks typical of adolescent boys: "When the regiments were filing past, Johanna and I sat on the garden wall, very grandly. Then we would throw pears and apples into the ranks. Great confusion would arise. An irate major turned toward his men and yelled, we popped quickly out of sight behind the wall, only to reappear and begin anew."

Although Frieda revered men and their activity, she was still a girl who faced a woman's destiny. Her mother had taught her kindness and social graces, but she also had to accommodate her masculine self to the expectations of her society. When she was fifteen, she left behind her scratched knees and uncombed hair and tomboy toughness, and welcomed dresses, ribbons, and gold chains. Her manners improved. A year later, in 1895, she tasted romance. Her distant cousin, sent to Metz to study military science at the Kriegschule, began coming on Sundays to her parents' spacious suburban house. His name was Kurt von Richthofen. "She was aware of him as she had never been aware of anybody before," Frieda later wrote of herself, and he responded "with a first trusting love." Slender, with close-cropped hair and perfect teeth, he was twenty-one and brought with him the radiance of morning sunshine. He and Frieda went for long walks, admired the newly opened irises, picked the first red and white strawberries, rowed on the Moselle River, played tennis, and enjoyed picnics of sausage, bread, and apples. He made her feel grown up and important. On Easter Sunday, when he turned to her in the mild spring night, "his lips, like butterfly wings," touched hers; but the social codes of the time curbed their passion.

On the surface Frieda's childhood swelled with emotional riches: her father's unbridled affection, her mother's indulgence, and her sisters' constant devotion. She never lost a secure sense of family. Yet beneath this happy exterior lay forms of estrangement, alienation, and disappointment that differed only in degree from those Lawrence experienced. About her parents, Frieda wrote: "Their own marriage was not so perfect." They were neither well matched nor tolerant of each other. Whereas Friedrich—like Arthur Lawrence—affected a brash self-confidence, his wife knew better. Both men were crippled by an inner weakness that rendered them vulnerable, crimped their self-respect, shrank their egos. Frieda believed that her father "had lost his faith in himself" and, like a failed vessel, had moored himself in old prejudices. Whereas Arthur drank, Friedrich gambled (once losing two hundred pounds) and took mistresses. Both were cowards, and both thereby lay exposed to their wives' wrathful tirades.

Frieda's parents engaged in long arguments. She remembered, "He had hurt [my mother] in many ways bitterly, but never did she complain about him to us, he was a father." Among Friedrich's mistresses was one, named Selma, who was more demanding than the others, wanting money—thousands of marks—for Friedrich's illegitimate son, conceived in 1897. Humiliated, the family complied.

Yet the daughters were learning from their father. To engage in an extramarital affair would, for Friedrich's daughters, be nothing less than a means of acquiring the same license and power that he had long assumed as his right. Unlike Victorian heroines such as Dora Copperfield or Tess Durbeyfield, Frieda eliminated guilt from the feminist equation. She saw desire on one side, power on the other, and nothing between. She would broker the two sides, not just to enhance her ego but to free herself from conservative social strictures. Friedrich's daughters understood early the risks of clinging to a failed marriage.

In the summer of 1896, when Frieda was not quite seventeen, her father found himself unable to pay the mortgage on their home; the debts of his gambling and mistressing eventually claimed his civil service salary. The house would have to be sold, two of the three servants let go, the family forced to relocate to an apartment in Metz. Janet Byrne says that the impending move was kept secret from Frieda, who was miserable when she found the family packing their belongings. A man had betrayed his wife and children. She would long remember his irresponsibility.

Yet life went forward. In the fall of 1896 the von Richthofens, although they were Protestants, agreed to send Frieda to a venerable Roman Catholic convent school named Saint Christiana, located a stone's throw from their new apartment. Reflecting the mix of Metz itself, the school welcomed both German and French children, although the number of French families had of course dwindled under German occupation. Frieda recalled that at the school "I did not learn very much. . . . I was a wild child and they could not tame me, those gentle nuns." She disliked school—its order, its discipline, its rectitude.

Well-bred German girls were expected to "finish" themselves at an appropriate school. Although the women's movement had begun, opportunities for changing women's education in pre-Weimar Germany were few. Wrote law professor Otto von Gierke: "The fate of the nation ultimately depends on the health and strength of the family," which women ably "beautify" with their physical and spiritual care; the renowned physicist Max Planck argued that nature itself "had given woman her occupation as mother and housewife." Late nineteenth-century theorists worried that women's lesser physical strength and more delicate psychology ill prepared them for serious academic study. In 1888 Oberschulrat Richter of Frieda's native Alsace-Lorraine cautioned that "there have been many complaints that the girls in upper girls' schools are overburdened."

But times were changing. After 1880 advocates of women's rights urged higher standards in girls' schools, more female teachers, and a curriculum that included religion, German language, French, English, history, geography, math, description of nature, principles of nature, drawing, writing, singing, needlework. Almost certainly, Frieda was offered instruction in these subjects, and would have spent nearly half of her class hours on German, French, and religion. Historian Juliane Jacobi-Dittrich writes that, for girls, "science, mathematics, and ancient languages, the core of higher education for boys in the nineteenth century, were never included." Else's friend Helene Lange was forced to spend long hours learning fancy needlework while boys were given the freedom to play outdoors. Organized in 1888, the Women's Reform Assocation campaigned for centers that would prepare women to enter the professions; they benefited not Frieda but Else, who in 1901 was the first woman to earn a doctorate (in economics) at the University of Heidelberg.

All three von Richthofen daughters attended the Eichberghaus, a girls' boarding school situated in the mountains above Littenweiler, near Freiburg, still run by Julie and Camilla Blas, the esteemed sisters who had taught Anna von Richthofen. Learned and kind, advocates of the outdoors, the Blas sisters did their best to inculcate good manners and an abiding interest in literature. But Frieda spent most of her time tramping about the Black Forest. Like her father, she was impatient and boisterous, and disliked drudgery.

At the close of the school term, when she had returned to Metz, Frieda met Lieutenant Karl von Marbahr, a Prussian soldier seven years her senior with whom she played tennis. Much later, he wrote to her (quoting

Lawrence's novel *Lady Chatterley's Lover*): "'She is nice, she is genuine, she does not know how nice she is.' That's how you were long ago, when I was very fond of you; a little bit naïve, ingenuous, and yet strong, but very feminine, no bluestocking." His use of "yet" and "but," almost together, gauges the surprising mix of qualities he found in Frieda. All his life he remembered her vigor.

When Frieda was seventeen, her scattered education coming to an end, her father's first cousin, "Uncle" Oswald (1847–1906), invited her to spend the winter with him in Berlin. Serving the empire as the German colonial secretary, he owned a fine apartment in an exclusive neighborhood near the Tiergarten. Berlin offered Frieda a bubbling social life—dances, races, balls, plays, the opera. But she wrote later that it was "no fun being a poor baroness" who had to buy gloves and shoes with the tiny allowance her disgraced father could now afford. At this young age she decided that elaborate and costly entertainments had little to do "with genuine living." For that she needed a husband. The fact that the German educational system had ill prepared such women as Frieda—had not developed their creative talent or their steadiness of purpose—meant that love affairs with men would play a disproportionate role in their lives.

## A Martyr in the Making

Who might have guessed that in 1898, when Frieda went to Freiburg to visit the Blas sisters, she would meet an Englishman named Ernest Weekley (1865–1954)—age thirty-three, respectable, upright, conventional, but also well educated, scholarly, exacting, and possessed of a fine sense of self-deprecating irony. In a curious way he was the male counterpart of Jessie Chambers. Both Weekley and Jessie came of simple, godly, working-class parents; both sought education as the escalator out of that class; both became schoolteachers; both expected far more of their mates than their mates could offer; both were cruelly disappointed. Their psychological makeup was that of the martyr.

Ernest Weekley, though poor, was very ambitious. Having earned a bachelor of arts degree from the University of London (the degree Lawrence declined to work for), he went for an additional year to the University of Bern to study German. In 1893 he progressed to Trinity College, Cambridge, to study languages, then to the Sorbonne for a final year to study French. Afterward, in 1897, he accepted a position as a lecturer in English at Freiburg-im-Breisgau University, a state institution situated on the slopes of the Black Forest.

Early in 1898 fortune smiled. He received a letter offering him not a lecturership but a professorship, paying £150 a year, at University College, Nottingham, which had opened its doors in 1881. Then a small urban institution at the city center, today its gray stone buildings perch like doves on an eminence to the west of the city. Weekley was euphoric. In Britain a professorship was a permanent (but not lucrative) position. He was appointed both professor of French and head of the Modern Languages Department. He needed only a wife and children to complete his happiness, to win him the emotional security that disciplined intellectual labor had not.

While he tramped through the German countryside, having yielded to the luxury of a brief holiday before he returned to England, Weekley paused at Littenweiler, a tiny village near Freiburg, where his friends the Schröers introduced him to an astonishingly beautiful girl on holiday with the Blas sisters. Her name was Frieda von Richthofen. Aglow with blond hair, perfect green eyes, frank expression, and infectious laugh, she must have seemed like a celestial gift to a lonely man. He was smitten. Her enthusiasm leavened his reserve; her buoyancy enlivened his quiet gravity; her charming whimsicality challenged his sturdy piety. Like her father she preferred *doing* things. She was active rather than contemplative; her energy sparked his taciturn good nature into a low, reluctant flame.

Except for the barrier of Weekley's stern moral code, they might have enjoyed an erotic idyll in the Black Forest, their flirtation shaking from them an affectionate tryst rather than a prolonged commitment. At nineteen Frieda was hardly ready to marry. Her robust, hearty, healthy nature had not been challenged; her desire for adventure had not been satisfied; her temper lacked seasoning; her prowling independence had not asserted itself. For a moment she must have felt as if Weekley's charm lay in a cavern whose recesses she might spend years exploring. If she could but enter, his dignified pedantry and self-righteousness would dissolve in the searchlight of her bold passion. She would conquer his aloof distance, humanize him, inspire in him a fulfilling sense of completion. Thus (as George Eliot would say) we all imagine first love—the beacon across the night sky tracing the path to inevitable happiness.

Frieda and her family were mesmerized by Weekley's *difference*; his foreignness may have seemed exotic, his British accent alluring, his large frame commanding. His respectability would have seemed reassuring after Friedrich's personal difficulties. If he had no liveliness, he had substance. If he lacked worldliness, he at least offered godliness. If he was bound by convention, he was also free from uncertainty. He knew what he believed, and his confidence would be a mooring for Frieda, who still yearned to experiment with limits. For the first time in her life someone constructed "firm ground" under her feet. As she wrote to Else, "I am attracted to him as I have never been attracted to anyone before."

On such *terra* Frieda and Weekley erected an engagement that lasted a year. It was followed by marriage on 29 August 1899 in the Blases' home near Freiburg, just after Frieda's twentieth birthday. Later that day, Week-

Frieda Lawrence, 1901 (Courtesy of the University of Nottingham Library)

ley's brother Ted performed a second marriage service at the little Anglican church nearby. Ernest felt entranced.

Afterward, the couple honeymooned in Switzerland. Frieda's recollection stressed the sexual uneasiness she and Ernest shared as they watched the sunny apple orchards and vineyards out of the train window: she feeling uncomprehending and "far away in her virginity" and he feeling "almost a virgin himself." Like many late-Victorian men, he was terrified by sex, his passions having been fiercely suppressed and nobly subordinated to his scholarship. As the happy couple sat on the train, which wound through the Alps to Lake Lucerne, "his body was held stiff and unbending." Fear seized him. To brace himself for the act to follow, he went out for a fortifying drink: "Go to bed, my child," he muttered in a frightened voice. Two hours later Frieda judged their conjugal bliss "horrible, more than horrible." After he fell asleep, a wave of degradation mixed with rage swept over her. She was a victim of their mutual inexperience. Embarrassed by the consummation he was compelled to achieve, he had not appreciated the supreme gift she had offered. She wanted passion, he delivered a rushed performance. In time, her loss became his. In 1912 Lawrence said to her: "You never got over your bad beginning with Ern[e]st."

☙❧

By November the Weekleys had settled into a small, dark, middle-class house in rainy, gray Nottingham. An industrial city of 110,000 people, it was surrounded by railway lines and factories lathered in smoke. Here the hosiery and lace industries employed a great many men and women, and new industries had begun to manufacture packaged cigarettes (Players), bicycles (Raleigh), and pharmaceuticals (Boots). Frieda was already pregnant. Ernest sallied forth busily to his lectures, sure of himself, aware of his success, proud of his discipline and perseverance. But whereas he scrupulously distinguished right from wrong, Frieda could never share what she later called "his rigid code of morals," which, like a warning light, checked her joy.

She learned the British routine of shopping in the morning, paying calls in the afternoon while the maid cleaned and cooked, presiding gracefully over the tea table and then dinner. She practiced the piano, tended the flower boxes, read George Eliot and Thackeray. In the evenings she and Ernest learned Italian together. But when she came down the narrow stairs too noisily, "he rushed out of his study and said: 'My God, I am married to an earthquake.'" His passion was for his work. Although Frieda loved his granite solidity and admired him still, she grew uneasy, insecure, and then bored. Often she was alone while he wrote French textbooks or taught night classes for those who worked, or spent his Saturdays in Cambridge, lecturing.

43

Frieda Lawrence and Ernest Weekley, her first husband (Courtesy of the Nottingham City Council Leisure and Community Services, Local Studies Library)

Occasionally she felt constrained, as if forced to run from the house, to run away like Connie Chatterley, escaping the dull confines of Wragby—until, rushing up Mapperley hill, Frieda waited for her sanity to return so she could go back to the dark little house and smell again her husband's books and pipe. But she felt imprisoned. His strange adoration froze her into a routine of dutiful obedience; her bountiful inner lights, one after the other, were going out.

What should she do? In her soul, energy and entropy began their battle. She minded most the *unwritten* English codes; they were like muzzles. Denied freedom, she longed "for things she . . . could not express," for a vocabulary to communicate with her deepest impulses, which lay far beneath convention. "It is mean," she wrote her sister Else at the end of 1901, "that people try to keep us women away by force from everything 'brainy,' as if one didn't need it just as much when one is married!" In fact, women were to be educated to become affectionate wives, adoring mothers, good companions, efficient housekeepers, and pious Christians. "Braininess," if encouraged, might impel women to depart from their traditional roles. In a state of subservience Frieda endured.

Yet domesticity provided its own generous rewards. In June 1900 their son Charles Montague was born; he had dark eyes, light hair, and was, she thought, "like Ernest in temperament"—"only livelier." She loved embroidering tiny clothes for him, telling him German fairy tales about princesses in distress, tossing balls to him. But later when she spoke German to him in a train or a tram, he would pull her skirt and, echoing his father's moral tones, whisper, "Don't speak German, people are looking at us."

Two more happy children arrived—Elsa in September 1902 and Barbara in October 1904. Enthralled, Frieda wrote later: "their eyes are so bright and their hair is so blond and they're so full of fun and it's such a joy to me that they love me so much." In 1993 Barbara remembered that around her mother, "[l]ife was wonderful, magical." For the children a competent teenage nurse named Ida Wilhelmy was hired, giving Frieda still more time alone: "[Ida] made my life so easy when the children were small," she remembered later. "I had only the fun of them."

Before long, a married neighbor, emancipated and mature, appeared. William E. Dowson (1864–1934), a well-to-do Nottingham manufacturer who had purchased one of the first automobiles—and who was godfather to Barbara—began driving Frieda away from urban noise and grime into primeval Sherwood Forest, where the great hoary oaks stood like mute observers above the bluebells and primroses. Briefly resuscitated—without her husband's knowledge—Frieda "felt alive again." Robert Lucas has said, "The affair, beyond setting a precedent, was of little significance to her." That may be. But it allowed her to test the value of fidelity as a social contract. She was not going to be "stuck in the old prejudices and taboos." Still in her heart a bold tomboy, she would test British moral codes, throw apples and pears into the midst of this repressive society, dive into the river of sensual abandon, even with Will Dowson, fifteen years her senior. She was determined to live fully.

## AN ADDICT'S WARBLING

Whenever she could, Frieda took her children to Germany. She hoped to recover the security she had long felt in Metz, where the comforts of family eased her anxiety. In 1901 she spent the whole summer in Metz. On one of her many journeys, she went to Munich to visit her sister Else and their schoolfriend Frieda Schloffer, who, between them, quickly immersed Frieda in the life of the *Kaffeehaus*, where she was thrilled by what she called the "ferocious" battle of ideas. The proponents of emancipation, to whom Frieda was drawn, were much like the 1960s radicals in America: they demanded an end to militarism, an end to competition, an end to sexual repression, an end to all suffocating bourgeois values. Stimulated by the new ideas swirling around her, Frieda was, she wrote, "a grateful audience." She heard spoken what for years she had felt inside. She was coming alive.

One man among the *Kaffeehaus* regulars utterly changed her life. Otto Gross, married to Frieda Schloffer, was a handsomely lanky man of medium height, with intense blue eyes and long, febrile, "piano" fingers like Franz Liszt's. The first vegetarian Frieda had ever met, he was an aggressive nonconformist. Born in 1877, institutionalized in Austria from 1913 to 1914, wholly neglected by 1919, he died in a sanatorium in 1920. But in the spring of 1907, when he met Frieda, Otto Gross, then thirty and immensely appealing, reigned over this cultural ferment, which bubbled most vigorously at the Café Stephanie, located in the Schwabing district of Munich. A Bavarian Greenwich Village, Schwabing was populated by a potpourri of outsiders—writers, poets, musicians, artists, and rebels of all stripes.

The renegade son of a famous criminologist, Gross had studied with Sigmund Freud; he had published *The Secondary Function of the Brain* in 1902 and a book on Freud's theories in 1907. In 1908 he was extensively analyzed by Freud's successor, Carl Jung, who admired his good friend's "unusual mind" yet discovered that Gross suffered from *dementia praecox,* known today as schizophrenia; it was highly resistant to treatment. But Gross, although he had earned a degree in medicine (in 1899) and was a carefully trained scientist, made himself into the poet of psychoanalysis. His ardent warblings of insight slid like wanton lyrics from the tongue of an addict. For most of his adult life he was addicted to morphine, opium, or cocaine, and by 1908 Freud believed that Gross had already entered "the early phase of toxic cocaine paranoia." A tender anarchist, Gross was committed to overthrowing nineteenth-century repression in all of its forms. In Frieda, whom he often called "the woman of the future," he found rich soil for planting his revolutionary feminist ideas. She too had begun to question the old order and to believe that it offered "no fun and no adventure and no mystery." It was, indeed, emotional *mystery* that would become one of D. H. Lawrence's central concerns.

Frieda was enthralled by the attention Gross lavished on her in the weeks they spent together. Although she shrewdly recognized that "[y]ou overrate me so much," she also reveled in the verbal delights he showered upon her—so different from the wry, sarcastic, sometimes smug conversation of Professor Weekley, who was, Frieda remembered in 1954, the year he died, "so cemented into his set ideas."

Gross gave Frieda a new faith. His letters—so passionate, seductive, intoxicating—supplied a warm glow of "music and light and refreshment."

Otto Gross, c. 1914 (Agentur für Geistige Gastarbeit / Harald Szeemann and Museo Casa Anatta, Monte Verita, Ascona)

About 1907, when Lawrence was completing his last year at Nottingham University College, Gross wrote to Frieda in the inflamed, prophetic rhetoric that he had mastered: "I *know* now what people will be like who keep themselves unpolluted by all the things that I hate and fight against—I know it through *you,* the only human being who *already, today,* has remained free from the code of chastity, from Christianity, from democracy and all that accumulated filth—*remained free through her own strength*—how on earth have you brought this miracle about, you golden child—how with your laughter and your loving have you kept your soul free from the curse and the dirt of two gloomy millennia?"

This was not the poetry that Frieda had heard in Nottingham. How triumphant she must have felt. "I had been longing for a cry of *real* passion," she told him, fired now "with enthusiasm for your ideals." They included the ideal of *Nichts verdrängen,* of repressing nothing, in order that sexual ties could be established that were neither possessive nor controlled, nor bound to patriarchal society's demand for monogamy. Gross believed (says Martin Green) that "[p]leasure is the only source of value" and that men's mastery of women "brought sin and shame into the world." Monogamy, though long established, violated the human instinct for social interaction. Gross's frequent seductions, which included both Frieda *and* Else, validated his philosophy. But even Carl Jung, who was sympathetic to Gross, found his affective life "abnormal" and his "sexual short-circuit . . . merely convenient." Sex rivaled drugs as an addiction.

Frieda was deeply flattered, even more so when Gross identified her "genius" as her capacity to insist on being herself. In his words, "You seem to have no idea what *genius* you have—how both power and warmth spring marvellously and irresistibly from everything you inspire with your own life." But Frieda, reflecting upon his words, may have sensed that Gross offered her only the inverse of what Weekley offered. For a woman to "inspire" men is to be put again on a pedestal, not as *wife/mother* but as *goddess.* Thus abstracted and simplified, she could be controlled by her new lover, to whom she gave herself, now, without scruples. She was, she thought, freeing herself.

When they shared a climactic night traveling by ship from Holland to England, Frieda felt a billowing awareness that "they were crossing over into an unknown world." That new world held not just glorious liberation but further anxiety, further uneasiness for Frieda in assuming the roles of wife and mother, which she also coveted. She was torn. Should she leave Weekley for Gross? Should she jettison duty and embrace abandon? The thought of Gross's helping her care for her three children quenched the glow in her soul. Gross lived only for his vision. He roamed above the turbulence of everyday life; his feet never touched the ground; he was as unpredictable as a rainbow. Finally, even though he "had given her her own soul," Frieda knew that she needed someone more reliable, more *sensible*, to justify her escape from the future that now lay ahead like a parched plain. She could not join her life to his. But she held passionately to Gross's letters as a badge of her courage. To Edgar Jaffe, her sister Else's husband (and a sympathetic friend), she wrote on 20 May 1907: "I had promised to burn all my letters from Munich, but I cannot do it; relieve me of my promise, I must still have something." The letters were a passport, valid for a lifetime, that entitled Frieda to believe that she had been specially chosen: "I believe I had what few women have, a real destiny."

As the year 1907 drew to a close, Frieda was twenty-eight. What lay ahead seemed miserable and grim. Still, she and Ernest, with their three children, soon moved to a finer home on Private Road in a neighborhood called Mapperley. Built of stone, the house had a large yard, more living space, and an indoor bathroom. Had she been ordinary, she might have been proud, vindicated in her domestic satisfactions, aware that a privileged life was the envy of those around her who survived on a pittance. Instead, she felt intensely alone, her revolutionized beliefs isolating her even from the Nottingham intelligentsia.

As if somnambulant, Frieda was now waiting. Year after year the months dragged like a fishnet trolling through a rough sea, trapping birthdays, outings to the seashore, visits to Germany, faculty gatherings, new books, piano recitals—as if, finally, they became barnacles on her memory, to be inspected but not to fire her soul's engine. Frieda's fully awakened sense of herself—that which set her apart—lay idle, as if it had washed up on the beach of her marriage to Ernest, faded by the sun of expectation and duty, dulled by the orbit of social calls, and patronized by Ernest's family. His prim sister Maude once scolded Frieda: "I know that you have strange views of life, selfish views as you know I think." Ripe for change, restless, chafing at the control and containment around her, Frieda waited. Five years passed. Her patience thinned, her hope waned, her disappointment festered. Her fine and generous spirit, her "genius," was dying.

# 4

# Their Adventure Begins

## 1912

Frieda waited restlessly in Nottingham, her adventure with Gross fading like a dream. Lawrence's prolonged illness in 1911 changed him too. It was as if he had shed a loose skin and come out fresh, his health sadly damaged but his soul awakened and infused with new strength. No doubt long talks with his mentor Edward Garnett—like Gross, "beautifully free of the world's conventions"—had heaved loose some of Lawrence's inert Midlands attitudes, had fostered a critical perspective on his youth, had given him access to freedom.

While still so ill and feeble, Lawrence stayed on with the Joneses in Croydon through the long Christmas holiday, convalescing, waiting anxiously for both his pulse and his temperature to stabilize. He pleaded for his strength to return: "I can't stand on my legs for my life," he told Louie Burrows on 17 December 1911; his heart raced "like a lady's watch!" He doubted he could teach again.

Finally, on 6 January 1912, his sister Ada, who had remained faithfully at his sickbed, took him to Compton's Boarding House, on St. Peter's Road in Bournemouth, a large seaside town set among heaps of dark pines which abutted the ochre sandstone cliffs. At Compton's, a place that harbored forty-five others, he was "a forlorn lost lamb"; but despite some initial bleating, he began to rework *The Trespasser*, writing in his bedroom beside a cozy fire, to chat with some of the friendly boarders, and to play cards and games in the billiard room. He planned to stay several weeks. Almost at once he felt better—"the air suits me." In those days sea air was routinely prescribed as a cure for the ill, although Bournemouth's frequent rain and heavy fog soon gave him a fierce cold that lingered fiendishly.

Already, Germany beckoned like a siren. Hannah Krenkow, a relative who knew he had been sick, asked him to come in April or May to Waldbröl near Cologne. He wanted to go, he told Louie on 12 January. If he absorbed a living knowledge of German, he could—if pressed—teach again. How much nicer (he no doubt thought) if someone could accompany him to this intriguing land. Who? His letters to Louie were less frequent now, and she must often have wondered if Germany would include her.

Edward Garnett, always solicitous and prompt in his attentions, had made an enterprise of encouraging nascent novelists. He had sponsored Joseph Conrad and had advised both E. M. Forster and H. G. Wells. He sent Lawrence books and literary news and agreed to read a chunk of the newly knitted *Trespasser* and criticize it: the rewritten novel exposed Lawrence's nakedness—"my most palpitant, sensitive self"—as nothing else had. With departure and change in the air, Lawrence planned to go to the Cearne (not to Louie's in Cossall) on Saturday, 3 February, to stay there for a few days, to savor dark beer in front of the roaring fire, and to discuss publication of the novel (his bills were mounting)—then go to Nottingham to see his married brother, George, on the eighth before returning to Eastwood a day later.

Once he arrived at the Cearne, he recognized that his most pressing obligation was to write to Louie. He needed to explain the transition he had undergone. It was not the letter she expected.

4th Feb. 1912
My dear Lou,
　　You will be wondering why I am so long in writing. I have been thinking what the doctor at Croydon and the doctor at Bournemouth both urged on me: that I ought not to marry, at least for a long time, if ever. And I feel myself my health is so precarious, I wouldn't undertake the responsibility. Then, seeing I mustn't teach, I shall have a struggle to keep myself. I will not drag on an engagement—so I ask you to dismiss me. I am afraid we are not well suited.
　　My illness has changed me a good deal, has broken a good many of the old bonds that held me. I can't help it. It is no good to go on. I asked Ada, and she thought it would be better if the engagement were broken off; because it is not fair to you.
　　It's a miserable business, and the fault is all mine.

D. H. Lawrence

This may seem a disturbingly cold letter to a fiancée. It records none of the prolonged anguish that Lawrence must have felt as he tried unsuccessfully to imagine with Louie a long married life. He blocked his feelings—made Ada the decisive agent.

From this point forward, Lawrence's illnesses will regularly disfigure a landscape, a place, a dwelling, even friends. It is as if he shed his illnesses with great effort, only to discover that the illness, like a parasite, had sought a fresh host, had attached itself anew and set up a virulent, independent life that remained threateningly close to him so that escape became his only means of survival. "I loathe the idea of school," Lawrence wrote in February. "I hate the whole Croydon crew violently." The Croydon teachers were allied with his defeat.

Unaware, Louie was caught in this process of emotional transfer. No doubt she felt victimized. In spite of her admirable passion—wedded, alas, to a narrow piety—Lawrence's regard for her was not strong enough or pure enough to keep her from being engulfed by his revulsion. His sister Ada found him annoyingly "flippant." That seems imprecise. He seems, rather, to have needed to cleanse his soul of the secretions of the past, "to pitch all my wits against her" in order to effect his release. His ardor for Louie, bled by his weeks away from her, had yielded to his need for friendship. His feelings embraced too little passion to justify marriage.

When on the afternoon of 13 February he met Louie in Nottingham—for a final talk—she had recovered her pride. Roused by Lawrence's irony, she turned angry rather than wistful, disgusted rather than tender, sarcastic rather than inviting, so that Lawrence easily freed himself. Having in hand a check for fifty pounds from William Heinemann, as royalty on *The White Peacock* (half his annual salary as a teacher), Lawrence paused at a critical crossroad. Cut free from the many ties that had held him, he was prepared to plunge into the flowery meadows of the future, which stretched as far as he could see. He was working steadily on short stories and had rewritten most of "Paul Morel," which had become, he said, "by far the best thing I've done."

But his soul, like Frieda Weekley's, had grown dormant as the weeks passed in Eastwood, where he stayed in Queen's Square with his sister Ada and their father. Following a visit to the emancipated Alice Dax, who had moved to the village of Shirebrook, Lawrence went in to Nottingham in March, stayed again with his brother in Laurel Street, and communicated with Professor Weekley, one of his teachers at Nottingham University College: Ernest Weekley had taught him French in 1907. "I had liked him, and he had liked me," Lawrence recalled some years later. Weekley invited his former student to enjoy a meal at his fine home on Private Road, where the professor and his family had lived for two years.

One Sunday in March, Lawrence came to lunch and altered forever the shape of his life. In her autobiography, *Not I, But the Wind* (1934), Frieda says that she had been "like a somnambulist in a conventional set life," isolated, even unbalanced (she thought) by the boredom that gripped her days. Her children, dear though they were to her, could not appease the hunger she felt within. Yet she was also a respectable woman with a position to uphold; she had a respected husband, now forty-six, who had just published a popular book, *The Romance of Words*; and she enjoyed an enviable degree of personal freedom within the suffocating cloak of her marriage.

When—on that fateful Sunday in March—Lawrence came to discuss a lectureship at a German university, he entered the Weekleys' house (Frieda wrote later) like an exotic bird, with "a long thin figure, quick straight legs, light, sure movements." As he and she talked in her room before lunch and watched, through the open French windows, the children romping on the lawn, Lawrence claimed that "he had finished with his attempts at knowing women." Eager to be amused, Frieda found his claim alluring; but she was surprised, then amazed, at the way he denounced women. He too was in revolt. At once she sympathized with this frail but lively man. His failure to connect vitally to others surely reminded her of herself. She had been stirred, as if Lawrence's long, thin verbal knife had reached the core of feelings associated with Otto Gross. Lawrence was a revelation.

Not long after, he visited again. Emboldened now, he said to her: "You are quite unaware of your husband, you take no notice of him." In fact, Lawrence had recently analyzed such a marriage in *The Trespasser* (published in May), understood the emptiness to which a spouse's inner coldness might lead, and recognized the necessity of escaping such a bond. When escape became impossible, Siegmund (in the novel) died. Frieda, who no doubt believed that she hid her boredom well and therefore disliked his criticism, was given a tart taste of the colliers' blunt mode of exchange. Refined, calculated delivery she could not expect; she could expect only the truth as Lawrence saw it. He was always fiercely honest. "That he came of the common people was a thrill to me," she said much later. "It gave him . . . lots of guts."

When he came again on Easter Sunday, 7 April, the children were hiding brightly colored eggs in the garden, acting out the kind of family tableau that gave Weekley the emotional stability he liked for his work. But in conversation with Frieda, Lawrence was equally direct this time too. He criticized her because, when she tried to make tea without the intrusion of servants, she could not even turn on the gas. Her ignorance in practical matters surprised him. But he was not surprised that he could see through the glass of her "hard bright shell," which foiled others from suspecting her domestic misery. His quick intuition, stripping surfaces, was a gift he never lost.

Thereafter they met often. Frieda winced at her own dilemma—to hide her lights under the marital cloak, or to thrust duty aside as an archaic prison designed for those without courage. One April day she and her daughters joined Lawrence at a train station in Derbyshire, then walked with him through the fields and woods that had been aroused by the spring. All at once, attraction shook into love: "We came to a small brook, a little stone bridge crossed it. Lawrence made the children some paper boats and put matches in them and let them float downstream under the bridge. Then he put daisies in the brook, and they floated down with their upturned faces. Crouched by the brook, playing there with the children, Lawrence forgot about me completely. Suddenly I knew I loved him. He had touched a new tenderness in me. . . . There had been nothing else for me to do but to submit."

Frieda's recollection is a key to Lawrence's creativity. A man intent on his work, while the image of water mysteriously connects him to both the woman's tenderness and her submission to him, becomes a motif in Lawrence's fiction, from "Daughters of the Vicar" to *Lady Chatterley's Lover*. The crouch is the image of vulnerability, for the fiercely proud man also needs protection from a vexing world. Frieda seems to have transferred to Lawrence some of the nurturing that she had offered her children, whereas he seems initially to have held back and embraced his mother's reserve: "I love you," he wrote on 6 May, "but I always have to bite my tongue before I can say it. It's only my Englishness." Although holding back feelings is a form of control, Lawrence tries to express the emotional truths that his working-class family had silenced. He blends male and female expectations: he yields, but resorts to a mental act (remembering "to bite") as a prod to express himself.

Fortunately, at some level Lawrence did not sense Frieda as vying with the revered image of his dead mother, Lydia. Lydia had been stern and sober, Frieda was gushing and garrulous; Lydia had been sexually repressed, Frieda was openly erotic, inviting Lawrence soon after they met to spend the night with her; Lydia had clung to her sons, whereas Frieda, having already discovered her "own intrinsic self," could release Lawrence to be as distinct from her as he could bear to be. Willing to sacrifice her children, Frieda aroused in Lawrence a very complex range of emotions: she was erotic, maternal, a comrade, but also competitive and egotistical. So dissimilar in background and temperament, the two of them would now engage in a difficult process of learning to accommodate their differences. Although splendidly matched, they soon cultivated their differences as readily as their similarities.

## To Germany

In the flush of their infatuation, they decided in mid-April to go to Germany together (as had George Eliot and George Henry Lewes in 1854, to kindle *their* lifelong union). But they hardly knew what might develop. Lawrence had resigned on 5 March, never again to think of teaching with anything but aversion. On 22 April he announced to Philip Smith, his Davidson Road headmaster: "I am probably going to Germany on the 4th May . . .

to Metz." Metz was Frieda's destination, too, for she wanted to attend the celebration of her father's fifty years of military service. Since the house would be full of grandchildren and relatives, Lawrence and Frieda could—without suspicion—stay together in a hotel for at least a week.

Although difficulties beset them at once, Lawrence wrote to Garnett the next day (23 April) to ask if he and Frieda could come to the Cearne on the following Saturday. Aware of the high social risk, he asked pointedly: "Are you *quite* sure you would like her and me to come to your house?" Having earlier described Frieda as "the finest woman I've ever met," Lawrence confessed he was extremely fond of her. After the weekend, Lawrence wrote Garnett again to say: "I am so anxious to know what Weekley will say. She is going to tell him today. . . . He will hate me. . . . He is getting elderly, and a bit tired. He doesn't want a wife like Frieda. . . . But he loves her, and in a jealous monogamistic fashion." It is tempting to think that this dismissal of "monogamistic" assumptions derives from Otto Gross. But Lawrence too was in revolt against "jealous" monogamy.

The couple's escape from England—set for 3 May, two months after their meeting—was now almost at hand. "I will come any time you tell me," Lawrence urged Frieda as he waited impatiently in Eastwood. He worried endlessly over her. He wrote again on 2 May, hoping she had money, for he could muster only eleven pounds—enough to take them to Metz but not far beyond. "I haven't told anything to anybody," he confided. For another month not even his sister Ada—much less the rest of his family—knew about Frieda. He knew the risks of scandal.

Their departure was full of troubled relief. In her memoirs Frieda says only: "We met at Charing Cross [train station at two o'clock] and crossed the grey channel sitting on some ropes, full of hope and agony. There was nothing but the grey sea, and the dark sky, and the throbbing of the ship, and ourselves." In Metz they went to the Hotel Deutscher Hof, occupying separate rooms, his true identity still hidden from her parents, who were later angry that their daughter had latched onto a penniless writer. Frieda was soon caught between Lawrence's intense passion for her and Nottingham's tugging pleas that she return at once to her three small children. She knew that if she did not return, she would lose them. Weekley would invoke English law forbidding adultery.

When Weekley realized that Frieda had left him, he exploded into a frenzy of anguish. Roiling with self-pity and then rage, he felt torn with deceit. By his own admission he was "insane for ten days" as he tried to rescue himself from the unexpected "shipwreck." On 10 May he received a letter from Lawrence: "Mrs. Weekley is afraid of being stunted and not allowed to grow. . . . [She] must live largely and abundantly. It is her nature." Inspired by this sincere if condescending explanation, Weekley waxed indignant and righteous: "All compromises are unthinkable," he informed Frieda on the tenth. "We are not rabbits," he added cruelly. "Let me know at once that you agree to a divorce." If she refused, he threatened, the ensuing scandal might cause him to lose his teaching post—their children might starve.

His was not the only voice. "What does all this mean?" demanded Weekley's sister Maude, who had taken the three children to London to stay with their grandparents. And from Lily Kipping, the wife of Weekley's closest friend, came this rending admonition: "[D]on't spoil your own life and the lives of all the others—the little girls without a mother, no mother's love, and Monty, he *must* have a mother to protect him. . . . [T]he children you brought into the world can't be cast off like this." For a while, these tremulous appeals (echoed by Frieda's own father and mother) rang in her ears like loud gongs, intensifying her distress.

The couple's love for each other, despite fierce opposition, gyrated into a flame: "I love you so much," Lawrence confided on 8 May, adding (a few days later), "I know I only love you. . . . And the promise of life with you is all richness." In a poem called "A Young Wife" Lawrence writes: "The pain of loving you / Is almost more than I can bear." Frieda, writing to Edward Garnett, said, "I love him with a 1000 different loves, I want everybody to love him[,] he deserves it. There is no fight between us, we want the same thing and our fighting will be against other people *never* with each other." Already, Frieda's courage and tigresslike temperament show themselves. She damns the proprieties, incurs the risks, and rejects (for now) the conventional cult of the child. To live "abundantly" is to lift the restrictions she had long tolerated.

❧

Suddenly, Lawrence was fleeing from Metz. As he explained to Edward Garnett: "[In Metz] Mrs Weekley and I were lying on the grass near some water . . . when we heard a faint murmur in the rear—a German policeman. There was such a to-do. It needed all the fiery little Baron von Richthofen's influence—and he is rather influential in Metz—to rescue me. They vow I am an English officer." Lawrence had inadvertently trespassed on military fortifications. With limited money and even more limited German, he went eighty miles north to Trier, near Luxembourg. There he stayed at the Hotel Rheinischer Hof; tramped around the Trier countryside, his eyes feasting on apple blossoms wafting across the valley in waves of pink smoke; and waited for Frieda to join him there. On 11 May he journeyed north to Waldbröl (the destination he had announced in April), a quiet village near Cologne, to see his cousin by marriage Hannah Krenkow, who had recently married. "We amuse ourselves a good deal with my German," he told Frieda on the thirteenth. In the cool mornings he wrote sketches of German life and spent hours revising "Paul Morel," soon to be renamed *Sons and Lovers.*

While Lawrence and Frieda waited to be reunited, they exchanged several important letters. As they prepared themselves for a life together, Lawrence insisted on a proper foundation for what he called their "marriage": no deceit, no lies, only truth. "My next coming to you is solemn . . . it is my marriage, after all, and a great thing—not a thing to be snatched and clumsily handled. . . . Dear God, I am marrying you, now, don't you see. It's a far greater thing than ever I knew. . . . I shall love you all my life." To him marriage was a new concept. The strength of his personal commitment had cracked the old core of him. The shock of freshly discovered feeling, part of his radical break with the past, gave Lawrence a motif that he would use in all his major works.

Although Frieda's replies have been lost, she may have told him bluntly that she demanded sexual fulfillment, that her conception of herself as a free, individual woman might embrace physical pleasure. Lawrence, forebearing though surely surprised, was stoical: "If you want [a man like Udo von] Henning, or anybody, have him. But I don't want anybody, till I see you. But all natures aren't alike. But I don't believe even *you* are your best, when you are using Henning as a dose of morphia." Her frankness jolted Lawrence, who had not yet told even his family about his great new love. Brenda Maddox believes that "Lawrence accepted with astonishing calm that he was a cuckold before he was a husband." The words "cuckold" and "astonishing" may be inexact to describe a man of twenty-six who sought— uneasily—to rid himself of the priggish moral codes enshrined by turn-of-the-century Britain. At this time (though not later) Lawrence longed for some kind of anarchic freedom in which cuckoldry would be irrelevant. He put passion ahead of morality.

By mid-May Frieda had gone to Munich to see Else, who, separated from her husband, Edgar Jaffe, was living in Wolfratshausen with Alfred Weber, brother of the famous German sociologist Max Weber. (At Heidelberg University Max had been Else's professor.) Frieda waited impatiently for Lawrence to join her, yet he seemed fearful and indecisive. If she had left her husband and children (she must have thought), at least he could leave his cousin in Waldbröl. If he did *not* join her, she was trapped, exposed as an adulteress, a cocotte. No wonder Lawrence could say, "You are far more ill than I am, now." She had risked much more. Gladly he had cast off teaching ("If I have to beg my bread, I'll never teach again," he vowed), but she had, with acute trepidation, cast off her family. The finality of the break, coming like a spear of lightning, shook her.

In such a fragile state they came together in Munich on 24 May, thrilled to be together yet exquisitely uneasy about the future. "After all," Lawrence wrote to Garnett, "Frieda isn't in any book, and I'm not, and life hurts." At first Weekley agreed to a divorce, then timidly shied away from the unsavory publicity that might flare. Through it all, Lawrence kept rewriting *Sons and Lovers,* having finished all but ten pages by the twenty-third. He was skilled at disciplining himself. A strange location never stalled his ability to compose.

## THE HONEYMOON

The weeks that followed, fired with emotional and physical activity, constituted the couple's honeymoon. Even though Lawrence and Frieda could not yet marry, both felt happy and intensely alive. After a night at Else's flat near Munich, they went on to Beuerberg, up the Isar valley in the Bavarian Tyrol. Although money was scarce, they stayed for eight idyllic days in the Gasthaus zur Post, Lawrence writing in "First Morning" that even the mountains "stand upright on our love." On 2 June he reported their whims to his Eastwood friend Sallie Hopkin: "In the morning we used to have breakfast under the thick horse-chestnut trees, and the red and white flowers fell on us. The garden was on a ledge, high over the river, above the weir, where the timber rafts floated down. . . . There are flowers so many they would make you cry for joy. . . . One day we went into the mountains, and sat, putting Frieda's rings on our toes, holding our feet under the pale green water of a lake, to see how they looked." Their new life together was full of surprises.

Both had awakened. Their rush of activity successfully hid the differences in temperament that would soon surface. To Garnett, Lawrence wrote on 2 June: "F[rieda], in a scarlet pinafore, leaning out on the balcony, against a background of blue and snowy mountains, says 'I'm so happy I don't even want to kiss you.' So there, you see, Love is a much bigger thing than passion, and a woman *much* more than sex." This playful comment illustrates what Germany offered that England could not—the opportunity for Lawrence to explore new regions of experience and to develop a critical perspective on his first twenty-six years, discovering how tight a noose England had thrown around him. "I have been fearfully happy," he told Arthur McLeod, still at Davidson Road School: "I tried several women—I did it honestly—and now, thank God, I have got a woman I love. You have no idea what it means. . . . I could stand on my head for joy, to think I have found her. . . . And I love her more every morning, and every night." This kind of passionate intensity could be sustained only when all the creative possibilities of "marriage" still seemed open to discovery and exploration.

Their relationship, however, soon derailed on the way Lawrence confronted the problem of Frieda's children. Later, Frieda remembered that when she "could'nt get on with their father (he did'nt know how I felt)," she had

loved her children even more. After she left and they were barred from seeing her, "Monty could'nt eat for 6 months and was sick—I am glad I did'nt
know that then—What hells L[awrence] and I went through anyhow!" It
pained Frieda to sacrifice the children—and pained Lawrence to recognize
how much she still needed them. He wanted her to choose him *because* she
wanted a life of freedom and independence; she wanted him, however, to
absolve her guilt by the force of his consuming passion. As Lawrence confided to Garnett on 3 July: "The children are miserable, missing her so
much. She lies on the floor in misery—and then is fearfully angry with me
because I won't say 'stay for my sake'. I say 'decide what you want most,
to live with me and share my rotten chances, or go back to security, and
your children—decide for *yourself*. . . .' And then she almost hates me, because I won't say 'I love you—stay with me whatever happens.' I *do* love
her. If she left me, I do not think I should be alive six months hence. And
she won't leave me, I think. God, how I love her—and the agony of it."

This pivotal letter reveals two strong personalities locked in combat as
they tried to shape the selves that would become marriage partners. These
selves were still unstable. Lawrence, freed now from his mother's hold, had
no wish to be dominated again; Frieda, used to having a man help her with
decisions, found choice difficult. To choose, in effect, meant stifling the
maternal feelings that were natural to her. Within Frieda's strength lay uncertainty; within Lawrence's strength lay rigidity.

In truth, Lawrence's ardor for Frieda whetted his ambition. Inspired by
the intensity of their honeymoon, he completed *Sons and Lovers* quickly
and on 9 June mailed it to William Heinemann, wholly aware (as he told
Walter de la Mare, Heinemann's assistant) that the novel was "not so
strongly concentric" as French-influenced fiction; he was also aware that
in its construction—it examined a family rather than one central consciousness—it might seem "loose" to some readers. He had had a similar
worry when he completed *The Trespasser.* Yet he knew his new novel was
"rather great. . . . Take my part with W[illiam] H[einemann]," he added
with mock playfulness, "and I'll say a prayer for you at every shrine I pass
in Bavaria."

Naturally, Lawrence was uneasy. Publishing decisions are often capricious. But like a cannon shot, Heinemann's letter of 1 July smashed the
couple's honeymoon. Declining to publish, Heinemann leveled three criticisms: the novel lacked unity, "without which the reader's interest cannot
be held"; its lack of "reticence" would sever sales to circulating libraries;
and it generated "no sympathy for any character in the book." Lawrence
was predictably angry: "I could curse for hours and hours—God help me."
He branded Heinemann a rotten Jew, inflaming a lifelong anti-Semitism.

To his credit Lawrence quickly recognized that he would have to rewrite *Sons and Lovers.* In spite of Heinemann's rejection, he told De la

Mare, "I maintain it is rather a great work." The word "rather" signals Lawrence's own cautious misgivings. And then a poignant postscript: "God helping me, my next novel shall be of the 'sweet' order. I must live." For he could not expect much money from his German sketches, which would soon appear in the *Westminster Gazette*. His situation resembled that of James Joyce, who in 1912 scraped by, teaching English in Trieste, while his manuscript of *Dubliners* went without a publisher. Although the proprieties had been tested by such recent novels as H. G. Wells's *Ann Veronica* (1909), publishers like Heinemann had yielded little ground.

While Lawrence and Frieda stayed in the tiny mountain village of Icking, twenty miles south of Munich, they continued to liberate themselves, even running through the beechwoods at night. In 1952 Frieda recalled that she sometimes spent the whole day in bed: "I think it rather shocked [Lawrence] that I was so undisciplined."

Suddenly their honeymoon flowered into a fine adventure. They agreed to a month-long trek over the Tyrol mountains in Austria. Then they would search for a warmer place in Italy, where, during the cold months, Lawrence could reconsider the criticisms of *Sons and Lovers* that Heinemann, De la Mare, and Garnett had offered. "I want to wander," he informed May Chambers Holbrook on 13 July. "I want to rough it and scramble through, free, free," he told Garnett. "I don't want to be tied down." He and Frieda would leave early in August, hiking first to Mayrhofen, about ten miles east of Innsbruck, then pause there for a week or two.

Before they departed, they swam nude in the Isar River just as, later, Ursula and Gudrun in Lawrence's masterpiece *Women in Love* suddenly throw off their clothes and slip naked into the water. To Lawrence, Frieda looked "fearfully voluptuous, rolling in the pale green water," and in July they welcomed Edward Garnett's twenty-year-old son, David (1892–1981), for a visit. Affectionately called Bunny, David had studied botany at the Royal College of Science and was loose limbed and open faced, sexually experienced, good looking, and very tolerant. Hoping to hear some lectures on botany, he had gone to Munich, where his handsome, tall, disenchanted friend Harold Hobson (1891–1974) was arriving from a jaunt to Moscow and planned to join him.

Taking the train to Icking on 24 July, Bunny was greeted by Lawrence, who seemed to him a slightly built figure with light movements and "beautiful lively, blue eyes . . . dancing with gaiety." Published in 1954, Bunny's recollection of Lawrence and Frieda, brittle with snobbery, assumes a patronizing tone: "His forehead was broad, but not high, his nose too short and lumpy, his face colourless, like a red-haired man's, his chin . . . altogether too large, and round like a hairpin . . . and the lower lip, rather red and moist, under the scrubby toothbrush moustache. He looked like a mongrel terrier among a crowd of Pomeranians and Alsatians, English to the bone. He was the type of the plumber's mate who goes back to fetch the tools."

After the pair had walked from Icking back to the borrowed house at Wolfratshausen, Bunny met Frieda and saw her at once as Lawrence's complement, comparing her to a German peasant woman he had observed in the train: "She had the same sturdy body, as strong as a horse, the same magnificent shoulders, but her head . . . and the whole carriage of her body were noble. Her eyes were green, with a lot of tawny yellow in them, the nose straight. She looked one dead in the eyes, fearlessly judging one and, at that moment, she was extraordinarily like a lioness: eyes and colouring, and the swift power of her lazy leap up from the hammock where she had been lying." The images suggest Frieda's unharnessed power (her swift leap is "lazy") to shape the forces around her; nevertheless, the "shaping" she left to Lawrence. Bunny found them wholly charming and, he said, "at once worshipped them." Equally delighted, Lawrence and Frieda were fascinated by his fearless swimming in the roaring Isar River and by his ravishing performances of Russian passion dances, which he had learned when his mother, Constance, had taken him to Russia.

Bunny remembered that Ernest Weekley, parading his distress, wrote nearly every day from Nottingham, begging his wife to return:

Frieda would hand the letter to Lawrence and say "See what he says . . ." Then Lawrence would . . . read it aloud. . . . Weekley's letters revealed the very worst and most contemptible side of his character. There was a stream of invective about Lawrence, and then appeals to Frieda's better instincts. How could she so demean herself as to elope with a miner's son? With a man who was not a gentleman? What would his friends in Nottingham be saying when they learned that she had so betrayed her birth and upbringing?

"Ernest is not so very grand himself," Frieda exclaimed, as Lawrence finished the letter and threw it aside. "To think that I was married for twelve years—yes, for twelve years—to a man who cares only what his neighbours will think!"

No one welcomed the arrival of these letters from England, forwarded by Frieda's mother. Weekley stirred up in Frieda "a perfect agony." Emotionally he was unable to let her go—and never remarried. In 1993 his daughter Barbara recalled, "He was a remarkable, kindly man," but toward Frieda "very unforgiving." In time he refused to allow even her name to be spoken.

Glad to be going south, away from such epistolary abuse, Lawrence and Frieda began their trek across rugged mountains, first those of the Tyrol, then the Alps. "We were happy in our adventure, free, going to unknown parts," Frieda remembered. On 10 August they arrived in Mayrhofen, staying at Mrs. Schneeberger's farmhouse. Above them hung "mountains draped in white chiffon clouds"; beside them ran a stream "as bright as glass." The couple spent their days outdoors—making fires, boiling eggs, and eating fresh gruyère cheese, Frieda boldly undressing and lying in the afternoon sun. In the evenings they sometimes drank with the peasants and danced. They planned to stay until 27 August, when they would go south into Italy by way of the Brenner Pass, which had served even the ancient Romans as a thoroughfare into Italy.

While they waited for Bunny and Harold to join them on Sunday, 18 August, Frieda captured the way she and Lawrence, to declare their separateness, embraced verbal sparring and jousting. She told Garnett, "Dont think me anything out of the way, please, I don't even prance theories or anything else of the sort any longer. L[awrence] says, he did it for me, I call him a liar, but there is some truth in it, I am afraid." The lioness and the light-footed deer: their quick sparks of difference, like a match and tinder, defined their coexistence, she mostly feeling (and sometimes grieving), he mostly conceptualizing and teaching: "He has taught me the feel and the understanding of things and people," she allowed; whereas he also reciprocated, writing on 19 August, "Let every man find . . . the woman who can take him and whose love he can take. . . . But the thing must be two-sided." What sustained them was mutual respect.

And then, from Lawrence, a hidden truth: "As a matter of fact, we are fearfully fond of one another, *all the more, perhaps, when it doesn't show.*" Their public sparring, which arose naturally as two strong people jockeyed for power, sometimes hid the bedrock affection that held them. "We want," said Lawrence to Garnett, "remarkably the same thing in life—sort of freedom, nakedness of intimacy, free breathing-space between us." The continuing problem would be to define that breathing space so that they preserved their bond yet made their margin of freedom wide enough for each to develop fully. At this point the freedom they desired combined complete self-revelation with a loosening of the possessive, "monogamistic" impulse they so detested in Ernest Weekley.

Bunny Garnett wrote two versions of the unforgettable August visit to Mayrhofen that he and Harold Hobson made. He observed that Lawrence, writing in the corner of the room, jumped up continually to stir the soup, or to make hilarious fun of himself, or to hear Frieda bubble over with joy at some sight beyond their window. "It never occurred to me, or I think to Frieda, not to interrupt him." Bunny also observed that "Lawrence liked Harold because of his uncompromising honesty and natural force [Lawrence called him "ripping"] and Frieda was not untouched by his good looks and masculine charm." Together the foursome set out to walk over the mountains for three days, after which Bunny and Harold would return to Munich. Both Lawrence and Frieda were in exceptional physical shape, light hearted, joyous, occasionally feisty.

All spent the first night in a hay hut, witnessing a violent thunderstorm, getting wet, braving the bitter cold. On the second day (28 August) they arrived at a rest house situated at 5,500 feet. While Bunny and Lawrence climbed the rocks toward the permanent snow line, Harold and Frieda (Bunny wrote) were left behind "to amuse each other as best they knew how." These words were a code. In 1980, long after Harold and the Lawrences were dead, Bunny revealed that Harold "was, no doubt most willingly, seduced. Frieda did not tell Lawrence about this until we had gone." (A year later, Bunny claimed, Lawrence told *him* about the seduction when he and Frieda stayed at the Cearne, Lawrence sadly commenting that "Harold is no gentleman.") The story may well be true; all recent biographers have accepted it. Fresh out of marital prison, Frieda was determined to deny Lawrence the power to establish the kinds of rigid boundaries that Weekley and his friends had prescribed for her; Lawrence, for his part, may have blamed Harold, whose "massive . . . egoism" even Bunny's mother was powerless to resist. But it is odd that Lawrence not only tolerated but encouraged Harold's continuing friendship. He articulated his own physical attraction to the younger man through Frieda. She completed what he may only have imagined.

The next day the foursome climbed to the Alpine pass called Pfitscher Jock and descended from drifted snow to houses wreathed in vineyards of black grapes. There they parted. Lawrence and Frieda went on to Sterzing, but they missed David "fearfully," Lawrence wrote to Garnett. He also expressed muted thanks for Garnett's arranging with Duckworth, a London firm, to publish *Love Poems and Others* within six months. The volume would earn Lawrence a few more pounds to swell the twenty-three pounds the couple had scraped together for their walking trip.

Their trunks having been sent ahead, they scrambled along the high road from Germany to Italy—sleeping in a cold hut on 1 September, nearly losing their way near Meran, cooking for themselves, bathing in the freezing streams, braving icy winds that cut like razors, and always shouldering rucksacks that held food, a spirit lamp, and methylated fuel. The towns of Bozen and Trient followed in turn. In Trient they could afford only a cheap, dirty hotel. There, tired and looking like tramps, they boarded the train for Riva. They also "quarrelled like nuts," possibly over Frieda's tryst with Harold, which (according to Lawrence's autobiographical novel *Mr Noon*) she revealed at the end of August.

Glad for a rest, they rejoiced when they reached Riva early in September. The town lay at the Austrian edge of Lake Garda, a few miles from the Italian border. "It is quite beautiful, and perfectly Italian," Lawrence told Garnett. The shimmering water of the lake was exquisite—an intense blue touched with purple—and everywhere black grapes hung from vines in heavy necklaces. Figs and peaches grew plentifully. "It is wonderful, and I love it," he exulted.

But two fears unsettled them: that Weekley would balk at giving Frieda a divorce, and that their money would not last the winter. So Lawrence was especially grateful that Garnett proposed to send fifty pounds from Duckworth as Lawrence's royalty on *The Trespasser*. The palatial and expensive Villa Leonardi, run by three women, cost a half-crown a day, or about four pounds a month. The Lawrences would soon need to relocate—and to economize.

Glad to help, the hotel manager sent them to a grand old Italian named Pietro di Paoli who lived in the lake village of Gargnano, about twenty miles south of Riva. He rented them the large bottom flat of the Villa Igéa for three pounds a month. Furnished, with dining room, kitchen, two big bedrooms, and a small garden full of ripe peaches, it looked "clean as a flower." Lawrence and Frieda arrived on 18 September, one week after Lawrence's twenty-seventh birthday. They stayed seven months.

If the shape of Lake Garda resembles an outstretched forefinger, then Gargnano sits on its knuckle, a tumble-down place stretched up against steep, rocky hills that gave way to lemon gardens on the slope behind. None of it was touristy. Gargnano offered warm, peaceful days for Lawrence's work, a therapeutic atmosphere for Frieda, a blue lake for bathing, olive gardens for evening strolls, and many opportunities for their love to ripen. Together they cooked spaghetti and macaroni over a charcoal fornello; fumbled in Italian with merchants and shopkeepers; bought figs and grapes for pennies a pound; shared the letters they sent and received; and discussed endlessly the quaint mores of the villagers, who were straight, muscular—and very poor. At this point their exile and poverty barely mattered. To Garnett, Lawrence marveled "how one can keep going further in love."

For Frieda, Lawrence made every familiar thing fresh. With him "nothing is ever stale or old," she told Garnett; underneath his quixotic surface he was "simple and real." "Everything he met," she wrote later, "had the newness of a creation just that moment come into being." Yet to Sallie Hopkin, Frieda wrote candidly that in spite of all the misery "Lawrence and I know we have done the right thing though there was a lot of wrong in it—My poor husband I simply dare'nt think of him."

With difficulty Frieda attempted to keep house. Having always had servants, she lacked training. When she scorched the pigeons and cried out, "What shall I do?" or flooded the kitchen when she washed the sheets, Lawrence "would come nobly from his work, never grumbling," and help her. Often in the cool mornings he would serve her breakfast in bed—eggs and sausage, toast and coffee—and sit and chat with her till dinner time, in spite of his deeply ingrained "horror" of loafing.

Gargnano, a village on the Lago di Garda, Italy, where Lawrence and Frieda lived 1912–13 (Courtesy of Domenico Fava [Collection of postcards D. Fava])

## "I've Written a Great Book"

He did not loaf long. As quickly as he could, he began "working like Hell at my novel," trying to shape it so that Paul Morel's psychological development would, first, honor his mother's powerful influence on him but, second, also reveal the subtle ways in which Paul's divergent behavior subtly criticizes his mother's crippling pressure to make him conform to her narrow, puritanical code. Lawrence had difficulty keeping the book focused on Paul. He needed to recast it afresh, and he welcomed Frieda's spirited assistance. "I lived and suffered that book," she recalled, "and wrote bits of it when he would ask me: 'What do you think my mother felt like then?'" During October he made immense progress. "I've got a heap of warmth and blood and tissue into that fuliginous novel of mine—F[rieda] says it's her—it would be. She saves me, but can't save herself," he joked to Edward Garnett. By the end of October he had recast four hundred pages and had made it vastly better. While he wrote, Frieda leaned on the windowsill and watched the impressive Italian soldiers strut by, or gossiped with her women friends. And she remained, she said, "an anarchist." Living in the long shadow of Otto Gross, she meant that only an anarchist would have chosen to live with an impoverished writer of genius rather than return to motherhood.

After weeks of sustained work, Lawrence completed his revision of *Sons and Lovers*. On 18 November he sent the manuscript to Gerald Duckworth in London, thrilled by the freshness and originality of the novel, certain that his genius had flowered. "I've written a great book," he told Garnett. Defending its form, which Garnett had criticized, he insisted he had "patiently and laboriously constructed that novel." To Garnett, Frieda also defended the novel's form, probably drawing on Lawrence's insights: "[A]ny new thing must find a new shape, then afterwards one can call it 'art,'" she argued, adding that Lawrence—"the only revolutionary worthy of the name"—was willing to take the English preoccupation with form and smash it. "[H]e dares to come out in the open and plants his stuff down bald and naked"—like "a real artist." Since she had relived the novel within her heart, and written out "bits" for him, and often contested his interpretation of a character's motives and actions, she naturally felt defensive. Given Garnett's reaction, Lawrence was grateful to have Frieda's powerful assurance at hand.

Garnett soon responded. He demanded a shorter novel. He wanted its exposition compressed, its repetitions lopped off, and its sexual explicitness curbed. The novel, he believed, had not yet achieved its potential. It needed many cuts, which he, with his sure eye, could make.

Lawrence was stunned. "I sit in sadness and grief after your letter," he admitted on 1 December. "I daren't say anything." The thought of further revision, not to say mutilation, must have seemed repellant. Normally "plucky" and independent, Lawrence probably realized that Garnett, serving as Duckworth's informal editorial board, controlled the novel's publication. "One must publish to live," he said bitingly to Hueffer on 10 December. No doubt Lawrence endowed Garnett with the qualities of the benevolent father he had never had, asking Garnett, for instance, if he approved of an idea for a novel (never written) about Robert Burns. "I feel always so deep in your debt," he worried on 29 December. These peculiar emotions exerted their own pressure.

"All right," Lawrence acquiesced, "take out what you think necessary." He was hurt. On this sanction, Garnett then shortened *Sons and Lovers* by about fifteen thousand words, cutting numerous passages about Paul's brother in order to tighten the narrative's central concern with Paul and his mother, culling inert passages that retarded the narrative's pace, and pinching the novel's sensuality. In one passage, for example, Garnett struck out the italicized words (following) that describe Paul and his married paramour, Clara Dawes: "Then he loosed her, and his blood began to run free. Looking at her, he had to bite his lip, and the tears of pain came to his eyes, she was so beautiful, and so desirable. The first kiss on her breast made him pant with fear. *The great dread, the great humility, and the awful desire, were nearly too much. Her breasts were heavy. He held one in each hand, like big fruits in their cups, and he kissed them, fearfully.* He was afraid to look at her. His hands went travelling over her, delicate, discriminate, fearful, full of adoration. *Suddenly he saw her knees, and he dropped, kissing them passionately. She quivered. And then again, with his fingers on her sides, she quivered.*" With a keen eye on the book's market, Garnett condensed the novel but also tamed Paul's fierce passion for Clara.

His editing has raised sharp questions. Should Garnett have returned the manuscript to Lawrence with the proposed cuts marked for inspection or approval? Conversely, is it reasonable to expect a busy man serving as an unpaid editor to offer a *second* set of comments if the only barrier to the novel's publication were twenty or so passages he could easily expunge or expurgate?

Wayne Templeton, like Mark Schorer before him, has judged Garnett a more competent editor than Lawrence. Garnett, he concludes, "turned a pedestrian . . . manuscript into a powerful . . . novel." But the editors of the recent Cambridge edition—Helen and Carl Baron—view Garnett's editing differently. They believe that he delivered Lawrence "an ultimatum" that Lawrence, without money or a secure reputation, could not contest: "I'm so afraid I shall have to take to teaching again," he worried on 24 December. The Barons judge Garnett's version of the novel "spurious," value Lawrence's own words as having ultimate textual authority, and discount both Lawrence's gratitude to Garnett for pruning done "jolly well" and

Lawrence's regret that his "prolix" style needed Garnett's scalpel to "barber" it. Both versions have merit. The longer version has greater artistic integrity; the shorter is more readable.

Despite its vexing problems, the novel had done much for Lawrence personally. Writing it may have altered his life. The clue to its therapeutic value appears in a letter Lawrence wrote to Frieda's sister Else on 14 December 1912—ostensibly about Frieda but really about himself: "If Frieda and the children could live happily together, I should say 'Go'—because the happiness of two out of three is sufficient. . . . But if Frieda gave up all to go and live with them, that would sap their strength because they would have to support her life as they grew up. They would not be free to live of themselves—they would first have to live *for her,* to pay back. The worst of sacrifice is . . . putting the recipient under the obligation of making restitution, often more than he could afford." This major insight helped Lawrence understand how his parents' raw incompatibility had turned him into an emotional servant who was "not free," whose emotional bondage required that he go on "paying back," "making restitution," honoring his mother's sacrifice to the point of yielding his "inner liberty" and his "pride." Such bondage had capped his soul's freedom and perhaps narrowed his emotional range.

One reason for his later wandering from place to place is clear: he constantly needed to escape from the fear that a fixed abode would subtly entrap him. The fact that he never saved the letters he received manifests the same impulse. Even though he was miserable when he rewrote the section about his mother's death, the novel helped him loosen the psychological fetters that had bound him to her. "If my mother had lived," he told Frieda, "I could never have loved you, she wouldn't have let me go." In his later years, short stories like "The Rocking Horse Winner" (1926) and "The Lovely Lady" (1927) show a sensitive son cruelly imprisoned by a mother who is unrelenting in her control. Such stories echo Lawrence's troubled past.

For the biographer *Sons and Lovers* has unique value among Lawrence's works. The first of its two major parts recreates Lawrence's family life; within it lies Lawrence's apologia for his mother. Yet the novel does more than settle the score with the man who (both Paul and his mother believe) violated her standards of principled behavior; for the novel also delineates turn-of-the-century working-class life as no one before Lawrence had done. Lawrence did for industrial small-town life what Thomas Hardy had done earlier for English rural life—with important differences. Uninterested in the sham aristocrats who fascinated Hardy, Lawrence paid closer attention to the psychic dynamics of the family and sought to analyze *dysfunctional* relationships. In an outline of the novel, supplied to Garnett on 19 November 1912, Lawrence talked about Mrs. Morel: "She has had a passion for her husband, so the children are born of passion, and have heaps of vitality. But as her sons grow up she selects them as lovers—first the eldest, then the second. These sons are *urged* into life by their reciprocal love of their mother—urged on and on. But when they come to manhood, they can't love, because their mother is the strongest power in their lives, and holds them." Like his brother, Paul finds his love funneled to his mother. Prevented by the incest taboo from openly expressing that love, Paul gives his soul to his mother and his passion to two women—first to Miriam Leivers, whose spiritual potency too much resembles his mother's moral hegemony; and then to Clara Dawes, a suffragette (like Frieda, separated from her husband) whose erotic openness might have offered Paul salvation—except that while his mother lives he is unavailable for any bond but physical love, so that by the end of the novel, his mother having died, he drifts toward death, alone, shorn of fulfillment. An intriguing scene in which Paul wrestles Clara's husband, Baxter Dawes, its erotic tincture scarcely concealed, reminds the reader that Paul, once he achieves a greater degree of maturity and insight, may require both male and female fulfillments.

*Sons and Lovers* holds in suspension two contrary forces, *control* and *freedom*, which intriguingly work themselves out. In technique Lawrence fuses both the impersonality of French fiction (so admired by Garnett) and a radically subjective rendering of his own experience. He has it both ways. He welds fact to injury, photograph to portrait, external restraint to internal outpouring. In theme he balances Mrs. Morel's implacable control with Paul's attempts to free himself from the fetters that (sequentially) his mother, Miriam, and Clara impose. What unifies the novel—and joins these oppositions—is Paul's remarkable sensibility. It allows him to observe attentively, to respond passionately, and to interpret intelligently.

The novel's most unforgettable scene, in which Paul approaches Miriam to claim her, illustrates these contrary forces as sexual passion confronts sacrificial pity: "He never forgot seeing her as she lay naked on the bed, when he was unfastening his collar. First he saw only her beauty, and was blind with it. . . . And then he wanted her, and threw off his things. And then, as he went forward to her, her hands lifted in a little pleading movement, and he looked at her face, and stopped. Her big brown eyes were watching him, still and resigned and loving; she lay as if she had given herself up to sacrifice: there was her body for him; but the look at the back of her eyes, like a creature awaiting immolation, arrested him, and all his blood fell back." To go forward and then to retreat comprises the novel's central rhythmic figure. The book's meticulous recording of psychic ebb and flow is moving and fresh. As Miriam uses her mind to transcend the physical horror of sex, Paul drugs his mind to focus on her alluring flesh.

What Ezra Pound said of James Joyce in 1914, he could as easily have said of Lawrence: he presents "subjective things . . . with such clarity of outline that he might be dealing with . . . builders' specifications."

Some critics regard *Sons and Lovers* as the pinnacle of Lawrence's achievement. Graham Hough believes that "*Sons and Lovers* remains his masterpiece to those who abide by the central tradition of the novel." Indeed, the novel's early chapters are unrivaled in their verbal precision and narrative mastery. "Absolutely, the opening half is the greatest thing in English fiction," declares Frank O'Connor. But the quality of Paul's insight is limited by his (and Lawrence's) youthfulness. Paul never understands, for instance, how industrialism has entrapped his father, numbing his soul as he hacks out the seams of coal. Lawrence's later novels will transcend the understanding that *Sons and Lovers* achieves and will probe, with more artistic dexterity, the inner mechanisms of British culture.

Now, however, Lawrence was ready to cast behind him both childhood and adolescence. He was ready to locate in marriage the basis of his newly defined self. In the placid months before World War I began, he grew alarmed by what he intuited as the incipient breakdown of the human spirit. His acute sensitivity detected a sterile spiritual force that disrupted the therapeutic calm that writing *Sons and Lovers* had brought him. Because he passionately believed in art as the purest means of measuring life afresh, he faced this disruption with great courage. But a central concern remained: How would art link him to Frieda?

# 5

# Exploring the Unknown

## 1913

What Lawrence wrote of Thomas Hardy's characters, he might have written of Frieda and himself: "These people of Wessex are always bursting suddenly out of bud and taking a wild flight into flower, . . . out of a tight convention . . . into something quite madly personal." As Lawrence and Frieda stayed on in Italy beside the Lago di Garda, mesmerized by Italian life, the weeks of "wild flight" stretched into months. Jeffrey Meyers nicely observes that "there were sufficient differences between [Lawrence and Frieda] to provide endless dialogue and stimulation." But as the novelty of being together faded and as their economizing turned from a challenge into an obligation, they began to struggle. In February 1913 Frieda wrote to Bunny Garnett in her inimitable way: "We are always just us two and we live so hard on each other[,] one day like the lions that ate each other, there will be nothing but two tails left." Their personal difficulties might be called setbacks except that Lawrence and Frieda always struggled forward into new phases. In their years together they always seem to have had a goal but rarely a direction. They seldom used others to guide them—for good reason. As Lawrence mused when writing to Arthur McLeod on 17 January, Frieda "sort of keeps me in direct communication with the unknown."

What does he mean? In composing *The Trespasser* and *Sons and Lovers* Lawrence had found a niche of new perception. He had discovered first that Siegmund and Helena, lying on the beach, comprise "two grains of life in the vast movement" of oceans, clouds, and circling spheres and then—with quick insight—that Paul and Clara, after making love, had pierced the *known* in order to discover "life wild at the source" where, dwarfed by a magnificent power, they comprise "only grains in the tremendous heave." This vast power overwhelms both the characters, who are in awe, and the narrator, who struggles to open new categories of perception for the reader.

In this struggle, even at the cost of dissension, Frieda's role was clear: to push Lawrence deeper into the mysterious union of man and woman. His artistic advance also stirred a profound spiritual advance. He aimed not to glorify God, as his Victorian predecessors might have done, and not to struggle toward a scientific rationalism, as some of his peers did, but rather to locate the spiritual mystery at the end of a long conduit to which his intuition, aided by emotion, would lead him—in concert with a person who was, herself, able to struggle independently toward the mystery. The question is, How did they do it? *Sons and Lovers* pointed the way. At work in the factory, Paul Morel feels "pure forgetfulness" (in manuscript) but "pure forgetfulness, when he lapsed from consciousness" (in proof). To lapse from consciousness opens the door to mystery. The critical difference between Lawrence *before* and Lawrence *after* he met Frieda is that he learned to locate mystery in the unconscious.

As Lawrence corrected the proofs of *Sons and Lovers* in February 1913, other changes were stirring. Despite the expense, he and Frieda needed to go to England so that Frieda could see her three children, now living in London with Weekley's sister and parents. Told repeatedly that their mother had deserted them, the children felt hurt and betrayed. Frieda's appeal for a divorce from Weekley had progressed, the judge having granted a decree *nisi*—"that is," Lawrence explained to Else, the divorce would be granted "*unless* something turns up"; if, after six months, nothing (and nobody) "turned up," the divorce would be absolute. Frieda would be free to marry again. But in 1913 only 1,037 divorce petitions were filed in the whole of England and Wales.

The difficulty of money remained. They needed two hundred pounds a year, Lawrence thought. How would he earn it? A country school was out of the question, not because he had left his post at Davidson Road School but (he told Edward Garnett, without arrogance) because Frieda's aristocratic lineage made it difficult: "I could get along with anybody, by myself, because, as Frieda says, I am common, and as you say, I am 1/5 Cockney. . . . But Frieda is a lady. . . . She is not a bit stuck-up, really more humble than I am, but she makes the *de haut en bas* of class distinction felt— even with my sister. It is as she was bred and fed, and can't be otherwise.

So, that really cuts out a country school. I mustn't [like Weekley] take her to England to bury her alive." Instead, he would need to write well, and Frieda would need to help him. Lawrence was grateful that Garnett thought his prospects "so good."

Garnett's assurance roused him to ponder new work while, as an artist, he faced a cruel conflict. He required money but could not write best-sellers: "I am a damned curse unto myself." In the slow winter months, he began two works, both of which came like a rip tide, rolling out of the depths of his experience with Frieda. "The Insurrection of Miss Houghton" was not to be visual, like *Sons and Lovers,* but all analytical, "really a stratum deeper than I think anybody has ever gone, in a novel," he told Garnett. After writing only half of it, he suddenly turned to a "lighter" novel that he called "The Sisters." This new work contained the seeds of a brilliant pair of novels, *The Rainbow* and *Women in Love.* They would occupy him for several years.

Frieda once adroitly remarked that Lawrence approached women "as if they were Gothic cathedrals." If she meant to suggest soaring heights and the sanctity of sublime feeling, her metaphor is apt, for in 1913 Lawrence was trying to enter a woman's consciousness ever more deeply. Using a different metaphor, he aimed to chart her impulses just as they swam from the inner pool of her subconscious self. As he worked on "The Sisters," he felt successive waves of joy and despair. Frieda gauged the work's striking originality when she wrote to Garnett: "I wonder how you will like L[awrence]'s new novel! I read it again and quite adored it; before, I wasn't sure. It's so quiet and different, you will be surprised."

When Frieda's sister Else visited Gargnano in March, she persuaded the Lawrences to come to Rome, where she was staying for a month. It was still Italy, which Lawrence loved. And Frieda wanted change. "We shall go first to Florence, then on to Rome," Lawrence reported to Garnett. "There we shall take rooms and stay for some months. We are neither of us coming to England," he added with resignation. Frieda would not, after all, be able to visit her children; Weekley had refused her plea. If she could not see them, at least she would be around others. Yet Lawrence had loved the Villa Igéa: "This has been my first home—and such a grand one," he said nostalgically to his sister Ada on 25 March. He doubted he would rise to such heights again.

The Lawrences' next move reveals their lifelong pattern of indecision about where to live. Socially marginalized, living at the edge of respectability, they spent, one might say, the next fifteen years visiting family or friends, or going to places others had recommended. The two complicating factors were, at first, Frieda's children and, later, Lawrence's health. Like magnets, these two exerted strong pulls, often in contrary directions.

## IN THE ALPS

Suddenly, perhaps deterred by the cost, Lawrence and Frieda decided to meet Else not in Rome but in Verona, then to return with her to Munich, where, in the village of Irschenhausen fifteen miles away, they could stay rent free in a summer bungalow belonging to Edgar Jaffe, Else's estranged husband, who taught at the University of Munich. After they arrived, Lawrence wrote to Ada: "We are in a lovely little wooden house . . . looking over to the Alps, which are white with snow—they are some ten miles away. It is quite near Icking, where I was last year." But after Italy's openness and warmth and freedom, Lawrence disliked Germany—it felt narrow and cruel, he told Garnett: not much different from the "beastly, tight, Sunday feeling which is so blighting in England."

Alone in the Alpine meadows, amid the primulas and blue gentians that inspired him, Lawrence continued to write "The Sisters," whose purpose and shape, he told McLeod, he had not *yet* grasped after composing 145 pages. Testing the limits of his imagination, the novel was more experimental than he had thought. It would radically readjust men's and women's sexual lives, and give verbal shape to the Unknown, to which Frieda had so fortuitously connected him. But the news that his *Love Poems and Others,* published by Duckworth in February, had sold only one hundred copies would have reminded Lawrence that, since he wrote mostly from within, the audience for his work might be limited. Admirably he was trying to match his internal *daemon* to external market pressures. In later years, when his expenses mounted, he became more pressingly concerned with this tension.

For a quick appraisal Lawrence sent Garnett what he had completed of "The Sisters." Ever dependable, "quick with nice news and slow with nasty," Garnett commented on Lawrence's remarkable, arrogant females and elicited Lawrence's explanation that in his first draft "it did me good . . . to depict Frieda's God Almightiness in all its glory." Ella Templeman, the protagonist, was (he added) a "portrait" of Frieda. But the portrait was crude.

While Lawrence considered how he would finish (or recast) "The Sisters," Frieda decided resolutely to make a move about the children, who for months had become, between the couple, like a drawn sword. As Lawrence explained to Garnett in May: "The idea is that Frieda sees her son Monty at St Pauls School, talks to him, arranges to see the little girls, keeps everything quiet from the father. Then the children shall say to their father 'We want to see our mother in Germany.'—It is a plan I don't like, setting the children between two parents." Confiding in Garnett, Frieda summarized—without any compromise—the long arguments she and Lawrence had waged: "Of course I don't think it's desirable that I should see the children in the street, but what can I do? I am entirely cut off from all, Ernest or the children. Ernest used to write my mother, not now. . . . If they ask Ernest, 'We want to see our mother,' I think he cannot say no. . . . [Lawrence] dreads my seeing the children; I feel them slipping away into nothing from me and I simply can't stand it and *won't* stand it!" Once she had seen her children, she and Lawrence hoped to return to Italy, after the summer heat had abated.

At last the published version of *Sons and Lovers* arrived. To Garnett, Lawrence declared himself "fearfully proud of it," but he also recognized that "[i]t's the end of my youthful period." Gone were powerful mothers and pale, inadequate male protagonists. They disappeared as Lawrence developed. But Garnett, having encouraged Jessie Chambers in *her* writing, also sent them her manuscript, called "Eunice Temple"—a version of her long and tormented relationship with Lawrence. She believed that Lawrence's fictional portrait of her as Miriam Leivers had been unjust—a displaced expression of his mother's jealous hatred. Repelled by *Sons and Lovers,* Jessie returned both the proofs of the novel, which Lawrence had proudly sent her, and his letter. She complained to Helen Corke that the portrait of Miriam was "a slander—a fearful treachery." It had shocked her brutally: "If I am to live at all," she added, "it will be necessary to put [him] out of my life—to ignore him entirely." To ease her enormous pain, she soon met a farmer, John Wood, whom she married in 1915, implicitly rejecting the artistic and intellectual "Bert" Lawrence.

Both Frieda and Lawrence were surprised when they read Jessie's manuscript. To Garnett, Frieda wrote first, on 17 May, reacting not with animosity but with pity: "Miriam's novel is . . . a faded photograph of *Sons and Lovers,* she has never understood anything out of herself, no inner activity, but she does make one ache! I only just realised the amazing brutality of *Sons and Lovers.*" Lawrence was shocked that he had inflicted such pain. Two days later he said to Garnett: "We got Miss Chambers' novel. I should scarcely recognise her—she never used to *say* anything. But it isn't bad, and it made me so miserable I had hardly the energy to walk out of the house for two days." Her novel probably shocked Lawrence into recognizing, more forcefully than before, the limits of his mother's perspective. Biographer Elaine Feinstein asserts that, in regard to Jessie, Lawrence finally "put any sense of guilt aside." That seems too easy. It is more likely that Lawrence used the seeds of new understanding, which Jessie had awakened, to inform "The Sisters," where mothers and daughters sometimes resemble Jessie and her mother—women bound not in coercive manipulation but in sympathetic connection. As Lawrence sought material beyond his own immediate experience, he saw with fresh eyes an alternative model for female bonding.

## "I THOUGHT I WAS MILD AND GOOD!"

The arrival of summer, even in the splendid Alps, brought stress. Because the couple spent most of their time alone, their problems were magnified by their isolation. Like Ted Hughes and Sylvia Plath, isolated at Court Green in North Devon, Lawrence and Frieda quarreled easily. On 1 June Lawrence said to Garnett, "The moving from Italy here upset us fearfully—I am even now not quite well, nor is Frieda." Lawrence believed that he *must* remain tightly disciplined in order to write and earn money, do the housework, and keep Frieda amused when she tired of reading books. Frieda was less focused, more hedonistic. She sewed, smoked, embroidered, slept late, enjoyed sweets—she caught life's feathers as they fell. But she was still a mother. Having been separated from her children for a year, she was determined to see them: no one must interfere. As Lawrence wrote pregnantly to Garnett on 10 June 1913, "I am doing as you say, letting her choose her own way," then added cryptically, "[b]ut Frieda has stayed a day or two in Wolfratshausen alone."

A disagreement had forced them to separate. To Garnett, Frieda explained: "I ran away from L[awrence] for two days after having broken a plate over his head, while washing up! I was astonished[!] I thought I was mild and good!" This simple explanation has aroused the ire of some writers. Margaret Anne Doody, for instance, argues that Frieda was a battered wife, Lawrence of course an abusive husband. Yet he benefited from these sharp exchanges, which kept him keenly aware of the dynamic range of emotions their relationship encompassed. His dependence on Frieda was also growing ("he cant bear to be away from me, hardly for hours," she told Garnett). Lawrence welcomed her buoyant solicitude but resented a dependence (even as he sought it) that resembled his tangled bond with his mother. Perhaps in that way he was unable to recognize how he transformed Frieda from a wife into a wife/mother. In turn, Frieda, deprived of her children, may have welcomed this more complex role. In her way she was as ambitious for Lawrence as his mother had been.

Their disagreement, despite its pain, fed Lawrence's writing. At this time he was attempting, within his own experience, to understand the origins of violence (which he would soon link to the forces that ignited World War I). Hence in June he worked on three German short stories, the finest being "Honour and Arms" (later retitled "The Prussian Officer"), which he called "the best short story I have ever done." This brilliant psychological study of violence traces an army captain's slowly developing hostility toward his twenty-two-year-old orderly. His hostility surges up from a frustrated *desire* for a young man who is warm, obedient, instinctual, unreflective, self-contained. "But the influence of the young soldier's being had penetrated through the officer's stiff discipline," wrote Lawrence, and before long, "a hot flame ran in his blood." Plagued by his unsatisfied and misunderstood urges, the officer intuitively understands the orderly as his complement, for women do not arouse the captain. Blocked by his military training from acting on his feelings, which are less and less suppressed, he punishes what he wants, lured by the thrill of deep pleasure that trails after the punishments like an ache. After kicking his orderly down the stairs, he feels his passion intensely gratified.

But during military maneuvers, the young orderly finally knots his courage, determined not to be torn to pieces. Surely he too thought of himself as "mild and good." Still, his instinct for self-preservation asserts itself blindly: his hands explode, his knee plunges into the officer's stomach, his palms press back the older man's strong neck until it crunches and blood floods the captain's nostrils. Like Frieda, the orderly, appalled by his sudden spurt of violence, runs away—to hide in the Bavarian forest. Soon he succumbs to a delirium in which all his sensations are magnificently distorted. In the story's final paragraph, when his dead body is placed next to his captain's, Lawrence fulfills the officer's desire and thereby exposes the story's rich psychological truth. Opening with the officer's rigid control, Lawrence concludes with the officer lying rigidly at rest. The story, puncturing codes of restraint, allowed Lawrence to mediate the extremes of love and hate.

☙

Having pondered imaginatively Frieda's sudden act of violence, Lawrence revealed to both of them the hostility that intense frustration could breed. Arguably, both wanted what was being denied. As early as *The White Peacock,* where Cyril is infatuated with George's muscular body, and then again in *Sons and Lovers,* where Paul tangles with Baxter Dawes, Lawrence had imagined physical intimacy between men. If Frieda fervently wanted to see her children, so perhaps did Lawrence, after the sustained intimacy of marriage, want a deeper intimacy with a man that would help assuage the angst he sometimes felt. Yet the bond he wanted, so difficult to define openly, was one that his marriage to Frieda did not seem ready to accommodate. He may not have been strong enough to insist on it; Frieda, despite her great tolerance, may have minimized his need for a supplemental emotional and physical fulfillment. Yet he needed it. Although the children slid a wedge between them, their quarreling developed partly from the unacknowledged conflict in that contested space between Lawrence's ability to define himself as potentially bisexual and Frieda's mild reluctance to accept that part of his nature. It is doubtful that, for all of their splendid openness, they ever directly confronted the critical difference that separated them. Instead, their quarrels may often have reflected their *un-*

*expressed* differences. It is no surprise that in July Lawrence could say to Constance Garnett's sister Katharine Clayton, "Frieda and I have quarrelled just as arduously as ever," and five days later, "Frieda and I are having a lull in the storm. I've no doubt the tempest will rage again soon."

By June their plans were firm. They would go to the Cearne for two weeks, where Constance Garnett could minister to them, then live by the sea for a month or so, after which Lawrence would attend his sister Ada's wedding in Eastwood while Frieda returned alone to Germany; her existence was still a secret from both his brother George, whom David Garnett thought a "Rasputin trying to be respectable," and his older sister, Emily, who would also have disapproved. These seven weeks would provide a social oasis in the couple's lonely isolation outside of England. In this oasis they would also meet two couples they would long regard with affection: Katherine Mansfield and John Middleton Murry, and Cynthia and Herbert Asquith.

At the Cearne the raspberries ripened, the air was fragrant with roses, and the house looked radiant in the early summer mist. At once Frieda warmed to Constance Garnett, and Lawrence welcomed the Cearne's homey distinction. On Monday, 7 July, Constance, sometimes disturbed by the Lawrences' arguing, wrote calmly to her husband, Edward, who now spent part of each week in London, that "L[awrence] and F[rieda] stay till Wed. when they propose going to Margate. . . . We have had a peaceful time— Lawrence very sweet—he is a nice person in the house—and F[rieda] rather trying—she won't let things drop. L[awrence] has been helping me by thinning the carrots." After Lawrence left the Cearne, he said mysteriously—but to Else Jaffe alone: "Garnett was awfully nice, but I don't like Mrs G." Something rankled. Fixed on translating Russian novelists, she had perhaps spoken bluntly. Yet Lawrence made complex demands on his friends, sometimes wanting an intensity of commitment that was unavailable, and he did not take criticism easily.

## Two Compatriots

On 9 July, Lawrence and Frieda went on their way to Margate, on the North Sea—not far from Dover—where for three weeks they took a small flat. They broke their journey to stop in London, where they met both Katherine Mansfield, who at twenty-four was three years younger than Lawrence, and her companion, John Middleton Murry, who was twenty-three. Both of them were enormously appealing.

Katherine had married George Bowden in 1909 but lived with him only a short while before she returned to her musical boyfriend, Garnet Trowell, by whom she had become pregnant; later she miscarried in Germany. Living with a disorder that for years she could not identify (it was

Katherine Mansfield and John Middleton Murry, c. 1914 (Courtesy of the Alexander Turnbull Library, National Library of New Zealand, Te Puna M tauranga o Aotearoa)

systemic gonorrhea), she was often ill. Responding in 1911 to Murry's call for contributions to a new quarterly magazine called *Rhythm* (later the *Blue Review*), which he helped found, she quickly joined him in his bold effort and, from Lawrence, enticed both a short story, "The Soiled Rose," and a pedestrian review of Thomas Mann's *Death in Venice*.

A 1913 photograph shows Katherine with a lovely face, shapely mouth and nose, dark liquid eyes, thick brows, and short dark hair. She dressed mostly in black and white. "I thought her so exquisite and complete," Frieda recalled, "with her fine brown hair, delicate skin, and brown eyes." Fond of intrigue, she also helped Frieda negotiate clandestine visits with the three children. Katherine's vibrant letters show her as passionate, romantic, lonely—and bitingly critical of others, her tongue like a razor. Her emotional insecurity made her attractively vulnerable but occasionally abusive. "Oh, I could lock you in a prison of my arms and hold you there— until you killed me," she wrote to Trowell in a typical letter of 1908. "Then, perhaps, I would be satisfied." Although Katherine lacked stamina and had published only one book of stories (*In a German Pension*, 1911), she was an accomplished stylist, always prepared to experiment with different tones and styles, to model voices and attitudes. She loved charades. She was more curious than her companion Murry, more committed to her art, more refined in her sensibilities—and a tougher critic. Like Lawrence, she was mostly self-taught.

Murry, an Oxford undergraduate when Katherine met him, was a small, square-jawed, good-looking young man, full of exuberance. Lawrence was immediately captivated. Murry had left Oxford with a second-class degree; had run up a printer's bill of £150, which he was paying off in installments; and, though ambitious and persevering, was now penniless. At least Katherine had an allowance of £100 a year from her rich banker father in New Zealand, although it could not support both of them; so Murry worked as a journalist for the *Westminster Gazette*. He was a capable writer—conscientious and versatile. Yet he was passive and surprisingly unsure of himself, displaying what Virginia Woolf called "a mania for confession." At first he welcomed the intense overtures of a more confident and productive writer like Lawrence.

The Murrys, who seemed "fearfully nice," had much in common with the Lawrences. Katherine and Frieda had left their husbands and were living with men to whom they were not yet married. Murry and Lawrence were commoners, hoisting themselves up on the ladder of talent and hard work. Katherine and Frieda were outsiders, Katherine a New Zealander, Frieda a German. Both women were exceptionally attractive; both revealed, adds Claire Tomalin, "the same streak of sexual anarchy." If Katherine and Lawrence were sometimes ill, defensive, and satirical, Murry and Frieda were healthier and more genial. The four of them looked upon themselves as rising stars, creating their own constellation above England's bourgeois horizons.

In London Lawrence and Frieda visited the Murrys at 57 Chancery Lane, and Murry remembered that "we rode in a bus to have lunch together in Soho, and . . . [soon felt] that we were made for one another." The Murrys (along with Gordon Campbell, an accomplished Irish barrister, tall and gaunt) soon came to Margate for the last weekend in July, bathed in the sea, and feasted on steak and tomatoes. As Murry recalled, "Lawrence was a really new experience. I was quite unprepared for such an immediacy of contact. In an astonishingly short time he knew all about me: all, at any rate, that I could tell him, and no doubt a good deal more. He seemed straightway to be taking charge of my affairs, unravelling the tangle. He . . . was very insistent that we should seize the opportunity of breaking away from England and coming to live beside him at Lerici in Italy." But the Murrys, though tempted, moved to Paris instead and did not join their new friends until 1916 on the desolate coast of Cornwall.

Like Frieda, Lawrence was adept at initiating friendships. While staying in Margate, he had written to thank Edward Marsh for a royalty check for three pounds (for the poem "Snap-Dragon," published in a volume of

*Georgian Poetry*) and invited him to call. A generous friend to artists, Marsh stopped by and, in July, wrote to his protegé Rupert Brooke about the Lawrences: "He looks terribly ill, which I am afraid he is—his wife is a very jolly buxom healthy-looking German, they seem very happy together." Scholarly and refined, Marsh took the Lawrences to tea at the home of his friends, Cynthia and Herbert Asquith, who were (thought Lawrence) "jolly nice folk—[he] son of the Prime Minister." Like Gordon Campbell, Asquith was a writer who had trained as an attorney, and he and Cynthia (who the next year would become Lady Cynthia) were at once more conventional and less complicated than the Murrys. Much has been made of Lawrence's flair for aristocrats, but he was intrigued for only a while and lost interest when he recognized that their social distinction did not penetrate to their mind or feelings.

The Asquiths treasured the Lawrences, who spent many hours in their company, talking, laughing, bathing in the sea, strolling on the sand under the white chalk cliffs, watching the gulls dip into the waves. Later, Herbert described Lawrence as "a brilliant talker, vivid, direct, unexpected, with a queer sardonic humour that was entirely his own." He often coined new phrases. From the start Cynthia admired Frieda: "Exuberant, warm, burgeoning, she radiated health, strength and generosity of nature." Frieda, in turn, found Cynthia "always a loyal friend, even through the war, when friends were rare." It might be thought that the Asquiths were too reserved and mild and discreet to be good companions. But Lawrence particularly admired Cynthia's strength, beauty, and clear-eyed intelligence. Her diaries show her to have been elegant and thoughtful.

Having attended Ada's August wedding to William "Eddie" Clarke (1889–1964), Lawrence returned to Germany by boat, sailing from London to Rotterdam on 7 August. "But I do miss Frieda," he confided to Katharine Clayton, whose son, Douglas, had become Lawrence's favorite typist. Meeting so many new people—the Murrys, the Asquiths, Marsh, Professor Walter Raleigh, Lord Elcho (Cynthia's father), the publisher W. H. Davies, Gordon Campbell, Grace Holman (Constance's sister)—he felt "worn out with whirling around." Frieda thought the trip had been good for him. It had boosted his confidence.

When they returned to Professor Jaffe's cottage in Irschenhausen, nestled in luminously blue Alpine mountains, to remain about six weeks more, they slept on the balcony, tramped through the pine woods at the back of the house, gorged on wild raspberries, and relished the cool purple gentians and autumn crocuses that sprinkled the meadows. While Lawrence waited restlessly to go on to Italy in September, he worked on a play, *The Widowing of Mrs. Holroyd*. He had read it to Frieda, he told Garnett. "It wants *a lot* of altering. . . . What a jolly fine play it is, too, when I have pulled it together." The play he rewrote is one of only eight he crafted during his lifetime—and one of the last works inspired by Eastwood's miners and their abusive relationships with their wives and children.

The play's most interesting biographical aspect is that it fuses the stories of the two women who still mattered most to Lawrence—his mother and Frieda—as they continued to help him sort out the kind of man he wanted to become. The outward straitened circumstances, full of domestic meanness, are Mrs. Lawrence's, but the courageous inward decision to leave an intolerable husband is Frieda's. The children, Jack and Minnie, are like Bert and Ada—frightened witnesses to their parents' discord. To her young rescuer, Blackmore, a skilled mine electrician the same age as Lawrence (twenty-seven), Elizabeth Holroyd cries: "I wanted to be a wife to him. But there's nothing at the bottom of him. . . . [There's] nothing that keeps him, no anchor, no roots, nothing satisfying." Although the play justifies their affection for each other, Elizabeth and her rescuer must share the guilt of Holroyd's death in the mines. Elizabeth imagines that marital strife caused a depressed Holroyd to linger behind the other miners and become trapped. Even so, Blackmore will return the next day and (one infers) soon take Elizabeth and the children to Spain.

The lingering weeks at Irschenhausen slipped by, Frieda less unhappy about her children now that she had at least seen them, Lawrence reworking some of his earlier stories for a collection. But he was eager to begin work again on "The Sisters." Refreshed, he began to tinker with it, sanguine that in his new coastal setting it would thrive. "I can feel myself getting ready for my autumn burst of work," he reported to Garnett in September, ripe with hope.

## "The Sisters" and Italy

Lawrence's move to his beloved Italy helped bring about the artistic change of "The Sisters." He would open himself in new ways. Though now only twenty-eight, he had embarked on twin adventures that would yield some of the happiest months of his life.

On 17 September Lawrence left Germany. From Irschenhausen Frieda had gone ahead to Wolfratshausen to see her sister Else. She wanted to visit her mother in Baden-Baden, then take a train to Milan, where she would meet Lawrence, who preferred to walk across Switzerland by himself, writing out slivers of "The Sisters" as he went. By the nineteenth he was floating down the Rhine River. By foot he went from Schaffhausen to Zürich— spending a mere three shillings a day—then, at a rapid pace, walked on to Lucerne, staying the night of 22 September in the charming Alpine village of Flüelen, on Lake Lucerne, before crossing the Saint Gotthard Pass (at seven thousand feet) toward Lugano and Como in Italy. Alone he walked thirty miles on 23 September through mountainous terrain, his stamina rarely flagging. On 26 September he met Frieda in Milan. He hated the city. Else's husband, Edgar Jaffe, who was staying on the Italian coast at the Albergo delle Palme hotel in Lerici, had started looking for a house that Lawrence and Frieda might like.

They were thrilled with the cottage they soon found in the tiny village of Fiascherino, near Lerici, and rented it for several months. Lawrence's spontaneous description, written to Garnett on 30 September, is worth quoting (though his sentences have been rearranged to make them coherent): "I am so happy with the place we have at last discovered. . . . It is perfect. One gets by rail from Genoa or from Parma to Spezia, by steamer across the gulf to Lerici, and by rowing boat round the headlands to Fiascherino. There is a little tiny bay half shut in by rocks, and smothered by olive woods that slope down swiftly. You run out of the gate into the sea, which washes among the rocks at the mouth of the bay. Then there is one pink, flat, fisherman's house. Then [higher up] there is the villino of Ettore Gambrosier, a four-roomed pink cottage among a vine garden, just over the water, and under the olive woods. There, D.V., is my next home. It is exquisite. The garden is all vines and fig trees, and great woods on the hills all round."

The furnished cottage cost a mere sixty lire a month, and the maid, Elide, only twenty-five more a month: about three pounds (or fifteen dollars) total. Elide lived in Tellaro, a fishing village twenty-five minutes away by footpath, along which Lawrence and sometimes Frieda, following the cliffs above the sea, would hasten to fetch the mail.

Across Lerici Bay lay San Terenzo, where the poet Shelley had once lived—the Lawrences could see his house—and the bay itself served as a naval arsenal. Frieda too recalled the pink cottage and the languid repose she felt there: "The cottage at Fiascherino had only three small rooms and a kitchen and I tried to make it look as cheerful as possible." They had their meals outdoors and from long walks returned only at dark, when they built a fire in the downstairs room. Sometimes, Lawrence would board a flat-bottomed boat moored in their little bay and row out to sea; on shore, Frieda watched like a hen and, in a rage, remembering that Shelley had drowned nearby, yelled at him, "If you can't be a real poet, you'll drown like one, anyhow." But mostly she spent lazy days lying in a hammock, watching the fishermen far below maneuver their red-sailed boats.

Alone while Lawrence wrote, Frieda quickly asserted her desire for freedom, and Lawrence surely had her in mind when he described Ella in a fragment from version two of "The Sisters": "A curious, rich lassitude kept her lying late in bed. . . . Ella sat in the sunshine, read, sewed, mused, and was happy." She rarely worked; "you know my reputation for laziness," she reminded Edward Garnett. When Lawrence was appalled by the cottage's dirty floors, he, not Frieda, got down and scrubbed them until the bricks flushed with a reddish hue.

In September, while they were still back in Irschenhausen, Lawrence had said to Garnett that Frieda is "cross with you, because you are cross with her." Garnett may have lamented her influence on "The Sisters." Lawrence added: "She says I've ruined her in everybody's estimation, by abusing her. I say I've only ruined myself." This exchange illustrates the ongoing friction that the Lawrences tolerated, and suggests that Frieda's willingness to compete with him for power sometimes led him to demean her to others. Then Lawrence's crux: "But I'll put her on a pedestal again." Presumably he meant to make amends in "The Sisters"—to interpret Frieda's character in prose as he rarely did, to her advantage, in person. He would exonerate her untrammeled passion.

For months, brooding over "The Sisters," Lawrence wondered how to incorporate the unknown to which Frieda had linked him. While he basked in the balmy Mediterranean weather, he began, after several false starts, to compose a second draft, of which today only seven printed pages survive. He was preoccupied less with recasting the first draft than reaching behind it, to discover the formative experiences of Ella, the character he later renamed Ursula Brangwen. To do so required a new kind of "interior" writing—no longer what the eyes saw but what the soul felt; no longer what other characters heard but what a character sensed behind the veneer of socialized consciousness. In 1913 this new emotional terrain in narrative had not been mapped. "The streets of London have their map; but our passions are uncharted," wrote Virginia Woolf in her novel *Jacob's Room*. In the new terrain the narrator *lost himself* in the act of exploring character. Narrative conventions were yielding to a kind of order, where Henry James's rules about point of view were being dismantled in just the way Georges Braque took apart the violin and the pitcher in his famous cubist painting of 1910.

Sitting on the rocks and listening to the music of the sea, then waiting for the setting sun to shake its milky gold and scarlet over the water, Lawrence sat out all day and, whenever he was moved, let the novel erupt from him. "It is *so* different . . . from anything I have yet written, that I do nothing but wonder what it is like," he told Garnett in October. Among the leaves robins sang all day, and for supper, when Elide was off, carrots simmered in butter might accompany their grilled steaks.

## Woman as Work of Art

Isolated, Lawrence and Frieda eagerly awaited their friends' letters. One day in October, Henry Savage, who had reviewed *The White Peacock*, sent along Richard Middleton's recently published *Monologues* (1913). The book elicited from both of the Lawrences a response that sharply clarifies the bold feminist ideas that Lawrence, braced by Frieda's daily conversation, was working out in "The Sisters." Two of Middleton's thirty-two skillful essays assess (simplistically) the suffragettes' demand that women abandon their role as subservient breeders. In "Why Women Fail in Art" he writes: "Men are born with the germs of character which they develop in passing from youth to maturity. Women are born with violent instincts, but with no character that they can call their own, and they spend their lifetime in endeavouring to acquire one." For Middleton that endeavor is unnecessary, since a natural woman expresses herself in her children, who are "her sonnets." In "The New Sex" he argues that for centuries men and women had effected a tacit compromise in which men were not to express emotion, women were not to think; that gains in education and jobs for women have negated this compromise and nurtured women's revolt against motherhood; and, finally, that women will soon join two opposed camps: "The one intellectual, energetic, independent, and supremely useless; the other emotional, affectionate, placid, and . . . motherly." A woman who wishes to be a man "is a fool."

To these reductive arguments Frieda responded forcefully, betraying not only her assumption that a woman should *naturally* be inactive, a support, an inspiration but also two further assumptions: that a woman, as a woman, can claim to be a work of art, and (though it sounds confused) that *equality* between the sexes could (in 1913) have saved a dissatisfied man like Middleton from suicide. She wrote to Savage: "I loathe my sex sometimes for being cowards and fools. . . . [W]omen should be satisfied to *be* and let the men *do*. We can *do* so much more *that* way—I hate the women for not having enough *pride* to be themselves[,] just their own natural selves, they must wrap themselves in false morals. . . . When M[iddleton] talks of women and art he is'nt quite fair, if a woman looks on herself as a work of art why belittle it? Is'nt that a form of aspiration, of perfecting herself, she may be stupid about it, but anyway she *tries*. But then, poor devil, he cant have met a girl, that was equal to him." It is clear that Frieda and Lawrence by now agreed that sexual dissatisfaction was the main source of crippled relationships, particularly in England: "It was really sex—unsatisfied sex—that killed him," Frieda imagined.

Lawrence's response, though aligned with Frieda's, is both more complex and more sweeping. He stresses physical satisfaction as the *sine qua non,* of course, but uses a surprisingly aggressive image to depict a woman's demands: "Frieda thinks they are stupid—Middleton's essays—particularly about women. I think myself he was stupid about women. . . . It seems to me that . . . in the long run [a woman] is not to be had. A man may bring her his laurel wreaths and songs and what not, but if that man doesn't satisfy her, in some undeniable physical fashion—then in one way or other she takes him in her mouth and shakes him like a cat a mouse, and throws him away." Seeking bold solutions to any problem he met, Lawrence, like Frieda, judged Middleton wrongly directed: "I think if you could have made him simply voluptuous, that would have been his salvation. . . . For it is so much more difficult to live with one's body than with one's soul. One's body is so much more exacting: what it won't have it won't have. . . . You should watch the free Italians, then you'd know what we've done. We've denied the life of our bodies, so they, our bodies, deny life unto us." Lawrence's critique of British civilization shows how far he had come. His critique rests on both Frieda's emancipation from middle-class codes of morality ("false morality" she calls them) and on his ability to free himself from a fixed home, regular employment, and the expectations of others.

Both, however, would have agreed with Middleton that in England the necessity of displaying "a wholly indecent reticence" toward sex makes writing about the body difficult. It is this reticence that Lawrence, warmed by the Mediterranean sun, was determined to crumble. As he reimagined "The Sisters," he listened for the "exacting" language of the body and sought for a way to elasticize reticent forms of expression without sacrificing his literary market.

One clue appears in a sentence that survives from version two of "The Sisters." Ella, ambivalently drawn to Rupert Birkin, begins to cry in agony, making "a sound she was unaware of, that came from her unproduced, out of the depths of her body in torture," after which she is cleansed and, restored to conscious awareness, confused with shame. Ella's journey inward to reach her "animal" instincts is like Lawrence's away from England to find an untrammeled voice for the deepest truths he had found. His response to Middleton's book was one of many preparations to map a road into the unconscious for his new fictional characters.

Some readers have thought that the new language Lawrence sought sprang from him like water from an opened valve. Yet he always worked in a context. A few months earlier he had read a new book by Jane Ellen Harrison called *Ancient Art and Ritual,* which seemed to him a revelation. "I got a fearful lot out of . . . *Art and Ritual,*" he confided to Henry Savage in December. Harrison, an acquaintance of Constance Garnett's at Newnham College, had proved her brilliance in the Philosophy Tripos of 1879 and had then studied archaeology at the British Museum. Her book, based partly on Sir James George Frazer's *Golden Bough,* inspired Lawrence to connect religion and art in fresh ways. She argued that great art blends "the individual and the general, the personal and the universal," which became one of Lawrence's overarching beliefs; she reinforced the value of a totem as an emblem of tribal unity (a forecast of the way Lawrence would link Will Brangwen and the hawk in *The Rainbow,* Gerald

Crich and the wolf in *Women in Love*), and most important, she argued that her contemporaries, having used science to conquer the world, were free to "trust intuition once again." In doing so, modernists could order the living tangle of experience by discovering "complexities of tone and rhythm hitherto unattempted." Harrison confirmed what Lawrence had already intuited. For the rest of his career these complexities of tone and rhythm would fascinate him.

As the autumn months slipped away, the Lawrences flourished in the Italian landscape and immersed themselves in the life of the peasants, who were welcoming and friendly. In the garden the fleshy oranges and lemons ripened, the last flowers blossomed, the dark olives dropped from the trees to be gathered. Occasionally Lawrence helped in the harvest. Elide, devoted and affable, cooked them two meals daily. She prepared the Italian staple *polenta,* which she made by sprinkling salted maize flour into boiling water until it thickened, and she concocted heavy pasta soups laced with strange vegetables such as *cardi* (like thistle stalks) and lots of local sardines. Desserts, requiring eggs and sugar, were a luxury. Frieda rented a piano, which was delivered by three men in a little bobbing boat, and she often sang folk tunes in her muscular voice. In the cool evenings, accompanied by the crackling of olive logs in the open fireplace, Luigi and Gentile, the peasants who lived in the pink cottage below the Lawrences', would sometimes come up, play the guitar, and sing their native songs. Sometimes all would gather to watch the battleships' eerie searchlights play in the harbor. "I love living by the sea," Lawrence exclaimed to his old friend William Hopkin in December, while Frieda purred to Arthur McLeod that "the freshness of this place, like eternal spring mornings[,] is amazing—and the food so jolly."

Excursions away from Fiascherino broke up the isolation of a couple who felt now, in Italy, "lost to the world." When the sea was calm, Lawrence would row Frieda over to Lerici. At the end of November, they were honored guests at a peasant wedding full of festivity and tipsy revelry. Occasionally they saw English friends such as Aubrey and Lina Waterfield, who lived twelve miles inland in a castle named Aulla; or visited the Pearses and the Huntingdons, both from Lerici, although Frieda poignantly records that after a time she said to Lawrence, "I don't want to be a fraud, let's tell them that we aren't married"; to which Mrs. Huntingdon, a staunch Catholic, replied: "I am fond of you both, and far be it from me to judge you, but I must tell you that I believe you are wrong, your life together is a mistake, a sin." Instead of being hurt, Lawrence said flippantly to Garnett: "When all our dark history comes out, I shall laugh." He was becoming as rebellious as Frieda.

Still, the nettles stung, and, though at a hearing on 18 October 1913 Weekley was granted a decree *nisi* (and custody of the children), Frieda was required to wait six more months for a final decree of divorce. When Christmas came, their only visitors were Elide's relatives, a dozen or so, who came on Christmas Eve to sing the Pastorella at midnight. Some weeks after Christmas came Constance Garnett, with a woman friend, to stay the winter months in Lerici, at the Albergo delle Palme. On 31 January 1914 she wrote to her son, David, that Lawrence "seems better—his voice much stronger and he doesn't cough—but he looks holloweyed and thin, of course. Frieda blooms like a rose."

Enchanted by his surroundings, Lawrence continued to labor over "The Sisters," which edged forward. Frieda valiantly encouraged him. "You are fighting the old standards, and breaking new ground," she urged when uncertainty spooked him; Constance Garnett reported, "He has plenty of pluck and is very industrious." On 30 December he told Garnett that the novel "is *very* different from *Sons and Lovers:* written in another language almost," and added on 6 January that the book's scheme had "widened and deepened." By the time he had finished 340 pages, the work had gained a fresh stillness, beyond struggle (he told Savage), deeper than change, penetrating to "the source, the great impersonal which never changes and out of which all change comes. I begin to feel it in myself." He had found a new stratum, a new surge of imaginative energy. He was relieved. The unknown had at last manifested itself. Yet he was troubled that readers might see his new fiction very differently from the way Frieda saw it. Would the public welcome the new "language" he had found?

# 6

# The Dawn of *The Rainbow*

## 1914

As 1914 unfolded, Lawrence alternated bursts of impassioned writing with the joy of days spent outdoors. He wrote as long as the unknown disclosed itself, then feasted on the many simple pleasures that Fiascherino offered. The wonders of Italy came in profusion. They were like blossoms before a frost.

One Saturday in February, he and Frieda boarded their little boat and spent the whole afternoon using a long, split cane to pry shellfish off the submerged rocks in the bay. They relished "the noise of the waves in the hollows, and the lift of the boat, and the sun and the smell of the things from under the sea." Even though they lived like princes on eight pounds a month—less than one hundred pounds (or five hundred dollars) a year—they gladly browsed among the rocks for their supper.

But also in February Lawrence realized that "The Sisters," although the second draft was nearly complete, would have to be rewritten. Suddenly "I knew it wasn't *quite* there," he told Mitchell Kennerley, the American publisher of his novels, on 7 February 1914. "And so I have begun it again"—the third version. This kind of exhausting revision became habitual. Two days later he told Arthur McLeod: "I knew that it just missed being itself. So here I am, must sit down and write it out again. I know it is quite a lovely novel really—you know that the perfect statue is in the marble, the kernel of it. But the thing is the getting it out clean." That was his new goal.

Lawrence invited Constance Garnett to read the old—and the fresh—versions while she spent the winter in Lerici. Very much like Lawrence, she had won a scholarship (to Newnham College, Cambridge, where she had excelled in the Classical Tripos), had taught for a term, had left teaching partly because of ill health, and could, writes her grandson, be both "gay and frivolous" but also "austere and almost puritanical." Lawrence valued her judgment, for she brought to her reading a rigorous training in Greek and Latin and her professional experience as a translator of Dostoevsky, Tolstoy, and Turgenev. She was also direct. On 24 February she told her husband, Edward, that she had offered Lawrence her reaction to his novel: "The characters aren't living at all, one doesn't believe in them, or take them at the author's apparent valuation. They seem simply invented to hang the pages of description of sexual experiences and emotions on to, and the theories about those emotions. And . . . the love part is ladled out so disproportionately that it isn't effective. It palls really because there's no light and shade. . . . Of course there are very good bits in it—and the underlying notion is good and strong—but it's so incredibly shapeless and inartistic—so sloppy in its presentation. I feel uneasy about his future if he can go off like that. But the new beginning he has made is very promising." Swept away by her dislike, she may have been tactless and hurtful in sharing her response with Lawrence, but her letter is important because it is one of only two reports that survive on the second version, the other being a report solicited by Kennerley. Her objection to the love part "ladled out so disproportionately" indexes her wish for a different kind of novel, the kind she assumed Edward would prefer; but she may also have been responsible for the quieter opening that Lawrence eventually wrote for his novel.

Lawrence worked on despite criticism, despite the days and days of spring rain that swept the Italian coast. The early narcissus, hidden among the rocks, and the anemones on the steep slopes sprang awake and shook in the March wind; almond and peach blossoms burst open like tiny mouths. Miming the deep urge to create, Lawrence hurled himself into version three, which he temporarily rechristened "The Wedding Ring" to reflect its evolution from a woman's character to the progressive socialization of her character. On 7 March he wrote to Henry Savage: "Does the spring unsettle you as it does me? Oh, the spring in Italy is the devil. You can feel the earth working with birth, and one's flesh is restless the same, and one's soul is worse."

The agony of creation sometimes made him want to lay down his pen and flee: "I wish I could just walk out of the house and into the hills, and on and on at my own sweet will." That was partly because Edward Garnett, still Lawrence's trusted mentor, had also criticized the second version of "The Sisters." Puzzled by Lawrence's rapidly evolving style, Garnett discerned three faults. First, he faulted the episode in which Ella used Ben Templeman to gain experience of men before she met Rupert Birkin. Second, he criticized the coherence of Ella's character—achieving coherence was always, for Lawrence as for Frieda, an artistic problem—compelling Lawrence at once to realize that he had unsuccessfully grafted Frieda's character onto Louie Burrows's. (Frieda's personal experience had not yet centrally anchored the novel.) And third, whereas Garnett still wanted "vivid scenes" like those he admired in *Sons and Lovers,* Lawrence did not: "I have to write differently," he insisted, capturing primitive forms of feeling and rhythmic changes in consciousness. "I am going through a transition stage," he added. He was composing scenes that required "everything vague." A contrarian, Lawrence would represent experience from another angle—its richness rather than its solidity, its subterranean texture rather than its concrete surfaces. He sought to represent the ebb and flow of the soul rather than the drama of personalities in conflict. Because his aim was new, it was difficult. He had no contemporary models to work from.

It is easy to imagine Lawrence and Frieda discussing the new novel, by turns irritated and grateful: Frieda recounting formative episodes in her life and imprinting the mark of her character on Lawrence's creative imagination, Lawrence prickly and cantankerous as he tried to control a novel that had already burst its banks.

In one of the best letters Frieda ever wrote—a response to Garnett—she gallantly took up Lawrence's cause (he was still too furious to write), examined her own motives, considered Garnett's criticism (without judging its merits, which she left to Lawrence), and, most important, reconsecrated herself as Lawrence's muse. She wrote at length:

> I have been so cross with you! You attacked me in your letter and I was cross but I am afraid you were right and made me realise my wrongs in a way—I had'nt cared twopence about L[awrence]'s novel; over the children I thought he was beastly, he hated me for being miserable, not a moment of misery did he put up with; he denied all the suffering and suffered all the more—like his mother before him; how we fought over this! In revenge I did not care about his writing. If he denies my life and suffering I deny his art, so you see he wrote without me at the back of him. The novel is a failure but you must feel something at the back of it struggling, trying to come out—

She quickly saw the importance of her undivided support:

> You see I dont really believe in *Sons and Lovers.* . . . It does not seem the deepest and last thing said. . . . I am going to throw my self into the novel now and you will see what a 'gioia' [joy] it will be—There is one triumph for us women, you men cant do things alone—Just as little as we can *live* alone. I have got over the worst, terrible part with E[rnest] and the children, so I shall enjoy L[awrence] writing—So dont pitch into me anymore, I have suffered very much for the love of men!

She offered, finally, a peculiar insight into Lawrence's continuing dependence on Garnett's judgment—it is the last time Lawrence will ever care so
much what another person thinks of his work:

I think it is rather nice of L[awrence] and intelligent to accept your criticism as he
does, because it is not easy to swallow criticism, but you need never be afraid . . .
because you are really the only man he has any opinion of . . . only your second letter was too cross, [though] perhaps it was a good thing too!

A good thing, she thought, because it compelled Lawrence to find "the
deepest and last thing said," the soul of the work that would reveal its religious core, where religious impulses and the unconscious were not
mingled but aligned, both saturated with mystery: for Lawrence, though
he knew (through Frieda) of Freud's work, rejected the scientific and
schematic dissection of the unconscious as too algebraic, too formulaic. "I
am not Freudian and never was—Freudianism is only a branch of medical
science," he told his London friend Gordon Campbell a few months later.
Freud crushed the butterfly while examining its wings.

Still confused and silent about Garnett's second letter, Lawrence had
gone on writing. To John Middleton Murry, who had written unexpect-
edly (having weathered Lawrence's haranguing letter about his character),
he confided on 3 April that he and Frieda were "really very deeply happy"
and that he had finished two thirds of "The Wedding Ring." In all, he had
drafted something like a thousand pages to reach the state where he understood what he had been "given" to say. "But now, thank God, Frieda
and I are together, and the work is of me and her, and it is beautiful, I
think." For fun Thomas Dunlop, the young British consul in Spezia, had
agreed to type the novel. Full of excited optimism, Lawrence asked him for
two copies—one for an English publisher and one for an American publisher like Kennerley.

## WOMAN TAKING HER OWN INITIATIVE

All the while, Lawrence had been mulling over Garnett's stiff-necked response. Though a mere eighty pages from the end (another two weeks'
work), Lawrence decided to define his stance with fresh precision. Now
that Frieda's resistance to him had muted and his depths could flow more
fully into the novel, he was sure it was "a big and beautiful work" that reflected them both. Sharply defensive when he wrote on 22 April 1914,
Lawrence made two points. First, he resented Garnett's insulting assessment of the novel's substance, an attack that appeared to parrot Constance
Garnett's patronizing assertion that Lawrence lacked nobility:

I am not after all a child working erratically. All the time, underneath, there is
something deep evolving itself out in me. And it is *hard* to express a new thing, in

sincerity. And you should understand, and help me to the new thing, not get angry and say it is *common,* and send me back to the tone of the old Sisters. In the Sisters was the germ of this novel: woman becoming individual, self-responsible, taking her own initiative. But the first Sisters was flippant and often vulgar and jeering. I had to get out of that attitude, and make my subject really worthy. You see—you tell me I am half a Frenchman and one-eighth a Cockney. But that isn't it. I have very often the vulgarity and disagreeableness of the common people. . . . But primarily I am a passionately religious man, and my novels must be written from the depth of my religious experience. That I must keep to. . . . Mrs Garnett says I have no true nobility—with all my cleverness and charm. But that is not true. It is there, in spite of all the littlenesses and commonnesses.

Lawrence vigorously measured his distance from the "father" whose respect he craved. It was as if Garnett had jeered at the author rather than at the work he had produced—a common failing among teachers. So Lawrence's second point is that he resented Garnett's disrespect for him as a man: "And that is why I didn't like the second letter you wrote me about the failed novel, where you rubbed it in: because you seemed to insult my real *being.* You had a right to go for my work, but in doing that, you must not hold *me* cheap in your own eyes."

For Lawrence, Garnett's criticism was tainted by his *ad hominem* arguments, although (to be fair) Lawrence invited that kind of response by stressing the way the revised novel contained "both of us." At bottom, Lawrence finally resented the Garnetts' class snobbery (very much alive in their son's description of Lawrence) and regretted that their snobbery diminished the value of their artistic judgments. Demeaning his working-class origins, they supposed that his new form of fiction lacked artistry. Because both copies of the typed manuscript have disappeared, we cannot judge the validity of their response. But Lawrence's sudden insight severed his relationship with the Garnetts; only its thin shell would remain. And although he could never forgive their arrogance, he would always remember their generosity and kindness. When he wrote again on 6 May, a little uneasy, he sincerely hoped his letter had not "hurt anybody." He had stated only what was necessary.

Now that he had nearly completed the novel, he needed to find publishers in England and America. All along he had assumed that Duckworth would publish it; indeed, he owed them another book. But to save Garnett trouble, Lawrence had earlier asked James B. Pinker (1863–1922) to act as his literary agent, and Pinker, approaching the London firm of Methuen, had secured for Lawrence a handsome advance on the novel's English rights— £300 (£150 on receipt of manuscript, £150 on publication). It was a sum "my heart aches after," Lawrence admitted. It tempted him (he reminded Garnett) because "I *must* have money for my novels, to live." "It is wearying to be always poor, when there is also Frieda," he added on 16 May.

J. B. Pinker, who spoke hoarsely in a Scottish accent, had become a literary agent in 1896 and had effectively represented Joseph Conrad, Stephen Crane, and Arnold Bennett. His round cherubic face, poised on a trademark bow tie, belied his professional savvy. Frank Swinnerton called him a "clean-shaven grey-haired sphinx." Lawrence would retain Pinker as his agent until 1919.

As June, the month of their departure, approached, the Lawrences decided to go to England, Lawrence walking most of the way through the mountains of Switzerland with an engineer named A. P. Lewis, Frieda going to Baden-Baden for two weeks of family visits. Her divorce decree, made final on 27 April, led her to hope that Weekley would now feel less injured—he had written her a milder letter on 9 May—and that he would allow the children, after all these months, to visit their mother. Gordon Campbell, an Irish barrister whose wife was away from London, had invited the Lawrences to stay in his South Kensington house. And although Lawrence, fed up with the legal system, informed Savage that a marriage "is after all only an impersonal matter, not a ceremony, but a mere legal contract," he and Frieda hoped to be married in London.

Meanwhile, the late Italian spring yielded its abundant treasures—wild orchids, rose-colored gladioli, ranunculi in bud, orange trees in full flower, and trees of acacia that opened like moonlight. Around their cottage the Lawrences had planted beds of anemones, and as Frieda wrote to the Waterfields on 8 May, "now they are just a joy of red and blue and cream with stripes." Lawrence added, "You have no idea what excitement it has been, going out to watch them every morning, and watering them every night." Creation was in the air.

About this time a flower of a different sort arrived from London. Ivy Low (1889–1977), a twenty-five-year-old novelist, gushed with enthusiasm. She had adored *Sons and Lovers,* written Lawrence a fan letter, and been invited to visit him in Italy. Staying with them in their pink Fiascherino house, she helped make marmalade, talked with Lawrence by the hour, accompanied him on his walks, was surprised by Frieda's passivity, and, although astonished by Lawrence's insights into other people, minded his dogmatic statements and his faultfinding. (Later, she thought him an incorrigible snob.) Through Ivy, he would soon meet two of her friends—Catherine (Jackson) Carswell and Viola Meynell—who would be vitally important to him in the years ahead.

In mid-May, on the eve of World War I, Lawrence finished his biggest novel yet, which had become not only long but also, he said, at times improper. After the Garnetts' apostasy, he needed support. From Frieda he got a major boost—a new and better title. On 9 May he explained to Garnett: "Frieda wants the novel to be called *The Rainbow.* It doesn't look it at first sight, but I think it is a good title." To Murry, who would in time prove even more apostate than Garnett, he added: "Can you understand how cruelly I feel the want of friends who will believe in me a bit. People think I'm a sort of queer fish that can write: that is all. And how I loathe it. There isn't a soul cares a damn for me, except Frieda—and it's rough to have all the burden put on her." Although Lawrence exaggerates, it is useful to remember his insecurity as he concluded his long work.

As the Lawrences were packing to leave Fiascherino, Garnett's second response to *The Rainbow* arrived. Like his wife, he was blunt. Still unsympathetic, he thought the psychology wrong. He wanted the novel to develop the "lines" of certain characters, as, indeed, some months later, he would reject (for Duckworth) James Joyce's *Portrait of the Artist As a Young Man* as "too discursive, formless, unrestrained." But now Lawrence was firm. Answering on 5 June, he retorted that since he sought now to represent the *nonhuman* elements in humanity, he was bored by the old-fashioned moral consistency of Tolstoy and Dostoevsky. He was more interested, he added, in what a woman *is* than what she *feels*. From the "futurist" artist F. T. Marinetti he had learned about the possibility of applying the laws of physics to emotional states, and so he drew upon the Chladni sand figures that he had perhaps seen demonstrated in college to suggest the way his characters' lives, properly represented, would create a rhythmic form "like when one draws a fiddle-bow across a fine tray delicately sanded, the sand takes lines unknown." His conception starts not with a scheme to be imposed (as in Thomas Hardy's novels) but with a series of intuitive glimpses into the characters' psyches, which are then harmonized with the narrator's fluid "map" of the world as he understands it—both then transformed simultaneously into language. The glimpse is deeper than before; the map is more radically subjective.

A more contemporary way to understand Lawrence's artistic aim is to draw on *chaos theory*, according to which random patterns replicate themselves at different scales: the jagged shoreline would, if drawn, reveal in miniature the pattern of the whole continental coast. In *The Rainbow* Lawrence connects the heavens and the underworld to his central character Ursula Brangwen—not as a simple link but as a replication of their energy. The rhythmic motion of tides and earth's rotation courses through Ursula, defines her deepest responses, and arouses her sexual fire. In chapter 11, for example, the wedding dancers among whom Ursula mingles form "a vision of the depths of the underworld, under the great flood." Soon, Ursula observes the moon observing *her*. The narrator says: "Out of the great distance, and yet imminent, the powerful, overwhelming watch was kept upon her . . . balancing all in its revelation." Ursula herself is the revelation of replicated energy, and despite her Midlands cultural history, she is the conduit of cosmic mystery. This replication of energies, distant yet imminent, manifests the workings of chaos theory in fiction long before it was articulated by mathematicians. It complements Lawrence's explanation that he traced his characters' egos through allotropic states of the same element, as diamond and coal are states of the pure single element carbon.

With great speed Lawrence was refining his vision. A comparison of Virginia Woolf's novel *The Voyage Out* with Lawrence's *Rainbow*—both were published in 1915—shows how bold he was. When Anna and Will stack the sheaves of grain, Lawrence brilliantly explores the complexities of tone and rhythm that Jane Harrison had anticipated in *Ancient Art and Ritual.* As Anna and Will work together and apart, "coming and going, in a rhythm, which carried their bodies in tune," drifting and ebbing like a wave, ever more closely, Lawrence sexualizes rhythm in a new way—not as Woolf does, with recurrent images of fear and loss, which sweep over her protagonist, Rachel, but with a firm link between personal and impersonal, human and celestial. In Lawrence's experiment with language, rhythm becomes one of the *technical* routes into the human unconscious. Locating layers of intuition and instinct that neither he nor his characters could name, his novel acquired extraordinary depth. Although he and Woolf never met (she glimpsed him twice), they would have in common several friends—Ottoline Morrell, Bertrand Russell, Dorothy Brett, and S. S. Koteliansky. These friends Lawrence and Frieda were about to meet.

The novel finished, a typescript completed, the Lawrences were ready to depart from Italy, staying away (they imagined) until October. The summer heat had already commenced. Had Lawrence divined what lay ahead when Archduke Franz Ferdinand was assassinated in Sarajevo and the conflict between Austria-Hungary and Serbia ignited into a European war, he and Frieda would never on 8 June have left their beloved pink cottage, perched like an impregnable castle on the cliffs of the Mediterranean.

## MARRIAGE

Although Lawrence disliked England, it offered opportunities that Italy did not. In England he could collect his early stories into book form; he could meet a dozen or so new friends, some of whom would become allies for life; he could, later on, imbibe the aura of Cambridge University; and in London he and Frieda could at last be legally joined. But after the war began, the Lawrences began a long slide downward, not into mere conflict but into emotional chaos.

On Monday morning, 13 July 1914, at the registrar's office off Kensington High Street, the Lawrences welcomed the long-awaited wreath of marriage. Frieda remembered Lawrence dashing out of the cab to buy her a new wedding ring: "I gave my old one to Katherine and with it she now lies buried in Fontainebleau." Although Frieda cared nothing about marriage, she thought Lawrence very glad they had now become "respectable married people." He wrote to Sallie Hopkin: "I don't feel a changed man, but I suppose I am one." Their witnesses were Gordon Campbell, with whom they were staying, and John Middleton Murry. Afterward they stood for a photograph that shows the married couple, flanked by Murry and Katherine, looking unperturbed. This moment, in retrospect, was one they surely savored.

Marriage brought Lawrence a new sense of responsibility toward Frieda's children. Still sequestered in Hampstead, they posed a daunting problem, which involved, said Lawrence, "scenes with indignant aunts" who had blackened the children's memories of their mother. On 17 July, while Lawrence prepared to visit his younger sister, Ada (living now with Eddie Clarke in the village of Ripley, a few miles from Eastwood), he wrote sadly to Garnett: "Frieda isn't going with me to my sister's. She is persisting in her efforts to get hold of the children. She has seen them—the little girls being escorted to school by a fattish white unwholesome maiden aunt who, when she saw their mother, shrieked to the children—'Run, children, run'—and the poor little things were terrified and ran. Frieda has written to her mother to come. I *do* hope that old Baroness will turn up in a state of indignation. Then we shall see sparks fly round the maggoty Weekley household." Frieda hoped to appeal to Weekley himself, to milk the affection he once felt for her.

Lawrence, his confidence high, worked steadily. While Methuen looked through the typed pages of *The Rainbow,* Lawrence revised twelve short stories for a collection that Duckworth—who had earlier refused to match the three hundred pounds that Methuen offered for *The Rainbow*—was now happy to publish. The Duckworth collection would include some of the best stories Lawrence would ever write: "Odour of Chrysanthemums," "Daughters of the Vicar," "The Shadow in the Rose Garden," "The White Stocking," and "The Prussian Officer." By October Lawrence was already correcting the proofs. Two months later an unsigned review in the *Outlook* called the stories brilliant and superhuman—and full of abnormal personalities: "All their thoughts are thought at a white heat. Their hates are of the corrosive kind. Their passions are volcanic." The reviewer had accurately sensed Lawrence's new fictional direction.

In London, Lawrence and Frieda met four new friends who, over the coming years, would prove unusually loyal: Catherine Carswell, Amy Lowell, Richard Aldington, and S. S. Koteliansky. Two of them, Carswell and Aldington, would later compose biographies of Lawrence. A neighbor of Ivy Low's, Catherine Carswell (1879–1945) was a middle-aged Scottish novelist who, when Lawrence met her in June, had just finished writing a novel (published in 1920 as *Open the Door!*). Enthusiastic about his fiction, she asked Lawrence for his criticism. He obliged by providing "thousands of notes and comments and opinions in the margin." He and Catherine met for a discussion and became friends for life. Tall, with brown hair; well read and well traveled; admirably sane and practical; once married to a man who had gone mad; and soon to marry again, Catherine lived in an old townhouse in Hampstead and reviewed novels for the *Glasgow Herald*. In her unpretentious home she made the Lawrences comfortable. Later, when she wrote about him in 1932, she remembered his "deep-set jewel-like eyes, thick dust-coloured hair, pointed underlip of notable sweetness, fine hands, and rapid but never restless movement."

Like Catherine, Amy Lowell (1874–1925), a plump, well-to-do imagist poet from Boston, admired Lawrence's work. When she visited London in July, she invited the Lawrences to dine with her in her elegant Berkeley Hotel suite where, at an elaborate meal, Lawrence met her friends Richard Aldington and his striking wife H.D., both imagist poets. Handsome and virile, Richard (1892–1962), then only twenty-two, was assistant editor of the *Egoist*. It was an avant garde magazine that, every other week, published (for instance) poetry by Lawrence and Amy Lowell, a serial novel by James Joyce, criticism by Dora Marsden and Ezra Pound, analyses of cubism by Wyndham Lewis, and studies of futurist music. In June appeared a fine essay by Aldington himself, called "Modern Poetry and the Imagists," in which he identified his wife's poem—beginning "The hard sand breaks, / And the grains of it / Are clear as wine"—as illustrating the imagist tenets of "hard, direct treatment, absolutely personal rhythm, few and expressive adjectives, no inversions, and a keen emotion presented objectively." A discussion of such tenets Lawrence would have found provocative.

Even though London's activity was stimulating, the English countryside beckoned. In July Lawrence was invited to join a walking party (fashionable at the time) of four young men. A. P. Lewis, a Londoner with whom Lawrence had crossed the Alps in June, may have proposed a foot tour of the Westmorland hills, where, at Barrow-in-Furness, his parents lived. To make a foursome, he may have invited two men who worked at the Russian Law Bureau: William K. Horne, who slipped quietly from Lawrence's orbit, and S. S. Koteliansky, who in time became Lawrence's most loyal and trusted correspondent. In appearance Koteliansky (1880–1953) was Lawrence's opposite. Broad-shouldered and powerful, he had dark, close-set eyes, a strong nose, and thick black hair brushed up and back. Although he spoke directly, even vehemently, he also liked to have fun. Leonard Woolf, Virginia's husband, remembered his "passionate intensity and integrity"—traits that Lawrence admired. A bachelor, Koteliansky had left the Ukraine in 1911 as a political refugee. At his basement flat on London's Acacia Road, he was both an orderly housekeeper

S. S. Koteliansky

and a good cook who in a flash could stir up mashed potatoes, sour herring, and very hot Russian tea. May Sarton, who knew him well, called him "the most *whole* man I ever knew."

When these four young men emerged from their rural jaunt on 5 August, they were stunned to find that war had been declared. Not for six months could Lawrence, writing to Cynthia Asquith, bear to sketch the scene of a holiday turned to madness: "I had been walking in Westmoreland, rather happy, with water-lilies twisted round my hat—big, heavy, white and gold water-lilies that we found in a pool high up—and girls who had come out on a spree and who were having tea in the upper room of an inn shrieked with laughter. And I remember also we crouched under the loose wall on the moors and the rain flew by in streams, and . . . we shouted songs . . . and I pranked in the rain on the turf in the gorse, and Kotilianski groaned Hebrew music—Ranani Sadekim Badanoi. It seems like another life—we *were* happy—four men. Then we came down to Barrow in Furness, and saw that war was declared. And we all went mad." He concluded poignantly: "The War finished me: it was the spear through the side of all sorrows and hopes." He went numb, intuiting the horror and devastation to come. In a little-known meditation entitled "With the Guns," published in the *Manchester Guardian* on 18 August, Lawrence concluded: "My God, why am I a man at all, when this is all, this machinery piercing and tearing?" Guns had no humanity.

## ANYTHING BUT THOMAS HARDY

Lawrence and Frieda were fortunate to have made so many new friends during their weeks in London, for in August the onset of war altered the economy and of course publishers' decisions. Alarmed, Constance Garnett wrote to her son, David, in September, "There will be a slump in books, no publishing, no reviewing going on—Duckworth says he shall publish nothing for 3 months." Strict economies would be demanded. Lawrence and Frieda would have heard similar reports from friends such as Murry and Aldington who earned their livelihood in publishing. Koteliansky, Lawrence said, faced "short wages, like the rest of us." An emergency was at hand.

These altered conditions explain why Lawrence did not vehemently protest Methuen's return of his *Rainbow* manuscript in October. They explain why he was willing to revise the novel still again before publication. Presumably Pinker, his agent, had written him that, in this state of emergency, Methuen may have been uneasy about publishing new books (in fact, Algernon Methuen had astutely ordered enough paper to print fifty thousand copies). It is likely that E. V. Lucas, Methuen's chief reader—and a director of the Methuen firm since 1910—sent along some pithy comments about what Lawrence called the novel's "flagrant love-passages." Revision must have seemed simpler than a contentious struggle, not least because Lawrence may have recognized that, without revision, the novel was probably unpublishable. Lawrence would never have bragged, as did his contemporary Arnold Bennett, that "[m]y first draft is always the final writing." Still, revision demanded time. In August Lawrence wrote to Pinker: "Here is a state of affairs,—what is going to become of us? You said Methuen signed the agreement for the novel—did he give you the cheque [for £150] at the same time? I ask because I am wondering how I am going to get on. We can't go back to Italy as things stand, and I must look for somewhere to live. I think I shall try to get a tiny cottage somewhere, put a little bit of furniture in it, and live as cheaply as possible. But to do that even I must know there is a little money coming from somewhere. . . . We can't stay here much longer." An alarm had sounded. Because of the war, even Frieda's parents could no longer send money.

As fast as they could, the Lawrences left London. In mid-August Gilbert Cannan, a novelist they had met through Murry, arranged for them to rent—for six shillings a week—a secluded country cottage in an orchard near Chesham. Located about thirty miles from London, and an hour by train, it was "tiny, but jolly," Lawrence observed bravely. He scrubbed and whitewashed the upstairs bedrooms while he and Frieda ate off the land—consuming eggs and cheese and bacon, and buckets of blackberries from the hedgerows. Frieda made excellent jelly.

After Gilbert and Mary Cannan brought novelist Compton Mackenzie for a Sunday afternoon visit in late August, Mackenzie wrote a fictionalized account that captured (or so he said) Lawrence's brusque treatment of Frieda and her gutsy assertiveness:

"Roll off that bed and come down, d'ye hear? The [Cannans] have turned up. Come on down and talk to them while I get tea.". . . He had wavy reddish hair and exquisitely delicate white hands. . . .

"I'm coming, [Lawrence]; don't be in such a state of excitement," [the visitors] heard in guttural accents of unvexed good nature. . . . She was a typical figure of Germanic womanhood, dressed in a floppy dress of some light material, her fair hair inclined to collapse like a badly made stook, her white teeth glittering in a wide smile, her forget-me-not blue eyes dancing with pleasure.

"I'm so glad you've come over. . . . [Lawrence] would scrub the floor, so I had to go and lie down.". . .

"Sit down and talk while I get tea," [Lawrence] commanded. He retired to the little kitchen at the back, and his wife plumped down with legs apart on a stool, bidding her guests accommodate themselves. . . .

"It will be a long long war," [she] declared. "My country is very strong. Much stronger than the English imagine. . . . I am a German woman, and I cannot help feeling proud of our German soldiers. . . . And it is quite wrong this English idea that we have begun the war," [she] went on . . . having to emphasize every statement. "I do not say the English have led Germany into a trap, though it is very easy for Germans to think so, and with them the hypocrisy of the English is famous. No, I do not quite blame the English for that. But what could Germany do when Russia has mobilized to interfere for this nasty little Serbia? We must be mad to allow such a thing."

Such bravado was alarming. But everywhere talk of war arose, much of it distressing to the Lawrences. On 6 August the Prime Minister, H. H. Asquith (Lady Cynthia's father-in-law), and his cabinet had approved sending the British Expeditionary Force, a small, well-trained professional army, to support the French. On 7 August Lord Kitchener, who alone expected a lengthy war, called publicly for 100,000 volunteers and got a fast response. On 22 August hostilities opened; the next day the Germans defeated the French army at the Battle of Charleroi in Belgium; on the same day, at Mons, the Germans killed 330 British soldiers. In the next three months the French and British forces were driven back to the outskirts of Paris, and at the Battle of Ypres alone the British Expeditionary Force suffered 50,000 casualties. Closer to the Lawrences in Chesham, four German cruisers on 16 December bombarded the coastal towns of Scarborough, Hartlepool, and Whitby, killing forty civilians and wounding hundreds more. Lawrence, reporting the news to Amy Lowell, said acidly, "I tell you the whole country is thrilled to the marrow, and enjoys it like hot punch." According to the war historian Martin Gilbert, the bombardment handed Britain a propaganda victory: "Henceforth the Germans were portrayed as the 'baby killers' of Scarborough." Propaganda against the evil "Hun" caught fire.

As Lawrence and Frieda fretted about the war, their money dwindled. Methuen's £150 advance, from which Lawrence was awaiting the final £50, would not last much longer, even if he and Frieda scrimped. The Lawrences were close to panic. Mary Cannan having written around about their distress, the playwright Alfred Sutro sent them £10, as did Edward Marsh. The kindness of novelist Maurice Hewlett brought an unexpected boon. Sponsored by Hewlett, Lawrence on 14 October was granted £50 by the Royal Literary Fund. For a few months the wolf could howl elsewhere. But if Lawrence was less than delighted, that may be because he knew that Joseph Conrad, accomplished though he was, had received RLF grants of £300 in 1903 and £200 in 1908, not to mention a Civil List Pension of £100 a year in 1910.

In the autumn Lawrence began writing a small book on Thomas Hardy, which a man named Bertram Christian had solicited for a series on contemporary writers, each volume to be fifteen thousand words. Although Lawrence's advance would be only £15, he told Edward Marsh the exercise might be stimulating. At once Marsh, ever generous, sent Lawrence the complete works of Hardy. Overjoyed, Lawrence danced about the room, frantic at the cost, until Frieda calmed him by saying, "'Never mind— never mind—take them—how lovely—oh how I shall revel—let him give them you.'"

Never before had Lawrence written a critical study. When he began it in September, while the "colossal idiocy" of the war framed his thinking, he saw that the book would be "about anything *but* Thomas Hardy." Lawrence was too sensuously creative to write a disciplined account of Hardy's work. (In fact, his book was not published in his lifetime.) Yet it is a vitally important work because Lawrence, as he studied the preeminent novelist of his day, hoped to understand Hardy well enough to accomplish three goals.

First, he hoped to use Hardy as a way of working out the critical principles that he could apply to another novelist's work. In 1932 Catherine Carswell pointed out that "though he was a valuable and astute literary critic, his critical point of view was not 'literary,' as the word is usually understood. He read that he might find out what the writer would be at, and having found out, that he might expound it to the writer. . . . It was this, with his astonishing patience, his delighted recognition of any sign of vitality and his infectious insistence upon the hardest work, that made him unique among critics. . . . If the writing under consideration was by an acknowledged master [like Hardy] it was just the same." Just the same because Lawrence (in Catherine's words) still concerned himself with "divining and revealing the underlying stream of life." That last phrase signifies what really interested Lawrence. He saw that each of Hardy's characters, manifesting a surging vitality, "suddenly bursts the shell of manner and convention and commonplace opinion, and acts independently, absurdly, without mental knowledge or acquiescence." The words "without mental knowledge or acquiescence" look tempting as a description of Lawrence's new conception of character. In truth, they are misleading. For it is *because* Ursula Brangwen really *thinks* in chapter 12 of *The Rainbow* that she can look at Wiggiston Colliery and, though recoiling in disgust from its capitalist underpinnings, defy "the great machine which has taken us all captives," or in chapter 15 pronounce the university "a little, slovenly laboratory for the factory." Lawrence's characters often analyze perceptively, but always with their feelings blended into their thought processes. For Lawrence the split between feeling and thought, initiated by Plato, was philosophy's worst legacy.

Moreover, Lawrence hoped to transcend Hardy's thematic dualities of social *versus* natural law, as they occur for instance in the conflict between Hardy's Alec d'Urberville and Alec's natural wife, Tess. Lawrence did not want to choose between but to reconcile opposites such as law and love, seeing them as equal truths, as a necessary *condition* of human life. In Keith Sagar's apt words, "Law and Love are the systole, diastole of the human heart." What unifies them is what Lawrence calls the Holy Ghost.

Finally, Lawrence hoped to separate his own fictional practice from Hardy's, and so identify what was unique in his own technical resources. From Hardy, for instance, he learned how (not) to construct a scene. He learned not to use plot revelations as springboards to human change (as

Hardy does in *Jude the Obscure*), because this form of causality seemed mechanistic, imposed from without. Rather, Lawrence learned to bring a scene to its height of emotional tension, then to use gestures of conciliation such as "Come here" or "He . . . touched her delicately" to drain tension and lead to closure. In other words, he learned to use a character's internal emotional life, as it sways rhythmically back and forth—now irritated, now enamored—to help him construct a novel like *The Rainbow*.

In Chesham the autumn of 1914 came cold and clear, like a smart slap, briefly awakening Lawrence and Frieda from the misery of the war. "We are not sad any more," he told Amy Lowell in November. "Now the days are brief but very beautiful: a big red sun rising and setting upon a pale, bluish, hoar-frost world." But by December the rainy, dark weather seemed hideous. "My dear God, I've been miserable this autumn," he cried. Coughing ominously, Lawrence was often ill with a lingering cold. The damp climate aggravated his bronchial condition. He was sliding into an emotional collapse that neither he nor Frieda could contain. It was a spiritual slump like none he had borne before.

# 7

# Crisis

## 1914–15

Lawrence had changed. The next year held the promise of a completed novel, fascinating friends, and a joyous marriage ripening into commitment. Yet the war—hostile to his ideals of personal liberty and social regeneration—had altered his feelings, had made him liable to outbursts, rages, tirades. To Gordon Campbell he railed against the "hideous stupidity of war" and the blow it heaved at sensitive people like himself. From this wound to his psyche, which festered for four years, came a rush of concentrated anger. An issue of *Poetry* "put me into such a rage," he told its editor, Harriet Monroe. Writing to Catherine Carswell on 31 October 1914, he apologized for "my tirades." On 18 November he told Koteliansky, who had come for a visit: "I hope you don't mind my tirades of Sunday." And Frieda told Amy Lowell that whenever Lawrence thought of Mitchell Kennerley, who had cheated him out of his *Sons and Lovers* royalties, "he gets in a rage with *me*." He was becoming a crucible of riled emotions.

Lawrence had changed in other ways too. He grew a red beard—a shield behind which he could take cover, a beard so warm and complete that it was like a skin over his nakedness. Much that is foolish has been written about Lawrence's beard, but it seems to have had two purposes: it was a bright badge of hostility to the war, and it signified a new maleness that his writing, from *Study of Thomas Hardy* forward, would exhibit—its stance more aggressive, its tone more definite, its themes more defiant.

Living so close to London, Frieda determined to scrap her role as the mother who had abdicated. She would accost Professor Weekley in Nottingham and, by her personal presence, coerce reasonable visiting rights. Feeling insecure, she persuaded Lawrence to go with her. On 5 December they went together to Ripley, about five miles from Eastwood, to stay with Ada and Eddie Clarke. A few days later, Frieda went to Nottingham and waited for Weekley, announcing herself to his landlady as "Mrs. Lawson." But the meeting was not a success. To Koteliansky Lawrence reported that "Frieda saw her husband—he was . . . quarrelsome—nothing decided." Because self-righteous people hate to be challenged, it is no surprise that Frieda's efforts yielded disappointment. To Amy Lowell, Lawrence gave "verbatim" the divorced couple's conversation:

"You—" said the quondam husband, backing away—"I hoped never to see you again."

Frieda: "Yes—I know."

Quondam Husband: "And what are you doing in *this* town."

Frieda: I came to see you about the children.

Quondam Husband: Aren't you ashamed to show your face where you are known? Isn't the commonest prostitute better than you?

Frieda: Oh no.

Quon. Husb.: Do you want to drive me off the face of the earth, Woman? Is there no place where I can have peace?

Frieda: You see I must speak to you about the children.

Quon. Husb.: You shall *not* have them—they don't want to see you. . . . If you had to go away, why didn't you go away with a *gentleman*?

Frieda: He is a *great* man. . . .

Q. Husb.: Don't you know you are the vilest creature on earth?

Frieda: Oh no. . . .

Q. Husb.: Don't you know, my solicitors have instructions to arrest you, if you attempt to interfere with the children.

As vile and painful as this sounds, it is likely that Frieda pressed her case much more forcefully than Lawrence has allowed. She would surely have argued that depriving the children of contact with their mother irreparably damaged their emotional health. In fact, Monty and Elsa were already siding with their disappointed father.

Against this cruel disappointment the Lawrences planned a gala Christmas Eve party. Weary of so much unrest, Lawrence felt (he said) like "kicking everything to the devil and enjoying myself willy-nilly." Koteliansky came to help Frieda, bringing with him cakes and two bottles of chianti. They prepared a succulent feast—boiled ham, roasted chickens, baked desserts, punch—and decorated the cottage with holly and sprigs of mistletoe. To this event came the Murrys (who lived at Lee, three miles away), the Cannans (who lived nearby in Cholesbury), the barrister Gordon Campbell, the young painter Mark Gertler, and Koteliansky (the last three from London). After the feast they went to the shaky-floored attic to dance and then to sing songs. Frieda remembered Koteliansky singing a mournful Hebrew song. "This occasion," she lamented later, "was the last time for years that we were really gay."

In the late autumn Lawrence, when not disheartened by the war, had been recasting *The Rainbow*, which Methuen had earlier returned. "I am working *frightfully* hard—rewriting my novel," he told Koteliansky. It needed only a final polishing, he told James Pinker when he sent the first hundred pages to be typed. (Although Amy Lowell had presented Lawrence with a Smith Premier typewriter in November, he was too busy writing to prepare a typescript; apparently Frieda could not do so either, though her efforts would have saved them money.) Lawrence anticipated finishing by the end of January. With the £150 that Methuen would then owe him, he would go to Italy. "I am tired of this country, the war, the winter." But other options might be needed. Ivy Low's friend Viola Meynell had offered them her cottage at Greatham in Sussex. By 5 January 1915 Lawrence had completed three hundred pages. As he warned Arthur McLeod, still teaching at Davidson Road, "It'll be a new sort of me for you to get used to. . . . I am coming into my full feather at last." He could not have anticipated how quickly his crowing would end.

Then a surprise. By 7 January Lawrence had decided, he told Pinker, to split the book into two volumes: "it was so unwieldy [in one]." If the first volume portrayed two sisters and their backgrounds, the second could focus on a pair of men who were *like* brothers. The two novels would be complements.

While his decision to split the novel gave him space to flesh out earlier generations of *The Rainbow*'s Brangwen family, Lawrence was also imagining a comparable location for himself and his friends. This ideal community he called Rananim. It was Koteliansky's Hebrew word to describe a concept of communal living which Lawrence increasingly saw as a solution—not so much to war or evil, but to the modern predicament of personal isolation and bureaucratic regulation. A small colony of twenty compatible souls might, Lawrence believed, band together for support and end their haggling with outworn institutions. "We will have no more *churches*," he proclaimed on 1 February. "We will bring church and house and shop together." In advocating this goal he may have been naive and idealistic. Yet many of his new friends also seemed adrift, discontented, ripe for a meaningful experiment in collective friendship.

Two of these new friends, well established and more stable than most, were looking to enhance the quality and intimacy of their own personal lives. Lawrence hoped that one of them, Lady Ottoline Morrell, might, with her immense power and influence, "form the nucleus of a new community which shall start a new life amongst us." This new life, based on integrity of character, would emphasize "the known, eternal good part in us." This titled woman commanded awe. Why?

Apart from Frieda, Ottoline Morrell (1873–1938) was perhaps the most extraordinary and flamboyant woman Lawrence would ever meet. David Cecil, an Oxford don who knew her well, said she spoke "in curious slow sing-song tones that rose up and down the scale from treble to baritone." The Duke of Portland's half sister, she had grown up at Welbeck Abbey, in Nottinghamshire, not far from Eastwood—a tall, lonely girl with an angular face and long, prominent nose, who wore exotic long dresses. After her marriage to Philip Morrell in 1902, she became increasingly fascinated by writers, painters, and assorted artisans. Leonard Woolf thought her "highly sexed."

In 1913 she and Philip, who was the son of an old Oxford brewing family (and a Liberal M.P.), bought a Tudor estate five miles from Oxford called Garsington, which they restored and redecorated over the next two years. Before repairs, the estate cost £8,450. With 360 acres of farmland, two farmhouses, and six cottages separate from the manor house, Garsington was a dream, a pacifist's haven—or a conspirator's den, depending on the stance of those who congregated there before, during, and after the war. Ottoline was its high priestess—benignly autocratic, full of lavish dispensations. The means of entry was accomplishment, the currency of exchange was impassioned talk, the outcome was a flurry of close attachments. Yet a busy black market of gossip often tarnished Garsington's inspired camaraderie. Ottoline's sympathy for others was genuine; her kindness and gallantry were enchanting. Lawrence thought her *"really nice."* At one time she even offered the Lawrences a cottage on her estate. Her weekend parties, with good food served attentively; with intensive talk about books and writers; with clever charades and sprightly dancing to Philip's pianola; with swimming followed by long strolls through the park; with lawn chairs beckoning under the ilex tree—all of these made an invitation to Garsington a plum to be savored. But Ottoline also plumbed a curious resentment in her guests. Her biographer Miranda Seymour concludes that "her need for [affection] drove her to lavish gifts and hospitality on those she loved in such a way as to put them uncomfortably in her debt." Her ardent friendship could be crippling.

Lawrence and Frieda met Ottoline in August; they were invited to lunch on 21 January as they left Chesham. At 44 Bedford Square in Bloomsbury, Ottoline maintained a salon where they met the cultured E. M. Forster (1879–1970), who was the same age as Frieda. Timid, well bred, reticent, and avowedly single, Forster secretly shared Lawrence's sexual ambiguity, having published several heterosexual novels but also in 1914 having completed a novel of homosexual love called *Maurice*—suppressed until 1970.

Garsington Manor, home of Lady Ottoline and Philip Morrell (Courtesy of Adrian Goodman)

(As Lawrence would discover, same-sex erotic relationships, even veneered with the narrator's disapproval, were invitations to legal action.) Enjoying the modest leisure that an inheritance bestowed, Forster, when he sent Lawrence a letter, must have wondered about his friend's class origins, no doubt intrigued by his broad Midlands accent, for on 28 January Lawrence replied: "I don't belong to any class, now. As for your class, do you think it could tempt me? If I'm one of any lot, I'm one of the common people. But I feel as if I'd known all classes now, and so am free of all. Frieda is a German of good family—in Germany she thinks herself very aristocratic. I have known Lady Ottoline's servants—gate keepers and cooks—at home. . . . Now I know Lady Ottoline. . . . And for each class, the other class seems to hold the secret of satisfaction. But no class holds it." Lawrence's fictional characters also break out of class confines, less to repudiate class distinctions than to enlarge their sense of personal freedom.

But before he and Frieda could know Lady Ottoline or Forster well, he found that he would be unable, during wartime, to return as he hoped to Italy. Instead, he gratefully accepted Viola Meynell's offer of her spacious cottage at Greatham, located on the eighty-acre family compound of her famous Catholic parents, Wilfrid and Alice Meynell, whose friends included Tennyson. Viola had a fine cameo face, like a doll's. The Lawrences, leaving Chesham on 21 January, spent two days in London, then went to Greatham, about forty-five miles southwest of London. Because the compound lay at the edge of the south downs, four miles from the nearest train station at Pulborough, the Lawrences would get full use of their walking shoes. A day after they arrived, Lawrence reported to Kotiliansky: "We got here safely last night, after a wonderful long drive in the motor car through deep snow, and between narrow hedges, and pale winter darkness. . . . The cottage is rather splendid—something monastic about it— severe white walls and oaken furniture—beautiful. And there is [a] bathroom and [hot water]. . . . I must say I love it." New places were usually full of allure. A few days later Frieda, having now *two* spare bedrooms, issued a warm invitation to their Russian friend: "Do come—and as the fare is so dear you are *not* to bring us anything—We are rich here, no rent, Viola wont even let us pay the servant—there is just the food, that's all—You will love it, it is so beautiful and white." Freed from paying rent, the Lawrences stayed at Greatham for six months, until 30 July.

Lawrence came to think of the winter months at Chesham as a time of exile, when he was ill tempered and unhappy, like "a corpse in its grave clothes." But as he approached the end of his rewritten novel, he grew more sanguine, and the beauty of the Sussex downs helped to raise his spirits, "the wind blow[ing] ripples on my blood," he told Kotiliansky, "as it rushes against this house from the sea, full of germination and quickening." The image of germination, of acorns falling down and opening new shoots, provided Lawrence with the closing image of *The Rainbow*. On 1 February he told Pinker that he had completed 450 pages (out of 700) and would "certainly be done by the end of this month." Like Thomas Dunlop before her, Viola Meynell had kindly offered to type the novel. Given its content, Lawrence knew that she would be "safer" than an agency typist and asked Pinker to return the manuscript pages in his possession.

As promised, Lawrence finished his novel by 2 March 1915 and laughed to Viola that now it was "off and away to find the pots of gold at its feet." Algernon Methuen wanted to include it in his autumn list, which would feature twenty-three new novels, so Viola (assisted by poet Eleanor Farjeon) worked diligently and finished the typescript on 29 May. But although Lawrence was a dreamer and increasingly a political revolutionary, he was nonetheless a tough realist, both unsentimental and savvy. When Frieda's father had suffered a stroke and then died on 29 January, Lawrence muttered, "You didn't expect to keep your father all your life." Now he said to Viola, "Tell me which parts you think the publisher will decidedly object to." Whether or not she did, Lawrence revised, sometimes extensively, her typescript, surely with one eye on Methuen's anticipated reaction. Lawrence responded to Frieda's comments, too, for on page 594 of the typescript Frieda scribbled, "Commonplace this!!" beside the words "in contrast with the corncrake in the summer grass, and the moon that shed down"—which likely led Lawrence to delete them.

Some weeks later, writing to Pinker, who wanted to see the fresh typescript, Lawrence framed his savvy differently, as a matter of honor and personal integrity: "I hope you are willing to fight for this novel. It is nearly three years of hard work, and I am proud of it, and it must be stood up for. I'm afraid there are parts of it Methuen won't want to publish. He must. I will take out sentences and phrases, but I won't take out paragraphs or pages." Lawrence was frightened. He had to protect his characters and *their* integrity; but he was penniless. "I heard the wolf scratch the door today," he told Pinker on 24 February. His strategy was therefore to censor his novel only to the point where Methuen would not *refuse* to publish. More than once he must have wished he could gauge Methuen's threshold of tolerance. Lawrence would not, however, have known that, since a mysterious illness in 1907, Algernon Methuen sometimes came to the office only one day a week.

## A ROMANCE IN THREE GENERATIONS

The novel that Lawrence sent to Pinker on 31 May, for immediate typesetting, is a historical novel. Chronicling three generations of the Brangwen family, Lawrence based it loosely on the Louisa Burrows clan. Still, he did not compose the novel chronologically but started with the third generation and worked back to the first. He adapted some of his and Frieda's most intense early experiences but braided other materials with them, so that the biographical strands are carefully disguised.

The third generation, which follows Ursula Brangwen from her birth in 1883 to her escape from college at the age of twenty-one, adapts many of Lawrence's experiences: for instance, Ursula's struggle as a spiritually confused adolescent, her rapid disillusionment with her professors' sham knowledge, her battle to teach well in a school that mechanized children and teachers more than it empowered them, and her need to slough off a parasitic lover. Frieda's early experience is also a well of inspiration. Like Frieda's father, Ursula's father, Will, set his heart on her and made her his own, criticized the way she trampled his seed beds, taught her to swim, and fought her attempts to break free of convention. As their collective early experiences merge within a single character, Lawrence creates Ursula from the angle of recollection. With superb artistic confidence he records the central episodes of her life. As she comes painfully to maturity, trying to adapt her sensitive intelligence to a hard and unresponsive society, she carries forward the challenge of woman becoming individual, self-responsible, courageous.

But she does more. Despite her inexperience, she embraces the feminist challenge of winning a place in the world of men without losing her gender identity. "For her . . . the liberty of women meant something real and deep." Ursula is a woman who confronts barriers without yielding her self-respect—or the reader's sympathy. Sensitive, proud, strong, Ursula rejects the "Sunday" world as one that obscures real mysteries with false religious myths. She acknowledges the authority of her teaching supervisor, Mr. Harby, without submitting to his will; she disciplines an incorrigible student without losing her own tenuous authority over her class; and she scrutinizes her colleagues and her dismal urban surroundings with unflinching rigor.

She can never forget the deepest call of her being: "Had she not come to hear the echo of learning pulsing back to the source of the mystery?" In order to hear this pulsing echo, she must dissect, sometimes brutally, her contemporary society—its religious scruples, its narrow morality, its embalmed professors. Nor will she spare her own shortcomings of imprudence, selfishness, and impatience. In a vicious Darwinian world she will survive. Unlike her fictional contemporaries, such as Forster's Lucy Honeychurch or Bennett's Hilda Lessways, Ursula brings to her task quick intuition, close observation, and a hotly critical stance.

Ursula's romantic life is equally full of challenge. Lawrence offers her two kinds of love, neither of them sanctioned by her society. At the age of fifteen Ursula acts upon her strong attraction to men when she meets her cousin Anton Skrebensky, a young man of twenty one, "with greenish gray eyes, a slender figure, and soft brown hair," clearly modeled on Frieda's cousin Kurt. It is no surprise that both men's lips feel as soft as butterfly wings. However, Ursula's sexual life soon "flamed into a kind of disease within her." In a chapter labeled "Shame," Winifred Inger, Ursula's college physical education instructor—muscular, athletic, and strong loined—offers Ursula an intimacy offensive to some readers. This lesbian encounter, superficially pleasurable, slowly—over several months—shakes Ursula free of feeling constrained by social or religious taboos. Yet she is also repulsed by Winifred, who resembles "moist clay, that cleaves because it has no life of its own." In some disturbing spiritual way Winifred is sterile. No longer intrigued by same-sex desire, Ursula, now a mature twenty-two, returns to Skrebensky for a deeper intimacy. The frank and sensuous physical details that describe their relationship alarmed the novel's first critics. Writing in the *Daily News* of 5 October 1915, Robert Lynd thought the book "a monotonous wilderness of phallicism."

But many years after the novel's publication, what still surprises is the intensity with which Ursula links her sexual consummation to the moon, her body's tumultuous craving seeming to rise up to the heavens, where she seeks a mysterious confirmation of her identity. In a letter to Henry Savage of 15 November 1913, Lawrence had defined sex as "the fountain head, where life bubbles up into the person from the unknown." Now he embodied this definition in a paramount scene in which "she turned, and saw a great white moon looking at her over the hill. And her breast opened to it, she was cleaved like a transparent jewel to its light. She stood filled with the full moon, offering herself. Her two breasts opened to make way for it, her body opened wide like a quivering anemone, a soft, dilated invitation touched by the moon. She wanted the moon to fill in to her, she wanted more, more communion with the moon, consummation."

This is the language of passion that Lawrence was crafting into a tool of revelation. His incantatory rhythms imply Ursula's goal. What she seeks is the impersonal force that courses through Skrebensky's body, but of which he is just the agent, just the husk around a potent vitality. She seeks what Lawrence once said all of us must seek: "Behind us all," he told Gordon Campbell in 1914, "are the tremendous unknown forces of life, . . . destroying us if we do not submit to be swept away." This powerful sentence holds a key contradiction: it requires those who seek truth to acknowledge their powerlessness against tremendous unknown forces while it demands their courage to undergo radical cleansing from within.

As Ursula learns to submit to radical change, she attempts to reach the limits of human experience, to go to the edge of the crater that is the Unknown, to peer in as far as possible before the ropes of rational knowledge hold her back. It is her uncanny second sight that sets her apart, makes her so critical of those around her, whose conceit blinds them to the blurred shapes hiding at the far edge of human awareness:

> This world in which she lived was like a circle lighted by a lamp. This lighted area, lit up by man's completest consciousness, she thought was all the world: that here all was disclosed for ever. Yet all the time, within the darkness she had been aware of points of light, like the eyes of wild beasts, gleaming, penetrating, vanishing. . . .
>
> She could see the glimmer of dark movement just out of range, she saw the eyes of the wild beast gleaming from the darkness, watching the vanity of the camp fire and the sleepers; she felt the strange, foolish vanity of the camp, which said "Beyond our light and our order there is nothing," turning their faces always inward . . . , ignoring always the vast darkness that wheeled round about, with half-revealed shapes lurking on the edge.

Impressed by Hardy's view of the unfathomable cosmos, Lawrence may have composed this passage of startled recognition in December 1913 when, after visiting the Waterfields at Aulla, he wrote to Lina that (in her paraphrase) "[i]t seemed to him as though wild beasts were circling round a fire and he was filled with a feeling of apprehension." Ursula develops Lawrence's insight. This tearing of the veils of secrecy, this sudden revelation of truth, sets Lawrence apart from contemporaries like Conrad and Woolf and prods him to look into the wild beasts' eyes, to recognize their energy and their fascination, and to trace the path they light into a central enigma of human existence: *how to reconcile what we know with what we feel*. For Lawrence, intuition is always prepared, if unhampered by rational prejudices, to strike the optimal balance between oppositions that are hard to reconcile. Whereas Conrad despairs at the loss of an underlying unity that would illuminate daily life, and whereas Woolf seeks unity in immediate sensory experience, Lawrence glimpses something beyond the mind that knowledge cannot reveal but that intuition, residing in the blood, can. He aims to show the way.

In one way Ursula's quest can be faulted. Because she is young and responds to stimuli so passionately, she sometimes fails to ask *why* her college lecturers were dull, or *why* Nottingham University College had been co-opted by a materialist society, or *how* her pastoral and agrarian assumptions led her to indict her uncle's coal operation in Wiggiston. In later novels Lawrence's more profound critique will appear.

At the novel's close, the rainbow that Ursula envisions, which harbors her hope for a man of strong character coming direct from God, is reinscribed into the two earlier generations. They too search for expression. Ursula's mother, Anna (also the name of Frieda's mother), passionately seeks the adventure into the Unknown, as intimated in the scene of her rhythmic stacking of oat sheaves, but too soon she yields to her role as breeder. Ursula's father, Will, though he also seeks the adventure in marriage, finds the church irresistibly attractive and settles too easily for a symbolic consummation in the cathedral's Gothic arch, which bears a social rather than a personal profundity. His soul flowers in religious icons. An organist and (like Louie's father, Alfred Burrows) a craftsman in wood, he strives for consummation in music, stained-glass windows, and wood panels of Adam and Eve. Within these limits he achieves a measure of fulfillment. It is not that Anna and Will fail but that they acquiesce to conventional satisfactions such as rearing children, enjoying varied forms of conjugal sex, and becoming accepted members of their society. They never transcend the roles prescribed for them.

Ursula's grandparents, Tom Brangwen and Lydia Lensky, born in the 1830s, were a different sort of generation. They were opposites meshing uneasily. In this way Frieda's personal experience was pivotal; for whereas Tom Brangwen is an agriculturalist attuned to the rhythms of the seasons, Lydia is, like Frieda, an outsider—a Polish woman, well born but without money, widowed rather than divorced, whose husband, like Otto Gross, was a doctor educated in Germany who had "great ideas of himself." Like Frieda, Lydia brings to the marriage a child (Anna) from her first marriage and is six years older than the man she marries. Their courtship, revealed in magical prose, reflects the simpler organization of nineteenth-century agrarian life, as when Tom, during Lydia's childbirth, takes Anna away from the house and calms her distress with the soothing sounds of the barn: "The child shrank, he balanced stiffly, rested the pan on the manger wall, and tipped out the food, half to this cow, half to the next. There was a noise of chains running, as the cows lifted or dropped their heads sharply; then a contented, soothing sound, a long snuffing as the beast ate in silence." In this first generation the rainbow is the imagined arch of connection between dissimilar cultures and personalities. Recognizing that the title "The Wedding Ring" no longer fit the third generation, Lawrence substituted "The Rainbow" because it had the power to connect earth and sky in an arch of hope, which matched the arch of conjugal connection that Tom and Lydia had built, and echoed the way Will Brangwen's religious experience in the cathedral was "spanned round with the rainbow," all three generations thereby folded into a unity. This massive, calming frame helped to stabilize Lawrence's emotions, which were gyrating in confusion.

## DIFFICULT FRIENDSHIPS

While Lawrence waited for his novel to be typed, set, and printed, he and Frieda—besieged by their poverty and the war—entered into a period of stressful friendship with others: with Forster, Ottoline Morrell, Koteliansky, David Garnett, and the intellectual giant Bertrand Russell. The culmination of it all was a crisis in which Frieda decided in May to have her own place in London. Lawrence, torn by his conflicts, felt betrayed.

In the difficult early months of 1915, Lawrence's relationship to Frieda changed. As he became more belligerent, he roused her to become more aggressive. And as the war advanced, her German ancestry made her own position more uneasy. Coincidentally, their good friend Koteliansky seemed to her not just to admire but to idolize Lawrence. As a result (she wrote on 19 February), she felt discounted and marginalized: "You think I do not count besides Lawrence, but I take myself, my ideals and life quite as seriously as he does his—This you will not allow, and it is our quarrel, you think I am conceited, I cant help that—but it hurts me very much when you think I do not count as a human being—But you do not think much of women." Still, at Lawrence's urging, Koteliansky continued to visit regularly, Lawrence always walking to meet him. Frieda apparently got used to his dislike, tolerated Lawrence's friendship, and exercised forbearance.

E. M. Forster, pale and modest, and as slight of frame as Lawrence, came to Greatham on 10 February and stayed for three days. It was a long visit. Lawrence considered him "very nice" yet, given his own turbulent state of mind, felt strangely antagonistic, annoyed by Forster's reserve. He exhorted him to express his manhood in the immediate physical action of taking a woman and thereby rediscovering himself. This was not advice that could be useful to a closet homosexual like Forster. That Lawrence recognized his friend's sexual preference is unlikely; it is equally unlikely that Forster, who believed that Lawrence "ignored his own homosexual side," would have divulged his own secret.

As Lawrence confided to Bertrand Russell on 12 February, he and Forster "were on the edge of a fierce quarrel all the time. He went to bed muttering that he was not sure we—my wife and I—weren't just playing round his knees: he seized a candle and went to bed, neither would he say good night. Which I think is rather nice." Some days later, on 24 February, Lawrence wrote to Mary Cannan that Forster's "life is so ridiculously inane, the man is dying of inanition. He was very angry with me for telling him about himself." Distressed by Lawrence's directness, Forster would have been offended by the imputation of waste, of settling too calmly for a stifling domestic life with his mother, Lily. In his diary Forster later voiced his hurt pride when he wrote that Lawrence "makes me feel that I am in a bad state. . . . I regret I cannot know him."

Like Marie Antoinette, Lady Ottoline herself sallied out for a day in the Sussex countryside, arriving at Greatham on 8 February and bringing along her confidant (and lover) Bertrand Russell (1872–1970), a small, witty, brisk man. The middle-aged son of an earl—whose promised appearance Lawrence found rather alarming—and the godson of Victorian philosopher John Stuart Mill, Russell had coauthored *Principia Mathematica* (1910–

13) and for many years enjoyed the exclusive society of the Cambridge Apostles, who met every Saturday for supper and erudite conversation. Unhappily married, he had channeled his disappointment into his scholarship and become "a sort of logic machine" until, in 1911, he met Ottoline Morrell, who with her bountiful love unleashed some of his ardent curiosity—and prepared him indirectly to appreciate a man like Lawrence.

Russell and Lawrence had many points of kinship. Both passionately committed to radical ideas, both pacifists, both at the height of their powers, they got on well together, despite Russell's shyness, and they struggled to make coherent the developing drama of Lawrence's Rananim community. Soon Lawrence, whose inner life simmered with stress, exhorted Russell to join him in the cause. Having observed the miserable lives of Eastwood's miners, having watched the Murrys struggle and flounder, and having himself felt the pinch of poverty as his reward for extraordinary discipline and hard work, Lawrence was incensed by Britain's unequal distribution of wealth: "But we shall smash the frame. The land, the industries, the means of communication and the public amusements shall all be nationalised. Every man shall have his wage till the day of his death, whether he work or not, so long as he works when he is fit. . . . Till then, we are fast within the hard, unliving, impervious shell." The "shell" is a variation of Ursula's lighted circle, to be smashed by the deeper echoes whose pulsing Lawrence could hear but whose relevance he could not yet shape into a program of social reform.

Russell, uplifted by Lawrence's visionary intensity, admired both his friend's habit of challenging assumptions and the energy and passion of his feelings. He invited the younger man to visit him in Cambridge for the weekend of 6–8 March, to see the ancient stone buildings and to meet the influential (if inscrutable) G. E. Moore and the brilliant economist John Maynard Keynes. Lawrence harbored some doubts. He worried that Russell patronized him: "I don't want you to put up with my talk, when it is foolish, because you think perhaps it is passionate." He implored Russell to "tell me when I am foolish and over-insistent." He must also have wondered if, at Cambridge, he could swim in that chilly cerebral sea. "Truly," he confessed on 2 March, "I am rather afraid." Elated at having finished *The Rainbow*, Lawrence nonetheless envisioned an outpouring of intellectual fellowship.

Yet the two thinkers faced an immense philosophical difference. Lawrence, relying largely on intuition, wanted a revolution of *sensibility*, something finally personal and interior and difficult to state; Russell, a rationalist and a logician, wanted a *social* revolution that would eliminate the need for war and (in his biographer's words) give people "more control over their lives, in politics as in work." Before long, these differences would develop into acrimony.

## A MATTER OF LIFE AND DEATH

Even though the visit to Cambridge was an extraordinary adventure for Lawrence, it was also disastrous, tinged with trauma. Partly Lawrence was put off by the elitist attitudes he encountered. But mostly he was stunned by having to confront, for the first time in his life, openly homosexual men. He was forced to see a side of himself that generated horrible homophobic anxiety. He looked at same-sex desire and recoiled in horror, as if he were Conrad's Kurtz looking into the pit of human degradation. Lawrence's soul had spoken when he wrote to Russell: "But sometimes I am afraid of the terrible things that are real, in the darkness," as if Ursula's "wild beasts" had come, lurking and prowling, into his ken. It is not enough to claim that Lawrence excoriated what he hated in his own nature. He knew it was there, but still he had no mode for expressing its "reality"; and without Frieda to anchor him, Cambridge had threatened his manhood, and made him come perilously close to the "dark passions—the subterranean universe . . . [that] I can't escape."

In his crisis Lawrence was made to confront the Dark Unknown in a new way, to acknowledge now (to Ottoline) that the darkness he had canonized contained evil. This surprise came to him first in a way hidden even from himself: it was followed by a grand seizure of repudiation.

Couched within Lawrence's letters is the predictable association of homosexuality and death. Cambridge sodomites such as John Maynard Keynes, the bookseller Francis Birrell, and the Bloomsbury painter Duncan Grant confounded him. Keynes, two years older than Lawrence, may have had a genius for economics but to Lawrence, who visited him in his rooms, he smelled morally foul as he stood there in his pajamas at midday; he was one of those who "must die" before they can rise. Braying that his recent appointment to the Treasury was a pleasure (his war work earned him six hundred pounds a year), Keynes lunched uneasily with Russell and Lawrence on 7 March. Says Keynes's biographer, Robert Skidelsky, "Both Russell and Lawrence attributed Keynes's frivolity to the 'sterilizing' effect of homosexuality."

But Lawrence soon sharpened his response. On 24 March he imagined a rat, slithering along in the dark: "I must always want to kill it," he thought, because it contained the principle of evil that he had envisioned "so plainly in Keynes at Cambridge," who, spreading contagion, had touched him, as if poisonously. But in a letter to Koteliansky Lawrence added curiously that Dostoevsky, too, whom he was reading, was "like the rat, slithering along in hate, in the shadows, [while] . . . professing love." And since (as we saw) Lawrence could not escape the dark passions of the subterranean universe, it is a surprise that he says about Dostoevsky: "I even feel a sort of subterranean love for him." The language is coded. If Lawrence can feel a subterranean love for the rat Dostoevsky, it is arguable that he felt something strong and potent, even if blocked, for the rat Keynes. His uneasiness turned to terror, for Keynes had acted out a nightmare of two men copulating.

This purblind sense of identification shocked Lawrence to the core. He remembered what had happened to Oscar Wilde. Accused of homosexuality by the Marquis of Queensbury for a crime described by the *Echo* of 6 April 1895 as "too horrible and too revolting to be spoken of even by men," Wilde had been sent to Reading Gaol for two years. Afterward he left for France, to die ignominiously. Part of Lawrence's nature revolted against the identification, and he sought to eradicate it in himself and in the sexually ambiguous David Garnett, who had for a while (unknown to Lawrence) been Duncan Grant's lover. "I have had a great struggle with the Powers of Darkness lately," he acknowledged to Ottoline on 8 April. He then generalized the insight that he could have applied to himself: "we refuse to acknowledge the passionate evil that is in us. This makes us secret and rotten." The passion that is rotten is Lawrence's unacknowledged alignment with men such as Francis Birrell and Duncan Grant, both of whom had been *Keynes's* lovers. These homosexuals made him dream of a biting beetle, like a scorpion, which (in his dream) he twice killed. In associating beetles with lust, Lawrence followed Dostoevsky, who in *The Brothers Karamazov* claimed that God gave insects "sensual lust." Frightened, he clung to Ottoline as a heterosexual protectress: "Dear Lady Ottoline, remember we must stick together. It really seems to me a matter of life and death." Using this frame, he implored young David Garnett to leave these homosexual "beetles," grow whole, love a woman, and marry her. In part it was Lawrence's own solution.

Brenda Maddox makes what appears to be a useful distinction when she tries to clarify Lawrence's homosexual panic: "But Lawrence was not, like Forster, a suppressed homosexual who did not have the courage of his desires. He is not so neatly categorized. Rather, he was a hypersensitive man unable to bring together the male and female components of his personality, and in the grip of a terror of losing the boundaries of self. In those weeks of collapse after Cambridge, Lawrence drew an almost psychotic picture of loss of identity . . . [and] he linked this death of self to homosexuality." Maddox is right to say that Lawrence cannot be neatly categorized, but her assertion that he could not unite male and female components of his personality misstates his difficulty. Having never acted on his homosexual impulses, Lawrence did not know the *nature* of same-sex passion. He feared the result. If he acted on his impulses, he might (he suspected) *become* homosexual. His anxiety was acute. Keynes, openly and rapaciously homosexual, parodied the kind of bond Lawrence had in 1911 innocently imagined between Cyril and George in *The White Peacock*, where, in a chapter called "A Poem of Friendship," male bodies that touch arouse not physical desire but affectionate love. Almost certainly Lawrence had never experienced, with another male, a sexual encounter that led to orgasm: he wanted (or at least *thought* he wanted) this experience to be Platonic, much as Clive Durham in Forster's *Maurice* insists to his lover "that their love, though including the body, should not gratify it," the sexual act becoming thereby "inexcusable" between men.

For Lawrence the polarities that matter now are not male/female components but fear of exposure and hope of protection. That is, he feared what might happen to him if a relationship with a man turned physical, yet he hoped that desire for a woman might remain wholly fulfilling and thereby offer protection. There is uncertainty, there is anxiety, there is blockage, but there is neither schizophrenia nor psychosis. For homosexuals the "coming out" process follows fairly consistent stages. In the first stage, writes Eli Coleman, individuals protect themselves with "denial, repression, reaction formation, sublimation, and rationalization" to avoid the crisis of confronting their feelings directly. Yet only by acknowledging same-sex feelings can this conflict be resolved. Lawrence struggles helplessly at this first stage. As he says of Ursula's affair with Winifred Inger, "It was the closed door she had not strength to open." Closure brought safety.

The power and difficulty of Lawrence's personal struggle are revealed in the revisions he made to the typescript and proofs of *The Rainbow*. In the examples below, he heightened certain homosexual characterizations of Uncle Tom Brangwen (canceled words appear in square brackets [ ], added or substituted words in pointed brackets < >):

"She could see him . . . bestial <, almost corrupt PROOFS>"
He "was handsome, with his [fine MANUSCRIPT] <womanish
    TYPESCRIPT> colouring"
He exuded a "[subtle MANUSCRIPT] <secret PROOFS> power"
He was "[loudly-dressed MANUSCRIPT] <effeminately-dressed TYPE-
    SCRIPT>"
Hidden was "[the grosser mould of his features MANUSCRIPT] <the
    strange, repellant grossness of him PROOFS>"

And when Ursula learns that Uncle Tom and Winifred have become lovers and will marry, the narrator makes Ursula's response more potently moral: "Their marshy, bitter-sweet [corrosion MANUSCRIPT] <corruption PROOFS>" gives her nausea. At the end of the novel, focusing now on Ursula, Lawrence preserved this thematic undercurrent by replacing "the brittle, marshy foulness of the old corruption" with the more neutral "the old, brittle corruption of houses and factories"; "marshy" and "foul" occupy the fetid ghetto of homosexuals. What such passages show is that Lawrence demonizes those qualities that he loathed in himself—partly for self-protection, partly to underscore Ursula's healthy heterosexual choices, and partly to reassure Frieda at a difficult time in their marriage. It is not (as Maddox believes) that "the war had released in Lawrence a terror that he might be homosexual"; it is rather that Lawrence's terror of his homosexual impulses was projected onto the deepening tragedy of the war.

In all of this turmoil, biographers rarely discuss Frieda's position. More tolerant than her husband, less threatened by same-sex desire, she wrote to David Garnett and offered him her own insight: his involvement with men weakened him, left him unable to stand alone, made him an appendage (as Frieda worried *she* might become): "I have learnt a great deal how much one has to use one's wits, and it is want of courage if we dont stick to the self, that God has given us." She hoped David might "collect [his] strength and direct it." Yet she accepted the possibility that he, like Ursula Brangwen, might want two kinds of love. She urged not a moral imperative, as Lawrence had, but friendly advice that neither echoed nor undermined Lawrence's: she provided a counterpoint to it. Recognizing the psychological damage inflicted on Lawrence, she tried to moderate and mitigate his fury.

But Lawrence's fury had only begun. About 20 April even Frieda, feeling trapped, wrote to Koteliansky that she wished she could creep into "a rabbit hole" to escape the human beings who abused her. "Lawrence," she allowed, "has spent two days trying to make me cross." A few weeks later Murry told Katherine he hated Frieda. In February Frieda had felt confident of withstanding the pressures that leaned like logs against her. Two months later her towering strength seemed shaken. Both she and Lawrence needed a mode of recovery. Just as Frieda wished she "could become an animal," so Lawrence was happy, he said, only when he was outdoors working with plants.

A serious fissure had opened in their marriage. Their emotional claims on each other were no longer complementary; they had discovered their respective limitations. Lawrence had entered, he told Ottoline on 14 May, "one of those horrible sleeps from which I can't wake": he was touched with delirium, hating the Germans who on 7 May had sunk the *Lusitania*, feeling as if he could kill them all. A few days later Frieda wrote to Bertrand Russell to decry Britain's "hate for the 'Huns.'" An exploding tension waited to engulf the marriage. In "England, My England," a short story he composed at this time, he wrote of Evelyn Daughtry and his wife, Winifred: "The reality was the tension of the silent fight between him and his wife. He and she . . . were armed and exerting all their force to destroy each other."

The Lawrences' solution was a brief separation. On 19 May Lawrence wrote bluntly to Koteliansky, the man who had become deeply sympathetic to him: "Friends are looking for another place for Frieda, also in

Hampstead. Probably she will go and stay alone in the[se rooms] for some time, if she gets them. She spends her time thinking herself a wronged, injured and aggrieved person, because of the children, and because she is a German. I am angry and bored. I wish she would have her rooms in Hampstead and leave me alone."

Lawrence's anger permitted him to simplify her predicament—to call her a woman "hopelessly unsatisfied," as if she wanted only motherhood when she had a man, only love when she had her children. In truth she wanted both—and saw no reason to choose. Lawrence, having both a wife and his work, was not required to choose a single form of fulfillment. This kind of inequality, Frieda told Ottoline, helped pitch her into a "deep rage." She hated dual standards for men and women. On 27 May she departed for London, staying with Dollie Radford, a friend of the Meynells, and hunted for a tiny flat, leaving Lawrence alone at Greatham, feeling alienated, disappointed, and (in his words) full of "corrosive darkness." That only hinted at what he would feel after *The Rainbow* was published.

# 8

# Disappointment

## 1915

"In the darkest night," Michel Foucault has written, "the glow of the dream is more luminous than the light of day, and the intuition borne with it the most elevated form of knowledge." At the end of May, as Lawrence prepared to leave Greatham (Frieda was already in London), he dreamt a frightening dream. Its portents, reflecting his disappointment, seemed weighted with somber meaning as the solar system's celestial order broke apart. "I dreamed last night," he confided to Ottoline Morrell, "that all the stars were moving out of the sky. It was awful. Orion in particular went very fast, the other stars in a disorderly fashion, but all trooping out of the sky, in haste, to the left hand. And some of them, low down, took fire. I was very terrified, more terrified than I have ever been." His dream manifests his bewildering anxieties. The disorder of the solar system reflects the disorder of his marriage, Frieda in particular having left "very fast," disrupting their domestic life. The stars, following Orion (by tradition a warrior), some of them exploding into flame, go "trooping out of the sky." They reflect the British troops' many losses, the dead departing "left" on a path of weakness.

Two elements of the dream stand as eerie portents, for as Lawrence himself said, "one can't run away from fate . . . even if it bites off [one's] nose." The stars that "took fire" anticipate the fate awaiting copies of *The Rainbow* in November, and the stars' unexpected exile from a powerful center anticipates the Lawrences' journey to remote Cornwall in December. But as art not only reflects but also anticipates life, Lawrence found himself on 8 September looking at the actual night sky exploding with luminous shrapnel and graced by a zeppelin high among the clouds. To Ottoline he wrote: "It seemed as if the cosmic order were gone . . . [as if] the Zeppelin is in the zenith of the night, golden like a moon, having taken control of the sky; and the bursting shells are the lesser lights. So it seems our cosmos is burst, burst at last, the stars and moon blown away." Lawrence's intuition guides first his dream, anticipating the chaos and destruction of war, and then—with greater surprise—his fiction. In his story "England, My England," a British soldier dies at the hands of the Germans, eerily anticipating the actual battlefield death of Perceval Lucas (an acquaintance on whom the story was based) about a year later, in July 1916. Lawrence must have felt that he possessed psychic gifts. His powers of intuition unleashed a new dimension of his character: rage.

While these events—attack on novel, journey to Cornwall, death of Percy Lucas—worked themselves free from the tangle of fate, the Lawrences' bond was changing again. For most writers, the days and weeks that follow the completion of a major work like *The Rainbow* empty into a crater of unrest or depletion. At such times Virginia Woolf was highly vulnerable to depression; to avoid such troughs Henry James learned to work on several projects at once. Paradoxically the relief of completion can bring despair. This axiom may help explain the Lawrences' marital discord.

But another explanation cannot be ignored. In their three years together the Lawrences had learned to accommodate the wide swings that characterized their emotional relationship. Lawrence was the doer, the provider, the leader, often the "voice"; Frieda admired his energy, savored her freedom, and knew that Lawrence accepted her lack of education and personal ambition. Yet she had not relinquished her personal *power* and continued to resist his ideas whenever she felt the least threat to her domain. Not surprisingly, they had reached the point where the freshness of their relationship had faded and where mutual dependency was as much a burden as a relief. Lawrence's poetic rhapsodies on Frieda's charm had ceased; her effusions on his genius came less often. They were undergoing consolidation. The pressures that other people put on their marriage sometimes obscured the deep commitment they had made to each other. Yet a sharp line of conflict, like the edge of a knife, wedged between them—and stayed there. Why?

The answer lies in three skeins of their shared experience involving a trio of people who greatly enriched their lives in late 1915. The trio included John Middleton Murry, Ottoline Morrell, and Bertrand Russell. That all three wrote prejudicial accounts of the Lawrences invites some adjudication. But all three raised the stakes that the Lawrences' marriage might not survive.

## Not a Man Yet

Murry is the most baffling of the Lawrences' friends. Exuding adolescent charm while he struggled to define himself, he became a kind of emotional politician. He loved Lawrence, respected his literary gifts, wanted to be his disciple, yet feared commitment. Although he possessed a luxurious sensibility, his integrity was too frail to allow his friends to harvest his goodwill. He hung back—bold while fearful, industrious while ineffectual, warm spirited while emotionally feeble. He was like a trellis on which nothing can climb. Infatuated by Murry's winsome charm, Lawrence was slow to understand him; he could not locate Murry's central core. Simplistically, Frieda saw his weakness in layers: "I think at the *bottom* he is pure, but on top not always," she told Gordon Campbell in March. But toward Frieda, Murry was mean. On 8 May he labeled her (to Katherine) "the Red Woman, the Whore of Babylon," and on the eleventh averred that Lawrence "is so lonely, with that bitch of a Frieda, always playing traitor, and hurting him in every secret and intimate part of his soul." Feeling protective, Murry wanted to take Lawrence far away, for a summer's holiday, to "see if I can urge him to the point of leaving her."

Surprisingly, Lawrence rarely mentions Murry in 1915. In March he thought his friend one of a tiny elite who could help him "understand the things I can't understand by myself." Murry was then a listener—interested not in ideas and purposes but in people. "All I wanted from Lawrence," he remembered, "was the warmth and security of personal affection," whereas Lawrence also wanted the two of them to become disciples of the same idea, champions of a new society. Murry tried to be what Lawrence wanted: "I was like a woman instinctively humouring her husband by accepting his arguments and principles." But Murry's core gave him no strength. He did not understand how to surrender his personality to a larger purpose. He was inert. With Lawrence he wanted only "a warm atmosphere of love."

Distressed, Lawrence accurately stated Murry's position to Cynthia Asquith: "He says he believes in what I say, because he believes in me, that he might help in the work I set out to do because he would be believing in me. But he would not believe in the work. He would deplore it. He says the whole thing is personal: that between him and me it is a case of Lawrence and Murry, not of any union in an *idea.*" Lawrence insisted on political activity for two reasons—he could justify his intimacy with Murry because activity helped to suppress the homoerotic component in their relationship, and he believed that social reformation could be achieved only by intense work. Although Murry had attended Oxford, he was still stuck in the ethos of the Cambridge philosopher G. E. Moore, whose *Principia Ethica* (1903) had deeply influenced all of Bloomsbury. Moore argued that mental states are only valuable in themselves and, of these, the best are the pleasures of human intercourse and the enjoyment of beautiful objects. As Maynard Keynes recalled in 1938, Moore believed that "nothing mattered except [those] states of mind . . . not associated with action or achievement." Murry, however, had not yet connected the contemplative cast of Moore's philosophy to the larger need (as Lawrence envisioned it) to reform society. Whereas Murry might settle for sentiment, Lawrence demanded a greater political concern than his friend could muster. He would be disappointed.

But Lawrence persevered in his commitment to a unifying idea. Perhaps he was mistaken when he decided to try to address the public directly, in a fortnightly magazine. Still, if the avenue of *The Rainbow*'s distribution were to close, he would have another outlet that did not depend on publishers. Issued to a few private subscribers, each number to be twenty-eight pages, printed in London's East End for five pounds, the magazine was called the *Signature*. Katherine Mansfield was to contribute satirical sketches, Murry a polemic on the individual soul, Lawrence a fantasia on reconstructing the world. Only three numbers appeared—in October and in November. But the experience of private publication later helped Lawrence gauge the effort required for *Lady Chatterley's Lover*. At work on the *Signature*, Murry proved a diligent and faithful ally. "Murry is going to be something very good," Lawrence confidently told the Hopkins.

Late in the year Lawrence began to see him more critically. When Murry returned from France, where he had gone to keep Katherine company after her brother was accidentally killed, Lawrence wrote to her (about Murry) on 12 December: "At the present I am not very much in sympathy with him"—especially with his supersaturated inner life. "I want," he added, "relations which are not purely personal," but grounded in purpose rather than personality, anchored not in what people are but in the new life they wish to create. Because Murry "runs away" from his fate and cannot stand firm, "he is not a man yet." Hearing from Katherine how unhappy she was in France, Lawrence confronted Murry, who wrote to his beloved on 20 December that, when he went to the Lawrences' flat for an hour, "Lawrence went for me, about you, terribly . . . that I was a coward, that I never offered you a new life, that I would not break with my past . . . that I had made you miserable, by always whining and never making a decision. . . . He says these things and I feel that perhaps some of them may be true." Murry was too passive and insecure to respond effectively to the Lawrences *or* to Katherine.

Still, Lawrence kindly arranged that Ottoline Morrell should invite Murry for Christmas at Garsington, where gossip amid close scrutiny of character would have stirred quite a debate about the Lawrences.

## A Bitter Thing, Only to Have Destroyed

In the last half of 1915 the relationship between Ottoline and the Lawrences was under similar strain. Lawrence wrote to Ottoline frequently, visited her several times (twice with Frieda), and came to think of Ottoline nostalgically, as a pastoral queen uniting an enchanted kingdom that was already slipping into the privileged past of Georgian England. Frieda, however, resisted Ottoline. It was not that she resented Ottoline's money, or was repelled by Ottoline's capacity for spiritual intimacy with her guests. It was rather that she mistrusted Ottoline's influence on Lawrence and worried that the older woman, given the opportunity, would prod Lawrence to leave her. This Frieda would not tolerate. But there is another reason. Frieda cared little for the past. She had been forced to abandon it, along with her children. She lived for the present. What Garsington represented to Lawrence—a glorious but evanescent era— Frieda did not value. It is unlikely that she hid her skeptical views.

On 15 June Ottoline wrote in her diary a long, disparaging analysis of the Lawrences. It is worth remembering that Ottoline viewed them from her own upper-class parapet. She valued civility, respect, personal courage, good manners, voices in moderation—*rational* exchanges. For instance, when she decided in 1911 that she could no longer deny Bertrand Russell the sexual favors he demanded, she discussed her quandary with her husband, Philip, not with temper or recrimination but with an iron strength. "You must [go] if you want to," he replied stiffly. She was in turn (she said) "terribly hurt" that Philip could envision her leaving him. The point is that their aristocratic code of behavior prevented dramatic displays. Through this aristocratic lens Ottoline saw the Lawrences. And Frieda, who had neither literary talent nor English blood to enhance her position, did not come into flattering focus. Frieda wanted complete liberty; Ottoline wanted complete control.

Although Ottoline offers the authority of an eyewitness, her expectations of how a husband and wife ought to behave compromise her judgments:

[W]ith Frieda one feels one is sitting with a tigress who will spring and rend either Lawrence or one of us at any moment. She was jealous that we all liked and admired Lawrence, or Lorenzo as she calls him, and that we did not consider her as important a person as he is. She even said in a loud, challenging voice, "I am just as remarkable and important as Lorenzo." Indeed, in all our talks she was very aggressive and self-assertive. I began to fear she . . . was already turning him against Bertie [Russell] because Bertie didn't flatter her. . . . Naïvely, I did not realize that the Lawrences were not happy here, but apparently she became jealous and they had a miserable time together, fighting and quarrelling all night. He came down on the morning of their last day looking whipped, forlorn and crestfallen, and she went off in a high temper to London.

Ottoline then assessed their marriage:

I shall always see that unhappy, distraught, pathetic figure standing in the hall hesitating. . . . Philip strongly urged him to assert himself and leave her. Of course he didn't. . . . He is very weak with her, although he abuses her to us and indeed often to her face he shouts abusive things, yet she will always win if she wants to; for she ha[s] ten times the physical vitality and force that he has, and always really dominates him, however much he may rebel and complain. He is by tradition and instinct faithful to a wife, and far too timid and sensitive to face life alone, for although he has the flaming ideas of a propagandist he has neither knowledge of the world nor the calm assurance that carries conviction. He soon becomes disappointed, angry, fierce and intolerant at not being attended to, and after a frenzy of angry barks he turns with a drooping tail and seeks refuge in Frieda, his "dark abode."

The whole passage strums a stereotype of the weak artist dogging the trail of the hardy vixen, as if they were like Stephen Crane and Cora, Somerset Maugham and Gerald Haxton, even Murry and Katherine. At its best, the passage reflects the inner despair that both Lawrence and Frieda felt as the war and its pressures dulled their desire for compatibility. But its prevarication is subtle, for it works out Ottoline's personal dilemma through the puppets whose cords she pulls: Ottoline the woman was indeed caught between "going" and "staying"; the "faithful" spouse acting "by tradition" was what she admired in herself; the yapping cur was the fiction that allowed her to master the scene she describes—to frame it as the kind of power struggle she enjoyed. Indeed, biographers have sometimes uncritically followed her lead in caricaturing the Lawrences, although Miranda Seymour acknowledges Ottoline's "unreasonable hostility" to Frieda. At some level Lawrence understood Ottoline's fervent need to patronize; no doubt Frieda saw it—and on his behalf resented it—for Lawrence admitted to Cynthia Asquith in September that "Frieda still abhors the Ottoline, and will have no relation at all with her."

On 8 November 1915 Lawrence went alone to Garsington. He and Ottoline planted purple irises in the wet stillness above the pond, drew close, she pouring out the incense of her sympathy at a time when Lawrence was *spiritually* vulnerable, his soul so sick as to be near collapse. He clung to Garsington's autumnal beauty, relished the connection he had forged with Ottoline, and at the end of his stay wrote to Cynthia Asquith about his deep hopelessness, which Garsington symbolized—"this old house, the beautiful shafted windows, the grey gate-pillars under the elm trees: really, I can't bear it: the past, the past, the falling, perishing, crumbling past, so great, so magnificent." Afterward, as a measure of his affection and appreciation, he sent Ottoline the handwritten manuscript of *The Rainbow* and said, "I don't want to see it any more." He hoped it would please her.

After lunch at the Lawrences' tiny flat in Hampstead on 19 November, Ottoline recorded her impressions in her journal. She reasserts the barking-dog analogy and discerns that Lawrence lacks Philip's political instincts, though of course Philip Morrell had been a Liberal M.P. since 1906 and, as a solicitor, had learned the value of caution. She wrote: "Lawrence is too impatient, he has not got the political instinct, which means that one must have endless patience, tolerance and wisdom. He is far too reckless and rapid in denunciation, and Frieda urges him on in his intolerant denunciations, and so he rushes about with one idea after another like an excited dog, barking and barking at an imaginary enemy, but he cannot put forward any solid ideas, and mere denunciations do no good." Again, he lacks moderation, restraint, proportion. Alongside this account it is useful to place Lawrence's comparable analysis of Ottoline and Russell when he wrote to Cynthia Asquith on 16 August; he skewers their patronizing and amused interest in him as ornament, entertainer: "They come to me, and they make me talk, and they enjoy it, it gives them a profoundly gratifying sensation . . . as if I were a cake or a wine or a pudding. They then say . . . [that] I am an exceedingly valuable personality, but that the things I say are extravaganzas, illusions. They say I cannot think."

For a while Lawrence was mesmerized by Ottoline's power and wealth, saw her kindness as redemptive rather than strangling, and sympathized with her emotional neediness. With understanding he had written to Cynthia on 16 November: "She has not found the reality, because it was not to be found till she had pulled the temple [of tradition] down." He added perceptively: "She has, in some sense, got away: but she has not got anywhere. She feels it bitterly. It is a bitter thing, only to have destroyed, not to have created." Ottoline was not a fighter or a leader, but rather a useful catalyst for change. After this visit Lawrence addressed her not as "My dear Lady Ottoline" but as "My dear Ottoline." For her part, hearing that Lawrence needed money to sail to America at the end of November, she sent him a generous thirty pounds (which was, incidentally, the wage that an experienced live-in domestic could earn for a whole year's employment). To nurture genuine talent thrilled Ottoline. But she must have wondered how her generosity would sit with Frieda.

The Lawrences, though wary, went to Garsington once more on 29 November—for what they thought was a farewell visit—and stayed until 3 December. Lawrence hoped that his fervent cry for a new beginning, even though he pitched it too shrilly, might reconcile the two women; for whether or not he sailed to America on the *Crown of Leon*, departing from Glasgow on 20 December, he was determined to leave London. His view of

Garsington is therefore tinted by nostalgia. On 5 December he wrote to Cynthia that Garsington is "so beautiful, one is tempted to give in, and to stay there, to lapse back into its peaceful beauty of bygone things, to live in pure recollection, looking at the accomplished past, which is so lovely. But one's soul rebels." The placid past, soiled by its reliance on privilege, offered no challenge. At Garsington the guests, resplendent in Ottoline's endless array of Italian "rags," played charades in the hallway. Humbly, Lawrence told Cynthia that, when they were not engaged in make-believe, he, Russell, Philip Heseltine (1894–1930), and an Indian named Hasan Suhrawardy (1893–1963) talked violently about politics and India: "I always shout too loud. That annoys the Ottoline," who preferred measured voices—and who on this visit found Frieda "devilish," "a wild beast," "madly jealous." She was out of Ottoline's control.

In other ways annoyance grew. When Lawrence and Frieda returned to London, he explained to Ottoline that despite the fine hours they had all spent together, the inevitable friction had festered: "Frieda hates me because she says I am *a favorite,* which is ignominious (she says), also she says I am a traitor to her." More clear-eyed than Lawrence, Frieda, though she fell too easily for flattery, refused to yield to Ottoline's "willed" generosity, perceived it as crippling, and surely inflamed Lawrence's later misgivings about Ottoline's character. This tense triangle, so unstable, would be dismantled in Lawrence's next novel, *Women in Love,* which he would begin four months later. There the rich, willful woman and the sensitive, intellectual man are, according to the novel's (suppressed) prologue, just uncoupling, their intimacy laced with friction. Lawrence's earnest advice to Ottoline, offered on 7 December 1915, consisted of solutions that Hermione Roddice, Ottoline's counterpart in *Women in Love,* will reject: "Only let go all this will to have things in your own control. . . . Do not struggle with your will. . . . Only drift, and let go—let go, entirely, and become dark, quite dark . . . only sleep in the profound darkness where being takes place again. . . . Only then you will act straight from the dark source of life, outwards, which is creative life." Lawrence often applied the principles he discovered in his fiction to the personal lives of his friends. Similarly, he counseled the young soldier-poet Robert Nichols: "Learn to be still and to trust yourself to the unseen loving forces of life."

Lawrence endeavored to help Ottoline, who was often unhappy. Their joint delight in poetry, politics, and Nottinghamshire enhanced their cozy, confidential talks. But Lawrence erred in assuming that her needs matched his. They did not. Ottoline needed people around her to suppress her ache of loneliness; Lawrence needed people to provide an audience. Ottoline was a listener; Lawrence was a lecturer. Her diary shows that although she was thoughtful and shrewd, she was also quick to judge her friends. Lawrence's letters, which constitute the diary he never kept, show him attempting to guide friends like Ottoline and Russell toward a new stage of fulfillment: he may have loved the past that Garsington represented, but he wanted to escape from it because it was tainted with the poison of "England," the land of persecution and dead spirits. The dualities that he finds in his writing he also finds in his personal life: England is the sinking pit of spiritual collapse; "Florida" (or any exotic place) is the land of salvation; and the journey becomes the means of negotiating the parts of the self that are in conflict. Lawrence's journeys always say more about him than they say about the country he leaves behind.

## ENEMIES OF MANKIND

Lawrence's ambivalence toward Ottoline Morrell extended, for different reasons, to Bertrand Russell, who in June had seemed to Lawrence almost like a brother, and in July *almost* like someone with whom he could swear a permanent brotherly allegiance. As a potential outlaw fighting Britain's elite, Russell was a man who might shape a new social and political system, who would, in his own words, *"change* people's thoughts." If each could adapt to the other's (wholly different) temperament, they hoped to present a joint series of lectures on peace and a new order of human life. But when Lawrence saw the lecture synopsis that Russell proposed, he was furiously disappointed. He believed that Russell's radical social program was timid, the philosopher proposing merely to criticize rather than to reconstruct society. For his part Russell ruefully explained to Ottoline that Lawrence "regards all my attempts to make him acknowledge facts as mere timidity, lack of courage to think boldly, self-indulgence in pessimism." Russell thought Lawrence "undisciplined in thought" and prey to "mad exaggeration." But Frieda's distaste for Ottoline may also have dampened Lawrence's enthusiasm for Ottoline's lover—and his platform.

When in September Russell offered Lawrence an essay called "The Danger to Civilization" (as a contribution to the *Signature*), Lawrence used the don's submission as a convenient way to break with him, arguing first that the essay, though plausible, was untrue; and second, perhaps responding to Frieda's hatred of repression, that Russell's character was defective and disordered: "You are simply *full* of repressed desires, which have become savage and anti-social. And they come out in this sheep's clothing of peace propaganda. . . . The enemy of all mankind, you are, full of the lust of enmity. It is *not* the hatred of falsehood which inspires you. It is the hatred of people, of flesh and blood. It is a perverted, mental blood-lust. Why don't you own it." Stunned, Russell recognized that Lawrence had demonized him, made him into an emblem of the old order's failures, the accusation of hatred reflecting Lawrence almost as much as himself. Lawrence soon recanted. In a delicious apology he wrote: "After all, my quarrelling with you was largely a quarrelling with something in *myself*, something I was struggling away from in myself."

But as these personal entanglements induced Lawrence's fiery fulminations, making him desperate to flee England and to find a fresh beginning in America, he remained, as always, a disciplined writer. In the October 1915 issue of the *English Review* he published "England, My England," which pointed a new direction in his fiction. Exhausted by the creative demands of *The Rainbow* and troubled by his marriage, Lawrence began a long series of fictional portraits of friends such as Cynthia Asquith and Ottoline Morrell. "England, My England," the first of them, composed while Lawrence was still living in Viola Meynell's cottage at Greatham, uses a powerful tactic that he may have learned from Charles Dickens. At the outset of the story, the narrator employs satire to distance the reader from the protagonist, then as death approaches the narrator moves inward to render that character with sympathy.

Some years before Lawrence began his story, Madeleine, one of the five Meynell daughters, had married Perceval Lucas, a man six years older than Lawrence who lived at Rackham Cottage, a mile from the Meynell family compound (and who was, it is worth remembering, a brother of E. V. Lucas, Methuen's reader of *The Rainbow* manuscript). Lawrence knew Perceval Lucas well enough to be troubled by the man's emotional emptiness and to judge him "a spiritual coward." The story he published exposed Lucas's failed inner life.

What Lawrence freshly saw—that personal weakness and cultural crisis are reciprocal, the one enabling the other—he would often see from this juncture forward. In "England, My England" evelyn Daughtry (renamed Egbert when Lawrence rewrote the story in 1921) provides the template for Gerald Crich, Mrs. Witt, the Woman Who Rode Away, and Clifford Chatterley in Lawrence's later works. Daughtry lacks responsibility for himself and his family, and the hard hatred between him and his wife, Winifred, restricts his energy. He becomes "a destructive spirit entering into destruction," an atrophied self that Lawrence had also detected in Lady Cynthia's husband, Herbert Asquith, about whom he wrote on 20 June: "The war is the only reality to him. . . . He ought [therefore] to die."

With calm inevitability Daughtry joins the war in France and is eventually stabbed to death by a German soldier. Just as for Lawrence the cosmic order had earlier collapsed, so has the moral cartilage of men like Daughtry. He is unable to bear his responsibilities as husband and father. The angle of identification between author and character begins to shift toward fable, the personal used to communicate the prophetic.

Lawrence now extends his cultural critique from Siegmund in *The Trespasser*, through Ursula's soldier-lover Skrebensky in *The Rainbow*, to Daughtry in "England, My England." These hollow men, though outwardly attractive, are crippled by their devotion to duty. Their Victorian sensibilities dim their inner lights of intuition and imagination. They deny themselves. When Daughtry's daughter Joyce falls on an iron tool he had left lying about and lames herself, the physical change in *her* works its way out as a psychological change in him: "[I]t was horrible to see her swing and fling herself along. . . . [Her] father could not bear it; he was nullified in the midst of life. The beautiful physical life was all life to him. When he looked at his distorted child, the crippledness seemed malignant, a triumph of evil and of nothingness. Henceforward he was a cipher. Yet he lived. A curious corrosive smile came on his face." Joyce's wound festers as a destructive spirit in her father. Satirical phrases like "curious corrosive smile" are later muted by the paragraphs that render, without irony, Daughtry's ebbing consciousness as he dies. This kind of incisive, fluid, metaphorical writing Lawrence found most congenial. To call the ending "curiously flawed" is to miss the way it unerringly captures Daughtry's *displaced* energy, his consummation reached when, moments before his own demise, he guns down three German soldiers.

It is no surprise that the story carries a message for Frieda. A husband who feels mistreated, rejected, and alienated will turn his intense frustration outward, committing murder if necessary to avenge his inner despair. Although Frieda would hardly have failed to hear the story's disguised cry, Lawrence's letters now comment very rarely on her feelings or behavior.

On 5 September 1915, after they had spent some days by the sea, Lawrence yielded and joined Frieda in London—in the tiny, dark flat she had taken at 1 Byron Villas, Vale of Health, Hampstead, not far from their vivacious friend Dollie Radford, or from Frieda's children. The rent was only thirty-six pounds a year. They bought a little furniture—a writing desk, some chairs. Lawrence's mood was buoyed by Frieda's infectious good humor, her provocative responses to all she had seen, and her enthusiasm for his writing. On many days he sat out on Hampstead Heath, in view of the rounded masses of trees and long, grassy slopes, and wrote philosophical essays for the *Signature*. Relishing the friends who remained, he frequently saw Koteliansky, Murry, and Katherine; welcomed Philip Heseltine, a twenty-one-year-old composer who thought Lawrence's novels "unrivalled in depth of insight and beauty of language"; and met three young painters who had studied at the renowned Slade School of Art—Mark Gertler, obstreperous and handsome; Dorothy Brett, a droll, deaf viscount's daughter; and Dora Carrington, whose shy blue eyes were like jewels set beneath straw-colored hair.

On 5 November the Lawrences attended a party for nine at Brett's studio, located in Earls Court Road, where they danced and drank to excess—a farewell for the Lawrences, who planned to depart for America on 24 November. According to Brett's account, they enjoyed supper on her balcony, then played charades. Lawrence spoke "Italian to Iris Tree. K[atherine] is sitting on the sofa clasped in some man's arms; Kotiliansky is singing on the balcony; Gertler and Carrington are squabbling as usual. While I, distraught [that some intruders had arrived], play the pianola fast and furiously, watching the party reflected in the bright woodwork of the piano. Some are dancing, some talking, all are more or less drunk." Versions of this tableau would be replayed at Garsington for years after the war ended. But on 8 November, just before Lawrence went by himself to Garsington, the blow fell.

## *"Peccavi! Peccavi!"*

Acting on a tip, the authorities suppressed Methuen's sale of *The Rainbow* on 3 November. Not until 5 November did Lawrence learn the news—and then not from Methuen. He was convulsed with anger. "I am so sick, in body and soul, that if I don't go away I shall die," he told Edward Marsh a day later. "I only curse them all, body and soul, root, branch and leaf, to eternal damnation," he seethed to Pinker. "It is the end of my writing for England. I will try to change my public." The only alternative was America, especially when a friend of Dollie Radford's dangled the possibility of a place in Florida; now, after some delays, they had their passports in hand.

What had happened to Lawrence's novel? After it was published, the National Purity League, led by Dr. Robert Horton, a Congregational minister, apparently alerted the police. To buttress its complaint, the League may well have cited two enraged reviews of the book—one by James Douglas in the *Star* (22 October), the other by Clement Shorter a day later in the *Sphere*. From the depths of Scotland Yard on 3 November came a detective, Albert Draper, ready to serve a search warrant on the Methuen establishment and sniff out the offensive copies of the book. Algernon Methuen was away from his office. Those in command thought that if they consented to the book's removal, they could avoid going to court. Draper's second visit, on 11 November, seemed to confirm this arrangement. But five days later Methuen explained to Herbert Thring, who had inquired for the Society of Authors, that he supposed the case "would not be heard in a public court, and we did not therefore obtain legal assistance or arrange to be legally represented."

Sir John Dickinson, the magistrate who heard the case on 13 November, asked Methuen—alas, in open court—why he had published such a book. According to Lawrence (remembering the details a decade later), Methuen behaved like a coward, claiming that "he did not know the dirty thing he had been handling, he had not read the work, his reader had misadvised him—and Peccavi! Peccavi! [he] wept." Methuen also alleged that his firm's readers had not understood the lesbian chapter called "Shame."

It would appear that Methuen was too busy making money to monitor his list. He offered no resistance when Dickinson ordered unsold copies of the book destroyed—all 1,011 (and close to half of those published). Although Methuen had once been a literary pioneer, he settled for security. A few months later, at the age of sixty, he was given the baronetcy he had coveted. But the company, bypassing bold new work, soon published many fewer fiction titles.

At Garsington, where Lawrence, utterly dejected, had gone on 8 November, the Morrells were furious at the magistrate's action. In the House of Commons on 18 November and again on 1 December, Philip Morrell pointedly asked the home secretary, Sir John Simon, why Lawrence had had no opportunity to rebut charges against the book, when his reputation and income would be affected. Simon adroitly replied that the police authorities had strictly carried out the law—an 1857 statute banning the sale of obscene publications—but agreed that Lawrence, if he believed himself unjustly accused, could arrange "for another copy to be seized . . . in order that he might defend the book." Though tempted by the prospect of a good fight, Lawrence had done with them, he told Ottoline on 3 December. "I am not going to pay any more out of my soul, even for the sake of beating them." In truth, the cold London winter had made him ill: on 16 November Philip Heseltine had written to the English composer Frederick Delius that Lawrence "wants to go to Florida for the winter, since he is, I am afraid, rather far gone with consumption." The dreaded word had been spoken.

What else could Lawrence, sick with what he called simply a violent cold, do to protest *The Rainbow*'s suppression? When W. L. George, a friend of Murry's and another Methuen author, alerted Lawrence that his novel had been suppressed, he suggested that Lawrence immediately join the Society of Authors. The group might take some action. Proposed for membership by Philip Morrell, Lawrence joined at once, but the Society, after weighing the issues, informed him that it "could not take any useful action." Even Morrell reluctantly agreed that taking the case to court would do no good. Lawrence was beaten.

He was determined to leave that "dark and hideous" place, London. Newspaper reports were equally grim. If the Lawrences had read the *Times* on 20 December, for instance, they would have read headlines like "German Cruiser Sunk," "German Gas Attack Foiled," and "French Air Raids on Metz Station" (forty bombs dropped on Frieda's own Metz-Sablons), and would have seen long lists naming 1,064 war casualties among the British armed forces. As Frieda recalled, "We were saturated with war." Lawrence had become profoundly restless, hating *The Rainbow*'s suppression, hating the war, hating his illness, hating "a house on my head."

Chafing against his despair, Frieda, now that she had seen her children and knew they were near—and not mistreated—suffered less from their absence. On 16 December Lawrence wrote to Thomas Dunlop, who in Lerici had typed a version of *The Rainbow:* "Mrs Lawrence has seen her children once or twice, and has almost ceased to fret about them." Feeling the maternal ties weaken, she would accept what she could not change.

It helped them both to have visits from young new friends. Heseltine, tall and blond, brought Michael Arlen (Dikrān Kouyoumdjian), age twenty-one, an Armenian Jew whom Murry cattily described as "the L's darling . . . a low swindler of a peculiarly hateful kind. Hair brushed back, semi-Oxford manner, probably makes his living in Leicester Square." Early in December, Aldous Huxley, also twenty-one, having met the Lawrences at Garsington on 29 November, came to their flat for tea. He was very tall, thin, and fastidiously intellectual. With Thomas Henry Huxley as his grandfather, his lineage was impeccable; in June he would—like his mother before him—take a First in English at Oxford. He was, he told Ottoline, "very much impressed" by Lawrence.

On 20 December the Lawrences transferred their lease on 1 Byron Villas, sold or stored the furniture they had collected, and prepared to spend Christmas week in Ripley with Lawrence's family, though he confided to Cynthia Asquith on 24 December that the limp resuscitation of his boyhood atmosphere grieved him: "Nothing is more painful than to be plunged back into the world of the past, when that past is irretrievably gone by." Too many unhappy memories flooded over him. His aversion led him to romanticize the future and, on the twentieth, to say to Katherine Mansfield, now living in France, "From the old life, all is gone. There remain only you and Murry in our lives. We look at the others [the Campbells, the Cannans] as across the grave. . . . We must look forward into the unknown"—and risk being born again.

With all their belongings stuffed into three small trunks, and desperate now for a new (and inexpensive) place to live, they heard of a farmhouse in Cornwall. On 19 December Murry had visited J. D. Beresford (whose novel *The House in Demetrius Road* Lawrence had read) to inquire if Beresford and his wife, Beatrice, would lend their farmhouse to the Lawrences. Not needing it till March, the Beresfords agreed, and Lawrence soon told Ottoline, "We'll go direct [from the Midlands], for my health." The Lawrences had scraped together about one hundred pounds on which to live. That, at least, is the figure Murry reported to Katherine on 22 December. When the Lawrences had thought they would sail on the tramp steamer *Crown of Leon,* Edward Marsh had sent them twenty pounds and (as noted earlier) Ottoline had sent thirty pounds; the *English Review* had paid perhaps ten pounds for "England, My England," and Duckworth had advanced perhaps fifty pounds for a book of Italian sketches proposed for 1916 publication, which Lawrence had worked on during the autumn. But

apparently the *Crown of Leon* did not sail from Glasgow to the West In-
dies in December, for the shipping tables in the December 1915 *Glasgow
Herald* never assigned it a berth. It may have been disabled. The Lawrences
did not seek out another ship because, Lawrence said to Forster, "I hadn't
the strength to go to America." His spirit had collapsed.

In London Lawrence had gained a good deal of notoriety, he told Thomas
Dunlop, and was much discussed. Both he and Frieda must have wondered
whether his notoriety would follow him. Could he go unnoticed to a remote, desolate area like Cornwall, on the southwestern ledge of England,
which, as it confronted the Atlantic, was bare and immemorial? His first
letter from Cornwall, to Koteliansky, dated 30 December 1915, began:
"We got here tonight—it is splendid." "Here I think my life begins again—
one is free," he exulted to Catherine Carswell. "We *love* being here," he
marveled to Beresford a few days later. Their long exile had begun.

# 9

# The Discovery of Cornwall

## 1916

The potency of Cornwall's presence awed the Lawrences. Defined by a rocky, rugged coastline, Cornwall in winter seemed barren and lonely and dark, its howling winds heaving off the Atlantic Ocean with percussive force. Big boulders stood like brave sentinels, asleep: Lawrence thought them impregnable, terrifying, "like solid darkness." Strong, white seagulls, with bent shoulders, swept through the sun's thin light, crying sharply. Inland, sloping fields groped mysteriously among granite outbreaks.

About the size of Rhode Island and a tenth the size of Switzerland, Cornwall was settled by the Celts and Saxons, who left behind a brooding past that appealed to Lawrence's love of elemental mystery, with its "flicker of pre-christian Celtic civilisation." In 1916 the north coast town of Padstow possessed fifteen hundred people, most of them fishermen, whose slate-roofed houses lined the narrow streets. Lawrence found the local people un-Christian and antisocial, as if harboring the souls of insects; yet he respected their fierce belief in magic and darkness. About four miles away, the Beresfords' cottage lay on the coast, in the tiny village of Porthcothan, which opened fanlike onto a bleak, bare landscape. In Cornwall Lawrence's human relationships seemed to shatter in the druidical darkness.

When the Lawrences arrived two days before the new year, they were struck by the silence of the Beresfords' large rooms and thick walls, the restless sea only a curtain preserving "such lovely silence . . . such peace," into which, Lawrence thought, he might escape contentiousness and begin to love again. His unhappy Christmas visit to Eastwood had subdued him. The farmhouse squatted low, its rooms overlooking a cove full of black rocks and towers of foam. "We can see the sea," he wrote to Dollie Radford, an accomplished poet who had been kind to Frieda in London, "and hear the sound of it." The wind, strong and fierce, boomed in the chimney, and the wild sea broke upon the ochre cliffs in smoking explosions, so unlike the sparkling sea at Fiascherino. "I have to hang on to L[awrence] on the rocks," Frieda wrote to Ottoline Morrell, "or he would be blown away like a little bit of foam right out to sea!" After walking with Frieda to Padstow—and then, on another day, across the rocky downs—a new sense of freedom stirred in Lawrence, and he felt he might be inspired to write again. The novel he would soon begin would capture brilliantly the group of people who were about to enter his life.

At this time the land Lawrence still yearned for was not Cornwall but Florida, that dreamy place of perpetual escape. Bruised, Lawrence no longer wanted to offer the world salvation but, he told Katherine Mansfield with sagging spirits, to "go like a thistle-down, anywhere, having nothing to do with the world, no connection." Even a month later he could murmur: "Something in me is asleep and doesn't trouble." Looked after by the Beresfords' efficient housekeeper, Emma Pollard, who made excellent breads, cakes, and puddings, Lawrence and Frieda had time to unveil a strategy. After Philip Heseltine arrived on New Year's Day, followed soon by the voluble Kouyoumdjian, Lawrence wrote to Barbara Low, Ivy Low's aunt: "We are trying to think of a plan of getting out of the country on a ship. . . . I wish I knew just *how* to do it." But he did not. On 7 January he was struck by another vile cold, which depleted him and, as he lay in bed, made him feel (he told Murry) "like a fox they have chased till it can't go any further, and doesn't know what to do." His soul's wound had spread to his body.

When Dollie Radford's son, Dr. Maitland Radford, came from London to examine Lawrence in late January, he may or may not have mentioned the hated word *tuberculosis*. Some days later Lawrence explained to Cynthia Asquith what the doctor had ordered: "He says the stress on the nerves sets up a referred inflammation in all the internal linings, and that I must keep very quiet and still and warm and peaceful. There was a sort of numbness all down the left side, very funny—I could hardly hold anything in my hand. But now, thank heaven, . . . I feel my old strength coming back." He was glad, for he had felt nearly disintegrated. He was not much better until the second week in February, and later in the month he lay on the brink of another collapse.

## Milk Casein

In 1916 the incidence of tuberculosis was still high, the treatments still experimental, the results still inconclusive. The disease Lawrence had contracted usually affected the lungs and so was called *pulmonary* consumption. The tubercle bacillus, isolated by Robert Koch in 1882, caused pulmonary tissue to ulcerate and gradually destroyed large patches of the lung. Without x-rays or skin tests, doctors could seldom diagnose the disease until the patient was already consumptive, his body tissues wasting away. Lawrence's symptoms (increasingly evident) included cough (with sputum), pulmonary bleeding, drenching sweats, fever, weight loss, and weakness. Since the tubercle bacillus can live for weeks in air or dust, particularly in dark, closed conditions like those at Haywood's factory or in a miner's cramped cottage, Lawrence probably contracted the disease by inhalation. The standard treatment demanded rest and fresh air. As early as 1840 George Bodington had said, "The application of cold, pure air to the interior surface of the lungs is the most powerful sedative that can be applied." Other treatments proliferated. Cod-liver oil therapy appeared in 1909, iodine therapy in 1912, treatment with gold in 1913, calcium therapy soon after; garlic, chewed and swallowed, seemed to help some patients, as did injections of cane sugar, introduced in 1918. From earliest times milk, because of its calcium content, was considered an effective treatment. To Ottoline, Lawrence wrote on 1 February, "I believe that milk casein stuff is *very* good." In fact, the kind of itinerant life the Lawrences favored, choosing (as they did) fresh-air country places, would have been as good for his tubercular condition as any treatment available.

Although a patient's body suffered, his mind did not. Richard Shryock writes that victims "remained alert, were often optimistic, and even seemed stimulated—presumably by low fever—into unusual mental activity." It is possible, he adds, that "pathology contributed to genius." Apparently Frieda enjoyed immunity, either natural or acquired. Studies showed that a great many spouses of tubercular victims remained healthy.

But Lawrence's consumption was not the only affliction in Porthcothan. Philip Heseltine dreaded a bill proposed in the House of Commons in January—and later passed—to make military service compulsory; and on 1 February Lawrence reported to J. D. Beresford that "the young men are all being called up now round here. They are very miserable." Yet Heseltine, though panicked, was full of excited vitality. He typed Lawrence's poems and motored over to Newquay and brought back his girlfriend, Minnie Channing. He called her Puma because of her fiery temperament, but she was affectionate and unobtrusive, with large, candid eyes, thick eyebrows, and pleasing lips. Soon Heseltine initiated a scheme he called Rainbow Books and Music, whereby he might publish privately, by subscription,

Lawrence's *Rainbow,* perhaps Murry's novel-in-progress, *Still Life,* and other books and music not sought by commercial presses. During the seven weeks that Heseltine stayed at Porthcothan, both Lawrence and Frieda responded to his enthusiasm and appreciated his generosity. "It has been nice living with him," Lawrence told the Murrys on 2 February, although a day earlier Lawrence had worried that "Heseltine and his Puma are not very happy." The Lawrences, their money ebbing, hoped Heseltine would share the expenses of a cottage, which they needed to find. But three days before they were to leave Porthcothan, Lawrence found Heseltine inflammable and overwrought, swaying violently between loving and hating his Puma.

As in 1911, when Lawrence was sick, so now illness changed him again, altered his priorities, made him demand less stridently that others change. He would trouble himself no longer with the world's entropy and disintegration. His brief confrontation with death having shaken his sensibility like an alarm, he sought solace in books and poems, the sun and the sea—whatever provided peace. Even a lack of cash no longer mattered. "I'm . . . existing on charity," he told Thomas Dunlop in January. "But I don't care. I have done the work, if they won't pay me properly, then they must support me improperly." Having enough money to last only three or four months in Cornwall, he nonetheless faced his poverty without complaint. His strength mattered more.

He was seldom idle. Even in bed he labored to make a living, correcting proofs and touching up the unpublished poems he had composed in Italy (Dunlop had forwarded the manuscript books that Lawrence left behind with their servant, Elide). In January 1916 Duckworth had sent him the proofs of *Twilight in Italy,* his book of essays. They would introduce English readers to the peasants Lawrence and Frieda had encountered in Italy—in churches, at the theater, at a rural lodging called San Gaudenzio.

Lawrence had taught himself how to penetrate an individual's and a family's psyche; now, in *Twilight,* he tried to penetrate a foreign culture, drawing on personal observation and informed comparisons with the British life he knew best. The second essay, "The Lemon Gardens," evocatively describes a family on the Lago di Garda. But when Lawrence revised it, he interpolated pages of cultural analysis—defining the Italian soul as receiving "the divinity of the flesh," seeking "supreme sensation," the Italian mind "subserv[ing] the senses." These speculative meditations also led him to denounce the way England "was conquering the world with her machines and her horrible destruction of natural life." Although some readers have disliked his free-wheeling judgments—which resemble those that populate his letters—it is hard not to admire his pictures of the Italian landscape: "The lake lies dim and milky, the mountains are dark-blue at the back, while over them the sky gushes and glistens with light. . . . The mountains melt suddenly, the light steps down, there is a glitter, a spangle, a clutch of spangles, a great unbearable sun-track flashing across the milky lake, and the light falls on my face." Lawrence's legato phrasing, smoothed by alliterative rhythms, positions the motion of dawn as would a camera, with spatial precision. In this book Lawrence discovered the margin between philosophy and fiction.

That was not all. Once Lawrence's manuscript notebooks had arrived from Italy, he saw that they contained enough material from the past decade to make a beautiful book of poetry he would call *Amores,* and he set to work revising early poems like "Discipline" and "The Wild Common." He settled finally on sixty poems that, he told Ottoline, comprised the "inner history of my life, from 20 to 26." He was now 30, Frieda 36. Though it is undated, the final poem in the collection, called "The Mystic Blue," suggests the direction toward which Lawrence's poetry had been moving—toward a natural voice using repeated enjambement along with analogies to nature which, like the powerful horses in *The Rainbow,* illuminated the human sphere. The poem opens with a mystery:

> Out of darkness, fretted sometimes in its sleeping,
> Jets of sparks in fountains of blue come leaping
> To sight, revealing a secret, numberless secrets keeping.

Although the triple rhyme perhaps forces the addition of "numberless secrets keeping," Lawrence skillfully breaks the rhyme at the center to throw emphasis on "To sight," with its hint of revelation. The final quatrain extends the middle stanzas but uses a syntax more difficult than usual:

> All these pure things come foam and spray of the sea
> Of Darkness abundant, which shaken mysteriously,
> Breaks into dazzle of living, as dolphins that leap from the sea
> Of midnight and shake it to fire, till the flame of the shadow we see.

Despite its difficulty, the closing lines gain a surprising energy from their one-syllable verbs, and the poem's final clause, which in the American edition reads "so the secret of death we see," expresses just the sort of revelation that Lawrence, despairing of his "beastly health," would have found consoling: rebirth lies mysteriously, like a phoenix, in the very motion of the dark sea.

Lawrence hoped that Constable or Sidgwick and Jackson would publish the volume, but both declined, Sidgwick enclosing some impertinent criticism with his refusal. Pinker thereupon secured Lawrence's reliable standby, Duckworth, who had published *The Trespasser, Love Poems,* and *The Prussian Officer* collection and whose loyalty Lawrence prized. The volume duly appeared in July, dedicated to Ottoline Morrell; the American edition, published in New York by B. W. Huebsch, followed Duckworth's two months later, Huebsch having earlier printed a kind of sur-reptitious edition of *The Rainbow,* slightly abridged, which he sold privately. Yet in 1916 *Amores* may have earned Lawrence only twenty-five pounds, not a large bulwark against the financial uncertainty ahead.

## A WILD, REMOTE PLACE

Leaving Porthcothan in February allowed Lawrence to reshape his idea of the Promised Land and to cast off the baggage of the old foul world along with his ill health. Change urged renewal. On 22 February 1916, appar-ently Heseltine motored the Lawrences about forty-five miles south to the tiny, remote village of Zennor, about fifteen miles from Land's End and only five miles from St. Ives, the coastal town Virginia Woolf would later make famous in *To the Lighthouse.* Lawrence told Koteliansky that Zen-nor was "a lovely place far down in Cornwall . . . very wild and remote and beautiful." A hamlet of seven houses, it seemed to Lawrence like an em-bodied Promised Land of the spirit, "as if a new heaven and a new earth would come to pass there." It was a cry he would often repeat.

After spending the early days of March at a little inn called the Tinners Arms, which Dr. Radford had recommended, the Lawrences looked for an inexpensive house. Stalked by their "prowling poverty," they guarded every shilling. Owners who asked large sums for a house "exasperate one past bearing," Lawrence complained to Beatrice Beresford. But at Higher Tregerthen, a short walk from Zennor, they found a two-room cottage, un-furnished, with a long scullery, and no indoor plumbing. The cottage lay at the edge of rough stony fields that led to a farm below, then down through gorse and primeval gray boulders to the Atlantic—a walk of fif-teen minutes. The rent? A mere five pounds a year. They would do without servants. A few yards away lay a larger cottage, with seven rooms—at six-teen pounds—which Lawrence at once invited the Murrys (still in France) to take, perhaps to be joined by Heseltine (whose discipleship, however, had been gutted by pique). Lawrence hoped that all three would soon join him and Frieda to create their Rananim and be contented and industrious together, without the distraction of quibbles and quarrels. For his little colony Lawrence at least tried to set a noble tone.

The practical matter of finding furniture showed Lawrence's resource-fulness. He wrote to all those who had stored the belongings he and Frieda had salvaged from Byron Villas—a camp bed, table and four chairs, mir-ror, blankets, eiderdown quilt, Persian rug, brass candlesticks that had be-longed to his mother, clock, saucepan, two portable Primus stoves that burned oil, a framed embroidery that Ottoline had worked—and then asked Dollie Radford to ship them by rail. "I wish I could afford to come to town," he apologized. "But oh dear, we are *very poor.*" While Dollie packed

The Lawrences' cottage (right), the Tower cottage (left), at Higher Tregerthen, Zennor, Cornwall

as best she could, Lawrence proudly made a rough dresser and shelves from scrap lumber given to him by the generous old Captain Short, their sixty-six-year-old landlord from St. Ives. Afterward, Lawrence and Frieda dashed to a sale in town to buy coco matting for the floors, a large wardrobe, and a chest of drawers for the upstairs bedroom. With a bed, table, and cooking stove from Captain Short, their furnishings were complete.

All around them, spring made the fields flush with green, the air tingle with scent, the dusk thicken with Celtic magic. Frieda, busy and contented, told Katherine that Lawrence had made buttercup-yellow curtains; on Thursday, 9 March, the gorse, happily in flower, "smelled hot and sweet in the sun," Lawrence told Ottoline, "and the lambs were leaping into the air, kicking their hind legs with a wild little flourish." At sunset the birds whistled in the sharp air. As he looked toward spring, he wanted to rise up and have done with miseries. Frieda agreed. She wrote to Dollie Radford two days later: "The world is so ugly now, that it seems more than ever one's absolute duty to be happy and nice with each other!" Lawrence was preparing himself to write. At the edge of a major work, he needed only Frieda's firm backing, the Murrys' friendship, and some warm, sunny days.

While the Lawrences awaited the Murrys' arrival from France—the exiles had promised to appear in April—Philip Heseltine made a different move. Although he had once judged Lawrence "a great and attractive personality," he and Puma turned nasty and, out of temper, wrote the Lawrences a pair of letters (now lost) whose vitriolic contents can be gauged from Lawrence's stunned reply, in which he agreed to "let the whole relation [between us] cease entirely." Knowing that Philip had the tongue of an adder, Lawrence added cautiously: "I only wish that you and Puma should not talk about us, for decency's sake. I assure you I shall have nothing to say of you and her. The whole business is so shamefully fit for a Kouyoumdjian sketch." Barry Smith, Heseltine's biographer, calls this letter "rather pathetic," but Lawrence had genuinely liked Philip, had perhaps confided in him, and may have thought him too unstable to absorb insult.

Why did Heseltine turn nasty? Two explanations are likely. Although Lawrence and Heseltine seemed initially to have a great deal in common— iron-willed mothers, strong traces of effeminate behavior, a ravenous hunger for "life," an aversion to Christianity, a hatred of the war, a rejection of conventional ways of earning money (Philip had refused to become a stockbroker)—they differed in one critical way. Lawrence was superbly focused on his work, having always a project either active or incubating, whereas Heseltine was wholly unable to follow a fixed course. Waffling between staying at Oxford, composing songs, and writing music criticism, he was a dilettante whose dabblings, like the Rainbow Books and Music scheme, soon exhausted his turbulent energy. He was an unreliable person all his life.

Beyond that was a petulance spurred by indecision. Desperately torn between his adoration for Juliette Baillot (whom he met at Garsington and who later married Aldous Huxley's brother, Julian) and his "licentious" feelings for Puma, Heseltine repeatedly sought advice from the more experienced Lawrences. They may have meddled unnecessarily (as David Garnett had thought when they criticized his choice of friends), or perhaps they thought they *must* interfere when they learned that in October Puma had become pregnant. Lawrence explained to Ottoline on 25 February that Heseltine "is exasperating because he is always in such a state of mad *reaction against* things, all mad reactions." Heseltine's extreme mood swings reflected what Barry Smith calls "an almost pathological inability to grow up."

One can guess what Frieda might have recommended. Given that both she and Puma discounted sexual purity, she probably urged him to choose Puma. Intriguingly, Barry Smith wonders if, in January, Ottoline perhaps showed Heseltine some of Lawrence's letters to her. On 22 April Heseltine wrote to Frederick Delius that Lawrence's "behaviour nearly landed me in a fearful fix—indeed, it was calculated to do so." Lawrence, concerned for Puma, had likely wanted Philip to recognize his own dark if uneasy attraction and marry her (which Philip did on 22 December 1916, six months after their son was born).

Certainly Lawrence felt betrayed by Heseltine, felt he had misplaced his affections. Lawrence relished Heseltine's charms, his sensitive if gushing adoration, his restless energy, his biting wit; would have welcomed his help with living expenses (Philip had £150 a year); and, as Lawrence pondered Philip's apostasy, must at least have wondered, as he welcomed the Murrys, how long *they* would stay.

The Murrys arrived about 5 April, on a cold, gray day, neither of them looking well. They were warmly welcomed. "I see Katherine and Murry arriving," wrote Frieda, "sitting on a cart, high up on all the[ir] goods and chattels, coming down the lane to Tregerthen." Katherine looked like an emigrant, her jackets cut fashionably short, her three-month idyll on the French coast—at Bandol—affirming her love for Murry, just as Lawrence and Frieda had gradually found, Lawrence told Ottoline, "a kind of new being, for each other, which is life." Lawrence and Frieda were relieved to have a sympathetic pair of outsiders to share with them the spring wonders in Zennor, where, Lawrence said in April, "it is marvellously beautiful, now the fine weather has come."

The foursome worked furiously to ready the "tower" cottage for the Murrys. Frieda remembered a frenzy of "painting chairs and polishing brass and mending old clocks, putting plates on the dressers, all the treasures we had bought." Lawrence labored at coloring the walls pale pink, cleaning and staining the floors, painting the handmade cupboard and shelves bright blue, and buying old, solid furniture in St. Ives. He found Katherine simpler and better, but Murry not much changed in any way. Yet for her part Katherine was wary. "I am very much alone. . . . I don't belong to anybody here," she soon confided to Koteliansky. The "huge stones" all around Tregerthen alarmed her; they were psychological obstacles, oppressive, a block to her creative power.

For a while peace reigned. "There in Cornwall," wrote Frieda, "I can remember days of complete harmony between the Murrys and us, Katherine coming to our cottage so thrilled at my foxgloves, tall in the small window seat." Attuned to the spring ferment, renewed by the friendship of those he loved, and feeling altogether better than he had for months, Lawrence began in mid-April the first draft of *Women in Love*, his richest and best sculpted novel, but also his darkest. He composed with lightning speed, sitting outdoors with his back against a granite boulder, a few yards above the cottage, with a view of the pale gorse framed by a blue sea, or, when the wind turned chilly, writing upstairs near the big window, in the bedroom that was, he told Catherine Carswell, "full of light and beauty." "I am quite happy here," he reported to Mark Gertler on 26 April. A month later he described for Amy Lowell the primroses, bluebells, foxgloves, and the sea-pinks which hovered like bees, the hawks, magpies, and foxes—and concluded: "I love it." The landscape, at once familiar and exotic, radiated energy.

## SEX IN STONES

On the morning of 20 May, a Spanish cargo ship named the *S. Manu*, cruising in dense fog, smashed into a rock ridge before running ashore at Tregerthen cliffs, where its foredeck went under. Frieda wrote to Cynthia Asquith: "We had a shipwreck, practically on our doorstep. . . . It *was* thrilling." Four days later Lawrence said pregnantly to Koteliansky: "I cannot tell you how it made me sad: it seemed a symbol of something, I don't know what." It became a symbol of their relationship with the Murrys, for on 4 May Katherine had written to Beatrice Campbell a surprising letter, about which two points are noteworthy. First, Katherine, frustrated by her inability to write in her new setting, may have been jealous of Lawrence's fluency—for on most days (she would have known) he was writing almost without pause, satisfied by his efforts. In truth, says Murry, she "distrusted the very idea of a community," only "pretending" to enjoy their camaraderie. Second, her biographer Claire Tomalin says without qualification: "Katherine was a liar all her life—there is no getting around this. . . . [S]he was a bold and elaborate inventor of false versions." In 1921 Lawrence bluntly told Mary Cannan, "[S]he's a liar out and out." Katherine's lively description of the Lawrences, in spite of its immediacy and apparent veracity, may well be "staged"—a sketch toward constructing a story about them, an imaginative portrait colored by disappointment and irritation:

> I want to talk about the L[awrence]s, but if I do don't tell Kot and Gertler for then it will get back to Lawrence and I will be literally murdered—He has changed very much—Hes quite "lost"—He has become very fond of sewing, especially hemming; and of making little copies of pictures—When he is doing these things he is quiet and gentle and kind, but once you start talking I cannot describe the frenzy that comes over him. He simply *raves*, roars, and beats the table, abuses everybody. . . . Frieda is more or less used to this. She has a passion for washing clothes—and stands with big bowls of blue and white water round her wringing out check tablecloths—and looking very much at home indeed—She says this place suits her. I am sure it does.
>
> They are both too rough for me to enjoy playing with. I hate games where people lose their tempers in this way—Its so witless. In fact they are not my kind at all. I cannot discuss blood affinity to beasts for instance if I have to keep ducking to avoid the flat irons and the saucepans. And I shall *never* see sex in trees, sex in the running brooks, sex in stones and sex in everything.

If this were a faithful portrait, it would affect one's sense of Lawrence's decency and self-control. But one's sense of them is quite different. Lawrence was comparatively happy at this time—his bond with Frieda secure (despite their friction), his novel progressing, his liking of the neighborhood genuine, his relative seclusion a joy. For his health's sake he had learned to curb his tendency to denounce what irritated him and to stay away from those whose presence taunted him: "I daren't come out of Zennor," he remarked to Beresford in August. "I feel such a terror of the world and its people, that when I get even into a railway train, I almost die of horror." He had created a cocoon to protect him from disruption while he wrote and then rewrote.

As Lawrence committed himself to a major new novel, he almost certainly knew that the character and quality of his imagination had changed. The possibility of harmonizing his artistic impulses with the social pulse of England had disappeared, foundering on *The Rainbow*'s suppression. As an artist (he said more than once) he would become "an outlaw," "a brigand," a bomb-thrower, an escaped gunman aiming "noiseless bullets." When he thought of the British public, "a sort of madness comes over me. . . . I hate the 'public.'" He had shed all outward concern for authority, had severed his ties to the past, had decided to stand alone. He wrote for himself now. Writing "naturally" at last, he was creating a book out of his free soul. He felt untrammeled by any compulsion to enlighten or entertain the reading public. Still, every firm stance has its effects—some uncalculated.

Lawrence's imagination had grown both deeper and darker. For one thing, having returned from a wintertime precipice when he felt like dying, he reconnected himself to the unchanging elements, the wind and rocks and sea, which helped strengthen him, offered him a brooding solace, and helped him "forget the rest of life," the terrible disturbances of the past months. In this primal métier he could recover his "original self" with confidence. He could more directly impugn the society from which he was now separated. Like a hero of myth, he had been washed out into the cold, dark sea; cleansed; and brought back "more unified, more and more a oneness." Out of this painful process was born the self that could now snap the entanglements of social relations, confront the spiritual nakedness behind them, and record the exposed truth.

Moreover, Lawrence's animosity toward the Establishment, whether it suppressed books or enacted conscription laws, could most readily be expressed in satire. In February Lawrence could admit to Edward Marsh—who, despite his generous patronage, had not liked *The Rainbow*—that "we have *often* laughed at you: because you are one of those special figures one can laugh at: just as I am, only I'm ten times more ridiculous. But I'm sure we've laughed kindly and affectionately." As satirical targets in his novel, Lawrence chose some of those with power who struck him as typical of his age. At one level he understood the value of friendship, appreciated the help of those who boosted his well-being, was grateful for the books and cakes and medicines they sent him. Yet his anger at England's oppression cooled his sense of obligation. Standing outside his time allowed him to discount some of the claims of common courtesy. "I am writing another novel . . . [in which] I am free at last, thank God. . . . Nearly everybody has dropped off from me—even Ottoline is *very cool*," he wrote to Forster on 30 May. "It is better to be alone in the world."

Frieda enjoyed her own animosity, simpler and more direct, which also empowered Lawrence's. It helped usher in the new hostility that enters Lawrence's creative work at this time. In February Frieda wrote to Cynthia Asquith: "I must say I am wild that not a single critic or writer has broken a lance for *The Rainbow*. That they attacked it[,] well and good, but not a soul, not a soul stuck up for it, it is maddening. I am full of black revenge!!" However softened by her sunny disposition, Frieda's vow of revenge sharpened Lawrence's aim on those who had bartered with his respect. Heseltine, in spite of his silliness and immaturity, had written to Ottoline on 28 January, "After living with the Lawrences for several weeks, I have come to the very definite conclusion that Mrs Lawrence has been most unjustly maligned behind her back . . . and, very naturally, she is unhappy about it." Frieda's quarrel with Ottoline lingered. Finally, goaded no doubt by Heseltine's gossip, she exploded. In May she wrote to Ottoline: "Now for over a year I was ready to be your friend—but steadily and persistently you have treated me with arrogance and insolence! It took me a long time to realise it. Your last letter to me was again cheap and vulgar—

You have told lies about me, you have tried to separate Lawrence and me because you wanted some sort of unwholesome relation with him—All the time you felt good and holy! This love that was between Lawrence and me was something that passed your understanding in spite of appearances, so with true irreverence you tried to interfere."

At Garsington, Frieda thought, Ottoline abused her power and only pretended that social barriers had fallen: "What a lie your democracy is, in your heart you want to override every body[,] you are not in the least aware of the neighbour's rights! Someday it may dawn on you what a good thing you have rejected in my genuine friendship." Whereas Frieda had scrapped the hypocrisy of middle-class bourgeois life, Ottoline had only refashioned it on a grander scale. A Victorian hostess *manqué,* she still clung to forms of etiquette that preserved the rungs of social stratification. About 21 May Frieda wrote to Cynthia: "I had a great 'rumpus' with Lady Ottoline, finally; I told her what I thought of her—All her spirituality is false, her democracy is an autocrat turned sour, inside those wonderful shawls there is cheapness and vulgarity." These were probably judgments that Lawrence and Frieda discovered in concert, but Frieda's letter would only have confirmed the judgments that Ottoline had disclosed to her journal in February 1916. There Frieda was called "robust and virile," "a Prussian Brunhilde," a woman who made Lawrence "succumb" to her.

Frieda's *virility,* Ottoline's *vulgarity*—these half-truths are the currency of angry people. They would not matter much, except that they go so far beyond what Frieda thought were simply differences in temperament that they boldly color the characterization in Lawrence's masterpiece, *Women in Love.* Those who had betrayed either Lawrence's or Frieda's trust would not be spared. In the new novel, which rushed forth in torrents of inspired prose, Garsington would become Breadalby, Ottoline Morrell would become the willful Hermione Roddice, Philip Morrell would become the insipid Alexander Roddice, Bertrand Russell would become the ponderous Sir Joshua Malleson, Heseltine would become the squealing Halliday, the Puma would become the foul Pussum, and so on. In his imagination Lawrence began to abstract these figures into symbols of calamity. As Lawrence worked on his new novel, these figures became the guiding lights by which his contemporary culture could be recognized. "[T]he stark truth is all that matters," he warned Mark Gertler in September.

As Lawrence satirized those who had been close to him, he believed that he was grounding his analysis on social and character *fact* as surely as field studies or empirical research served a scientist such as Edward Tylor, whose two-volume *Primitive Culture* (1871) Lawrence had been reading. Lawrence has sometimes been criticized for lifting his characters from life. Anthony Burgess, for example, cites Lawrence's tendency, in characterization, "to draw the essence out of himself, impose appearance out of a mixture of fancy and real people, and introduce habits or actions observed among his friends and enemies." That is not so. Lawrence swiftly leaves "appearance" behind and, going below a character's surface awareness, pierces to the knowledge that a character *cannot articulate* and, there, isolates a spiritual kernel. All around him Lawrence had seen his contemporaries grinding out their conflicts—Ottoline's deploring the Easter 1916 uprising in Dublin while vilifying Frieda; Heseltine's desperate clash of sympathies toward women; Bertrand Russell's public lectures on the social transformation of England coupled with his interior psychological sterility; the homosexual Forster's novels about heterosexual love; Katherine's desire for a bond like marriage crushed by her impulse to escape it; and Murry's entrapment in his own aimless welter of emotions.

In his new novel Lawrence would define these assorted clashes as comprising a psychological determinism. He does what Joyce and Woolf do not: he amalgamates these clashes into a *systemic* social illness previously unacknowledged. The impulses that led to World War I lie embedded in characters like Halliday and Pussum, and Gerald and Gudrun, whose personal struggles mirror what patriotic British soldiers were, for instance, carrying out in September 1916, on such Belgian battlefields as Passchendaele, where the British suffered a quarter-million casualties. This reciprocal understanding, expanding what Lawrence had discovered in "England, My England," will constitute a major contribution.

## THE HEATHER IS OUT

Once Lawrence had finished the first draft of his novel, about 4 July—and knew its contours—he decided that, to save money, he would type the novel himself, making one carbon copy. He still had the L. C. Smith typewriter that Amy Lowell had given him a year earlier. As he typed he revised extensively, often expanding his work. Once the Murrys had departed (they left in June), Lawrence assumed their lease and typed in their "tower" sitting room, estimating for Katherine that "it will take me just *three months* to type my novel." To revise as he typed compounded his labor. He was soon exhausted. He began, instead, to write the final draft in pencil. "It is 4/5 done now," he told J. B. Pinker, his agent. "This is the fourth and the final draft." He meant that the material he had not used in *The Rainbow* comprised the first draft; the material from a later effort (which included the canceled prologue), the second; the full holograph manuscript composed in spring 1916, the third; and the version he typed in the summer and fall (and finished by hand), the fourth.

When the weather was bright and inviting, he and sometimes Frieda went out to help the Hockings (who owned the farm below) harvest their hay, or they worked in the garden that Lawrence had planted. On 3 July

1916 he wrote to Captain Short: "I have cleared your garden thoroughly. The things are growing splendidly." Murry recalls Lawrence's expertise with plants, his "kneeling on the ground, parting the leaves of his parsnips to show us what goodly roots he had grown." The garden yielded plentifully. Stanley Hocking, who lived below with his family, remembers Lawrence's "[c]arrots, parsnips, peas, lettuce, parsley, and what he was most fond of, spinach and endive."

There were other pleasures. In mid-August, when Barbara Low visited, they strolled down to the sea to go swimming in the Wicca Pool cove: "It was splendid also yesterday, waves *mountains* high: but not so hot as the time before," he told her on the seventeenth. The waves lifted him and flung him to shore among the rocks, which seemed both exciting and alarming. In September Frieda wrote to Cynthia to report on their "jolly summer, when we have been able to forget everything, it's the only way nowadays. . . . [T]he heather is just out and we have [had] some beautiful days." They hoped to forget not only the war but also the Murrys' treachery. Wandering on the cliffs, Lawrence and Frieda found small, round mushrooms. Well into September the wild blackberries ripened, hanging thick on the briars; the Lawrences made ten pounds of jam, some jelly, and perhaps blackberry cobbler. They probably shared their treats with Mrs. Hocking, a widow with several children still at home, one of whom Lawrence would become especially fond of.

Much has been made of the Lawrences' poverty while they lived in Cornwall. What, one wonders, *were* their expenses in relation to their income? What did Lawrence mean when he told Katharine Clayton in October that he and Frieda had "just enough to scratch along with"? Whereas a writer like Virginia Woolf had inherited about £400 a year, Lawrence's income was much less; he appears to have had £172 in 1916, or, on average, £14½ a month. If September were typical, their month's expenses can be estimated as follows:

| *Expense* | *Cost in Pounds Sterling* |
|---|---|
| rent and taxes on two cottages | 2 |
| clothing (e.g., stockings) | 1½ |
| coal for heating cottage | ½ |
| flour, sugar, meat, potatoes, rice, and fruit | 2 |
| milk, butter, eggs, cheese, cakes, and sweets | 2½ |
| soap, candles | ½ |
| tea, cigarettes for Frieda | 2 |
| writing, typing, and carbon paper; typewriter ribbon | 1 |
| postage (for fifteen letters), miscellaneous, gifts | 2 |
| transportation to Penzance for excursion | ½ |
| SEPTEMBER 1916 EXPENSES | £14½ |

Stanley Hocking remembers that although the local shops supplied the Lawrences with bread, cheese, and jam, his mother supplied their chief necessities from the farm—"butter, milk and eggs, an occasional chicken or rabbit." They appear to have spent nothing on electricity, telephone, medicine, doctors, dentists, books, retirement—and very little on clothing, gifts, and transportation. They spent what they earned. They lived frugally, at the sharp edge of discomfort; their penury, though not extreme, was real; and they seem to have acquiesced to their wartime fate.

Once the Murrys had left Tregerthen, saying the climate ill suited them, the Lawrences must often have felt hurt—even if they felt partly to blame. No doubt Murry had criticized Lawrence for his rows with Frieda, and departed feeling that he had bid them goodbye forever. In July, complaining that Murry no longer wrote to him, Lawrence told Koteliansky that Murry had been horrid. Frieda thought him venomous. The Murrys "weary me, truly," Lawrence concluded. "You shouldn't say you love me," Lawrence accused him later. "You disliked me intensely when you were here." Leaving for London on 16 September to see her children, Frieda renewed her friendship with Koteliansky and Gertler, and together they surveyed their disappointment with the Murrys.

But the Murrys left the Lawrences a legacy—a desire to examine their own relationship more fiercely than before. "Frieda and I have finished the long and bloody fight at last," Lawrence wrote to Murry in October, "and are at one. It is a fight one has to fight—the old Adam to be killed in me, the old Eve in her—then a new Adam and a new Eve. Till the fight is finished, it is only honorable to fight. But oh dear, it is very horrible and agonising." They were trying to snuff out the resistance each had to the other, trying to convert the need to control into a willingness to accept. The process of change was "horrible and agonising" because some changes needed to be subterranean, where Frieda's strength and Lawrence's irritability still clashed.

Four days later Frieda wrote Koteliansky a long letter which, while it expresses her vengeful spirit, shows how quickly the Murrys—once the Lawrences' "only real friends in the world"—had shed their glitter and become as truant as Heseltine and Puma: "To me they have been so mean—especially Jack[—]wherever they have been, they have turned people against me, tried to regard me as a 'quantité négligable'. . . . You know I love Katherine, but I blame her when she believes Jack, when she knows better herself." Roused from her indolence, Frieda could be surprisingly confrontational. She understood that Katherine spoke through Murry by not opposing him in his "vileness": but of course Frieda and Lawrence could still taunt each other in order to exercise their personal power, so that one might, in turn, see how Murry could criticize both of them—Lawrence for belittling his friends, and Frieda not for her silence but for leaping into the fray and turning a difference of opinion into an argument. Both couples worked as complementary pairs. The truth is that Frieda may have enjoyed a marital quarrel ("I am no angel myself," she acknowledged in the same letter) as much as Katherine enjoyed hearing Jack unsheathe his rapiers of spite.

Catherine Carswell, who visited the Lawrences for about a week in late September, had a different view. She justified their "rows" as healthy and praised their complementarity: "He had chosen . . . a woman from whom he felt he could win the special submission he demanded without thereby defeating her in her womanhood. Sometimes it seemed to us that he had chosen rather a force of nature—a female force—than an individual woman. Frieda was . . . mindless Womanhood, wilful, defiant, disrespectful, argumentative, assertive, vengeful, sly, illogical, treacherous, unscrupulous and self-seeking. At times she hated Lawrence and he her. There were things she jeered at in him and things in her that maddened him—things that neither would consent to subdue. But partly for that very reason—how he *admired* her!" Lawrence's refusal to yield was one of his mother's supreme qualities, rediscovered in Frieda. For Carswell he admired what he could not change even as he sought to change it. This contradiction provides a clue to the exceptional balance of forces Lawrence locates in *Women in Love.*

However, it is hard to agree that Frieda's "female force" was elemental or that submission strengthened her "Womanhood." Carswell's analysis inverts Mansfield's satirical letter to Beatrice Campbell. Doubtless the truth lies elsewhere. Because the Lawrences were thrown together for so much of every day in a small cottage, and subjected to a sustained intimacy that few ever experience, their natures chafed. As Frieda wrote to Catherine in October, "And L[awrence] and I had to fight each other, he being an artist wanted *many* things." The emphatic *many* is oddly indirect. That the Lawrences fought mostly in front of others (as Frieda later claimed) points to a stratum of unresolved insecurity in both of them that was difficult either to acknowledge or to eradicate. Like Murry, biographers such as Elaine Feinstein believe that their quarrels recreated, for Lawrence, the friction between his parents. That may be—he, like his mother, taking the high moral road and working diligently; Frieda, like his father, doing as she wished and smoking cigarettes, as he had drained pints of ale. The difference however is twofold: Frieda's modest pedigree and personal power gave her leverage with Lawrence that his father never enjoyed, and Lawrence's kindness and compassion saved him from his mother's icy complaints.

Still, the Lawrences sometimes offended because they were not circumspect, did not gauge the reactions of those around them. Nor was Lawrence prudent in offering to send Ottoline Morrell the manuscript of his new novel, which (he must have known) would offend her.

William Henry Hocking in the fields at Higher Tregerthen (Courtesy of Kitty Rogers)

## WILLIAM HENRY

Into this furnace of frictions came a new, unsettling force. A man. He interested not Frieda but Lawrence. His name was William Henry Hocking (1883–1962). After Murry's rejection of Lawrence's notion of sensual bonding, which he called *Blutbrüderschaft,* Lawrence transferred his desire for male camaraderie to Hocking, a thirty-three-year-old farmer who lived below. Since almost nothing has survived from William Henry's point of view (no letters, only a brief BBC interview, no response to Edward Nehls in the 1950s, children unresponsive to interviewer C. J. Stevens), the biographer's knowledge of the bond shared by the two men is certainly partial, and the temptation to speculate is very high.

In the Hocking family William Henry was the oldest of seven children—the butt of family criticism because he kept irregular hours in the fields, the antagonist of his much-younger brother Stanley, and the family member most dissatisfied with his lot. William Henry helped his mother, widowed since 1901, to keep up the small tenant farm on which they grew hay and turnips for their cattle and sheep, and wheat and potatoes for themselves. All the wheat had to be scythed by hand. A photograph of William Henry holding a scythe shows a tall, lanky, handsome man—a sort of Heathcliff with taciturn features and agrarian dress, and hints of sulky sadness about his eyes and mouth. Apparently he was thoughtful and sensitive.

To Barbara Low, Lawrence first mentions him in August as a Cornish farmer who desires the intellectual life and whose family therefore despises him, toward whose contempt however "he is very plucky, holding to his own half-lights." He wanted Lawrence to "give him wings." He wanted fulfillment. William Henry therefore became a replacement for Murry as well as a rural version of Lawrence's youthful self. In September Lawrence acknowledged the complication: "It is true, I still run away from him—and *cannot* ask him to the house," as if uneasy that an attraction might develop between them, so that "one *does* avoid him" and his "burden," as if he offered Lawrence some conflicted hope of intimacy. For many months he continued to do so.

Although Lawrence could have brought his friend to London and introduced him to cultured people, he declined. Partly he had gotten a cold and felt wretched, and partly he needed a safe distance from the London "set" he was then writing about; for in September he had heard from Koteliansky that some Café Royal habituées had sat mocking his *Amores* poems until Katherine Mansfield boldly intervened. At once, Lawrence introduced the episode into his novel.

Alas, autumn in 1916 came early to Cornwall, enveloping the Lawrences in a wet bleakness unlike the booming wind and roaring sea they had prized when they had come to Cornwall almost a year earlier. On 11 September Lawrence wrote to Barbara Low, "The heather is already fading on the hill, the wind from the sea is quite cold and strange, one can smell the northern oceans." The days of mid-October came windy and wild. Frieda wrote to Dollie Radford that the dreary wetness was so oppressive when she returned from London that she found Lawrence sick and in need of her nursing. "November and December will be worse," she added. She wished she could take Lawrence to a drier place. Winter seemed already to have come: "The heather on the hills is dead, the bracken is dry and brown, and blowing away to nothingness," he reported. "Already the fowls stand bunched-up motionless and disconsolate under the stacks, out of the wind, the sky is all grey and moving." He soon felt frustrated that it had rained every day for nine weeks. "I feel so wretched as the winter comes on," he told Pinker. The atmosphere all over the country seemed dark and painful, the shorter days brooding and lonely.

Cornwall had profoundly affected the Lawrences. It had ground their hopes against their poverty. It had opened their eyes to human betrayal. And it had left them stunned by the spiritual torpor around them. As Lawrence alternately typed out and revised by hand the finest novel he had yet composed, the book seemed to him "big and fearless—yes, I love it," he told Ottoline, regretting only that he would have to publish what "everybody will hate, save me." Big in conception, fearless in presentation, disliked by those who discovered themselves in it, the book was as utterly different from contemporary novels as it was thoroughly rooted in contemporary culture. Every major character in the book expressed some dimension of Lawrence's recent experience.

# 10

# *Women in Love*
# The Masterpiece
## 1916

*Women in Love* is Lawrence's most highly accomplished, most complex, most rewarding novel. Superbly organized, it is like a great cathedral, its scenes paired, counterpointed, and echoed in such a way that the novel achieves an extraordinary balance. Lawrence wrote it at an optimal point in his artistic life, when he was able to balance his intimacy with Frieda, his illness, his anger, his longing for a male *Blutbrüderschaft,* and his fascination with the forces of darkness and fate. In unexpected ways Lawrence's life—and Frieda's before he met her—enriches and informs his novel.

As the novel rushed from him, Lawrence must have felt in direct touch with some inspiring force that yielded its secrets. But he needed a typescript that Pinker, his agent, could send around to publishers like Methuen, whose contract for *The Rainbow* had stipulated first refusal on his next novel. An inveterate reviser, Lawrence could rarely let a finished page stand. Just as he hated "to go back to the past," so he could not return to a page of manuscript or typescript without transforming it. Hence, when he needed to economize and type *Women in Love* himself, he found himself in a thicket of revision. For her part Frieda dreaded typing. "Poor as we were," she wrote later, "he never expected me to do it."

Yet readers today seldom recognize the extent to which money may determine even the way a writer revises. Lawrence found typing to be like teaching—mechanical and exhausting—and by 21 August it had made him ill. He asked Pinker to order a typescript so that he could go on "scribbling out the final draft in pencil." But Pinker's charge must have been too steep, for on 12 October Lawrence told Amy Lowell that the constant typing took tremendous effort. He could not go on. Instead, he wrote and corrected the last third of the novel by hand, in ten notebooks, deftly inserting the café incident involving Katherine Mansfield and *Amores*. At last Pinker agreed to prepare a typescript (original and carbon) in his office. On 6 November Lawrence told E. M. Forster that he had "finished the sequel to the *Rainbow*—rather wonderful and terrible," then informed Pinker that the first batch of typescript had just arrived. As Lawrence revised, Frieda helped him copy revisions from one typescript to the other. Impressed by the novel's brilliance, she was always delighted (wrote Ottoline Morrell) by those ideas that "were anarchic and rebellious."

Ever since the novel was published in 1920, it has tantalized readers. Lawrence found its "seed" in two letters of July 1916 to Catherine Carswell. He claimed that most works offered too little *resistance* "to bring that solid equilibrium which is the core of art." He wanted an absolute "reached by the sheer tension of life stubborn against death, the two in opposition creating the third thing . . . art." Such an equilibrium of forces anchors his new novel, mainly because he and Frieda had now achieved the balance of harmony and friction necessary to stir his creative imagination to its richest outpouring. He had recently described the two kinds of love that intrigued him—frictional love and creative love: "Frieda's letter is quite right, about the *difference* between us being the adventure . . . this is creative life. And the reacting of a thing against its different, is death in life. So the act of love, which is a pure thrill, is a kind of friction between opposites, interdestructive, an act of death. . . . But there must be an act of love which is a passing of the self into a pure relationship with the other, something new and creative." This passage describes the balanced motion of Lawrence's novel—one couple seeking love as a path to death, the other couple seeking love as a creative, regenerative force. These two young couples are stirred into action by a pair of "fifth wheel" satellite characters who act as foils. The first of these, Hermione Roddice, is "a man's woman" of malevolent charm whose worldly riches permit her, in a kind of "friction," to go among them; the second, "a woman's man," is a bisexual named Loerke whose malevolence derails their Alpine adventure.

The two couples at the novel's center turn out to be strikingly different. Gudrun, brazenly beautiful, has returned home from London to teach art in the ugly colliery town of Beldover, in the English Midlands, while she tries to decide, at age twenty-five, whether to make marriage her "inevitable next step" or to wander alone, seeking sensation. Her sister, Ursula—a year older, less beautiful but sunnier—has taught for some years at the Willey Green Grammar School, her bright flame of life enmeshed now in the dreariness of instructing large classes. Both want change.

At the outset the two sisters find themselves attracted to two genial men who would like to have been brothers. Rupert Birkin, a district school inspector of about thirty, generally called Birkin, is strikingly vital, strong willed, brave, and by turns engaging and acerbic; he is trying to end his affair with the flamboyant Hermione Roddice, "the most remarkable woman in the midlands." Birkin, drawn to Ursula, piques her, even annoys her. But in this novel of multiple attractions, Birkin is also drawn to the oldest son of the district's chief mining family, the Criches. Tall, good looking, fair haired, forceful, and masculine, Gerald Crich, also about thirty, has been educated in Germany and now reigns as czar of the mines. He appeals to Gudrun. Restless and provocative, Gudrun feels as if Gerald had inoculated her and "changed the whole temper of her blood." But as each couple wrestles to discover grounds for commitment, they split apart, like a seed from its fruit. Birkin and Ursula ultimately find grounds for marriage; Gerald and Gudrun find in their frictional bond a pit of hard resistance.

Each of these characters stands at a fascinating angle to Lawrence's biography.

## BIRKIN AND URSULA

Rupert Birkin, the novel's fount of ideas, is often called Lawrence's mouthpiece. Kate Millett calls Birkin "Lawrence himself," Anthony Burgess repeats Millett's identical words, and to Sheila MacLeod "Birkin is certainly his mouthpiece." But to argue this congruence is to miss the complexity of Birkin's characterization. Lawrence shapes him into a synthesis of elements from Lawrence's past *but elevated one level:* hence, Birkin is a school inspector (a teacher no longer); has been ill (but does not have consumption); has two hundred pounds a year of his own (precisely the figure Lawrence tells Pinker *he* needs in order to be secure); can afford to chuck his job in midyear (Lawrence pleaded illness to leave his in midyear); has lodgings in both Nottingham and London (beyond Lawrence's means); can afford to buy a chair at a place like St. Ives and cast it off (Lawrence would have been more frugal); and has developed an intense friendship with Gerald which culminates in a magnificently sensual wrestling match in the chapter called "Gladiatorial" (which Lawrence's friendship with Murry could not in 1916 accommodate). Birkin is Lawrence not only elevated but also inspired. He is the kind of man Lawrence admired—ferocious in his integrity, attuned to his instincts, insistent on the (painful) truth, able to shatter false assumptions, and empowered to judge people and social processes. He has the acumen of a literary critic, the understanding of a philosopher, the intensity of a prophet.

But for Birkin this intensity produces a passionate dislike of the world. A spiritual emissary who seeks a new vision of society, he is maniacal about change and demands it from others. He castigates Hermione's willful perversity and causes her to erupt, her attempt to kill him with a lapis paperweight providing a striking instance of violence. Ottoline Morrell, the model for Hermione, surely confided in Lawrence her rage for power, such that sometimes (she wrote in her journal in March 1916) "I feel that I have a terrible strength inside me and that if I let it I could crush anyone." Similarly, Birkin presses Gerald to acknowledge his hollow purpose and empty goals. Later, reversing the motion of the lapis, Birkin stones the moon's reflection in order to combat symbolically Ursula's female will. "I wouldn't give a straw for your female ego," he cries to her. "I want you to drop your assertive *will*" and "let yourself go." Once she understands his need for freedom within intimacy, he urges her to leave her job as schoolmistress and join him.

In all of these efforts Birkin is articulate, resourceful, and charismatically persuasive. He is also maddeningly inconsistent and thereby escapes being a prig, instead coming alive as a fiercely intelligent outsider. Like Lawrence, Birkin has thought deeply—about love, marriage, fate, death, patriotism, sexuality, religion, and art. Like Lawrence, he freely denounces whatever evokes his disapproval; other characters criticize his need to be "always shouting," "want[ing] to *dictate*," inviting a "dreadful reaction" to his milieu. Although Birkin shares many of Lawrence's gifts, he lacks Lawrence's keen sensitivity, his profound reliance on intuition, his simplicity, and his humor.

The weakness of his characterization is that Lawrence chose not to imagine Birkin's parents, childhood, adolescence, education, or professional training—all of them untouched in the novel. Readers have therefore tended to supply *Lawrence's* background to fill the narrative gaps. That would not much matter, except for one crucial case involving draft material. At some point in 1916, Lawrence also wrote for his novel a prologue (which he later canceled). In it the narrator imagines Birkin's sexual desire for men competing with his desire for women: "Although he was always drawn to women . . . yet it was for men that he felt the hot, flushing, roused attraction which a man is supposed to feel for the other sex." In the novel Birkin insists that the two desires are complementary, the bond with men "additional to marriage." But the discovery of the canceled prologue in 1963 has invited biographers such as Jeffrey Meyers and Brenda Maddox to assume that the prologue states *Lawrence's* position. To do so, however, discounts the literary angle of Birkin's creation, in which the elevation and inspiration that refine his character permitted Lawrence to consider, for Birkin, sexually conflicted drives that are more nakedly outlined in the prologue than Lawrence would ever have allowed in describing himself. The most that can be said is that the prologue records a phase of development that both Birkin and Lawrence wanted to shed but never fully left behind. In short, Lawrence never lost his belief in love between men but gradually gave up believing that it might include a completed sexual act.

Ursula Brangwen is created differently. She does not want two loves, nor does the salvation of the world much interest her. Full of tolerance, she is a mild version of Frieda, embracing normalcy, safety, common sense. Elaine Feinstein writes that "Ursula has a jolliness which instantly recalls Frieda; she enjoys everything." When Ursula clings to her own sense of what is right and punctures Birkin's more extreme pronouncements, she seems robust and healthy. Lawrence builds her character on Frieda's personality while disguising Frieda's Germanic origins (England and Germany were still at war). Hence Ursula sews, takes walks, makes visits, talks engagingly, and criticizes as needed. Like Frieda, she becomes a domestic support for her husband.

To camouflage Frieda's Germanic origins, Lawrence places Ursula as a teacher in a Midlands town like Eastwood. Her past must be jettisoned: "She wanted to have no past," Ursula thinks later. Her commitment to teaching soon yields to a bigger conception of life's purpose. She can leave her class in midyear because she implicitly rejects a rote, regimented system of instruction. Over time she has developed her own core of beliefs. She values integrity, hates abuse of animals, resents being patronized by Hermione, sees through falsity. She has courage, humor, style, confidence, self-respect, and a giant appetite for life. If she has few scenes in which her striking blend of qualities can be articulated and tested, that is because she is less complex and exacting than Gudrun. Two features—her insistence on her own set of values and her desire to be acknowledged as more than an appendage to a gifted man—are part of what Frieda brought to Lawrence. In December 1916 Frieda happily wrote to Koteliansky: "to my satisfaction I am a nicer person [in *Women in Love*] than Gilbert [Cannan] made me" in his *roman à clef* entitled *Mendel*.

Ursula makes a good partner. Her hunger for perfect love and fulfillment guides her toward the body's mystery, as when she and Birkin make love under the stars in Sherwood Forest. Her roused sexual appetite transcends conventional intercourse: "There were strange fountains of his body, more mysterious and potent than any she had imagined or known, more satisfying, ah, finally, mystically-physically satisfying. She had thought there was no source deeper than the phallic source. And now, behold, from the smitten rock of the man's body, from the strange marvellous flanks and thighs, deeper, further in mystery than the phallic source, came the floods of ineffable darkness and ineffable riches."

"Further than the phallic source" is a code that anticipates anal intercourse. Part of Ursula's courage is to recognize it as a means to freedom:

"She was free, when she knew everything, and no dark shameful things were denied her." One useful way of explaining this shame is to observe that Ursula encourages Birkin to do to her what he might wish to do to Gerald—and what Gerald might wish to do to Birkin's squealing friend Julius Halliday, into whose effeminate softness Gerald "might plunge with gratification." Brenda Maddox says that Frieda yielded to Lawrence's desire for anal intercourse in order to satisfy him. But the truth may be simpler: that Lawrence wanted to strip away every bodily shame in order to purge the deep fear of rejection that sexual partners bring to each other.

## GUDRUN AND GERALD

The other couple, their sensuality veering toward violence, are more firmly positioned in history. Their deepest urges echo the violence unleashed by World War I, whose ferocity parallels their licentious behavior. The brightness that filters through the novel's exterior dims against the corruption and violence and death that represent displaced expressions of the war. These forces mirror Lawrence's contemporary society: "They want [a disaster], the people in this country . . . in their vile underneath way," he angrily told Cynthia Asquith on 11 December 1916. On the Somme battlefield, from July to November alone, almost 100,000 British soldiers had died; the Germans had lost many more.

Yet the war appears peripheral in the novel. As Lawrence told Cynthia back in February, "The war . . . has gone out of my imagination." In *Women in Love* the slight military action belongs to Gerald Crich and is placed in the past, when Gerald served in the Boer War (1898–1902) and then resigned his commission. Lawrence could not imaginatively comprehend the brutality and slaughter of war. When he was called to Bodmin on 28 June 1916 for a physical examination, he told the doctor he had *had* "consumption" (a rare mention of the word) and got a complete exemption. But he recognized in November that the soldier-spirit "means an endless process of death." It was the deathly *process* that interested him now.

Unlike Ursula and Birkin, Gudrun and Gerald drift toward violence and death as they discover more and more clearly how the deepest strata of their natures are fields of gravity that pull their vital, purposive selves toward collapse. Their buds of psychic growth wither. For them the unknown is not a creative energy and not an access to mystery; it is *fate,* a force that repeatedly darkens the novel. "There's one thing about our family," Gerald confesses to Birkin. "Once anything goes wrong, it can never be put right again—not with us." And even Birkin, remembering that Gerald had accidentally shot his brother, disbelieves in accident: "It all hung together, in the deepest sense." This "deepest sense" Gerald cannot fathom; the unknown offers him no escape.

Lawrence had long sought direction from the unseen powers of darkness. But now he makes a clear advance on his use of the unknown in *The Rainbow*. There the unknown had offered Ursula power, fulfillment, and access to the *Wille zur Macht* (will to power) that Birkin alludes to and that Gerald desires; the unknown had connected Ursula's soul to the cosmic forces surging outside her, in unison with the calls emanating from her subconscious affective life. Now, in *Women in Love,* Ursula says to Gudrun, "I believe what we must fulfil comes out of the Unknown to us." The spiritual hell that Lawrence had endured over the past year made him see something new: the *complexity* with which darkness and light, sex and death, reason and madness are joined. With greater maturity now, he recognized the way all simplicities deconstruct themselves. He also recognized an essential paradox of human existence: that binaries of good and evil are false—that love can harbor destruction, that knowledge can corrupt, that beauty hides ugliness, that institutions which empower also constrain. In short, he recognized that contradictions—deep, unsolvable contradictions—are central to the human condition.

In *Women in Love* this insight yields a brilliant sequence of symbolic scenes, each one powerfully illustrating the paradox of truth and falsity, love and hatred, gain and loss, life and death. One vivid scene—of Gerald riding his horse—can illustrate them all. As heir to the Crich empire, Gerald is both immensely attractive and confusingly destructive, his face "beautiful and soldierly," his body "full of male strength." Still, while his insecurity festers like an unhealing wound, he must reaffirm his control, manifest his will, assert his supremacy. Fascinated by him, Gudrun—out for an afternoon walk with her sister—watches Gerald ride his Arabian mare toward a rushing train, loaded with coal from his mines. Gerald aims not to exercise his horse or to consult his foreman, but to assert his dominance over the mare, to certify her usefulness to him, to reinforce his patriarchal prerogatives. As he gouges the mare's flanks with his spurs, which puncture her flesh like swords, she, terrified by the rattling noise of the cars and driven to frenzy, tries to escape. She cannot. The Brangwen sisters are equally terrified. "'Let her go, you fool, you *fool*—' cried Ursula," almost hysterical.

In describing Gudrun's response, however, the narrator moves in fresh ways. He uses repetition to excavate the layers of Gudrun's alarmed and thrilled response to the animal's subjugation, and he discovers her sadistic and masochistic impulses as she feels the "indomitable soft weight of the man, bearing down into the living body of the horse." One layer after another (body, thighs, calves), Gudrun imagines Gerald's sexuality and discovers that her vicarious pleasure in the mare's suffering taps a mysterious stratum in herself that she can sense but never articulate. In this stratum pain becomes pleasure, lust becomes beauty, wounds sanctify and ennoble the flesh, the phallic spurs arouse orgasm. "The world reeled and passed into nothingness for Gudrun."

The interior portrait of Gudrun draws unmistakably on Katherine Mansfield. As her biographer Claire Tomalin says, "Lawrence's [fictional] account of her is acute," the portrait is "warm and affectionate," and "something of the essential Katherine" shapes Gudrun. This, though helpful, leaves gaps. Nor is it enough to say, with Jeffrey Meyers, that "Lawrence uses Katherine as an inspiration rather than as a precise model for Gudrun." Lawrence was fascinated by Katherine's profoundly critical attitude toward life. In November 1916 he wrote to Catherine Carswell that Turgenev "seems so very critical, like Katharine Mansfield." In the novel "she's always on the defensive," says Birkin, "she challenged the whole world," she was full of "contrariness," her very life "goes by contraries." But Lawrence quickly goes beyond obvious links: that, for instance, both Katherine and Gudrun have "a certain amount of money." He chooses Katherine's most elusive qualities, her most intriguing, those he understands least well, and ponders them in his most inventive fashion to create a portrait that is *judged* just as Katherine would judge, her charming exterior providing only a mask. It is a mask for her rapacious desire hidden by aloof cynicism.

Thus, at an indirect angle to his own life, Lawrence understood Katherine's essence. He saw it as unlike his own essence—his own bearing love, hers bearing "an act of death." In *Women in Love* Gudrun, though initially attractive, soon elicits the reader's skepticism. Her desire to hatch "new schemes for going away," her discovery of her sullen cruelty, her increasing contempt for a conventional man like Gerald (who, in her hands, becomes as passive as Murry in Katherine's) all cause her to be inexpressibly restless. As Katherine went off with Murry in June—leaving Tregerthen and running, Lawrence said, "away from herself—but also from Murry"— so at the end of the couples' Alpine holiday, Gudrun goes off with the sinister Loerke, seeking a temporary haven, her restlessness as insatiable as her sexual appetite or her mockery. Where she goes, she tells Loerke, "depends which way the wind blows." Her destiny is to wander.

On the surface Gerald Crich is less complex than Gudrun. A typical industrial entrepreneur, cushioned by family power and personal magnetism, he is a figure like Evelyn Daughtry or (later) Sir Clifford Chatterley. He gradually turns to pulp. His driving purpose is not self-fulfillment but work: "I suppose I live to work," he tells Birkin, "to produce something." His faltering "I suppose" points to his lack of moral courage in drawing the elements of his nature into cohesion. He worries, for instance, that marriage may not satisfy his emotional needs. "I don't believe a woman, and nothing but a woman, will ever make my life," Gerald allows, hoping that Birkin can suggest an alternative. Although Gerald is drawn to Birkin, he is like Murry: he can express his attraction only in confused, crippled ways. Caught in a net of social pressure and personal indecision, he dangles commitment before Birkin: "I don't believe I've ever felt as much *love* for a woman, as I have for you—not *love.*"

Yet Gerald is oppressed with death wishes. When his sister falls off a boat, he plunges into the icy current of Willey Water to rescue her, but fails. The "terrible hopelessness of fate" eclipses him. Subsequently denying his physical attraction to Birkin and the stability it might bring, he encounters various forms of death or emasculation. The death of his father, Thomas, though long expected, shakes his confidence. Gudrun chases his bullocks; but when he admonishes her, she strikes him across the face, crying, "And I shall strike the last [blow]." When he tries to subdue an enraged rabbit, his arm—like hers—is scored with gashes. One of the novel's finest passages portends his doom: "But it was as if he had had knowledge of her in the long red rent of her forearm, so silken and soft. He did not want to touch her. He would have to make himself touch her, deliberately. The long, shallow red rip seemed torn across his own brain, tearing the surface of his ultimate consciousness, letting through the forever unconscious, unthinkable red ether of the beyond, the obscene beyond."

This is difficult writing. One explanation is that such knowledge, normally kept hidden by convention and taboo, leads the characters to spiritual collapse. But Lawrence liked to defy convention. A more persuasive explanation points away from spiritual collapse to vaginal obscenity. Gudrun's ambivalence toward Gerald, his anxiety in having "to make himself touch her," his quick perception that the "long, shallow red rip" might become a "soft" red vagina, his sudden "knowledge" that her hard female power might "tear" and rip with her clitoral beak: all of those fears open into a sexually terrifying crevasse called "the obscene beyond." There his annihilation might take place. There his doomed spirit might expire. Typical of Lawrence's artistry, this scene of opened or cut flesh parallels a similar scene in which Birkin proposes to Gerald a *Blutbrüderschaft*. A ritual scene to establish a mutual blood-brothership, created by cuts and the exchange of blood, the one Birkin proposes, updated to a mere verbal commitment "to swear to love each other," frightens Gerald. He insists on leaving it "till I understand it better"—likely Murry's precise words to Lawrence in May 1916.

The reciprocal link between Gudrun and Gerald is strengthened as Lawrence explores his uncanny knowledge of Katherine Mansfield's private malady—her systemic gonorrhea. The "sharp inoculation" that Gudrun feels when she first sees Gerald develops in such a way that Gudrun's interior horror, once they mate, also becomes Gerald's. But although he is initially the sadist and she the masochist, they exchange roles partway through the novel—when she becomes "one of life's outcasts" and he, an outcast to himself. As the dénouement unfolds, she taunts him: "Fancy your actually having said [that you love me]." Torn by her cruelty, he is yet fascinated by her power even as he withers under her assault. Tottering, his spirit as broken as his own mother's, Gerald wanders away from the lodge near Innsbruck where the two couples have gone for their winter holiday. Emptied of inner vitality, he sinks upon the snow and dies. The ice crystals image the contraction of his frail emotions.

## THE PAST RETURNS

Part of Lawrence's brilliance in portraying Gerald is that he draws (as expected) on his own recent experience, but he also anchors Gerald's character in the historical Thomas Philip Barber (1876–1961). As a boy, Lawrence occasionally saw this man around Eastwood. Son of the local squire, Thomas Barber had accidentally killed his brother in 1890, had witnessed a double death at Moorgreen Reservoir in 1892, and had served as a captain in the Boer War in 1900. At an historical angle Lawrence grafts this personal recollection of mines and mine owners onto his inferences about the "interior" Murry. Even though these two perspectives are at odds, Lawrence remembers with painful clarity the way his father had failed him, then enlarges that notion of failure to include the way the mine owners coarsened and exploited the lives of employees *like his father,* then complicates that notion with his recent attraction to and disappointment with Murry. He forges a composite portrait angled both historically and erotically.

Beyond that, Frieda's experience also influenced Lawrence. In 1951 she said about the novel, "Ursula is mostly me, Gudrun: Katherine, a little my sister [Johanna], and the setting the Burrows." Later she added: "Yes, the outer setting of Women-in-Love is Louie Burrows, but the inner relationship is L[awrence]'s and mine, like the ring scene, where I throw the ring at him, *that* happened." And to a critic named Edward Gilbert she wrote: "Those [fictional] episodes are practically true." But one striking aspect of the Criches has received no comment: the way the Thomas Crich family boldly encapsulates the Ernest Weekley family and then, later, the way Gudrun and Loerke explore what might have happened had Frieda left Weekley not in 1912 (when she did) but in 1907, when she almost did. As Lawrence pondered his own Eastwood past, he also pondered Frieda's past, then joined them.

Lawrence was scarcely acquainted with the Barber family. Just as Rupert Birkin has been stripped of a family in *Women in Love,* so the Crich family's inner dynamics have few antecedents in Lawrence's experience. To fill this gap, Lawrence grafted the emotional truth of the Weekley family onto the Criches. After Frieda left Nottingham, she would have talked to

Lawrence by the hour of Ernest and the children, and Lawrence always felt that Ernest, despite his unrelieved distress, was a decent man: "I like him," Lawrence claimed. The fictional portrait of the Crich family ingeniously works out the parallels.

Sometimes coming home "tired to death," Ernest Weekley was so busy lecturing at the University of Nottingham, even teaching night classes to workers' associations, that Frieda, despite loving her children, grew bored and dissatisfied. Thomas Crich, too, "was sorry for [his wife, Christiana], her nature was so violent and so impatient." Unable to escape her husband's generosity and pity, Christiana opposes him silently: "And because she was his prisoner, his passion for her had always remained keen as death. . . . Within the cage, she was denied nothing, she was given all license." Just as Thomas Crich "loved her with intensity," so Lawrence wrote to Edward Garnett on 3 July 1912 that "[Weekley] is *fearfully* in love with F[rieda]." And so, in Nottingham, she had remained an Angel of the House—even given "license" to go with her neighbor, Will Dowson, for long drives in Sherwood Forest. Birkin says to Gerald:

> "You can see how much marriage is to be trusted to—look at your own mother."
> "Do you think mother is abnormal?" [Gerald wonders.]
> "No! I think she only wanted something more, or other than the common run of life. And not getting it, she has gone wrong, perhaps."

Lawrence presciently defends Frieda's decision by imagining in Christiana Crich what Frieda might have become.

The parallels extend to her children. The oldest child in both families is a tall, responsible son. Montague, said Frieda, was "like Ernest in temperament." Gerald Crich, educated in Germany, takes over the mines from his father, then refines his father's work with "a vision of power." Because the older daughters are married, only three Crich children remain at home: a boy and two girls—the same configuration as the Weekley children. When Lawrence completed the novel in November 1916, Frieda's two daughters, Barbara and Elsa, were twelve and fourteen—almost the ages of Winifred and Diana Crich, Gerald's younger sisters. Winifred Crich is "a girl of thirteen or fourteen" and, like Barbara Weekley, an artist with an "instinctive critical faculty" and "her father's dark hair and quiet bearing"; Winifred "avoided her mother," just as Barbara, when a girl, had been taught "to run away if we saw our mother." Like Elsa Weekley (Frieda's older daughter), Diana Crich was "a handsome girl a little older than Winifred," "just in her teens," probably fifteen or sixteen, "a fretting, negated thing." Lawrence envisioned Frieda's increasingly dysfunctional family. The Crich children are gradually crippled by their parents' inadequate nurturing, and a futility ferments inside them that robs them of their courage to live.

Lawrence's use of Frieda's experience extends to her German lover, Otto Gross. Lawrence had never forgotten that, for Frieda, the affair with Gross remained an electrifying experience, and in the novel's dénouement he created a German artist named Loerke who borrows surface features from the painter Mark Gertler (1892–1939)—as others have noted—but who, underneath, surprisingly recreates Gross. Lawrence grafts Gertler's Jewish artistry onto Gross's bisexual identity. The later development of *Women in Love*, then, partly derives from Frieda's affair with the ecstatic but erratic Gross. In 1912 Lawrence reported to Edward Garnett that Weekley "never says anything against [Frieda] herself, only against the previous lover, a German, who put these 'ideas' into her head." In the novel Gudrun discovers the conclusion to Frieda's potential experience with Gross. After Frieda met Gross in Munich, in 1907, and after he invited her to run away with him to Holland, she seriously considered his offer. But the risk to her and her three children was too great.

In *Women in Love* Loerke becomes a strangely perverse version of Gross. Both have "thin hair," a "thick . . . moustache," and a "rather shapeless mouth." Both are "like a child." Both hate their fathers. Loerke rejects his indigent father, who "wouldn't work for anybody." Even Sigmund Freud certified Gross's "hostility to his father." Perversity is their link. Whereas Gross regularly indulged in cocaine and opium, Loerke enjoys inflicting pain on a sixteen-year-old model named Annette. Whereas Freud believed that Gross had an "abnormal affective life," and whereas Carl Jung believed that Gross had "infantile identification blockages of a specifically homosexual nature," Lawrence extrapolates this same tendency in Loerke by bonding him to a young male lover named Leitner. The two men, although they had "lived together in the last degree of intimacy," now despised each other.

Just as Gross urged Frieda not to return to Nottingham, Loerke says to Gudrun, "You cannot go back to teaching . . . that is impossible. . . . You are an extraordinary woman." Loerke views Gudrun as a soul mate and, reciprocally, "something in Gudrun seemed to accord with him." Gudrun had long been ready to try a new form of life. When Loerke says to her, "But come. . . . Come to Dresden," one can hear Gross writing to Frieda, "Come, Frieda, come to me." "You know the bliss you would confer upon me *if* you were to come to Holland." Like Frieda, Gudrun recognized that Loerke "would only want her to be herself": and although his poverty attracts her, Gudrun, like Frieda, knew that "[i]n the last issue he cared about nothing." To follow this man would be to submit to an inexorable drift toward instability, both physical and emotional. Indeed, Birkin thinks Loerke "almost like a criminal," and that is what Gross became in 1913 when his father had him arrested in Berlin as a psychopath and then confined. Gudrun's life as a vagabond, as part of the "German Bohemian life" of "free individual[s]," was, according to Lawrence's intuition, the life Frieda might have known. At the novel's close Gudrun thinks she might "be going to Munich, to a girl-friend she had there." That is where Frieda went in 1907, when she left Nottingham for Munich—she went to see her girlfriend Frieda Schloffer. These parallels suggest the acute insight with which Lawrence could intertwine life and art.

For Lawrence, Frieda's beguiling biography suggested a way of conceptualizing repressed Eastwood types like Thomas Barber, then giving them license to act out the darker sides of their natures. Lawrence's ability to imagine what Frieda might have experienced before he rescued her offered him an artistic method of exploring two sides of a character's life—the old shaping environment that compressed opportunity and the opposed environment that released a character to act. Both directions were fraught with danger. To close off one's inner self is to die prematurely, as Gerald does; to release one's inner forces, as Gudrun does, is to risk chaos. In *Women in Love* Lawrence perfectly balances these opposed forces. As Frieda aged, she realized that Lawrence had extracted the essential truth from their personal experience: "When I read [*Women in Love*] now, I can hardly bear it," she wrote. That was perhaps because Lawrence had captured both her actual and her potential experiences in a single work.

Lawrence's masterpiece unceasingly probes the mysterious connections between life and art. Given that the major characters are all aligned to his and Frieda's personal lives, Lawrence sought to understand artistically the core of psychological distress in those he knew. Yet the novel's publication remained a worry; he needed a commitment from someone who dared to publish the book as it stood.

## FINDING A PATRON

After Lawrence and Frieda finished correcting the two typescripts—sending one to Pinker for circulation, one to people like the Carswells for comment—he sank quietly into a kind of spiritual torpor, as if he understood from the inside Gerald's feelings of despair. The world, he told E. M. Forster in November 1916, seemed full of "sewer-rats, with all the[ir] foul courage of death and corruption." To search for the good in others would imprison him, he thought, in a lie. Seeing the worst, Lawrence spit out his lapsed friendships: "I have done with the Murries, both, for ever—so help me god . . . [and] with Lady Ottoline," he announced to Koteliansky the next day. He felt the urge to cast England behind him and to find "a place in the far west mountains [of America]," nearer to freedom, nearer to the "new" unknown, he told Catherine Carswell.

To relieve the Lawrences' solitude came two Americans, Esther Andrews (*c.* 1885–1962) and Robert Mountsier (1888–1972), both of them journalists, she hoping to do a book about women and the war, he representing the *New York Sun*. In Cornwall they stayed in Penzance and St. Ives but came several times to see the Lawrences in Higher Tregerthen and returned for Christmas; Esther lingered for several weeks. "He is over here," wrote Lawrence, "to interview the leading authors," apparently explaining why Mountsier came to see Lawrence, who had actually met him a year earlier. The new couple, who lived together briefly, seemed "really nice, gentle . . . [and] more innocent than children," Lawrence thought. Mountsier was tall and shy, with a quiet modesty; Andrews, who had briefly attended the Yale School of Art, was tall and attractive and husky voiced, spoke like an actress, and rejected the notion of marriage. They were a version of what Lawrence and Frieda had been in *their* first two years together.

As Christmas approached, the Lawrences' money ran out. It was time to ask for help. In October Frieda wrote to Amy Lowell: "I know how really generous you are and I ask you to help us a little—It would be so infinitely welcome just at the moment." Lowell kindly sent sixty pounds, and Lawrence appealed again to Pinker, who at once sent fifty pounds. To Lowell Lawrence wrote: "One is so moved by the kindness: the money, after all, is necessity, but the kindness is given." Financially the Lawrences were fixed for about six months. They could now afford to travel to London—Lawrence to consult a doctor and an oculist, Frieda to see her children—and even to visit the Midlands. Lawrence had not seen his family for a year.

The dark weeks passed like fitful sleep. Lawrence roused himself to tell Koteliansky in November: "One only wanders through the dim short days, and reads, and cooks, and looks across at the sea. I feel as if I also were hibernating, like the snakes and the dormice." Koteliansky sent him an Italian *Baedeker,* in case he and Frieda were allowed, in wartime, to go to Italy ("most probably not," Lawrence guessed). But a letter from Ottoline Morrell on the 27 November broke the sleep. She had heard—probably from Murry—that she was the villainess of *Women in Love*. Lawrence offered to send her the manuscript. To Catherine Carswell he wondered aloud: "Do you think it would really hurt her—the Hermione? Would you be hurt, if there was some of you in Hermione? You see it really isn't her at all—only suggested by her." In time the carbon copy of the typescript wended its way from the Carswells to Esther Andrews to Barbara Low to H.D. and finally to Ottoline Morrell, who, when she read it in January 1917, went (she said) "pale with horror, for nothing could have been more vile and obviously spiteful and contemptuous than the portrait of me that I found there. It was a great shock. . . . I wrote to Lawrence to protest, but his only answer was that Hermione was a very fine woman." Ottoline thought her portrait libelous, and to show her hurt she decided that she would never see Lawrence again. To give her some protection, her husband, Philip, a solicitor, threatened legal action.

But as 1916 closed, Lawrence's major worry was not libel but finding a publisher—any publisher—for his work. On 19 December he nervously communicated a plan to Cynthia Asquith, who was well connected: "I have finished and sent in the novel *Women in Love,* which is more or less a sequel to the *Rainbow.* It is a very fine piece of work, and I will stand by it for ever. But there is the same danger ahead as ever: it is, perhaps, almost as likely to be suppressed as was the *Rainbow:* which seems to me monstrous, a serious and profound piece of work like that. . . . Do you know anybody of any weight or importance, who would take it under his, or her, protection, so far as to accept a serious dedication? It is a much finer book than the *Rainbow,* and I would rather it were never published at all than insulted by petty dogs as that [book] was." It is the first of many strategies that Lawrence hoped might secure publication for the novel that he regarded as "a masterpiece."

But with the holidays came a prolonged sadness. David Lloyd George—who became prime minister on 8 December, having ousted Lady Cynthia's father-in-law, H. H. Asquith—addressed Parliament in stirring words that, when Lawrence read them in the *Times,* infuriated him: As England awaited possible peace terms, said Lloyd George, "we shall put our trust in an unbroken Army rather than in a broken faith. (Loud cheers.) . . . Just look at it. An absolutely new Army. . . . It has passed through a fiery furnace, and [become] fine steel." Exasperated, Lawrence cried, "The man . . . mechanically does what Germany does." The Christmas spirit died in his heart. Even as he and Frieda sent a lapis lazuli pendant to Dollie Radford and an agate letter opener to Koteliansky, Lawrence felt "awfully downhearted—down altogether," and wrote to Gordon Campbell two days before Christmas that, except for Frieda, he felt isolated and cut off—fulfilled and happy in his solitary self yet having "*no connection* with the rest of people, I am only at war with them." He could only hope that the political tide would turn, that the existing social frame would smash so it could be rebuilt, and that travel restrictions would ease so he and Frieda could leave England.

It was probably Frieda who insisted that, despite their poverty, they must have a joyous Christmas party to raise their spirits. Bearing a basket of fruit, Esther Andrews and Robert Mountsier came, as did the entire Hocking family from the farm below. In the tower cottage once occupied by the Murrys, the Lawrences served a supper, sang English and German folk songs, and afterward played games. The festival mood faded quietly. The evening was like a match struck against a gloomy expanse of darkness.

# Suspicion

## 1917

As the new year opened, Lawrence and Frieda were not alone in braving the privations of war. Others they knew were also affected. Lawrence's mentor, Edward Garnett, had enlisted in the British ambulance unit and worked briefly for the Red Cross in Italy, but found when he returned home that his editorial position at Duckworth was gone. Constance Garnett continued to translate Dostoevsky, publishing thirteen volumes from 1912 to 1920. After a stint of relief work in France, their son, David, became a conscientious objector and labored on a Sussex farm. In London, Katherine and Murry now lived apart, she taking a Chelsea studio by herself in order to write, he working in the War Office as a translator until, in November 1917, sick with pleurisy, he crept to Garsington to recuperate. Bertrand Russell, too old to be called up, had begun giving eloquent pacifist lectures and in 1917 headed the radical No-Conscription Fellowship. E. M. Forster, working for the Red Cross in Alexandria, became a volunteer searching for missing soldiers. Meanwhile, at Garsington—itself a refuge for COs—Philip Morrell offered farm work to Bloomsbury pacifists like Clive Bell, who had won exemptions from the Military Service Act. All of these writers had defined themselves in relation to the war. The difference between them and Lawrence is that Lawrence fought the war internally, within his spirit, as if it were a trench where grenades of angry passion exploded. Demolishing his faith in Britain, the war made him crave escape. His deepest instinct opposed it.

Although Cornwall had initially soothed Lawrence's sense of himself, now the place tethered him. Eventually he felt trapped. J. B. Pinker had had no success in placing *Women in Love*, not even with Duckworth, Lawrence's stalwart supporter. The firm of Constable, rejecting the novel on 23 January 1917, had complained that Lawrence's "destructive philosophy" and his "expressions of antipathy to England and the forms of English civilisation" would, while soldiers' lives were being sacrificed, antagonize readers. Without a contract for the novel, Lawrence had little confidence that his writing would flower. His friendship with Robert Mountsier and Esther Andrews helped him think that on American soil his literary gifts might flourish. He needed some *deus ex machina*. "I want to go clean away, for ever," he told Gordon Campbell in January. "I feel it is finished in me, with this side of the globe. . . . Here one is thwarted, cribbed, stunted, body, soul, and spirit, there is no peace of being." The repeated rejection of *Women in Love,* including Ottoline Morrell's "frenzy" when she read it, made him unable to write for England. Philip Morrell had even accosted Pinker and threatened libel if the novel were published without revision.

America beckoned, offering the Lawrences a possible site for their Rananim; for America, which seemed vast and free, had not yet (not until 6 April) declared war on Germany. Closer to home, the war hounded Lawrence's spirit: "Yesterday two ships were submarined just off here: luckily we didn't see them: but Stanley [Hocking] watched one go down, and the coastwatchers saw the crew of the other struggling in the water after the ship had gone: all drowned: Norwegians, I believe. My sister writes a ghastly story from Glasgow, of a new and splendid submarine on her trial trip in the Clyde [River]: she dived and never came up, all watching expecting her. But I cannot bear it, it makes me tremble. It . . . is the maximum of evil." Lawrence saw the enemy coming closer, savage and unpredictable. The weeks as they passed seemed to him scarcely bearable—made worse by the cold wind and snow.

Lawrence hoped that Edward Marsh, soon to become Winston Churchill's private secretary, could help him and Frieda renew their passports. He wrote Marsh four letters in January. On the twenty-ninth came the reply that, although Frieda's birthplace would pose some difficulty, Lawrence could probably leave for America if he produced convincing evidence. To Pinker on the same day, he cited evidence of ill health, inability to earn money in England, and the need to place his literary work in America. The real reason was less commercial than spiritual—to escape a kind of panic that oppressed his very breathing. Given that Frieda "flatly refuses to go [by] English boat," he hoped they could sail in March on a Dutch ship departing from Falmouth, thirty miles away. Of course his passport was not renewed—"a bitter blow," he told Mountsier in February, so bitter that he thought "foul inward poison" would kill him.

To combat such feelings he turned instinctively to the land. On 9 February he had written to Gertler, "If we have to stay here, I shall become a farmer" and help William Henry Hocking just below, "whom I like." A few days later he happily observed the doves and lambs down at the farm, their spontaneity a reviving force, "a sign that life will never be destroyed." In February Lawrence helped William Henry with the spring chores— probably assisting the ewes to give birth, cleaning the stables and spreading manure over the fields, repairing the harness, hauling rocks turned up when the fields were plowed, setting out broccoli and cabbage as soon as the first garden was dug, cutting seed potatoes for planting.

Staying busy helped him forget the war. "Now I am going to garden," he told Koteliansky on a day of glorious March sunshine. "I believe we are really going to be pinched for food." He asked his friend to send him *The Culture of Profitable Vegetables in Small Gardens,* a pamphlet that recommended "incessant stirring of the soil," liming, manuring—as well as the most prolific varieties of thirty-two vegetables, including oddities (which Lawrence planted) such as *salsify* (enticingly called vegetable oyster) and *scorzonera,* both of them tap-rooted plants to be dug in late autumn and served "with white sauce." To accommodate so many varieties, Lawrence decided to have two gardens near the house, with flowers and vegetables, and a larger garden in the field below. Although he was certainly too outspoken in his hatred of the war, he no doubt thought that his patriotic gardening would shield him from suspicion that he and his German wife were spies.

Yet Lawrence had never stopped writing. He labored at two projects— a book of poems and a collection of short essays. Working against despair, he culled from his old notebooks the last and best of his poems, sixty-one in all. They made, he told Catherine Carswell, a "conclusion of the old life in me" and consisted of poems so "intimate and vital" that he shrank even from giving them to Pinker for circulation, waiting till April to do so. He thought at first of calling them *Poems of a Married Man,* but later chose the title *Look! We Have Come Through!* By 18 February he had prepared a fair copy, which he sent for comment to Carswell and the young American poet H.D., whose judgment he respected. The essays, which he called "The Reality of Peace," were new and short and (he thought) very beautiful. He sent them to Pinker on 19 March for placement in the *English Review,* where four of the seven appeared over the next few months, yielding the author twenty guineas (twenty-one pounds). To find peace, Lawrence wrote, requires "that we yield up our will to the unknown" and so make ourselves "new and vivid." In lyrical, hortatory prose, punctuated by biblical cadences, Lawrence developed a distinctive mode of writing that would long appeal to him.

The third "Peace" essay, for instance, climaxes in a fervent prayer that, while apostrophizing death, directly explores Lawrence's recent concerns: "Sweet, beautiful death, come to our help. Break in among the herd, make gaps in its insulated completion. Give us a chance, sweet death, to escape from the herd and gather together against it a few living beings. . . . Break for us this foul prison where we suffocate in the reek of the flock of the living dead. Smash, beautiful destructive death, smash the complete will of the hosts of man, the will of the self-absorbed bug. Smash the great obscene unison. . . . Smash humanity, and make an end of it. Let there emerge a few pure and single men—men who give themselves to the unknown of life and death and are fulfilled." His fervor gauges his desperation. Crawling with repulsion for bugs and obscene visions, his prayer is like a curse on his enemies. Invoking the aid of forces outside his control, he pleads for purification and, fearful of the herd, demands separation from the plague spread by the human will. Even though he would acknowledge—in July—that "[t]he herd will destroy everything," he hoped these essays might make a new path toward peace and hope. They were his form of battle.

## THE PULL OF LONDON

The sunny days and warm greenness everywhere stimulated both the Lawrences. They wanted to go up to London—but separately, Frieda to see her children, Lawrence to see his family and friends. In late March she departed, stayed with Dollie Radford in her tiny house, and returned home about 30 March. Apparently her children reported their father's hypocrisy, for she wrote to Koteliansky on 1 April: "I was *disgusted* to find that Ernst who poses as a tragic figure to the children, takes Gladys [Bradley] (she is a handsome, coarse girl) out to dinner, flirts with her, but keeps of course the last respectability." She minded not his need for companionship but his pretense.

While she was gone, Lawrence gardened happily, waiting for the daffodils and primroses to come out among the trees. Esther Andrews came to visit and apparently stayed about a month in the tower cottage, departing by 11 May. Both Jeffrey Meyers and Brenda Maddox speculate that she and Lawrence may have become lovers at this time. That seems possible, although somewhat unlikely in view of Lawrence's fidelity to his marriage and his intense attraction to William Henry. The anonymous memoir that Mabel Dodge Luhan included in *Lorenzo in Taos* (1932) probably came from Andrews: the details suggest intimate knowledge of the cottage at Higher Tregerthen, and she had read *Women in Love* in manuscript. If Andrews judged Frieda sunny and rich, "living only in her emotions," she saw Lawrence as a verbal geyser: "The first time I ever saw him, he talked for a whole afternoon, almost steadily. . . . He talks as brilliantly as he writes, and as frankly. Have you read *Women in Love?* Because that *is* Lawrence—his word. It is his final philosophy. It pours out of him like an inspired message, and no matter how much you may differ when you are away from him, or how little able you are to follow his own particular mysticism, he makes you believe it when he is with you." This kind of swooning discipleship could not have inspired Frieda's goodwill or bolstered her sense of herself; later, perhaps fearing that Lawrence had been pursued, she felt antagonistic toward Andrews.

When Frieda returned from London, her vivid anecdotes about their friends stirred Lawrence to make his own trip. On 14 April he left for the Midlands (the train journey took all day) to see his sisters at Ada's home in Ripley and to visit his staunch Eastwood friends, Sallie and Willie Hopkin and their daughter Enid. After two days, he had a revulsion: "I hate the Midlands," he told Koteliansky. In London he went to 5 Acacia Road, the home of Koteliansky and his landlords, Sonia and Michael Farbman, and their daughter Ghita. On Friday he saw Pinker (probably for lunch) and Austin Harrison at the *English Review,* then visited Dollie Radford and later Catherine Carswell. For good reason he did not telephone Lady Cynthia: on Sunday he collapsed for two days with sickness and diarrhea. But by Wednesday he was able to go out to Dollie Radford's tranquil duplexed cottage, at Hermitage, in Berkshire, where he stayed until Friday, walking through the woods, watching a jay in flight, and admiring the primroses as they lit the dusk. In the other half of the duplex lived young Hilda Brown (b. 1911) and her parents. She recalled her mother's first impression of Lawrence as "a very sick man"—tall, slim, pale faced, with sad eyes above his red beard.

For Lawrence, returning home was a joy. His seeds had sprouted, the early cress was ready to cut, the cuckoo called, the woods were in flower, and he felt (he told Cynthia) "as if the young grass growing would upset all the cannon on the face of the earth." But on 28 April Frieda was so ill with colitis that he had to write for the doctor, who prescribed *koumiss,* or fermented milk, a folk remedy for settling the stomach. Years later Frieda wrote: "Once when I had colitis in Cornwall *yoghourt* cured me, when nothing else would."

Lawrence had planted his lower garden with carrots, peas, spinach, endive, broad beans, scarlet runners, kohlrabi, squash, leeks, and melons, all planted in perfect rows, all requiring intense hoeing and weeding. Frieda must have helped. In 1953 William Henry recalled that Lawrence planted "about every kind of vegetable that I knew of at the time—and some that I didn't know." The gardening book had inspired him.

But while the garden grew, so did Britain's need for young men to fight in the trenches that lined Belgian battlefields such as Messines or Ypres.

During May 1917 German planes began to bomb Britain and on 13 June killed 162 civilians in London. Lawrence's antagonism to the war was fierce, undying, and vocal. When first called to Bodmin to be examined, a year earlier, on 28–29 June 1916, he felt humiliated: "I beg all my stars that I may never see Bodmin again. I hate[d] it so much," he told Dollie Radford the day he was given a rejection. Now the stakes were higher. The new Military Service Act had empowered recruiters to dredge deeper into the pool of those who had not been called. Hence in June 1917 Lawrence received a notice for reexamination. Frieda was frightened. The man who had just pleaded with Death "to escape from the herd" was ordered to appear in Bodmin on 23 June. Although Lawrence could not have been surprised, he felt keenly the trespass on his security and privacy: "I have a bad feeling about Bodmin," he told Murry. Quickly he wrote to Dr. John Rice (probably the physician who had treated Frieda), secured a certificate about his ill health, and mailed it to the officials. They decided to see him for themselves.

Lawrence's anxiety was now acute. Although he hated London and had little money, he decided to consult urban specialists who, he hoped, might certify his unfitness and free him from a Bodmin-style exam. Accordingly, he took the train to London; stayed with the ever-gracious Dollie Radford, a frail but intrepid woman who reminded Lawrence of his mother; probably saw a specialist on Friday, 15 June, or the following Monday; and may have returned to Cornwall the next day. He was disappointed: "I don't think I got much good out of the doctors," he told Dollie. Near the end of his resources and thereby at the far edge of hope, he dejectedly took the train to Bodmin on Saturday the twenty-third. Frieda, feeling estranged in the country, worried that if he were conscripted, she would be interned in a camp. Two days later he announced hollowly that he had been rejected again, given a C-3 rating, and declared unfit for military service (although he was conscriptable, as needed, for light, nonmilitary work). For Frieda he detailed the pathetic sight of men stripped to their shirts, their privates probed, their human qualities ignored as they moved along like cattle: "The war seemed to drive Lawrence to utter despair," she wrote in her autobiography, *Not I, But the Wind*. Apart from Frieda, he had nothing to hold to but his solitary self.

## How to Spend Eternity

As the summer months arrived, Frieda was happy all day long. But Lawrence, feeling entrapped by the war, believed he was simply marking time. Refusing to be depressed, he occupied himself with three projects: helping a young composer named Cecil Gray, whom he met through Philip Heseltine (the latter had returned briefly to Cornwall "on the verge of utter collapse"); struggling to get his books published; and working outdoors, harvesting his vegetables and the Hockings' hay.

Cecil Gray (1885–1951), a Scottish dilettante basking in two hundred pounds a year from his parents, had tired of London and, in Cornwall, had sought his friend Heseltine, with whom he had shared a studio in Battersea and a love of contemporary music. Like Heseltine, he had rejected a career in business and the military had rejected him as C-2. For a mere five pounds a year Gray had rented an old house pretentiously called Bosigran Castle, located near Pendeen, on a coastal summit about four miles from the Lawrences. Tall and broad, unmarried, age twenty-one, Gray seemed nice and congenial, Lawrence thought. Eager to break their isolation in Higher Tregerthen and skilled at bargaining in the St. Ives markets, the Lawrences offered to help Gray furnish Bosigran with used furniture. For less than ten pounds Lawrence had located tables, chairs, bed, mattress, chest, and lamp. When Gray moved to Bosigran in June, bringing along his piano, he began to see the Lawrences frequently, and in July and August the Lawrences spent days with him, often singing Hebridean folk tunes such as "The Seal Woman's Song." For a while, Gray wrote in his autobiography, *Musical Chairs*, "We were, in fact, almost one household: when I was not visiting the Lawrences, they were visiting me." The Lawrences tolerated well Gray's priggish conceit.

The problem of money remained. Cecil Palmer, who had thought he might publish *Women in Love*, declined it in mid-August and wrote that he wished he were rich enough to print it privately. Pinker, unsuccessful with *Women in Love*, had sent the manuscript of Lawrence's poems, *Look! We Have Come Through!*, to Chatto and Windus, a distinguished firm founded in 1855, which had published Swinburne, Wilkie Collins, R. L. Stevenson, and many others. On 18 July 1917 Chatto, impressed with the poems, nibbled. They offered a conditional acceptance. They wanted to add the volume to their autumn list but proposed five deletions ("a process of refinement," they coyly called it). They offered an advance of twenty-one pounds and a 15 percent royalty on all English sales, leaving the door open to Benjamin Huebsch for an American edition. Lawrence was delighted with their offer but infuriated by the request to delete one of his favorite poems, "Song of a Man Who Is Loved," written (Frieda said) in 1912 in Icking. The publisher, when asked to reconsider, was adamant: "[I]n view of past history . . . the continuously sexual tone of the volume should be modified." "Past history," of course, referred to *The Rainbow*'s suppression.

The objectionable poem has a quietly conversational tone, which is so direct as to seem unmediated, its desire for refuge so clear as to be like the call of a hurt child for its mother. Still, the word *breasts*, providing a frame around the poem's veiled anguish, would have startled Chatto's reader:

Between her breasts is my home, between her breasts.
Three sides set on me space and fear, but the fourth side rests,
Warm in a city of strength, between her breasts.

All day long I am busy and happy at my work
I need not glance over my shoulder in fear of the terrors that lurk
Behind. I am fortified, I am glad at my work.

I need not look after my soul; beguile my fear
With prayer, I need only come home each night to find the dear
Door on the latch, and shut myself in, shut out fear.

I need only come home each night and lay
My face between her breasts;
And what of good I have given the day, my peace attests.

And what I have failed in, what I have wronged
Comes up unnamed from her body and surely
Silent tongued I am ashamed.

And I hope to spend eternity
With my face down-buried between her breasts
And my still heart full of security
And my still hands full of her breasts.

To view the poem as revealing "infantile solipsism," as Brenda Maddox does, misses its achieved sense of resolution and equipoise—not yet the *transcendence* that Lawrence imagines at the end of "The Reality of Peace," when love interacts "in such intimate equipose with hate that the transcendence takes place," but rather the enveloping security that Frieda continued to offer. Yet her power of protection is unlike that of Lawrence's mother, who in "Death-Paean" was imagined as a militant and virile Viking; instead, Frieda is protectress and anchor, "city of strength" and pillar of acceptance: his wrongs, already atoned, come "unnamed from her body," eclipsed by the fervor of her love.

## RUDDY AND HANDSOME

And what of William Henry? While Chatto's printer worked on the proofs, Lawrence worked in the hay, helping William Henry during July, August, and September. The two men spent many hours together, binding sheaves of wheat and building ricks of hay and sometimes, on Thursdays, driving to the Penzance market. Stanley Hocking remembers that Lawrence, though not strong, "loved coming down and doing what he could [to help]." The family welcomed Frieda too: "We loved for Frieda to come down in the fields, but my sisters [Mabel and Mary] were a bit uneasy . . . feeling that Mrs. Lawrence was a lady." No doubt Lawrence remembered the joy of helping the Chambers boys in 1908, just before he started teaching in Croydon. Frieda remembered that Lawrence "could talk by the hour with William Henry, the farmer's elder son, ruddy and handsome," and that sometimes, after being with William Henry, Lawrence would come home "and want to quarrel with me." Because she spent so many evenings alone, she would have preferred that William Henry visit Lawrence in their cottage.

What of Lawrence's emotions? In this period of his life, so much is coded that readers, perplexed, have wondered what happened when Lawrence and William Henry were alone. How far did their intimacy go? Did attraction flare into love? To put the issue differently: Did they consummate their friendship in a sexual act? The answer matters, for if sexual consummation took place, then Lawrence was not a secret but an active bisexual, technically unfaithful to Frieda. The point is subtle: Frieda's occasional *sexual* infidelities did not, in her view, constitute marital infidelity, for in her heart she was always firmly committed to Lawrence as her husband. For Frieda sexual fidelity was not the axis of marriage; for Lawrence it was. As he said later, in 1929, "sex is the clue to marriage," a defining component; sexual fidelity provided marriage with its firmest anchor.

Several biographers have thought consummation likely, and at first glance the evidence might suggest it. The prologue Lawrence canceled from *Women in Love* (probably composed in April 1916) connects a Cornish male to sexual appetite. When Rupert Birkin beholds a strange Cornishman, he sees his dark eyes, "like the eyes of a rat, and . . . full, heavy, softly-strong limbs." Twice before, Lawrence had used the image of the rat as a metonymy for homosexuals like "Keynes at Cambridge" and for Loerke, the slinking "rat" in *Women in Love*. Yet Birkin is undeterred, unguarded: "Then again Birkin would feel the desire spring up in him, the desire to know this man, to have him, as it were to eat him, to take the very substance of him. And watching the strange, rather furtive, rabbit-like way in which the strong, softly-built man ate, Birkin would feel the rousedness burning in his own breast, as if this were what he wanted, as if the satisfaction of his desire lay in the body of the young, strong man opposite." Birkin is aroused by androgynous "softly-strong" limbs, the man's furtive male behavior arousing a strong physical urge toward sexual "satisfaction." To "eat" the man and to take his "very substance" may encode a desire for oral sex. In a letter of 27 July to Eunice Tietjens, Lawrence clarified his belief: "Desire is holy, belonging to the mystic unknown, no matter *what* the desire."

Mesmerized, Lawrence wrote of this friendship again in 1922, after he had left England. In his novel *Kangaroo* he included a "Nightmare" chapter that recounts his protagonist's life in wartime Cornwall. Admitting that the chapter contained "my own long 'war' experience," Lawrence invited biographers to plunder it for details about his sexual and emotional life. The novel's protagonist, Richard Lovat Somers, infatuated with his Cornish friend John Thomas Buryan, admits spending more time at the Buryan farm than with his wife, Harriet (Frieda), sometimes "lying in the bracken or on the heather [with John Thomas] as they waited for a wain." Actively withdrawing from Harriet, Somers expresses solidarity with the farm people, who hated "her beauty, her reckless pride, her touch of derision." Somers fights her attempts to interfere. A personal crisis emerges. His marriage cannot protect him from the powerful feelings that have arisen.

What happened when Lawrence and Hocking were alone? Did they— as both Jeffrey Meyers and Brenda Maddox aver—succumb to their strong desire for each other? A critical passage from *Kangaroo* is full of codes that, when translated, suggest an aroused state that leads Somers "over the border," the spirit of arousal "invading him" and "making him savage," an intense "longing" for sexual experience flooding over him; and yet, when the two men put up the sheaves, as did Anna and Will in *their* mating dance in *The Rainbow*, John Thomas, with his nervous gestures and quick brown eyes, felt "full of fear," especially a "fear of the unseen . . . of death":

And as Somers sat there on the sheaves in the underdark, seeing the light swim above the sea, he felt he was over the border, in another world. . . . [H]e could feel it invade him in the savage dusk, making him savage too, and at the same time, strangely sensitive and subtle, understanding the mystery of blood-sacrifice: to sacrifice one's victim, and let the blood run to the fire, there beyond the gorse upon the old grey granite: and at the same time to understand most sensitively the dark flicker of animal life about him . . . [so that] he no longer saw its sickeningness. . . . Then would come John Thomas with the wain, and the two men would linger putting up the sheaves, linger, talking, till the dark. . . . John Thomas, with his nervous ways and his quick brown eyes, was full of fear: fear of the unseen, fear of the unknown malevolencies, above all, fear of death.

The Cornish farmer's fear of death encodes his fear of yielding to his impulses, whereas Somers's willingness to look beyond the "sickeningness" of dark animal life encodes his willingness to respond. When Lawrence wrote an essay on Whitman in 1919, he clarified the sequence of Whitman's merging with others: "For the great mergers, woman at last becomes inadequate. . . . So the next step is the merging of man-for-man love. And this is on the brink of death. It slides over into death. . . . It always slides into death." For Lawrence conventional associations of guilt and fear compact into a form of extinction long associated with homoerotic behavior.

Other evidence, though suggestive, is not conclusive. That John Thomas is a slang name for the penis suggests that in the narrator's mind lies a strong sexual association. According to C. J. Stevens, who interviewed the Hocking family, a relative named Arthur Eddy once said: "I don't know if I ought to tell you this or not, but William Henry told me one day that Lawrence was [homosexual]. . . . He said Lawrence used to come down to the farm and talk to him about it a lot." In his own way William Henry sought to protect himself. He apparently destroyed the letters Lawrence sent him. Older than Lawrence (but scarcely the "innocent native son" Meyers thinks him), he married in June 1918, not long after the Lawrences left Cornwall, publicly affirming his heterosexuality. Frieda's later reflections on Lawrence's behavior in 1916, which she divulged to Murry in 1953, suggest that Lawrence wanted "the homosexuality" from Hocking, the "deeper [spiritual] thing" from Murry: "I think the homosexuality in him was a short phase out of misery—I fought him and won—and [I think] that he wanted a deeper thing from you." She then makes a concession that biographers have missed: "I am aware . . . of the elements in us, that we consist of," suggesting her awareness of Lawrence's bisexual "elements" but not her acceptance of them.

In spite of this suggestive evidence, it is unlikely that the two men consummated their friendship in a sexual act. There is Lawrence's own statement, made in 1918 to Katherine Mansfield, that, although he believed in the inviolable pledging of one man to another, he had "not ever met or formed such [a] friendship." But the most persuasive reason is that so powerful an experience would—for Lawrence—almost certainly have found its way into his art. His attraction to Frieda, for instance, had exploded into *Love Poems and Others,* parts of *The Rainbow,* and much of *Women in Love.* After Virginia Woolf engaged in erotic encounters with Vita Sackville-West—"I *have* gone to bed with her (twice)," claimed the latter—Woolf soon wrote the extraordinary *Orlando* (1928) to commemorate their affair. But in Lawrence's case the imaginative work after 1917 does not reveal any such tribute to William Henry, although Lawrence may of course have felt betrayed or found the sexual act so disappointing as to inspire no literary response. Still, given Birkin's intense need for a physical relationship with Gerald, a physical consummation between Lawrence and William Henry would have resulted in some extraordinary works written before Lawrence's 1919 essay on Whitman's love of comrades. Perhaps he remembered Oscar Wilde's saying that "criticism is the only civilized form of autobiography," for one acceptable outlet for Lawrence's intense feelings came in the series of critical essays later called *Studies in Classic American Literature* (1923); there he could interpret other writers' experiences rather than assess his own. This link between life and art helps explain the exceptional richness, integrity, and sense of risk these essays reveal. *They* enshrine the erotic fire that William Henry aroused.

## A Sudden Blow

While the autumn mists of Cornwall blew in from the Atlantic, and while Lawrence gathered in the last of the gourds and shell beans, he and Frieda relished their fragrant soups bubbling on the tiny oil stove and the crisp silence of the shorter days. Gratis, Lawrence was still helping to bring in the last of the hand-tied sheaves of wheat, and still savoring the Hockings' *croust,* or afternoon tea served in the fields. He and Frieda had achieved a kind of contentious perfection in their lives, their quarreling the yeast of their emotional engagement with each other. "There has been a curious subtle mystic invisibleness in the days, a beauty that is not in the eyes," he wrote to Koteliansky on 23 September. The forces of Lawrence's personal life had fused into an equilibrium, however narrow and temporary, which satisfied him. He and Frieda saw only the Hockings and (sometimes) Cecil Gray. Otherwise they lived in solitary and uneventful peace. In late September Lawrence happily finished the proofs of the *Look!* poems, which were published two months later.

One afternoon as the Lawrences returned from Kate Berryman's store in Zennor, coast guards suddenly sprang from behind a hedge and demanded to see their rucksack: "[Y]ou have a camera in there," they cried. While Lawrence gasped with rage, Frieda lifted out the loaf of bread and insolently held it under their noses. She may have been unwise. Other clues gathered ominous significance. Frieda remembered once sitting with Lawrence on the sea rocks, feeling intoxicated by the air and sun: "I had to jump and run, and my white scarf blew in the wind. 'Stop it, stop it, you fool, you fool!' Lawrence cried. 'Can't you see they'll think you're signalling to the enemy!'" In August Catherine Carswell's letter to Lawrence had been held back and examined: "I only got your letter today, Monday [the 13th]—and it is dated 9th." Later, Lawrence acknowledged that foreign letters had sometimes arrived at the cottage: "Of course," he told a friend in October, "my wife was corresponding with her people in Germany, through a friend in Switzerland."

Suspicious by now that his letters were being opened, Lawrence had— about the twenty-fifth—perhaps unwisely written Gray a letter in Italian. One evening at Bosigran, coast guards, who had been listening under the windows, spotted a bedroom light, foolishly left burning by a new housekeeper from London. Frieda shivered with fear: "I had before this been under suspicion of giving supplies to the German submarine crews." The locals had long feared that the odd outsiders, she an assertive German and he a bearded writer, might be spies, and they may have resented Lawrence's outspoken hostility to Britain's war effort.

A few days later, on 11 October 1917, two men came looking for the Lawrences. They called first on the Hockings, who were no doubt alarmed that they might attract suspicion by mere association. "I was full of fore-boding," Frieda said. The next morning—the twelfth—four policemen came to the cottage and delivered an official ultimatum: *The Lawrences must leave Cornwall in three days.* Frieda remembered their angry words:

"And what is the reason," [Lawrence] asked.
"You know better than I do," answered the captain.
"I don't know," said Lawrence.
Then the two awful detectives went through all our cupboards, clothes, beds, etc., while I, like a fool, burst into a rage: "This is your English liberty, here we live and don't do anybody any harm, and these creatures have the right to come here and touch our private things."
"Be quiet," said Lawrence.

Judged dangerous to national security, they were banned from entering any coastal region or major port and ordered to report their location to the police. That same day Lawrence wrote to Lady Cynthia: "This bolt from the blue has fallen this morning: why, I know not, any more than you do. I cannot even conceive how I have incurred suspicion—have not the faintest notion. We are as innocent even of pacifist activities, let alone spy-ing in any sort, as the rabbits of the field outside. . . . It is *very* vile.—We have practically no money at all—I don't know what we shall do."

Hoping to return, they left the cottage and its furnishings intact and took only their personal belongings. Like felons, implicitly condemned and publicly shamed, the Lawrences crept away to Dollie Radford's bur-row in Hampstead, where they could declaim their astonishment and rage to their London friends. "When we were turned out of Cornwall," Frieda acknowledged, "something changed in Lawrence for ever." Like a wall that had toppled, some deep sense of security had vanished. He had lost his country. "One grasps for support," Lawrence cried to Gray a day later. The wave of suspicion had washed him away from the granite boulders, gar-dens, and flowering gorse that had secured him. Even dark-eyed William Henry was too frightened to write. The Druidic magic had died. Never again would Lawrence see Cornwall.

# 12

# Wartime Castaways

## 1918–19

During the next six months the Lawrences' sails went down. Without a steady income, they borrowed flats and cottages where they could, as if huddling in lifeboats that pitched in the swollen seas of war. It was not just the war or their poverty that brought them low; it was also that Lawrence could no longer write for a British audience he detested. He became discontented, petulant, irascible. Frieda thought it "torture . . . to live with him." She told Willie Hopkin that "Lawrence's soul seems one big curse." Yet even as he endured a protracted restlessness, he persevered in his writing, completing *Studies in Classic American Literature,* his most penetrating book of criticism, and shaping two collections of his verse. The Lawrences, however, felt lost, like transients.

On 20 October 1917 they moved from Dollie Radford's cottage in the village of Hermitage to H.D.'s flat at 44 Mecklenburg Square. There they relished visits with H.D. and her husband, Richard Aldington, when he was (briefly) on leave from the army. But they hated being followed by security detectives who apparently held damaging reports about them from Cornwall.

Two things kept them afloat. Friends often entertained them. In November, for instance, Cynthia Asquith took the Lawrences to Mozart's *Abduction from the Seraglio,* and for the occasion Frieda made an evening dress and brought along a vibrant, deep-voiced American girl, also elegantly clothed and living at the same address, named Dorothy "Arabella" Yorke (1891–1971). Along with the poet H.D., Arabella had replaced Esther Andrews as a female acolyte. When he was not being entertained, Lawrence still nurtured his dream of sailing away to an Isle of Happiness— this time in the Andes. As he told Cecil Gray on 29 October, "It has become so concrete and real, the Andes plan, it seems to occupy my heart." For Lawrence the image of home, soothing his uneasy soul, had been displaced from Eastwood to a spot on the globe accessible only by the imagination. "One must have *something* to look forward to."

When the Aldingtons required H.D.'s space, the Lawrences moved within London to the small flat of Cecil Gray's mother, at 13 Earls Court Square. Its middle-class mustiness led them to be off again, this time to Chapel Farm Cottage, Dollie Radford's country duplex at Hermitage, where the Lawrences arrived on 18 December. It was their favorite nest. But they stayed only ten days before going on to Ripley, as if in flight again, to stay with Ada's family and to ring in 1918. Ada wanted them to take a cottage in Derbyshire, near her and near Lawrence's boyhood haunts, which she hoped might prove secure and settling.

By now few coins jingled in the Lawrences' cup. On 8 February Lawrence (although he signed Frieda's name) wrote to Mrs. Mary Hutchinson, declining an invitation to her Valentine's party: "We should have liked to come, if we had not been so hard up just now, and railway fares so high." On the twelfth he reckoned they had "exactly six pounds nineteen shillings in the world: and not a penny due." To Lady Cynthia he confided his dream of arriving in Italy, that coveted place where one could live cheaply in the sun. Even Frieda began to worry about money. She helped Lawrence gather firewood from the nearby forest, where trees were being cut for trench props, and she appealed once more to Amy Lowell for funds: "We are very poor at present, even for us [a] low watermark . . . that's why I cant tell you, how glad it makes me that Hilda A[ldington] said you would help us again!" Lowell sent two hundred dollars. Koteliansky, knowing their cup was empty, sent ten pounds, as did a friendly London barrister named Montagu Shearman, whom they had met through Mark Gertler. To Lady Cynthia, who was scarcely well off, Lawrence capitulated on 18 February and, brushing aside his scruples, accepted her help: "Yes, it will be nice if you can send me a little money from somebody. At first I had a bit of a revulsion, from mixing up my friendships and money matters. But one is really too tired for these squeamishnesses—they are false. I would give you money, if I'd got any."

When Dollie Radford needed her duplex, the Lawrences dipped into their tiny hoard and temporarily sought room and board from Bessie Lowe, who lived nearby. She urged them to visit a pair of interesting young women, Cecily Lambert and Violet Monk, who, though sadly inexperienced, were having a rustic adventure. Their attempt to farm without the aid of men intrigued Lawrence. A week later the Lawrences returned to Chapel Farm Cottage. In the meantime, Lawrence had bravely rushed to London to consult a young publisher, age twenty-six, named Cyril W. Beaumont.

Lawrence had invested far too much in *Women in Love* to let it languish. If Pinker had had no success in placing it, Lawrence felt he must act directly on its behalf. It is not that he went behind Pinker's back but rather that he sought a publisher like Beaumont beyond the mainstream market, on the far banks of Pinker's connections. Lawrence keenly wanted the book in print, even if it had to be done privately. On 6 March he saw Beaumont at his little shop in Charing Cross Road and learned sadly that the young entrepreneur did not wish his name attached to the novel. Although willing to facilitate the printing of a thousand copies, Beaumont would require—up front—part of the £375 he estimated as printer's costs. Lawrence was staggered by this sum. Prices had risen sharply during the war. Lawrence hoped that Cynthia's wealthy diplomatic friend, Prince Antoine Bibesco, might offer a subvention to launch the work. He would not. When no one came forward to help, Beaumont returned the manuscript. Lawrence had not yet found a patron with the right mix of courage and cash.

Knowing that Dollie Radford needed her duplex, the Lawrences sought another lifeboat. They had liked living in Hermitage: "It is very nice here—Hardy country—like *Woodlanders*—all woods and hazel-copses, and tiny little villages that will sleep forever." But in Hardy's *Woodlanders* (1887) Giles Winterbourne, becoming homeless, lives outdoors without the support of his family, whereas Lawrence knew that if he and Frieda went to Derbyshire, Ada, whose tailoring business had flourished, would support them. But he suffered from anxiety: "A real panic comes over me, when I feel I am on the brink of taking another house," he told Cecil Gray in March. "I truly wish I were a fox or a bird—but my ideal now is to have a caravan and a horse, and move on for ever, and never have a neighbour."

In these weary, unsettled spaces Lawrence had been revising some poems and writing some new ones for Beaumont, who wanted to print a collection on a hand press and to pay Lawrence the extravagant sum of ten pounds. Lawrence promised him "impeccable" lines—nothing to scare even Cynthia Asquith, to whom Lawrence would dedicate the little volume of eighteen poems. Pinker having made the final arrangements, the agreement was signed on 21 May. But not until 20 November 1919 did Beaumont publish the book, entitled *Bay*, printing 120 copies on handmade paper, 50 copies on cartridge paper, and 30 copies on costly Japanese vellum, the vellum signed by the author and his illustrator, Anne Estelle Rice. It was the first of Lawrence's books to be issued by a private press in an expensive format.

In *Bay* the erotic perfume of *Amores* and *Look! We Have Come Through!* yields entirely to dark, poetic meditations on war and death, waning moons and aching eyes, annihilation and torn hearts, bleeding suns and monotonous sands. Lawrence, now chastened, sings with injured, poignant lyricism, his close rhymes punctuated by questions, as if—dazed—he were contemplating the "[s]word [of death] that severs the question from us who breathe" ("Obsequial Ode"). One of *Bay's* best poems, "On the March," reflects not the thud-thud of soldiers' boots but the Lawrences' restless shifting about, "with numb feet," along repetitive roads. Cleverly, the poem ends its quatrains with a sequence of adjectives that trace the weary hostility that the poem expresses: *strange* road, *long* road, *wan* road, *dead* road, *old* road, then *last* road; for it may be "oblivion" to which, in the closing stanza, they march:

> If so, let us forge ahead, straight on
> If we're going to sleep the sleep with those
> That fall forever, knowing none
> Of this land whereon the wrong road goes.

The poem's surprise is "wrong road," the road of war and disintegration, the road Gerald Crich takes, the road marked with error, crossed with emptiness, dark with despair. The Lawrences, "out on the open road," marching in "coiled, convulsive throes," may have felt similarly dislocated, as if the British soldiers' plight were lived also by those who stayed at home, kept "at bay" by the war.

## A FAMILY RETREAT

On 5 April they went from Berkshire to Ada's cramped little house in Ripley, where she lived with her husband, Eddie, and young son, Jack. Negotiating on their behalf, Ada—ever solicitous—took them to see what Lawrence called a furnished bungalow, on the brow of a steep valley near Cromford, a nice place with pleasant grounds and two rough fields. Located about twelve miles from Ripley and fourteen miles from Derby, the bungalow was called Mountain Cottage. Here the Lawrences, arriving on 2 May, stayed for almost a year, as if stranded on a hilltop island. Ada paid the rent of sixty-five pounds and supplied twenty pounds toward food.

From Ripley Frieda went to London to see her children—probably on 6 April, probably by train, probably staying with Dollie Radford. As Lawrence reported to Gray on 18 April, "[I]t all went off quite pleasantly and simply." Her daughter Barbara remembers that "we were allowed to see Frieda occasionally. Coming up from the country one spring day, she arrived at a London station carrying large twigs of apple blossom, to Monty's embarrassment. We went to a matinee performance of *Figaro*, with Beecham conducting, and then to tea at Lyons, where Frieda gave us each ten shillings. In the Ladies Room Elsa said to me anxiously, 'You are not to like Mama, you know, now that we have got ten shillings.'" Their father returned the money to Frieda.

A few days before they vacated Chapel Farm Cottage, a singular event occurred. On 21 April 1918, only seven months before the war finally ended, Frieda's cousin, Manfred von Richthofen, "the Red Baron," after eighty successful air strikes, was shot down near Amiens and buried the next day with full military honors. On the twenty-third the *Times* reported that "all our airmen concede that Richthofen was a great pilot and a fine fighting man." Just one week later, Lawrence's extraordinary powers of intuition had, it seems, registered his death, as if an owl falling into enemy territory had been young Manfred himself. Although perhaps unaware of the pilot's death, Lawrence wrote to Mark Gertler on 28 April: "We went for a walk this evening through the woods—and I found a dead owl, a lovely big warm-brown soft creature, lying in the grass at my feet, in the path, its throat eaten by weasels. It sticks in my mind curiously—as if something important had died this week-end—though what it can be I don't know."

These deaths hinted at further change in the dynamics of the Lawrences' marriage. Lawrence was becoming dependent on Frieda's expansive good nature as a means of exploring his own darker nature, both husband and wife balanced in a querulous but creative opposition. This balance has often been misunderstood. Lawrence clarified its nature when he wrote to Gertler: "In some blind and hypnotic fashion I do a few bits of poetry—beyond that, I am incapable of everything—except I dig and set potatoes, and go walks with Frieda—who is actually forbearing to demonstrate her impertinent happiness, and daring to know her monstrous angry unhappiness. I don't pretend to be 'happy'—and for the moment don't want to be. I am much too angry. My soul, or whatever it is, feels charged and surcharged with the blackest and most monstrous 'temper', a sort of hellish electricity—and I hope soon it will either dissipate or break into some sort of thunder and lightning, for I am no more a man, but a walking phenomenon of suspended fury." From this taunting passage one can extrapolate a mode of interchange—not the creative excitement of their early years together, nor anything like its opposite, a soured antipathy, but rather a creative opposition that thrives on the certainty of a counter-response. If Frieda is happy, Lawrence will press her to acknowledge "angry unhappiness"; if Lawrence feels blighted, Frieda will insist on her gratitude for what little they have. They walk together in fascinated contrariness, each accepting the legitimacy of the other's claim but rarely acknowledging it. They suspend their agreement, which dissolves in the silence they also share. Frieda's total lack of cynicism permitted Lawrence to indulge in moods of intense darkness, confident that she would respond to his "suspended fury" by disarming it, redirecting it. Frieda, certain of his literary powers, would have urged him to write even as he professed that he could not. She assumed the function that Miriam in *Sons and Lovers* had provided for Paul: "She brought forth to him his imaginations."

Once installed at Mountain Cottage, the Lawrences invited family and friends to visit. Ada brought her son, Jack (1915–42), and Emily brought her daughter, Peggy (1909–2001); even Lawrence's father came, as did the Hopkins—Willie, Sallie, and Enid. Despite Lawrence's passion for being alone, he came to appreciate his ties to the past and to like mingling with his family, for they were like a drug that dulled his need to argue and provoke discussion, and helped soothe his restlessness. Arabella Yorke, a warm and gracious house guest, arrived about 13 June and stayed for two weeks: "[W]e became very fond of her," Lawrence told Sallie Hopkin. While Arabella visited, the Hopkins also came. Enid later recalled an evening with the Lawrences (probably 22 June 1918) when the beauty of the hills could not compete with Frieda's piano technique: "I remember one night in [late] spring we were at Mountain Cottage near Cromford in Derbyshire, my parents, myself, Lawrence's sister Ada and brother George, and a friend named Arabella York[e] and some friends of mine, when Frieda came in wearing a most extraordinary hat and dress—both of which Lawrence had made for her. He was quite a good seamster and at that time used to trim all her hats and make many of her clothes. Lawrence decided to walk over the hills and asked for volunteers to accompany him. A light rain was falling, so only my father and I, Arabella York[e] and one of my friends [probably Kitty Allcock] decided to brave the weather. It was quite a wonderful walk, with Lawrence as usual elaborating on the beauty of the hills in the misting rain."

After refreshments had been served, Frieda sat down at the piano, lit a candle on either side, and persuaded the group to sing English folk songs: "I sat at the open window. There was a moon, and I can remember so plainly the view down the hillside to the road, the mountains further away and the perfume from the lilies-of-the-valley coming up through the open window. And I remember the group around the piano in the candlelight, Frieda singing with a cigarette hanging out of the corner of her mouth. And Frieda, who was not a good pianist, every now and then would strike wrong notes. After several of these Lawrence would lose his temper and scream at her, Frieda would scream back, and it would be a free-for-all for a moment. The whole scene was very dramatic, as we stood in mid-chorus wondering what would happen next. Suddenly it was all over, and Frieda would settle down and go back to playing, and we would all start to sing again."

It is interesting that even so sympathetic an observer as Enid (she was twenty-three at the time) would recall a few moments of quarreling rather than the food or decor—or conversation or songs. The Lawrences' frequent "trespasses" against English propriety had an incalculable effect on their guests. It is not that the Lawrences feasted on friction but rather that, unlike those around them, they maintained a permanent space between them where verbal sparring was at any time permitted. Their love for each other fostered neither acquiescence nor charity but bald competition for power. And competition shone brightest around a bemused audience. "Do you know," Lawrence told Sallie on 26 June, "I quite suffered when they had gone away on Monday—and usually I am so glad to be alone."

## Ways to Survive

The Lawrences' summer months were spent in choppy waters. Lawrence felt "disagreeable, even with myself, these days," he told Cynthia Asquith, and on 26 June he told Gertler: "I don't work—don't try to—only just endure the days." A grant of fifty pounds from the Royal Literary Fund, facilitated by Cynthia's friend Charles Whibley, briefly eased their financial anxieties but left Lawrence feeling peevish and ungrateful, as if he resented some obligation buried in the bequest. Although he felt ambivalent about handouts, he could not yet prostitute himself to write popular fare.

Somehow he still hoped to earn his own money. To that end he cobbled together a plan with three parts: he could place separately some of the essays from *Studies in Classic American Literature*; write a textbook on European history, which had been proposed by Vere Collins at the Oxford University Press; and perhaps snare work as a writer or reviewer. The first part of the plan was comparatively easy since, by summer 1918, he had finished most of his *Studies:* "I think," he told Pinker, "we may really sell these essays, both in America and in England. . . . Will you send [Austin] Harrison this first essay at once?" Entitled "The Spirit of Place," the essay was promptly accepted for the November 1918 issue of the *English Review*. The spirit of place that Lawrence analyzes may have been stimulated by his move to Cornwall at the end of 1915, its bleak "otherness" as striking as its isolation. While reading the American literary classics, Lawrence finds a fresh insight—that Britain's insular mode of feeling has, across the Atlantic, been superseded, become distinct, as the vital magnetism of the new region inspires a new literature. Drawing on his analysis of power in *Women in Love,* he argues that America's Pilgrims sought not religious liberty but a "tyrannical sense of power . . . to annihilate all living impulses," their repressive Christianity a weapon in fulfilling their goal. They sought to bend the spontaneous self to fit the mechanical will, Lawrence insists, whereas "if we have one spark of sanity, we know that we can never possess and direct the life-mystery." The seven essays that followed this one in the *English Review*—on such topics as James Fenimore Cooper's novels,

Edgar Allan Poe, and Nathaniel Hawthorne—make bold claims in confident language; and as a whole the *Studies* essays have been called "the crucial study of American literature."

About his own life Lawrence discovered that the literary conflicts he found in these essays were deeply personal in origin: for instance, the split between the tale and the teller—between the author's message "from his own moral consciousness" and the message "from his unconscious or subconscious soul"—corresponds to the sharp division in his own character. It is not that Lawrence's life "was the expression of profound emotional disorder," as Eliseo Vivas says, but rather that Lawrence's ambivalence operated at so deep a level that he could neither escape its pressures nor block its varied flowers of expression.

In case the *American Literature* essays proved not to be lucrative, Lawrence reluctantly accepted a proposal from Vere Collins that he write, for Oxford University Press, a textbook on European history for schoolchildren. It was the second part of his plan. By 26 July he had already completed three chapters. They were rather long, he worried, although he intended (he warned his editor, Nancy Henry) to endow education with "deep, philosophic reverence." He loathed "the broken pots of historical facts," he explained, and labored instead to grasp imaginatively the "thread" of significance. Lawrence drew freely on his sources, for instance, turning Edward Gibbon's prose in *The Decline and Fall of the Roman Empire* (1776–88) into a rapid, concentrated version of European history, as when he works over Gibbon's description of the Huns. Here is Gibbon: "They were distinguished from the rest of the human species by their broad shoulders, flat noses, and small black eyes, deeply buried in the head; and as they were almost destitute of beards, they never enjoyed either the manly graces of youth or the venerable aspect of age." Lawrence, injecting a staccato vividness, freshly characterizes the Hun as "little, short in build, but very broad and powerful. His head was big and like an animal's, with coarse, straight black hair. Tiny black eyes sparkled deep in the flesh of the flat face, the great wide mouth opened and shut. There was no beard, only a few bristles here and there." Whereas Gibbon built up detail across a huge canvas, Lawrence simplified and vitalized—like Cézanne. He also understood the market value of a disguise. Complying with the suggestion that a pen name might improve sales of the book, he chose "Lawrence H. Davison."

And if these two initial ventures had no success, Lawrence had mulled over a third: he was at last prepared to look for work. He knew that in July, Cynthia Asquith, feeling strapped, had taken a job as secretary to Sir James Barrie (she held it for twenty years). What might Lawrence do? Two trips to London—one in August, the other in October—gave him time to probe some possibilities. On 12 August 1918 he and Frieda arrived at Koteliansky's flat, primarily so that Frieda could see her children again, and brought what food they could. Indeed they savored Koteliansky's friendship: "You, my dear Kot, are a tower of strength," Lawrence told him on the twenty-seventh, "a real tower of strength to us both," and added wryly: "Frieda quite loves you since open enmity is avowed." Koteliansky had groused at Frieda's disrespect for her husband.

Finding London detestable, she and Lawrence left to spend the weekend with Barbara Low and her sister Edith Eder (Dr. David Eder, the Freudian psychoanalyst, was in Jerusalem); went back to the ever-peaceful Chapel Farm Cottage to spend a day or two with Margaret Radford, Dollie's daughter, who was "there alone—very seedy"; then caught a train on Monday, 26 August, to visit Catherine Carswell, her barrister husband, Donald, and their infant son, John, who were vacationing at a vicarage at Lydbrook, near Ross-on-Wye in Hertfordshire. There the Lawrences stayed about a week. They happily took long walks in the forest, carried the infant boy, and enjoyed picnics in the green riding. These memories, he told Donald on 1 September, were "worth a lot, really," especially when the stone vicarage suggested to Lawrence the outline of a story he called "The Blind Man." Returning to Mountain Cottage they braved blustery winds and beating rain—early signs of autumn.

The Lawrences' money, spent on train fares and costly food, was slipping away despite their severe economies. Lawrence still had no job. A reminder of his situation came on his thirty-third birthday. Official papers arrived calling him up for medical reexamination: the war marched on. Furious, Lawrence blurted out to the poet Robert Nichols: "But having been badgered about as I have, kicked out of Cornwall, and pushed about by the police, I'm damned if I will move one step at the bidding of such filthers." Yet they might force him to accept employment. "Yes," he told Nichols, "I am very nicely stranded—like a fish chucked up above high-water mark, and gasping." The next day the metaphor flipped as Lawrence contemplated the kind of work he might do: "I want to burst this sort of cocoon that I'm in—it is likely to prove a shroud if I don't," he exploded to Cynthia Asquith. Perhaps, he thought, he could do political work for the Independent Labour Party, which had fiercely resisted the war and welcomed recruits. Unable to endure simply sitting still at Mountain Cottage all winter, Lawrence would make his own move. He was ready. He wanted to "do what I can," he informed Koteliansky.

After the medical examiners had finished with him on 26 September, Lawrence, speechless with fury at being pawed by "swine," learned that the military doctors had placed him in Grade 3, which meant that he could be called up for sedentary labor. But Lawrence was determined, he told Cynthia, to find work—"I want a job under the Ministry of Education." He needed her help. "I shall come to London next week," he concluded, hoping to act before the authorities could press him into service. A job would ease both his military and his financial worries. "Tell me," he exhorted Mark Gertler, "if you hear of anything."

Accordingly, on Monday, 7 October, the Lawrences came to Dollie Radford's Hampstead flat at 32 Well Walk—Dollie was away, her husband (mentally ill) confined to a nursing home. From there, using Donald Carswell's connections, Lawrence sallied forth to see George Freeman, deputy editor of the *Times Literary Supplement,* who, Lawrence told his old friend Arthur McLeod on the sixteenth, "will give me some work for the *Supplement*—perhaps both *Literary* and *Educational*—because I am so hard up." For Freeman he soon composed three essays that he called "Education of the People." They reflect his haste and worry. Freeman soon returned them as "rather matter for a book than a supplement."

That didn't matter. Suddenly Lawrence's urgency to find work abated when he learned that Britain lay at the edge of peace: "I don't care about anything, if there's peace," he declared in late October, about the time Martin Secker published Lawrence's verse collection, calling it *New Poems* (though they were mostly old). Peace, sought for so long as to seem elusive, arrived in stages. Plagued by troop desertions and sagging morale, Germany's Kaiser Wilhelm stubbornly resisted surrender. The German chancellor, Maximilian, Prince of Baden—appointed only a month earlier, and now confronted with relentless Allied successes in battle—soon accepted President Wilson's Fourteen Points as the basis on which to begin peace negotiations. The armistice agreement was signed at Compiègne, north of Paris, on 11 November 1918, the day after Wilhelm fled to Holland. The agreement required Germany to withdraw troops behind 1914 frontiers, surrender military matériel, and make reparation for damages to Belgium and northern France. Frieda's native Metz was returned to France. Her mother wrote, "Papa's complete life's work in enemy hands! Thank goodness he did not live to see the break-up!"

A few weeks earlier, when Frieda, weakened by a cold and a sore throat, came down with influenza, Dr. Maitland Radford had urged her to stay in bed. While she was ill, Lawrence saw much of Katherine Mansfield, who soon reported to Dorothy Brett that he was "his old, merry, rich self, laughing, describing things, giving you pictures, full of enthusiasm and joy in a future where we become all 'vagabonds.'" Murry, now her husband, felt marginalized; he was no longer willing to participate in their gay talk of a new life, which had once provided such solace. But as soon as Frieda was better, about 22 October, she and Lawrence fled again to Chapel Farm Cottage, where the trees looked resplendent draped in saffron and chestnuts had fallen in the woods. There, on Thursday, 7 November, the day of uprisings in Munich, news of peace negotiations trickled into the hinterlands. The "marvellous Peace report on Thursday night," Lawrence told Catherine Carswell, aroused great celebrations. The Lawrences left for

London to join the revelry at Montagu Shearman's flat, where on 11 November the vibrant David Garnett, accompanied by his companion Duncan Grant, found Lawrence darkly somber and looking ill.

Enjoying perfect weather, stirred by memories of the vicarage at Lydbrook, soothed by reports of peace, driven no longer to write twaddle for the *Times*, Lawrence began some of the finest stories of his middle years. The conditions were at last favorable. By 4 December 1918, when he and Frieda were installed again at Mountain Cottage, he had completed "The Blind Man" and sent it to Pinker for placement. "The Fox" followed within a week.

## TWO WAYS TO TOUCH

Lawrence's sudden release from the pressures of job hunting expressed itself in two stories of release which illuminate each other. Both concern soldiers returning from the war, both were written in November and December, and both are set in dark, lonely cottages that resemble Mountain Cottage. There, for instance, the night of 28 November seemed (Lawrence said) "very dark, moving with misty rain," the place "very lonely," so that he needed, he told Katherine, "a little reassuring of some sort." These two themes—dark, lonely setting and the need for reassurance—shape both stories. At the same time, his fiction was evolving in such a way (he said) that he could now "cross the threshhold of the human psyche." That was also, he knew, a way to cross the threshold of same-sex intimacy.

There is more. As in *Women in Love*, the angle of literary creation continues to shift inward, but with an important difference. Whereas the inner lives of the two stories' protagonists, named Bertie and March, one male and one female, possess Lawrence's psychological complexity, the surface features of their lives are masked. At once Lawrence moves deeper into his psyche but uses a fuller disguise.

In both stories the protagonist rejects same-sex intimacy, as if Lawrence were still grappling with the rejection implied in Murry's and in William Henry's rebuffs of his ardent offers of friendship; at this time neither man would even answer Lawrence's letters. Yet both stories center on *touch*, that most sensual of senses. In "The Blind Man" Bertie Reid, a rich Scottish barrister, has some of Lawrence's features: he is "thin and worn," having "thin, white fingers" and a "childlike intuition," a man who has "friends among the fair sex—not lovers, friends." When he comes through "the rainy dusk" to visit his close friend Isabel Pervin, he finds that her husband, Maurice, a big fellow with heavy limbs like Gerald Crich's, had been blinded in Flanders and now seems disoriented. In the new complexity of Lawrence's work, the Birkin/Gerald friendship is reversed. At the story's close it is Maurice who approaches Bertie. Hiding in the barn and "trembling in every fibre," Maurice gathers up Bertie's thin fingers and presses them eagerly onto his scarred eyes, making Bertie swoon, as if struck with terror, as if his shell had cracked and his soft tissue were scorched with pain; whereas Maurice, in need of passionate friendship, was filled with "hot, poignant love" and feels transformed by their encounter. The insecure, handicapped married man has found a fulfillment. His courage has dissolved his fear of touching another man's body. By inverting these roles, Lawrence could explore his own frustrating ambivalence to Murry and to William Henry. Turned into a "lone wolf," Lawrence saw his capacity for friendship contract: "I begin to despair altogether about human relationships," he lamented to Katherine in December.

"The Fox" develops inversely. It opens directly into same-sex intimacy and moves resolutely away from it, as if it were unhealthy. The close bond between the two women in the story, Jill Banford and Ellen March, is destabilized by male predators whose power is irresistible. Living on a farm at the edge of a wood, the two women eke out an existence, threatened (like Lawrence and Frieda) by poverty and by the encroaching loneliness of the dark evenings, both of them huddled against the rigors of wartime rationing and a marauding fox—until at dusk, one August night, March, taking her gun, looks straight into the eyes of the fox and is daunted, mesmerized by his gaze: "She was spell-bound," "possessed by him." The look in his eyes touches her soul with revelation, makes her (like Maurice) tremble, weakens her masculine defenses (gun, trousers, long stride), and releases her, all vulnerable, to the twenty-year-old Henry Grenfel—the fox in human form. Having returned from the war, with all its instability, Henry seeks out the farm where he once lived with his grandfather, stays on to help the women, takes charge of the gun, and soon releases March from her vague dissatisfaction: "She need not go after [the fox] any more."

The difficulty is Banford. Anxious and bespectacled, she clings to her companion. The guilt that March feels releases itself in a dream where touch triggers pain. As March approaches the fox (in her dream), "she wanted to touch him"; instead, "whisk[ing] his brush across her face," his fiery tail sears her mouth, awakening her. Whereas in "The Blind Man" Bertie folds into himself, March opens outward, though hesitantly, responding to the caress of Henry's voice, "like the softest touch of a cat's paw"; at dusk one late November day, he proposes. Even as March resists him (by imagining Banford's fury), she feels a "swoon" pass over her. Inwardly she wants a man.

The biographical significance is clear. Frieda had rescued her husband from the attraction of another man. Lawrence's art had told him a truth he was loath to acknowledge. "Never trust the artist. Trust the tale," he had counseled his readers in his revised "Spirit of Place." He was redefining his sexuality, asserting the primacy of marriage.

"The Blind Man" was published in the July 1920 *English Review* and probably earned him five guineas; the first version of "The Fox" was published in *Hutchinson's Story Magazine* in November 1920, earning him a princely thirty pounds, and like "England, My England" it was later expanded and revised. Financially, too, Lawrence was rebalancing his life.

## FRIEDA'S TENDER MERCIES

After the awful strain of the war, Ada Clarke was determined to make the Christmas holiday festive and memorable for her extended family. She was well aware that her brother and his wife, after the privations they had suffered, wanted to leave England. Lawrence captured his sister's generosity when he wrote to Katherine two days after Christmas. The rationing imposed by the war gives way to his sensory delight in food and drink: "At Ambergate my sister had sent a motor car for us—so we were at Ripley [twenty minutes later] in time for turkey and Christmas pudding.—My God, what masses of food here, turkey, large tongues, long wall of roast loin of pork, pork-pies, sausages, mince pies, dark cakes covered with almonds, chiscakes, lemon-tarts, jellies, endless masses of food, with whiskey, gin, port-wine, burgundy, muscatel. It seems incredible. We played charades—the old people of 67 playing away harder than the young ones— and lit the Christmas tree, and drank healths, and sang, and roared—Lord above."

Yet these splendid Christmas festivities did not bode well for the next few months. The influenza epidemic, about which Lawrence had been worried, suddenly struck him. In February a bad cold sent him to bed and no doubt sapped his resistance, so that, hit by that "putrid disease" influenza, he suddenly collapsed about 10 February. Ada, who in Croydon had ably nursed him once before, insisted that he would recover more quickly in Ripley. Although Frieda likely objected, Lawrence sided with Ada, whose doctor feared he might die. For three more weeks he was bedridden. An exhausted Frieda wrote to Koteliansky on 24 February: "I feel two hundred years old—have'nt slept at all. If you hear of *anything* nice in the world tell him." She suggested a box of chocolates: "he is so thin, the doctor says, and must have plenty of sugar."

Gradually Lawrence was able to consume the grapefruit, brandy, and port that Koteliansky sent, and drink the champagne supplied by his uncle Fritz Krenkow in Leicester, but not until 6 March could he creep down the steps to tea. He felt very feeble: "I am quite at the end of everything here," he told Murry, who had written to boast that he had been appointed editor of the revived *Athenaeum* and would welcome some prose from Lawrence. Spiritually exhausted, Lawrence cried to Cynthia Asquith: "I have only one desire—to go out into the world, to wander." This statement forecasts the pattern of his final decade.

Whenever his strength returned, he wanted to go to Germany with Frieda to see her family. The task of negotiating Lawrence's moods—and then his sister's officious nursing—depleted Frieda. Because so few of her letters have survived from 1918 and 1919, we must infer more than we would like from Lawrence's letters. His wry comment to Beatrice Campbell on 10 March cannot be ignored but surely reflects affection rather than surliness: "I suppose I'll get strong enough again one day to slap Frieda in the eye, in the proper marital fashion. At present I am reduced to vituperation." His jest sounds coarse. But that comment was followed four days later by comments to Koteliansky that, shorn of their context, will seem astonishing: "My sister goes with us [on 17 March] to Middleton. I am not going to be left to Frieda's tender mercies until I am well again. She really is a devil—and I feel as if I would part from her for ever—let her go alone to Germany, while I take another road. For it is true, I have been bullied by her long enough. I really could leave her now, without a pang, I believe. The time comes, to make an end, one way or another. If this illness hasn't been a lesson to her, it has to me."

To cite this letter as evidence of Frieda's raw assertiveness may be wrong. In every marriage angry, irritated partners sometimes say—and write— things that are better left unexpressed because they represent such a small truth about the relationship. Lawrence's illness would have aggravated his irritation with Frieda. (Did her exhortations that he get out of bed and be cheerful conflict with Ada's protectiveness?) While he was ill and weak, the combative energy he prized in Frieda lost its appeal.

Moreover, it is worth remembering that Ada had grown up in a family that specialized in excluding the likes of Arthur Lawrence. As Lawrence and his sister reverted to their earlier family roles, with Ada supplying money (and perhaps, on occasion, reminding Frieda of her generosity) and with Frieda gradually feeling alienated, it is no surprise that tempers flared. Frieda's tender mercies, which no doubt allowed some carelessness in following the doctor's instructions, were replaced by Ada's more dependable ministrations. Caught between them was a vulnerable Lawrence.

These lingering conflicts were reflected in the Lawrences' plans to leave England, Frieda hoping to depart in June ("Frieda sits as if on needles, till we can get away," Lawrence told her sister Else), while Lawrence preferred July or August, probably not from obstinacy but because only in March had he begun "taking shaky walks" in the bitter wind. He worried that the long journey by train might strain his health. While they argued (knowing the lease on Mountain Cottage would soon expire), they began to pack their bags. On 25 April they had agreed to go again to Chapel Farm Cottage in Hermitage, where the climate was milder and the woods and flowers more plentiful, and where also Margaret Radford would be on hand to welcome them. In the weeks that remained, Lawrence needed only to build up his strength—by chopping wood, gardening, and carrying water from the outdoor well—and to revise the European history book, which he managed to finish by 23 April: "then I hope speedily to receive the [promised] £50," he told Koteliansky, adding bitterly, "There is a sum for you!" But such work, although it was a squandering of his talent, must have contributed to his sense of irritation and uncertainty, "as if," he told Amy Lowell, "the days were stones that might start sliding under one's feet," allowing "no past to stay one, and no future to wonder over." The yearlong return home had ended; it would never be repeated.

## ROSALIND BAYNES

At Chapel Farm Cottage the Lawrences knew they would soon have the cottage to themselves, could visit neighbors they liked—the Browns next door, Mrs. Lowe nearby—and could, before leaving England, invite their London friends to visit. They awaited now only passports and enough money to travel. With no major work at hand, Lawrence felt almost free—and well enough to write stories: "I promise you," he assured Pinker on 30 April 1919, a few days after they arrived at Hermitage, "that for the next six weeks I will write nothing but short stories, if the short stories will come." Lawrence had not been a lucrative property, but he sent Pinker "Fanny and Annie" and "Monkey Nuts."

At the end of May, their friends began to arrive: Barbara Low, who helped Lawrence make blue linen jackets for himself and Frieda; Ivy Low (now Litvinov), who had visited them in Italy; the Carswells; and then Murry. In early June, accompanied by Ivy Low, the Carswells arrived for the Whitsun holiday. For about one pound Mrs. Lowe, close at hand, gave them room and board, and milk for their son from the goat tethered behind her cottage. Although Catherine remembers a rainy outing to Silchester to see the Roman ruins ("We missed the last train back, and had to walk a long way home"), she recalls that Lawrence often sat quietly on a chair in the garden, shaded by an apple tree, and, with a pad on his knee, wrote his stories. Afterward, they all went "wooding" among the bluebells, collecting faggots for their fires. "With all he had to do, in and out of the house," Catherine observed, "he found time to help [Mrs. Lowe's] daughter every day with her lessons." He never let visitors impede his writing.

In late June, Murry suddenly arrived—"like a bolt from the blue," Lawrence slyly alerted Koteliansky. He sought a cottage where Katherine might try to recover from her advancing tuberculosis. Murry recalls sitting "glum and unresponsive" as Lawrence predicted a gloomy future for industrial England. On Sunday morning that same weekend, the pair of young women from Grimsbury Farm—Cecily Lambert and Violet Monk, on whom Lawrence had based "The Fox"—conducted a wagon ride and picnic. The Lawrences brought Murry. Frieda was dressed in a check shirt, blue jacket, and huge brimmed hat. Cecily Lambert remembers her as "large and striking." She had gained weight. Lawrence wore drainpipe trousers, his new blue linen coat, and a white floppy hat. Murry dressed in regulation flannels. The Lawrences, vibrant and amusing, could be counted on to enliven a party. But in September Lambert recalled a different kind of liveliness. Swayed by a temper turned diabolical, Lawrence castigated Frieda for misusing Violet's sewing machine, called her "lazy and useless"; after he ordered her to scrub the kitchen floor, she called forth "every insult she could conjure up." Witnesses listened and remembered but seem not to have shared with the Lawrences the terrible fright these outbursts caused.

During the summer months Lawrence found himself shifting about like a gypsy without a caravan. Moreso than Frieda, he liked the challenge, welcomed the change, and adapted quickly. As Frieda became more stolid, he became more restless. "My wife like an unhappy hen flutters from roost to roost. But I like not to have a home," he told an acquaintance. He had hoped to go to New York and brave a lecture series that his American publisher Benjamin Huebsch might arrange; he hoped eventually to settle with Frieda in America, "in some log hut out west." To Cynthia Asquith, who was ill and depressed, he wrote on July 1: "The great thing is not to give in—not to lose one's sense of adventure." But if the lecture tour did not materialize he would, he thought, accompany Frieda to Germany. She told Cynthia: "I [too] feel like setting out for new adventures."

In July he went to London twice, apparently by himself, the first time to apply for Frieda's passport and to see friends like Nancy Henry and Vere Collins at Oxford University Press. Collins took him to see Helen Thomas, a woman living in Kent whose husband had died in the war and who later remembered his shrieks of anger when Collins suggested that science might allow life to be "generated in a test-tube" and his amused mimicry of a psychoanalyst treating a patient: "and in the role of doctor he asked intimate questions, and in the role of patient answered them," illustrating for his listeners the threats of such probing. Later he went to London again—to escape Margaret Radford's invasion of Chapel Farm Cottage—and stayed with Koteliansky, where he gladly set the table and washed up after meals.

On Monday, 28 July, the Lawrences moved again, this time borrowing Myrtle Cottage from Rosalind Baynes (1891–1973), whom he had come to admire at the home of her cultured sister and brother-in-law, Joan and Bertie Farjeon. Rosalind, beautifully molded, with the complexion of a

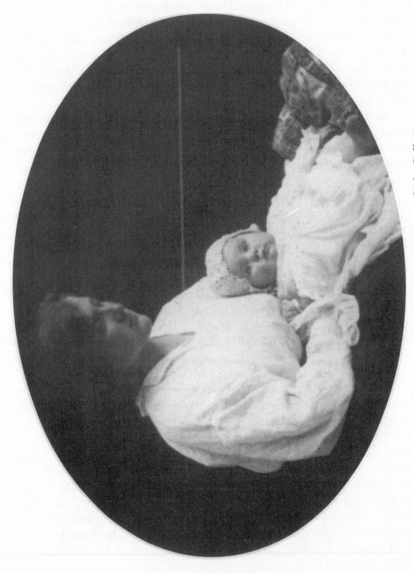

Rosalind Baynes with her daughter, Brigit (Courtesy of John Coffey)

russet apple, was a sculptor's daughter in her late twenties who had married a surgeon named Godwin. They were near divorce. Rosalind, like Lawrence, knew the fraying edges of marriage.

Rosalind's brick cottage, located nine miles from Hermitage in the village of Pangbourne, was large and spacious, with a high, pitched roof. Lawrence liked it: "I have been working in the garden all morning, Frieda busy about the house," he told her on 1 August. The pears and apples were starting to ripen. During the day he worked to smooth and tighten Koteliansky's translation of Leo Shestov's small book of philosophy, *All Things Are Possible*, whose Russian irony Lawrence found delectable; after he contributed a brief foreword, he placed the book with Martin Secker, the publisher of his *New Poems* (and a man whose loyalty never wavered, even though Lawrence complained that he offered "filthy [financial] terms" for the books he published). In the afternoons Rosalind drove the Lawrences around the countryside in a pony trap; they rode old bicycles; they walked for hours in the silent countryside. One day, while a group of her friends picnicked in the woods, Rosalind heard Lawrence and Frieda singing the German folk song "Wo hast du Dien schönes Töchterlein?" ("Where Do You Have Your Beautiful Daughter?") in voices that were "shrill, penetrating, unforgettable." But sometimes Lawrence visited the two young women he had befriended at Grimsbury Farm, sawed logs for them, milked their nanny goat, hacked thistles out of their fields, or—indoors—concocted rich goats' milk puddings or skillfully stewed wild mushrooms in milk and butter, which he served over toast. He was a lively guest.

In August, both of his sisters came with their families for brief visits, as did eight-year-old Hilda Brown, who lived at Hermitage in the cottage adjoining Chapel Farm. Hilda remembers the Lawrences entertaining her—Lawrence with stories of long walks in Cornwall; Frieda with stories of her native Germany: of festive parties, nurses who always accompanied her and her sisters, and (plucking a leaf from her days as a tomboy) the way "she pushed her sister down a stone staircase." To help occupy Hilda and his niece, Peggy, two years older, Lawrence urged them to construct a child's garden, with walls of brown mud, twigs for trees, and flower heads for borders and beds. He gave each of them a prize.

⁊⁊

Leaving England was a priority. Until peace agreements were ratified, Lawrence could not apply for Frieda's passport. He mailed her application about 15 August. She was very anxious. At last a policeman arrived on 23 September to verify her application and confirmed that "the passport would come all right," Lawrence informed Koteliansky. It came on 7 October. But for reasons that are unclear, Lawrence decided not to go with Frieda. Later she said that he wanted to avoid Germany "so soon after the war," although probably the expense barred them from going together. Sometime in September Lawrence knew that he really wanted to return to Italy—he thought strong sunshine would improve his health, and Italy was still inexpensive. For years he had longed to return.

But it is possible that the Lawrences' marriage was under increased strain, perhaps because of Lawrence's increasing fondness for the appealing, emancipated Rosalind Baynes. Toward Frieda the tone he adopted in his letters was still prickly, as when he wrote to Cynthia Asquith on 16 September: "Frieda, who still insists on 'feeling' her trials, gets very cross, or weeps, when the letters come from Germany. She has her mind set on going: and she can't go. Another quandary." He sounds impatient. And Cecily Lambert reported that in September, when the Lawrences stayed briefly at Grimsbury Farm, they occupied separate bedrooms, "and when I suggested to Frieda that it would ease things if they shared one, her reply was that she did not wish to be too much married." Maybe Lawrence's frequent coughing kept her awake. Although previous biographers offer no clue, Mark Kinkead-Weekes alone thinking "they needed more space and independence," Lawrence and Frieda had probably reached the point where they simply slept better apart, to accommodate Frieda's girth and Lawrence's cough.

As their departures from England approached, Lawrence was happy—finally—to settle the publishing of two books dear to him. They were *Women in Love,* still "the best of my books," and *Studies in Classic American Literature,* the fruit of "five years of persistent work." It was a difficult task. "I'm almost having to kick myself into making an effort for my own rights," he lamented to Koteliansky. He had grown increasingly disenchanted with Pinker's meager efforts on his behalf.

Lawrence was sure he could place his own work. Once he had acted for himself, he found it natural to continue. In New York, his publisher B. W. "Ben" Huebsch (1876–1964) favored contemporary writing. Son of a German rabbi, he was an idealist who had bravely published James Joyce—and then Lawrence's *The Rainbow, Amores,* and *Look! We Have Come Through!* Now he proposed issuing *New Poems* with a short foreword to secure an American copyright (technically, he explained, the foreword would make it "a different book"). Accordingly, Lawrence sent Huebsch an essay about the beauties of free verse, especially Whitman's, whose poems penetrated "so near the quick"; then he offered Huebsch *Studies in Classic American Literature,* the book of essays he had just completed, crowned now with a vigorous and controversial essay on Whitman that "no one in the world has seen." In it, Lawrence bristles against Whitman. He acknowledges the poet's pioneering efforts to deny the notion that the soul is superior to the flesh, but he attacks Whitman's desire to merge with others—slaves, prostitutes—because merger, Lawrence says, violates the soul's need "to keep clean and whole . . . to preserve its own integrity." Above all else Lawrence valued personal integrity.

But Lawrence also guessed that Huebsch, because of *The Rainbow*'s suppression, regarded him as "a risky venture" and had probably passed on the chance to publish *Women in Love* when Pinker (presumably) had sent him the novel. Consequently, guided deftly by Douglas Goldring, a young London writer, Lawrence sent the latest revised copy of his manuscript to Thomas Seltzer in New York. Seltzer agreed to publish the novel and to pay an advance of fifty pounds. A Russian Jew like Koteliansky, Seltzer (1875–1943) was a tiny, adventuresome man barely five feet tall who, over the next five years, would publish twenty of Lawrence's books. Pinker sent his agent's copy of the manuscript to the hospitable Martin Secker, who agreed to publish the novel in England. In placing the American edition himself, Lawrence hoped to dodge Pinker. But Lawrence soon realized that Secker must print *Women in Love* not from the old typescript that Pinker had submitted but from the typescript, recently revised, that Lawrence himself had mailed to Thomas Seltzer in New York. Astonishingly—after years of discouraging rejections—Huebsch also wanted to publish *Women in Love* and cabled Lawrence the stunning news that "Pinker never submitted [the typescript]." Lawrence, no doubt close to panic, admonished Seltzer on 2 November to return the novel at once unless he had started printing. Already Lawrence's business dealings were becoming tangled.

## THE END OF AN ERA

Frieda departed for Germany on 15 October. Her passport included a photograph of a woman dressed in what was almost certainly the blue linen jacket that Lawrence had fashioned for her, cut rather large, fastened with large buttons, a pale scarf folded under its broad lapels, her face crowned by a straw hat. Some of the fierce pride has drained from her features; now forty, she has aged. By 30 October she had arrived in Baden, her trunk having been stolen. Lawrence heard from her again on 4 November: "She says food *very* scarce there," he told Cecily Lambert, and of course the appalling number of deaths had left behind a "sad, different Germany," its economy torn apart by unemployment and inflation, its grand militarism "*utterly* gone." Her family, Frieda said, was now poor and famished.

Lawrence, alone now, was bound for Italy. He needed to decide how to travel, where to go, and whom to see. He wrote to Compton Mackenzie (1883–1972), a novelist on Secker's list whom Lawrence had met in Chesham five years earlier: "[P]erhaps [I'll] spend the winter with Compton Mackenzie on Capri," he told Huebsch. Other tasks remained. He needed

Frieda Lawrence, passport photo, 1919 (Courtesy of the Gersheim Collection, Harry Ransom Humanities Research Center, the University of Texas at Austin)

to pack his trunk, sell his books, and bid adieu to family and friends. After visiting the Midlands in mid-October, he was stranded indoors with a cold when he returned to Chapel Farm Cottage, but heard from Rosalind Baynes's father of a farm in rural Italy to which Rosalind hoped to take her children for the winter, to be shielded from the shrapnel of an impending divorce. Lawrence pleaded that he and Frieda be allowed to act as her scouts.

On 4 November Lawrence went to London to say farewell, brought all his luggage, stayed with Koteliansky, went to the French and Italian consulates to get his required visas, and spent an evening with Richard Aldington, who recalled, "He was in that state of animosity which comes to a man when he finds himself alone against the world." At 8 A.M. Friday, 14 November 1919, waving goodbye to Koteliansky, he boarded a second-class train from London through Paris to Turin; his trunk he had sent ahead. Martin Secker, on his way to see Mackenzie, joined him for the trip. Just in time, Huebsch sent twenty pounds which Lawrence, before he departed, probably converted into a thousand Italian lire. He did not reach Turin until 8 P.M. the next day, the trip *"slow slow—slow,"* he warned Rosalind, who planned to follow soon. Stopping off in Turin, he decided to go for a day or two to the Albergo delle Palme in Spezia (the same hotel he had in 1914 chosen for Constance Garnett), then seek out the glorious city of Florence. There he would await Frieda's arrival. A whole era had closed.

෨෴෴

As the Lawrences reached the end of the decade, where a long-awaited beginning opened up before them, they must have sensed how much they had changed since that Sunday in 1912 when Lawrence had knocked at Professor Weekley's door and met the woman who would reshape his life, who would help him clarify the integrity he sought, who would give him a new vision of human possibility. Yet the intervening years had seriously frayed their marriage. Why, then, did Lawrence and Frieda stay together after 1919? It is a central question. There were no children, no possessions to divide, no established community to help them honor their vows; parting would have been easy. Richard Aldington says that in November Lawrence "seemed not to care if he never saw [Frieda] again"; yet Aldington adds that "these two were as certain to stay together as a river to run to the sea." His remark, with its tired simile, merely skirts the complex truth.

Coming from such dissimilar backgrounds, Lawrence and Frieda had gradually shaped their cultural differences into a creative opposition of temperaments. Expansive and easygoing, Frieda played the role of vigilant defender of her husband's creative flame. She encouraged him, though she did little to help him. In 1909 Jessie Chambers had sent Lawrence's poems to Ford Madox Hueffer at the *English Review*; yet Frieda never marketed Lawrence's work—she had neither the initiative nor the skill. By 1919 she no longer even copied Lawrence's manuscripts to save him time; instead, he enlisted Koteliansky and Rosalind Baynes as copyists. Frieda reverted to the role of the incorrigible schoolgirl who earned her reprimands. Yet she remained a powerful catalyst. As much as his mother, she gave ferment to his sensibility, inspired him, envisioned herself as a muse for his genius. Even as she helped him less and less, she believed what he believed—that she *enabled* him to create. That is one reason why he stayed with her.

After seven years together, they prided themselves on their ability to define their lives at the edge of economic survival. That the market for Lawrence's work had so deteriorated angered them but also helped them redefine their ambition. They no longer sought any form of outward success; indeed, they rejected creaturely comforts. They redefined success in multiple ways—as communing with nature and making visits to responsive friends; as plying the domestic arts, especially decorating, sewing, embroidering, and gardening; and as having the liberty to pursue whatever interested them. Their poverty, though real, seems primarily to have narrowed the range of their tolerance—to have given them a kind of antagonism toward privilege, toward the kind of ease bought with wealth. The path they had chosen became a moral imperative for judging others.

Lawrence, alert and responsive to the events around him, but especially to kinds of friendship, had countered the privations of the past with razor-sharp insights into the cultural failures of England and America. In particular, he intuited the contemporary drift toward spiritual emptiness. To attack it, though, he chose an unexpected approach. He took the concept of the family, extended it not to relatives but to friends, then vigorously fought any form of external coercion on that redefined family unit. He distrusted forms of social or political organization anchored in the past or tied to history, because they tended to kill the deep, spontaneous impulses of the individual self. That Lawrence would decide to sell most of his library before he departed for Italy suggests an extraordinary willingness to live for the future. He and Frieda leveraged all the vicissitudes and privations as they came and—as a way of life—accepted this buffeting by the unexpected. They rarely talked of returning to a former residence.

The quality of Lawrence's inner emotional life had also changed. After about 1916 almost no one records the Lawrences holding hands, kissing, hugging, or showing affection. By 1919 both Joan Farjeon and Cecily Lambert remember the *impatience* with which Lawrence treated Frieda. Some erosion of respect coarsened their interchange. That Lawrence had been rebuffed by both Jack Murry and William Henry Hocking seems to have baffled him. They made him seek Frieda's protection but also allowed him, deep within, to link her to these failures. The fact that he and Frieda no longer preferred to share a bedroom suggests that their sexual life had changed, that intercourse may have been infrequent, that veiled irritation had replaced sexual responsiveness. The erotic electricity of the earlier years had gradually eased into friendship, but it was friendship that depended on intimate understanding and fed on moments of mutual surprise. More than their camaraderie, more than their mutual dependency, it was their capacity to surprise that kept them interested in each other.

If their sexual attraction had diminished, their travels had opened them to a cosmopolitan world. In a marketplace of ready rebuffs, Lawrence—no longer free to explore difficult themes in challenging forms like the novel—began to prefer commentary on contemporary mores. The fruits of his travels provided readier copy than work that required, for instance, historical research. The European history textbook, with so much of it necessarily cribbed from Edward Gibbon and others, had left him with a jaundiced view of such work. Increasingly he took the analytical method to encompass dissection of psychological and social motives rather than the dissection of culture which an academic writer like Michel Foucault, much akin to Lawrence (though a generation later), made into an industry. Whereas Foucault spent hours poring over the archives of research libraries in order to cross disciplinary boundaries, Lawrence looked lyrically and meditatively across the contrasts and contradictions within a culture, as he did, for example, in "The Whistling of Birds" (1919), a poetic rhapsody on the shock of winter erupting into spring, and on its human application, as "[w]e [too, like birds,] are lifted to be cast away into the new beginning." Lawrence's archive was intuition. His store of memories, easily freshened by travel, transcended what he found in books. He was impatient with any kind of cant. While he honed, alone, a style that was fertile, sensory, penetrating, and sharp, Frieda gave him something else—a driving desire to explore and enjoy simple pleasures like gathering mushrooms or making sheepskin coats for Rosalind's daughters. She also gave him a tenacious willingness to tackle basic human questions and then to draw quick, opinionated, even brusque conclusions.

Molded by this rich set of experiences, bound together by needs met and unmet, and bedeviled by a series of vexing privations, the Lawrences sought the freedom of Italy. They were ready to inaugurate a decade of profound change.

# PART TWO

PART TWO

# 13

# The Sun Rises Again

## 1920

The moment Lawrence entered Italy the landscape beckoned. It seemed bathed in warmth. Stirred by his surroundings, Lawrence found himself drawn "further and further south," pulled toward the healing power of the sun. Strong and supple, its penetrating rays seemed to crumble the cold pillars of British rectitude. No doubt he hoped that southern Italy, with its radiant sun and pellucid sky, would inspire him to write, to interpret the experience of those who, as they fled England, would embrace the challenge of Italy. Not many months would pass before Lawrence's exiled fictional characters Alvina Houghton and Aaron Sisson would savor Italy's freedom.

On Saturday night, 15 November 1919, when his train reached Turin, Lawrence climbed out with his suitcase and went to Val Salice to visit a rich English couple, Sir Walter Becker, thirty years Lawrence's senior, and his wife. Lawrence had been sent by a mutual friend. Finding himself in alien territory, he and Becker squared off in disagreement, Lawrence told Cynthia Asquith. As "the impotent old wolf" growled about "security and bank-balances" (the standbys of the rich), Lawrence advocated "naked liberty." But even as he was awed by the Beckers' great luxury, he dismissed them as "parvenu"—mere crust on the cheese. For his part Becker, reacting in 1925 to Lawrence's acid portrait of him in *Aaron's Rod,* lamented that he had inspired "such shockingly wearisome tirades."

When Lawrence's train, going south, stopped at Lerici on Monday, 17

November, Lawrence got out and—spending two nights at the Albergo delle Palme—visited friends he and Frieda had liked six years earlier when they had lived at Fiascherino. Although, as he told Cecily Lambert, he found everything "different—not so gay any more," he marveled at the sea under his window and, far beyond, "the blazing blazing sun."

On board once more, Lawrence watched as the cultivated plains slipped by, without hedges or boundaries, speckled with oxen ploughing the dark, velvety earth; he saw stands of silvery poplars sliced by straight canals of blue-green water; and in the exposed sweep of plain and sky, so unlike England, he felt that he had escaped from the old, tight conditions of his past. Snap, snap, snap went the ligatures that had bound him.

When he reached Florence (his temporary destination), he stopped at the moderately priced Pensione Balestri, at 5 Piazza Mentana, to await Frieda's arrival. "I've got two friends here," he wrote to his niece Peggy, "so am not quite alone." The two friends were Norman Douglas (1868–1952), a Secker author who had secured him a cheap room, and Maurice Magnus (1876–1920). These two men were the most charming homosexuals Lawrence had ever met. Far from feeling repelled by them, Lawrence welcomed their lively humor, their fastidious quibbling, and their love of Italy, his terror of gay men having collapsed into guarded tolerance. He would certainly have seen aspects of himself in both the burly, masculine Douglas and the mincing, effeminate Magnus.

Douglas, much older than Lawrence, was a tall, solidly built man with thick white hair parted in the middle, eyes as blue as Lawrence's, and an angular face that reflected his aristocratic origins. A 1912 photograph shows him dressed in a well-tailored suit, his vest setting off his high white collar, above which, from his mouth, hangs a cigarette. Born in Austria, he trained as a scientist before joining the British Foreign Service (1893–96); in 1898 he married his first cousin Elsa and, with her, had two sons, Archie and Robin, before he divorced her in 1903. By then he was thirty-five and free to move to Italy and redirect his abundant energies, yielding now to his rapacious sexual interest in boys. He preferred virgin buds of thirteen or fourteen. Once he had spent the last of his inheritance, Douglas returned to England and, while employed as assistant editor of the *English Review* (1912–16), met Lawrence, whose short stories he admired. His *South Wind*, published in 1917 by Martin Secker, brought Douglas both strong sales and a reputation for sardonic wit. Moving to Paris the same year, at least as poor as the Lawrences had ever been, he borrowed money from friends (he proved an excellent companion) and continued writing books of whimsical hedonism. He arrived in Florence on 20 September 1919, where he stayed rooted for eighteen years.

Maurice Magnus was different. A small, portly man in his forties, American, fastidiously dressed, with dark, curly hair above a round face, and touched with an air of timidity, Magnus was the son of an adoring mother. In that way he resembled Lawrence. In other ways he did not. Long before, he had left his wife, and, smitten now with Douglas, he acted as Douglas's concubine. Hating women, he was the kind of man who could say to Lawrence, "How lovely your hair is—such a lovely colour!" In 1916 he had enlisted in the French Foreign Legion, was sent to North Africa, soon recognized with horror the foolishness of his choice, and, deserting, fled to Italy. He was trying to turn his Legion experience into a memoir (for which Lawrence would later write a trenchant introduction). He was, Lawrence said in a pregnant sentence, a man who "knew all the short cuts in all the big towns of Europe." A Catholic convert, he would soon seek shelter at the Monte Cassino monastery.

While Lawrence waited for Frieda to clear her passport and come south from her long visit with her mother in Baden-Baden, he savored Florence and its extraordinary culture, roaming among its galleries, quaint streets, and assorted shops. His large, sunny room—located near the Ponte Vecchio, the most ancient bridge of the city—looked out onto the swollen Arno River, which cut straight through the city. "Florence is beautiful," he wrote, "and full of life and plenty;" and it struck him, he told Koteliansky, as "*much* better than England—not that pressure." The crown of Italian culture, Florence had for centuries excelled in architecture, sculpture, and painting. Lawrence would have admired the Gothic Duomo, with its multicolored marble faces, sixteenth-century palaces designed by Vasari, sculptures by Donatello and the della Robbias, frescoes by Ghirlandaio, and (at the Uffizi Gallery) paintings by Botticelli, Titian, and Leonardo da Vinci. Above all, he loved Michelangelo's *David*, which stood near the Palazzo Vecchio.

Lawrence discovered that at the Balestri he could live comfortably for only two pounds a week. Although someone stole his fountain pen, he liked the easy-going people, the good red wine, and the insouciance in every face. From his window he could watch the horses and mules trotting across the Ponte Vecchio, the drivers hidden under big green umbrellas, the heads of the animals warmed by gray bonnets. He dined out with friends, went to the dentist, walked a great deal, tasted the sights, and amused himself with Douglas and Magnus. "One loafs one's life away in Italy," he mused to his sister Emily.

At last Frieda, revived by her trip to Germany, wired that she would arrive on 3 December and that her lost trunk had been recovered. Leaving Florence on the ninth, they would stop briefly in Rome before trekking on to Picinisco, in the mountains of Italy, "at least to see what it is like," perhaps staying the winter. When Frieda arrived at four o'clock in the morning, looking (as expected) "a good bit thinner . . . but very well in health," Lawrence insisted on a ride through the city. As Frieda remembered, "'You must come for a drive with me,' he said, 'I must show you this town.' We went in an open carriage, I saw the pale crouching Duomo and in the thick moonmist the Giotto tower disappeared at the top into the sky. The Palazzo Vecchio with Michelangelo's David and all the statues of men, we passed. 'This is a men's town,' I said, 'not like Paris, where all statues are women.' We went along the Lungarno, we passed the Ponte Vecchio, in that moonlight night, and ever since Florence is the most beautiful town to me, the lily town, delicate and flowery."

The months they spent apart had eased their differences and renewed their commitment. But Frieda was uneasy in this "men's town," and she used a code to veneer the pederasty that Lawrence may well have described: "The English there in Florence had still a sense of true hospitality, in the grand manner. And yet it struck me all as being like 'Cranford' only it was a man's 'Cranford.' And the wickedness there seemed like old maids' secret rejoicing in wickedness." In Florence the village gossip of Mrs. Gaskell's *Cranford* (1853) grew a sinister mold, and much later Frieda regarded Douglas's sexual practices as heinously foul. But it is peculiar that Lawrence, who must have heard Douglas rhapsodize about his boys, makes no criticism. Did he listen in fascinated horror? But just as Frieda recalls that he was "deeply disturbed by Magnus," so he must have been by Douglas, the pederast; and a month later, when Rosalind Baynes arrived at the Balestri with her children, Lawrence worried that Douglas's presence might be unsavory, for he told a friend who lived near Florence, "I've half a feeling he's making new scandals for himself, and I don't want her in any way to be touched or frightened." Lawrence probably knew that Douglas had been expelled from England after he picked up a schoolboy in the Natural History Museum.

Departing for Rome, the Lawrences remained there only three days— the city was impossibly crowded and expensive—before they sojourned in a house belonging to Orazio Cervi, who had modeled for Rosalind Baynes's father. It squatted below the village of Picinisco, radiant with sunlight in the wild Apennines, a good hundred miles south of Rome. When they arrived, they were stunned. Picinisco was inaccessible and "staggeringly primitive," Lawrence warned Rosalind on the sixteenth: "You cross a great stony river bed, then an icy river on a plank, then climb unfootable paths, while the ass struggles behind with your luggage. . . . At the moment a terrible commotion, bagpipes under the window, and a wild howling kind of ballad, utterly unintelligible—Christmas serenade. . . . If the weather turns bad, I really think we must go on, to Naples or Capri."

The conveniences were so minimal they could not stay. Writing ahead to Compton Mackenzie, who had recently put up their publisher Martin Secker, Lawrence hoped to borrow Mackenzie's small cottage on Capri, the mountainous but warm island twenty miles from Naples. On the twenty-

D. H. Lawrence, passport photo, 1919 (Courtesy of the Gersheim Collection, Harry Ransom Humanities Research Center, the University of Texas at Austin)

third they left Picinisco, walked five miles to catch a bus to Cassino, and, once on Capri, spent Christmas Day moving into a balconied apartment situated at the top of the Palazzo Ferraro, high above the Bay of Naples. To reach the Mediterranean demanded a mile's steep descent. The weather, stormy but mild, appealed to the Lawrences, although they lamented Italian prices: "butter 20 francs, wine 3 francs a litre the cheapest,—sugar 8 francs a kilo, oil 7 or 8 francs a litre . . . and so on. With the exchange at 50," he told Catherine Carswell on 4 January 1920, "it is just possible [to stay here], and only just."

The island of Capri teemed with interesting people. Often the Lawrences dined with Compton Mackenzie, the rich Scottish novelist who, suffering from sciatica, a nerve disorder that affected his lower body, had first come to Capri in 1913. He now owned a cottage and some land, and lived in a fine seaside villa, earning advances of fifteen hundred pounds on his books. Narrow chested like Lawrence, Mackenzie had an angular face and tight mouth that made him look more reserved than he was. Lawrence half admired the aesthetic figure Mackenzie created for himself and wrote him a number of intimate letters, the kind one novelist could write to another about the craft and publication of fiction. Two years older than Lawrence, an Oxford graduate, the author of a heralded novel called *Sinister Street* (1913), a man of some talent and more confidence, Mackenzie very much liked Lawrence—enough to offer him advice about negotiating with publishers like his close friend Martin Secker. With Mackenzie, Lawrence also had long discussions on the maladies of the Western world. But Mackenzie, annoyed at the way Frieda provoked Lawrence "with boisterous laughter to pull people to pieces," could not decide if Lawrence was a portent, a phenomenon, or a freak. Mackenzie's wife, Faith, recalls that, to amuse themselves, Lawrence and her husband would sing "Barbara Allen" and "Sally in Our Alley" as the poet John Ellingham Brooks pounded out an accompaniment on Mackenzie's Erard grand piano.

The Lawrences soon made friends with another novelist, Francis Brett Young, and his wife, Jessica, who had already settled into Mackenzie's cottage. Although Brett Young's enthralled discipleship to Mackenzie riled Lawrence, Brett Young was a doctor who, like Lawrence, had left his original profession. Both had resolved to live by their pens; neither had much money. In *The Young Physician,* a variation of *Sons and Lovers* which Secker had just published, Brett Young portrays the crisis brought on by the death of his protagonist's mother. But Lawrence was not impressed by Brett Young's talent, and today his novels seem full of shallow introspection—sometimes ponderous, always dull. Lawrence liked the lively Jessica Brett Young better.

To the Lawrences' surprise they also found Mary Cannan (1867–1950). They had liked her very much when she and her husband, Gilbert, were frequent visitors to Chesham in 1914 (she had also been married to James Barrie). Now she was divorced and lived by herself. Lawrence called her "a disappointed creature." Cultured and full of anecdote, vibrant but insecure, her eyes rolling from side to side as she spoke, she clung to the Lawrences and quickly pumped them full of the cosmopolitan gossip that swept Capri like a sirocco. They spent New Year's Eve with Mackenzie's wild crowd at Morgano's Café, where, Frieda said, "the local people came with a band and danced the Tarantella." At first the Lawrences were amused by all the spiteful scandal swirling about the flamboyant set of internationals harbored there, and even planned to stay a few months. But gradually Frieda came to dislike the gossip that flourished in Capri.

They stayed only two months. On 11 January the little local steamer, penetrating the storms, brought Frieda a Christmas present from Germany, "a beautiful scarf: which at the moment she is showing to the servant," Lawrence regaled Violet Monk on 12 January, "who sings out *Come è bello!—come è be-e-e-ello!*—Isn't it lovely. I expect the dear Liberata will be donning the scarf when we are out." But although he enjoyed writing letters to English friends like the Grimsbury women and the Hopkins, Lawrence felt lazy: "Italy is a lazy country," he informed Cecily Lambert. "One meets people, and lounges till the next meal; and so life passes."

Still, even as postal and rail strikes kept him from working, he reveled in the Italian weather, so different from the gray skies and cold rain of English winters: "[T]he weather is wondrous fine—brilliant, hot sun, brilliant, beautiful. [Today] I watched him go down red into the sea," Lawrence wrote to Cynthia Asquith. By the twenty-ninth the strikes were over. The headline in Milan's *Corriere della Sera* on 30 January read, "La fine dello sciopero ferroviario" (The End of the Railway Strike). Italy's railway workers had settled for a six-hundred-lire payment and an eight-hour workday. All the while, Lawrence had been thinking hard about what he might do next. Finally, he knew.

First, he broke with his agent, James Pinker, so that he could place his own work. Weary of the vagueness and complaisance of agents and publishers, he was determined to have "every point of agreement between myself and my publisher precise and explicit," he warned Thomas Seltzer in America. Lawrence believed that he could protect his own interests in ways that Pinker had not. But Lawrence had no secretary, no files, no typewriter, no legal training; he struggled with an unreliable Italian post; and, although scrupulously honest, he was not skilled at compromise. His decision to act for himself was unwise; it gave him little pleasure and stole energy from his creative work.

Then, knowing that his remaining hundred pounds would not last, he began to write, first composing "six little essays on Freudian Unconscious" for wry, gentle Ben Huebsch in America, and then working again on a novel called "The Insurrection of Miss Houghton," which, he told Secker, "has lain in Bavaria since early 1914" (he expected it any day from Germany), and whose brisk plot, he hoped, would deflect the censors' attention. But he also wanted to begin serious work in an atmosphere more congenial than Capri's. By 5 February, when he and Frieda had taken a little excursion down the Amalfi coast and admired its extraordinary beauty, he realized how weary he was of Capri, of Compton Mackenzie's urbane influence, and of Mackenzie's mewing assortment of "semi-literary cats." Although he loathed the expense of moving again so soon, he had to "clear out," he told Catherine Carswell, "to Sicily, I think." All along, he had wanted to go south. Having joined the Brett Youngs to visit the temples at Agrigentum, in Sicily, Lawrence now borrowed J. E. Brooks's *Baedeker* and, three weeks later, left to explore the island and its possibilities.

Lawrence's decision to break with England had far-reaching effects. Now that he was free of Pinker, he could act decisively. When Murry, in London, rejected Lawrence's further contributions to the *Athenaeum,* his slap was both a professional and a personal blow. Frieda almost certainly shared Lawrence's fury. Stung by the rejection, Lawrence branded Murry "a dirty little worm." Katherine, who had probably seconded Murry's judgment, seemed—Lawrence spat at her—to be "stewing" in her own deathly consumption. He had finished with them. These breaks with the past asserted Lawrence's newfound freedom, which Italy invited—a conception of the self bursting constraints and bristling with unleashed energy. These breaks also expressed Lawrence's strong belief that, in literature, he would yet "have [his] day." To that end he asked Robert Mountsier, a friendly face from the dark Cornwall days, to become his American agent.

## COMING TO LIFE AGAIN

On 26 February, accompanied by the Brett Youngs, he left—without Frieda—for Sicily, the largest of the Mediterranean islands, famous for its cloudless skies and mild winters. About the size of New Hampshire, Sicily exported almonds, oranges, and lemons and boasted snow-capped Mount Etna, at eleven thousand feet one of the largest volcanoes in the world. Just nine years earlier, it had erupted; even in 1920 it puffed flame at night and smoke by day. Perhaps Brooks's *Baedeker* led Lawrence to the village of Taormina, full of Greek and Roman ruins, full of exquisite views of Etna in the distance and the blue sea below, bursting with peach and almond blossom and tall wheat rippling up the green slopes like pale fire. Taormina, Lawrence wrote Brooks, had "more space, more air, more green and succulent herbage" than Capri, where the parched dryness seemed to snare the island's gossip.

By 3 March Lawrence had found a house he loved. Called Fontana Vecchia ("old fountain"), it lay north of the village. Built around 1650, its stone walls were a foot and a half thick. It had several rooms on two floors, a handy kitchen, a big vegetable garden, two terraces, and an ancient fountain that still gushed near the garden and supplied the house. Looking east and resting on a steep, rocky slope high above the sea, the house seemed like a fortress. He rented it for a whole year. The cost: 2,000 francs (about $110 or £30). Although it had been built by the Hubrecht family of Holland, it was now owned by a prosperous young peasant named Francesco "Ciccio" Cacopardo. On 8 March Lawrence wrote to Compton Mackenzie: "Frieda loves the house"—as did Mary Cannan, who had come along and lodged at the Timeo Hotel; Lawrence himself felt "very grand" in the house and garden, with its mimosa and eucalyptus trees—all "really lovely." The Lawrences' frequent walks turned up pink-and-white almond blossoms, asphodels, anemones, and wild narcissi. Nothing escaped Lawrence's notice. "Living in Sicily after the war years," Frieda remembered, "was like coming to life again."

But as Lawrence was finding a place that would support his creative life, he encountered afresh the problem of publishing *The Rainbow* and *Women in Love,* still his favorite novels. In New York, Thomas Seltzer, a bold little entrepreneur, would not relinquish the manuscript of *Women in Love* to his rival Ben Huebsch, and instead promised Lawrence the prompt arrival of proofs. "Let us go ahead," Lawrence acquiesced on 9 March and signed Seltzer's contract. Nor was arranging for publication in London any simpler. At first Lawrence approached Martin Secker, who offered three hundred pounds for *Women in Love* and two hundred pounds for *The Rainbow*—without royalties. Lawrence bristled. If he believed in the future of his books, why settle for lump sums and throw away his future earnings potential? He therefore approached the stalwart but timid Duckworth, who wanted Lawrence "to leave out a chapter of *The Rainbow*" (probably "Shame"). Lawrence refused. Limping back to Secker, Lawrence wrote him on 22 March: "[I]f you still offer me the same terms, I'll take them." He knew he would need money to travel when the hot weather drove him and Frieda from Taormina. Still, he told Mackenzie, he hated "to lose all my rights over the books." The job of literary agent was harder than it looked. Lawrence was therefore relieved when Secker wrote kindly on 28 March, proposing to publish both novels on a royalty basis: a shilling per copy on the first two thousand, one shilling sixpence up to five thousand, and two shillings thereafter. Lawrence then courageously asked for (and got) an advance of one hundred pounds on each book. He was never timid.

While these negotiations went forward, an unusual domestic scrape occurred, of the kind that Lawrence both cultivated and despised. Mary Cannan's former husband Gilbert wrote from New York, where he had gone to lecture, to say that he would collect money from Lawrence's pub-

Fontana Vecchia ("Old Fountain"), above Taormina, Sicily (Courtesy of Salvatore Galleano)

lishers (though Lawrence doubted his honesty and apparently wrote him to say so, perhaps expressing, at the same time, Mary's animosity toward her own "dirty little worm"). To the Lawrences' astonishment, Cannan suddenly appeared in Taormina on 8 April with the money bulging from his wallet:

Yesterday I heard a fumbling on the terrace—and there Gilbert at the foot of the stairs, in a brown hat rather like yours [Lawrence wrote sardonically to Mackenzie]: gave me quite a turn: thought it was somehow you-not-you. He came express from Rome in one of his tantrums because of the nasty letter I'd written him—fume!—But . . . in his indignation he disgorged a cheque for £75—SEVENTY-FIVE POUNDS STERLING—as the equivalent of $300 which he had collected from Americans for me. Benone! Fortune so had it that *for once* Mary wasn't here to tea: and that he had taken a room at Domenico, as being a *little grander* than Timeo. He is tout américain . . . pocket book thick, fat, bulging with 1000 Lire notes—'these beastly hotels'—'Oh yes, picked up quite a lot of money over there'—'Oh yes, they seemed to take to me quite a lot.'. . . However, we parted as friends who will *never* speak to each other again.

This tense parting marked another break with Lawrence's English past—as decisive as his break with Murry. On the same day Frieda wrote to Mackenzie: "I was sorry, there is *nothing* left [of Cannan's friendship]." His posturing had met an unappreciative audience.

But this was not the only rustling on Lawrence's terrace. If Cannan had at last pressed a check into Lawrence's ready hand, Maurice Magnus (one might say) deftly slipped it out. Lawrence's three encounters with Magnus are surprisingly veiled in his letters, as if they were secret and unsharable, and it would appear that, through Magnus as agency, he was able to confront some of his hidden erotic feelings, to give them voice without exposing them. For Lawrence the matter was less one of shame than of privacy.

Responding to Magnus's invitation to visit him—alone—at Monte Cassino, a vast monastery one hundred miles from Naples, Lawrence decided, perhaps against Frieda's wishes, to yield to the monastic experience. From 19 to 21 February he stayed with Magnus in the stone-cold, hilltop monastery, founded by Saint Benedict in 529 (and completely destroyed in 1944), and was escorted through the cathedral and crypts and morning mass, and perhaps exposed to some of Magnus's sexual secrets: for when Lawrence later wrote about Magnus, in the mesmerizing *Memoir of Maurice Magnus* (1924), he chose language usually reserved for a heroine aroused by a man: "I felt it acutely, a kind of appeal . . . I felt it so strongly," he said, when Magnus appealed to him "with a tender, intimate look," whispering "ecstasies in my ear" as they tiptoed about the dark, silent church, Magnus behaving "like a woman who isn't quite sure of her lover." In truth, Magnus was—soon enough—unsure of more than Lawrence. He had passed bad checks; the Italian police sought him; and so he fled Monte Cassino and rushed to Taormina, "straight to you," he whispered as he stood in anguish on Lawrence's lower terrace, under the creamy bignonias. Though feeling ambivalent, Lawrence agreed to help. He paid Magnus's most recent hotel bill but was relieved when the parasitic American boarded a ship for Syracuse.

When Mary Cannan wanted to visit the isolated island of Malta, directly south of Sicily, she enticed the Lawrences to come with her by agreeing to pay their passage. When they paused in Syracuse, in May, whom should they discover but Magnus, penniless in a good hotel, needing to sponge only one pound this time. Once they reached Malta, they met again, and Lawrence and Magnus spent an afternoon together out of the dazzling heat and dust, drinking whiskey and soda, talking intimately. A letter that Magnus wrote to Norman Douglas, dated 18 July 1920, shows the kind of emotional (but not sexual) intimacy that Lawrence and Magnus apparently won from each other. According to Magnus, Lawrence opened his heart: "He is looking for bisexual types for *himself*," Magnus reported, but Lawrence, innocent no longer, apparently believed that he had "[a]rrived too late—[and] regrets it. Never speaks of it." This strong suggestion of unfulfilled sexual potential would fit into the full range of Lawrence's character. But he could not explore it directly: he was married, uninterested in paying male prostitutes (as Magnus did), and anyway could use his fiction to explore—more conveniently—his unfulfilled sexual needs. And here was a novel, still unfinished, in which his regret could be translated into desire.

"We love our Fontana Vecchia," Lawrence wrote to Amy Lowell, "where we sit on our ledge and look far out, through the green, to the coast of Greece." For many months his health was good. The sun had energized him; his tuberculosis seemed almost arrested by the climate. Inspired by the calm, sleepy slopes above Taormina and by the marital peace at home, Lawrence had been far busier than usual. While he agitated over negotiations with publishers, he had begun to rewrite the manuscript of the "Miss Houghton" novel that had arrived from Germany on 12 February, jettisoning the work he had done in Capri, where the drought was both climatic and creative. The novel, he often said, amused him; and he judged it morally quite proper. By 9 April he was more than half done: "I like it so much," he confided to Mackenzie. In the brilliantly sunny days he sped along and, by the end of April, had chosen the title "The Lost Girl." Because of the unreliable post, he decided to have the manuscript typed in Rome (for a hefty twenty-two pounds) so that he would have a typescript for Secker and another one for Seltzer. On 5 May, just as the hot weather dazed the island, he finished the novel.

For the biographer *The Lost Girl* is a curiosity. Its most tantalizing clue is Lawrence's. While he was reading the typescript in June, he wrote to Mackenzie: "It's different from all my other work: not immediate, not intimate—except the last bit: all set across a distance." This "distance" arises from Lawrence's sunny narrator, who playfully sketches the English background of savvy merchants and penurious defeat from which Alvina Houghton, stewing in idleness, must escape. What is new is the tone of a sentence like, "Surely enough books have been written about heroines in similar circumstances." Both Alvina and the narrator slowly free themselves from the restrictions that surround them, the narrator initially mocking narrative conventions, his female protagonist ignoring the wisdom of the British middle classes.

Now close to thirty, Alvina, discarding the dull suitors of Woodhouse, feels herself "withering towards old-maiddom." The rescue she needs comes dashing on horseback out of an odd, Dickensian troupe of performers in the town. The rescuer's name is Ciccio ("CHEE-chee-o") Marasca. The most alluring of the troupe, he is tall, loosely built, Italian, and full of expressive gesture despite his silence. Only twenty-five, he sees Alvina as Henry Grenfel earlier saw March in "The Fox," his dark eyes "looking

right into her, beyond her usual self, impersonal." Fascinated by his passion, Alvina feels hypnotized and powerless in his presence, "as if she had
lost her soul." And when he returns to Italy, she follows him to his native
village of Pescoca-lascio. Then the novel becomes "intimate" and eloquent. Like a transcript, it recreates the ten days that Lawrence and Frieda
had spent in Picinisco—the biting cold, the primitive conditions, the lack
of comfort, the long journeys for the post, the bagpipers' Christmas serenade. For Alvina, now married and pregnant, Lawrence imagines the elemental rhythms of mountain life that he would have experienced had he
remained in Orazio Cervi's isolated house. It is a curious ending.

Alvina, a character without erudition or subtlety, works out one aspect
of Lawrence's sexual potential, discarding security and respectability for
passion and erotic adventure. It is no accident that Lawrence's young
Taormina landlord, Ciccio—whom Lawrence calls in a moment of unguarded intimacy his "darling" landlord—is also the name of Alvina's
lover. He is the reincarnation of Magnus's good-looking Maltese men who
will, Magnus tells Lawrence, "do anything you want." Alvina is less forceful than either Ursula or Gudrun. In her quest she pierces through nothing
more than cultural differences of accent and attitude. She seeks experience
but not understanding. She is so hungry for affection that she accepts a relationship that offers little more than a mysterious male's sensual excitement. For Ciccio desire becomes demand; for Alvina sensual satisfaction
means surrender and annihilation.

But if Alvina's quest for salvation reaches neither the depth of Ursula's
in *The Rainbow* nor the complexity of Ursula's in *Women in Love*, that is
partly because Lawrence, knowing that in 1920 neither of these novels
could be openly purchased, had aimed instead to write a novel that was familiar in strategy and light in spirit. He hoped it would sell. He aimed not
to uncover dark layers of the soul but to fuse English sterility with Italian
insouciance. He wanted Alvina to free herself from her father's mercantile
concerns, her mother's invalidism, her guardian's propriety, and the townspeople's pettiness in order to discover the mysteries of another culture.
Books like *The Lost Girl*, Lawrence confided to Mackenzie in May, "are
the crumpled wings of my soul. They get me free before I get myself free."
They spoke his soul's language. They constructed the Pegasus who carried
him away from poverty and war—and possibly unsatisfied desire.

After Lawrence completed *The Lost Girl* and knew that Martin Secker
was thrilled with it, he and Frieda waited patiently, amid the heat, for their
money to bulge the wallet that would fund their escape from the long,
scorching days at Taormina. Frieda wanted to go again to Germany, from
August to October, to see her mother, the dark fir trees, and the dewy
grass; Lawrence, hating hot Italian trains and the expense of long journeys,
and fearing that Germany might be "inhospitable to foreigners," thought

instead he would go to Venice, perhaps reconnoitering with Rosalind Baynes, perhaps meeting his Cornish friends Irene and Percy Whittley in Milan, then walking with them by cool lakes and moist woods, from Lake Como to Lake Garda. "Sounds wildly extravagant," Lawrence demurred to his young friend Jan Juta, "but when I'm alone I'm a gnat of economy." "We should have to be economical," he warned Mrs. Whittley on 16 July; that meant carrying a spirit kettle and a saucepan.

What intervened were dozens of business letters. Secker still anxiously awaited the corrected manuscript of *Women in Love*; serial rights to *The Lost Girl* and *Women in Love* had not been sold; *Dial* magazine wanted stories like "Rex" (which brought in fifty dollars); and Lawrence still needed to place the book manuscript of *Studies in Classic American Literature* in both England and America. He knew that he could correct the proofs of Seltzer's *Women in Love* as he traveled.

While he waited to leave Taormina, he remained intensely alive to the Sicilian landscape, delighted by the ripening almonds and fat green figs, glad for the profusion of apricots and cherries, enchanted by the come-and-go of the peasants along the little road skirting Fontana Vecchia, where (Lawrence wrote) he and Frieda could see "the many goats stepping down the hill, the asses coming slowly, and processions of girls with great bundles of bright corn on their heads. So the peasant life threads almost through our fingers, perhaps the best of it. This frail streaming contact is what I like best: not to know people closely." This is a revealing statement. At such a remove, Lawrence could appreciate the working-class life that linked him to his own roots. The vicarious participation in age-old rural rhythms—of beasts and grain gatherers—he had also loved in Cornwall: the threading of the grain and hay through his fingers. But Lawrence had been hurt by *too* close a proximity to one particular peasant, William Henry Hocking. Now he wanted contact that was *frail*, unthreatening, without emotional risk. He would not repeat the unsettling experience in Cornwall.

And how might Frieda have spent her days in Taormina? Sleeping later than Lawrence, who rose early, she would have helped him with the housework. By 1920 she had become, she said, quite a good cook and, on Sundays, when Lawrence lighted the big kitchen stove and began roasting the beef and baked potatoes, she got out the flour and "made cakes and tarts, big and little, sweet pies and meat pies and put them on the side-board in the dining room." No doubt she hoped these high-fat, high-sugar dishes would help Lawrence, now thinner than ever, gain weight. On weekdays, over a charcoal fire, she stewed fruit or fresh tomatoes (in season, they were only twopence a pound), or sugared the juicy red mulberries that Lawrence picked. While he wrote his novels, she would have helped wash up, done some sewing, perhaps mending Lawrence's socks, then read whatever Lawrence was reading or whatever he had written. Because his writing so vividly reflected their daily life together, Frieda says that she "read every day what he had written." Occasionally she wrote letters or went into the village. At teatime, Mary Cannan might come along for a gossipy visit, bringing some delicacy she had found; for she had money. And when the hot summer days cooled into evening, Frieda would have joined Lawrence for a stroll. Always she discussed everything with him, in a rhythm of shared irritation or pointed disagreement spliced with amused tolerance and mimicry.

## The Orgasmic Rupture

By the end of July, when the smoldering heat had become oppressive, Lawrence and Frieda had made final plans to visit the young South African artist Jan Juta (1895–1990) and his Welsh friend Alan Insole in the hilly village of Anticoli, near Rome, then on 12 August proceed by train to Florence, then go to Milan to the Hotel du Nord. From there Frieda would go on to Baden-Baden (a journey of twenty hours!) to stay with her mother in the comfortable Ludwig-Wilhelmstift for widows, and to visit her two sisters, Else in Berlin and Johanna in Munich. On the seventeenth Lawrence would join the Whittleys (she a teacher, he a banker), coming from London to join him for a week of mountain hiking and camping around northern Italy, all of them reaching Venice on the twenty-fourth. And then, when they had departed, Lawrence would just wander—"as if," he told Rosalind Baynes, "I might drift off anywhere," even into something unpredictable.

When the Lawrences left Sicily, they found travel conditions awful—trains slow and crowded, food expensive, the heat suffocating. But Lawrence enjoyed his holiday—the alpine rains, the cool nights, bathing in Venice, the extended "picnic à trois" with the Whittleys, and finally rediscovering the ambience of Florence. Lawrence reached the city on 2 September. Almost at once he went to the ancient, rambling Villa La Canovaia, three miles outside of Florence, set on the first bluff toward Fiesole, the villa's high wall shielding it from intruders, its garden terraced up the sunny hillside, its rooms musty with old furniture but enlivened with chickens, cats, puppies, and goats. The Canovaia he borrowed from Rosalind Baynes, who, when an explosion shattered its windows, had relocated into Fiesole proper. Camping at the Canovaia was "great fun, even alone," he told Irene Whittley on 8 September, the day the grape harvest began.

In surprising ways Lawrence's break with the constraints of the past continued to guide his behavior—and his art. On the verdant slopes of Fiesole and in the Canovaia's garden, where its cypresses hung with nightingales and fireflies, Lawrence was stirred to write a series of poems about the natural world. What is astonishing about these poems—published in 1923 in the collection *Birds, Beasts and Flowers*—is the way they separate the narrator's strong personality into two voices. One voice broadens observation into philosophy, as in "There is only one evil, to deny life"; the other, a gnomic voice like an amused troll's, devours the life of an object so intensely that it yields up its inner self in a flare of revelation.

For the biographer the most revealing are four poems on fruits—"Pomegranate," "Fig," "Grapes," and "Medlars and Sorb-Apples"—which are narrated by a forceful, feisty narrator who uses each fruit to negotiate the space between his narcissistic self and a hostile world outside. These poems are neither nature poems nor meditations on nature; they are sexual explorations into the mysteries and seductions of female anatomy, brazen in their juicy delight, daring in their excursions into forbidden zones, perfectly controlled by their seeming innocence. "Pomegranate," for instance, defiantly searches out the fruit's "fissure" and discovers there how lovely it is "within the crack." "Fig" is more explicit. In Ken Russell's film of *Women in Love* (1969), Birkin declaims the poem to Hermione and her guests as a zany affront to country-house society. Indeed, "Fig" details the vulgar "put[ting] your mouth to the crack" to eat the rosy, moist, honeyed fig. Gliding to the fig's "symbolic" female secret, the poem, in long, thick lines, tastes the strange-smelling sap and the secret scarlet "through the fissure," the crimson "through the purple slit / Like a wound," Lawrence's simile bruising the erotic with pain. But the fig's secret, framed in a layer of moral significance, lingers "through moist, scarlet lips / That laugh at the Lord's indignation." The poem's final, interrogative, "What then, when . . . bursten figs won't keep?" pleads for the release of the narrator's helpless sexual urgency, even as it splits his marriage covenants.

What provoked this sudden fascination with female genitalia? Why did ripe fruits suddenly tantalize Lawrence? In August he told Rosalind Baynes he hoped to "linger with you" in Florence. Apparently he did. When he visited her at her villa in Fiesole, they walked together, talked of love, bought sorb apples, cooked supper. On Sunday, 14 September, their attraction took an unexpected turn as each of them, in the warm autumn glow gleaming with fireflies, opened cautiously but eagerly to the other, each of them uneasily folding their erotic secret into a pocket of private memories. "It is something quite special and lovely, the time, the place, the beloved," Lawrence whispered to her as the sunlight slid off into the pungently perfumed night. The moment was exquisite.

In Lawrence's poetic sequence on fruits, figs decay into the medlars' "rottenness." It is a rottenness the narrator loves "to suck . . . out"—such delectable "excrementa" of autumn drenched with fragrant sweat and soft mystery. And then the dark, crucial lines:

A kiss, and a spasm of farewell, a moment's orgasm of rupture
Then along the damp road alone, till the next turning.
And there, a new partner, a new parting, a new unfusing into twain,
A new gasp of further isolation,
A new intoxication of loneliness, among decaying, frost-cold leaves.

The shock of this sexual meeting is profound, orgasm a "rupture" of his commitment to the sanctity of marriage. What follows is not an expected fusing but "a new unfusing into twain," its poignancy leaving the narrator gasping with the "intoxication of loneliness." These powerfully felt lines expose the cruel power of attraction and the equally cruel power of separation:

Going down the strange lanes of hell more and more intensely alone,
The fibres of the heart parting one after the other,
And yet the soul continuing, naked-footed, ever more vividly embodied
Like a flame blown whiter and whiter
In a deeper and deeper darkness
Ever more exquisite, distilled in separation.

What "embodies" the soul also tears it asunder, with inexorable force. This tearing force is a somber development of Gudrun's "passion of cruelty" in *Women in Love*. It is a sudden, bold confrontation with Gerald's horrible *tearing* of the membrane that lets ooze in, like a bursten fruit, "the obscene beyond." It is a realization that the most exquisitely painful of all human experiences is the moment of satiation bursting into dissolution and separation. No wonder Frieda hated these poems when she read them.

But the question remains, Was the affair consummated? Rosalind's memoir suggests (but only *suggests*) that it was; Lawrence's poems (although not his letters) appear to confirm it, as does *Aaron's Rod*, the novel he completed in 1921, in which a married man yields to a married woman but finds the experience a violation of his troubled marriage. At this time both Lawrence and Rosalind were vulnerable—Lawrence living apart from his wife, Rosalind estranged from her husband, Godwin. Both of them had chosen self-imposed exile from England, Lawrence escaping an oppressive culture, Rosalind the nasty publicity over her impending divorce. Calm and attractive, athletic and independent, the daughter of a prominent Royal Academician named Hamo Thornycroft, Rosalind had been taught to value spontaneity over duty, to revere beauty over Victorian morality, to find freedom more satisfying than restraint. Age twenty-nine, she had always loved to bicycle, camp, hike, explore unfamiliar terrain. She saw her life as an adventure. In 1912 the gifted English composer Arnold Bax described her as a person who "radiated a wonderful sympathy," a "wonderfully intuitive understanding"—a person who possessed "a very deep emotional life hidden under the calm exterior that [she showed] to the world." After her husband, inflamed by patriotism, impulsively joined the RAMC in 1915, Rosalind was unfaithful, and when her third daughter, Nan, was born of a tryst that Rosalind initiated with her handsome childhood friend Kenneth Hooper, Godwin sought a divorce. Except that she kept her three children, Rosalind became a version of Frieda Weekley in 1912, awaiting a divorce she would not contest.

Yet Godwin himself had been unfaithful, and as his own father had written in March 1919, "Rosalind knew all about Godwin's free and easy ways with both sexes long before she married him," as if, warned at the outset, she should have continued to acquiesce. But she found she could not accept her husband's behavior. She had wearied of *his* infidelities in a way that Lawrence had not of Frieda's: whereas Rosalind grew jealous and hurt, Lawrence was acquiescent and yielding. She and Lawrence would have spent many hours talking over the problem of infidelity in marriage, the perplexing ways of calculating its emotional effects, the value of exile to vanquish gossip, and a child's claim to a home free of marital discord. She would have found Lawrence's own "intuitive understanding" immensely comforting.

Lawrence, however, seems never to have considered leaving Frieda for Rosalind Baynes. Accordingly he proceeded with his plan to meet Frieda in Venice, to stay there a week or two, near Juta and Insole, and then to touch down in Rome before landing again in Taormina. On 28 September Lawrence left Florence, and in Venice he lounged on the dank waterways with Juta and Insole, who for a month had hired a gondola and a gondolier; he went to the deserted Lido alone—"take my lunch and sit and watch from the sand hills, and bathe"; he gazed at the brilliant sun as it beat back the first touch of autumn's chill.

Meanwhile, Frieda had relished her months in Germany. She had gone to Munich, Lawrence told Mackenzie in September, and feasted on "peasant drama and marionettes and [a] return to innocent bare-footed dance under heaven," but she had also reported "very bad feeling between French and German." And with great enthusiasm, she had urged Lawrence to come to Baden-Baden, but he had declined—too late in the year and, he reckoned, too expensive. But he longed for her return. A few days before Frieda arrived, he was, he told his Dutch friend Marie Hubrecht, already "a little tired of wandering about" and felt now like settling to work. Frieda proclaimed her own joy at their reunion: "We are glad to be together again."

Departing from Venice on 14 October, the Lawrences left for Florence and Rome, then braved the exhausting journey to Fontana Vecchia. They relished the peace, silence, and anonymity which their house, high above the rainy sea, afforded. "What a dash we had!" Frieda told Réné Hansard, Juta's sister, about 30 October 1920. "We are enjoying the peace of

[Taormina]—and so lovely it has been, not too hot, we have had some long fine day walks right behind into the hills—Everybody is very charming since we are back—but we have been very quiet and much alone out here." Frieda added a rare mention of her children, who were now almost grown: "I heard from my children's aunt—They are well and Barby the youngest is accepted at the Slade but she must wait till there is room for her—Monty plays football for Oxford—So they are all right anyhow." They seldom wrote to her.

The Lawrences had been home only a short time when they had news about Maurice Magnus, whom they had not seen since Malta. Leveraging his name and his pride, he routinely overspent his income, then on 4 November watched in horror as the Maltese police, whom he feared, suddenly approached him in the street. They were preparing to arrest him for defrauding an innkeeper in Rome. Feigning that he was improperly attired, Magnus rushed into his little rented house on Strada San Pietro, locked the door behind him, and drank a bottle of hydrocyanic acid, which he chased with water. An hour later he was dead. Three days short of turning forty-four, he had killed himself. Wounded and fragile, a consummate parasite, a gentleman stripped of his dignity, he died at almost the age when Lawrence himself, at forty-four, would be dead. Still, he had touched Lawrence, and Lawrence continued to feel "connected with him." But Magnus's suicide may also have warned Lawrence of the risks of such a life. Part of Lawrence's alarmed, allergic reaction to Magnus, as expressed in his *Memoir of Maurice Magnus,* emanates from the doomed man's character, as if Lawrence could neither expiate his sordid influence, nor expel his lingering presence, nor understand his defeat. He remained a puzzle. Fourteen months later Lawrence composed a rancid requiem for this self-defeated man. Of the many ways in which Lawrence broke with England, his requiem for Magnus was the strangest.

# 14

# Farewell to Fontana Vecchia

## 1921

Home again, Frieda was like Lawrence—glad to rediscover Taormina's autumn delights: the quiet simplicity, the fine sea views from the balcony, the long walks among sloping terraces where oranges ripened, and even the October rains. But like Lawrence she was also feeling uneasy about Italy's postwar politics. The world, she thought, seemed "in a worse state than ever." On 18 October 1920, the day they returned to Taormina, Lawrence warned Robert Mountsier, now his American agent, "I think Italy will inevitably revolute." Lawrence had been worrying over Italy ever since Oxford University Press, before issuing his *Movements in European History*, had requested a chapter on Italian unification, which he supplied at top speed. The yeast in Italian politics imaged his own internal restlessness, which, though it happily produced several completed works, also yielded a profound need to cast Europe behind.

Lawrence could tell writer Eleanor Farjeon that, with the proper introductions, he would "really join . . . the revolutionary socialists." But he might have scorned what he found. The truth is that the leaders of the Italian government could not make a successful transition from wartime controls to peacetime growth. Social classes were so diverse, and special interests so numerous, that national unity could not be brokered while blocs of power collided. Nor could political leaders such as Francesco Nitti and his successor Giovanni Giolitti control galloping inflation. By late November Lawrence could warn his friends that goods were scarce even as prices soared. Against the pound the lira had fallen off a precipice—from thirty in March 1919 to one hundred in December 1920. "The natives are . . . in a temper over the exchange," he admitted in December. By February 1921 prices seemed absurd.

Such a road to Italy's ruin demanded a detour. Revolution seemed imminent; strikes interrupted production; unions swelled with almost two million recruits; peasants in the south seized whole tracts of land; and then in late 1920 a recession stalled the country. Into this political fray, on a mighty steed of salvation, rode Benito Mussolini (1883–1945). Intelligent and militant, energetic and bellicose, he used his newspaper, *Popolo d'Italia,* to coalesce assorted ex-officers and students into a Fascist movement. In 1920 it employed armed squads to crush the peasants' unions and to restore law and order to Italy. A year later the Fascists had become a strong-armed political party, even sweeping the middle classes off their feet. Food reappeared on shelves; mail was delivered; trains ran on time. By October 1922 Mussolini had become Italy's prime minister.

This political agitation left the Lawrences uneasy. "I am cogitating," he told Mary Cannan, who had gone to Monte Carlo to gamble, "whether to take this house for another year." Knowing that his lease on Fontana Vecchia expired in March, he wondered if he might prefer a more isolated island like Sardinia, about two hundred miles northwest. While he fretted, Frieda relished Taormina's sea breezes and rich vegetation: "[R]oses bloom and narcissus and mimosa and carnations and the oranges are nearly ripe," she told Sallie Hopkin, "and we have just had the first new carrots."

Into the lush muddle of Taormina's seasons came Christmas. Although Lawrence and Frieda cooked a huge turkey in their newly installed oven, Lawrence's most cherished Christmas gift came from America: Thomas Seltzer's handsome, long-awaited edition of *Women in Love.* It made Lawrence feel that he and Seltzer would be "friends for life." Seltzer reciprocated by calling the novel not only Lawrence's best but one of the best ever written. Despite its price of fifteen dollars, it sold well. Secker's edition, ugly by comparison, did not appear for another six months, but before he would publish it, he proposed "two or three excisions" in the text, so that, for example, Lawrence obligingly altered a passage about Loerke and his companion Leitner from "lived together in the last degree of intimacy" to "lived together, sharing the same bedroom."

Secker's fear was a portent. Tipped off earlier by Cecil Gray, Philip Heseltine—Lawrence's erstwhile friend in Cornwall—decided that he recognized himself and his wife, Puma, in the novel's portrait of Halliday and Pussum. Angrily he wrote to his solicitors, urging them to "press the claim for damages in respect of the libels in copies already sold." Approached on 2 September 1921, Secker agreed to circulate no more copies until Lawrence had altered the text. The author unwillingly disguised the two characters—"since you wish it"—but alas, Secker, to avoid further difficulty, paid fifty pounds in damages to Heseltine and ten pounds, ten shillings in solicitors' fees. Enraged, Lawrence, believing that Heseltine had extorted the money, wrote to Secker in November: "Heseltine ought to be flushed down a sewer, for he is a simple shit." Strong language for Lawrence.

Meanwhile, Sardinia still beckoned. To help celebrate the new year of 1921, Lawrence and Frieda decided to judge Sardinia's suitability for themselves. On 4 January, before dawn, they sailed from Palermo (Sicily's capital), stopped in Trapani, and landed in Cagliari, a terraced town that rose steeply from the harbor to the cathedral, reminding Lawrence of Malta. As they journeyed inland on slow trains punctuated by primitive hotels, they marveled at the striped peasant costumes, the ridges of moorlike hills, the hard bread in Mandas, the high-pitched shrieks that scattered the sheep from the tracks, and the stark freedom everywhere. Frieda called it "a fascinating trip," but Lawrence believed that, despite the island's fascination, the place was unfit for them.

A week later he began writing out a little diary of the trip. Finished in just one month, it became *Sea and Sardinia*. Among Lawrence's travel writings, it is the most satisfying—its peppery prose redolent with acute observation, its veracity undisputed, its tone bantering, its method unsparingly honest. But it bears on the Lawrences' marriage in a disquieting way. Frieda, never named, becomes "the Queen Bee," later just "the q-b," a strong woman—even once "an interfering female"—who often jostles against the book's narrator and softens his fascinated repugnance to much that he encounters. When, for example, the couple pause in Trapani, the narrator is accosted by a ragged, dirty girl nursing an infant:

I had my big hat down over my eyes. But no, she had taken her seat at my side, and poked her face right under my hat brim, so that . . . I thought she would kiss me. . . .

"Too much for me," said I to the q-b.

She laughed, and asked [the girl] what the baby was called. . . .

I gave the fat boatman two liras, two francs [to take them back to the ship]. He immediately put on the Socialist-workman indignation, and thrust the note back at me. Sixty centimes more! . . . I [said to him]: "Per Dio, we are in Trapani!" He muttered back something about foreigners. But the hateful, unmanly insolence of these lords of toil, now they have their various "unions" behind them and their "rights" as working men, sends my blood black.

The q-b's kind indulgence leavens the narrator's scorn; her mitigating presence charms his irritation into suppressed anger rather than haughty indignation. Yet, throughout, the q-b is kept at a marked emotional distance, as if on a marital leash, its jangling a reminder that, even now, the couple sometimes sat at the edge of a quarrel. In Sardinia the scenery is everywhere more appealing than either its inhabitants or the Queen Bee.

But Lawrence's dash to Sardinia had not quelled his spirit of restless adventure. He told friends that he had loved floating on the sea, that it had always been his "heart's desire to have a boat." *Sea and Sardinia* voices Lawrence's ardent longing for what he calls his Dream Ship: "To find three masculine, world-lost souls, and, world-lost, saunter and saunter on along with them, across the dithering space, as long as life lasts! Why come to anchor? There is nothing to anchor for." Did he have in mind Jan Juta, Alan Insole, and Robert Mountsier as shipmates? Whatever, the dream collided with Lawrence's own sense of inadequacy. In a rare aside to Mountsier he wrote that, although wanting a ship, he recognized his ineptness "at making casual acquaintances." He desired a masculine persona to negotiate the world of men, or (better yet) a secure man to accompany him. When Mountsier did finally find a boat that would whisk the Lawrences away from Europe, their reaction was mixed: "Frieda is scared, she says[;] I am not," he told Mary Cannan. Soon the Dream Ship disappeared over the horizon.

The pattern of Lawrence's life was now fixed. While he and Frieda balanced their domestic responsibilities with a busy social life (mostly tea parties), all of it regulated by bursts of rapid writing, they also kept alive their yearning for adventure by always having in mind a new place to go. An abandoned farm near Westminster, Connecticut—offered by Carlota Thrasher, an American woman Lawrence had met in Florence—became the 1921 equivalent of Frederick Delius's abandoned farm in Florida, which had seemed so alluring in 1915. "I must come to America," Lawrence cried to Mountsier in February. He hoped to bring along two recently married Sicilian peasants, Vincenzo and Ciccia, to manage a proposed peach orchard, whereas he thought Mary Cannan might manage bees and strawberries, and sell honey and jam to make a tiny living.

This dream gave Lawrence enormous zest, a steady fund of imaginative energy, and a way to curb his increasing displeasure with those who surrounded him. He despised Scandinavians in Taormina, bolshevist Italians, Jews of every description, editors, publishers: *anyone* who had ever tried to cheat, belittle, or discredit him. Sometimes only a thin veneer of politeness saved Lawrence from angry hostility.

This dream could excite Frieda too. Although both of them loved Fontana Vecchia, they also wanted to go away to an *unfamiliar* Promised Land, populated with congenial people who had also escaped from the straitjacket of contemporary existence. Yet sudden illness intervened to dash the dream. "Frieda today has a wire [from her sister Else] that her mother is very ill," Lawrence reported to Mountsier on 3 March 1921. Determined to go to Germany, Frieda, struggling to pack, persuaded Lawrence to accompany her as far as Palermo. They left on 11 March. Once he had deposited her on the Naples boat to Rome, he returned on the fourteenth to a house that, without Frieda, he said, felt "very empty." With little money and less patience, what itinerary could he devise? Having no plan frustrated him. Since he admitted that he had no pressing work on hand (except to send off the typescript of *Sea and Sardinia*), he could easily have gone with Frieda. Surely she pressed him to come along. But underneath—and stoking his indecision—was a personal crisis in which he needed, he said, "to come unstuck from the old life and Europe." Yet he could not. The Dream Ship was a metonymy for freedom, escape, another new beginning.

He also knew that Frieda, who found Germany "cold and depressing," might want to stay all summer to help her mother recuperate from her heart ailments. In these circumstances America seemed so far away, the farm so great a leap, the investment of borrowed money so unsettling, that Lawrence agreed to renew his lease on Fontana Vecchia for another six months, until September. The cost: a thousand lire plus four hundred for the new oven. "It is very cheap," he told Mary Cannan—a mere fourteen pounds, or fifty-six dollars, at the current exchange.

Roiling with uncertainty, Lawrence decided to find fresh stimulation. Leaving Taormina on 9 April, he went briefly to Palermo to see Ruth Wheelock, a young woman at the American Consulate who had typed *Sea and Sardinia* and with whom he may have scoured the docks for a ship he could lease; then on to Capri, where he probably stayed with J. E. Brooks, an Englishman he liked, and where he was introduced to an extraordinary American couple named Earl and Achsah Brewster.

The Brewsters—born in 1878, a year before Frieda—were painters who had lived in Europe since 1910, when they married and came to live in Italy. With them everywhere came their daughter, Harwood (1912–1990). Whereas Earl, lithe and open faced, radiated kindness, Achsah's smooth features exuded a silken sweetness. Generous in spirit, placid in temperament, refined in manner, they uniquely complemented the Lawrences: they absorbed Lawrence's intensity (and later Frieda's virility), yet intrigued him with their own more meditative quest for spiritual nourishment. They never scolded, never raised their voices, and rarely criticized others. They were noble but not stuffy, learned but not pedantic, attractive but not physically desirable. Brewster recalled that when he first met Lawrence, they went with a group to bathe at the Piccola Marina: "It was a typical day in southern Italy, with sun, sirocco and haze. We lay on the rocks, but Lawrence did not bathe, declaring that he did not enjoy it." The next morning, when Lawrence joined Brewster for a long walk, they talked of the problem of human suffering. Lawrence urged him to "turn to the deepest life within your-

Lawrence and Brett (in front), Harwood, Achsah, and Earl Brewster (in back), Capri, 1926

self . . . to your solar plexus." That evening, seated before a fire at the Brewsters' home, Torre dei Quattro Venti, Lawrence recounted one humorous anecdote after another, and Brewster found him "vivacious, gay, extremely witty, with a light tactful touch." Earl would prove a steadfast friend.

Lawrence trekked on toward Germany. From Capri he continued to Rome, where he presumably saw his handsome young painter-friend Jan Juta and Juta's girlfriend, Elizabeth Humes, and discovered that Juta was ready to sail to Sardinia to paint eight illustrations for *Sea and Sardinia*—but not with Lawrence. The reason is unclear. Lawrence, surely disappointed, went on to Florence, where he met novelist Rebecca West in the company of Norman Douglas and another expatriate, Reggie Turner, before he embarked on a "devil of a journey" to Baden-Baden. He arrived at his mother-in-law's retirement home on 26 April.

Now that Frieda's mother had improved, the Lawrences found a peasant inn at Ebersteinburg, three miles outside of Baden-Baden, where they could enjoy themselves—for a while. Surrounded by cool forests and fine country, the inn had good food—fat sausages, fresh asparagus, and early strawberries—and cost, for both of them, a mere seventy marks a day (less than nine pounds, or thirty-six dollars, a month). They occupied separate rooms. In Germany the old order seemed to Lawrence "completely gone," a "great blank" where the young men had been, the people, though penniless, law abiding and clean and orderly—especially when compared to the Italians. Yet the Germans seemed to Lawrence "inwardly tired and very sad."

Happily nursing her seventy-year-old mother, Frieda pined to stay all summer. But Lawrence, still restless, told Mountsier he doubted he could stand it more than a month. He urged his agent to join him and Frieda for a walking trip through the Black Forest.

At first, Mountsier—as slight as Lawrence, balding, always ready to express an opinion—proved very useful. He was aggressive and exacting, even as he shamelessly inflamed Lawrence's anti-Semitic prejudices. His valiant attempt to untie the knots in Lawrence's American publications—he sought out Seltzer and Huebsch and Kennerley, and worked strictly in accord with Lawrence's wishes—had a valuable side effect: it made Lawrence acutely aware that he needed a British agent too. In Curtis Brown (1866–1945) he found a reliable man—twenty years his senior—who would represent his work until 1932. Courteous and efficient, "more obedient than the impudent Pinker," Curtis Brown had established a literary agency in 1916 that was thriving. In April he and Lawrence signed a five-year agreement. But the generalized distrust that now pervaded Lawrence's feelings extended also to Curtis Brown. "Keep him in his place," Lawrence admonished Mountsier on 1 May. "Let us never give an inch to these people." They were antagonists.

Lawrence's restlessness was taking new forms. He was developing a new resistance to middle-class pieties, willing to discard love and charity, eager to embrace power. In a letter of 3 June 1921, he hoped, he said, to "spit in the eye of love" and, more boldly, to "spit in the face of anybody who tries to insult me." The tenor of Lawrence's letters changes. Fresh annoyances now erupt more frequently. Whereas his letters had once expounded philosophical issues—the nature of democracy, the basis of love, the virtue of comradeship—now more space is given to business matters. Whereas friends like Ottoline Morrell and Edward Marsh and Katherine Mansfield had once elicited philosophy, wonder, and intense meditation, now friends like Compton Mackenzie, the Brett Youngs, and Mary Cannan elicit responses that are cynical, jocular, and ornamented with gossip. Lawrence's youthful idealism has gone. A loss of belief in *love* anticipates a deeper loss of faith in humanity, especially in the goodness of women. This loss Lawrence soon worked out in his novel *Aaron's Rod*.

## LIKE BROTHERS

Lawrence's aggression emptied into the two books on which he had dabbled for many months. *Aaron's Rod* and *Mr Noon* express the newly disrupted phase of his life; they now absorb the unsettled state of mind that arose from his frustrated energy.

Having begun *Aaron's Rod* in 1917, he had set it aside, picked it up again in the hot Sicilian summer of 1920, but found, as it crept along in "ever-diminishing spasms of fulfillment," that it simply halted, awaiting inspiration—which came in one small burst the following September. When half done, the novel then stuck in a swamp of indecision. Lawrence's Florentine tryst with Rosalind Baynes that month had inspired free verse rather than satirical fiction. He could not finish *Aaron's Rod* because he could not, in the guise of his protagonist, Aaron Sisson, imagine a way out of marriage. Underneath, perhaps he did not want to.

Whereas Alvina Houghton in *The Lost Girl* meanders on her way to marriage, Aaron, a handsome man of thirty-two, is her opposite. He leaves his wife, Lottie, and their daughters near the opening of *Aaron's Rod,* plunging away from his past "in a delirium of icy fury." Then, like Lawrence in 1919, he pauses for a time in London before getting a passport. Eager to shed his English skin, he alights at Novara (Turin) and then gropes his way at night to the stately home of Sir William Franks (Sir Walter Becker) and the small talk of tedious people, before going to Florence in the company of two amusing gay men who introduce him to other amusing gay men, such as the misogynist James Argyle (Norman Douglas) and little Algy Constable (Reggie Turner, a kind but nervous man who gave elegant dinner parties). There, amid harangues about wives who impose their wills on their husbands, Lawrence's inspiration ran dry.

Suddenly, in May, sitting in the woods near his hotel at Ebersteinburg, amid big, straight, strong trees full of phallic power, he returned to the novel whose end he had never sighted. In a burst of sustained work, he finished it about 1 June 1921. While he composed, he must often have wondered how he could save *Aaron's Rod* from being his most randomly organized, even his most egocentric novel. "You will like it in bits only," he warned Mary Cannan.

In this novel Lawrence does what he had never done before: he splits himself into two male characters, at an autobiographical angle that permits him a dual solution to the problem of marriage. Whereas Aaron Sisson can walk away from marriage, troubled by few second thoughts, his friend Rawdon Lilly can embrace marriage while damning its possessiveness. The fact that the narrator always refers to Aaron by his first name, and Lilly always by his surname, indicates that the two men, when joined, form a whole. In these twinned characters Lawrence works out the intense conflict of his own 1919 experience. It is the conflict between marriage as battlefield and prison (Aaron) and marriage as a form of freedom in which, says Lilly, he and his wife, Tanny, are (paradoxically) "free of each other, and eternally inseparable." While Aaron is working class, readily speaks the Midlands vernacular, and becomes ill with influenza (aspects of Lawrence *in* England), Lilly is an outspoken intellectual, a writer who is worldly and emancipated, and a sophisticated traveler (aspects of the Lawrence who *left* England); and so the two men (says the narrator) are "like brothers," even springing from "the same class." Both have separated from their wives (Tanny is "visiting" Norway), and both Aaron's flute and Lilly's pen become twin instruments of self-expression—twin *portable* instruments, so that both characters can depart from England carrying their livelihoods in their luggage. Refusing to worship women, both deplore the reality that "two men [cannot] stick together, without feeling criminal, and without cringing, and without betraying one another." This concern had long been Lawrence's own.

The problem of how men should relate to each other is also linked to the problem of how men can stay married. After Aaron and Lilly are reunited in Florence, on Argyle's balcony, Aaron, desiring the assurance of a father figure, senses Lilly comfortably at the back of him, like a pillar. He also feels a complementary surge of sexual desire for the wife of a marchese he has met. American, brown haired, fair skinned, about forty—and safely married—she is a version of Rosalind Baynes. Imagining her as his "younger sister," Aaron finds her both seductive and repulsive, his attraction for her tinged with the loathing of incest, and when they make love, he feels "blasted" afterwards and knows he must tell her (as perhaps Lawrence told Rosalind) that, even though fidelity was not a law *he* must obey, his ten-year marriage to Lottie had made any other woman "a violation" to him. A violation?

That is a curious explanation, since Aaron has no intention of returning to his wife, but it probably explains why—when he is drawn once more, a few days later, to make love to the marchese's wife—his revulsion is complete and why he felt neither unburdened nor relieved but "stunned, withered" by the experience—so much so that he vows to avoid her. To characterize Aaron, Lawrence draws on Thomas Hardy's *Jude the Obscure* (1895), a novel about which he had thought deeply. Both Aaron and Jude are intelligent, working-class men who leave their unsuitable wives and whose attraction to seductive married women brings them long frustration and, for Jude, death by tuberculosis. Women offer no release.

But Lawrence's abiding hopefulness—it makes him perennially attractive—colors even this novel. The concluding dialogue between Aaron and Lilly, who stroll in the country outside Florence, is the novel's best part, prefaced by an extraordinary dream in which Aaron is split in half, fractured, fragmented—like his flute when it gets smashed in a café. Aaron feels himself at an end, with only "a thread of destiny" attaching him not to a woman but to Lilly. At the close Aaron assumes the passive role normally assigned to women in Lawrence's fiction; Lilly assumes the prophetic role played earlier by Birkin and later by Mellors. Castigating love, craving power, Lilly urges Aaron to change—to submit himself to Lilly's leadership, unfold a new destiny, and "have a shot at a new mode." Aaron, in search of a new kind of family, has at last found a caring father; Lilly has found a dutiful son. It is wrong to call *Aaron's Rod* "a homosexual novel," as Jeffrey Meyers has done. But it *is* a novel that affirms Florence as "a town of men"; that positions women in the roles of hostess or seducer, and dislikes them in both; that seeks, instead, the convivial company of men; that creates a homosexual ambience without homosexual acts. The early scene in which Lilly heals Aaron by massaging his body seems less sexual than therapeutic—and is never repeated.

*Aaron's Rod* is, finally, a novel that positions Lawrence the man with unusual precision. He wanted to be married, but at a distance (in separate bedrooms) and to a submissive woman; he wanted to be allied emotionally with men, but to be both leader and follower. That is why the character splitting works. Yet the fact that Lilly has no format for Aaron's submission shows how vague all of this was to Lawrence, how hard it was to imagine. They have no vehicle for accomplishing their mission. Hence in the novel men talk but rarely act. The novel's indeterminate ending images their uncertainty.

But what of that other novel with which Lawrence had struggled? While laboring at *Aaron's Rod*, he suddenly began a picaresque novel about an impetuous young man named Gilbert Noon, who, as a bachelor school-master, resembles Lawrence but whose antics with Emmie Bostock are not Lawrence's but those of George Neville, his old Eastwood friend and fellow teacher. By January 1921 Lawrence's comic novel, now two-thirds done, felt "peppery," he said, and leaped with "wicked joy." Like *The Lost Girl,* it holds up a Midlands town to amused scrutiny, then rejects it in order to precipitate Gilbert Noon's departure from England. Most surprising is the veiled irritation with its readers that *Mr Noon* expresses:

> It doesn't matter what you do—only how you do it.—Isn't that the sincerest of modern maxims?—And don't we all do it nicely and *con molto espressione*? [the narrator asks]. You know we do. . . .
>
> Ah, dear reader, you don't need me to tell you how to sip love with a spoon, to get the juice out of it. You know well enough. But you will be obliged to me, I am sure, if I pull down that weary old scarecrow of a dark designing seducer. . . . There is no harm in us any more, is there now? Our ways are so improved: so spiritualised, really. What harm is there in a bit of a spoon?

With the narrator as his guise, Lawrence discharges his pent-up venom toward publishers, reviewers, and readers who demanded conventional fiction, while he preferred experimentation, and so he plays lightly with the conventions of romantic "spooning." In February, when the strain of writing *Mr Noon* chafed against his sensibility, he finished only the first of three projected volumes—and it was not published in his lifetime. In spite of its ebullient charm, it was too sardonic and lightweight, too smug toward its characters, and too uncertain of its genre to attract a publisher.

## The Austrian Alps — and Beyond

Once *Aaron's Rod* was finished (Lawrence had asked Violet Monk in England to type the first part), and once Frieda's family had visited them in Ebersteinburg, the Lawrences were ready for a holiday that would lead them slowly back to Taormina. After much vacillation, they agreed to walk partway to Austria to see Frieda's younger sister, Johanna, at her summer villa, then ramble on to Florence, reaching Taormina by October. Rushing to join them, Robert Mountsier arrived in Ebersteinburg on Tuesday, 5 July 1921, eager for their jaunt together.

On Sunday the trio took the train from Baden-Baden to Freiburg, where Frieda had attended the Blas sisters' boarding school and had often tramped through the Black Forest nearby. In Freiburg they began their journey on foot, going southeast toward Lake Constance, passing through the dark fir trees of the wilderness, then coming upon majestic waterfalls and splendid mountain views. They walked perhaps fifteen miles a day for five days until they reached Lake Constance on 14 July, by which time the heat was oppressive. Lawrence must have been in fine health, preparing the food, deciding their route, managing the frontier. That Frieda may have been a welcome buffer on the journey is suggested by Lawrence's remark to Seltzer, at the end of July, that "Mountsier read the first half [of *Aaron's Rod*] and didn't like it: takes upon himself to lecture me about it. Says it will be unpopular." Seeing Mountsier every day, he confided to Rosalind Baynes, gave him a strong distaste for Yankees.

After a respite to visit the picturesque town of Constance and an annoying delay for passport clearance, they crossed the lake to reach the Austrian town of Bregenz, then took the night train to Innsbruck and on to Zell-am-See, a resort in the Austrian Tyrol near Salzburg, where Johanna and her family—on holiday from Berlin—welcomed the tired travelers on 20 July. "Much cooler here," Lawrence reported to his sister. The Lawrences stayed at the Villa Alpensee, whose red and white geraniums graced the large balconies, stacked one above the other.

Zell-am-See, exquisitely situated in view of the snow-tipped Alps, lay on clean, sparkling Zeller Lake. When bathing and boating did not occupy them, the Lawrences joined the excursions that Johanna, her husband, Max von Schreibershofen, and their two children had planned. One day, they climbed the Hundstein to see the snowy peaks. Another day—29 July—they boarded a horse-drawn carriage to reach Bad Fusch, then went on foot to the big glacier at Ferleiten, walking under the great, sloping white mass and hearing the water roar downward like thunder. High up, the Alpine flowers—lavender gentians, dark harebells, tawny monkshood—displayed their exotic beauty. The next day Lawrence wrote to Seltzer, "Perhaps when I am cajoled into a good mood, I will write you a Tyrol story." As soon as he was settled again in Taormina, he would begin a superb story that used a Tyrolian glacier and lake as its setting.

Lawrence soon tired of the family *ménage*. "Frieda quite loves it [at Zell-am-See]," he told Catherine Carswell, "and is quite bitter that I say I want to go away." Even though he had now received the complete typescript of *Aaron's Rod* to revise, he felt strangely impatient and had trouble working in Austria. He said later that he had been "awfully depressed" in Austria. Here we must speculate—that Frieda, perhaps unhappy with her portrait as Tanny in *Aaron's Rod*, may have marginalized Lawrence, bonding tightly with her sister's family.

When the weather ran to rain and cold, he longed to move on to Florence. There he had arranged with Nellie Morrison, a writer who was the Brewsters' friend, to borrow her flat at 32 Via dei Bardi, located across the river from the Uffizi Gallery. "I have been so happy these three months in Germany, and one month in Austria," he wrote bravely to Anton Kippenberg, who planned to publish German translations of Lawrence's best novels. Then he added: "But now I want to go south again." He and Frieda arrived on 25 August, dead tired, to stay in Florence almost a month. Their well-furnished flat was dark, cool, and quiet, and they liked taking their meals on the terrace, watching at evening the "[s]wallows with spools of dark thread sewing the shadows together," as Lawrence wrote in a fine poem on bats. Visitors arrived—Mary Cannan on the thirtieth, the Whittleys about two weeks later. It was not a time for work.

With the Whittleys, the Lawrences left Florence, going to Naples, where they parted wearily, the Lawrences stopping at Capri to visit the Brewsters before arriving in Sicily on 28 September and rushing to Fontana Vecchia. Their relief was palpable: "[W]e are so thankful to be back, to be still," Lawrence wrote to Irene Whittley. "The very silence is heaven, after all the turmoil. Never again will I dash about as we dashed this year. I feel worn to ribbons." With its calming sea views, bright sunshine, and warm nights, Fontana Vecchia seemed utterly compatible. They had come home.

Yet Lawrence would not stay long. He had enjoyed the Brewsters so much—their calming Buddhist views and meditative temperament still intrigued him—that he urged them to organize a foursome against the empty future of Europe. The three Americans were on the verge of sailing to Ceylon, where, at the Buddhist monastery at Kandy, Earl planned to study Buddhism and the Pali language of the earliest scriptures. Lawrence pledged to follow the Brewsters east on his way west, to America, where he hoped to find a little farm, perhaps in the Rocky Mountains, "away from the body of mankind." The Dream Ship was still alive, but the Lawrences' shipmates would no longer be crewmen but passengers on a commercial steamer. Frieda had nixed the sailboat.

While the Lawrences waited to feel destiny's rudder move them, they settled into the daily domestic round. Their deep affection for each other, though it is rarely recorded, constituted much of what was meaningful in their lives. They savored the last figs and grapes, sliced the late melons, sampled the first pomegranates, and delighted in the new spinach and cabbage and carrots, even as they lamented the lack of milk and butter (the island's goats had not yet delivered their kids). They went to Miss Elizabeth Fisher's for tea, to Mr. Wood's to hear a sappy violin performance, then to Miss Rosalie Bull's for her welcome-home tea for the expatriate community now returning for the winter. They took long walks into the countryside, shopped in the half-deserted Corso, even admired the red, yellow, and pink roses. Still, they were a little bored.

With the return of autumn, Lawrence was glad to be working again. In October he began "The Captain's Doll," an accomplished story full of wry humor, whose biographical resonances are richly disguised. Outwardly, Frieda's sister Johanna provides the model for the story's protagonist, Johanna zu Ressentlow, an Austrian countess who, reduced to penury after the war, makes and sells dolls with her friend Mitchka, who is herself a

German baroness like Frieda. Johanna—nicknamed Hannele—has become the mistress of a married man named Alexander Hepburn, just as the real-life Johanna had become involved with a banker named Emil von Krug, whom she later married. Cleverly, Lawrence recasts this von Richthofen situation but insouciantly splices into it a wryly disguised portrait of Compton Mackenzie, whom he had met in Capri, as Captain Hepburn. Both Mackenzie and Hepburn are Scotsmen, both are about forty, both are (or were) officers in the army, both have slender chests, both have made marriages in which their wives are not really wives but, as Hepburn says, "very good friends," such that a spouse's erotic "slip" signifies nothing; indeed the Hepburns had been married for seventeen years, the Mackenzies sixteen (in 1921). The story works out the conflict within the triangle created by Hannele, Hepburn, and Hepburn's wife—most amusingly when Mrs. Hepburn, boasting of her second sight, confides to Hannele that her husband is involved with Mitchka.

But the story's genesis yields few clues to its internal motivation. Inwardly, it adapts from *Aaron's Rod* the theme of a man becoming free of a manipulating spouse. This is its angle to Lawrence's life. At a subconscious level Lawrence imagines ways of freeing himself from Frieda for a different kind of relationship; but at the same time he draws boldly on another von Richthofen biography—that of Frieda's sister Else, whose husband Edgar Jaffe had just died the preceding April, freeing *her* to embrace Alfred Weber, whose mistress she had become. Hence in the story Mrs. Hepburn, having come abroad to monitor her husband's behavior, accidentally falls from the third-story window of her hotel room and dies. Her death is barely mourned—just as, in Lawrence's rewriting of "The Fox" in November, Jill Banford's accidental death allows her friend March to feel "glad she was dead." Mitchka, the Frieda figure—the "Baroness"—dies too, in a Salzburg riot; it is part of the postwar collapse.

When the two surviving characters—Hannele and Hepburn—go to an Austrian summer resort near Salzburg—it is just like Zell-am-See, with "a lovely little lake in the midst of the Alps," and, away beyond, a glacier—Hepburn, weary of being alone but also weary of that "tiresome word Love," finds Hannele. He takes her on an all-day excursion to a glacier. There each can test the other's physical and psychological endurance. The test is akin to "the rampant, insatiable water" that, as the couple toils up the mountain, roars around them "like a beast," awakening a "silent hostility" between them. Near the glacier, their hostility flares into a confrontation. Whereas he insists that she love him, she determines not to be bullied. And yet, when they reach the top, it is Hepburn who—victorious—mounts the glacial ice-beast, while Hannele watches. This symbolic battle for mastery and dominance cannot end until Hannele agrees "to honour and obey" Hepburn and to append "the proper physical feelings." It is a version of what Birkin finally offers Ursula in *Women in Love*—a marriage that preserves the carefully chiseled independence of an insecure man. Here Lawrence inverts the cry of the Victorian woman, who, living as a doll-like Angel of the House, feared the gendered simplifications that men thrust upon her in the name of Love. Like Hepburn, Lawrence fears the way a woman's love will squeeze his essential maleness into a *role*, will make a *doll* of him (as Hannele once makes of Hepburn), and so diminish his strength. This fear of women intensifies as Lawrence's physical strength slowly declines. The intransigence it creates is remarkable in the fiction, just as it must have been in life:

> "I'll come to Africa with you. But I won't promise to honour and obey you," [Hannele says at the close].
> "I don't want you otherwise," he said. . . .
> "But won't you have me even if I love you?" she asked him.
> "You must promise the other," he said. . . .
> "But anyway I won't say it *before* the marriage service," [she responded tartly].

Hannele yields—but only by a thread. Her resilience will easily match his tenacity. This new level of conflict and accommodation may well reflect the Lawrences' marriage. It is worth saying that in the story these half-masked antagonisms replace the kisses and fondlings of conventional romance. Love has been redefined as a contest of wills.

## MABEL AND THE TAOS INDIANS

Stealing as quietly as a shadow came a new figure in 1921, arising like a wordless imprecation out of the American Southwest. Mabel Dodge Sterne was already a minor legend. Iron willed, wealthy, magnetic, and also neurotic, she was a patron of the arts who used her bountiful allowance from her mother, Sara, to create a kind of arts brokerage. Long acquainted with Europe, she had in 1913 written about another minor legend, Gertrude Stein, whose brother, Leo Stein, Lawrence had met in 1919 near Florence. Between Mabel and Lawrence there was already a connection of sorts.

Born in Buffalo, New York, in 1879—the same year as Frieda—Mabel was almost as robust and vital as Frieda. Though smaller and plainer, Mabel had dark hair, cool gray eyes, and a voice like a viola's. She exuded warmth. An only child, she enjoyed wielding influence and sought out attractive men, often effeminate men, whom she could control. But like Dorothea Brooke in George Eliot's *Middlemarch*, she also had a great desire to do good. She liked causes—the cause of modern art, for example—and had come to believe that the Indians of the American Southwest were endangered. Settling in Taos in 1918 with her third husband, Maurice Sterne, Mabel had chosen the Taos Pueblo—a tribe of six hundred—as her hobby. And having just read and admired the excerpts from *Sea and Sardinia* that had appeared in the American magazine *Dial*, she was praying fervently for a gifted writer like Lawrence to come and interpret her Indians, their festivals, and their sun dances—to erect a verbal shrine to their waning vitality.

She wrote enticingly to the Lawrences, offering them a furnished adobe house and promising to supply their needs. That promise was important. After months of traveling, Lawrence had little money, he needed spiritual nourishment, and Mabel's Taos seemed poised to supply it. For Lawrence, Taos emitted the call of fate: "I want to go," he told Brewster in November. "The Indian, the Aztec, old Mexico—all that fascinates me and has fascinated me for years. *There* is glamour and magic for me." Equally thrilled, Frieda warbled to Mabel: "We are so keen on coming!—both of us—the mountain lakes and the piazzas and Indians, and I am very grateful to you for giving us the impetus to a *real* move and putting our noses onto the spot where I'm sure we want to go." For Lawrence, Taos offered an escape from spiritual exhaustion; for Frieda, a gateway to a richer happiness, for she too may have begun to feel a little constrained, even with Lawrence.

Although January would not have been soon enough for Lawrence to leave, he and Frieda had trouble finding a suitable ship. In their initial enthusiasm they had hoped to take a merchant ship from Palermo to New Orleans or Galveston, Texas. But that proved difficult, and Lawrence grew impatient. His letters complain of the tedious people, the high prices, the disaffected peasants, the crime, the horrid weather, the political unrest. With the approach of winter, Taormina had shed its beauty. "I shall be glad to go," he told Mary Cannan on 5 December.

While Lawrence ardently sought a ship, feeling unbearably tired of Europe, the thought of leaving prompted a highly creative phase in his life. He wrote rapidly, recomposing stories like "The Horse-Dealer's Daughter" and "England, My England." By the end of December he had assembled enough material—some old, some new—for a collection of three novellas that included "The Captain's Doll," "The Ladybird," and an expanded version of "The Fox," published in both England and America in 1923, and also for a book of short stories, published by Secker in 1924 as *England, My England*. He stirred himself to compose his trenchant *Memoir of Maurice Magnus*, unique in being the only biography he ever wrote. One by one, he was closing the shutters of his creative shop. He would take with him only some translation work. He imagined it would be restful rendering into English some novels and stories by Giovanni Verga, a Sicilian writer who, at age eighty-two, had just died.

Although good news was rare, he learned of some friendly recognition in Britain: he had won the James Tate Black Memorial Prize of one hundred pounds for *The Lost Girl*. It would help fund their getaway from Europe. From Mountsier he also learned that he had accumulated income of eighteen hundred dollars in America. He and Frieda had new clothes tailored—three new dresses for Frieda, Lawrence's brown suit turned inside out to look new. To celebrate the Christmas season, Frieda baked hundreds of delicious dainties. Yet when Christmas Day arrived, Lawrence stayed in bed with a cold, which turned to influenza and then, as the new year began, to lingering headaches and listlessness. His passport photo, taken in Florence a few months earlier, showed a fully bearded, well-groomed man, his brow now furrowed, his suit rumpled, his face, acquiescent and worn, showing a sad repose.

Having waited almost on the edge of his suitcase, Lawrence suddenly halted. Frieda was surely dismayed. A letter from Earl Brewster had touched a quivering nerve: Lawrence decided to go *east* before going west; to seek a measure of peace before he sought again the fray of action. "Dio Mio," he cried to Brewster, then wrote at once—even to Koteliansky in London—about ships to the port city of Colombo, located in what was then Ceylon (now Sri Lanka). Earlier in the month Lawrence had thought his life's goal was not meditation but "some sort of action and strenuousness and pain and frustration and struggling through"; now, however, he realized, at Brewster's prompting, that life is ultimately grounded in sorrow, that one must build upward from the contemplation of that philosophical position. "I think one must for the moment withdraw from the world, away towards the inner realities that *are* real," he wrote Catherine Carswell on 24 January: "and return, maybe, to the world later, when one is quiet and sure." He needed rest, peace, time to grow a new skin. Frieda thought he was not yet strong enough to face America. Two days later Lawrence wrote to book second-class berths on the SS *Osterley*, which sailed from Naples on 26 February and would reach Colombo on 13 March, then continue to Australia. The cost: seventy-four pounds each. "Isn't it thrilling?" he asked Rosalind Baynes. He anticipated elephants, palm trees, and dark people. It was the stuff of dreams.

Like casting England behind in 1912, like leaving for Cornwall in 1915, like escaping to Italy in 1919, the adventure of going to Ceylon in 1922 offered Lawrence the possibility of a glorious spiritual rebirth. But for a man now so bruised by experience, a rebirth would be difficult: so many negative attitudes had attached themselves to his mind, so many betrayals rankled in his consciousness, so many dashed hopes lay on the shore of his memory, that a rebirth might require immense efforts of openness and forgetfulness. In his 1919 story "The Horse-Dealer's Daughter," Mabel Pervin, weakened by the emotional burdens of her home life, sinks suicidally into a dark pond until a young doctor offers her a rescue and possible salvation. The pond is a metaphor for the ocean. Was Lawrence strong enough—and secure enough—to make the journey from the intolerable weight of experience to its erasure on the other side of the Pacific?

The first stage of this long journey was set. At a farewell party the Lawrences gave for themselves, Frieda heaped the tables at Fontana Vecchia with fruit, cakes, and pastries. On 20 February, accompanied by four trunks, they went to Palermo to stay with Ruth Wheelock before moving to the Hotel Santa Lucia in Naples. The second stage ensued on 26 February as they boarded the *Osterley* in Naples, only minutes before the gangplank was pulled up, and went to their luxurious cabin. As they chuffed out into the evening sea, they no doubt guessed that they would never again see Fontana Vecchia. Its fragrant roses, blue sea, and bursts of almond blossom would soon become bouquets of memory.

# 15

# The Voyage Out

## 1922

As early as 1913, Lawrence had welcomed the adventure into the unknown, away from consciousness and into the mysterious union of man and woman. Now, in 1922, the adventure changed. Now it took him into the geographical unknown, where the mysteries of new locales replaced the mysteries of personality.

During the long voyage to Ceylon, which lasted fifteen days, Lawrence was inundated with sights, smells, and sounds that sped by like frames in a film. He felt himself drawn to the edge of "some queer dream." His old categories of satiric response broke away and left him freshly astonished. Astonished by Port Said and its beggars and scribes, its old men reading the Koran, smoking their chibouks in the cafés. Astonished by the wondrous Suez Canal, eighty-eight miles long, and its Arabs wandering on camels through the red-and-yellow desert sands. Astonished by the sharp sand hills, gold and pink, undulating like a dream as the sun slid behind the desert and left the sky burning in flames of pink and green. Astonished by Mount Sinai, rising above the Red Sea, looking as rusty as dried blood, naked, without trees, the air hanging hot and stifling. Astonished by the flying fish, silvery in the salty light, which flew gaily in the wind, like butterflies, across the Arabian Sea. In brilliant letters to Frieda's mother in Germany, he evoked the wonders of a world he had never known before.

On board the *Osterley* he and Frieda chatted with the friendly Australians, but Lawrence also spent time on deck translating Giovanni Verga's *Mastro-don Gesualdo* (1888), a novel about the defeat of an ambitious Sicilian peasant. Frieda was fascinated, she said, by traveling around the world. They decided, before landing in Colombo, that they would go on to Australia, a shipmate named Anna Jenkins having invited them to Perth. After Australia they would cross the Pacific, landing in San Francisco, and then cross the mountains to Taos, New Mexico. That long voyage, though costly, would constitute their grand world tour.

Earl Brewster met them on 13 March 1922 and brought them by train into Ceylon's interior, to Kandy, which is today a compact merchants' town of produce markets and small shops selling garment overruns cheaply; at the outskirts the commercial district turns quickly, like a green eclipse, into coconut plantations and truck farms. Ceylon's history would have interested Lawrence, for it had become one of Britain's crown colonies in 1798 and soon developed large tea, rubber, and coffee plantations. An island the size of West Virginia, Ceylon rises up out of the Indian Ocean southeast of India. From 1907 to 1908 Leonard Woolf, Virginia's future husband, lived in Kandy, helped to administer its colonial government, and found the whole region "entrancingly beautiful," lying halfway between the low country and the high mountains. Shortly after the Lawrences arrived in Kandy, they witnessed a Buddhist ceremony called the Perahera, celebrating the visit of the Prince of Wales. Frieda remembered the ceremony's smell of coconut torches, the wildly beating tom-toms, the oily scent of dark men, and the procession of lumbering elephants decorated with long tassels and tinkling bells—all of it strangely barbaric.

Overlooking Kandy Lake, the Brewsters' isolated, hilltop bungalow—a mile from town—was capped by a zinc roof and encircled by a broad veranda that almost touched the jungle of breadfruit and palm trees. Agile monkeys bounced about in the trees, vipers slithered out of holes, and brightly colored birds shrieked and cackled, rattled and exploded, all day; at night they idled like tiny machines. Frieda remembered that the sliding noises on the roof and the sudden jumps in the dark disturbed them all: "How could one rest under such a darkness that was so terribly alive!" At first the Lawrences, suffering from the heat and the sensory assault all around them, felt stupefied. "We are almost too dazed yet to know what we feel," Lawrence told Irene Whittley on the twenty-fifth. Enthralled, Frieda loved the exotic atmosphere of swaying palm trees and swarming, dark-brown people. In April she wrote to her mother: "Yesterday we came back from a motor trip through the countryside—it was wonderful—through tropical forests and villages and Hindu temples—the charming little black children running around just as God made them, wearing only a bracelet or footband or waistband."

In the afternoon, when Brewster had finished his studies, Lawrence would join him for long jungle walks, to see the white Buddhist temples gleaming amid the fragrant champak flowers and, from time to time, to yield the pathways to the dark, lumbering elephants hauling timber. Achsah Brewster's painting *Homage to Buddha* (1922) shows her rapt adoration of the Buddha's hilltop bliss, over which she casts the brooding maternal affection that characterizes her artwork. Frieda scoffed at her pictures "of huge St Francis's and unbirdy birds and white chiffon clouds of garments round her [subjects'] solid flesh." She preferred naked children to Achsah's spiritual romances.

But very soon Lawrence felt he did not belong among these dark native people. Buddhism, denying the soul, seemed to him barren. Worse, the nauseously sultry climate drugged his desire to work. "My being requires a different physical and psychic environment," he told Brewster. To help explain his reaction, he imagined that the island's intense ultraviolet sunlight decomposed his blood; he worried that his creative powers might fail. Perhaps, he claimed later, he had contracted malaria.

Yet Lawrence liked being with Brewster and relished their camaraderie. "I would rather work with you, each doing something with our hands, than to talk together," he admitted. Working in unison, in an enfolding silence, Lawrence could subtly recapture the bond his father had found underground with other miners, a physical intimacy like that which arises on a rugby or soccer team, providing a ritual form of bonding. He began to feel a fresh appreciation for male solidarity. When he was not translating Verga's collection of stories, *Novelle Rusticane,* he would fashion bright materials into garments or help Harwood Brewsters pack her doll carriage or wander to the merchant's booth and buy blue sapphires for Frieda.

"Can't stand Ceylon," Lawrence announced to Anna Jenkins, an Australian socialite, on 3 April. He loathed even the tropical fruits. As his body succumbed to the heat and the cloying food, he lost weight. Achsah recalled that he was so ill he could scarcely move. Drawing on a thousand dollars of his accumulated American royalties, he proposed taking another ship, the *Orsova,* leaving Colombo on the twenty-fourth, arriving in Fremantle, Western Australia, on 4 May, then going to Perth to see Anna Jenkins before risking a big city like Sydney, which lay in the eastern colony of New South Wales. Lawrence's bold plan was to go on and on, spending recklessly if need be, until he found a place he liked. "And if I like none of the[se] places," he warned Koteliansky on 17 April, "I shall come back to Europe with my mind made up, and settle down permanently in England or Italy. So there's the programme." Fueled by the urge to travel, he was an engine of unfulfilled desire.

## AUSTRALIAN KANGAROOS

Australia surprised the Lawrences. It was bigger, more open, more pristine than they had imagined. To Frieda the Australian bush seemed like a different world: "The quiet is good for us," she told her mother on 10 May; "we are sitting in the quiet bush all day long, only now and then a flock of parrots, a couple of horses, a horseman—otherwise all is still and green and warm, and the nights fresh and cool." To Lawrence the bush, at the edge of civilization, seemed "like a dream." To him the land stretched vast and empty, still uninhabited; the air smelled strong and new, "fresh as silver"; and the sky rose high and blue, "as if no one had ever taken a breath from it," he told Frieda's mother five days later. When they reached Perth on 4 May, late in Australia's autumn, Anna Jenkins took them to a guest house at remote Darlington, sixteen miles east, managed (in part) by Mollie Skinner, who turned out to be a novelist in the rough. Her frontier romance, *The Boy in the Bush*, Lawrence rewrote in 1923, supplying his inimitable psychic exploration and giving the book harmony and unity. He arranged for it to be published a year later by both Secker and Seltzer. To Mollie Skinner, who had been a nurse, Lawrence seemed sympathetic and fragile but more reserved than Frieda, who usually placed herself at the center of conversation, recounting their most amusing travel experiences. Anna Jenkins also drove them into the eerie, untamed Australian wilderness for a picnic lunch. Lawrence had tasted the outback.

Tired of wandering, Frieda needed a long rest and at least a temporary home, a semblance of what she had once known in Nottingham. Lawrence had never owned a home, and the home he had known best—the home of his youth—had been tainted by his mother's death in 1910. The idea of "home" was repugnant. Lawrence preferred "to keep moving on . . . round the world." Frieda, however, insisted that they settle for a while near Sydney, the big port city on the east coast toward which the Lawrences now voyaged. "I love trying things and discovering how I hate them," Lawrence told Brewster on 15 May.

That odd sentence rings with a hard truth. What does it mean? Lawrence's familiar response of liking a place and then finding that it had made him sick—starting in Croydon in 1911—had left him with an enduring psychological mechanism. It was a mechanism of fascination followed by disgust. But beyond that, he "hated" things in order to combat Frieda's opposed way of finding how much she liked new places. Their oppositions were still functioning as a synergy. If she could marvel, he could withdraw into silence; if she could gush, he could dampen; if she could rave in delight, he could be repelled. These dependable oppositions defined the couple, sparked their responses, but also probably cramped Lawrence's emotional flexibility, intensifying his animosities. Indeed, Frieda may have waxed with animation, *assured* that he would spring in recoil. This psychological mechanism left a permanent mark on his writing.

The Lawrences went now from the southwest to the southeast corner of this continent the size of the United States. From 18 to 27 May they traveled close to twenty-five hundred miles in their voyage on the *Malwa*. Sydney's splendid harbor—shielded by two cliffs broken by an inlet—impressed Lawrence. But like any big city, Sydney seemed so expensive—when Lawrence had now less than fifty pounds in his pocket—that he and Frieda fled by train. "We'll look out the window and where it looks nice we'll get out," they agreed, clutching the "To Let" pages of the *Sydney Morning Herald,* which advertised "THIRROUL—Fur[nished] Cott[age]s to Let. Winter T[er]ms."

Traveling through mining country to Thirroul, a ramshackle town forty miles south of Sydney, the Lawrences climbed out with all their trunks on 28 or 29 May and within two hours had found a small furnished house built on a low cliff above the Pacific Ocean. Called "Wyewurk" (or "Why work?"), it cost only one and one-half pounds (about seven dollars) a week, but since it was filthy, they agreed to wage war on the havoc they found within—and the rats that crept about. "So," Frieda remembered, "we . . . cleaned and cleaned as we had done so many times before in our many temporary homes! Floors polished, the carpet taken in the garden and scrubbed, the torn canvases removed [from the porches]." They apparently did all the work themselves. Luckily, beef, apples, butter, and fish were cheap and plentiful. The couple could easily afford to stay. Lawrence wrote to Frieda's mother on 30 May: "The heavy waves break with a great roar. . . . We have only our little grassy garden—then the low cliff—and then the great white rollers breaking, and the surf seeming to rush in right under our feet as we sit at table. Here it is winter, but not cold. But today the sky is dark, and it makes me think of Cornwall. We have a coal fire going, and are very comfortable." Frieda, he added, was contented with her new house and, by spreading bright cloths and displaying a few objects, had beautified the main room. She felt rejuvenated. As in Cornwall, they could seabathe in complete privacy. Although high temperatures averaged 65 degrees Fahrenheit, the midday sun was hot. Frieda felt attuned to the quiet, leisurely rhythm: "We took long walks along the coast, lonely and remote and unborn . . . , finding shells for hours that the Pacific had rolled gently on to the sand."

Lawrence loved reading the weekly *Sydney Bulletin.* In June 1922 the newspaper would have taught him much about Australia that he could not have learned from his brief firsthand experience. "Let the Majority Rule," an article of 22 June, concluded that "the majority must govern, if democracy is to endure." A quaint column called "Aboriginalities" printed tales of outback life—of the terrifying shriek of an Australian screech owl, of the nest-building rat, of the "mopoke" bird, of adders that bite cows' udders, of a fanged brown snake over nine feet long, of the tonu fish that eats humans. Lawrence was amazed by the odd and the extraordinary in Australia. He would come to imagine Australian politics as equally strange.

Warning Mountsier that he would soon need another seven hundred dollars, he decided, while he and Frieda rested in Thirroul, to write a novel. He had unfettered time, and he had many crisp impressions of this vast continent that had inspired his ambivalent response. Its miles and miles of bush seemed lost, forlorn, empty. "I don't really like it," he said at first, "it is so raw—so crude." It was so unfamiliar that he longed for Europe and its civility. To Koteliansky he added that, because Australia reminded him of the Midlands of his boyhood, "the life [seems] very familiar and rough— and I just shrink away from it." He had traveled so far from England that he recoiled from the incidental reminders of his provincial past.

But Lawrence soon began to like Australia. It seemed to be "a kind of dream" suffused with magic. Frieda loved the open, unspoiled country. To her mother on 22 June she exclaimed that she loved the sunshine of early spring, "always beautiful, like Paradise before the Fall!" On most mornings Lawrence wrote steadily—in one of the three small bedrooms or on the wide veranda—while Frieda dealt with the tradesmen who unobtrusively delivered bread, meat, and fish. Around noon the Lawrences bathed in the ocean and strolled along the sunny beach; showered outdoors; then, while Frieda napped, Lawrence wrote letters or read the *Sydney Bulletin*. Later he helped her cook, bake, or sew; they took turns reading books like Louis Berman's *The Glands Regulating Personality*; they went out walking to buy milk and butter from the simple, easygoing farmers; and they took excursions to the Sydney Zoo or to places like Wollongong, ten miles away. At Taormina, Capri, and Ebersteinburg, at Zell-am-See and Ceylon, people surrounded the Lawrences, sought them out, entertained them. Now Lawrence was alone and apart, without invitations. "The sea is extraordinarily good company," he admitted to Brewster. He thought it felt "lovely . . . to know nobody in the whole country." He could disappear into Australia.

Yet their close daily intimacy, despite its frequent joys, cost them dearly. Frieda appraised the cost when she wrote to Mabel Dodge Sterne, who was already building the Lawrences an adobe house in Taos: "By the way *dont give* us too little a place to live in, we are much too quarrelsome—it's quite fatal—We . . . must'nt be too much on top of each other or we get on each other's nerves." It would be wrong to read Frieda's remark as evidence that she and Lawrence were incompatible. Rather, as Lawrence became less tolerant, squeezed into a mode of dyspeptic irritation, silence became the means of healing himself. Silence allowed him to converse with the elements, which soothed him. Silence converted his irritability into energy rather than frustration.

But at a deeper level he was redefining himself, seeking a new form of separation, isolation, singleness—apart from the exhaust of love, apart from the chain of physical desire that followed temptation. He had taken his childhood sense of acute difference and placed it at Thirroul, near the mines. He was still the outsider, still activating the familiar protective mechanism of rejecting others before they rejected him. Separation and silence bred not just the conditions for creative work but also a way to negotiate a distasteful democratic world. His next novel would take up this theme of human separateness caught in a web of communication (letters, newspaper bits, conversations), then broker the new forms of conflict it yielded.

By 3 June he had already begun writing. He called his new novel *Kangaroo*. At first he prayed to complete it by early August, when he wanted to sail away from Australia. But in his self-imposed isolation, he wrote at top speed and completed the novel on 15 July. He aimed to find some truth about Australia that would release him from the anxiety and spiritual torpor that had oppressed him in Europe. He also aimed to do what he had always done with such precision: to capture the landscape and the exotic atmosphere of a new place. Beyond that, he aimed to capture his day-to-day life with Frieda and then (this is a real surprise) to set that life within the country's political upheaval.

New in Lawrence's fiction is his extraordinary fidelity to their combined experience. In *Kangaroo*, more so than in any other novel he wrote, Lawrence composed the early chapters almost as a transcript of his rich domestic life with Frieda—from the sight of a shark's black fin to the queer taste of brown honey to the occasional fierce quarrel. Whereas in *Aaron's Rod* the Frieda character (Tanny) had been exiled to Norway, here she occupies a central place, shaping day-to-day choices, her voice alive with energy and opinion.

Parallels abound between the Lawrences and the novel's central couple. Richard Lovat Somers, a bearded writer slight of build, derived from common stock of the English Midlands, had once lived in Cornwall. His wife, Harriet, mature and handsome, dressed in Bavarian peasant costume, is his opposite—gushing, genial, an upper-class European. Her courage separates her from other women. She provides her husband with both male fierceness and female softness and (surprisingly) becomes both "the only man as well as the only woman" in Somers's life. Well-traveled itinerants, they soon settle into a seaside bungalow paid for by the week and take separate bedrooms. They plan to sail on to San Francisco "by August." Together they want not just to taste but to understand the vast, uninhabited land of Australia, to discover "its secret."

Another secret is Lawrence's waning sexual desire. Although Lovat and Harriet once make love after Lovat runs naked in the rain, the event is summarized in a few sentences. Yielding to Rosalind Baynes in 1920 had inspired Lawrence to recognize "[a] new gasp of further isolation, / A new intoxication of loneliness." Somers's recognition that their good friend Victoria Callcott is available for sex invites not lust but recoil. Somers refuses "involuntarily"—physical desire "would no longer carry him into action"—and the dream that follows at once forces him into a dark sack (displaced vagina) while a theft (violation) occurs. The possibility of extramarital sex inspires horror.

Some of the later chapters have aroused a different kind of speculation. How could Lawrence—a newcomer to Australia and her politics, a man with few Australian contacts—have concocted a novel of bold political intrigue? Did he fuse shipboard talk of Australia with his reading of the *Sydney Bulletin*? The truth is that, after he wrote *Aaron's Rod*, Lawrence could muster no enthusiasm for love and sex in fiction. He sought an alternative in a special kind of male bonding shown in revolutionary activity. The details of such activity Lawrence may have learned from either William Siebenhaar, a Dutch civil servant and an anarchist whom he met in Perth; or, on board the *Malwa*, from Father Maurice O'Reilly, a self-confessed rebel involved in Australia's 1920 civil riots, although Lawrence, ever resourceful, probably invented most of the details.

But in his speculative book *Lawrence and Australia,* Robert Darroch goes much further. He theorizes that Lawrence made the acquaintance of two important figures—W. J. R. Scott, a colonel in the King and Empire Alliance who divulged many details about a secret Australian "army," and Charles Rosenthal, a Sydney architect and former soldier who was the group's president. Darroch's theory, though often plausible, has been sharply criticized. Lawrence scholar Bruce Steele, for example, judges it "without foundation." Relying on firsthand evidence, a local historian named Joseph Davis—though sympathetic—doubts "the whole Darroch thesis." Perhaps the most revealing evidence comes from Frieda. In an unpublished letter of 9 August 1922, written just before they left Australia, she tells her mother: "We didn't know any well-educated people here."

The novel's central mystery—will Somers join a political group?—is intriguing. Somers's dabbling in politics, though it may sound strange, is cleverly presented. It comes in strands, like clues in a thriller. From them Lawrence creates two paths of the same theme—the inside and the outside of male bonding.

Inside is Somers's attempt to bond with two strong men—Jack, a follower; and Kangaroo, a leader. The Somerses' next-door neighbors in Sydney, Jack and Victoria Callcott, are intoxicatingly friendly. But Jack's well-guarded secret is that he, with his brother-in-law William James, has joined a group of men who yearn for political power. As Jack whets Somers's interest in the group, an electric current develops between the two men that parallels the suppressed attraction between Gerald and Birkin in *Women in Love*. Like Gerald, Jack boasts broad shoulders, is "handsome, well-built, with strong, heavy limbs," whereas—like Birkin—Somers is "sensitive all over," a gentleman exuding a "quiet finesse." As they perform a rite of Australian "mate-ing" by the roaring twilit ocean, and achieve "a sort of embrace," Jack urges Somers—an articulate if zany intellectual—to join the party of "diggers" (servicemen returned from World War I). Somers would be "a sort of queen bee to a hive," "a power behind the throne." But he would have to swear allegiance to their leader.

When Somers meets their leader—a well-educated Jewish lawyer and self-styled messiah named Ben Cooley (a.k.a. Kangaroo)—he at first swoons before the older man's charisma and paternal protection, and pledges to be his follower. The truth that Somers recognizes in himself is the truth that Lawrence often proclaimed at this time: "only in the fight would his soul burn its way once more to the knowledge, the intense knowledge of his 'dark god.'" The political "fight," involving dinners and secret meetings and riots, is mainly a device that allows Somers to strike deeper than before into his own identity; to "strike at communion out of the unseen"; to freshly tap his unconscious in order to acknowledge the dark gods as the most ultimate and satisfying source of knowledge. What these dark gods offer remains vague. Somers is, as Sheila MacLeod says, "feeling his way towards that which cannot be defined, that which can only be apprehended intuitively." The dark gods seem to offer access to fulfillment beyond fear, beyond social conditioning, beyond some unnamed terror. But the novel, even as it encodes a sense of homosexual panic, is a superb portrait of a man struggling to balance his strong marriage with his unfulfilled needs. That balancing effort requires Somers to reach a cruel recognition. It is that Kangaroo, the man he might have loved, has—once an anarchist shoots him—an unexpected problem: A bullet has wrecked his body's plumbing. This plot device allows Somers to repudiate the temptation of sodomy.

Somers painfully acknowledges the secret cravings that he must deny; he defends himself against them by demonizing the object he might desire. His desire and his fear, once they collide, lead him back to marriage—but at a cost: Harriet will have to endure Lovat's frustration. Hating to be excluded from these efforts at male bonding, Harriet uneasily tries to mediate between her husband's male and female components, even as she prizes his marvelous creative energy; she will puncture his pride so that she can mediate with ever more finesse. It is the same battle that Frieda fought in life. In a passage canceled from the manuscript of *Kangaroo*, Harriet wounds Somers—much as Constance Garnett had wounded Lawrence in 1914—by saying, "'Ignoble, that's what you are. . . . You have none of the qualities that make a man noble.'" The "inside" of male bonding is fraught with contradiction and disappointment.

The outside of this theme quite differently informs the book's second half. It follows the "diggers" group from loose confederation to tight solidarity, and it follows the separate Socialist group from inert presence to fiery public speech. Somers, emotionally insecure, hovers always at the edge of commitment. He wavers between embracing Kangaroo's fascist vision of love and working for the Socialist movement led by the spiderish, brooding Willie Struthers. Somers, unsure whether either movement will ease his earlier fixation on marriage and the family, resists both. Although Lawrence's organizational powers slacken in the book's second half, Somers's resistance gives the narrative a fine tension between the inner and the outer themes.

When at last Somers confronts his potent memories of the war years—in the "Nightmare" chapter—he undergoes a slow catharsis, a cleansing that he (like Lawrence) has long awaited. His pent-up fear and fury pour out like lava, cleansing him of his immense hostility, allowing him, at last, "[t]o be alone from it all. To cut himself finally clear from the last encircling arm of the octopus humanity. To turn to the old dark gods, who had waited so long in the outer dark." This is Somers's breakthrough, the means of refreshing his soul. His insight resembles insights that Lawrence had earlier discovered—with one important difference: now Somers makes primary his isolation and aloneness, his need to connect to the dark gods first alone, then (when possible) with others: first as an act of religious faith in the unconscious, then in an act of possible human connection. Sensing Kangaroo's impending death from the anarchist's bullet, Somers puts the whole continent in perspective: "He fled away to be by himself. . . . His great relief was the shore"—precisely the place that Lawrence had found healing. Australia is the geographical equivalent of Somers's new identity. Australia becomes finally a metaphor of rebirth, of discovery, of acknowledging the larger truth that self-knowledge is the core of identity. It has little connection to politics. Cleansed, purified of the loathsome past, temptation put safely behind him, Somers is ready to leave Australia.

## THE TRAIL TO TAOS

The Lawrences had remained in Australia only three months. The novel finished (and mailed to Mountsier), the trunks packed, the reservation on the RMS *Tahiti* confirmed for 11 August, the Lawrences took the train to Sydney a couple days early, probably knowing they would never return. The *Tahiti*, crossing the Pacific to San Francisco by way of the beautiful Cook Islands and Tahiti, had only sixty passengers in first class. The long voyage—twenty-five days—would have allowed them to become intimately acquainted. Lawrence thought the small ship "like a big boarding-house staggering over the sea," but Frieda wrote to her mother that "on the ocean one plays, one dances, one flirts without limits," and adds, "A nice Frenchman is sitting next to me! 'Madame, let me be your slave!!!'. . . It is a very delightful ship!"

Arriving in San Francisco with less than twenty dollars in his pocket, Lawrence wired Mountsier for money. The expensive Palace Hotel cost seven dollars a day, and with their new shipboard friends they wanted to motor about, attend the cinema, and dine at good restaurants. A cafeteria was a novelty they had never before encountered. Although the city's noisy clashing of iron and its glowing lights surprised the Lawrences, Mabel Dodge Sterne had sent them good news. Graciously calculating their penury, she had mailed them train tickets and refused any rent for the adobe house she had built for them. "When you leave San Francisco you are my guests," she told them.

Boarding the train on 8 September, they crawled across the hot American desert toward Lamy, a small town fifteen miles south of Santa Fe, New Mexico, where, two days later, Mabel, standing on the platform in a dress of turquoise blue graced by silver jewelry, met them. Her brown eyes were warm. "She has eyes one can trust," Frieda said to herself. Beside Mabel stood Tony Luhan, a silent, handsome Indian, wrapped in a blanket, who had become Mabel's lover. Both of them were still married—Mabel to the painter Maurice Sterne, who (at Mabel's urging) had left Taos four years earlier, Tony to a Taos Pueblo woman named Candelaria Romero.

That night Mabel took the Lawrences to the Santa Fe home of her friend Witter Bynner (1881–1968), a skilled poet who soon became one of Frieda's staunchest allies. Bynner felt cool toward Lawrence, whose shrill voice and satiric barbs seemed to him less enchanting than Frieda's hearty ebullience. "In her," he wrote later, "were none of the physical timidities and reservations which made one questioningly aware of her husband's personality. . . . She never had to insist that she was there." The next morning Lawrence and Frieda awakened early, washed the previous night's dishes, and cooked and served an ample breakfast before Mabel collected them in her car.

Motoring toward Taos, fifty-five miles north of Santa Fe, where the flat desert slowly ascended to the Sangre de Cristo Mountains, winding through canyons and gray sagebrush, through plateaus and pinion scrub, the Lawrences might have recalled the train rides they had taken from Colombo to Kandy, or from Sydney to Thirroul. All three journeys furthered the adventure into the geographical unknown. In all three the Lawrences sought a fresh level of stimulation to replace the weariness they had felt in Europe, sought to discover in simpler societies fresh springs of the human unconscious, and sought to find in the world's frontiers supreme expressions of the dark mysteries of life. In Taos they would not be disappointed.

# 16

# The Lure of the Indians

## 1922–23

Located on a high plateau, Taos today is a mecca of fringe artists, a town of small shops and summer festivals, a place of leathered ranchers and quaint entrepreneurs; but in 1922 Taos comprised an extended village of eighteen hundred people. Mabel Sterne's compound lay at the edge of town, a mile from the main plaza. Three miles away, the Taos Pueblo had settled eight centuries earlier in a small adobe village; they irrigated some cornfields and kept cattle and horses. These Indians, steeped in centuries of spiritual intimacy with the land, conveyed a tantalizing remoteness, their gaze revealing more than their words. Whereas Lawrence had only tasted the Australian bush, now in the American Southwest—and below it, in old Mexico—he hoped to seize upon what these sun-baked cultures had developed that Europe had lost. He wanted to discover the secret of their collective racial identity. Deep inside himself, he hoped to awaken some of their allure. And even in Australia he had wanted to write an American novel. Now he would have his chance.

On 11 September—Lawrence's thirty-seventh birthday—he and Frieda arrived in Taos, ready to start what Frieda called a "new life." Living two hundred yards from Mabel's house, they needed to get used to the air at seven thousand feet, to make the ample house their own, to get acquainted with the Indians. Mabel quickly posted Lawrence for five days to the Jicarilla Indian Reservation, where he watched the Apaches dance: "I shall never forget . . . when I first came into contact with Red Men, away in the Apache country. . . . It was something of a shock. Again something in my soul broke down, letting in a bitterer dark, a pungent awakening to the lost past, old darkness, new terror." Accompanying him were Tony Luhan and Mabel's childhood friend Elizabeth "Bessie" Freeman (1876–1951), from Buffalo, New York, who lived now in Palm Springs. At once Lawrence liked America's fierce grandeur, its great open spaces, its rough freedom.

This freedom also had an economic dimension, for Lawrence was fast shifting his publishing allegiance to America. In England, Martin Secker, overly cautious, had annoyed him. But Lawrence's American publisher, Thomas Seltzer—full of enthusiasm—had placed "The Captain's Doll" with *Hearst's International* for the princely sum of $1,000 and had fought off an attempted "vice" coup by John S. Sumner. A moral zealot, Sumner had seized copies of Seltzer's limited edition of *Women in Love* but, in court, had failed to secure a conviction. Seltzer, now emboldened by his triumph, promptly issued a new $3 edition of *Women in Love* on which Lawrence would earn a 15 percent royalty on all copies over 5,000. (Some months later Seltzer reported triumphantly that "*Women in Love* is a big seller. It [has] already sold over 12,500 exclusive of the limited edition and I have ordered a fourth printing.") Seltzer was also preparing to issue several more of Lawrence's works in close succession: *Fantasia of the Unconscious,* a speculative work on harmonizing the regions of the self; the stories "England, My England" and "The Captain's Doll" (with "The Fox" and "The Ladybird"); *Birds, Beasts and Flowers*; a freshly revised *Studies in Classic American Literature*; Lawrence's translation of *Mastro-don Gesualdo,* and finally *Kangaroo,* which Lawrence now considered "the *deepest* of my novels." For 1922 Seltzer totaled Lawrence's royalties at more than $6,000. The Lawrences no longer hovered at the edge of poverty. With confidence Lawrence could now say that he had £500 in the bank, could offer to lend money to his friend Koteliansky, could repay £15 to Ottoline Morrell and £20 to Edward Marsh—small amounts he had borrowed during the war—and could often send money to Germany for Frieda's family, who still felt impoverished. Seltzer's enthusiastic letters encouraged Lawrence to feel more secure financially than he had ever felt before.

The Lawrences soon acclimated themselves not only to the thin mountain air but to a western style of life. They even learned to ride horses. Later, Lawrence told Mabel that he fondly remembered "how you and Tony taught F[rieda] and me to ride on Granfer and my little Zegua." With Frieda and sometimes Bessie Freeman, he loved galloping across the open desert and scrambling up the slopes among the piñon bushes. "[Y]ou should see me," he exulted to Earl Brewster on 22 September, "in your white riding breeches, a blue shirt, a cowboy hat, and your white tie, trotting on a bay pony with an Indian, across to the Pueblo. Frieda too." Encountering the desert on horseback was unlike any of their prior adventures—a glimpse of time sloping back into a new dawn. In the house they occupied, with its four rooms and kitchen—all tastefully furnished with Indian rugs and paintings—Lawrence and Frieda could see the bluish-green mountains a few miles away, make peach jam, and cook the wild plums that the Indians brought. Lawrence could also revise the typescript of *Kangaroo,* which Mountsier had sent him from New York. In the evenings, they could, when they wished, visit Mabel and such guests as Alice Corbin, Witter Bynner, and Nina Witt. Lawrence disliked only one thing: "living under the wing of the 'padrona,'" who, though kind and generous, seemed to exert her will like a painful pressure. Mabel seemed smothering.

Over the next two months the Lawrences tried to adapt to the strange experience of living so close to Mabel and her entourage of guests and servants. Mabel kept everyone vibrantly busy—viewing Indian dances, taking motor trips, bathing in hot springs, riding to distant canyons. She must often have reminded Lawrence of Lady Ottoline Morrell, the aristocratic Edwardian hostess whose collection of artists had in 1915 proved so scintillating. Both Ottoline and Mabel were sensitive and intelligent, both were gracious but insecure, both had unfulfilled artistic yearnings, both had taken lovers, both were willful in displeasing ways, both insisted on gratitude as the wage for their generosity, and both expected Lawrence to ennoble their sense of themselves. Mabel even proposed that Lawrence write a novel about her discovery of Taos, and he almost succumbed. Much later, after Lawrence died, Dorothy Brett, who knew both women well, said: "What kind of a person was Ottoline Morrell[?]—oh my hat—a sort of Mabel—only a sick one—a woman of passion!! so called—a permanent invalid from headaches and heartaches— fascinating and rather terrible." But there was one other difference between these two powerful women. Despite her majesty, Mabel was a bully. She used her money and her patronage as a dam to control the flow of other people's lives.

## THE GEOMETRY OF CONFLICT

Brewing in this cauldron were two explosive triangles; in both, Lawrence was the valence between strongly opposed forces. The first triangle arose when Mabel began to compete with Frieda for Lawrence's attentions. It was a classic struggle for power. Frieda explained it best: "One day Mabel came over and told me she didn't think I was the right woman for Lawrence and other things equally upsetting and I was thoroughly roused and said: 'Try it then yourself, living with a genius, see what it is like and how easy it is, take him if you can.' . . . When Lawrence came in, he saw that I was unhappy, and somebody had told him that Mabel's son John Evans had said: 'My mother is tired of those Lawrences who sponge on her.' This may have been pure malice, but Lawrence was in a fury too . . . and he said: 'I will pay the rent of the house and I'll leave as soon as I can.'" He then admonished Frieda to be more vigilant: "It's your business to see that other women don't come too close to me." He needed Frieda's protection.

Was Lawrence tempted by Mabel's physical charms? It seems not. He admired the paradox of her energy and her silences, her magnetism and her boredom, yet judged her a perfect *strega,* a witch. But Mabel wanted to believe that Lawrence had finished with the primary sex impulse. In a letter to Leo Stein she said that Lawrence was unable, with Frieda, "to develop this impulse on other levels," while Frieda aggressively barred "this [sort of bonding] with anyone else." Whatever the case, Lawrence sent Mabel a blunt ten-point manifesto on 7 November. Its key point is this: "I believe that, at its best, the central relation between Frieda and me is the best thing in my life." Judging Mabel "antagonistic" to his central relation, he would leave.

Where to go? A few days earlier—on 31 October—the Lawrences had gone to the 160-acre ranch that Mabel had given to her twenty-year-old son, John, who was, like his mother, spoiled and headstrong. Located in the foothills of the Rockies, about sixteen miles from Taos, the downsloping Lobo ranch struck Lawrence as extraordinary, with its stands of timber and its two little abandoned cabins, where one could have, he said, "the world at your feet and the mountains at your back." Nestled in this remote, snowy forest, the Lobo seemed a good solution to Mabel's interference. But a few days later the Lawrences conceded temporary defeat; the heavy snow had made repairs difficult, then Mabel required that one cabin be kept vacant for John. Ever resourceful, Lawrence introduced himself to the Hawk family, who lived on a large spread two miles below Lobo, and discovered that for one hundred dollars he and Frieda could rent a place on the Hawks' Del Monte Ranch and spend the winter. The place was a rough, five-room log cabin, with little furniture and no indoor plumbing, a quarter of a mile from the house occupied by the Hawks, who were sturdy, refined cattle ranchers. "Perhaps," he wrote Mabel, "we'd better accept that [offer] and simplify everything." He preferred essentials.

To combat the lonely isolation at Del Monte, the Lawrences asked two Danish painters, both young, to join them and, for fifty dollars, to rent an adjacent three-room cabin. A man who remained Frieda's friend for life, Knud Merrild (1894–1954), age twenty-eight, was a skilled designer of bookplates, posters, and ceramics. Sedate and solid, athletic and good looking, he appealed to the Lawrences. In his art he preferred an abrupt, angular style that in 1922 seemed uniquely modern. Kai Götzsche (1886–1963), age thirty-six, was taciturn but agreeable—and equally radical in his art. With Merrild, he had studied painting at the Royal Academy of Fine Arts in Copenhagen. He was patient, hard working, modest, and uncomplaining. From New York the Danes had driven across country as part of their own world tour, camping along the roadsides, and—having gone to Taos to paint the Indians—were taken up by the gruff Taos painter Walter Ufer, who one evening introduced them to the Lawrences. According to Merrild, who wrote his account in 1938, the famous English novelist and his wife seemed simple, pleasing, and obliging as they talked animatedly of Australia and Tahiti. Frieda, the Danes decided, was herself a genuine personality, not just a second to her brilliant husband.

Driven by Götzsche in his dilapidated Ford, the Lawrences left Taos for Del Monte on 1 December 1922. Conditions at Del Monte were as bleak as those back in Italy's Picinisco: the men were forced to haul water, chop cords of wood, and scare off rats. Still, Frieda proudly told her mother that "Lawrence never felt so good during the winter." For her part she loved Del Monte—the cellar full of apples, the thick cream on the Hawks' milk, the low-hung pines on the wild hills, the hot midday sun, the coyotes that howled at night. With the Lawrences gone from Taos, the triangle that Mabel had constructed now collapsed. "Thank God . . . the parting was friendly," Lawrence groused to Mountsier. A few months later, however, Frieda admitted to Bessie Freeman: "I still like Mabel . . . but Lawrence and she hated each other."

The second triangle, involving three men, was quite different. It was professional. While living in Sicily, Lawrence had been glad to have Robert Mountsier look after his work, despite his agent's hostility to Jews; and although in 1921, in Austria, Lawrence had found him trying, he nevertheless urged Mountsier to visit him in Taos and pay the three hundred dollar train fare from Lawrence's royalties. Mountsier agreed. Meanwhile, Thomas Seltzer and his wife, Adele—Jews who adored *The Rainbow* and *Women in Love*—had proved such sincere and committed publishers of Lawrence's books, and such eager and solicitous friends, that Lawrence urged them to come to Taos for Christmas: "Don't come if you mind roughness," he wrote. "Otherwise it's great fun, and very beautiful wild country."

Although Lawrence had tried to arbitrate the differences between his publisher and his agent, he failed. Mountsier spitefully haggled for a 15 percent royalty on all copies of Lawrence's books, whereas Seltzer felt that the petty haggling and mistrust affected his good work on Lawrence's behalf, and he urged his prized author to jettison the despicable Mountsier. Lawrence was torn. He liked having an agent, but he minded Mountsier's tepid enthusiasm for his work; he didn't trust publishers, but he liked the Seltzers.

To everyone's astonishment both the Seltzers and Mountsier came to Taos in late December. They had to be put up not at Mabel's—her houses were full for her son's wedding and for Christmas—and not at Del Monte, with its primitive accommodations, but at the Hawks' big house, where they could have a room with breakfast. Luckily the visitors overlapped for only one day. While the Seltzers visited for a week, from Christmas to New Year's, Lawrence and Frieda were gracious hosts. They made mince pies and Christmas puddings, bought fifteen fresh chickens, baked delicious breads, built roaring fires of pine logs to repel the icy mountain nights, sang English Christmas carols (Lawrence rendered "Good King Quentin" especially well), entertained their guests with mimicked American accents, played with Bibbles (a black pup Mabel had given them), invited the Danes to join them in the evenings and smoke, toured the Taos Pueblo, visited Witter Bynner in Santa Fe—and all of them probably journeyed to Manby Hot Springs ten miles away, where they could bathe in the soothing water. Thomas and Adele were entranced.

Lawrence and Seltzer mostly talked shop. Seltzer, for instance, had arranged to send Lawrence a copy of James Joyce's infamous *Ulysses* (1922), which Lawrence, who found it tiresome, would have criticized. And Seltzer, who prided himself on his steadfast loyalty to Lawrence, declared his readiness to publish all of Lawrence's works in a uniform edition, including the out-of-print titles published in America by Kennerley and Huebsch.

About Mountsier, however, Seltzer was adamant. Because (he must have said) you can trust me to publish you decently and to treat you fairly, why have an agent, especially one who does not believe in your genius? Lawrence no doubt hedged: Mountsier's help with manuscripts and contracts was scrupulous. But after the Seltzers departed, Mountsier lingered at Del Monte for four long, trying weeks before going to Taos. On 1 February 1923 Lawrence told Seltzer: "Mountsier left on Sunday. I wished it. Whatever friendship I felt for him before, I don't feel now. I have told him I want single control of all my money. But I haven't yet broken with him as my agent, because I feel he tried." The next day Seltzer's letter of 26 January arrived. He had given additional thought to Mountsier's utility: "I should feel miserable if we were 'contractors of business' only, just as you would. With you I absolutely refuse to be that, and that alone. As to my being 'innerlich' loyal to you, you know that I am, don't you? You don't want me to make protestations. But I want to say this, the relation between us with regard to your books is perfectly natural . . . any interference by a third person is unnatural, unnecessary, and creates needless fuss and inconvenience both to you and me. It must be stopped even if the feelings of somebody are hurt, and the only way to do it is to put an end to it once for all. No half measures will do."

The ax had fallen. No doubt Frieda agreed that Mountsier's agency came at too high a price. Lawrence replied at once: "On the main point, of Mountsier, I do agree with you. I have this minute written to him— Mountsier—that I wish to break my agreement with him, and that in future I wish to handle all my business personally." The deed was done. Lawrence would now depend on Seltzer's honor and loyalty as never before: "I put my trust in you." The second triangle had collapsed, firmly, inevitably, but without the violent scenes that Mabel had created. Yet all the friction in America had left Lawrence bitterly disappointed. Feeling churlish and annoyed with all Americans, he wanted to leave Del Monte's brutal winter winds and go south: "Feel I must go now. Want to go down to Mexico City via El Paso," he wrote Seltzer on 7 February. He imagined that in old Mexico, with its Catholic veil lightly spread over the ancient, passionate rhythms of the common people, he might find a more hospitable climate in which to write.

## THE CHARMS OF MEXICO

In the cold, snowy February before their departure, the Lawrences must often have talked of Katherine Mansfield. Her husband, John Middleton Murry, had written a desperate letter to say that she had died on 9 January in Fontainebleau. Gonorrhea and tuberculosis had taken her life. She was only thirty-four. To Murry, Lawrence wrote that her death left "something gone out of our lives." "It grieved us both deeply," Frieda wrote to Adele Seltzer. The Lawrences had liked Katherine's cynical, worldly elegance. Her death also soothed some of Lawrence's long-festering animosity toward Murry, now pitiful and alone in his grief.

While living in New Mexico, Lawrence wrote a series of five poems about animals and birds, which he added to Seltzer's forthcoming American edition of *Birds, Beasts and Flowers* (1923). These creatures awaken the narrator's affection and respect but also kindle a blunt resistance, as if his relationship with them were as prickly and difficult as that with humans. With one difference. He now seldom wrote poems about living people but only about the ghosts of humans. In a mode of affectionate antagonism, he poetically encounters his little dog Bibbles, a powerful eagle, a metallic blue jay, a lone red wolf, a proud lioness. Typically he isolates the uniqueness of each one, then entangles it in the narrator's moral judgment. He both strokes and slaps at the same time.

The most meditative is the haunting "Mountain Lion." It catches Lawrence's disillusion with Mabel and Mountsier even as it gleams with the visual attributes of the lion, now dead, which a foolish Mexican has trapped:

Lift up her face,
Her round, bright face, bright as frost.
Her round, fine-fashioned head, with two dead ears:
And stripes on the brilliant frost of her face, sharp fine dark rays,
Dark, keen, fine rays in the brilliant frost of her face.
Beautiful dead eyes!

Like the death-paean he had written just after his mother died in 1910, and like what he no doubt felt now for Katherine Mansfield, this poem reveres a splendid female, proud, invincible, her resolute selfhood preserved, her integrity untouched by death. As the mesmerizing body of the lioness invites the narrator to protect her in lines of poetry, to preserve her tawny, sacred, female singleness, he recognizes that

> . . . in this empty world there was room for me and a mountain lion.
> And I think in the world beyond, how easily we might spare a million or two
> of humans
> And never miss them.
> Yet what a gap in the world, the missing white-frost face of that slim yellow
> mountain lion!

The loss is dual: it is personal, but it also reflects Lawrence's gradual and more profound retreat into a pensive solitude. Even in remote Australia, even in the isolation of Del Monte Ranch, humans despoiled the ecosystem and ravaged the social landscape with their words. But Lawrence's reverence for animals also had a dark side. Merrild, among the most objective of memoirists, reports that when Bibbles went into heat and abandoned her loving master in order to mate, Lawrence was enraged by her disloyalty and kicked her. Occasionally touched by hysteria, he had this time seriously misplaced his demand for fidelity.

To prepare for the sojourn in Mexico, Lawrence asked Thomas Seltzer to send him *Terry's Guide to Mexico,* which, when it arrived in February, gave the Lawrences their most important introduction to the country about which they knew almost nothing. In the 1923 edition, written when tuberculosis affected millions, one page likely set the whole course of the Lawrences' visit, for Lawrence had long wanted to live away from cities: "Certain of the towns in this favored [temperate] zone are natural, open-air sanatoriums, and the warm, still days and cool, sleepful nights are tonics which bring many a sufferer (particularly from tuberculosis) back to health. One of these health stations is *Guadalajara,* with an almost perfect climate. . . . Other towns in this land of eternal spring . . . are *Orizaba, Oaxaca, Cuauhtla,* [and] *Cuernavaca.*" From Mexico City the Lawrences would—accordingly—sample nearby towns like Cuernavaca, journey west to live in the region around Guadalajara, return six months later, and finally go south to Oaxaca, a city full of Zapotec and Mixtec Indians.

Hating to go alone, yet knowing that the Danes had sold too little of their art to afford such a trip, Lawrence asked Witter Bynner and his slight young friend Willard "Spud" Johnson (they were a couple) to come along a little later. Bynner, tall and bald, was urbane and Harvard educated; Johnson (1897–1968) was neat and winsomely attentive. Both were good company; both were lively and courteous. Their sexual preference seems not to have mattered, although Frieda clucked once to the heterosexual Danes: "Bynner is an old lady and Johnson a young one." She called them "the Bynners."

In 1923, with a population of six hundred thousand, Mexico City comprised a mass of imposing buildings like the Palacio Legislativo and the marbled Teatro Nacional (as they were then called), which were set near a maze of hovels, like vast warrens, all sprawling in a huge oval basin that today traps the exhaust of VW taxis, buses, and factories. When the Lawrences reached the city on 23 March, they went first to the Hotel Regis, recommended in *Terry's Guide* as a popular, modern hotel with five hundred rooms; disliking it (perhaps it was too expensive), they went the next day to the Hotel Monte Carlo, located near the city center, where, for only four pesos a day (two dollars each) they could have a room and good food. The Italian-run hotel was friendly and pleasant (today its fine entrance hides shabby, spartan rooms). The Lawrences liked the ramshackle, unpretentious, noisy vibrancy of Mexico, even though Lawrence found the city raw and threatening—and evil.

Once Bynner and Johnson arrived, they no doubt used *Terry's* "How to spend 10 days in Mexico City" to identify the best local sights. Lawrence would have acted as their manager. They went by tram car to Xochimilco and the tranquil floating gardens, to the ruined monastery El Desierto de los Leones, and by motor car to the famous pyramids at Teotihuacán, where in one of the temples huge stone snakes with turquoise eyes coiled at their feet. They took photos of each other. And they visited the tawdry Thieves Market, with its ropes and saddles, belts and baskets, pots and dishes. They went to the National Museum to view the Aztec relics and to government buildings to see, in progress, the huge Diego Rivera murals.

On 1 April they went to the impressive Gran Plaza de Toros, which seated twenty thousand, to witness a bullfight, which Terry had warned was an "unadulterated spectacle." The Lawrences were brutally shocked. To Adele Seltzer, Frieda wrote on 8 April: "We saw a big bullfight—A wild and low excited crowd [and] 4 bands, then a nice young bull and the men with their mantles dodging it so quickly, the bull jumped the barrier and the attendants jumping so cleverly was fun—but then oh horrors, blindfolded horses led up to it by picadores who prick the bull with lances. The bull of course thinks it's the horse that hurts him, and with his horns he goes for the horse—I know no more, I fled and Lawrence white with rage followed me—My last impression—a smell of flesh and blood and a heap of bowels on the ground—Vile and degraded the whole thing." Lawrence would soon use this potent event in his fiction.

After exploratory visits to Cuernavaca and Puebla, Tehuacán and Orizaba—all of them hot and politically unstable—Lawrence had seen enough.

Witter Bynner, 1928 (Courtesy of the Ansel Adams Trust and the University of Arizona)

Willard "Spud" Johnson, 1932 (Photograph by Will Connell, Courtesy of the Harwood Museum of the University of New Mexico)

The political turmoil alarmed him. By December 1920, when General Obregón became president, stability had begun to return to Mexico. Most revolutionary leaders were dead (Emiliano Zapata had been murdered the year before) and others such as Pancho Villa had retired. But the redistribution of land under Obregón had provoked armed conflict between landowners and starving peasants. Frightened by what he saw and heard, Lawrence wrote to the Danes on 21 April: "In these states [around Mexico City] almost *every* hacienda (farm) is smashed, and you can't live even one mile outside the village or town: you will probably be robbed or murdered by roving bandits and scoundrels who still call themselves revolutionaries." For Lawrence the sites for a possible home were narrowing. Bynner's friend Idella Purnell, who lived with her dentist father in the small western city of Guadalajara, may have praised the surrounding plateau, or (more likely) Lawrence recalled *Terry's* cheerful commendation of the area.

"I am going this evening to Lake Chapala," Lawrence announced to Seltzer on 27 April, "to see if we might like to live there a while." Cooled by the Pacific breezes, Guadalajara lay 325 miles northwest of Mexico City, and on holidays Guadalajarans often came out to Lake Chapala to bathe, boat, dance, and bask in the cooling breeze. In a long rhapsody on the region, *Terry's Guide* says, "The views over the lake on moonlit nights are very beautiful."

Taking the train to Ocotlán, Lawrence apparently boarded a steam launch to come down the lake—seventy miles long, twenty miles wide—probably reaching Chapala village on the evening of the twenty-ninth and going straight to the recommended Gran Hotel Arzapalo, which looked out over Lake Chapala and charged four pesos (two dollars) a day. (A contemporary photo displayed today in the Gran Hotel Nido shows a smallish two-story structure, embellished by fine arches along the inside corridors.) Making inquiries on the thirtieth, Lawrence found a house two blocks away, at Number 4 (today 307) Calle Zaragoza, rented it, and moved in on 1 May, the day he sent Frieda a telegram that read: "Chapala paradise. Take evening train. Purnells will meet you in Guadalajara." Accompanied by Bynner and Johnson, Frieda arrived the next morning, thrilled by Lawrence's choice. Located on a quiet street about three hundred feet from the large lake, the one-story house had six rooms, a wide veranda, and a private patio surrounded by green banana trees and blooming oleanders. Frieda quickly laid out her embroideries and spread her colorful serapes on the floors, and made it a home. She had learned to bring with her just enough decorative accents to make a new place familiar. The weather was sunny and hot but cool at evening, when the Lawrences bathed in the shallow lake. Everywhere it was very dry. Hiring a nice Mexican "Isabel" to cook and clean for them (she lived with her children at the back), they were forced to speak Spanish.

Lake Chapala, Mexico, today (Photograph by Michael Squires)

Surprisingly, Lawrence liked Mexico better than New Mexico. Despite worries about water, food, hygiene, and thieves, the Mexican people were generous and acquiescent, patient and stoical. Lawrence immediately set to work, having intended all along to find a place where he could settle long enough to compose the draft of a novel. This was his chance.

In the mornings, by the waterfront, he sat under a willow tree to write. He could see the low mountains in the distance, Scorpion Island straight ahead, a few fishing boats scattered across the tranquil expanse of pale-brown water, and, nearby, Indian women washing their clothes. By noon each day he preferred to leave the intense sun, and after a hearty lunch of rice, fried fish, and mangoes or guavas, he often spent his afternoons reading novels like Pío Baroja's *César o nada*. As soon as he and Frieda were settled, Bynner and Johnson arrived from Guadalajara, where they had gone to see Idella, Bynner's former student at Berkeley, and her father. The two men settled at once into the Hotel Arzapalo and—while Lawrence wrote—spent the days by themselves, frolicking with local boys in the warm lake. In the evenings Lawrence and Frieda might walk two blocks to the main plaza, or meet Bynner and Johnson for supper at one of the hotels, or saunter among the lakefront vendors and occasionally choose a colorful serape as a gift. On many Sundays the Purnells arrived. But at night a *mozo* slept outside the Lawrences' bedroom doors and, with a pistol at his side, guarded them.

Near the end of their six-week stay, Lawrence took time out from his novel to travel with Frieda around the lake. They went a hundred miles, looking for a hacienda to rent near Ocotlán: "Feel like making a little life here on this lake," he told Thomas Seltzer. But the country, bone dry, seemed to him still very dangerous and politically unstable. Reluctantly he gave up hope of a little Mexican banana farm which Götzsche and Merrild might help him manage. Rananim would have to wait: "We have to be a few men with honour and fearlessness," he urged Merrild on 27 June, "and make a life together. There is nothing else, believe me." Fearless artists rather than politicians, Götzsche and Merrild in the flesh had replaced Jack Callcott and Ben Cooley as potential comrades. As art sometimes anticipates life, so the two iconoclastic characters Lawrence had created in *Kangaroo* prepared him to respond to the Danes.

## QUETZALCOATL: "THE MOST SPLENDID THING"

The novel on which Lawrence made steady progress was turning into a favorite. "It interests me, means more to me than any other novel of mine," he told Seltzer in June. Reading it as it came, Frieda thought it "the most splendid thing he ever did." Lawrence called it "Quetzalcoatl," after the Aztec deity representing a feathered snake. Its themes and characters have inspired much debate among readers, especially since, more than a year later, Lawrence greatly altered *Quetzalcoatl* when he rewrote it as *The Plumed Serpent.* Biographers usually sidestep the effect of Chapala on Lawrence's imagination. It gave him not a new source of mystery but a new site of sinister majesty that reflected his inner turmoil at this time.

*Quetzalcoatl* records Lawrence's encounter with Mexico in a direct, concise form, wholly appealing in its easy lyricism. At once he made a bold decision. Whereas he had chosen male protagonists for *Aaron's Rod* and *Kangaroo,* for his new novel he chose a female protagonist named Kate Burns, almost his age (she's thirty-eight, he's almost thirty-eight). Well built and strong, with full white limbs, she offers an amalgam of his and Frieda's experience and temperament. In *Quetzalcoatl* Lawrence joins Frieda's life story (aristocratic parentage, previous marriage, children left in England) to his own sharp sensitivity; he blends Frieda's womanliness with his own critical intelligence; he fuses Frieda's distaste for a crumbling Europe with his own search for religious rebirth and responsive manhood.

This is the angle from which he worked. He layers their joint experience, expressing Frieda's exuberant vitality but equally venting his own splenetic irritation with a country that elicited both fascination and disgust. In short, *Quetzalcoatl* reflects the Lawrences' growing closeness as a couple—not their harmony (harmonious they were not) but their intimacy; not their fusion but their creative separateness, which invited squabbling. Hearing Frieda complain how much she hated her husband's outbursts of temper, Witter Bynner urged that Frieda begin attacking Lawrence before he could humiliate her, and as she did so, she wrested from her husband a new level of respect that may account for Kate's surprising independence in *Quetzalcoatl.*

As the novel follows Kate into central Mexico, she witnesses a ghastly bullfight in Mexico City, journeys (like the Lawrences) to Chapala, takes a house with servants, and begins to discover the manifold miseries of contemporary Mexico. Her discoveries strangely intoxicate her and soften her repulsion for the country's heat and filth and cruelty, for initially "[s]he had imagined Mexico a pure pastoral patriarchal land." But as she listens to the Indian men sing the hymns of Quetzalcoatl, the freshly resurrected god—part bird, part serpent—her optimism parallels Lawrence's own when, thinking about the Indians, he wrote to Frieda's mother on 30 May: "If they only had a new faith, a new hope, they would perhaps be a new, young, beautiful people."

In the novel, that new faith takes root in two extraordinary men—a visionary and his follower. The visionary Ramón Carrasco—dark, mysterious, handsome, but also an educated historian—recognizes that the Catholic rites, imposed centuries earlier on the Indians, have obscured the Indians' rightful gods—Quetzalcoatl, Huitzilopochtli, and Tlaloc. Ramón sets out to bring them back, to bring back the Indians' natural religious passion and to banish the icons of Jesus and Mary. His faithful follower, General Cipriano Viedma, is a military commander passionate about Mexico's future. Lean, bearded, black eyed, educated at Oxford, he swears to help Ramón. In a scene that is like a spiritual orgasm, Ramón touches him with a blessing, after which Cipriano swoons: "and from the depths of him a dark fountain of life seemed to rise up. He felt this dark fountain rising strong, till . . . he felt whole again." Whereas in Lawrence's earlier novels, female characters usually serve as agents of male wholeness, now men do so for themselves. This change is important. It reveals how Lawrence begins to marginalize women even as he makes them—as protagonists—more central in his fiction. They are more important in the narrative but less important in the thematic development. Lawrence's frightened response to powerful women like Frieda and Mabel made him enhance their roles as he diminished their significance. Patriarchal codes asserted themselves now more subtly in his work.

As Jack and Kangaroo had mesmerized Somers, so these two Mexican men mesmerize Kate. The creamy brown skin of Ramón's back, for example, "made her shudder" with sensual awareness as he emanates "a fascination like a narcotic, the male asserting his pure, fine sensuality against her." Aroused from her torpor by these two men and admiring their ambition, Kate, though weary now, senses that she—even she—might somehow participate in the life of the Mexicans. But how?

The novel's two strands—the sensual and the religious—run parallel, and in both, the characters flirt with what is new—Kate with two exotic men; Ramón and Cipriano with the incipient religion of Quetzalcoatl. All three characters, in spite of their altruistic motives, want—like Lawrence—to revive their own sagging spirits. What Lawrence does especially well is to capture the complex human rhythms—ebbing, halting, flowing—by which these sagging spirits open themselves to revitalizing forces. Though tempted by Cipriano's offer to make her both his wife and the goddess Malintzi, Kate has a great deal of Frieda's mature common sense. She will not compromise her female integrity by becoming a symbol in a patriarchal mythology. "You are a woman of will," Ramón's wife says to Kate. Flooded with memories of England, her white-haired mother, her son, and her daughter, she recognizes that, however alluring Cipriano's proposal, she cannot be a part of Mexico, old or new. She must go. Not for sixteen months would Lawrence rewrite *Quetzalcoatl* as *The Plumed Serpent,* and by then his attitude toward Frieda had vastly changed.

*Quetzalcoatl* ends just where Lawrence found himself in early July 1923: poised to leave Mexico yet highly ambivalent about returning to Europe. Kate enacts Lawrence's personal dilemma. "The novel is *nearly* finished—near enough to leave," he told Bessie Freeman on 27 June. Frieda had long assumed that he would go with her first to England, so that she could see her children, then to Germany where both of them could visit her beloved mother, Anna. He had repeatedly agreed to her plan. But when they went north to New York, via New Orleans, to stay with the Seltzers—first in New York City, then in a rural New Jersey suburb—Lawrence wrote Merrild a letter full of pregnant meaning: "I am not very keen even on going to England.—I think what I would like best would be to go back to Mexico," he said on 15 July. A serious butting of wills was imminent. It would alter Lawrence's novel.

## "I WILL NOT GO BACK TO HIM"

New York City, criss-crossed with traffic and intrigue and money speculation, had long piqued the Lawrences' interest. Yet they were soon disappointed. The city seemed dreary and dead. Arriving on 19 July, they went to the Seltzers' apartment at 219 West 100th Street, where Thomas handed Lawrence proofs of three books: *Kangaroo, Birds, Beasts and Flowers,* and *Mastro-don Gesualdo.* Lawrence was surely impressed that Seltzer would lavishly issue three books almost simultaneously. When Lawrence expressed the need for a quiet place to work, the Seltzers rented a nice cot-

Thomas Seltzer, who published twenty of Lawrence's books (Courtesy of Lawrence Levin)

tage in Dover, New Jersey, for the summer. In the placid New Jersey hills, amid old oaks and maples, Lawrence worked hard all day; Seltzer took the train out in the evenings and on weekends; and, feeling subdued by the Seltzers' deification of Lawrence, Frieda imagined herself as a "poor little night light" next to her husband.

Beneath this placidity lurked danger. Beset by doubts, plagued with confusion, weighted with work, Lawrence felt unable to go to England with Frieda. He must have felt intensely frustrated. "Can't get myself to go to Europe.—God knows why," he lamented on 1 August. Frieda was indignant. He had promised and, she thought, had no excuse but stubbornness. She felt acutely disappointed.

Why did Lawrence balk? Why did he recoil from England? To answer, it is worth remembering that he had once before demurred in this way. In 1919, while Frieda went to Germany, he had gone by himself to Florence, staying near Norman Douglas and Maurice Magnus. Now, while Frieda went to England, he might go to Los Angeles, join Götzsche and Merrild, and go south, perhaps "pack with a donkey in the mountains," he told Catherine Carswell. That three men might create an alternative family and make a temporary life together appealed to him. That "solution" calmed him, although he may not have fully understood its meaning—or even shared it with Frieda. Three men against the world, united in affection and trust, bound in work and quiet respect. It was an empowering ideal.

But Lawrence eventually offered a very different reason. Torn by the domestic struggle with Frieda, worn by their friction, he needed a respite. To his old friend Amy Lowell he wrote on 18 August, the day Frieda sailed on the *Orbita:* "This New York leaves me with one great desire, to get away from people altogether. That is why I can't go to Europe: because of the many people, the many things I shall have to say, when my soul is mute towards almost everybody." Murry bereaved, Koteliansky depressed, his sisters content in a provincial life he despised—all would expect a cheerful camaraderie and evenings enlivened by happy *raconteurs*. Frieda could rise to the occasion; he could not. More important, the pronouncements expected of him he wanted to save—for the rewritten version of *Quetzalcoatl,* which he hoped soon to re-work. It is likely that Frieda misunderstood Lawrence's internal conflict between his creative and his critical selves. She tended to simplify.

Whatever the exact cause, the Lawrences separated. The rupture between them reflected Frieda's sudden assertiveness and Lawrence's willful intransigence. For both of them, yielding had become more difficult, less certain of a compatible outcome, more fraught with risk. Their affection and love for each other had not died but had paled into a strained friendship. For either to yield was a badge of failure.

On board the *Orbita,* Frieda was irate. During the ten-day voyage she wrote several letters that index the precarious state of their marriage. To Bynner she wrote circumspectly on 19 August: "I do hope my journey won't be useless, especially as far as my children go. Lawrence wouldn't come, he is going to wander. Where we meet again, I don't know." But to Adele Seltzer a week later she was forceful and blunt. She had had time to consider her feelings. Her dockside parting from Lawrence must, at best, have been bittersweet, and he may have charged her with disloyalty: "I feel so cross with Lawrence, when I hear him talk about loyalty—Pah, he only thinks of himself—I am glad to be alone and I will *not* go back to him and his eternal hounding me, it's too ignominious! I will *not* stand his bad temper any more if I never see him again—I wrote him so—He can go to blazes, I have had enough." Fed up with Lawrence's verbal abuse, weary of his spiritual indecisiveness, still angry that he had refused to come with her to Europe, Frieda snapped. Unaware even where Lawrence had gone after he left New York, she no doubt felt relieved to be on her own. On the day she landed in Southampton, he—going in the opposite direction—had already reached Buffalo, New York, on his way to California. Soon they would be nearly six thousand miles apart.

# 17

# Reconciliation

## 1923–24

Lawrence's art often forecast his life, and his characters' preoccupations often became his own. The unconscious sources that bubbled up into the rich material of his novels readily fed his conscious decisions. His life and his art shared the same stimulus. As Kate refused Cipriano's offer of marriage in order to escape from a place that distressed her spirit, so did Lawrence disappoint Frieda, going off alone on a journey of defiant self-expression. It was his midlife crisis. Kate, pressured by Cipriano's presence, felt that "something had turned to iron inside her"; Lawrence, pressured by Frieda's urgent appeal to return to Europe, felt that "[m]y heart goes like lead when I think of England or Germany." Both Kate and Lawrence seek a place where they can avoid performing roles—she a role in an alien mythology, he a role in the drama of the Returned Genius—and so can escape these coils of constraint. To register her disagreement, Frieda performed her own drama of the Outcast Mother restored. Yet as she and Lawrence came apart, even separated, their world a little smashed, they were in truth preparing themselves for reconciliation. On both sides of the Atlantic, the year ahead would measure the fraying of their marriage. Not for a long time had they acknowledged their love.

When Lawrence left the Seltzers in New York City, he went first to Buffalo—to see Bessie Freeman and Mabel's queenly mother, Sara—before boarding the train for Los Angeles, where he arrived on 30 August 1923.

Merrild and Götzsche met him. They had found work in nearby Brentwood, decorating a personal library for Harry and Olivia Johnson, whose coffee table proudly displayed Lawrence's *Captain's Doll* with Merrild's bold jacket design. Lawrence stayed in the area for almost a month—having supper with the Danes, watching them work, enjoying a picnic at Topanga Canyon, viewing the eclipse of the sun on 10 September, visiting an ostrich farm, going to the circus. But he was restless and lonely without Frieda (who rarely wrote), and when he went with the Danes to a dance hall—as host of a night on the town—he turned from an amused participant into a sarcastic chaperone. Three recently discovered letters from Lawrence to Frieda, written in late September, reveal his chagrin.

Still, he found compensations. Once Götzsche had agreed to accompany him to Mexico, where they would straggle along its wild west coast, Lawrence was rejuvenated by the thrill of an adventure across sparsely settled territory. The pair left Los Angeles on 25 September, destined for Guadalajara. As they passed the "broken, lost, hopeless little towns" along the way— Alamos, Guaymas, Navojoa, Mazatlán, Tepic, Ixtlán, all sizzling under the ferocious sun—Lawrence felt he had come "over the brink of existence" to the end of the world. For his part Götzsche found Mazatlán "unbearably hot, day and night," and the road to Tepic gutted and rutted beyond belief. Lawrence told Adele Seltzer that after his Mexican ordeal he was visibly thinner. His health had suffered.

In Guadalajara they went to the faded Hotel Garcia, whose manager, Winfield Scott, Lawrence had met and liked at the Hotel Arzapalo in Chapala. On many days Lawrence walked the six blocks to 150 Calle Galeana, where Dr. Purnell had his dentist's office and where, upstairs, behind grated windows, Lawrence and young Idella Purnell talked poetry by the hour. Yet it was a sad time. Lawrence was still angry that Frieda had refused to join him in Mexico, and he redirected his hostility on all around him. The hotel was depressing. Even Chapala, he thought, had changed: "I went to Chapala for the day yesterday—the lake so beautiful," he told Thomas Seltzer on 22 October. "And yet the lake I knew was gone—something gone, and it was alien to me." It was he who had changed. The narrow, bustling streets of Guadalajara offered little to interest him—and no place for Götzsche to set up his easel and record the quaint, picturesque street life. For temporary work Lawrence at least had Mollie Skinner's novel *The Boy in the Bush* to recast. It filled only his mornings.

He had hoped to spend the winter on a little Mexican hacienda and (most important) to revise *Quetzalcoatl*, but he and Götzsche soon tired of each other and the hotel. Lawrence decided that he might just as well return to England. Frieda, with her stronger will, had prevailed. "I had a cable yesterday," he wrote Merrild on 3 November, "asking me to go to England. So there's nothing for it but to go." Going seemed inevitable. So he and Götzsche, though hating to leave the majestic mountains and fiery sunsets of the west, went straight to Mexico City, found a ship departing from Vera Cruz, and boarded the *Toledo* on 22 November. Lawrence headed to England, Götzsche to Denmark. Just before leaving, Lawrence wrote a poignant letter to Mabel Luhan (she had married Tony) which indexed his new frailty: "Send me some strength then on my way. My need is perhaps greater than yours. Give me your strength, and I'll fight a way through—little by little. Don't you see I find it very hard." He felt vulnerable, as if he were coming to some crisis. For almost a month he wrote no more letters.

Meanwhile, Frieda, having boarded her ship on 18 August, had discovered that traveling alone wearied her too. Although she missed Lawrence, she was too exasperated to feel much affection; yet without him she felt empty and disorganized, perplexed by the dozens of decisions she had to make by herself. It helped that Lawrence had given her some money and offered her an "allowance" if she wished. He loved her still. Always full of goodwill and generosity even when he seemed obstinate, he had written to his closest friends in London—Koteliansky, Murry, and Catherine Carswell—asking them to look after Frieda. "You know what a vague creature she is," he alerted Murry. To console himself after the death of Katherine, Murry—aided by Koteliansky as business manager—had founded a new monthly in London called the *Adelphi* and fervently hoped to publish Lawrence's work. Frieda would be on hand to observe its operation for herself. With Murry in tow, Koteliansky apparently met her ship and took her to his "cave" on Acacia Road for a few days, after which she went to stay briefly at Mary Cannan's flat in Hyde Park. Then she moved again. Renting a room in Mark Gertler's house for three weeks, she relocated on 7 September. And there, Gertler reported, "she sleeps and"—rolling his eyes to Ottoline—"god knows what else." There Frieda could also invite her children for a long-awaited family reunion. Being alone did not deter her from her plan of seeing her son and two daughters, going to Germany for the month of October, then renting a flat in Hampstead where (she hoped) she could welcome Lawrence with a grand celebration. It had been more than four years since he had walked on English soil.

On 28 September she left for Germany in the company of Murry, whom she had always liked, despite his squirming ambivalence toward Lawrence. He was going to Switzerland to recover some of Katherine's belongings at Sierre. But on the way—unsure of what lay ahead, hungry, drawn to Murry's good looks—Frieda suddenly proposed that they become lovers. Too weak to resist, too vacillating to be principled, too muddled to be sober, he yielded. He too was lonely.

Those who criticize Frieda believe she was simply unfaithful and crassly pragmatic, supposing that if Lawrence had really left her, then she might plot her future with Murry. She would have justified herself as Somers justifies Harriet's potential disloyalty: "For her too honour did not consist in a pledged word kept according to pledge, but in a genuine feeling faithfully followed." But that argument hid a serious risk—that the physical consummation at the center of an affair might bind the lovers with a secondary emotional connection strong enough to compromise the bond of marriage. It was a risk that both Lawrence (with Rosalind Baynes) and now Frieda (with Murry) had taken. Inevitably it seems to have led to some deterioration of feeling and respect. Frieda thought Murry worthy of her love, yet she acted unwisely, and their affair may ironically have infected Murry with a sense of guilt that would henceforth make him cringing and uneasy around Lawrence.

But Germany offered Frieda a healthy distance to put her marriage and the affair into perspective. (Indeed, her trip allowed Murry to return to London and resume his earlier role as lover to Dorothy Brett, a forty-year-old painter he had seduced in April, a few months after Katherine's death. Although Frieda complained that Murry treated Brett "*vilely,*" she seems not to have guessed the whole truth.) Reunited with her beloved but impoverished mother at the Ludwig Wilhelmstift home for aged ladies in Baden-Baden, she wrote to Martin Secker on 8 October, thankful for publishers' profits: "For once yesterday with one of Lawrence's pounds I gave the whole house of old women and young girls a feast—It was wonderful to think that just for once they really had had *enough.*" In Germany postwar inflation, soaring to crisis proportions in 1923, had reduced government benefits for widows to almost nothing. In November one U.S. dollar bought 4.2 trillion marks.

Frieda's frequent visits with her three children, now virtually grown, helped to vindicate her trip to London. Many years later, in her autobiography, she acknowledged that "they didn't want me any more, they were living their own lives," and that, separated from Lawrence, she felt lost. Her admission has led Jeffrey Meyers to think that she was "alienated from her children." At the time, however, their visits enchanted her. Writing to her mother on 5 November, she exulted that the children, who had visited the previous afternoon, had charmed both her and Murry. Monty, an Oxford graduate, ready at age twenty-three to take up a post he coveted at the Victoria and Albert Museum, impressed them both with his sobriety. Elsa and Barbara were attractive and graceful, and Frieda gave each one a stylish hat from Paris. Barbara, a student at the respected Slade School of Fine Art in London, had fled her father's nest and would soon be engaged. "I have had a great time with my children," Frieda wrote Thomas Seltzer on 9 December; "they are so jolly and young and natural and you can imagine what a pleasure it is to have them in my life again, when they eat my 'Leberwurst' out of the kitchen and take my 'glad rags'!"

## THE HOMECOMING

In 1924 metropolitan London was extraordinary. The largest city in Europe, it burst with new roadways, railways, docks, tube lines, factories, car production, and airplane manufacture. The British Empire Exhibition of 1924, covering 220 acres at Wembley Park, featured such giant structures as the Palace of India and offered a panorama of the grounds on a circulating train. Lawrence's impending arrival in this thriving city had inspired Frieda to spruce up her rented flat at 110 Heath Street in Hampstead. She chose flowering azaleas. But when Lawrence arrived at Plymouth on 12 December and came on to her flat, he felt as if he had entered a tomb. Even though his good friends the Carswells had taken the flat below, the rambling old house with its William Morris wallpaper, the worn china cups, the yellow urban air oozing with fog, the dismal winter streets that were dark by late afternoon, the dreary gray days of rain or snow, the reappearance of friends long gone—these remnants of the past made him ill. He languished in bed with a bad cold and perhaps a mild attack of malaria. Only Frieda seemed to him really nice, and he reviled *her* for dragging him back to England.

It was an awful winter. Lawrence wanted to leave. But a proposed formal dinner to celebrate his return awaited his consent, which he reluctantly gave. Frieda and Murry apparently suggested that it take place in a handsome private room at the Café Royal; according to Frieda, "Murry is responsible for the 'drinks.'" Several of Lawrence's closest friends were also invited—Koteliansky and Brett, Mark Gertler and Mary Cannan, Catherine and Donald Carswell. (Interestingly absent were old friends like Cynthia Asquith, Edward Marsh, Barbara Low, E. M. Forster, and David Garnett.) Because the published accounts of the dinner vary so much, only a few things are certain: Lawrence, a sensitive and gracious host, eventually asked each person in turn for a commitment to go with him to New Mexico and inaugurate a new life. Most were equivocal. Brett says she told him she would follow him anywhere (her need to serve was immense), and after Koteliansky stood and repeatedly toasted the man of genius, smashing wine glasses to raise the emotional stakes, Murry crept from his seat, sidled up to Lawrence, and kissed him in an effusive display. According to Catherine, Lawrence remained "perfectly still and unresponsive" while Frieda, who always minded rites of deification, sat "aloof and scornful." A final round of wine, fermented with more effusive testimonials, suddenly made Lawrence ill. After he fainted at the table, Koteliansky and Murry carried him to a taxi, up the steps to the flat in Heath Street, and into bed. For Lawrence, so private, so exacting, so vigilant, it was a moment of supreme embarrassment.

When he was well again and had gone (by himself) to the Midlands to celebrate the New Year with his sisters, he and Frieda left for Paris on 23 January 1924 to spend two weeks at the Hotel de Versailles. It was a vacation. In the winter sunshine and frost, Paris seemed draped in loveliness. Frieda went to a dressmaker to order new clothes; they visited Josephine Bonaparte's chateau at Malmaison; they went to Fountainebleau, where Katherine, holed up at the Gurdjieff Institute, had died; they savored the food and wine; and they met Sylvia Beach at her famous bookshop, Shakespeare and Company, where she stocked lots of Lawrence's books. In the mornings he occupied himself writing short stories, one of which has unusual biographical interest.

Not long after Lawrence arrived in London—and probably a few days after the formal dinner—he divined that Frieda's interest in Murry had been touchingly warm and vivid. Whether or not Frieda broached her feelings, Lawrence quickly realized that her interest had been reciprocated. One reason he wanted desperately to leave England is that he felt betrayed by Murry. In Paris he soon began a story about his feelings. Called "The Border-Line," it is one of the most personal stories Lawrence ever wrote. Recreating the triangle with Murry, it adopts Frieda's point of view and, calling her Katharine Farquhar, follows her on a journey from Paris through Strasbourg to Germany. Lawrence, splicing jealousy with malice, uses her story to discover an important emotional truth.

Katharine's first husband, a Lawrentian figure named Alan Anstruther—thin, strong, unyielding, with red hair and blue eyes—had fought her valiantly until, after ten years of marriage (exactly the time the Lawrences had been married), the couple had "ceased to live together." After Alan's death in the war, Katharine succumbed to the spell of Alan's close friend Philip Farquhar, a clever journalist (like Murry) whose dark good looks and potent sense of offering wrapped Katharine in a cocoon of "subtle, cunning homage." Unable to resist, she married him. In Philip, Lawrence neatly captures Murry's talent for cringing sentiment, which appealed to a woman like Frieda. Philip offers Katharine what Alan would not: a supreme sense of her female self.

The story transcends realism. In one of Lawrence's first attempts to use the supernatural, he allows Katharine, visited in Strasbourg by Alan's ghost, to recognize the truth about her two husbands. As she waits to cross "the border line" between France and Germany (countries still dislocated by the war), she confronts a more wondrous border between life and death. This surprising turn in Lawrence's fiction is forged out of his own emotional crisis. The story, expressing his struggle, suddenly transforms itself. It turns into a *disguised letter to Frieda* designed to illuminate her potential choice between Murry and himself. As Katharine, she realizes the supreme value of comradeship:

And as she walked at [Alan's] side through the conquered city, she realized that it was the one enduring thing a woman can have, the intangible soft flood of contentment that carries her along at the side of the man she is married to. It is her perfection and her highest attainment.

Now, in the afterwards, she knew it. . . . And dimly she wondered why, why, why she had ever fought against it. . . . The strong, silent kindliness of him towards her, even now, was able to wipe out the ashy nervous horror of the world from her body. She went at his side, still and released, like one newly unbound, walking in the dimness of her own contentment.

The story communicates to Frieda what Lawrence was perhaps too proud and emotionally reserved to tell her directly. In December Frieda had cried out angrily to Koteliansky: "*Why* can't [Lawrence] say he will be glad to see me?" In January he had complied, writing her a love letter in story form that would both acknowledge his deep affection and guide her to appreciate his exceptional qualities. If this sounds egocentric, it is because he wanted his marriage to survive. Feeling insecure about the strength of Frieda's commitment, he wrote to her indirectly because, in the words of the story, both characters are "too proud and unforgiving" to make themselves vulnerable by protestations of love. Indirect forms of communication were easier to initiate—and accept. The chasm between them could close.

They could now make plans. Leaving Paris for Germany on 6 February, Lawrence and Frieda expected to stay two weeks with her mother and younger sister, Johanna, then return to London, sail in March to America, and go once more to Taos, New Mexico. There both Lawrence and Frieda hoped that Mabel, now much chastened after their quarrels, might have transformed herself into a finer friend. In America Lawrence had to pay his income tax by 15 March but for some time had been worried about his income from Thomas Seltzer, who no longer wrote reassuring letters. Lawrence hoped that nothing had "gone wrong with him or his business." He needed Seltzer's money.

Returning from Germany, Lawrence and Frieda stopped in Paris long enough to visit Versailles, the opulent seventeenth-century palace built by Louis XIV, and to gaze at the stately cathedral at Chartres before they reached London. There they paused for a few days at Garland's Hotel and had a nice surprise: Dorothy Brett (called just "Brett") would accompany them to America on the *Aquitania*. She was grateful to escape a place where, all winter, she had worried that she might be pregnant with Murry's child. Her allowance of five hundred pounds a year from her father, Viscount Esher, would make her independent of the Lawrences' charity. Though partly deaf, Brett was oddly attractive, having round pink cheeks, a receding chin, and a shy, girlish manner that hid the passionate core of her being. On 1 March her painter friend Dora Carrington, coming to say goodbye, shared her reaction with writer Gerald Brenan: "Lawrence was very rude to me of course, and held forth to the assembly as if he was a lecturer to minor university students. . . . 'We lead a very primitive life [he says], we cut our own wood, and cook our own food' [—] 'and Lawrence makes the mo-ost beau-ti-ful bread'. Frieda always comes in like a Greek chorus, the moment D.H.L. has stopped speaking." This unfriendly vignette deftly measures the kind of antiphonal response the Lawrences thought entertaining. Not all were amused by his pompous declarations.

Thrilled to be pulling up anchor, Lawrence, Frieda, and Brett left London on 5 March. When they arrived in New York City six days later, in gale winds and blinding snow, they split up—Lawrence went to a hotel, Frieda and Brett to the Seltzers' small apartment off Broadway. There they learned the truth about Seltzer's publishing business: he had lost seven thousand dollars in the previous year, partly in legal costs to defend his books; had paid Lawrence no royalties since October; and was struggling to stay afloat. Lawrence blamed Seltzer's wife, Adele, and her "bad influence"; she wanted bestsellers. But the truth is that Seltzer's business was undercapitalized, so that when sales fell, he had no protective cushion and could not even advertise his list. Wisely Lawrence asked the American branch of Curtis Brown, headed by A. W. Barmby, to look after his work; they, not Lawrence, would enforce his contracts and demand that Seltzer pay. Braving the crowds in New York, the three travelers attended a concert, went to the theater, had tea with Willa Cather in Washington Square, and sauntered along Broadway. On 18 March they left by train for Taos and the great experiment of Rananim in the West.

## Frieda's Ranch

When they arrived in Lamy, Witter Bynner and Spud Johnson greeted them and, after a brief reunion, got the travelers into the coach to Taos. Astonished by the landscape, Brett had never before seen a desert that resembled the ocean, its snow-clouds rolling like long, white breakers, and, above it, majestic mountains rumbling into the sky, topped by tall pines stippled with bright snow. Awakened by the stark grandeur around Taos, they went directly to Mabel Luhan's big adobe house. Some things were just the same—the grand fireplace with its cluster of chairs; colorful Mexican blankets, folded and hung; and comfortable beds. Mabel, who arrived from San Francisco four days later, had changed. Once dominating and manipulative, she seemed calmer and more tolerant now. On 4 April Lawrence explained to Seltzer that he and Frieda resided in the two-story house across the field, Brett in the studio nearby; all three took their meals in the big house, where Amelia, the jolly Mexican cook, presided over the stove. "Mabel is wiser, has had a very bad time last year"; she is now "much nicer really," he informed Seltzer. For her part, knowing how much the Lawrences loved the Taos landscape, Mabel—in her own way as generous as Lawrence—offered them an incentive to stay. She gave them the ranch, with three cabins, where they had camped a year earlier. She had bought it in 1918 for twelve hundred dollars. Located above Lobo Mountain seventeen miles away (and two miles from the Lawrences' beloved Del Monte), it had 160 acres and unrivaled views of pine forest above and gray desert below. Eventually they named it Kiowa Ranch.

Lawrence called it *Frieda's* ranch. He disliked the concept of ownership and believed possessions posed a burden of responsibility that hampered one's freedom to change. He wanted the life impulse to be untrammeled. For him the ranch seemed to invite sturdy pioneers—people who could link themselves to the land and carve meaning out of its obstacles. He, Frieda, and Brett decided to move from Taos to Kiowa on 5 May—the onset of spring—and begin repairing the main cabin. Lawrence was eager. "I feel," he told Seltzer, "more than I ever did, that I should like to be right away from the world." The pale green of the cottonwood trees and the dense green of the alfalfa fields seemed magical. The Lawrences took with them two Indians (probably Candido and Tony's nephew Trinidad) and a skilled Mexican carpenter named Richard. Laboring every day, they felled and stripped logs; repaired the cabin's foundation and rebuilt its walls; chinked the rooms, making them ready for plaster; hinged the cupboards; made adobe bricks for a new chimney; and whitewashed the board siding. They rebuilt the corrals for the horses and repaired both a two-room cabin for Mabel (in case she visited) and a tiny, one-room cabin for Brett. On 12 May Lawrence reported to Mabel: "Thundering like the devil, and fierce rain. . . . Ponies neighing, trees hissing, Richard scuttling." Two days later Frieda, overcome by work at an altitude of eighty-six hundred feet, told Mabel that she had rested in the hammock all afternoon, healing herself in the sun. Various photographs (probably taken by Brett) show Lawrence on horseback, looking thin and fit; Frieda with a turban around her head, looking contented; and two black-braided Indians, strongly built, standing in repose behind their outdoor work table, flanked by the Lawrences. Frieda wrote happily to Adele Seltzer: "Well, we sit on my estate with 6 Indians, Lawrence making adobe bricks and working hard, It is a lovely place—I give Mabel Lawrence's Manuskript of Sons & Lovers, which my sister [Else] told me she had!" By giving Mabel the manuscript of Lawrence's third novel, Frieda proudly paid for the ranch, which she kept to the end of her life.

By June the hardest work was behind them—shingling the cabin roofs, clearing the rats' nests from the rafters, scraping the muck from around the spring, and opening the irrigation ditch from the Gallina Canyon several miles distant. Brett, learning to be self-sufficient, chopped wood and fished.

Lawrence, Frieda, and the Indians who helped them, Kiowa Ranch, 1924 (Courtesy of the Department of Special Collections, Charles E. Young Research Library, UCLA)

Only their own labor was cheap. Early in June Lawrence reckoned he had spent almost $500 on renovations. "I'm being very economical," he chided Seltzer, who had again warned Lawrence that book sales had slumped. Ever resourceful, Lawrence now depended on the income from his short stories—for instance, $175 from *The Smart Set* and £40 from *Hutchinson's Magazine* for "The Border-Line." *Quetzalcoatl*, far from being ready, could not now be completed until he returned to Mexico and immersed himself in its aura: "I think we shall stay [on the ranch] till October," he wrote Catherine Carswell, "then go down to Mexico, where I must work on my novel." That plan left them with the prospect of a long and pleasurable summer—riding their horses, named Azul, Poppy, and Bessie; walking in the cool pine forests at evening; going down to Del Monte for the mail and the milk; and, for Lawrence, slipping into the early-morning woods to write. Despite his frequent headaches, he loved the privacy and the adventure, the unspoiled primitiveness of the ranch.

Still, it would be wrong to think that Lawrence yielded gently to the vicarious joy of ownership. In a way his love of the ranch was altruistic. The ranch elicited his courage and fortitude—and the resourcefulness of both Frieda and Brett. Living so far from cities and hotels, they had no choice but to do their own work. Lawrence did not mind hard manual labor. He had told Earl Brewster that, when they were together, he preferred working to talking. He relished his work with the Indians—instructing, constructing, learning, sharing, savoring the strange camaraderie. At his side, like a desert spring, Frieda provided nourishment: guardian and maternal power, she also offered a corrective to his every excess of language and behavior. He had—without her—already tried bonding with the Danes and now acknowledged some kind of failure; he rarely even corresponded with them.

But by starting afresh with Frieda and Brett, he could recenter his strongest intuitions. Bringing into harmony a wife, a small group of friends, and a way to bond with men very different from himself, Lawrence had rediscovered his vital center. This sense of rediscovery gave him uncanny access to a cultural unknown—namely, the Indians' mysterious unity and the influence of the cosmos upon them. After Lawrence went to Santa Fe in April to witness the impressive Santo Domingo Rain Dance, he captured its power in an essay called "The Dance of the Sprouting Corn": "And the mystery of germination . . . is accomplished. The sky has its fire, its waters, its stars, its wandering electricity, its winds, its fingers of cold. The earth has its reddened body, its invisible hot heart, its inner waters and many juices and unaccountable stuffs. Between them all, the little seed: and also man, like a seed that is busy and aware. And from the heights and from the depths man, the caller, calls: man, the knower, brings down the influences and brings up the influences, with his knowledge: man, so vulnerable, so subject, and yet even in his vulnerability and subjection, a master, commands the invisible influences, and is obeyed." The rhythmic dancing achieves closure between earth and sky, uses the language of the body to articulate a faith in the cycle of renewal, and makes room for the Koshare jesters to weave together the dancers' eloquent supplications. For years Lawrence had struggled to define the mystery of manhood, in novels from *Women in Love* to *Quetzalcoatl*. His understanding had evolved from a repressed erotic communion between men, to a bonding that subsumed the erotic flow into work, channeled it, shaped it into a kind of cosmic rhythm, at once meaningful and mysterious. As if gelded, the erotic component of male bonding had for Lawrence now become spiritualized. Displaced from the body onto landscape or ritual, it was no longer a direct force but a tranquil presence. The Indians gave Lawrence a way to decenter sex and take it out of the body.

Yet for the biographer a perplexing question remains. Why did Lawrence's new fiction, written in the halcyon summer of 1924, express his renewed sense of self in such altered ways? Why did it, in spite of its burnished eloquence, continue to mine the spitefully satiric vein of "The Border-Line" and its companion stories, "Jimmy and the Desperate Woman" and "The Last Laugh"? Lawrence's mental health holds the answer. The awful winter months had sapped his vitality, made him weary, discontented, and at the core, lonely. The hard work at the ranch in May and June fearfully strained him even as it leavened his spirits. The healing landscape could not erase the profound sense of inner defeat that had come over him after Frieda's departure and infidelity while they were separated. To Bynner he wrote candidly in July that he knew "most people naturally dislike me." Something had changed. Never again would his writing have the same luminous fusion of psychological penetration of character with a landscape sensuously rendered. Spiked with flippancy or laced with aggression, his art shifted now to the edge of anger. And with that striking change he advanced to the late phase of his creative work.

## SERENITY AND RAGE

Two long stories fully express his new style. *The Woman Who Rode Away* and *St. Mawr*, both begun in the gorgeously beautiful days of June, reflect his rankling distrust of Frieda now projected onto Taos women like Mabel Luhan and her close childhood friend Nina Witt. Both stories show women leaving a marriage that has not so much failed as gone hollow; both show women coming to the end of difficult physical journeys; and both find sexuality unappealing.

*The Woman Who Rode Away*, despite its technical perfection, has angered feminists. Its treatment of the heroine has seemed vindictive, a "masterwork of misogyny," a "barbaric" tale. But the story's art has such serene power that one is forced to look further—to the use of sun-and-moon mythology as a frame—in order to understand how Lawrence can so well contain both his serenity and his rage.

In the story, set in the mountains of Mexico, the Woman Who Rode Away closely resembles Mabel. Both relish their female power; both live with servants in adobe houses; both bore sons in their early twenties; and both are fascinated by Indians, the Woman feeling "it was her destiny to wander into the secret haunts of these timeless, mysterious, marvellous Indians": just as Mabel had gone into the Taos Pueblo. The Woman's female power brings with it a spasm of madness, like a death wish, that propels her toward the Chilchui Indians, their inscrutable gods, and their need to offer a sacrifice.

Here the story changes. Led by Indians into the mountains, the Woman prepares for a slow transfiguration from arrogance to submission, and when, in the cold of winter, an herbal drink heightens her senses, "[t]hen she could actually hear the great stars in heaven, which she saw through her door, speaking from their motion and brightness, saying things perfectly to the cosmos, as they trod in perfect ripples, like bells on the floor of heaven, passing one another and grouping in the timeless dance, with spaces of dark between." Soothing her fear with thoughts that connect her to a timeless world, Lawrence sequences the Woman's preparations for death with a sober control, a cool exactness. He builds inexorably toward the moment when the Woman is led to the Indians' sacred altar within a cave—like one Lawrence himself saw near Arroyo Seco, high above the village—and toward the moment when the chief priest watches to fix, in nature, the orgasmic moment when the dying sun shines through a long shaft of ice into the hollow of the cave and deep into the cave's orifice, at which time the priest lifts his long phallic knife, made of obsidian, and, as the assembled tribe watches, prepares to sacrifice the Woman and reclaim the racial power so long denied his people.

It is a shattering climax. Its fusion of displaced sexual intensity, willing victim, and cultural apotheosis ranks among the strangest and most disturbing of Lawrence's work. Although the story has the severity and compression of a fable, it disturbs because the Woman is so clearly an instrument in the hands of men, like Lawrence, whose sexuality has been rechanneled outside themselves and whose fulfillment lies in an act of violence rather than an act of love. As these men restore the tribe's spiritual potency, they unlock a pair of cosmic secrets: social unity is more profound than individuality, and the violence inherent in male bonding must somehow be purged. The story expresses, finally, Lawrence's extreme longing for the companionship of men. It is a very personal story given a mythic shield, its disciplined restraint a tight lid on its seething fury.

The other story, *St. Mawr*—longer and less brilliantly unified—portrays women and men separating from each other, the power struggle becoming so intense that to be alone is more appealing than to be connected. Human sexuality turns distasteful, ugly, coercive. Lou Witt, who is a version of recently divorced Nina Witt, discards her playboy husband, Rico; Lewis, a groom for Lou's horse, flees Lou's aggressive mother. Midway, when the story shifts from England to America, Lou rejects the imagined overtures of Phoenix, an Indian who would prostitute himself to a white woman. The story's sexual force is again rechanneled, concentrated now into the sleek, handsome, vital horse named St. Mawr, "beautiful, with his poised head and massive neck, and his supple hindquarters." He alone offers no threat. Making her way from England to the Kiowa Ranch, Lou retraces Lawrence's own journey a few months earlier. At the ranch, she discovers—as Lawrence had discovered—some deeply essential goal, a wild spirit in the landscape that "soothes me, and it holds me up."

Most interesting is the way Lou settles into this wild landscape, relieved to be alone with her exhausted mother, without any desire for others, grateful instead to root herself in its history and spirit. Like the Woman Who Rode Away, Lou rejects her initial boredom by riding away on a horse, coming not to a village of Indians but to the home of settlers, taking as her tonic not a secret herbal potion but the sudden discovery of her place in the cosmos. Like Lawrence, both women freshly acknowledge larger forces outside themselves and achieve their nirvana. In doing so, they illustrate one of Lawrence's postwar truisms: they discover a female identity that prizes acquiescence over willfulness.

༄

As the summer passed, the Lawrences' days slipped by like shuffled cards. Lawrence relished the flowers and the pristine beauty of the desert, Frieda the lazy days of hot sun and cool nights. For these months Brett's absorbing account, *Lawrence and Brett,* is the most valuable. A keen eyewitness who kept a diary, Brett records Lawrence's fluctuating moods, but she also revels in the gossip of minor insult that Mabel, so incomplete in herself, inspired in those she befriended. Stubbornly partial to Lawrence, Brett caricatures Frieda as a chain smoker lying in bed most of the summer, unable even to make bread by herself. But Frieda read and knitted, rode horseback for her exercise, and cooked most of the meals. In time she found Brett's patronage annoying and never sympathized with her deep loneliness, exacerbated by poor hearing. But Brett was perceptive in ways Frieda was not and, in her quiet subservience, knew how to find the essential Lawrence. She gradually turned herself into the "man" Lawrence had always wanted to work beside. She felled logs for the new porch, hauled them, trimmed

293

them, shot rabbits for meat, saddled the horses, loved to ride, dressed as a cowboy, and carried a knife in her boot. She became his best friend. Her masculine qualities perfectly complemented his feminine qualities; she had no need to criticize him; and because there was no sexual struggle to complicate their bond, they became buddies, looking out for each other but at a measurable distance. They were comfortable and close without being intimate.

Restraint did not characterize another close relationship that Lawrence formed—with Clarence Thompson, one of Mabel's protégés. Tall, blond, gay, age twenty-six, Clarence, who had already provoked friction at one of Mabel's Saturday evening parties, carried up to the ranch his roused attraction to Lawrence. A graduate of Harvard, he wore a velvet tunic—deep red—whose sleeves jangled with silver Navajo buttons. Brett records her irritation that, in front of others, Clarence made "googoo eyes" at Lawrence, a flirtation she found an "impertinence," even though Lawrence merely sniffed at the sexual bait.

But the hard work and high altitude eventually made Lawrence ill. On 2 August, already a little congested, he spat bright red blood. His lungs had hemorrhaged. Frieda, astonished and alarmed, and stoutly resisting his wishes, sent for Dr. T. P. Martin from Taos. Fearing pneumonia, the doctor had brought warm blankets for transporting the patient in his car. But after he had gone, Brett rushed in to hear Frieda say, "Nothing wrong; the lungs are strong. It is a touch of bronchial trouble—the tubes are sore. I am making him a mustard plaster and you must ride down tomorrow to Rachel [Hawk at Del Monte] and borrow some mustard from her, as I have no more." The plaster, which brought heat to the infected parts, was thought to speed healing. Frieda also asked Mabel to bring up aspirin and another home remedy—"some camphorated oil."

Unfortunately the infection lingered. A few days later Lawrence complained to Mabel of a swollen throat and a sore chest, and hoped she could bring him "a good gargle for my throat: it hurts like billy-o! this evening." Rachel Hawk sent a bottle of Listerine. Although barely recovered, Lawrence recalled that, long before, he had accepted Mabel's invitation to visit the Hopi Indians in Arizona and to witness their exotic Snake Dance. On the thirteenth he and Frieda left the ranch, toting food and camping gear, and joined Mabel and Tony for the five-hundred-mile drive over sizzling mesas and through vast canyons whose great red cliffs stood up like desert warriors. At last, on the eighteenth, they saw the dances at Hotevilla— "priests dancing with live rattle snakes in their mouths—weird rather than beautiful," Lawrence told his sister Emily. Home again, Lawrence felt exhausted. He was unable to work. His persistent illness now hastened his desire to go south for the winter.

It helped that autumn came early. Snow capped the mountains again,

Dorothy Brett dressed as a cowboy (Courtesy of Center for Southwest Research, University of New Mexico)

the days grew calm and sunny, the landscape crept with color: the alfalfa field—Lawrence told his niece Peggy—turning "all mauve and gold, with dark michaelmas daisies and wild sunflowers." Each day his eye harvested new treasures. Into this tranquil setting came a sudden cable: Lawrence's father, Arthur, had died on 10 September, one day shy of his son's thirty-ninth birthday. Lawrence's grief was thin, cool, and impersonal: "It is better to be gone than lingering on half helpless and half alive," he told Emily. "But it upsets one, nevertheless: makes a strange break." To help with the funeral expenses, he sent his sisters thirty pounds. His father, who for years had lived with Ada, was seventy-eight.

By the time six inches of snow had fallen, Lawrence knew it was time to leave Kiowa—to go, he told Frieda's mother in October, "where the Maya Indians and the Zapotecs live." Although Seltzer still teetered on the brink of bankruptcy, Barmby in New York had squeezed a little money out of him. By careful economizing the Lawrences had saved two thousand dollars for their trip south. Brett would come along. As the three of them packed their large trunks, they began to close the ranch for the winter, boarding up the windows, taking their valuables and furniture down to Del Monte for storage, and arranging with William Hawk to board their horses from December until the alfalfa rose green again in the spring, at which time the Lawrences planned to return. They left Kiowa on 11 October 1924—Brett eager, Frieda sad, Lawrence joyful. They paused in Taos, then on the twentieth crossed the Mexican border at El Paso.

Just one year earlier Lawrence and Frieda were estranged; now they returned to Mexico together, some of their differences healed while others were born of Brett's presence. It was a year of extraordinary change. Lawrence had discovered that his absence from Frieda might tempt her to place her affections elsewhere (with extraordinary effects on his fiction), but he had also discovered that he was happiest when he was mostly alone, in a savagely beautiful landscape. Frieda, tired of itinerant living, had found what she had long craved—a home of her own, a base camp to which she could always return. She might say in September that she felt always on the edge of a suppressed growl, but she had become much calmer, having tested Murry's mettle, reclaimed her children, and returned to Lawrence. Despite the frayed edges of their marriage, she felt more complete and fulfilled than she had for years. Brett, awakened by the aura of New Mexico, had found that breaking from her privileged British past had allowed her to shed her old skin and to adopt a new identity, finding both new subjects for her painting and a special fondness for the Taos Indians. From the height of the Rocky Mountains all three figures saw themselves afresh—as hardy, courageous, and self-sufficient. As they crossed the Mexican border, not one of them anticipated the terrible collapse that would send them hastening back to Kiowa.

# 18

# The Mysteries of Oaxaca

## 1924–25

Oaxaca . . . a place of "brilliant sun all day long: and a nice little easy town"—that is how Lawrence described it. But to most readers Oaxaca connotes a place of mystery—wholly unfamiliar in name, people, customs, and landscape. Pronounced Wa-HA-ka and located 320 miles south of Mexico City, it is today a much larger town of 220,000 people—lively but subdued, pleasant but uneasy, peaceful but rebellious, affluent amid scandalous poverty. A place of subtle contradictions, it is quite unlike larger Mexican cities like Guadalajara, which stridently mix noise, hustle, and colonial charm. Spread out flat in a broad valley, bordered on all sides by mountains barnacled with tin shacks, Oaxaca—even today—retains the distinctive Indian influence that so appealed to the Lawrences. The Zapotecs and Mixtecs still plow the immense flat fields with mules and oxen; still bring their rugs, woven in complex geometric designs, to the outdoor markets; and still roam the zócalo, peddling wares only a few blocks from the Hotel Francia where the Lawrences stayed. At the end of 1924 Oaxaca would test Lawrence's belief in the purity of primitive cultures.

Arriving in Mexico City on 22 October 1924, they went again to the Regis Hotel but then moved on, with Brett, to the family-run Monte Carlo, where Lawrence had happily stayed before. For a daily rate of two dollars, they had the best rooms and enjoyed the Italian cuisine. While they waited to learn if the rail trip to Oaxaca was safe from roving bandits, who had long plagued rail travel to the hinterlands, Lawrence used his letters of introduction to meet some old and new literary lights. In suburban Coyoacán Mrs. Zelia Nuttall invited them again to her hacienda, adorned by gardens of roses and bougainvillea. A noted archaeologist and the author of a book on world civilizations, she knew all about the violent uprisings that had greeted Plutarco Calles as he prepared to take over the Mexican presidency on 1 December, when he would succeed Alvaro Obregón. Calles was a zealous reformer. He demanded land reform all over Mexico and eventually redistributed eight million acres from large landowners to peasants. Closer to home, on 31 October, wearing a boiled shirt and jacket, Lawrence attended a dinner given in his honor by the P.E.N. authors' club, and spoke briefly about male solidarity, about becoming "men together, before we are artists." Sitting next to him was a twenty-four-year-old poet named Luis Quintanilla. Dazzled by Lawrence's presence and intrigued by the way he bent his head forward, "as if in constant meditation," Quintanilla took Lawrence to meet the renowned Edward Weston, who photographed him on 4 November. With Lawrence, Quintanilla roamed the maze of side streets in Mexico City until Lawrence's excessive hostility toward Mexico ruptured their friendship.

Soon bored with the sprawling city, eager for a warmer place, and complaining that they had gotten colds, Lawrence and Frieda hastened away on 8 November. With Brett they went by rail to Esperanza, boarded a narrow-gauge train to Tehuacán, then continued on to Oaxaca the next day in "a wild queer lonely journey in a steep gorge"—all for thirteen dollars each. Astonished by so many armed guards, Brett felt uneasy: "The train to Oaxaca twists and turns so that after an hour we are hardly any distance from Tehuacán: we still can see the little town shining in the distance. Again we drop down to the tropical belt. The heat is stifling. We buy sugar cane and suck it. . . . All the stations are pock-marked with bullets and there are ruined villages and houses everywhere. At every station, rows of silent men in clean white clothes sit along bits of broken walls, their . . . glinting eyes watch us unceasingly."

Going straight from Oaxaca's train station to the Hotel Francia, they took huge, cool rooms that, although they faced the street, were also near the hotel's central patio, graced with a fountain and trees. When Brett's ear trumpet, a primitive hearing aid, was stolen, a local tinsmith, who quickly improvised, made her another. From the Lawrences she was learning resourcefulness.

Intrigued by Oaxaca's strangeness and seeing hardly a tourist anywhere, the trio strolled about town in the hot sun while the Indians stared and stared, and sometimes murmured after Lawrence, "Jesucristo!" In the covered market three blocks from the Francia, they savored the sights of fruits and vegetables piled high; sturdy wicker baskets, leather huaraches and bright serapes in tiny stalls, each with its own vendor; roses heaped into a crescendo of color; rising stacks of woven wool rugs; and squawking ducks and chickens. Brett's photograph of Lawrence and Frieda at the market shows Lawrence gaunt but well dressed in a pale suit, his head covered by a straw bowler, and Frieda—now almost stout—in a long plaid housedress, her head also clad by a bowler. They liked the exotic atmosphere even as they sometimes shrank from the squalor they saw.

But Lawrence needed a quieter place than the Francia to finish the *Quetzalcoatl* novel which, he told Curtis Brown, had often been on his mind. He had not worked on it for a year. Within a few days he took a letter of introduction to Father Edward Rickards, whose brother Constantine, the vice consul of the British embassy in Mexico City, Lawrence had met and liked. Father Rickards, born in Oaxaca and now a parish priest, agreed to rent them a wing of his rambling house at 43 Avenida Pino Suarez, twelve blocks from the Francia. The Lawrences at once liked its spacious quietness. A long house flanked by a wide verandah and a shaded inner garden with tall trees, its walls came right up to the narrow sidewalk; the heavy iron grates on the high windows offered protection from thieves— and are still intact today, as are the foot-thick walls inside, designed to withstand Mexico's frequent earthquakes. The rooms were big and bare, and the climate so temperate that Lawrence thought they could live mostly out of doors, spending only the nights in their separate bedrooms.

Leaving Brett at the Francia (to give them more privacy), the Lawrences moved to Pino Suarez on 18 November and, from Rickards' friends, borrowed a table and rocking chairs and at the central market bought blankets and pottery. Father Rickards introduced them to Rosalino, a young Zapotec Indian who became their *mozo* (servant). He ran errands, carried their basket to the market, delivered letters, and tidied the grounds.

At first the Lawrences found Oaxaca a small, friendly town of thirty thousand. But gradually it seemed choked with intimidation and suspicion. In the countryside the outbreaks of rebel violence made them fearful to venture out. "This is a strange country, quite fantastic in its wild politics," Frieda wrote on 3 January 1925. Three days later Lawrence reported feeling "never quite safe, always a feeling of being hemmed in, and shut down." They would stay only the winter.

In spite of the risk, they enjoyed their many excursions. With their neighbor Donald Miller, a mining engineer, they went to the marvelous ruins at Mitla, thirty-three miles east, where the walls and floors and steps of an Indian temple had been excavated, and where the dead rulers were laid in tombs that, until they were pillaged, contained prized artifacts for a life after death. Most interesting were the geometric designs on the walls, a fretwork full of repetition and severity, like drum beats captured in stone. Courageously, Lawrence and Brett would go out into the fragrant morning desert, deep in solitude, she sitting under a low tree painting a canvas like *The Road to Mitla,* he under another tree writing his novel or composing essays he would call *Mornings in Mexico.* On most afternoons at four o'clock, Brett boarded the mule tram and arrived at the Pino Suarez house for tea. In the evenings they came into town and sat in the zócalo, sipped their drinks, waited for a band to play, watched a procession of Indians holding aloft their Chinese lanterns like ghosts in the pale light, or went to a party hosted by one of the few Americans in Oaxaca. One evening they all watched the film *Thief of Baghdad.*

But in January a mutiny caused their Rananim to founder. Frieda apparently resented the camaraderie that arose between Lawrence and Brett, and whenever she quarreled with Lawrence, Brett took her idol's part and sometimes even made fun of Frieda. Triangles, eternally unstable, need only jealousy to speed their collapse. And at some point the balance of marital power shifted, probably when Lawrence returned to Frieda just one year earlier. Now Frieda defined herself as the dominant partner. With her mouth set hard and her eyes darting about, she could make Lawrence feel guilty and ashamed. She decided she would not allow a female saboteur on the premises without a struggle. So Lawrence, hating these domestic scrapes, wrote Brett a letter about 9 January, which Rosalino delivered to the Francia: "The simplest thing perhaps is to write, as one can't shout everything. You, Frieda and I don't make a happy combination now. The best is that we should prepare to separate: that you should go your own way. I am not angry: except that I hate 'situations', and feel humiliated by them. We can all remain decent and friendly, and go the simplest, quietest way about the parting. . . . I am grateful for the things you have done for me. But we must stand apart." Shocked, hurt, and miserable, Brett nevertheless came to tea that day but left in the face of Frieda's silent hostility. In despair, Lawrence soon appeared at Brett's hotel window and begged her not to return to the house. Worried that he would again become ill if Frieda did not relent, Brett agreed to return to the Del Monte ranch above Taos and spend the late winter in one of the Hawks' cabins. Palpably relieved, Lawrence said, rushing away, "I will go and tell Frieda."

With Brett now at the edge of departure, Frieda could be more direct. To avoid being misinterpreted, she wrote Brett a letter to articulate her feelings and one morning personally delivered it to the hotel. She had not, however, gauged Brett's girlish inexperience and incredulity. Frieda announced that two people immensely attracted to each other should complete their attraction and become lovers. Brett was stunned. "But Frieda," she countered, "how can I make love to Lawrence when I am your guest; would that not be indecent?" After Frieda left, Brett wondered, "And what is the correct behavior in a triangle?" The wry calculation behind her question confirms the emotional complexity of the triangle. Lawrence wanted intense friendship; Brett, whatever emotional commitment Lawrence would offer her; Frieda, a minimum of meddling in her marriage. Their goals collided. Lawrence was too frail, perhaps too conflicted, to lay down a grid of correct behavior. It was easier to yield. He needed to get on with his work. At the train station on 19 January 1925 Lawrence shook Brett's hand, Frieda accepted her kiss, and then, waving and waving, she was gone. Lawrence, though greatly distressed that she was traveling alone, went home to write.

## ILLNESS IN *THE PLUMED SERPENT*

He wrote quickly. He hoped, he said, to finish by the end of January, having already "a good deal done from last year." By 29 January he could tell Martin Secker he was completing the last chapter but added that, "at the bottom of my heart, I'd rather not have it published." Why not? To answer that question invites speculation on why Lawrence rewrote *Quetzalcoatl*— why he created a fresh novel that taunts feminists, annoys biographers, and divides readers into passionate camps.

Called *The Plumed Serpent* when it was published in 1926, the rewritten work, full of irritated action and reaction, freshly reflects Lawrence's psychological crisis. The emotional upheavals of the preceding year clarify the transformed novel as nothing else does. Disillusioned by his return to Europe, disappointed in close friends like Murry, Götzsche, and Merrild, uneasy about his health, oppressed by Mexico's political turbulence, stung by the latest domestic scrape, Lawrence altered much in his revised novel—its tone, its mythology, and especially its characterization of Kate. Now she becomes less assertive, more introspective, more yielding—less like Frieda, more like Brett. Because Lawrence had often suffered from strong females, he now disbelieved in giving them power that was not anchored in male enterprise.

Having just turned forty (like Lawrence), Kate feels herself "cross[ing] a dividing line." The age of forty had closed an era, had made her cast away youthful spontaneity and accept responsibility, caution, even loneliness. Like Lawrence, Kate has turned bitter, the path ahead (she thinks) "black and empty." She loathes Mexico City, detests the vulgar spectators at the bullfight, finds people repulsive. Aztec artifacts oppress her, make her irritable while the spirit of the place waxes cruel and destructive. To Juana, her servant, she wanted to say, "For God's sake, leave me alone." In ways like this the novel has been freshly shaded with illness.

Once the novel's opening bullfight and tea party have categorized those who are either poor or powerful, Lawrence repositions Kate in relation to the men around her. At dinner with Ramón, Cipriano, and others, she finds herself in the presence of men not her equal but "passing beyond what she knew, beyond her depth." Kate, ardent with admiration, impresses such men by dissolving into tears about the memory of her second husband, an Irish leader who died young, having (like Lawrence) "ruined his health." For these men she defines herself emotionally. Suffering nobly, she invites their interest not in her intellectual acuity, which she mostly hides from them, but in her vital presence: "Her great charm was her soft repose."

What has happened? Although the revised novel is more pointed and polished, and its narrator more trenchant and assertive, it creates a different Kate—a woman whose resistance weakens, whose energy declines. Tortured by malaise, weighted with strange weariness, sometimes paralyzed by fear, she responds most fully to those who are strong—Cipriano displaying his "magnetic power," the boatman flush with "great strength," Ramón exhibiting his "powerful will," the man guarding her house with "wild strength." More passive now, she yearns for someone—even unknown gods—"to put the magic back into her life." She craves salvation. Yet the salvation of love is no longer enough; she needs a messianic hope, which Ramón and his followers can inspire.

Outside this narrative space, a rebirth evolves in which Kate has no part except as an observer. Ramón acts as the idealized embodiment of Lawrence's yearning for male comradeship—this time as the leader, not of a small band of followers but of a cultural revolution. As before, Ramón hopes to replace the outworn creed of Christianity by reviving the god Quetzalcoatl. On a personal level he too must strip away his Christian ties. Rejecting his wife, Carlota, growing distant from his two adolescent sons, spurning the established political structure, Ramón mobilizes a systematic change in consciousness that Lawrence—when he was well—had always dreamed of doing. Supremely healthy, Ramón has a fierce integrity, a natural ability to command, and an imaginative grasp of what Mexico, deep down, needs. In this man's presence Kate feels "dizzy," "dazzled" by his white jacket and trousers, touched to the quick by his remote godliness and superbly sensual body. No matter how much she resists his male prerogative, she recognizes—and accepts—the honor of serving him. She has tired of opposition.

To say that Kate is seduced by a fascist ideal, as some writers have said, is to miss the point that she has nowhere else to go: the pull of her family, so powerful in *Quetzalcoatl*, now almost disappears. Like Lawrence, she has no home. Gradually she becomes like Brett—a woman with weak family ties and a "moderate income," a woman ready to serve a man who will claim her allegiance but leave her body untouched. A single comparison can illustrate. In *Quetzalcoatl* Kate saves Ramón's life during an attack by local bandits, after which she simply returns home. But in *The Plumed Serpent* she soon feels "numbed" by her experience, as if the threads that bind her to humanity have snapped: "Never had she been so alone, and so inert, and so utterly without desire." Only a little flame in her innermost soul wants to live. "She wanted," she says, "to live *its* life, not her own life." Who is responsible for this new flame? Not herself now, but Ramón: "Ramón had lighted it"—Ramón, the married man who likes her, feels comfortable with her, can talk openly to her, but shows no sexual desire for her. Having given him the responsibility of transfiguring her life, Kate has made the same choice that Brett had made a year earlier. In Oaxaca Frieda may have asserted her will over both Lawrence and Brett, but in the revised novel Lawrence and Brett—like Ramón and Kate—have the best of possible relationships: ennoblement without entanglement.

*The Plumed Serpent*'s closing chapters show Kate, now bound to General Cipriano, acting out a role of "supreme passivity." She willingly embraces Cipriano's wish that she become the Quetzalcoatl deity, Malintzi. She is the Woman Who Rode Away rescued rather than sacrificed by the Indian gods. Yet all of the luminous beauty of Lawrence's prose—its incantations, its hymns and chants, its sultry evocations—cannot rescue Kate from seeming, near the close, both shallow and incoherent, as if Lawrence's own illness, while he wrote the last part, had changed her. Spiritually exhausted and now, finally, "just a woman," Kate yields to a man she scarcely knows and, at times, barely respects. Although she can still resist Cipriano, she derives a sense of passive power from his embrace, and his magnetism is so great that she allows herself to become the wife-goddess of Huitzilopochtli, then marries Cipriano legally. The double ceremony cuts her ties to her past, nullifies her "European" individuality, and gives her a new sense of passive fulfillment.

Sexually she is also transformed. With Cipriano as her teacher, she learns not to strive for external clitoral stimulation but to lie passively, awaiting the deeper vaginal fulfillment that Cipriano prefers: "And he, in his dark, hot silence would bring her back to the new, soft, heavy, hot flow when she was like a fountain gushing noiseless and with urgent softness from the volcanic deeps." The key word is "noiseless." Some readers believe that Lawrence has stripped women of their sexual equality and tied them to beds of male pleasure. But a biographer may use the life to construct a more plausible reading. Lawrence—weaker now, his potency endangered by illness, his pride still smarting from Frieda's liaison with Murry—had come to resent her sexual assertion and, as in his story "The Border-Line," used the novel to convey a message to Frieda. His own sexual experience may have been diminished by a woman forcefully manipulating him. It is no surprise that Cipriano, by "instinct," recoils from any kind of direct clitoral stimulation. On the final page Kate's tears measure her desire to be loved intensely, by a strong, dark man outside the boundaries of conventional relationships, in an emotional region beyond "thought," in a nether world of loosened inhibitions. In that world the inhibitions that separate Kate from an Indian disappear. In Lawrence's imagination Mexico is a region hot with helpless desire, where he can yield to his thwarted wish for spiritual and sexual wholeness. In a novel, he confided to Mollie Skinner a few months later, "one can live so intensely with one's characters."

## A Mysterious Malady

Lawrence finished revising the novel about 1 February 1925. He had not felt well for two months. Perhaps, he thought, the malaria he had contracted in 1922 in Ceylon had recurred. Like many travelers to Mexico, he also worried that the hot midday sun had harmed him. Within a few days he felt worse, "as if shot in the intestines," he told Amy Lowell. Whether he had malaria, influenza, typhoid fever, or dysentery is not clear. He was soon dehydrated. Greatly alarmed, Frieda watched as he lay on his bed; it seemed (she thought) that he could not extend the thread of his life. "But if I die," he told her, "nothing has mattered but you, nothing at all." The Americans in Oaxaca rallied to assist Frieda; a doctor gave him quinine shots to combat malaria; a missionary's wife brought soup and, at his bedside, prayed. "I never wanted to come here," Frieda wrote to her mother, "but Lawrence seemed bewitched by his Mexico." Finally, unable to stand, Lawrence was moved by stretcher back to the Francia, where friends could assist Frieda more easily.

Lawrence now despised Mexico. He fervently hoped he and Frieda could depart quickly, catch a boat to England, then proceed to Germany. On 24 February 1925 they climbed aboard the narrow-gauge train from Oaxaca to Tehuacán—Lawrence in his illness jostled brutally all the way, Frieda deeply depressed—then went on to the deluxe, expensive Hotel Imperial in Mexico City, where they had a private bath in their top-floor suite of rooms. He was extremely ill. "I was a month in bed," Lawrence wrote to Quintanilla on 3 March, "and can still hardly crawl through the days;" "I get thinner and thinner." Frieda, too, was ill, her prolonged anxiety lowering her resistance. Then a sudden shock: "One morning I had gone out and when I came back the analyst doctor was there and said, rather brutally, when I came into Lawrence's room: 'Mr. Lawrence has tuberculosis.' And Lawrence looked at me with such unforgettable eyes. . . . And I said, 'Now we know, we can tackle it. That's nothing. Lots of people have that.'" But the doctor, probably drawing inferences from a sputum analysis, warned Frieda that Lawrence would not live long. She had to be cheerful and strong—no more difficulties or depression, no more petulant stubbornness.

"Take him to your ranch, that is the place for him," the doctor urged Frieda. She agreed. "He says I *must* stay in the sun," Lawrence told his sister Emily. When he was better, they left Mexico City on 25 March—with a basket of food packed by the Conways, a Scottish couple they had met— and took the Pullman to Santa Fe. Before they left, Frieda acted on a possible problem. She warned Brett not to follow them from her Del Monte cabin to the Kiowa Ranch: "I think it would be a strain if you came to our ranch, both for L[awrence] and me. . . . You will hate me for [saying] this, but I have my life to live and the responsibility [of Lawrence's recovery]." The strongest of the three, Frieda again prevailed.

At the El Paso border came trouble. Health officials created an ugly scene—and, as Lawrence told Amy Lowell, "nearly killed me a second time." He faced "[s]heer degrading insult!" he said later. But Frieda fought them valiantly, and after two days of haggling—and the help of the American embassy—they were allowed to enter the United States.

On 5 April 1925 they at last reached their beloved ranch, where snow glittered in the brilliant sun and where Frieda happily arranged her house once she had fixed a warm log fire. But Lawrence was still so ill that, feeling only half alive, he hardly cared whether it was day or night. He slept for hours at a time. In order to help, Trinidad and his wife, Rufina, came up from the Taos Pueblo; they chopped wood, hauled water, fetched supplies. Frieda cooked. Soon Lawrence was able to take short sunbaths on the front porch he had helped to build and to watch the squirrels and, nearby, the spreading quilt of new anemones. Gradually the long rest and the spring sunshine began to heal him. Writing in pencil, he sketched a biblical play he called *David,* which poignantly voices Samuel's struggle to transfer his allegiance from Saul to David, but also voices Saul's madness and despair. "Brush me again with the wings of life," Saul cries to heaven. With this play, Frieda said, Lawrence "wrote himself back to health."

For Lawrence, recuperating so slowly, a whole era had ended. The great sea voyage begun in 1922 was over. The ranch, so pure in the sunlight, was a destination where every new morning brought with it a gift of spiritual peace and solitude. Frieda was watchful but not intrusive, Brett visited but not every day, Mabel had gone to New York. These were days to savor. "It made him deeply, almost religiously happy to feel better again," Frieda wrote.

Badgered by a bad cough, feeling spent by lingering weakness, Lawrence knew he would have to guard his health—no more chopping or hauling, no more digging or saddling for many weeks. To avoid riding horseback, he retrieved two of his horses (Aaron and Ambrose), bought a buggy from the Hawk family, and employed Trinidad as his driver. In time he could walk short distances and help plant the garden and irrigate the fifteen-acre alfalfa field near the house. In April he had hired a crew headed by Scott Murray to dam the stream running through Gallina canyon and pipe water into an irrigation ditch, thence two miles down to the ranch, "and by tomorrow," Frieda told her mother on the twenty-eighth, "our water will be a cool river along our meadows." Each day Lawrence redirected the irrigation pipe onto a new stretch of parched brown earth. Often he was needed to supervise: the corral needed rebuilding, the barn a new roof, the cabins a coat of protective adobe mud.

Glad to be self-sufficient, the Lawrences decided to make Kiowa a real farm, realizing a dream they had long harbored. On 2 June a black cow named Susan arrived. Almost daily, Lawrence—now stronger—chased her through the woods, scolded her vociferously, and milked her morning and evening; from the milk Frieda made two pounds of butter a week. From eleven hens came several eggs a day; Frieda could bake as often as she liked. Her nephew Friedel Jaffe (b. 1903)—Else's tall, dark, twenty-one-year-old son—came for the summer, stayed in Brett's old cabin, and helped with the chores. Trinidad and Rufina had been sent away, for money was tight after the Lawrences' splurge at the Hotel Imperial in Mexico City. They still lived mostly on what small royalties could now be squeezed out of Thomas Seltzer, whose business had all but collapsed.

Finally, in June, Lawrence felt well enough to look over the typescript of his Mexican novel, which had consumed so much of his spirit; to make revisions; and (now that his agent had found him a new publisher) to accede to Alfred Knopf's wish that he translate his quaint Mexican title "Quetzalcoatl" to *The Plumed Serpent*. Perhaps because Ramón and Cipriano had acted out Lawrence's personal dream of close male bonding in the service of a religious idea, Lawrence told a friend that the novel "lies nearer my heart than any other work of mine." But there were lighter moments, too. Interviewed by journalist Kyle Crichton, Lawrence fondly reminisced about Hueffer, Garnett, Mansfield, and Murry, then served tea, homemade bread, and raspberry preserves made from Brett's hand-picked berries.

Brett records an exchange that shows how, as the summer of 1925 progressed, Lawrence felt stronger and therefore more contentious. Having invited Rachel and Bill Hawk for supper, Lawrence assigned Frieda the job of roasting the chicken. But when he began to carve it and found it still raw, he burst out furiously at Frieda:

"It's no good," you storm. "Unless I do everything myself, it is always wrong, always. I have to do everything myself if it is to be any good."
Frieda shouts back at you: "If you would only keep out of my kitchen and stay where you belong, you wouldn't get in my way and spoil everything." To and fro the battle goes. Rachel is laughing in sheer delight; Bill is grinning from ear to ear; but I switch off my machine.... Then someone has the bright idea to fry the chicken. It is hastily cut up and put in a frying pan. The smell is wonderful. Peace slowly descends on the party, and amicably and with great enjoyment we feast on the chicken, the squabble forgotten.

Quicker than anything else, an audience brought the couple to the edge of an argument. Lawrence's struggle for perfection had its counterpart in Frieda's easy carelessness, which dependably invited his correctives. For years friends

Lawrence near the Del Monte Ranch, Taos, New Mexico

had laughed away their discomfort, but the arguments were a reminder that Lawrence still needed to assert his fraying power in the marriage.

By midsummer the Lawrences had settled on their travel plans. In the autumn they would (though with great sadness) leave the ranch and, from New York, board a ship for England, go on to Germany to see Frieda's mother, then go south for the winter: "I feel very much drawn to the Mediterranean again," Lawrence wrote his sister Emily. His nostalgia for Italy had returned. Uneasy about Brett, who had nowhere to go for the winter and who feared traveling alone, Lawrence suddenly accosted her one evening after she had come for supper: "Look here, Brett. . . . You have plenty of money. . . . Why don't you go to Capri?" So it was settled. Clutching a letter of introduction to Earl and Achsah Brewster, she would go there for the winter to see Italy. Lawrence could perhaps meet her there, by himself. She was full of hope.

## ONE OF THE MYSTERIES OF FATE

Once the Lawrences had lashed some of their belongings to ceiling hooks (to foil the pack rats), carried some to Del Monte for storage, and found homes for their animals, they were ready to depart. Boarding the train for New York on 10 September, they arrived three days later in a city steaming with heat. As usual, Lawrence felt uneasy and dislocated. Nina Witt gave them one floor of her three-story house near Washington Square, from which they could sally forth to see friends and publishers. They met Alfred and Blanche Knopf at their impressive offices on Fifty-seventh Street and heard Alfred scold them for letting a private publisher (the Centaur Press in Philadelphia) issue a volume of Lawrence's essays called *Reflections on the Death of a Porcupine*. They had lunch with the Seltzers, Adele crying piteously to Frieda, "All I want is to pay our debts and die," though Seltzer, bruised by Lawrence's defection to Knopf, soon complained to a friend that "Lawrence is using his wonderful gifts on material that is rotten." One night friends drove them to the Long Island shore, lit a big bonfire, and roasted mutton chops; Lawrence liked having nothing in sight but endless sand and the dark, gleaming foam.

They saw others. On 18 September they had supper with Lawrence's first bibliographer, Edward D. McDonald, who a few months earlier had published a bibliography of Lawrence's writings; his wife, Marguerite, who came along, recorded her impression of the Lawrences dining at the Algonquin Hotel:

Lawrence was neatly, even conventionally dressed in a light tan tweed suit—there was some quality about his light springy way of walking, a kind of alertness that drew all eyes—someone "alive" had come in. The attention Mrs. Lawrence drew was partly because she was a handsome woman, glowing and very sure of herself.

But also her costume, to say the least, was a bit unusual. She wore a dress of un-bleached muslin she had made at the ranch . . . its sleeves trimmed with narrow black fur. Over her shoulders she wore a beautiful embroidered silk shawl Law-rence had bought for her in Ceylon. She had good shapely feet and ankles which showed off to advantage in the black satin slippers which, she said, a friend had just bought for her at A. Miller's. On her head was a broad pink straw hat which threw an attractive rosy shadow on her face.

Making no mention of Lawrence's recent ill health, Marguerite noticed largely the couple's natural distinction: they were neither elegant nor fa-miliar but confident, remarkable, and friendly.

When the Lawrences boarded the SS *Resolute* on 21 September 1925, they faced a dull eight-day voyage in the cramped second class. In London, staying for several days at Garland's, a nice, old-fashioned hotel, they vis-ited more friends and publishers. While Frieda saw her children, Lawrence spent a day with Catherine Carswell in a damp, ugly cottage in Bucking-hamshire; they had lunch with Compton and Faith Mackenzie, spent a day in Bridgefoot with Martin Secker, who supplied Lawrence with galleys of *The Plumed Serpent* (he corrected them at once), then went north to the Midlands to visit his sisters, Emily King and Ada Clarke, both of whom had prospered—Sam King working as a shopkeeper, Eddie Clarke as a tai-lor. Although Lawrence enjoyed the motor excursions around his native Derbyshire, keenly observing all that had changed, he found the rain so de-pressing, the dark skies so gloomy, and England so lifeless that he was grateful to leave. In London again, Lawrence told Catherine that the hor-rors he recalled of his Midlands childhood had nearly engulfed him; he had a sad lunch with his old friend Cynthia Asquith and her husband, Herbert, but when Frieda—in a hurry—went ahead to Germany, Lawrence was alone.

Without the burden of negotiating another triangle, he was able at last to meet Middleton Murry by himself. But he reported sadly to Brett that there was now "nothing between us." It was the same conundrum as be-fore: Murry emotionally unavailable for anything but a meager bond, Lawrence cruelly disappointed by the lack of a deeper commitment. The only way they could get close was to argue about Murry's book on Jesus, which Lawrence disliked. Affection was disguised in disagreement. As Murry's biographer, F. A. Lea, says, "Of that intuitive knowledge of what others are thinking and feeling . . . [Murry] exhibited hardly a trace." He was Lawrence's opposite.

Lawrence followed Frieda straight to Baden-Baden, via Ostend and Strasbourg. Settling with her into the inexpensive Hotel Eden, they found Frieda's mother, now seventy-four, noticeably older and slower but still very lively. Although they played whist and laughed with gracious amuse-ment at the faded German nobility, Lawrence spent much time alone, tramping through the hills, absorbing the fragrant autumn landscape, viewing old castles, and, in the distance, glimpsing the waters of the Rhine.

Their visit refreshed them both. But for the winter months they had planned all along to go to Italy and the Mediterranean—just *where* they did not yet know. Secker's charming wife, Rina, suggested they go to Spotorno, a small, sunny, coastal village on the Italian Riviera, where her parents lived. It sounded ideal. They arrived on 15 November. After a few days at the Hotel Ligure, they found, high above the village, the four-decker Villa Bernarda, with lots of rooms and a balcony overlooking the Mediterranean, and felt almost as if they were back at Fontana Vecchia in 1920. But in truth, guided by one of the mysteries of fate, they found much more than they expected. They found a handsome Italian, age thirty-three, married, with two young children—a lieutenant in the Italian Bersaglieri who was himself ripe for change. His name was Angelo Ravagli. He would transform their lives.

# 19

# What Lawrence Discovered

## 1926–27

For Lawrence, returning to Italy was like returning home—not to the English Midlands, where the dismal grayness and the pinched lives depressed him, but to the Italy he had discovered in 1912, when he and Frieda had walked over the Alps to the Lago di Garda and started a new life together. In Italy he had defined himself as a professional writer. Italy had come to mean freedom, spontaneity, uninhibited people. Now, in sleepy Spotorno, the sunny hills and sparkling Mediterranean still suited his temperament and made him feel healthier and happier than he had felt for months. His bronchial congestion seemed less severe, and (he said) the Mediterranean sun seemed like "the love of God." That is a jarring image of reconciliation for a feisty man who in September 1925 had turned a mere forty. He seldom complained—except about Jack Murry, that "incorrigible worm" whose perverse charm still taunted him.

Lawrence and Frieda let the lazy winter days slip by. On the sunny balcony at the Villa Bernarda, they sat out and saw the village roofs straggle in steps down three hundred feet to the water's edge; took splendid walks through the stony, untamed hills behind the villa; and often entertained Martin and Rina Secker, who had come from England to Spotorno for a month's holiday. As Lawrence watched the sea glitter brightly, washing in and out of its bays, he said to Edward McDonald: "I feel at home beside [the water]." But lying in the folds of Italy's warm sunshine and soft air was a contrary force—another worm, like Murry, curled beneath the flower petals, turning and turning till Frieda saw it, all feathered and fine—the plumed serpent coming to life in sunny Spotorno.

Outgoing and full of charm, Angelo Ravagli (1891–1976) had been married for six years to Serafina Astengo. She was older than he and taught Italian literature and history at a high school in Savona. Since 1915 he had served in the Bersaglieri, an infantry regiment of the Italian army. In Spotorno, ten miles south, he helped his wife manage the Villa Bernarda, which she had inherited from her uncle. It was Angelo Ravagli who showed the Lawrences the Bernarda; it was he who took their payment of twenty-five pounds for a five-month lease; it was he who strutted by in his dress uniform for Frieda to admire: "I am thrilled by his cockfeathers," Frieda chortled to Brett on 8 December, then confided that "he is almost as nice as the feathers!" Short and stocky, the son of poor Italian peasants, he had dark hair, good features, and an open smile; like Frieda's father, he had joined the army to find a career. His son Stefano remembered that "he was conscious of being attractive, and he loved women."

Ravagli found his way to the Lawrences on most weekends. On one visit he cleaned the soot from the stovepipe so they could enjoy a warm fire in the kitchen stove (it was their only heat). Often he found Lawrence using indelible inks to paint decorative designs on silk handkerchiefs, one of which Lawrence presented to Serafina, whom he liked. On Sundays, trying hard to learn English, Ravagli would bring along his lesson book so that Lawrence could help him with his pronunciation. The fact that they did not get far suggests their uneasiness around each other. In a letter of 1957 Ravagli was quick to differentiate himself from Lawrence who—he remembered—was always busy "doing housework" at the Bernarda. Toward Frieda, though, Ravagli displayed a vigorous virility.

In truth, the past was being reborn. Piece by piece, figure for figure, the tableau of March 1912 was repeating itself—the busy, successful writer-professor; the bored housewife with children close by (in December, Frieda's daughter Barbara was staying in nearby Alassio); a vibrant younger male, intriguingly foreign to the bored housewife. One Sunday the vibrant male enters her home and makes an unforgettable impression. He is active, practical, vigorous, and very physical—sailing paper boats in a small brook or skillfully cleaning the stovepipe. The busy writer-professor, impotent to abort the relationship, seems not to notice as the younger male gauges his future. As sure as Lawrence had been ready to leave England in March 1912, so was Ravagli ready to leave Italy with a charming woman. But there was a difference: Frieda was reluctant to consider the same step again. She remembered what it had cost.

The Lawrences had not lived long in Italy before Lawrence captured, for Frieda's mother, a typical moment of their day. In his stylishly irritated way, he enlivens Frieda as well as old Giovanni, the caretaker who lived on the Bernarda's bottom floor and ran errands: "Now it's evening: we're sitting in the kitchen, high up under the roof; the evening star is white over the hills opposite, below lie the lights of the village like mandarin oranges, small and bright. Frieda has gobbled up her whipped cream from Savona at one gulp, now she complains that she hasn't kept it to enjoy with coffee and cake after the meal. She is sitting by the stove reading. The soup is cooking. In a moment we'll call downstairs, into the depths: Come on Giovanni! Food's ready. Then the old man runs upstairs like a happy dog, nose in the air, smelling, sniffing." Lawrence's kindness to the old peasant is matched by his petulance toward Frieda, whom he playfully chides for her great appetite. Her appetite may have created other complications, too, for Lawrence's capacity for sexual performance had decreased markedly after his illness in Oaxaca. According to Richard Aldington, Frieda complained frequently after 1925 that Lawrence "had become impotent." The evidence of Lawrence's fiction—the flagging interest in sexual acts in *The Woman Who Rode Away, St. Mawr,* and *Quetzalcoatl*—confirms this date for the probable onset of Lawrence's impotence. It is difficult to imagine the Lawrences' dialogue on this painful topic, but for Frieda it was a new concern, one full of confused possibility, especially when Ravagli's attentions became more ardent.

Meanwhile, Barbara Weekley, having also cast England behind her, came to Italy—partly to paint new subjects and partly to see her mother and Lawrence, both of whom came to her pension in Alassio. "Pa prefers she shouldn't house here," Lawrence laughed to Brett, who—staying with the Brewsters in Capri—now received his most intimate letters. When Barby visited Spotorno, the three of them painted together, the Lawrences eager to hear Barby's gossip about her father, her aunt, and her grandmother, whom she once described as a "blind old woman, full of hate," who nurtured "the hostility we children had shown to our mother." Barby's sister, Elsa, once said to her, "You and Lawrence encourage each other to be spiteful about everyone."

Before long, Lawrence had turned her spiteful gossip into a lengthy story called *The Virgin and the Gipsy,* which he finished in January 1926. He took Frieda's vague remark about her two daughters—"All I want of them is to learn to get something out of life"—and used it to generate an amusing story of a well-protected daughter named Yvette, who, in order to experience *life,* meets a sophisticated couple named the Eastwoods (a lightly satirized version of Lawrence and Frieda), and—through them—a gypsy named Joe Boswell. Fashioned of "English" materials, this cluster of ingenue, sophisticates, and an outsider is a rough-draft version of *Lady Chatterley's Lover,* which Lawrence would start in October. Biographically, the most interesting part of Lawrence's story is not the meeting of

Yvette and Joe, or the flood that joins them briefly; it is Barbara's portrait, through Lawrence's merciless lens, of her father (as the rector), her aunt Maude (as Cissie), and her grandmother (as Granny Saywell). The rector's feeble rectitude—"he was fanatically afraid of the unconventional"—and Granny's devious manipulation of others reveal Lawrence's animus toward the family from whom Barbara (and Frieda) had escaped. The liveliest figure is Granny: "Under her old-fashioned lace cap, under her silver hair, under the black silk of her stout, forward-bulging body, this old woman had a cunning heart, seeking forever her own female power." Frieda, who liked the title "Granny on the Throne," must have relished Lawrence's acidly flippant portraits. But the story, because it so closely divulged Barbara's confidences, was not published until after Lawrence died.

## TWO WOMEN CLASH

Once in Spotorno, Frieda made plans of her own. She invited both her daughters, now tall, blossoming girls of twenty-one and twenty-three, to stay with her; and, although the evidence is slim, she did not, in the early months of 1926, discourage Ravagli's flattering attentions. As planned, Barbara and Elsa came in February with an older woman, Eileen Seaman, who in 1929 became Elsa's mother-in-law. Surprisingly, all three went to the tiny Hotel Ligure nearby, for Lawrence had already invited his favorite sister, Ada, and her friend Lizzie Booth. Since he had issued his invitation first, he refused to put his family into a hotel. Tensions mounted; Lawrence got the flu—and a "bronchial hemorrhage like [that] at the ranch, only worse," he told Brett; Frieda grew ever more upset; and a cold rain trapped them inside the dismal cage of the Bernarda.

Forced to bed for a week, Lawrence could not control the conflict that erupted between Frieda and Ada over who was mistress of the kitchen—and who was nurse to Lawrence. (The eruption resembled one in 1918, at Mountain Cottage, when Lawrence complained bitterly of his wife's tender mercies.) When Frieda could stand no more of Ada—who shrieked at her one morning, "I hate you from the bottom of my heart," and locked Lawrence's bedroom door against her—Frieda jumped ship. She joined her two daughters at the Ligure and said finally, "Now I don't care." She had endured enough. She refused life at the edge of marital chaos.

A week later Lawrence, with Ada and Lizzie in tow, fled to Monte Carlo. Angry at Frieda's obstinate behavior, Lawrence did not yet recognize the extent to which her feelings, freshly awakened by Ravagli, may have fired her need for independence. In early March, for instance, she wrote vehemently to Koteliansky about Christ: "Had he said to me: 'Woman, what have I got to do with thee,' I would have boxed his ears and said: 'That's what you have to do with me!'" She understood her own tempestuous nature, which could explode like a grenade. Lawrence, bruised and "muddled up" and still shaken by flu, felt compelled to "go away by myself for a bit, or I shall give up the ghost," he protested to William Hawk, his Taos neighbor.

But go *where*? He found Monte Carlo boring and saw no easy exit from his difficulties; he needed uncritical friendship, understanding, sympathy. After he accompanied Ada and Lizzie along the Grande Corniche to Nice—on 25 February—and after the women caught the train home, Lawrence took a single room at the Hotel Brice and wrote sadly to Ada: "I sat on the beach all the afternoon—still and sunny—then had a cup of tea. It *does* feel a bit lonely now, when I can't walk round and find you in your room. And I was awfully sorry we had all this upset: I was so looking forward to your coming and having a good time." The "upset" soon found its way into his creative work.

That very day, from Nice, Lawrence sent his London agent a short story he had just written. Called "The Rocking Horse Winner," it is one of his most poignant. Although it reflects his great anxiety, the story also gauges the way Ada stirred up memories of home and the lengths to which he would go, in childhood, to please his mother. He had recently recalled how his mother would manipulate him by saying, "You used to be such a dear good boy, Bertie."

The story's protagonist, a young boy named Paul, is—like Dickens's orphans—spiritually alone. To fill this void, Paul tries desperately to earn his mother's love, which, he understands, means *earning money*. But Paul, like Lawrence, is a special boy, endowed with extraordinary powers. As Lawrence exhibited uncanny insight into people, Paul exhibits uncanny perception—in this case, knowing which horse will win the Lincoln or the Leger, well-known races. In private, he rides his rocking horse until, with a sudden orgasm of knowledge, he *knows* the winner and can, in turn, offer his mother the money she covets. Alas, she is insatiable. One night, riding harder than before, he utters the name of the Derby's winner—*Malabar* (roughly, bad place)—then slips into a coma: "He neither slept nor regained consciousness, and his eyes were like blue stones. His mother sat, feeling her heart had gone, turned actually into a stone." The story, though clearly a fable about materialism, is told without a trace of Dickens's sentimentality for victimized children. The unfeeling mother had got her money at the price of her son. The message of Lawrence's fable is clear: cold-hearted women prey upon those they pretend to love. The chiseled portrait of the cold-hearted wife and mother who disregards her unlucky husband and drives her innocent son to madness has deep biographical significance. Despite his best efforts, Lawrence could not provide what his wife/mother Frieda wanted. Ironically, the story earned him an impressive sixty-five pounds—enough to rent the Bernarda for a whole year.

While Lawrence waited in Nice for some sign of where he should go, no doubt with tender thoughts toward warm-hearted women, he also waited for his anger at Frieda to subside. He considered going to Florence or to Spain—alone. But suddenly, on 26 February, he sent Brett a telegram—*Vengo a Capri*—to say he was coming. He longed for the unconditional support of friends. When his cable arrived, Brett was thrilled. He was coming without Frieda. She could spend endless hours alone with him—exploring the caves and outbreaks of rock, picnicking, or drinking cold beer at the end of a hike. In Capri Lawrence went first to the Brewsters at Quattro Venti—their grand white villa—arriving shortly before they sailed to India; with Brett he visited old friends like Faith Mackenzie and J. E. Brooks. At Quattro Venti, Brett recorded seeing Lawrence with a letter from Frieda sticking out of his pocket. It had upset him. The letter may have exalted Ravagli; it may have barred Ada from a return visit; it may have shown again women's obsession to do what Lawrence most decried—"to have their own way." Whatever it contained, the phrasing in Brett's memoir soon becomes peculiar and suggestive—Lawrence (in the guise of charades) turning into "the responsive male" and Brett later seeing him "looking at me, looking at me," as if entranced. A sexual undercurrent festered. Yet Lawrence, she says, acknowledged the excruciating pain of his existence—he found climbing steps exhausting, was weary of marital friction, and felt far from rich. He welcomed escape.

About 10 March he accompanied Brett to Ravello, a rocky, seaside perch east of Capri, where they joined two refined English painters, Millicent Beveridge and Mabel Harrison, for some pleasant days together. Lawrence and Brett took adjoining rooms in the Hotel Palumbo annex. He had not sent Frieda his address until the first of March. His feelings were like the weather he described—"still uncertain . . . stormy, then too hot, then too cold."

Before long, something unexpected happened. Brett's account, published in 1933 but expanded in 1974, is the fullest; Lawrence's, more perplexing, requires decoding. In 1974 Brett bared the details of a failed sexual experiment that has disturbed many readers:

Lawrence suddenly walked into my room in his dressing gown. "I do not believe in a relationship unless there is a physical relationship as well," he said. I was frightened as well as excited. He got into my bed, turned, and kissed me. I can still feel the softness of his beard, still feel the tension, still feel the overwhelming desire to be adequate. I was passionately eager to be successful, but I had no idea what to do. Nothing happened. Suddenly Lawrence got up. "It's no good," he said, and stalked out of the room. I was devastated, helpless, bewildered.

All the next day Lawrence was a bit glum. . . . That night, he walked into my room and said, "Let's try it again." So again he got into my bed, and there we lay. I felt desperate. All the love I had for him, all the closeness to him spiritually, the passionate desire to give what I felt I should be giving, was frustrated by fear and not knowing what to do. I tried to be loving and warm and female. He was, I think, struggling to be successfully male. It was hopeless, a hopeless horrible failure

Despite the passage's ring of authenticity (the two friends had tried precisely what Frieda had urged in Oaxaca), biographer Jeffrey Meyers disbelieves Brett's account, calling it a compensatory fantasy: "Lawrence's behavior in Brett's bizarre anecdote is completely out of character. He was never promiscuous or unfaithful to Frieda after their marriage. He was not at all attracted to Brett. . . . He would not, in any case, have wanted to reveal the sexual difficulties that had developed as a consequence of his disease. . . . Three of Brett's close friends—Lady Juliette Huxley, Julian Morrell Vinogradoff and Harwood Brewster—have confirmed in recent interviews that Brett's late story was certainly a fantasy." The problem is that Meyers, who had not read Rosalind Baynes's memoir about her affair with Lawrence in 1920, cannot relinquish his belief that Lawrence held rigidly to his marriage vows, and he interviewed women who shared his conception. Lawrence's letters therefore become the key documents. Can they yield their secret?

The next day, when Brett found Lawrence packing in great distress, she offered to leave. She pretended she needed to visit Naples to confirm her status as an immigrant from Italy to the United States. After she departed, Lawrence wrote her frequently—evidence that their friendship really was indestructible. The italics below interpret what we believe Lawrence's letters imply. The first, of 18 March, is cautious, calming, and philosophical; for Lawrence didn't know what Brett might think or do:

> Glad you got safely back [*to Capri*]. I'm sure it's better for you there, where you have a few friends, than mooning [*about what happened*] in an unknown place.
> One has just to forget [*the failed experiment*], and to accept what is good [*— our enduring friendship*]. We can't help being more or less damaged [*by my advancing impotence, by your inability to arouse me sexually*]. What we have to do is to stick to the good part of ourselves, and of each other, and continue an understanding on that. I don't see why we shouldn't be *better* friends, instead of worse.

Tormented by her feelings, Brett wrote Lawrence in mid-March, probably pleading that she wanted to be near him, felt lonely without him—and begged to join him. He responded with the ultimate insult: "Don't be Murryish, pitying yourself and caving in. It's despicable. . . . Rouse up and make a decent thing of your days, no matter what's happened [*between us*]. I do loathe cowardice, and sloppy emotion." He surely believed that this letter—urging dignity and discipline—would cool her ardor. He hated "scenes." He had also had time to consider Frieda's outstretched olive branch.

After he returned to Spotorno on Easter Sunday (3 April), arriving like the Easter Lamb into a fold of friendliness, he wrote again to Brett: "And now, I think we should find Frieda much more tolerant [*of our relationship*]." This is a crucial sentence. We think it means that Lawrence had intuited her attraction to Ravagli and, by his pregnant silence, given her permission to conduct a discreet affair, even though—said Barbara Weekley—he thought Ravagli "just a cheap nothing." In return, Frieda may have offered Lawrence permission to see Brett on his own terms, for Frieda soon wrote to Brett: "And if you are fond of Lawrence why the dickens should I mind? I dont a bit!" The evidence that an emotional realignment had taken place lies in the double triangles that form the subject of Lawrence's major novel, *Lady Chatterley's Lover,* which he would start as soon as he and Frieda had resettled, well away from Spotorno. One additional piece of evidence is that the name *Ravagli* (pronounced Ra-VAL-le)—*read backwards as el-lav-ar*—easily converts to *Oliver,* the first name of Lady Chatterley's seducer. Such coding typifies Lawrence's complex art.

## SETTLING DOWN

After all the anxieties both had endured, it is no surprise that Lawrence and Frieda were undecided where to go when their lease on the Bernarda expired. No doubt frank discussions about their marriage—and the revised expectations that each might make of the other—eventually led to some kind of truce and perhaps new freedoms for both, for on 23 April Lawrence confided to Brett—in code—that he now felt "absolutely numb to the soul, what with cold rain *and the rest of things."* Two days later he mused to Rachel Hawk, "It is always better to give way, rather than break something [like marriage] which shouldn't be broken." Although Frieda had wanted to take her daughters to Germany, she may have decided that Lawrence was more important. He wanted a base in Florence so that he could visit the Etruscan tombs and artifacts at Cortona, Volterra, and Tarquinia for a book he envisioned on this pre-Roman culture whose remains intrigued him. Frieda, knowing that a new book was vital to their income, supported him. Warily, they were coming together again.

Finally, Lawrence, Frieda, and her daughters went from Spotorno to Florence, then into the Pensione Lucchesi, an "old-maidish place" costing only three pounds a week, where Lawrence could again see friends like Reggie Turner and Nellie Morrison, whom he had liked in 1920, when he had lived briefly in Florence. Through Turner he also met again the bookseller Giuseppe Orioli (1884–1942), called Pino, an avid homosexual who would soon become Lawrence's ally in a grand publishing venture.

The moment Elsa and Barbara left for England—on 28 April—the Lawrences rushed to find a nearby villa. They had heard about a place they might rent, located seven miles beyond Florence. On 29 April 1926 they took the half-hour tram from the central Duomo all the way to Vingone (the terminus), then walked twenty-five minutes up the hill to a big, square, white house. It was, Frieda said, "so perfectly placed" that she yearned for it. Lawrence glowed with excitement: "We both like the spot *immensely*." For twenty-five pounds they took the Villa Mirenda for a whole year—as a *pied à terre*—and kept it for almost two. It was the queen of their homes. Even today it has hardly changed.

Austere but handsomely situated in the tiny village of San Polo Mosciano, the Mirenda had two ideal qualities: it was in the country, away from foreigners; and it was near a beautiful city—a cradle of European culture. From a cavalry captain named Raul Mirenda, the Lawrences rented just the top floor. It had six large (if bare) rooms, brick floors, high ceilings, two gardens, pine woods behind, and excellent views of the Arno valley below, with peaceful slopes of grapevines and olive trees swaying gracefully in the sun. "I am really very fond of Italy," Lawrence told Rachel Hawk in May; "the flow of life seems rich and easy." In all its forms, he believed, the sheer physical flow healed and sustained life, and it thrived best in Italy.

A restrained joy sprang from their decision to relocate. The Lawrences settled into the Mirenda, visiting Florence once or twice a week, buying pots and pans for the kitchen (and brackets to hang them), painting the chairs and shutters green, carpeting the big sitting room, and whitewashing the walls. Frieda rented a piano and sang German songs. Together she and Lawrence picnicked by the stream and, indoors, embroidered a sketch of a peacock, a kid, and a deer. When they walked in the soft pine woods, they could hear the nightingales trilling and the peasants singing as they worked.

Relieved to be alone with Lawrence after months of stress, Frieda reveled in the life around her, especially the flowers that, even now, linked their sensibilities: "The spring that first year was a revelation in flowers . . . and as usual in our walks we took joyful possession of the unspoiled, almost medieval country around us. By the stream in the valley were tufts of enormous primroses, where the willow trees had been blood red through the winter. On the edge of the umbrella-pine woods, in the fields, were red and purple big anemones, strange, narrow-pointed, red and yellow wild tulips, bee orchids and purple orchids." Frieda shared Lawrence's assumptions about nature and its relation to the world, her catalog of flowers like a lyric. Especially in her autobiography, *Not I, But the Wind*, her memory works in flashes, like photographs in an album, all neatly separated. And so, in a neat compartment, she may have kept her attachment to Ravagli. Janet Byrne says that Frieda sometimes "lied freely" when she later constructed a portrait of her marriage to Lawrence, but it seems rather as if Frieda had taught herself early to compartmentalize her experience—and

The Villa Mirenda, near Florence, where *Lady Chatterley's Lover* was written (Photograph by Michael Squires)

then vividly recalled those parts that were least painful. Frieda naturally dwelt on happy times. "I am so rich in caring for people," she told Brett.

Remembering the heat of Italian summers, Lawrence decided to defer his research trips for the Etruscans book. He and Frieda had agreed to go to Germany to celebrate her mother's seventy-fifth birthday on 14 July, then to stop in England for the hot month of August. Instead of writing, he took up Frieda's German translation of his play *David*—on which she had labored at the Bernarda—and spent many days typing and correcting it: "such a sweat, typing German and making revisions," he told his sister Emily on 14 June.

All this time, while he stored up impressions from his own recent experience, another novel was teasing his imagination. It was stirred by two events. First, his sisters had warned him of an impending coal strike in Britain, designed to block proposals for cutting wages and restoring a forty-eight-hour workweek. In fact, the strike was called on 30 April 1926, followed by a general strike on 4 May. Lawrence may have seen the *Times* report on 1 May: "The coal crisis looks like a deadlock. Weeks of negotiations on hours and wages are heading to no solution." King George proclaimed a state of national emergency, and Lloyd George feared that Britain had come "to the verge of disaster." Beset with overproduction, the coal industry—experts thought—needed to be reorganized to regulate its output. Although the general strike ended on 12 May, the miners and mine owners remained deadlocked for another six months. Lawrence first mentioned the strike on 1 May. Fearing a class war, he told Ada that "altogether it feels like the end of the world." A few months later, when he visited the Midlands, he saw "families living on bread and margarine and potatoes—nothing more."

A second event, oddly related to the strike, was a visit that Lawrence and Frieda made on 2 June to see the Sitwells—he a baronet since 1862 (and hence called Sir George, she Lady Sitwell). From time to time the Sitwells lived at Montegufoni, their thirteenth-century castle outside Florence, which Sir George had bought in 1909. It had a hundred rooms. Although Frieda never mentioned the Sitwells, Lawrence frequently did and judged them "such an odd couple." He jeered at Sir George's conceit but agreed to visit the couple at Renishaw, their Midlands estate, in September, when the grown Sitwell children—Edith, Osbert, and Sacheverel—would be at home: "so we might run over," he alerted Ada in June. But in September, when they tried to do so, the Sitwells were not at home. Lawrence could only stare at the stark, imposing front of the mansion and imagine the life inside.

Coming slowly into focus were several of Lawrence's major concerns—the unsettling themes of infidelity and impotence, the miners' hostility to their masters, and a conceited upper-class family. Although these potent raw materials would eventually fire his imagination, he faced a new problem: how to weave them into a novel when he didn't feel like working. A languor—not seen before—seeps through his letters: a mix of irritation, ennui, and disgust. "Secker and Knopf want me to write another novel, but I'm not going to lay myself waste again in such a hurry. Let the public read the old novels," he snapped when he wrote to Brett, who in June had returned to the Kiowa Ranch. Even as Lawrence worried that sustained work had wasted his strength, he was unusually contented at the Mirenda, the summer drowse stilling his energy and ambition. The persistent purr of the cicadas dulled his impulse to write for money.

Two weeks in Germany and eight in England marked only a long pause in Lawrence's contemplation of his novel. While Frieda visited her children in London—seeing them often—Lawrence went alone first to Scotland, to visit Millicent Beveridge, then to see his two sisters at a seaside resort in Lincolnshire, where strike talk would have been on all their lips; as soon as his sisters had gone, Frieda arrived for two weeks at a bungalow he had rented near Mablethorpe. She swam in the surf while he, fearing a chill to his so-called bronchials, watched. This was the coast he had known as a boy, and he found it not distasteful but "bracing and tonicky," while to his surprise he found himself now drawn to "the common people"—to their strength and modest purity. His stance toward England was softening. "For the first time for years," he told Koteliansky on 2 September, "I am rather glad to be at home in England."

Their sojourn past, the Lawrences reached the Mirenda on 4 October, in hot weather, just in time for *vendemmia*, the immemorial grape harvest. The peasants, driving a team of white oxen, hauled masses of sweet grapes into the basement of the Mirenda, moving through the landscape like figures in a myth. Lawrence's visit to England, just concluded, had given him first-hand evidence of the miners' plight, shown him the gulf between workers and owners, and exposed him to his sisters' lamentation over losses in their retail shops. Soon after he settled in, two sets of visitors arrived, both of them highly stimulating in their discipline and intelligence. Richard Aldington and Arabella Yorke arrived first. They had known the Lawrences since 1914. They lived together because Richard's wife, H.D., had refused him a divorce; a busy critic, Richard would soon begin his splendid wartime novel, *Death of a Hero*. Although he found Lawrence sharp tongued and brutally frank, he admired his friend's energy, swift intuition, and gift for mimicry. Soon, Aldous and Maria Huxley arrived in their new six-cylinder Itala, which could bolt ahead like a demon; Aldous, like Richard, was hard at work on an ambitious novel called *Point Counter Point*—using Lawrence and Frieda as material. After they left, Lawrence walked alone in the soft hills, admired the fragrant pines and pink cyclamens, and let the days drift by in a haze of seeming inertia.

But his mind was bristling with ideas, and he was revising his notions of class and marriage. Living a few hundred yards from the Mirenda, his eccentric British neighbor, Arthur Wilkinson (1881–1957), a benevolent expatriate, a radical socialist who had come to Florence with his family, recorded a Sunday afternoon tea—on 24 October 1926—when the Lawrences were their guests. His account reveals the kind of tense conflict that now energized Lawrence's emotions: "The Lawrences came to tea by appointment, and we had a nice spread and made him specially comfy in 'his' green chair and the electric fire, and we gave her 'her' box of cigarettes. The talk soon got on to Revolution and stayed there and was really impassioned. We all generalised a bit—but he did so tremendously and swears by his class, and death and damnation to the other class. He's done with them. 'They're hard—cruel—cruel' (*crescendo*). He was so rude and cross to her, and she retaliated with spirit—'Why didn't you marry one of your own class then?' she said. 'You'd have been bored stiff.' Says he, very sad and vinegary, 'I may have my regrets.' And she retorted, 'Well, you can be off, you can go now if you like.'" Lawrence's irritation and regret are matched by Frieda's quick defense. *Would* he have been "bored stiff" with a woman of his own class? A day earlier, he had decided to find out.

About 23 October he took his notebook, fountain pen, and a cushion and walked into the pine woods behind the Mirenda, lured by the pure sun and the cool breeze and the perfect peace. There he began *Lady Chatterley's Lover*. It would become his most famous novel.

Yet he started it as a mere sketch; its subject had not yet fully gripped him, its shape lay dormant. "I am working at a story," he told Martin Secker on 27 October, but shrank from a long effort. Still, he was intrigued by the coal strike: "I am always thinking about the strike," he told Ada a day later. As he began writing, Lawrence had "come back home," back to Nottinghamshire and Derbyshire, relocating Renishaw just outside Eastwood—precisely where he had located Shortlands in *Women in Love*—and drawing externally on the Sitwells. As a family, they interested him only as a metaphor of class snobbery. He took the family structure, purged all of its members but Sir Clifford and his Aunt Eva (an alcoholic like Lady Sitwell), and put Clifford and his attractive wife, Connie, into a large, brooding estate renamed Wragby, where two things link them to the Sitwells at Renishaw: their isolation from the common people and their close proximity to the coal mines.

Lawrence's brooding thoughts began to shape themselves into characters from opposed classes. Connie Chatterley, molded by the aesthetic of the upper-middle class, has traveled, knows literature and art, values civility; but she has the shallow self-assertion that Lawrence thought the privileged classes cultivated. (Clifford, paralyzed by a war injury, is consumed by self-pity.) Oliver Parkin, proud of being a miner's son, at once reveals the assumptions of his own class—he talks only in dialect, defines himself as a laborer, and scorns the upper classes—but he shows the tenderness and loyalty that Lawrence thought the privileged classes had lost. As Connie and Parkin meet at his well-hidden hut in the woods and discover the intense splendor of the sexual act, both must alter their assumptions about class. Like Kate when she finds herself drawn to Cipriano, Connie and Parkin must measure their tolerance for a person so unlike themselves. For both, what is tacitly forbidden is full of attraction.

To enrich this material with personal meaning, Lawrence does a bold thing: he sees himself as Clifford, a writer and a cripple who clings to his wife for support, and he sees Frieda as Connie, needing a sexual fulfillment her husband can no longer provide. Yet Lawrence sought a strategy to hide this autobiographical layer, wrapping it in layers of his *literary* past. For instance, the gamekeeper Parkin is indebted to figures that Lawrence had earlier created—to the rough vitality of Arthur Pilbeam, the manly gamekeeper in "The Shades of Spring"; to the physical beauty of Ramón; and to the secure manliness of the gypsy, Joe Boswell. The point is not that Lawrence, uninspired, limply reworked earlier materials—as some readers have thought—but that he absorbed such a range of autobiographical influences that every character is (in odd ways) a composite. Every character is cleverly disguised. Unlike Lawrence, for example, Clifford has money and pedigree (he is a baronet like Sir George); unlike Frieda, Connie, though trapped in a sexless marriage, is soft and demure, patient and elegant, her interior life resembling that of Rosalind Baynes, whose father, like Connie's, was a Royal Academician. Similarly Mrs. Bolton, that fine purveyor of Tevershall gossip, draws on the garrulous William Hopkin, Lawrence's longtime Eastwood friend; the change in gender provides the perfect cover.

Writing almost every day in November 1926, often outdoors, Lawrence used the secluded pine woods behind the Mirenda as a metaphor for Connie's forays into the woods of Clifford's estate, where she and Parkin can privately have sex and even fall in love but—like Frieda and Ravagli—cannot fathom a way to be together while Clifford lives. Lawrence aggressively confronted his own worst fears. He understood Frieda's earthy needs, yet he allowed in his fiction only an *affair* between a titled woman and a rather ordinary man who, like Ravagli, had been in the army. Frieda must have been stunned when she read the story in manuscript.

When he finished the novel's first draft, on 26 November, he rested and, in the quiet autumn days, turned for relief to painting. He had always liked copying works of art and had long amused himself by helping Brett with her paintings or advising Barbara Weekley on hers. When the Huxleys had come for lunch on 28 October, they had generously brought along some spare canvases and left them. Aldous had come to see Lawrence in London in August, and when both realized they were wintering in Italy—both

Maria and Aldous Huxley, c. 1928 (Courtesy of the Huxley Estate)

loved bright sunshine—they arranged to meet in Florence. Aldous had known Maria since 1916, when Ottoline Morrell had employed her to tutor her daughter Julian; and in 1919, she and Aldous had married and, on the lavish money he earned from his writing—for his stories, as much as a thousand dollars each—they had traveled extensively. Aldous, renowned

325

as an intellectual, was tall and soft spoken; Maria, small and wiry, was "like Ottoline's Cinderella daughter," Lawrence said; their son, Matthew, age six, had stayed in Cortina with a governess.

After the Huxleys left the Mirenda, Lawrence began painting in the cozy sitting room he and Frieda had furnished. One of his first paintings, *Boccaccio Story,* surprised those who viewed it. As Frieda wrote to Edward McDonald about 6 December: "We live quietly here in our cinquecento villa, have made such a beautiful room covering old chairs ourselves, painting everything—Lawrence has painted a picture a Bocaccio story of the gardener and the nuns!! O shades of Queen Victoria! Then he has written a short novel also very reprehensible!" The painting she cites shows three nuns coming upon a gardener who, having fallen asleep in the nude, lies fully exposed. Capturing the shock that male sexuality induces, the painting is a visual equivalent to the novel Lawrence had just finished, for when Connie comes upon the keeper's body as he washes outside his cottage, she is equally shocked: "The white torso of the man had seemed so beautiful to her, splitting the gloom . . . like a revelation." Frieda's choice of the word *reprehensible* to describe the new novel is a surprise, since the novel develops only four explicit sexual encounters. Yet the sexual act has immense restorative power—as if Lawrence, unable to satisfy Frieda in life, will do so in fiction.

## Bottomless Pools

At once Lawrence saw the inadequacy of the first version—its rushed meeting of the unfulfilled lady and the brusque keeper given no context, its episodic plot driven by caprice rather than vision. Bravely, on 1 December, he began the second version, writing now in a tiny, patient, perfect script, page after page, the novel bubbling slowly out of him—he told Brett on the nineteenth—swimming up from the "bottomless pools" of his imagination, eloquent and articulate. By reconsidering the rise of illicit love, he found a way to impose a structure on the steady flow of the novel.

A series of additions, carefully placed, would make Connie's plight a reflection of England's poisonous attitudes. Inspired, Lawrence began to add material to justify Connie's affair. He introduced her burly father, Sir Malcolm, who warns her that she risks becoming paralyzed by her wifely duty to Clifford, and that her life with her husband might become "dreary, dismal, priggish." He introduced five visitors to Wragby—intellectuals who, like Aldous and Maria Huxley, arrive near Christmas, celebrate the life of the mind, and talk abstractly about the resurrection of the body, making Connie pray that *her* body "should not go dead." And he introduced the narrator's long, intense exposé of the faults of modern life—sex, power, gossip, and class hatred—inducing the reader to fear their effects on a young woman voluntarily imprisoned in her marriage.

Beyond these carefully calculated additions to the novel, Lawrence began to reinvent the gamekeeper. He quickly discarded the simple, working-class Parkin and began instead to make him a more complex figure capable of offering Connie more than a freshly awakened sexual body. When Connie stumbles upon the white torso of the man splitting the forest gloom, Lawrence now quadruples the length of his earlier scene and allows Connie a realization that had earlier been hidden. Now she discovers a religious awe in the man's flesh, "a pure loveliness, that was alive, and that had touched the quick in her. It was as if she had touched God, and been restored to life." To justify this profound impact, deeper now than a revelation, Lawrence must rebuild the gamekeeper's character so that beneath his commonness lie depths to be discovered.

Two examples capture Lawrence at work, enhancing Parkin's character. Whereas Parkin, on duty in the woods, had wanted to "avoid his fellow-men, *and then pounce* on them" when they trespassed, Lawrence revised the manuscript so that Parkin would "avoid his fellow-men *rather than pounce* on them"; they are no longer *prey* but *danger.* Feeling vulnerable, Parkin tries to escape further damage to himself. Similarly, about halfway through the second version, when Parkin and Connie have come together in the forest, his speech, no longer limited to pure dialect, becomes "almost correct," signaling his ability to shed his early conditioning. Yet he still lacks the power to offer Connie a firm alternative to her insipid life with Clifford and his nurse, Mrs. Bolton, with whom Clifford has gradually forged "almost a sort of marriage." With that "marriage" the double triangles cited earlier are complete; as Lawrence had linked the triangles in life, so Connie links them in fiction.

The second change in the gamekeeper's character is more interesting. All his life Lawrence had been concerned—even preoccupied—with the ways in which a man could absorb female elements into his code of manhood. Paul Morel, Rupert Birkin, Richard Lovat Somers—all wrestle with the problem of masculinity, trying to redefine it in order to join female sensitivity to male strength and discipline. When the theme was sounded years earlier, in *Sons and Lovers,* Paul had said to Miriam, "It is I who ought to be ashamed—like a spiritual cripple. And I am ashamed." But Parkin is troubled not by oedipal conflicts, as Paul was, but by an emotional insecurity that arises partly from his marital strife (his estranged wife has been unfaithful), partly from his feelings of personal inadequacy.

Near the close of the second version, Lawrence made a discovery. He saw that he could double-strip his characters—take off their clothes to reveal their sexual depths, then take off their psychological defenses to reveal their emotional depths. Jobless after Clifford turns him out of the wood, inadequate in a man's world, Parkin is ashamed "that he should have to come to [Connie] for help in his life." Lawrence may have felt the same when he returned to Frieda at the Bernarda. "'If I'm handicapped I'm handicapped,'" Parkin laments, poignantly begging Connie to "be tender to me!" When Lawrence rewrote this passage in the manuscript, he made explicit the gamekeeper's insecurity: "The idea that he was too womanly was terribly humiliating to him." Angry at the implied insult to womanhood, Connie forcefully defends his hybrid personality: she insists that he protect his sensitivity and his "gift of life" even as he might manage a farm she would buy him with her inheritance. Without Connie to defend him, the gamekeeper feels he might die. In his torment he reflects Lawrence's own dilemma of the preceding year.

This crisis of identity anticipates Lawrence's very personal letter to Earl Brewster, written on 27 February 1927, recording his anger at the "sex swindle" of modern life, when one is a great deal "swindled out of one's proper sex life." Usually read as a simple gloss on Lawrence's marriage, this letter goes further. The crisis that Lawrence and the gamekeeper share is that both have been doubly denied, by wives whose infidelity cheapens sex, and by a society that openly discourages strong attachments between men: and so, Lawrence tells Brewster, he puts a phallus into his paintings—and into his novel—to signify the "deep, deep life which has been denied in us." A mystery even when denied, the phallus becomes a source of beauty, its repression inspiring its celebration. For Lawrence the phallus—whatever else it may be—symbolizes his personal loss.

And then comes the passage—in Connie's voice—that probably records the compromise that Lawrence and Frieda, needing a new agreement, had reached: "Promise me you'll be true to the feeling that is between you and me. And if you do ever go to other [sexual partners], go nicely and gently, and be grateful to them. *And don't tell me.* If you keep your heart gentle, I shall know I haven't lost you. The other won't matter, *if you need it.*" The fact that the same message appears earlier in the novel, when Clifford tells Connie that "'you are your father's daughter'" and that an affair won't matter "[i]f you need it,'" shows how urgently the characters sought compromise. As Clifford early wants Connie's promise of fidelity, so later does Connie want Parkin's inner fidelity. Some moral confusion results. Which is right—to stay or to leave, to honor a commitment or to break it?

As a result, Lawrence grew dissatisfied even with the second version of *Lady Chatterley's Lover.* It ended with too much uncertainty, it stood too close to his personal set of circumstances, and it waffled on a central matter—whether emotional fidelity was as powerful as sexual fidelity. Preferring more distance between himself and his characters, he wanted them to work out a salvation different from his own. By 25 February he told his magazine agent, Nancy Pearn, "I've done all I'm going to do of my novel for the time being." Knowing it had also become "very improper," he concluded that he would need to rewrite it still again. But even though Frieda said he was "awfully well this winter," and even though he cherished the solitude of the Mirenda and the hills around it, he needed a long rest and a major diversion from work.

Before he had finished the second version, Christmas arrived. Pietro, a young Italian who worked on the Mirenda estate, stole a pine tree which Lawrence and Frieda then decorated with candles and ornaments, and on Christmas eve they invited two dozen local peasants—who had been especially kind—to a festive party. The Lawrences served sweet Marsala wine to the adults, enticed the older girls to sing and dance, and gave the children small gifts—wooden toys and bags of Florentine sweets. A few weeks later, Earl Brewster—back from India—arrived for a visit and agreed to join Lawrence in his Etruscan walk. In the early spring days Lawrence yearned to stroll through the ancient Etruscan sites around Florence and Rome, looking at cave walls, talking to caretakers, lingering over museum artifacts, and sharing his vivid impressions with Brewster, whose exterior calm he much admired.

In truth, the preceding months had been among the most tumultuous of Lawrence's life—the protracted conflict with Frieda, her involvement with Ravagli, the liaison with Brett, his marriage rebuilt on a smaller foundation. The placid, dependable peace at the Mirenda, almost a marvel in itself, helped him to accept whatever had happened. His one strong hope was that his creative energy would surge so strongly that he could, once more, rewrite his passionate, tender novel—and finish it finally. But as the days lengthened and the flowers burst open, a shock greater than all those he had endured awaited him at the Mirenda. As the clock ticked, a different kind of worm—internal, tubercular—made its way, like a doomed moth, toward the light of the long, Italian summer days.

# 20

## Lady Chatterley's Lover
## The Last Novel
### 1927–28

Spring came early to the Mirenda. The yellow aconites and purple anemones sprinkled the hillside paths, and the primeval surge of the fragrant earth stirred both the Lawrences. Their thoughts turned to travel. In mid-March Frieda departed for a long visit to Baden-Baden, to see her family—and perhaps, on the way, Angelo Ravagli. A few days later, on 21 March, Lawrence left the Mirenda to join Earl Brewster in Ravello for the first leg of their walking trip. The two men hoped to trek through the Etruscan sites on the coast north of Rome. This would be Lawrence's last walking trip. Never robust—and now almost frail—Lawrence was often troubled by a deep cough. Death, strung from his life's clock like a weight, pulled steadily at him. But now the pull took on a fresh malaise—what in April he called "a queer sort of recoil, as if one's whole soul were drawing back from connection with everything." Yet against that recoil he fought with all of his ebbing strength. He fought most fiercely for the final version of *Lady Chatterley's Lover,* his most courageous novel.

Some weeks before the walking trip began, Cynthia Asquith sent Lawrence an odd request. For a collection she had proposed, she wanted a murder story. Lawrence complied with "The Lovely Lady," a story that links death and life, adultery and salvation—the very themes that had permeated Lawrence's own life. Older and richer than most of his characters, Pauline Attenborough, at seventy-two, clings to her youth, loving soft candlelight and feeding off her son Robert, a poor barrister whom she has charmed into decoding old Mexican documents—her pet project. Controlled by his mother, he has become a neuter in a cage. Like Parkin, Robert "was ashamed that he was not a man."

Yet Lawrence's bitingly funny satire holds out a perverse surprise. While Pauline enjoys her afternoon siesta outdoors, in her courtyard, her niece Ciss—who lives with her—calls down a drain pipe, startling the lovely lady, who thinks the eerie voice belongs to her dead son. Frightened, she leaks a confession to Ciss—that she, Pauline, had seduced an Italian priest, Robert's father. The result? A child who now looks suspiciously (and hilariously) like Angelo Ravagli: "medium-sized, rather broad and stout, though not fat," his "creamy, clean-shaven face" secretly suggesting an Italian priest's. Armed with this revelation, Ciss exposes Pauline as a fraudulent beauty, an old witch who looks collapsed and haggard in the bright electric light, "squirming inside her shell." Having thereby freed the unfortunate son, Ciss hopes that he is not too damaged to begin to love her.

Robert is the grown-up version of Paul, the struggling boy in "The Rocking Horse Winner"; Pauline, the hard-hearted mother, has a strange biographical relevance, for she is only four years younger than Lawrence's mother would have been had she lived. It is not that Lawrence attacks his mother but that he still felt confounded by the feminization his mother had imposed on him, and saw Ciss's assertive behavior—like Connie's for Parkin, or Frieda's for himself—as a key. Yet in all three cases the damaged man remains potentially crippled. This abiding sadness weights Lawrence's late fiction. Its pain is palpable.

The ten-day walking trip with Earl Brewster, begun in early April, had two goals: it provided material for another new book (and thus some income), and it allowed Lawrence to recover something from the past that he felt he had lost, something to heal the contrary forces that had led to his parents' discord. In the Etruscan tombs at Cerveteri and Tarquinia, at Vulci and Volterra, death and life were strangely reciprocal. From the tombs of those carefree people, who flourished in central Italy a good five hundred years before Christ, splashed an effervescent sense of life entirely different, Lawrence thought, from the forced mental consciousness that the Greeks had prized. Lively and fresh, the Etruscans cultivated "ease, naturalness, and an abundance of life." Especially intriguing by the tomb doors were the phallic stone symbols—some life size, some much larger—that Lawrence and Brewster found. For Lawrence these phalluses not only symbolized the sexual life denied to men like himself but also provided an image of resurrection that now gave him his fullest sense of emotional satisfaction. These phalluses affirmed his fragile male identity. Such artifacts, together with the combs and jewelry and armor that he found in local

Etruscan museums, stirred in him a peculiar sense of awakening. "I liked [them] immensely," he told his publisher Martin Secker.

After visiting the Etruscan ruins, Lawrence was never again stirred by the artifacts of a foreign culture. Some profound change had worked through him. He began turning inward. He described the change as a change "in the psyche," but it went deeper than that. It was a refocusing of interest, a gigantic centripetal force that turned him back into the past. Travel, he said, had lost its glamour. He worried about his sisters and their children in England, and eagerly awaited their letters. In May and June he rarely ventured away from the Mirenda: "[W]e hardly see anybody— which is what I prefer," he told Frieda's sister Else on 1 June. "Frieda grumbles sometimes, but when people come, she doesn't want them."

Feeling that he had "never been right" since he collapsed in Oaxaca in 1925, he began to withdraw from the external world, and he winced at the "slow bitter revocation" of what he had once been. He seldom relished new books, and in June his American friend Christine Hughes and her daughter struck him as ugly tourists when he showed them the sights of Florence. "God, . . . how glad I will be to see the last of them," he cried to Brewster. It is as if Frieda's recent betrayal had worked its way outward from his heart, subtly numbing his sensitivity, subtly eroding his assurance, subtly redirecting him to the themes of his boyhood.

One of these themes, religious exaltation, had once seemed immensely appealing. In the spring he painted a large canvas, three feet square, that he called *Resurrection,* depicting a gaunt, bearded man released from his tomb, and he wrote a story called "The Escaped Cock," which takes literally Christ's resurrection, makes him a stranger in a fresh phenomenal world, and lets him recant his role as a divine prophet. Both works are pointed critiques of Christianity. Both also show Lawrence rejecting his mother's strict Protestant religion, toppling the myths of his childhood, and asserting a new vision of the afterlife. When Lawrence came to extend "The Escaped Cock" in 1929, doubling its length, he boldly made the risen Christ possessor of a risen phallus capable of mating with the mythic Woman of Isis—and he thereby offended many readers by forcefully denying Christ's supposed sexual purity. Angry at the denials he had himself endured, Lawrence refused to sanitize the historically sanctioned portrait of Christ's redemption. He would make Isis do what Brett earlier could not: massage warmth and potency into the frail limbs of a sick man and cause him to say, "I am risen!"

## RIPE PEACHES

Savoring the hot days of early summer, Lawrence and Frieda broke the long afternoons with a pleasant siesta. Outwardly they lived at the edge of contentment. In the garden the red roses poured forth their funereal scents, and the friendly peasants, charmed by the Lawrences' warmth and simplicity, brought them fresh asparagus, peas, beans, and potatoes. Soon the big red cherries ripened, and in July the peaches, as if they would burst, hung full and heavy in the garden. Except for rising prices, all seemed well. Lawrence composed six sketches he would publish as *Etruscan Places*, hoping to make this small book "as popular as I can make it," and wrote long letters to Earl Brewster, who had earned Lawrence's trust and affection. But Benito Mussolini, Italy's dictator since 1926, had now summarily altered the exchange rate so that one British pound bought not 150 lire but 90, thereby pricing Italian goods out of the world market. In June Lawrence complained that prices in Italy were double those in England. He saved money by lying quietly at the Mirenda.

But in the quiet summer flared a worry far worse than soaring prices. Lawrence's lungs, perhaps inflamed by swimming with the Huxleys at Forte dei Marmi, seemed to burst. Frieda remembered that on the hot afternoon of 6 July,

Lawrence had gathered peaches in the garden and came in with a basket full of wonderful fruit—he showed them to me—a very little while after, he called from his room in a strange, gurgling voice; I ran and found him lying on his bed; he looked at me with shocked eyes while a slow stream of blood came from his mouth. "Be quiet, be still," I said. I held his head, but slowly and terribly the blood flowed from his mouth. I could do nothing but hold him and try to make him still and calm and send [to Florence] for Doctor Giglioli. He came, and anxious days and nights followed. In this great heat of July nursing was difficult—Giulia [the servant girl], all the peasants—helped in every possible way. The signor was so ill—Giulia got down to [the village of] Scandicci at four in the morning and brought ice in sawdust in a big handkerchief, and milk, but this, even boiled straightaway, would be sour by midday.

A decade earlier, when Lawrence had been ill, milk casein had helped, and now Frieda tried boiled milk. Its protein might repair his damaged tissue. For his part Dr. Giglioli prescribed bed rest and Coagulin, which was thought to speed coagulation; he may have urged Frieda to place an ice bag on Lawrence's chest wall; and he recommended that Lawrence go to a higher altitude, where the drier air and the lower atmospheric pressure were supposed to relieve congestion. Alas, little helped. Mark Caldwell, a specialist in tuberculosis, says that "the vast majority of treatments devised before antibiotics, though subjected to scientific tests by the lights of the era, were probably worthless."

"I really get depressed," Lawrence admitted to Koteliansky, lying in his hot bed day after day, believing now that his illness, like a systemic poison, had come "from chagrin—chagrin that goes deep in." Work was out of the question. On the eighteenth he took a walk in the hills, then paid dearly for it. More blood gushed from his lungs. Alarmed at his relapse, Frieda wept. When Dr. Giglioli ordered Lawrence back to bed for another week, Pino Orioli and his friend Reggie Turner came to visit, as did Arthur and Lillian Wilkinson, the Lawrences' neighbors. Soon the Huxleys arrived, Maria with a big bouquet of lotus flowers, Aldous writing to his father that Lawrence's "long standing tuberculosis" had by now quelled his violent outbursts and left him "touchingly gentle."

On 4 August the Lawrences escaped from Florence and its sweltering heat, not to return for more than two months. Taking the night train, they went first to Villach, Austria, a resort town near mountains and lakes, where they met Frieda's sister Johanna, now married to Emil von Krug, an amiable German banker. "It's like heaven, to be cool again," Lawrence wrote; and Frieda, swimming and taking excursions across the lakes, felt "very chirpy among the mountains again." On rainy days Lawrence translated more Verga, this time some stories that Jonathan Cape would publish the following year as *Cavalleria Rusticana and Other Stories*. By 1 September 1927 Lawrence and Frieda had come once again to Irschenhausen, to Else's wooden chalet in the Isar valley, which Lawrence had not seen since 1913, when he and Frieda had stayed there and walked in the cool pine forests, now grown tall. In the cupboard Lawrence was amazed to find his own advance copy of *Love Poems and Others*. He was returning to a familiar environment, as he had a year earlier, when he went to the Midlands.

"I am a good deal better," he informed Koteliansky, though much of his vitality had slipped away. He drank plenty of goat's milk, and in the evenings, with Else, he and Frieda played patience (solitaire), or embroidered, while sampling the malt beer that von Krug had sent. After a month, the Lawrences went on to Baden-Baden to see Frieda's mother. There Lawrence allowed himself to be examined by a doctor who concluded (Lawrence told his sister) that the "catarrh [is] clearer on the lower lungs, but still not clear at the top, and bronchial passages [still] inflamed." So Lawrence resolved at once to get better—"and I'll really try to do that and nothing else," he vowed—and suffered through a week-long "inhalation" cure, spending an hour each day breathing the cold steam from radium springs. He would simply rest and heal; he even fancied that he might "never want to write another book."

## ILLNESS AND ITS DEFEAT

Arriving at the Mirenda on 19 October, after the Wilkinsons (with a motor car) met them at the station, the Lawrences rejoiced to be back in Florence, where the days opened cool and sunny, and gentle clouds mottled the afternoon sky. Settled into familiar surroundings, Lawrence had much to ponder. How long might his energy last? How long before his creative powers slipped? How long would Frieda endure his illness?

In the quiet autumn the Lawrences kept busy at small things. Having hired a piano, Frieda began to learn Handel's *Messiah,* and in the evenings she made a jacket out of Johanna's velvet coat, its new silver buttons flashing with a Florentine look. Lawrence painted *Jaguar Leaping at a Man,* typed out poems for a collected edition of his poetry that Secker had proposed, played cards with the Wilkinsons, and played patience. Although he still felt feeble and coughed too much, he was able to find mushrooms in the damp valleys and walk through the hills without gasping for breath. But nothing enraged him, he told Richard Aldington, "like not getting well," and in a vision of his life's end, he grieved that he "couldn't spit in the face of the narrow-gutted world and put its eye out." That pugnacious image, written on 18 November, eight days before he began *Lady Chatterley's Lover* all over again, indexes the new stance—feisty and furious—that allowed Lawrence to combat his illness. In a mood of both elation and despair, he tackled the novel again. Although his handwriting was looser and larger, his strategies were more calculated and his message more potent. He intended now to shock.

Two points explain why Lawrence suddenly returned to *Lady Chatterley's Lover,* which he had not touched since the spring. Because his income had dwindled, he needed to publish a new novel. Train fares, hotels with separate bedrooms, inhalation cures, lake excursions, dentists, concerts—all had been expensive. Whereas others got rich, he reminded his sister that "my earnings aren't much, nowadays." Michael Arlen, whom the Lawrences had known in 1915, suddenly turned up in Florence on 17 November, and when Lawrence discovered that the suave Armenian writer had, in America, made nearly a million dollars from his novel *The Green Hat,* he felt a shivering envy. Equally annoyed, Frieda lamented to Secker at the end of 1927: "It is sad that we get no richer, do you know that Lawrence has'nt had a 100 £'s from all his books, that you have [issued], this [whole] year?" With such a tiny income from his books—and not much more from short stories and articles—Lawrence needed to make *Lady Chatterley's Lover* a success. His visits to Austria and Germany for just two months had cost him close to £75.

There is more. Lawrence certainly knew that *Lady Chatterley,* now "under lock and key," would be labeled indecent. He could not therefore use ordinary commercial publishers whose cuts would spoil the novel's erotic beauty. Late in October, however, Norman Douglas had written that he was busy in Florence privately printing a book—and doing all the work himself. Could Lawrence do the same? With Orioli's help, and with luck, he might earn £700 or £800—"which would be a windfall for me," he said dryly. He could publish the novel exactly as he wished in Florence, where book production was cheap and where he could avoid both interfering editors and sensational publicity.

Standard accounts make his work on the novel sound easy but intense. True, he completed the final draft in just forty-four days, between 26 November 1927 and 8 January 1928. But few readers are aware of the profound impact of Lawrence's hemorrhaging and subsequent illness on the final version. Medical disorders determined many of the changes Lawrence made when he recast the novel. In July and August he had suffered so much (he told Koteliansky) that he found it "terribly difficult to write intimately." Somewhere he could hear death's rattle. It is no surprise that he wove into his novel a new pattern of illness and despair, of malady and malfunction.

As early as chapter 1, Clifford's father, Sir Geoffrey, "died of chagrin"— precisely the malady Lawrence thought *he* suffered from; Connie, her body ailing from her soul's malaise, becomes frail and pinched and, like Lawrence, feels miserable about "getting thinner." Just as Frieda's older sister, Else, arranged for Lawrence to see a doctor in Baden-Baden, so does Connie's older sister, Hilda, arrange for her to see a doctor in London. He urges Connie to recover her vitality, to be amused, to avoid depression; Lawrence, too, wanted a "really amusing" tonic. Doctors assist those who cannot heal themselves. That is why Clifford, though sadly crippled, never consults a doctor; he uses his employees—his colliery managers and his nurse, Mrs. Bolton—to infuse him with new life. They extend his ego.

Even when Lawrence introduces an entirely new character, the playwright Michaelis, he cites the man's malfunction. Like Michael Arlen, Michaelis is a rich outcast who gives Connie a false sexual outlet before she meets the gamekeeper (named Mellors in the final version). But if Clifford can no longer ejaculate, Michaelis suffers from premature ejaculation and "was finished almost before he had begun"; he could not "keep anything up." Michaelis wants no intimacy—only an affair that will briefly enliven his loneliness. His material riches, like Michael Arlen's, lie on the surface; underneath he is as maimed as either Arlen, whose testicle had been removed, or Clifford, whose war wound has paralyzed his lower body.

Although Clifford gradually acquires a virulent energy—bossing, managing, bending others to his will—the most surprising change is that Lawrence now shapes Clifford in his own image: both men are satirical writers, both are familiar to the public, both are impotent, both are married to women who are sexually unfaithful, and both—having nearly lost their lives—are plagued by illness. After Christmas, while Lawrence wrote the novel's last chapters, Frieda described his semi-invalid condition to her mother: "If Lawrence is doing well and if it's a nice day, he gets up; otherwise he eats his breakfast in bed." Often he was "very exhausted." Just as Lawrence's tubercular cough kept him awake at night, so Clifford dreads the nights "when he could not sleep." Clifford's sleep disorder requires the same treatment as Lawrence's for tuberculosis: malted milk. Brought nightly by Mrs. Bolton, it reduces Clifford's anxiety.

But if Clifford is crippled, his bullying tone, which so annoys Connie, recaptures his power, and a muscled *tone* is precisely what Lawrence adds of his own personality to the narrator, whose presence is most keenly felt in the final version. Never a neutral observer, the narrator now aggressively interprets the Chatterleys' world. He is opinionated, angry, and sardonic: "The [reading] public responds now only to an appeal to its vices," he insists in a typical sentence, echoing what Lawrence himself wrote to a friend on 23 December. Judgment pervades *Lady Chatterley's Lover.*

For her part Frieda was astonished that Lawrence "identified himself with both Clifford and Mellors." That took courage, she thought. But in the final version it took something else too: an artistic ability to transcend both Lawrence's personal history as a miner's son and the two earlier Parkin figures. Whereas in version two Parkin was strong but insecure, Mellors is different—now confident and iconoclastic but weakened by long illness. Born in 1885, the same year as Lawrence, Mellors, despite his damaged health, has traveled, observed his surroundings, and thought deeply about the world's disappointments. Like Lawrence, he tires easily and coughs in the cold wind. His lungs are vulnerable: "That pneumonia took a lot out of me," he confesses to Connie, who observes how ill he's been. After he dislodges Clifford's motorized wheelchair, which sticks amid a patch of bluebells, he looks "paler than Connie had ever seen him," and he concedes that illness "left my heart not so strong—and the lungs not so elastic." He cannot heal himself.

But Mellors's physical state is offset by his tough-minded intellectual force. His years in the army have given him perspective: he can see through surfaces, judge motives, criticize his shallow culture. Though damaged by his war experience, brutalized by his brief marriage to Bertha Coutts, and saddened by the state of the world, Mellors has nevertheless salvaged three things: his disdain for material success, his clear-eyed view of women, and his self-respect. He is a fierce judge. Bertha—a partial (and tawdry) portrait of Frieda—is a sexual predator five years older than Mellors who has run away with another man and who, when she was married to Mellors, had insisted—like Frieda—on having her own bedroom. Like Frieda, she has now "grown heavy." Brazen and coarse, Bertha turns into the character "equivalent" of the novel's new verbal register—slang. Both express a profound disrespect.

In Mellors Lawrence delivers his most powerful punch against illness. Although Mellors's sexual prowess has earned him masses of comment, he has a gift: he can engage in sex without shame. The vital forces of sexual feeling rout illness and despair. As Lawrence explains in "A Propos of *Lady*

*Chatterley's Lover*," an essay he wrote in 1929, the sexual act links Connie and Mellors to the most central rhythms of the universe. Sex leads Connie to be reborn as "a woman," Mellors to be broken open, and both of them to enter "the moving cosmos." Nourished by its energy and health, they can replenish themselves from the "sources which flow eternally in the universe." The power of sexual renewal mimes nature's cycles of renewal—day, lunar month, season, year. At its center, desire—the engine of restoration—drives their renewal.

Lawrence constructs *Lady Chatterley's Lover* to capture the stages of emotional recovery. He is both careful and deliberate. His architectural precision shows itself in his sequencing of the novel's erotic scenes. The first stage, daytime intercourse, occurs when the pheasant chicks hatch in the secluded wood. The second stage, intercourse in the afternoon and early evening, allows Connie to discover the transfiguring tide of female orgasm, when she opens herself to the "primordial tenderness, such as made the world in the beginning," and yields all of herself "in the flood." The third stage, intercourse at night, allows the couple to pause and discover the power of sex to heal their antagonistic words. And the fourth stage, anal intercourse—discovered during a night of sensual passion—takes Connie on a journey to the heart of herself, to the last recess of shame, where in the jungle of her body every secret is pried open. Each erotic stage strips Connie more fully of her resistance to a fully disclosed relationship. She loses her cold, derisive will, which—after encountering Michaelis in chapter 5—had "stiffened" against physical intimacy. With rapt intensity she explores Mellors's body—in her mind, where she can fantasize about his potency. At last, when she dissolves her fear of the deepest organic shame, she reaches her goal: to share her ultimate nakedness with a man.

Critics often argue that Connie and Mellors relegate love to sex, that Connie submits too easily to Mellors's chauvinistic attitudes, and that Lawrence fails in his attempt to purify the language of sexual description. Indeed, Lawrence took great risks in writing the novel. Perhaps he should have included more expressions of Mellors's tenderness—sharing with Connie his own burden of fatherhood, showing interest in her past, recalling his father and mother. Instead, once they are friends, he tends to lecture her. Yet these critical arguments also minimize the most fundamental stimulus of the novel's creation: the use of sex to battle illness. Every cure has its cost. Far from being "one of Lawrence's inferior works," as Brenda Maddox claims, the novel aims to identify those behaviors that can renew potency, revive health, and awaken wonder at the human body. Even flowers gathered to decorate the nude body celebrate the spontaneity of the spirit. The novel's singular skill makes its gender politics—who dominates, who submits—less central than its deeper drive toward renewal, which has a clumsy propulsion of its own. Silence, touch, opening buds, secret entrances, sensual mysteries—all become vehicles of empowerment. They quiet the keen will, turn struggle into peace, and allow Connie and Mellors to become "utterly unknowing" in a silence that was "unfathomable." Words cannot mediate the spiritual health they find.

But that spiritual health has a hidden biographical component. Readers who have followed Lawrence's fascination with male love will wonder both how the novel expresses it and how anal intercourse (as the zone of gay men) completes heterosexual passion. Sheila MacLeod worries that the couple's final phase of lovemaking includes an act in which it is not necessary that Connie be a woman. "No," she concludes, "it is Mellors and not Connie for whom this episode is necessary." That is a brash claim. Certainly the episode is necessary for Connie to complete her own sexual awakening. No erotic zone will be taboo for a woman who wants, in her zeal for liberation, to become a *different* woman. And, yes, the episode is necessary for Mellors too—not to master Connie or to manipulate her body but to allow him to express the range of his sexual desire with a woman who wants what he wants: total bodily intimacy. Her love for him accepts his complex sexuality without needing to define it. Securing Connie as his half-willing participant in anal intercourse, he heals the psychic split that—earlier—had troubled Paul Morel in *Sons and Lovers*. Mellors's bisexual component—he is a man with "too much of the woman in me"—has now been simplified. This simplification, reflecting the spread of Lawrence's illness, shows how he eventually gave up on same-sex intimacy and moved its core activity to heterosexual lovemaking.

Lawrence's personal experience may also have altered the novel's ending. The narrator openly admits that barriers of blood and culture can block relationships from developing. He recognizes, for instance, the power that antagonists like Hilda wield. When Connie leaves Wragby, going to Scotland to be with her sister, Mellors can only write to her. It is as if Connie, like Frieda, could receive only letters from her paramour—no visits. When Ravagli came to see Frieda in 1927, Lawrence demanded to see his papers certifying his summons to a courtmartial in Florence. Lawrence must often have pondered Ravagli's effect on his marriage. The fact that Connie and Mellors can only hope to be together at the close means that Lawrence could not predict the outcome of infidelity. It baffled him.

Still, Mellors's concluding letter has two qualities that characterize both himself and Lawrence: a hard-won insight into the embattled self and a voice remarkable for its pungent compassion. It is a voice like no other in English fiction. Mellors writes: "My soul softly flaps in the little pentecost flame with you, like the peace of fucking. We fucked a little flame into being. Even the flowers are fucked into being, between sun and earth." The brave use of "fucked," the delicate image of flowers, and the wistful allusion to the pentecost sum up Lawrence's final creative phase. They capture his strict Protestant heritage, its subsequent repudiation, and—mediating the two—his abiding love of nature, which transcends ideology. It is a voice of complete resignation.

Lawrence's final rewriting of *Lady Chatterley's Lover* allowed him to make recovery more central but to make the novel's themes more explicit, to assault contemporary mores more daringly, to affront the hidden timidities of his readers more aggressively, and—most important—to awaken a counterforce of unflinching honesty and truth. Many readers prefer the final version, despite its psychological and thematic simplifications, because it so vigorously defends sexual openness and because it takes so many artistic risks. Never again would Lawrence possess such concentrated imaginative energy.

## THE UPWARD CLIMB

Another form of renewal now lay just ahead. For Lawrence, emaciated by illness and feeling dangerously "near the brink of the abyss," the struggle to get a typescript, to print the book, and to distribute it provided one of the finest challenges of his life. Like Dickens, he would be more than a novelist; he would be an entrepreneur, a scrupulous businessman. But in the world's view he would be a pornographer.

Even before he had finished the manuscript he wrote not to a typing service but to Nellie Morrison, his writer-friend in Florence, to ask her to type as much of it as she could but to tell "nobody." He insisted on publishing his novel "uncastrated." But when she balked, after typing just five chapters, Lawrence—retrieving his manuscript—sought the skilled help of another old friend, Catherine Carswell, who engaged several amateur typists to help her and sent him regular batches of typescript.

Meanwhile, Lawrence thought that the foggy lowlands around Florence had worsened his cough. When the Huxleys invited him and Frieda to join them in Switzerland, at a sunny winter resort named Les Diablerets, thirty-five hundred feet above sea level and not far from Lake Geneva, he gladly accepted, despite the expense. He and Frieda would have their own four-room chalet, with maid service. Feeling sure that the altitude would be a tonic for his cough, the Lawrences arrived by funicular on 20 January 1928 and found not only the Huxleys but Aldous's brother, Julian, his wife, Juliette, and their young children. The Huxley brothers, tall and vigorous, were good skiers; Maria and Juliette, looking petite and chic— Maria sophisticated and worldly, Juliette rather prim—were sympathetic listeners when, each afternoon, they all gathered for tea. Lawrence and Frieda, although they occasionally went tobogganing or joined the Huxleys for picnics in the snow, chiefly stayed indoors. While Frieda, her body

Les Diablerets, Switzerland, where the Lawrences went in January 1928 (Courtesy of the Archives and Rare Books Department, the University of Cincinnati)

large and loose, cooked or lay on her bed reading books like Andre Gide's *Corydon*, Lawrence, feeling better, worked at a feverish pace—reading proofs of *The Woman Who Rode Away and Other Stories*, revising his early poems, writing letters, and correcting the typescript of *Lady Chatterley's Lover*. Maria, ever generous, agreed to type the novel's last seven chapters in Les Diablerets.

Juliette Huxley, in her memoir, recalls the Lawrences coming to tea and staying to advise Juliette's mother on her embroidery or to join in the lively discussions. But scientific topics like evolution enraged Lawrence—"they may be facts but not truths," he would shout, his face going red. He preferred to talk amusingly about his Mexican travels, about Mabel Dodge Luhan and her escapades, about Brett and her quirks, about the *grand dame* Ottoline Morrell, whom all the Huxleys had known well; in short, he talked about the women who had altered his fate. Juliette remembers that Frieda, who preferred the Mirenda to the glaring snow, at first lay resentfully on her bed but gradually allowed Lawrence to arouse her nest-building instincts. Gathering some bright wool, Frieda would stitch a cushion cover or decorate the window. But she may have been bored; harboring a secret lover, she wrote very few preserved letters in 1928.

One afternoon Lawrence, annoyed by Julian Huxley's imperious manner, broke his reserve and told Juliette, with encouraging noises from Frieda, that her husband was "an expurgated version of a man." Too repressed to risk a discussion, Juliette nonetheless recognized the accuracy of Lawrence's insight. She fought back when Lawrence asked her to read the typescript of *Lady Chatterley's Lover*, which she promptly denounced, saying he should call it "John Thomas and Lady Jane"—penis and vagina—because "that was really all it was about." Exploding with laughter, Lawrence tilted his head and let his blue eyes twinkle, well aware, though, that he was wholly alone in his crusade. Juliette had let him taste the bitter outcry to come.

Some weeks before the Lawrences left the Swiss resort to return to the Mirenda, Lawrence had decided to expurgate the two carbon copies of his novel—for Martin Secker and Alfred Knopf. (Their public editions would at least protect his copyright.) But Lawrence went color blind, he says, and could not tell the purple of impropriety from the pink of naughty suggestion. He expurgated only the obvious. He altered, for instance, "penis" to "passion"; "her mound of Venus" to "her intimate body"; "a good cod on you" to "good spunk in you"; "my lady's fucker" to "my lady's paramour." He knew it was a vain attempt.

Still, Lawrence's splendid moment arrived on 9 March 1928. After he had lunch with Pino Orioli in Florence, the two men went to the Tipografia Giuntina, a little printer's shop at 4 via del Sole where, Lawrence vouched, "nobody understands a word of English." Performing all work by hand, Mr. Franceschini, the printer, delivered a specimen page the next day and soon prepared fifteen hundred leaflets that Lawrence could begin sending out in batches of ten or twenty—to friends like Mabel Luhan, Christine Hughes, and the Huxleys, who would know others likely to buy and then appreciate the book. In a single week in March, Lawrence wrote at least eighteen promotional letters to his friends. His letters are proud and defiant. They insist on a distinction he would often repeat: "I don't call my novel a sex novel. It's a phallic novel"—that is, not cerebral but warm and spontaneous. "I feel very bold," he told Koteliansky. He was also firm. He frowned on giving away any copies, or allowing booksellers a commission over 15 percent, or sending copies before payment. By the last day of March, so many orders had reached Orioli that Lawrence could chide his British agent Curtis Brown, who believed that Lawrence had risked his reputation: "Looks like I'll sell the thing all right."

Annoyed at the cold and rainy weather, often tired, sometimes dispirited, Lawrence nevertheless kept unusually busy in March and April, choosing handmade paper for the novel, ordering binding paper, drawing a phoenix design for the cover, and correcting the proofs, whose words danced exotically to a foreign tune—"dind't, didn't, dnid't, dind't, din'dt, didn't like a Bach fugue," he lamented. The proofs came quickly until the printer, who was short on type, realized that he would have to print half the book, then break up the type in order to print the second half, whereupon Lawrence decided to print two hundred extra copies on cheap paper. He could give them as gifts.

Giuseppe Orioli, June 1935 (Courtesy of the Library of Congress, Prints & Photographs Division, Carl Van Vechten collection)

At this time Frieda almost disappears from Lawrence's letters. After her daughter Barbara and her sister Else came for a visit, she went to Alassio, near Spotorno—ostensibly to see Barbara but really to rendezvous with Ravagli. Gone five days, 11–16 April, she had what she called (in code) "a few beautiful days." Lawrence did not reproach her. "Every heart has a right to its own secrets," he told her one evening. He knew what she needed—and what he couldn't provide. But the truth was more painful: she had grown tired of nursing her sickly patient. A few months earlier she had told her mother that perhaps Lawrence would visit Capri by himself so that she could sail to Germany—"save your money so that you can pay for me," she urged. Although Juliette Huxley claims that Frieda's periodic prowls left Lawrence "vulnerable like an orphan," her claim is doubtful. In Frieda's absence Lawrence could provide his own social life. While she was gone, for instance, a young friend named Margaret Gardiner—the sister of an admirer—arrived at the Mirenda. Though appalled by his illness, she also recalled both the lunch that he prepared—stew, boiled potatoes, grapes, red wine, and figs—and the delicate mockery and gaiety that brightened his bitterness. She remembered that he was "immensely proud" of his wife.

## GOING STILL HIGHER

The Lawrences, though they felt obliged to go to Switzerland for his health, did not leave Florence until 10 June. They were delayed by the printer. He was slow to stock the handmade paper, slow to deliver proofs to Lawrence (who corrected some batches twice), then slow—it seemed—to print. More than once Lawrence exclaimed, "I wish the printer would hurry up." Yet the book was in production only three months, and by the time the Lawrences departed, Orioli—rotund and witty—had received orders for more than five hundred copies from England alone, including some from booksellers like Alan Steele, who ordered eighty copies but who also wondered if the novel were salacious. America, guarded by zealous customs agents, seemed even more risky as the American orders started trickling in.

The Mirenda's end was near. In deference to Frieda, who loved it, Lawrence leased the old house for another year but now as a place to store their heavy trunks. And before the Brewsters arrived in Florence to join them in their next jaunt, Lawrence packed seven of his largest paintings—having sent all of the smaller ones with his old friend, Enid Hopkin Hilton, a few weeks earlier—and shipped them to the Warren Gallery in London, where Dorothy Warren, Lady Ottoline's niece, was (she said) "longing to have your show."

Florence was almost a place of the past. The train journey to Switzerland was one of Lawrence's last adventures. With a compartment to themselves, all five travelers—Earl, Achsah, Harwood, Lawrence, and Frieda—sang old Protestant revival hymns like "Throw Out the Life-line," whose final verse roused their spirits:

> This is the life-line, oh, grasp it today!
> See, you are recklessly drifting away;
> Voices in warning, shout o'er the wave,
> "Grasp the strong life-line, for Jesus can save."

Exhilarated, Lawrence stood up, pretended to lasso the drowning souls, and pulled them safely to shore. He loved the spectacle.

When they reached Grenoble, they motored up to a rustic inn at St. Nazier, a spot that was brimming with spring flowers. Soon the proprietor told Brewster that because Lawrence had coughed all night the group would have to leave: the law prohibited tubercular guests. Frieda was furious. As Lawrence wrote to Orioli on 21 June, "[T]he insolent French people actually asked us to go away because I coughed. . . . I felt very mad." Undeterred, they went straight to the Grand Hotel at Chexbres-sur-Vevey in Switzerland, where the view over Lake Geneva resembled a Turner canvas and saved the hotel from dullness.

Lawrence often felt good enough to work. On his little balcony he wrote the extension of *The Escaped Cock* and then, for London newspapers, began a series of four-page pieces collected a year later as *Assorted Articles*. Earning as much as twelve guineas for each piece, he could, after coffee, turn out one in part of a morning. One of the best is "Insouciance," which he completed on 27 June. Built on the opposition between a healthy intuitive outlook and a diseased love of abstraction—between a sensitive man and a white-haired English lady perched on the adjacent balcony— the essay adroitly entwines them until, "[b]efore I know where I am, the little white-haired lady has swept me off my balcony, away from the glassy lake, the veiled mountains, the two men mowing, and the cherry trees, away into the troubled ether of [Mussolini and] international politics." She has cut the thread of his sensuous life. His tart moral: "I am not allowed to sit like a dandelion on my own stem." But Lawrence's range has narrowed—to an opinion, acerbic and brusquely sardonic, that he could effortlessly conjure out of his wide human experience. He often read these pieces aloud to the Brewsters, whose mild delight pleased him. Frieda, he allowed, was "by no means the soul of patience." She minded people coming to him as if he were a shrine.

Nor was she fond of nursing: "[I]t's so terrible always this anxiety, never any peace," she cried to Lawrence's sister Emily, who would soon arrive with her daughter, Peggy, for a visit. For one whole week Frieda escaped to her mother in Germany. Lawrence, frugal but never tight, did not begrudge her the money to travel. When she returned, they all felt like going still higher into the Alps. They ascended to the edge of the snow, at Gsteig, above four thousand feet, the Brewsters into a hotel, the Lawrences taking (on 9 July) a primitive four-room chalet one mile uphill from the village and only eight miles from Les Diablerets, where, in February, Lawrence had thought the altitude so beneficial to his chest. At the chalet "the air is really good" and the views of the mountains "rather lovely," almost "like being in another world," he wrote. The peasants provided most necessities—firewood, eggs, butter, milk, and honey—and under the pines they built him a rough table and a seat so that he could sit alone in the cool mornings, while Frieda slept, and paint or write. In spite of the climbing— "I simply gasp going uphill"—he and Frieda stayed two months, until mid-September. "I do so want to get rid of my tormenting cough," he told Ada in despair.

Though he yearned to get well, he felt worse. His disease had progressed. A photograph taken in August 1928 shows sunken cheeks collapsing beneath a full head of hair. Yet he wrote more letters now than ever before, 150 from Gsteig alone. Their content had changed from intense wonder at new places to practical concerns like changing address, reporting his health, depositing checks, paying bills. These could be the letters of almost any displaced person, except for one thing: their blunt precision.

Lawrence with his sister Emily, in Gsteig, Switzerland, August 1928 (Courtesy of the University of Nottingham)

"If I sign any [copies]," he snapped about Secker's forthcoming *Collected Poems,* "we must divide the proceeds of the signing—else let them go unsigned." In most matters he was decided, sure—and a little jaded. Life's wonder had crumpled.

While the Lawrences stayed in Switzerland and then visited Frieda's mother in Baden-Baden, they delighted in figuring out ways to supply subscribers with copies of *Lady Chatterley's Lover* (published in July) while outwitting government authorities. Orioli's small packages invariably reached England. There, when frightened booksellers refused their copies, good friends like Enid Hilton, Aldington, and Koteliansky rescued and then distributed more than a hundred "refused" copies. Loyal but scared, Koteliansky would stick inside each package a label that read, "Sent by Pino Orioli, 6 Lungarno Corsini, Florence." But in America Lawrence learned that customs agents had seized perhaps half of those Orioli had mailed. Maria Cristina Chambers, an admirer from Long Island, New York, wrote Lawrence on 9 August that although her friends' copies arrived, hers did not. He grew alarmed. Some had been confiscated: "Damn the Americans—damn and damn them," he cried. He soon realized that he had two choices: authorize a small firm like the Vanguard Press in America to photograph his edition, or wait and risk pirates launching their own editions and stealing his rightful profits.

Inexperienced and ill, Lawrence was slow to respond. By the time he found a satisfactory publisher for a cheap paperback edition—not until March 1929 did he find Edward R. Titus—the pirates had already issued three editions, one with his forged signature. But at least Titus's edition, which Lawrence called the Paris Popular Edition, would supply him (and later Frieda) with a steady income. By March 1929 the Florence edition alone had piled in his lap a little pot of gold: £1,240 ($6,200)—enough to fund four or five years of living in hotels. Although Lawrence felt he had lost many of his friends by publishing *Lady Chatterley's Lover,* he had found financial health for the first time in his life. Yet fate held its own cruel revenge. When the unexpurgated public editions of *Lady Chatterley* finally appeared in 1959 in America and 1960 in England, not one of Lawrence's own family benefited. His sisters' children watched in horror as some of the novel's huge profits bulged the pockets of Angelo Ravagli's children.

But that was after Lawence's novel had become the slogan of sexual freedom, the bomb that shattered the walls of 1950s repression. His notoriety as a sexual pervert dates from October 1928, when he and Frieda found themselves on an island called Port Cros, ten miles off the southeast coast of France. The question of where to go for the winter of 1928–29 had nagged them incessantly. Frieda clearly preferred the Mirenda; Lawrence, though sometimes pining for the ranch in New Mexico, sought a sunny place outside Italy—away from Ravagli: "[S]omething bleeds me a bit, emotionally, in Italy," he admitted, for he knew that Frieda "secretly hopes to get me back to Italy." Before they were forced to choose, Richard Aldington, who had helped distribute the novel, invited them to come to an island fortress, not far from Toulon, which Aldington and Arabella Yorke—and their friend Brigit Patmore—had rented from a French magazine editor. The high fortress, capped with arbutus trees and wild lavender, comprised two acres enclosed in a low, thick wall and with a moat out-side it. Inside, in a row, squatted four small bedrooms beside a great room with an open fireplace. "It's quite fun—only ourselves," Lawrence said. He left for Port Cros from the coastal town of Le Lavandou; Frieda joined him from Florence, where she had gone for a week to close the Mirenda and—said Aldington—to sneak a visit to Ravagli.

When the Lawrences arrived on 15 October, their friends were shocked. Aldington thought Lawrence much too ill to join in their walking or bathing expeditions: "I used to listen to his dreadful hollow cough at night, and wonder what on earth I should do if he got worse. . . . Luckily his marvellous vitality made yet another recovery, but naturally he was not in the best of spirits and apt to be bad-tempered. His talk was too often on a lower level than his best, too personal and satirical, sharp with the reck-less hatred of those about to die." Brigit Patmore, still a beauty at forty-six, had left her husband. Now, Lawrence discovered to his astonishment, Arabella was not the only one at Port Cros drawn to Aldington's vigor and masculine charm. Before their shocked communal eyes, Brigit and Ald-ington rekindled a liaison that had begun years earlier, when Aldington was only eighteen. Later, when everyone had left the island, Aldington confided to Brigit that he guessed the Lawrences "came to my bedroom [one night] and found me not there." Creating a row, Arabella denounced his disloyalty and may have enlisted Lawrence's sympathy, for he and she occupied the same position in their respective triangles. In dismay Law-rence said later, "But since [Port Cros] I don't write to him."

That was not all. From Frieda, Lawrence caught the flu, spent two days hemorrhaging, awakened in the mornings with his pajamas saturated with sweat, and by 29 October realized that the warm, moist climate had churned his cough into a stream of sputum. Before the Lawrences left on 17 November, the mail boat brought some press cuttings about his novel. One evening they read them aloud, bemused by shining gems like "a liter-ary cesspool," "a landmark in evil," "the foulest book in English litera-ture," "[the fruit] of a poisoned genius." Brigit Patmore remembered,

Beside the fire there was a heap of light branches, rosemary, thorn and myrtle. They were used to kindle dying embers, but a devil suddenly came into Lawrence and he threw a branch on the flames. It crackled beautifully and he threw another and another. Fire filled the whole hearth-place, licking over the edges.

"What are you *doing*," cried Frieda. He didn't answer but two more branches went into the flames. "Look out! It'd be a cold night in the open if you burnt us out." No answer, but quicker, more branches, more thorns. Painful smoke and lovely perfume began to fill the room. But each protest only made him add more fuel in a sort of rhythmical rage. His fury died out with the swiftly burnt herbs, and having served up his enemies symbolically as a burnt sacrifice, he never bothered about them again.

Lawrence was glad to leave Port Cros. Arriving in Bandol, a pretty coastal village ten miles from Toulon, where white boats bobbed and palm trees waved and orange lamps glowed at night, the Lawrences paused. They decided that the inexpensive Hotel Beau Rivage, with its friendly staff and excellent seafood, suited them well. For two persons it cost only eighty francs (about three dollars) a day. They would stay the winter. Lawrence felt weak, worse in health than ever before, scarcely able to paint or write, and still pained by the entrails of infidelity that curled in the sunny days like offal. It is doubtful that he and Frieda confronted each other on this score; his debilitating weakness and her confused loyalty would have ensured silence on the topic that rankled them both. After shifting about for several months, Lawrence needed rest, ease, and contentment to battle his irritation and indecision. He wanted to wander but found his health like a leash. As his fighting spirit sagged, he seemed lonely and dispirited. He had fifteen months to live.

# 21

# The End and the Beginning

## 1929–31

To Lawrence the winter days, unfolding on the southern coast of France, seemed sunny and mild. His bedroom window on the second floor of the Hotel Beau Rivage looked out over the broad bay; the hotel, centrally located in Bandol, was gracious, placid, and comfortable. He seemed contented. He was forty-three, Frieda forty-nine. They had lived together for almost seventeen years. But a change had altered their lives: "After the Mirenda," Frieda wrote, "we seemed to live chiefly for his health. Switzerland and the sea one after the other seemed to do him most good." Frieda's brief account of these winter months omits her boredom, whereas Lawrence repeatedly describes her as "uneasy" and "fidgetty." She had much to think about but almost nothing to do. She pined for a house of her own. Lawrence however wanted no ties—partly because he never wanted to risk returning to a place where he had been ill, partly because moving on nipped Frieda's temptation to stray. (Lawrence remembered what taking the Villa Bernarda had cost him.) A wedge of frustration had lodged in their marriage, translated emotionally into a power struggle—Frieda so large, vital, and healthy; Lawrence so frail and weak but strong willed: both at times struggling against each other to the point of a standoff. They needed a place to live. She wanted Italy, he preferred Spain. As the winter lazily passed, they sat still for four months, unable to compromise. While Lawrence clung to the shreds of his life, Frieda would listen through the open door for his breathing, hour after hour, sometimes all night long, and—though dreading the end—surely wondered what sort of fresh beginning awaited her in the dawn after his death.

Knowing no one in Bandol, the Lawrences depended on visitors for their social life. Apart from Barbara Weekley, who arrived for a week after Christmas, three young men came to visit—disciples who offered Lawrence sincere homage. He liked all three. To the young his passionate voice was a cry for action. By now he was a prophet, a mystic, a legend.

The first to come to Bandol was Rhys Davies (1903–78), a superb Welsh novelist with heavy features—he looked like Igor Stravinsky—whose grandfather had mined Welsh coal. The themes of his first novel, *The Withered Root* (1927), echo those of *Sons and Lovers*. Reuben Daniels's sharp-tongued mother, the village's strict chapel influence, and the novel's working-class realism remain authentic even today. Reuben's father, though he is more admired and sympathetic than Walter Morel, angrily protests the wage that merely "bought him a little bread and a miserable dwelling." When Davies arrived from Nice on 29 November 1928, Lawrence thought him quiet, yielding, and tolerant. Brenda Maddox's tawdry suggestion that Lawrence "divined Davies's homosexuality" and may have sought a "flirtation" seems very unlikely; Lawrence now regularly overlooked the homosexual preferences of others.

Davies, missing no detail, found the Lawrences cheerful and charming. Taking breakfast in his room, Lawrence worked all morning, sitting up in bed, watching the sun slide across the Mediterranean, writing numerous little poetic *pensées,* which he called pansies. Before lunch—the main meal—they often met for an apéritif in a nearby café, then went to the hotel for soup or salad, fish and vegetables (with wine), coffee and dessert. Because walking usually tired Lawrence, the afternoons and evenings unfolded in easy idleness. While Frieda napped, Lawrence dawdled at the edge of the sea or wandered onto the jetty; naked boys played on the beach, as they had in Chapala. Lawrence would ask Davies about his Welsh childhood, then rail against the economic poverty of his own early days. Once he said that he respected his father far more now than when he wrote *Sons and Lovers.* Meeting them on the beach, Frieda agreed, declaring *Sons and Lovers* "an evil book, because of that woman in it, his mother." In the evening they would sit in Frieda's room, on the bed or in a chair, and talk. Later, Davies trenchantly assessed the Lawrences' marriage, using the same lioness image that David Garnett had applied to Frieda in 1912: "Frieda had a lioness quality that could meet [Lawrence's] outbursts with a fine swing and sash: when really stung, she would shake her mane and grunt and growl; sometimes she charged. . . . [H]er spirit was direct and generous, and his was laughing, malicious and subtle. Their notorious brawls were grand. She would lash out, and, gathering his forces with confident ease, he met her like a warrior. He would attack her for smoking too many cigarettes, having her hair cropped, taking a wrong line of thought, eating too many cakes in a café in Toulon, or trying to be intellectual or aristocratic. He kept her simmering, subtly; for a natural inclination to a stout German placidity threatened to swamp her fine lioness quality." But Lawrence was glad for Frieda's assurance; it cushioned his sharp tongue. Without her, he risked sounding like a shrew; with her to provide a genial curb, his conversation had bite and sting but no cruelty. She regulated his animosity.

In the *Pansies* volume of 231 poems, which Lawrence finished on 28 February 1929, his creative juices begin to run dry. His vibrant intensity sours now into flat, categorical statement—by turns bitter, wry, and pungent, yet enlivened by an amused conversational fire. The volume's major theme is simple: all of us have been let down by a society that worships money, elevates class, and prizes cerebral emotion—and no one has been let down more than Lawrence. (Frieda is not mentioned.) Man is intrinsically so much better than the system allows him to be, Lawrence argues. Two tiny poems capture him in the wake of physical decline—patient, acquiescent, alone, as he often was in his later life:

> I cannot help but be alone
> for desire has died in me, silence has grown,
> and nothing now reaches out to draw
> other flesh to my own.

And then more poignantly, using a favorite image, the ocean, he writes:

> I have no desire any more
> towards woman or man, bird, beast or creature or thing.
> All day long I feel the tide rocking, rocking
> though it strikes no shore
> in me.
> Only mid-ocean.—

The final, stark, lonely line evokes the quiet closure of death. Tossed from the boat of mainstream culture, Lawrence has valiantly struggled to stay afloat. Only his body yields.

When his manuscript of *Pansies* was (temporarily) seized by Scotland Yard, Lawrence exploded: "How sickening this dirty hypocrisy!" He dutifully retyped the poems, sent Martin Secker an expurgated typescript that appeared in July, but allowed Charles Lahr, a friendly London anarchist, to publish an unexpurgated edition in August. In its review the *Times Literary Supplement* identified the book's central effect as "a comprehensive hatred."

The second young man who came to Bandol that winter was P. R. Stephensen (1901–65), a tall, lanky, athletic Australian who had taken his degree at Oxford. Forceful, impulsive, anarchic by nature, he was, says his biographer, "a man's man: an all-round chauvinist." Backed by a London bookseller named Edward Goldston, he was, though still in his twenties, about to inaugurate the Mandrake Press. On holiday with his friend Davies, he appeared in Bandol on 18 December. Stephensen wanted to print an expensive limited edition of Lawrence's paintings and to preface it with an essay Lawrence would write on modern painting. Energetic and fearless, he would attempt (Lawrence hoped) "to make a hole in the bourgeois world" and pull down its walls. For his part he admired Lawrence's courage and heroic loneliness and, with Lawrence as his guide, envisioned "constructive hatred more clearly as a prolegomena to action than ever I did before." Lawrence's cry had not fallen into midocean.

In January Lawrence duly composed an introduction to his twenty-four paintings, which Stephensen reproduced, using a four-color process. Lawrence's critical essay shows him fully charged. He grapples with Bloomsbury art critics like Roger Fry, laments the way earlier painters fought their intuitive understanding of the body, and strongly endorses Paul Cézanne (who had died twenty years earlier) as a painter who transcended clichés in order to startle viewers into seeing what is new. Lawrence praises Cézanne for his willingness to rely on intuition as the means of seeing afresh the world of substance—and hence to see not a fruit called an apple, but the "appleyness" of the fruit. Cézanne tried, that is, to see an object not just from the front but all around. "The true imagination," Lawrence concludes, "is for ever curving round to the other side, to the back of presented appearance." It aims for wholeness of vision. Indeed, Lawrence's painting *Leda*, completed a month earlier, hides the nude woman's face so that what is alive is not her "personality" at all but her womanly body, fully formed, molded with tawny tints. She looks like Frieda.

Delighted by Lawrence's brisk and perceptive introduction, Stephensen spent £2,000 to produce the volume of paintings. He printed 500 copies to be sold at 10 guineas each and a special edition of 10 vellum copies to be sold at 50 guineas each. His prices astounded Lawrence. But all were sold.

Unlike Davies and Stephensen, the third man to come, a handsome young Californian named Brewster Ghiselin (b. 1903), was then a student at Oxford. Adrift during his winter vacation, disillusioned with current modes of academic study, he came to Bandol looking for Lawrence and found him on the beach, sitting alone on a tree-shaded bench, huddled inside an overcoat, quietly watching the sea. The two men talked about the beaches of California, the ranch in New Mexico, the working class in England, and Keats's poetry. At Lawrence's invitation Ghiselin moved into the Beau Rivage until he returned to Oxford in mid-January. On some days they visited the teeming market in the church square to buy yellow apples and sweet tangerines, look at the racks of clothing, or admire the fish heaped in baskets; or sauntered among the fishermen mending their brown nets; or strolled out to see a flock of goats grazing near the roadside. One afternoon when Lawrence felt able, they climbed the hills above Bandol, winding among the olives and pines, Lawrence's "quick attention accent[ing] every scene and event," Ghiselin recalled. And on the afternoon of 10 January 1929 they took the bus to Toulon, ambled through the port, remarked on its sailors and cats, drank coffee and rum in a dockside café, then meandered through the dark streets, buying roasted chestnuts. Although Ghiselin felt revived by his visit, he never saw Lawrence again.

After his departure, the Lawrences felt lonely. They wanted visitors. They were also solicitous to old friends like Ottoline Morrell, who had been ill. On 25 January Frieda wrote her a letter that reflects both her generous optimism and the core of her philosophy: "I wish there were something to soothe those pains of yours, I feel [it is] sitting still in the sun and letting the good spirits of the universe carry them away—I dont believe in big towns, they take one's inner peace and the relation with all abiding things—But you will get well, I am sure—Lawrence is really so very much better, it is surprising how one can heal, miracles happen if one lets them!" Frieda is touchingly naïve as she applies Lawrence's self-help remedy to Ottoline, who suffered from necrosis of the jaw, from deafness, and (emotionally) from having sold her beloved estate, Garsington, six months earlier.

After Aldous and Maria Huxley stopped for a brief visit, Lawrence's sister Ada Clarke came in February, bringing with her a swell of unrest. She stayed for eleven days. Beset by a midlife crisis, ready to abandon the Midlands life she had patiently constructed, fed up with the depressed retail "trade" in Ripley, where she lived, Ada filled Lawrence "with tortures of angry depression." Her unhappiness was only a version of his own. On 22 February he confessed to the emotional change that Ravagli's coming had wrought. This man had altered his own relation to Frieda: "The things that seemed to make up one's life die into insignificance, and [a person's] whole state is wretched. I've been through it these last three years—and suffered, I tell you." This frank statement recalls the partial collapse of his marriage three years earlier. Both he and Ada felt deeply disappointed.

By March the Lawrences had agreed to leave sunny Bandol, where Lawrence had not (he proudly told Mabel Luhan) spent a single day in bed. In Toulon he bought a new gray suit, fashionable new shirts, smart new shoes, and a brimmed hat, hoping for reincarnation as "a dashing body that doesn't cough." After all the dithering, the Lawrences had decided to go to Spain, to the island of Mallorca, not far from Barcelona, which their 1929 German *Baedeker* described as "a quiet resort in winter and spring," its mild climate rarely disturbed by rain. On 11 March they departed, Frieda going first to Baden-Baden to see her mother for two weeks, Lawrence to Paris to arrange for a cheap edition of *Lady Chatterley's Lover* designed to rout the three or four pirated editions then available. To this Paris edition, which Edward Titus eventually supervised, Lawrence wrote a brief introduction, "telling them all what I think of them." Bravely he tried to shield himself against the city's dirt, noise, polluted air, and crowded streets.

Looked after by Rhys Davies, who accompanied him to Paris, Lawrence stayed four long weeks, mostly at the Hotel de Versailles. His haggard eyes made blue sockets in his pale face, while the raw March wind tore at his frail frame. His letters allude to his ill health, but Davies has left a far more candid account. One night, lying asleep in the connecting hotel room, he heard Lawrence's violent, writhing cough, rushed into the room—frightened that a hemorrhage would follow—and at the sick man's bedside suddenly saw that Lawrence could treat himself: "His leather bag of homely medicines lay open beside his bed. When I suggested calling a doctor he flew into a rage. He asked me to sit quietly by the bed for a while. He needed the aid of some human presence. The fit of anger seemed to be good for him, and soon he was calmer, lay back exhausted, unspeaking but triumphant." Why did he refuse a doctor? Long ago he had learned that doctors meant money, that self-treatment protected both his pride and his pocketbook. Worse, a doctor might confront him with a shocking diagnosis and insist on a sanatorium. Aldous Huxley recalls that when Frieda returned from Germany, Lawrence—now buttressed—refused to seek medical treatment, even though Huxley found him "a great deal worse" than he was in Les Diablerets a year earlier—"coughs more, breathes very quickly and shallowly, has no energy," and, though talking animatedly for an hour or two at a time, showed only a semblance of health.

But that semblance of health often reappeared, and Frieda seemed to call it forth more quickly than anyone. Resourceful in her own way, she would organize money-saving picnics in her hotel room, which kept Lawrence from having to brave the outdoors. As Davies recalls, "She would go out with a basket and return with delicious pâté and vegetable salads which we ate from paper napkins and cartons; cheese, apples, one of those long batons of bread, and wine in our tooth glasses, made the feasts all the more festal for Frieda's broad *hausfrau* gaiety and her eye for the best items in food shops."

Lawrence was often busy. With Davies he set out to find a publisher—finally Titus—to issue a cheap edition of *Lady Chatterley*, from which Lawrence would reap half the profits. And without Davies he visited two distinguished couples, the Huxleys at nearby Suresnes and, with Frieda, the Crosbys at Moulin du Soleil, a restored mill at rural Ermenonville. The Huxleys, who entertained Lawrence for the week of 18 March 1929, were solicitous and kind but were caught in their own social spin; Lawrence quickly tired of seeing people. "These big cities take away my real will to live," he said ominously.

The Crosbys, Harry and Caresse, were far more flamboyant than the Huxleys. Rich and spoiled, a hedonist even in the twenties, Harry had once paid one hundred gold dollars for the manuscript of Lawrence's unexpurgated story "Sun," and when he impulsively bought the old mill at Ermenonville, he wrote an IOU on the white cuff he ripped from Caresse's shirtwaist. He was both romantic and eccentric—he had acquired tattoos on the soles of his feet, smoked a pipe of opium to pave his way to Nirvana, and nicknamed one of his dogs Clytoris. A 1928 photograph of the Crosbys shows Harry, at thirty, looking anxious and thin, his intense eyes gleaming like demons; at thirty-five, Caresse looks genial and tolerant, her ravenous sexuality subtly cloaked. The Lawrences spent the last weekend in March at the mill, Lawrence soaking in the sun while Frieda played records on the Crosbys' gramophone. They could scarcely believe, some months later, that Harry had shot himself in a New York City hotel as his mistress, also shot, lay dead at his side. But Lawrence at once fathomed Harry's deed as "the last sort of cocktail excitement," the culmination of a series of escalating personal risks, piled like dominoes on the slope of a short life.

## THE CHATTERING OF CASTANETS

The Spanish island of Mallorca had long appealed to Frieda. Larger than Capri, and much quieter, Mallorca was the size of Cornwall or Rhode Island. "It's so clean and shiny and glamorous here!" Frieda told Davies. Lawrence liked it too. At their small hotel, the Príncipe Alfonso, centrally located on the harbor, their rooms (16 and 17) abutted the Mediterranean. The sea shimmered brilliantly in the cool breeze. Frieda could swim, and the climate seemed wonderful—"about the best in Europe," Lawrence announced to the Brewsters. In the fields nearby grew olive trees, grapes, and corn, but with precious little rain, the crops struggled. Mule-drawn trams traversed the capital city of Palma, and away from the city stretched good roads for motor-car excursions to such sites as the Miramar chateau.

Soon after they arrived, on 17 April, Lawrence took ill with what appeared to be malaria, "and my teeth chattered like castanets—and that's the only truly Spanish thing I've done," he laughed to Davies, who had returned to England. But his sudden illness meant that Frieda could forget about a home in Spain. Anyway, she scarcely tried to speak Spanish. They would stay on at the Alfonso, despite its cost. Incredibly, Lawrence's hotel bill for the week of 29 May has survived. It shows that a week cost him £10 (282 pesetas). Beverages, which were extra, included beer, wine, and vermouth, and, because he sometimes invited local residents for lunch, he paid for three additional dinners and a good red Rioja wine on the twenty-ninth. The slowly passing weeks allowed him, he told Harry Crosby, "to be very successfully lazy," and days spent resting under the pine trees of a lonely bay made him loath to leave the island. But Frieda, weary of itinerant living and aware that Lawrence was now comparatively well off, wanted to settle somewhere, preferably (of course) in Italy: "I *must* have a house of my own now," she cried. Finally, Lawrence agreed: "I'd best have a proper place to live in," he admitted to Secker. He was now too ill to wander.

Meanwhile, in London, Dorothy Warren had been holding Lawrence's paintings for months—holding them without telling him when she would show them publicly. She annoyed him; he found her unreliable. But she and Stephensen finally agreed that his sumptuous book of Lawrence's paintings and her show at the Warren Gallery should coincide. Her exhibition opened to the public on 15 June 1929 and Lawrence received his *Paintings of D. H. Lawrence* a few days later. (Described as "very nice indeed," it would earn him five hundred pounds, an impressive sum for one book.) When Lawrence and Frieda finally left Mallorca on 18 June, Frieda went to London to see the long-promised show—and her children. She journeyed to Kent and stayed briefly with Stephensen and his lady friend, Winifred, then moved into the Kingsley Hotel on Hart Street. Lawrence, grateful still for the Mediterranean sun, went to be near the Huxleys at Forte dei Marmi, a city west of Florence, and invited Orioli to be his guest at the Pensione Giuliani, where they could take all their meals under a huge shade tree. Orioli's lively gossip amused him.

No one who saw the twenty-five paintings—some of them boldly provocative—would have been surprised that trouble lurked. Even Frieda thought that the paintings "looked a little wild and overwhelming" in the gallery's delicately furnished setting. They had a daring insouciance. From Renoir Lawrence had learned the luxurious modeling of the human body, as in *Contadini* (1928), a sensuous painting of an Italian peasant whose dark head and nude torso link him to Mellors. From Cézanne Lawrence had learned to reduce the landscape to shapes, as he does in *Red Willow Trees* (1927)—a personal favorite of his—in which the rounded trees and the nude buttocks of the three men frame a peninsula of land at the center, which looks like the uncircumcised phallus that Lawrence had admired in Etruscan statuary. In his painting the landscape projects what the three men hide.

Newspaper critics found the paintings flagrantly individual. The *Daily Express* thought that Lawrence's ugly subjects might make viewers "recoil with horror," and the *Daily Telegraph* urged British authorities (who could invoke the 1857 Obscenities Act) to close a show both "gross and obscene." Curious spectators, each paying a shilling, quickly swarmed to the Warren Gallery. Lawrence learned that thirty-five hundred people had seen the show in the first week alone. Bloomsbury sniffed at his paintings. Lytton Strachey, the eminent biographer, found them "wretched things" and lamented that he had seen "some pricks visible, but not a single erection."

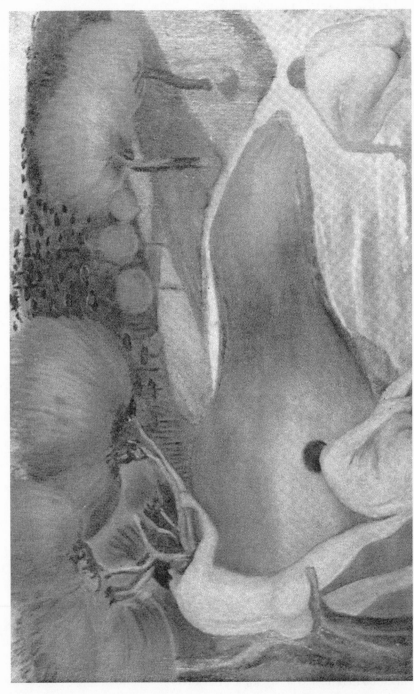

*Red Willow Trees* (1927), painting by D. H. Lawrence (Courtesy of Laurence Pollinger Limited and the Estate of Frieda Lawrence Ravagli)

On 4 July the Warren Gallery gave a champagne party for Frieda. She wore a bright shawl, a spray of lilies, and red shoes. "I had a terrific time there," she recalled later, "feeling no end of an important person." Her experience scripted a role she liked more and more—the role of guardian and champion of her husband's work.

On the fifth, however, two detectives arrived at the gallery and, spotting pubic hair on some of the nudes, demanded that Philip Trotter, Dorothy's new husband, close the exhibition at once. He refused. An hour later, four burly men arrived in a police van and confiscated thirteen of the paintings, including *Contadini*. Aghast, Frieda remained in London to hear what action the gallery's attorney would recommend. She wanted the paintings back without delay, and urged Dorothy and Philip to compromise—agree never to show them again—in order to rescue them from the cellar of the Marlborough police station. Frieda knew for sure what Lawrence soon wrote: "I do not want my pictures to be burned, under any circumstances," he enjoined Dorothy, who—for her part—relished the publicity. Lawrence would have remembered the fate of 1,011 copies of *The Rainbow*. When the case came up on 8 August, the magistrate released the pictures but charged the Warren Gallery five pounds, five shillings to destroy four copies of the paintings book, which had been for sale in the gallery.

Although Lawrence rested quietly on the beach at Forte, he was unable to protect his body. On 6 July the food or the water attacked his digestive system just as he reached Florence to gather his summer clothes from the trunks Orioli had stored. Alarmed by seeing how limply Lawrence lay, Orioli put him to bed, then—worried that Frieda might go blithely to Germany to see her mother—telegraphed his distress. She came at once. Sadly, from London Frieda had seldom written to Lawrence. She had been too busy seeing family and friends. She had learned, she told Mabel Luhan in May, to "leave him alone and give him as much as I can but make no demands—not of any sort." Still, her epistolary silences disturbed Lawrence. When she arrived in Florence on the eleventh, he had anticipated what she would do. He told Orioli: "Do you see those peaches in the bowl? She will say, 'What lovely peaches,' and she will devour them." So it was. "After my first look at Lawrence," Frieda added, "when his eyes had signalled to me their relief, 'She is here with me,' I felt my thirst from the long journey and ate the peaches." In fact, her appetites would not be denied. A touch selfish, a touch careless, she could sometimes put her own needs first.

After she and Lawrence left Florence for Germany, where they went for two months to escape the Italian heat, Frieda celebrated her fiftieth birthday on 11 August, joined by her mother and their close friends. It would be Frieda's last birthday with Lawrence. Showered with roses and chocolates, she enjoyed trout, duck, and champagne. "[N]ine people—very nice," Lawrence recounted for his sister Emily. But beneath the surface he thought

Frieda oddly tentative, "afraid of the next step." Altogether, he told Maria Huxley the next day, "I just leave her alone." She was depressed about Lawrence. His energy was streaming away. He could not take walks, felt miserable in the cold German climate, and—he told Orioli—hadn't the strength to do a thing. The doctor he consulted advised living by the sea, avoiding both exertion (which aggravated his cough) and dust (which blocked the absorption of oxygen). He felt wasted, and, in his slow descent, powerless: "[I] can't fight any more."

In fact, Lawrence had changed a great deal. His letters—he averaged two a day in the last year of his life—suggest how his interests had narrowed. Worries about his health had eclipsed his concern for the world. What once seemed a challenge became an annoyance—finding a house, traveling, negotiating with publishers, writing articles. Now he cultivated a *generalized* repugnance for the world of men, and his delight in human relationships vanished. People like Frieda's mother now irritated (even enraged) him, their health a galling reminder of his decline. It is not that Lawrence felt isolated but that a great loneliness had overtaken him. Even in his marriage to Frieda some of the joy had withered, the affection gone slack.

Miracle cures like the Gerson Diet offered Lawrence the cruel hope of recovery. "So now for a new diet and a new man," he wrote blithely to the Huxleys, confident that the Gerson Diet of raw food and porridge without salt—which his new doctor urged—would buttress his health. But not until he and Frieda reached France—on 23 September—did he feel better. Within days Frieda had found a real estate agent in Bandol, Lawrence's beloved seaside village, and then located the Villa Beau Soleil, only a ten-minute walk from the Beau Rivage. Ready for new occupants on 1 October, the stucco house had six rooms and a sunken marble bath, central heating, and a large sunny terrace overlooking the Mediterranean—all for a thousand francs a month ($40 or £8). Strong sunlight "has a soothing and forgetful effect on [me]," he told Caresse Crosby; he was grateful to see the sparkling Mediterranean again. He needed it. Frieda sadly acknowledged the change: "Lorenzo is often depressed, it's hard to put up with, I suppose for him too."

## The Beau Soleil Stands Empty

Sometime in October, Lawrence finished his poem "The Ship of Death," creating a spare final statement. It offers no Christian consolation. It opens with a plea, followed by lines that ripple over the ends:

> Oh build your ship of death, for you will need it.
> Now in the twilight, sit by the invisible sea
> Of peace, and build your little ship
> Of death, that will carry the soul

On its last journey, on and on, so still
So beautiful, over the last of seas.

When the ultimate day comes, the long-awaited journey ends in

Oblivion, the last wonder!
When we have trusted ourselves entirely
To the unknown, and are taken up
Out of our little ships of death
Into pure oblivion.

His intuition confirms a simple truth—that a lifelong exploration of the unknown at last confronts a final mystery: *oblivion,* the unknowable. He will not speculate on what is beyond reason and intuition. Only the journey, however arduous, has mattered.

As the autumn months passed, the envelope of Lawrence's life closed tighter. He spent his mornings sitting up in his bed, looking balefully at the Mediterranean, its dancing waves a comment on his own feeble condition. Yet he loved the view. Occasionally he would totter to a cluster of dark pines near the house, then creep back, exhausted. When the Brewsters came from Capri to be near him, they would take him for short motor drives as they searched for their own country villa; Achsah brought flowers to cheer him and, like Lilly in *Aaron's Rod,* Earl came daily to give him coconut-oil massages, his affectionate silence a welcome reassurance. Even their cook, Mme. Martens, prepared mustard and linseed plasters to try to heal him.

But the life-thread was too thin. All these remedies having failed, Lawrence grew weaker. "I am in bed again here, feeling pretty rotten," he alerted Caresse on 15 October. "I expect I shall have to go into a sanatorium for a time, unless I pick up very soon." The thought of writing and publishing repelled him. On 1 November he completed an extension of "A Propos of *Lady Chatterley's Lover*" but—though thinking the essay beautiful—he loathed publishing it. Even the pot of money he had earned hardly mattered, although it now included ten thousand francs from the Paris *Lady Chatterley,* enough to rent the Beau Soleil for close to a year. The money, he knew, was for Frieda—the bubbling spring from which her new life would need to flow. She yearned to go back to the Kiowa Ranch, but not by herself.

For now she could only implore him to get well. "Everything flourishes," she would tell him—"plants and cats and gold-fish [—] why can't you?" Baffled, he would reply: "I want to, I want to, I wish I could." Frieda's words sound unfeeling, but all other remedies had failed: only his tenacious will could be lured into further combat. A friend named Frederick Carter, who had interested Lawrence in the symbols of the Apocalypse, came to see him in November and found him dressed in gray trousers and blue jacket, his conversation still penetrating but acrid with gossip. "Now don't be spiteful, Lorenzo," Frieda called out, laughing, as he weakly began an anecdote about the novelist H. G. Wells. People wearied him.

Beaten now, thwarted by destiny, his tenacity overpowered, he had at last no choice but to go into a sanatorium. The idea seemed poisonous—the inmates coughing and spitting blood, their condition a cold sentence of despair. "It's so bitter for him," Frieda wrote the day before they departed. Rigid with self-discipline, unwilling to sentimentalize his own slow collapse, he commanded Frieda to bring him his papers. He tore up most of them; the others he made tidy; but he did not make a will. On 6 February a hired car drove up to the Beau Soleil. On the floor of his room lay almond blossoms that Achsah, tireless defender of beauty, had brought—her graceful gesture a final salute to the man and artist she revered. Rigidly silent, Lawrence climbed into the car to make his last journey.

From nearby Toulon he, Frieda, and Earl took the train to Antibes, then a car to the Ad Astra sanatorium in Vence, a hilly town on the Mediterranean coast of France. There he lay in a room painted a harsh blue, his windows covered with yellow curtains, his balcony in full view of the mountains and sea. Earl stayed with him for two weeks, brought him masses of orange flowers, and, before leaving for India, heard Lawrence say that he longed to return to New Mexico. Others came—Barbara Weekley, the Huxleys, Ida Rauh from New Mexico, the di Chiaras (friends of the Huxleys), Jo Davidson the sculptor, the Aga Khan and his wife. They tried to amuse him, bringing flowers and cheerful conversation, but he did not rally. Nor did he respond to the treatment that Dr. Medinier, his physician, recommended. On 23 February Ida wrote to Mabel Luhan: "Lawrence is sinking very rapidly and I see very little hope for him." He weighed ninety-eight pounds.

Frieda was relieved not to have the full responsibility for his care. She was not a skilled nurse. One day Lawrence surprised Barbara when he said, "Your mother does not care for me any more, the death in me is repellent to her." Earlier he had hurt Frieda when he said, "I could always trust your instinct to know the right thing for me, but now you don't seem to know any more." She knew nothing about death—only about forms of living. Still, one night he wanted her to stay with him, to sleep on the long chair in his room, and when she agreed, his eyes turned warm and grateful. Yet what Frieda remembered was her powerlessness: "I knew how Lawrence suffered and yet I could not help him."

At last, when both of them realized that he was rapidly losing weight, that he could no longer write, and that even the Ad Astra had done him little good, Frieda rented a villa in Vence—the Villa Robermond—and took him there in a taxi on 1 March for his last desperate attempt to heal himself. His lungs were so scarred that he was like a ship with shredded sails, crawling helplessly across a long sheet of sea. Helped up the villa's steps, he lay on the narrow bed, exhausted. He was too ill to eat much. The next day Frieda sat and read him a biography of Columbus. In the afternoon, tortured with pain, he cried, "I must have a temperature, I am delirious"; to Maria Huxley, who sat holding his head in her hands, he cried, astonished, "I see my body over there on the table!" As his misery intensified, his resilience failed: "I must have morphia," he gasped. Barby ran for a doctor, who came with an injection. Lawrence began to breathe more peacefully. Frieda held his left ankle. "Hold me, hold me," he had pleaded earlier. "I don't know where I am." Gradually gaps came in his breathing, wider and still wider, until his face became a mask, his jaw sank. Stunned, Frieda walked up and down beside his room, astonished that he had died so calmly, without pain or struggle.

Then she saw that he had changed. He looked proud and manly and splendid, his face tearing from death's grip a new poise, a new dignity, without a mark of anguish. She dared not touch him now. He had gone from her. In triumph, he had joined the elements—the rich earth, the shimmering sea, the luminous sky. The earth's body could reclaim him now.

Two days later he was buried in the cemetery at Vence. The funeral was simple and cheap; his sisters sent masses of mimosa that covered the coffin. There was no service, no series of tributes, no music—just a plain oak casket lowered silently into the earth. Only Lawrence's close friends came: Aldous and Maria, Achsah Brewster, Barbara Weekley, Ida Rauh, Robert Nichols, the di Chiaras, and Edward Titus—and at a distance some unknown admirers and reporters. "It was all beautiful and dignified because there were only people there who loved him deeply," Frieda wrote to his sisters on 4 March. Afterward, she placed all the flowers on the grave. They were what he loved.

## Frieda Struggles

Letters and telegrams arrived in profusion. Around the world Lawrence's death was reported in major newspapers. In a front-page story the London *Evening News* hailed Lawrence's power as a writer. The *Glasgow Herald* called him a "brilliant novelist and poet," and in the London *Daily News* Robert Lynd, who had once attacked *The Rainbow,* praised Lawrence for showing more fire and energy than any other English novelist of his generation. Old friends consoled Frieda. "I believe no one could have given him the things he needed as well as you did," wrote Barbara Low. David Garnett, a friend from almost twenty years earlier, professed that he had *loved* Lawrence. Although Frieda felt reassured, she astutely recognized the immense weight she shouldered. The world's response to Lawrence's death showed her how important it would be to protect his memory. Inside her, his essence grew larger and larger.

At once, decisions confronted her. Because Lawrence had died intestate, how much money would she have? Could she afford to travel? Who would administer the estate—she? or Lawrence's family? What unpublished material should she release? And to whom? Most important, where should she live?

She knew all too well how Lawrence had resisted external compulsion. He had never wanted a circumstance to interfere with an intuition—had never wanted a cerebral plan to curb a truthful impulse. His distrust of professional medicine extended even to the law. With consummate tact, Frieda had never urged him, even in his final illness, to make a will. She informed his sisters: "He had made no will, but said to me—I suppose I leave everything to you but if my sisters want any thing, you'll give it them." His grudging "I suppose" gauges his deep ambivalence to possessions. Hoping to oblige, Frieda asked his sisters if they wanted either his clothes or his watch. She had been advised to burn his clothing, and shortly after his death the French authorities came to disinfect the Villa Robermond.

Frieda paused to think of her future. Having given Lawrence her unstinted strength and confused devotion, she now wanted a return. She wanted not just the majestic memories that she could so readily recall but the financial profit that his work had not yet earned. She knew that the Paris *Lady Chatterley*—and its German translation—sold steadily. "I will make them pay now," she said with bravado. A few days after his death, Frieda confided to Emily: "I have something over 4000 £s; its just possible, that there will be quite a lot of money later on, if affairs are properly managed; in which case, I will gladly give you and Ada some of it."

Frieda had a great deal to do—seeing a slow stream of mourners, packing up her belongings at the Beau Soleil, then coping with the awful news that her daughter Barbara had been diagnosed with tuberculosis of the bone. Her back would have to be put in plaster. Some months later Frieda was forced to acknowledge that Barby had also suffered a nervous breakdown, sobbing, "My poor mother her child is dead." Still, she told Emily, she firmly recognized her mission: "I must live and do my share for him yet."

Writing from New Mexico, Mabel Luhan gave Frieda a shock. A draft of Mabel's book, *Lorenzo in Taos* (1932), portrayed the Lawrences as squabbling and mean. "How it upset me!" Frieda told Brett. And to Mabel she complained that "the positive achievement of us all you don't put in your book." Mabel's typescript had a profound effect. Alone among those who knew him, Frieda would harvest the wonder of Lawrence's legacy and, if necessary, sanitize him in order to forestall such treachery as Mabel's. One might say that Frieda froze Lawrence's memory when she finished reading Mabel's typescript.

Believing that she understood Lawrence even better now that he was dead, Frieda adopted a defiant stance. She believed that the world had refused to acknowledge his genius. She would promote it. In her distinctive way she would reconstruct his vision of simple living and spiritual truth, of protesting sham values. His fight would become hers. As she wrote to Brett, "But for *me* he made a new heaven and earth anyhow and I stick by it—I will live for it." She would take him west, back to the ranch. "I want to come to New Mexico," she told Brett, "and what would console me would be to build him a little temple there ourselves, I know the place at the ranch, high up beyond the spring." But her dream, though it freshly energized her, stalled in new complications.

Lawrence's brother George, whom Lawrence had not seen for fifteen years, decided to intervene. On behalf of the family he wanted Frieda to have the income from the estate only during her lifetime. Feeling aggrieved, Frieda balked at what might have seemed a reasonable compromise. Her reasons are unclear. She knew that Lawrence would have objected to George, who had once, during the war, railed against the Germans and avowed that they "ought to be killed." But she seems primarily to have believed, ever more forcefully, that the royalties *and* the copyrights *and* the manuscripts should be hers. "Firmly fixed in my mind," she told A. S. Frere-Reeves, a London publisher, "is that Lawrence wanted me to have everything." She seems to have felt neither greed nor spite but, as the custodian of his flame, a new sense of power, even as she admitted to Ottoline's husband, Philip, "I dont know in the least how to behave legally."

In the interim she and George were named co-administrators, but after a time he refused to authorize royalty payments to Frieda. Finally, in 1932, her London solicitor, C. D. Medley, brought suit against George and used John Middleton Murry's testimony to persuade the court that Frieda was Lawrence's sole heir and deserved the entire estate, valued then at £2,438. The court's decision in November turned Frieda into the family's antagonist. An exchange of bitter letters left them unable to be civil. "I had some respect for [Ada]," Frieda told a friend in October, "I have *none* left." She thought Ada deceitful. For her part, Ada very much blamed Frieda. Repulsed by her greed, she asked Frieda "never to write to me again." For the rest of her life, Frieda never spoke to Lawrence's family— her hatred ran deep—and Lawrence's niece recalled that George, with thick sarcasm, "always referred to [Frieda] as 'My Lady.'"

Frieda knew that important material remained unpublished. When Aldous Huxley suggested that he might select some of Lawrence's letters for publication, and introduce them, Frieda was grateful. Enid Hilton offered to make a typescript, and Aldous arranged that the book would appear in 1932 from William Heinemann, where his friend A. S. Frere-Reeves was the director. But beyond the letters, there were late poems, the Apocalypse, a study of Thomas Hardy, the Etruscan sketches, some early plays, and an assortment of manuscripts that could be put on the market. Frieda, trying to be an intrepid literary broker, astounded A. S. W. Rosenbach, an American dealer, when she asked twenty-five thousand pounds for all of Lawrence's manuscripts. After Norman Douglas came with Orioli to see Lawrence's grave, he warned Frieda to be wary of her grand "illusions" and on 29 March wrote her a sobering letter: "Don't make any mistake: now is the moment to print everything that DHL ever wrote. In a few years' time there will be very little demand."

Confused, Frieda went to London four times in the year that followed, meeting with Percy Robinson, solicitor for the estate (he now sided with George); with Martin Secker, Lawrence's longtime publisher; with Frere-Reeves, who offered her an advance of two thousand pounds for the rights to Lawrence's unpublished work; and with Laurence Pollinger, the young literary agent whom Lawrence had trusted. In business matters Pollinger was efficient, experienced, and tactful, displaying just the qualities that Frieda lacked. She could muster enthusiasm or fierce anger but not finesse. Even Lawrence thought her impulsive. Her rich understanding of emotional complexity did not transfer to contractual complexities, which daunted her. She would need help.

For a year she roamed Europe, shifting from London to Paris to Baden-Baden, back to Vence, back to Florence. She saw mostly old friends—Ottoline and Philip Morrell, David Garnett, Enid Hilton, Middleton Murry (often), Michael Arlen, Orioli and Douglas, her son Monty and his fiancée, Vera, and of course the Huxleys. The social whirl appealed to her. In this volatile period all who spent time with her valued her friendship and savored her stories, but some were struck by her impetuous behavior. Her fear of exhausting her money—she had quickly received one thousand pounds from the royalty account—did not curb her yen to travel. She also had medical bills for both Lawrence and Barby, not to mention rent for the Villa Robermond and, later, because Barby needed a different house to recover her mental stability, the Villa Les Aspras. Frieda had roots nowhere. In July she told Brett that she was "frightened" to be alone.

When she got news in mid-November that her mother was very ill, she went straight to Germany. Alas, she arrived two hours after her mother's heart failed. In less than a year, she had lost the two people for whom she had had the greatest affection. She became anxious, agitated, even reckless. Lawrence had often said that Frieda needed someone who would keep her balanced. What she needed was a man. As Aldous Huxley wrote to Brett, "Since L[awrence] is no longer there to keep her in order, she plunges about in the most hopeless way." Even Orioli—always genial and accommodating—was annoyed when she asked him to travel to Savona and arrange for a certain attractive Bersaglieri officer to leave Italy with her. Orioli unkindly called her "a nymphomaniac."

For a year after Lawrence's death, Frieda had rarely mentioned Angelo Ravagli's name in her letters, but she had spent time alone with him and treasured his "genuine warmth for me." Bored in the Bersaglieri, Ravagli, enamored of Frieda, reckoned his chances for career advancement were slim. Ravagli's son Stefano, interviewed in 1998, recalled that when his father first met Frieda in 1925, she was a married woman and, as such, represented no threat to his Italian family. Good looking, powerfully attracted to women, Angelo had already had many affairs. But after Lawrence's death, Stefano remembered, "Frieda was in great trouble; she was very disorganized. She needed somebody who could help her manage the Lawrence estate. My father went along with her as her business partner. It was right. It was his opportunity to see a new part of the world." He wrangled half-a-year's unpaid leave from the army. It may have cost Frieda five hundred pounds.

Soon she was set to depart for America, the place she had longed for. "I am thrilled at coming," she told Mabel Luhan. In early May 1931 she traveled to Genoa and, with Ravagli in tow, stepped aboard the S.S. *Conte Grande*. Her life was about to change. She had always felt overshadowed by Lawrence. She had always worried that her development into a woman of purpose and maturity, of charm and interest, had been eclipsed by the approbation accorded him. Now, at fifty-two, she was free to redefine herself as an emancipated woman, full of robust joy, standing on the precipice of a new life. But what connected her most intimately to Lawrence was the piece of property that both of them had cherished—the Kiowa Ranch in New Mexico. They had often talked of returning. She would go there.

# 22

# A New Life for Frieda

## 1931–37

When Frieda and Angelo stepped off the ship on 20 May 1931, they stepped into a country caught in a depression that lasted for ten years. As the American economy collapsed, unemployment rose from 3 percent in 1929 to 24 percent just three years later, and in the same period industrial production fell 45 percent. Stocks were hit hardest. From their peak in September 1929 to their trough three years later, stock prices fell an astounding 83 percent. In the midst of this debacle, Frieda and Angelo arrived in New York City, spending one week at the Prince George Hotel on Twenty-eighth Street; seeing friends like the seasoned photographer Alfred Stieglitz, who owned an art gallery on Madison Avenue; visiting gentle Ben Huebsch at the Viking Press, which would eventually publish most of Lawrence's work in America; and checking on Lawrence's manuscripts at Curtis Brown's branch office in New York, where they met the repellant Samuel Roth. He offered Frieda one thousand pounds to sanction his piracy of *Lady Chatterley's Lover* and to bless his dramatization of the novel, which she thought "so terrible that I cant take his money." They rushed away to New Mexico, hopeful that Mabel Luhan and her entourage would be amicable. "O dear, how *mixed* my feelings are in coming," Frieda acknowledged on 23 May. She wanted to make Taos her new home—she loved its freedom and simplicity. But she hardly guessed how complicated her simple sheltered life would become.

Almost six years had passed since Frieda had been in Taos, and she was naturally worried about what had happened to her beloved Kiowa Ranch. Although Dorothy Brett had been left in charge, Frieda mistrusted her—and had flatly told her so—believing that Brett, always fiercely loyal to Lawrence, might ridicule her when she arrived. Brett, hoping to avoid conflict (while secretly thriving on it), had spent two weeks dispersing the pack rats, scrubbing the rough interior of the cabin, and making tidy a place that still had no running water, electric lights, or bathroom. Money was scarce, people were broke, and banks everywhere were collapsing. The Depression had scarred New Mexico, too. "The largest bank in El Paso popped . . . and another at Las Cruces," Brett informed Stieglitz.

Frieda's arrival, long anticipated, stirred great interest. Both Mabel and Brett recorded their reactions. After Christine Hughes drove the couple from Santa Fe to Taos, Mabel telegraphed her intimate friend Una Jeffers that Frieda seemed "VERY JOLLY" and her Capitano "FASCINATING." But beyond this fine welcome lay Mabel's deep ambivalence to Frieda—a grudging acknowledgment of her *gusto* and warmth but a dislike of her sexual energy and her sentimental husbanding of Lawrence's memory. Again, Mabel sensed a rival.

Brett, affronted by what she observed, felt like a wounded bird. In June she confided to Stieglitz, whom she adored, her exasperated account of Frieda making a new life at the ranch. That account, shaded by her own unconsummated relationship with Lawrence, bristles with pain: "Nothing would do but she must go straight up to the Ranch, had I the keys, so much anxiety to get the keys[;] with no food, no blankets, she hired a man in the town, would'nt wait for me, I had a flat tire, and went off, got some food from the Hawks and their blankets. I went up next day and took her a few tins. Then the following day I took them to Taos, met Mabel and Tony speeding up with Tony's station wagon, for her to buy. The man did'nt like it, so they bought Tony's La Salle for $800 which was a bargain, and the man is an appalling driver, he goes at a terrific pace and does'nt know how to stop the car. To go up there, to see that man (quite a nice man too) in Lorenzo's blue shirt, his white trousers, that wont button on him, gives me a pain." Intensely jealous of Frieda, Brett lashed out recklessly while she enshrined her own 1926 tryst with Lawrence as the central experience of her life. Unable to acknowledge Frieda's ebullient, passionate candor, Brett erected a simple contrast of chaste and unchaste: "I feel I am more truly his widow than Frieda. That one week of intense living, two nights of tragedy, have given him the only widow he is likely to have. . . . I have outwardly done all I can to make her comfortable, inwardly I vary from bitterness to laughter, to see her throw the spoons at [Ravagli], to watch his calmness, where Lawrence would have blazed. . . . Mabel and I shiver for Lorenzo—that chaste sensitive man—struggling to pour his chastity into

Mabel Dodge Sterne Luhan, c. 1930s (Courtesy of the Gersheim Collection, Harry Ransom Humanities Research Center, the University of Texas at Austin)

that Prostitute—His power was so great that he kept Frieda straight—by fighting—the moment he is dead she reverts—she was a prostitute with her first husband—she is now."

In the naïve hope that her candor would protect her, Frieda disregarded the emotional stew that her return had set bubbling. She could not alter the fact that Mabel and Brett, who were writing about Lawrence, wanted to anchor their recollections in a past that Frieda, now living with Ravagli, challenged. Frieda wanted to write too, but at her own pace. Because she was less disciplined than they, she thought she could write her memoir even as Angelo wore Lawrence's clothes and slept in his bed. Her desire for the company of a man distracted her. "Angelino . . . makes me forget my life with Lawrence, that life of otherness, how wonderful it really was!" she confessed to Mabel. Her confused feelings surprised her.

Yet it would be wrong to call Angelo Ravagli an opportunist, a gigolo, or a parasite on the Lawrence legacy. On the surface he was all of these—but he was much more. In many ways he was a typical soldier—simple, genuine, inarticulate, pragmatic, and hedonistic. But he offered Frieda stability and security; he also offered her an open sympathy that Lawrence had rarely shown after 1926, and a warm, sensual European charm. He was always genial. Brett judged Frieda "much happier" with him than she had been with Lawrence.

Mabel, herself happily married to a tall, stolid, inarticulate Native American named Tony Luhan, saw the newly arrived couple as well-matched sparring partners. Always a trenchant judge, she saw Ravagli as "the muscle and brawn kind, very determined and selfwilled . . . [who] shouts that Mussolini is the greatest man in the world today—and the greatest that has ever lived! This enrages Frieda—she screams—throws the knives and forks at him—shakes her fist." Although Frieda looked much older, her vitality fascinated Mabel, who recognized candidly that Frieda had used the profits of Lawrence's "painful exposés of their love" to build a new life.

Mabel could not see that Frieda had reinvented herself. The challenge that Lawrence had posed—of adventure encased within a stern moral code—had given way to a different challenge, to a grand venture unfolding within a more permissive code. After Lawrence's brooding depths, Frieda relished Ravagli's florid Italian flair, well captured in Mabel's description of a "Venetian" party they gave at the ranch in July 1931:

We found the whole place illumined with home made lanterns in green, red and white—very Italian! Long tables laid in the leveled and smoothed placita before the house . . . and *loads* of lovely food!
A large illumined and transparent sign before the place read: "Una noce in Venezia!". . . To a gramophone seven or eight couples danced on the smooth earth. Angelino is a marvelous dancer—moving tenderly and gravely through the most subtle patterns of the modern step. There is something of the noble child about him and a beauty of cheerful health. We all like him. He never misses an opportunity to seize one's hand under the table; and dancing with him is a somewhat embarrassing thing, though one cannot show a sign in the face of that candid happy creature—upon whose wide brow and wide apart brown eyes lies no slightest con-

sciousness of anything but amiable and affectionate delight. It was funny to watch Brett circling slowly in his arms with an intent look upon her face. Frieda was simply a magnificent Walkyrie with her blond hair flying, dressed in a white-squaw dress—of purest buckskin all trailing with little bells, teeth and strings of fringe. She was wild with pleasure at her party—at the lights—and the music. Brett and Frieda and I sat at one moment in a row! "Here we are!" she bellowed in her lusty voice! "We three! Wouldn't Lawrence be *astonished* if he could see the ranch tonight!" "Perhaps he can," replied Brett in a sinister voice. "That is the danger!"

Mabel brilliantly enthrones the regal new Frieda, trimmed in buckskin, triumphantly central, and now embracing Ravagli's "work hard, play hard" philosophy. What has changed is the seductive duplicity of hands gently squeezed under the table. But even that jarring image, which Mabel coyly records, exhibits the codes of the place. At that time (one resident remembered), Taos was "a place where people could do what they wanted," and because of its extreme permissiveness, "Taos was a sort of mecca," recalled Eya Fechin, the daughter of Frieda's close friend Tinka Fechin. Yet Taos was something else—a little Capri set in the American Rockies, a place where intrigue and gossip shaped its appeal. Clasped hands in clandestine places heralded even stranger events. Mabel remembered the sudden appearance of a youth named Parke, age eighteen, whom Frieda had befriended. Getting directions from Mabel, he walked all night to reach the ranch, then came to lunch stripped of his clothes. Gently, Frieda sent him on his way. He was the first of many odd creatures who would turn in wonder to Frieda.

## WE MUST GO BACK

At the ranch six months passed quickly. Angelo and Frieda had cleaned, repaired, gardened, and recaptured the simple life. Now they had to go. They could neither risk overstaying their visas nor ignore the fact that the Italian army had recalled a professional soldier on leave. On 16 November 1931 they departed for New York City, just as the gusting west winds socked the mountains above Taos, stripped the last leaves from the aspens, and showered the first snow over the treetops.

Although Frieda and Angelo remained in Europe for almost a year and a half, they were very restless. Frieda embroiled herself in getting Lawrence's books away from Thomas Seltzer's nephews and in settling Lawrence's estate; Angelo tried to free himself from the army. "I do hope I shall have enough money to get him out," Frieda confided to Mabel. Both she and Angelo longed to return to the openness and peace of the ranch. Yet because Frieda would need to help him support his family, and because he dreamed of building a more comfortable house near the old cabin, they would require a steady supply of money. Frieda would need to develop her bargaining skills.

But Europe provided compensations. In England, Frieda liked social-izing, liked being Lawrence's widow; she felt important. During 1932, ex-cept for long visits to Germany and Italy, she spent her time in London, at the Kingsley Hotel or at her quarters at 10 Hammersmith Terrace on the Thames River. She had lunch or tea with an array of friends—Murry, Dorothy Warren, Brett's brother Viscount Esher, Ottoline Morrell, Law-rence's South African friend Jan Juta, and the Bernard Shaws. Guided by Laurence Pollinger, her agent, she pored over the baffling details of the contracts he prepared for her signature, which soon included Pocket edi-tions; Colonial editions; French, German, and Spanish rights; film deals; and Aldous Huxley's edition of Lawrence's letters.

Though Frieda was eager to shore up Lawrence's literary reputation, she meant to live well. She thought Lawrence wanted her to thrive: "As for Lorenzo, I sit at his grave and smoke a cigarette," she wrote Brett on 14 May 1932, from Vence, "and I feel his strong spirit of love round me in the air and coming up from the earth—and then it is as if he said: 'Now you go away and live and attend to your jobs.'" One job was to keep alive Lawrence's memory and to promote his work; another was to secure a comfortable in-come for herself. Surviving royalty statements allow us to estimate it. In 1933, for instance, she earned, after taxes and agent's commission, at least $20,000 (about £4,500), which included £3,000 from the sale of film rights to *Lady Chatterley's Lover,* and in 1934 at least $6,000 (then about £1,200), which did not include Lawrence's U.S. stock certificates, trans-ferred to Frieda in August. Near the end of 1932, when she learned that the French translation of *Lady Chatterley's Lover* had sold 200,000 copies, she exclaimed to Mabel: "Can you see me as a business woman? When Lawrence always paid the little there was to pay and I never had a purse?"

Yet Frieda soon tired of London and waiting for her court case to be heard. Finally, after many annoying delays, old Judge Merrivale listened intently to Frieda tearfully describe Lawrence's last wishes, pondered Murry's declaration that Lawrence had made a will in 1914, and read depositions from Norman Douglas and Pino Orioli describing how they once heard Lawrence say that he hated his family. After contemplating this testimony, the judge handed the victory to Frieda. She got everything. "It was a real triumph," she exulted to Douglas Clayton, an old friend who had typed Lawrence's early stories. She and Angelo had freed themselves from the grip of what felt like a dying civilization. "I am *sick* of towns, sick of busi-ness, sick of Europe," she cried. They departed from Genoa on 25 April 1933, having struck a bargain. With her finances flourishing, Frieda agreed to pay Angelo a salary of one hundred dollars per month for his assistance;

Lady Ottoline Morrell and Frieda Lawrence, 1932 (Courtesy of Adrian Goodman)

his army pension would go to support his family, still living in Spotorno. A new phase could begin.

∽⟐

That second spring in Taos bestowed on them a splendid sense of renewal. To Brett, Frieda seemed much gentler now—less truculent. Supplied with money, seemingly replenished, confident and smartly dressed, Frieda and Angelo began to build a new home, located only a few dozen yards down-hill from the cabin that Lawrence had lovingly repaired in 1924. As soon as Frieda had decided on the rooms she wanted—especially a big kitchen—Angelo, helped by local workmen, began to position the logs and erect the house. He worked hard. In a simple memorandum he recorded, "Today, May 30, 1933 we started to build the New House in Kiowa Ranch." His extraordinary stamina made construction go quickly while cheap labor limited Frieda's cost. In August she told Pollinger that she had spent only five hundred pounds (less than twenty-five hundred dollars) on the new house. Cooking squash-blossom omelets, gardening, washing, feeding the lambs, making butter from the milk of her Jersey cow—these chores occupied her all summer. Harold Jay Snyder, a Lawrence collector and enthusiast who visited Frieda at this time, observed that she stayed busy "sewing and reading and fixing up [her] hacienda."

Yet she was also determined to write her memoir of Lawrence, which she had started soon after his death. It had cost her a good deal of anguish. She had struggled with its organization. Unlike Brett, she had not kept a journal of her years with Lawrence—she had only memories. Earlier she had told Mabel, "If I really write it with all the honesty and courage that's in me, it *wont* be a pretty book, but rather terrible." But she rejected that approach—she wanted to remember the inner beauty of her life with Lawrence. His writings had confirmed her stature as a woman. (Although she might have welcomed the help of a skilled writer, Angelo, who mangled written English all his life, could not assist her.) Inspired to write simply and concretely of their experience together, she gave the world a portrait of Lawrence that sparkles with immediacy and authenticity, that unfolds in fragments of lyric beauty, that prizes especially the valor of their pilgrimage together. Her brief account, though always vivid, is not comprehensive. "Yes," she admitted to Mabel, "the book ought to be more in detail, but then it comes, as it comes."

The book finished at last, Frieda chose the precise mode of publication and number of copies that Lawrence had chosen for *Lady Chatterley's Lover.* The Rydal Press, operated by a rich *littérateur* named Walter Goodwin, published her book privately in Santa Fe, in a beautiful limited edition of one thousand copies. Priced at $7.50, it appeared in June 1934 as *Not I,*

*But the Wind.* Her companion took Orioli's role, sending out circulars that instructed buyers to "Address all orders to Capt. Angelo Ravagli / care of Mrs. D. H. Lawrence." He sent 150 circulars to Harold Jay Snyder alone. The book sold well. In October Viking published a cheaper, slightly shorter trade edition, and four months later, in England, A. S. Frere-Reeves excitedly published the British edition for Heinemann and paid Frieda well. The reviewer for the *New Republic* praised Frieda's style for its dignity and directness, though he thought she included "too little of her [own] story." But Frieda never overcame her disappointment with the Viking Press. "My dislike of them," she told Alan Collins, later the New York agent for Lawrence's work, "came when I was publishing my own book with Lawrence's letters to me, which I never dreamt I had signed away to them, never meant to do so—They threatened me right away with a lawsuit—That seemed unforgivable." Frieda mistrusted publishers for the rest of her life.

In Taos, as the autumn nights grew colder, Frieda and Angelo decided, in spite of the expense, to spend the hard winter months of 1933–34 in a warmer climate. It was a pattern they would follow for years. Although at first they had wanted to go to Carmel, California—to be near the ocean, near Mabel and Tony, and near their mutual friends Robin and Una Jeffers—they suddenly changed their plan, motored east, and in December sailed from New Orleans to Buenos Aires. A loan gone sour had upset their plan.

Angelo, always ready to make himself agreeable to others, had struck up a friendship with a shyster named Nick Luciani and his wife. They were strange—she a schemer; he a quixotic dreamer whose charm hid pebble-hard eyes. But Angelo and Luciani had bonded, and when Angelo asked Frieda to lend the dreamer eleven hundred dollars to make wine, she did. "People take from me as if I were the sun and not a human being," she once quipped. Although the full truth may never be known, the sheriff suddenly came to arrest Ravagli, who was charged, she explained, with a "confidence trick" to solicit women. An alien resident, Ravagli felt vulnerable. Nor was Frieda exempt. She was soon accused of stealing a bag of trinkets that Luciani's wife had planted in her house. Frightened by the couple's clever machinations, Ravagli wrote a full account for his Taos lawyer, Floyd Beutler, then fled. Frieda soon followed. Driven in the La Salle by the ever-kind Knud Merrild, who (with his Danish wife, Else) had been visiting for ten days, Frieda joined Angelo in Alamosa, Colorado.

Her published account of the months that followed, as they wandered south, is crisp with Lawrentian observation. She projects a voice of clear-eyed tolerance as she observes other creatures on the wing, buffeted by fate and winter winds: "[We] fly along in the La Salle. There is a dead rabbit in the road; two huge birds rise from it, slowly; their enormous wings lift. The mountains are left behind. It is all open road to the next town now. A terrific wind is blowing across the plain. Shivering cattle try to shelter behind a sandbank or a tousled haystack. With a swish of wings, a great flock of tiny birds rises just in front of the car, birds thick as a swarm of bees. Are they flying south, as [we] are, away from the cold?" Blowing wind and whirring wings illustrate the rhythmic flow that Frieda could create. Wasting no words, her writing rises not out of an overarching design but out of spontaneous bursts of recollection. That is her strength and occasionally her weakness.

After a month on board a freighter, the SS *Delmundo,* Frieda and Angelo reached Buenos Aires, Argentina, where Frieda met his relatives—his brother Giovacchino, his sister Gina, and her husband, Ferruccio Castori—who lived together in a dreary apartment. Although diabolically hot, the city was luxurious with flowers and shrubbery. Frieda and Angelo went out to the carnival, where nimble gauchos danced, and one day in a bookshop saw a huge display of Lawrence's books. Yet, panting to leave the heat and Angelo's unhappy relatives, they finally left Argentina but found themselves stranded for almost a month in Rio de Janeiro, Brazil, where they stayed at the old, rambling Hotel dos Estraneros—swimming in the mornings and gambling at night—until they could board their ship home. Frieda mostly lay in her cabin and embroidered tropical birds on blue linen or treasured again Fenimore Cooper's *Last of the Mohicans,* which she and Lawrence had read together in 1916, searching then for the magical flavor of America.

The Lucianis having disappeared, Frieda joyfully returned to the ranch with Ravagli. Her sojourn had given her a fresh appreciation of New Mexico, a country that, she wrote, "suits my very soul." She liked the practical help of her American friends and their ready assault on sham, and for years she depended on Diego Arellano, her faithful helper who in any weather delivered food and mail to the ranch. In the abundant spring sunshine, work seemed like fun: planting fruit trees, making rows in the vegetable garden, shaping flower beds in front of the house—and planning how to memorialize Lawrence's remains. "I . . . enjoy most looking after things here at the ranch, like my life with Lawrence was," she informed Pollinger.

## A RECIPE FOR LAWRENCE'S ASHES

By the midthirties Frieda realized that she had the resources—both a trusted person and the money—to "complete" her life with Lawrence. She had long wanted to bring his ashes to the ranch he loved and to put them permanently in a small memorial chapel. Now she could. To the grave in Vence, France, she sent Ravagli on 5 December 1934. Helped by Frieda's loyal friend Martha Gordon Crotch, whose Vence gallery had once exhibited Lawrence's paintings, Ravagli disinterred Lawrence's body, arranged for its cremation in Marseille on 13 March, and in April, sailing on the

*Conte di Savoia,* brought back the ashes to Santa Fe, where Frieda, ill with double pneumonia, had gone to recuperate. Over the years amusing (and amazing) stories were told about his throwing the ashes overboard or leaving them on the railway platform at Lamy (or elsewhere), or dumping them at Ray Otis's house in Santa Fe. But the ashes, stashed in a box, seem to have arrived safely, Ravagli delivering them to a grateful Frieda, who felt she had now achieved a lasting peace. Soon, however, she found herself mired in the dirt of gossiping friends.

If Frieda was too kind and generous to take much pleasure in gossip, the same cannot be said for others of her circle. By 1935 Mabel, whose interference could range from thoughtful to poisonous, had made meddling an incurable habit. Once, for an April Fool's joke, she sent to Edward Bright, whose marriage was none too stable, a telegram that read, "Meet me"—and signed Frieda's name. Now, knowing that Lawrence's ashes had arrived, Mabel disliked the apparently callous way they were treated. A plot slowly hatched. Some of Mabel's sympathizers would steal the ashes and scatter them over the desert, giving Lawrence to the world. Mabel co-opted Brett, who in winter needed Mabel's social orbit; but two recruits—Frieda's daughter Barby and Barby's husband, Stuart Barr—soon thickened the plot.

Long Frieda's favorite, Barby wanted to show Taos to her new husband. Tall and good looking, Stuart was a Scottish journalist and would-be politician. The couple came to visit Frieda in June 1935, spent the summer, and helped her decorate the little hillside temple that she and Ravagli had built. It featured a stained-glass window above the altar. But Barby soon grew jealous of Frieda's "Angelino" and worried that he would fleece her mother. Infuriated that Frieda, to reward his faithful service, had granted him a share of her estate, the couple unwisely took their fears to Mabel, who—telling them how Angelino ridiculed Frieda behind her back ("the old woman," "silly old fool")—fanned their concerns into bright coals of resentment. Already feeling insecure, Frieda explained to Mabel that "I left him only the ranch and enough to make up for his salary, after all he gave up his career to look after my affairs, and he has done that faithfully and efficiently. The rest of everything, the bulk goes to the children. If Barby wants the ranch, she can arrange it with Angelino when I am dead." Their meddling annoyed her. But when Barby, convinced that Ravagli was a swindler, accused him to his face and demanded proofs of his honesty—and then threw a glass at him when he said something she misunderstood—he slapped her. Chaos erupted at the ranch. Frieda was hurt and bewildered. Hating treachery, she demanded openness and truth—and loved Angelino, despite what he said to others.

Frieda's anxiety reached such a pitch that, feeling already maligned, she despised the tale that now came to her—that Lawrence's admirers (Brett and Mabel included) wanted to steal the ashes. To deter them, Frieda apparently decided to mix the ashes with mortar and sink the whole into the raised altar of the little hillside temple where the ashes would be safe from marauders. If Frieda's decision sounds ludicrous today, it reflects her fury at disloyal friends. Blaming Mabel and Brett equally, she severed her social connections to them. Nonetheless, on 15 September 1935, around a huge bonfire that perfumed the sky, she held a ceremony to consecrate the ashes and made it simple and beautiful, graced by the songs of three Indians who were recruited at the last minute. Her enemies stayed away.

For sure she and Ravagli would spend the winter elsewhere. In November they decided—after he returned from Juarez, Mexico, where he had gone to get on the "quota" of legal immigrants—to drive west to Hollywood. There, a few years earlier, the poet Hart Crane had found Hollywood a "greasepaint pinkpoodle paradise with its everlasting sunlight." But there the Merrilds lived, and there Frieda hoped to interest the thriving studios in filming Lawrence's novels. Perhaps she could also write. Although Frieda too found Hollywood a "queer superficial amusing place—[where] movie people lead a dog's life," she liked the pepper trees, the tall cypresses, and the great open markets with avocados and oranges. The smell of the market at night, she wrote, "will always be Hollywood to me." Yet how expensive Hollywood was! Although she and Angelo had lived cheaply at the ranch, Secker's publishing firm in London had unfortunately collapsed, and although the firm of William Heinemann had then taken over all the Lawrence titles, her income from publishers was disrupted.

Wisely, Frieda—now in need of money—had kept back a major asset: Lawrence's beautifully handwritten manuscripts, some of them still unpublished. They were her capital. In Hollywood she and Ravagli eventually met Galka Scheyer, a colorful Hollywood agent who led them, early in 1936, to a handsome man who would become indelibly linked to Lawrence's manuscripts. His name was Jacob Zeitlin (1902–87).

Many years younger than Frieda, Jake Zeitlin—having grown up poor in Fort Worth, Texas—was struggling to establish himself as a Los Angeles bookseller at a time when buyers were scarce. Jake remembered Frieda as a frank, vigorous woman with lots of vitality, "whose presence you were aware of. She was straightforward and uninhibited, with no pretense about her. If she was offended by something you said or did, she told you right away. But she had a lot of kindness in her too, and trusted everybody." Given his wide knowledge of people, Jake also thought Frieda naïve. She very much depended on Ravagli, whom Jake judged good looking, outgoing, neat, and clean. "I could see where Frieda was taken with him. She

D. H. Lawrence chapel, Kiowa Ranch, as it looked in 1953 (Courtesy of Louis Gibbons)

seemed to dominate in lots of ways—and he deferred to her—but she depended on him in all practical matters. He was a very practical man. He had no sentimental attachment to these manuscripts [that she owned], but he was very much concerned that she get the most out of them." Jake agreed to try to sell Lawrence's holograph manuscript of *The Rainbow* for seventy-five hundred dollars, and she agreed to his commission of 15 percent. A quick sale would help her bring her sister Else (and family) from Germany to America.

In Jake's Los Angeles bookshop, his friend Lawrence Clark Powell (b. 1906) met Frieda and Angelo on 1 April 1936. On that date Powell wrote in his journal: "I liked her immensely. We talked a good deal in the shop and then at lunch. She is a bit more than buxom, her voice is German and hoarse, her face is weathered, fine. She is alive and hearty and warm-hearted. I know her life so well that I talked easily with her of many people and places; so that she later told Jake that I knew more of Lawrence than anyone she had met. . . . We are now her agent in the disposal of some of L[awrence]'s mss. she has. Yesterday I did a description of 'The Rainbow' and at this very hour JZ is trying to sell the ms. to Hugh Walpole for $7,500.00. If he succeeds I will get credit, and cash too."

Powell found Ravagli appealing but highly sexed: "Her Italian ber-saglieri . . . has been with her ever since Lawrence's death 6 years ago last month. He is short, husky, curiously boyish, shy, faun-like—a little too much of the goat in him." Fifty years later he remembered Ravagli as manly and forthright, but as an aggressor who had made advances even to Powell's young wife, Fay: "He was volatile, genial, a very companionable guy. But I spotted him. He was a wolf, really—a satyr. He screwed anything he could. Frieda tolerated it because he was a very sturdy mainstay and companion and handyman."

Frieda prized Lawrence's manuscripts, loved to look at them and touch them, and to remember where they had been written; but she knew, as Jake had insisted, that if they were sold, they should all be kept together for students of Lawrence. Laurence Pollinger had arranged for Bumpus of London to exhibit the manuscripts in 1933, after which they had lain in a vault at the Westminster Bank. Jake hoped that Stanford University, some three hundred miles up the coast from Los Angeles, might safely import them and mount an exhibit, which he subsequently arranged with Nathan van Patten, the library's director. On 28 April 1936 Jake, Frieda, Angelo, and van Patten met for lunch at the Biltmore. Eventually, from 21 September to 31 October, the library exhibited Lawrence's manuscripts, typescripts, proofs, paintings, and photographs. Inspired by this unique collection, Jake sought a knowledgeable person to prepare a catalog of the manuscripts—to help sell them. Long before he could do so, though, Frieda welcomed to the ranch a married couple from Harvard University. They wanted the manuscripts far more than Jake did.

## THE TREASURE ROOM YIELDS

It is extraordinary that a major research institution like Harvard did not, when given the chance, pay twenty-five thousand dollars for the complete collection of Lawrence's manuscripts. That was the special price Jake and Frieda had set. Probably, in 1936, Lawrence's literary reputation seemed too uncertain. Although Harvard's decision seems obtuse today, one man singlehandedly developed the university's (tepid) interest in Lawrence. His name was Harry K. Wells (1911–76), known everywhere as "Dan."

Blond and blue eyed, tall and forceful, Dan Wells had ambition, energy, intelligence, and money. Only twenty-five at the time, he and his intrepid wife, Jenny—she was twenty-three and a graduate of Vassar—had spent 1935–36 roaming across Europe in search of Lawrence's letters; they had visited Catherine Carswell and Koteliansky in London, William Hopkin in Eastwood, and Else in Heidelberg; and they had purchased Bertrand Russell's DHL letters for $1,000, bought those Orioli possessed for another $1,000, and acquired still another set of DHL letters from Enid Hilton. A graduate student at Harvard, Wells planned to write the first critical biography of Lawrence. To that end he and Jenny visited Frieda in August 1936, stayed in the original Lawrence cabin for ten days (taking their meals with Frieda), looked around, and for $2,500 bought a sixty-acre ranch nearby. Dan copied all of Lawrence's letters that he couldn't buy. One of Jenny's photographs shows an outdoor picnic in Frieda's front yard—Dan looking trim in a white shirt and tie; Frieda, next to him, lounging in the grass and laughing; the other guests forming a circle around them.

When Wells returned to Harvard, he arranged for Jake Zeitlin to ship the manuscripts for a grand exhibition in Harvard Library's Treasure Room and then for the university to invite Frieda to give a lecture on 11 December, paying her $250. Her topic was Lawrence's poetry. Frieda told Jake she was "thrilled" that Harvard might buy the manuscripts. For two months Frieda and Angelo stayed in the Wellses' house in Concord, an easy drive from Harvard. Interviewed in 1998, Jenny Wells Vincent remembered the pleasure their winter's visit brought her: "Angelino made bread one time and put it to rise on the radiator, and when he came back, it had dripped all down the radiator. But he made awfully good bread. Frieda did embroidery; she did two samplers—I still have them—and she knit a baby blanket for a friend of mine who was pregnant. We had quite a few people coming in to visit us. Meeting Frieda and Angelino was a very exciting moment for some of our younger friends."

Having seen the Lawrence exhibition at Harvard, one young person who came to the Wellses' Concord bungalow was Frederic A. Fisher Jr., then a twenty-six-year-old student at the University of Chicago. On 29 December he found Frieda blond and merry, dressed in a plaid Bavarian outfit, her eyes glistening with shiny wateriness. "She was full of a clean, salty gusto," he remembered. Smoking Camels, she talked of Bertrand Russell's emotional immaturity, Middleton Murry's mushiness, and Aldous Huxley's cold intellect, and told Fisher with pride that she and Ravagli, on their trip east, had spent only $96.50. Fisher was mesmerized by her.

Once Harvard had decided not to purchase the collection, the manuscripts—177 items in all—went back to Jake, who signed a sales agreement with Frieda on 18 March 1937. Still keen on a catalog, Jake at once

A picnic at the Kiowa Ranch, 1936, Frieda Lawrence third from left; original cabin in background (Courtesy of Jenny Vincent)

approached Larry Powell, who had been studying Lawrence for years. Larry had earned a doctorate at Dijon and in 1932 had traveled to Vence to visit Lawrence's grave. Where Jake was loosely built and genial, Larry was slight, intense, and a highly trained scholar. Because he was then attending library school in Berkeley, he needed the hundred dollars that Jake would pay him to prepare the catalog.

But almost a year would pass before Frieda returned to Los Angeles. After some waffling, she reaffirmed her wish to appoint not Dan Wells, whose Lawrence phase was ending, but Jake Zeitlin as her sales agent. Jake had celebrated their renewed agreement with a party on 31 March, after which she and Angelo were free to depart for Taos, and Jake could await the day, two months later, when Harvard at last, after six months, released the precious manuscripts from the Treasure Room.

To compile Jake's catalog, Larry Powell worked for a month in an unheated bank vault—it was like a tomb—where the manuscripts had been placed. "Make the catalog readable, for God's sake," Jake had warned him, so he spliced in bits of biography from the published memoirs, aware that all of the venture's participants needed money. The Depression had greatly diminished their livelihoods.

Published in November 1937, with a foreword by Aldous Huxley, *The Manuscripts of D. H. Lawrence: A Descriptive Catalogue* made a splendid bibliographical monument to Lawrence. Frieda, delighted, naturally asked Jake to set prices. Highest were the holograph manuscripts in Lawrence's impeccable script: *The Rainbow* $2,500 (quickly reduced from $7,500), *St. Mawr* $1,000 (eventually given to Huxley and destroyed in a fire), the *Last Poems* notebooks $1,000, "The Prussian Officer" and "The Captain's Doll" $500 apiece, and sketches like "The Dance of the Sprouting Corn" $100.

Back in Taos again, Frieda made plans for enlarging and improving the structures at the ranch. Always busy, Angelo planted a big garden, then fields of alfalfa and oats, brought back the horses from the Hawk ranch nearby, and settled in for the short growing season. Frieda felt restored and revitalized at the ranch. But she had invited the Huxleys to spend the summer of 1937 in the Lawrence cabin where the Wellses had stayed the previous summer, and there she wanted Angelo to install a bathroom—and, in the main house, to build a room for Lawrence's paintings and to add a garage. Arriving about 1 June, the Huxleys—Aldous, Maria, and their son, Matthew—stayed for three months. Aldous found Frieda a great deal calmer now, and he found Ravagli a decent, middle-class Italian who efficiently managed her affairs. She also invited Knud and Else Merrild in July, and Jake in August—and, with Jake, set a new price of $30,000 on the whole manuscript collection. With no bidders in sight, however, Jake re-

Frieda Lawrence at the San Cristobal Valley Ranch, 1937 (Courtesy of Jenny Vincent)

gretfully began the slow, systematic dispersal of Lawrence's manuscripts, which continued for the next twenty years. By September, Jake had already garnered $2,900 in commitments from Bertram Rota, a buyer in London, and from T. E. "Ed" Hanley. An aficionado of the circus, Hanley was an eccentric industrial baron from Bradford, Pennsylvania.

In the midst of the Depression, Frieda made a bold move. She had become acquainted with a young German couple named Edward and Hanni von Maltzahn. When they wanted to sell their ranch, four miles from Taos, and return to Europe, Frieda bought it on 28 October 1937 for the extravagant sum of $4,500. Ravagli groused because the German couple had paid only $900 for it. But as Frieda explained to Witter Bynner, who lived in Santa Fe, "I also bought Mal[t]zahn's place as an investment and as an act of friendship. His wife has bought an old ruin of a castle in Austria and he wants to go. [His place] is 300 acres and he has made it nice, but it will mean more to look after for Angelino." Frieda wanted a place off the mountains where, in the winter, she would feel less isolated.

But for Ravagli, too, Maltzahn's ranch offered advantages—a nice shed that he could use in his new pottery venture and a place that was not steeped in Lawrence's aura. Long fettered by his dependence on Frieda, he sought a way to earn his own money. Back in 1933, according to Mabel, he had left a note on Frieda's desk that read, "*non posso vivo como uno fungo*" (I can't live as a fungus). Now he had a plan. When he went to Italy for the winter of 1937–38, he could, while visiting with his family, learn a new craft. At the Maltzahn ranch he would have a place to work and easier access to markets. Amazingly, Lawrence had already written Ravagli's life story in *Lady Chatterley's Lover*: "I'm not keen on coming to live on you, being kept by you," Mellors tells Connie. Like Ravagli, Mellors is a father who leaves his family and, at the novel's close, is learning to farm. Just as Connie's capital will affirm Mellors's integrity on the fringe of a capitalist system, so Frieda's capital would launch Angelo's new livelihood.

Frieda called the new ranch Los Pinos (The Pines). Its purchase initiated the second phase of their life together, a phase of consolidation and contentment. Her feuding with Mabel and Brett would soon end. Now fifty-eight, Frieda had at last found what she wanted: a highly sexed companion, a place of her own, a good income, and a wide circle of friends. But there was a risk. It was that she would drift from the combat of ideas into serene comfort, from living at the edge of stability to worry about ownership. Feeling overwhelmed after Lawrence's death, she had perhaps overcompensated for the pain she had felt. A different partner—one who faced no barriers of language, one who carefully skirted philandering— might have helped direct her energy more skillfully. She surely wondered whether her generous spirit would find voice in another volume of autobiography. She surely wondered whether, firmly planted in Lawrence's shadow, she could escape it with a fresh identity. She surely wondered whether she could still lift the wings of freedom that had once allowed her to soar from one emotional frontier to another. Now, suddenly, she had to ponder another question—whether Angelo would return from Italy, where his wife and three children eagerly awaited his return. Their claim on his affections was at least as great as Frieda's.

# 23

# Frieda and Angelo at Los Pinos

## 1938–46

While Angelo Ravagli stayed in Spotorno with his family, Frieda moved to Albuquerque, staying in a comfortable tourist court where she hoped to write at length about her childhood and her later life with Ravagli—segments left out of *Not I, But the Wind*. She wrote often to Italy—friendly letters about whom she had seen and what she had done, but they were not love letters. She usually signed them "Always your friend" or "With many greetings"—not knowing whose eyes might see them. Frieda also wrote to Ravagli's wife and children and once chided him: "You don't say anything about your wife and how it is!" Ravagli's struggle to balance his commitments can only be imagined, but Frieda, when she acknowledged his emotional ties in Spotorno, professed herself "glad you love the children." Still, she felt uneasy. In February 1938 she finally admitted her fear: "Perhaps I am stupid, but sometimes I feel you will not come back"—in which case she would feel overcome with misery. She had left him the upper ranch in her will, had offered him sexual license, had given him money, and had bought the lower ranch, Los Pinos, partly for him and his pottery. She had grown deeply attached to him.

Pinched for money, Mrs. Ravagli and her three children—Federico, Magda, and Stefano—had accepted Ravagli's liaison with Frieda as a long-term career assignment, a furlough from family life, a kind of business venture. Yet they had needs, too, and Ravagli may have complained, because Frieda bristled after he reached Spotorno: "You never think of money, except when you think of Italy." His relations with his family, after years of neglect, had suffered. Despite his kindness and generosity, their lives had gone on unfolding without him, and now he was just a visitor. He had gone home to learn pottery, but his family soon realized that he would probably carry his new skill back to Taos—and stay. He was genuinely fond of Frieda, she gave him the freedoms he desired, and, set up by her money, he could become more independent than before. In time, he came to like what she liked—tending the farm animals, welcoming visitors to the Lawrence chapel, wintering in a warm climate, and relishing good friends. But Frieda's tolerance of his affairs would soon complicate their lives.

The mild Taos winter of 1938 had made Frieda eager to leave Albuquerque. On 10 February, Teddy Maltzahn—in blue jeans and long hair—gathered Frieda and her belongings and drove her to Los Pinos, her new ranch in the tiny settlement of El Prado, four miles north of Taos. He acquainted her with the house, then—miserable at leaving ("he cried and he said, how he loved me!")—he departed with his wife, Hanni, for Austria. Now alone, Frieda thought Los Pinos incredibly beautiful. On one side the dark sagebrush plains stretched like a desert carpet to the Rio Grande River; on another side rose the majestic mountains that sheltered the upper ranch; and on still another side ran the ancient Pueblo settlement from which Frieda could lease water. She hoped to graze sheep on her land. The house delighted her, too. "It is surprisingly beautiful," she told Ravagli. "The big room really splendid and the simplicity of this landscape I love. . . . I *know* this place is a good investment, I don't care what anybody says. . . . But I wish you were back. Come soon," she pleaded on 16 February.

With Angelo still in Italy, Frieda was glad to hire two men to help her. Diego Arellano was caretaker of the upper ranch until his untimely death in 1939; J. J. "Joe" Montoya, who lived in El Prado, helped Frieda in essential ways—built simple furniture for her house, took her shopping or drove her to the upper ranch, ran errands, and worked outdoors. His wife, Juanita, baked Frieda's bread and later cleaned for her. Using money from the sale of Lawrence's manuscripts, Frieda hoped to build a bathroom at Los Pinos. Luckily, the collector Ed Hanley soon offered her $3,000—paid in installments—for a group of seven Lawrence manuscripts. That was only $1,500 less than she had paid for the Maltzahns' big ranch a few months earlier.

Sailing on the *Rex,* Ravagli returned to Taos about 15 April 1938. At once he constructed a kiln and began to turn the outdoor shed at Los Pinos into a potting center. Before long, however, Frieda needed to be driven west. She had promised the Huxleys that by 12 May she would come to Los Angeles for Occidental College's production of Lawrence's biblical play, *David*. She and Angelo stayed only a few days, probably with the Huxleys, who, a year earlier, when their earnings plunged, had migrated to Hollywood. There Aldous, with his famous name, had gotten lucrative work as a writer of MGM filmscripts. In 1938, for instance, he adapted Marie Curie's life, earning an astonishing eighteen hundred dollars a week. As Hugh Walpole once remarked, Hollywood writers "are all on a raft together in the middle of the cinema sea and nothing is real here but the salaries."

Among the Huxleys' closest friends were Edwin and Grace Hubble, who lived in Pasadena. A Rhodes scholar, Edwin was a tall, powerful, taciturn astronomer who in 1929 first discovered that the galaxies of the cosmos are rushing apart in the wake of the Big Bang, and who had recently published books on the nebulae and cosmology; Grace, the patrician daughter of a West Coast banker, had graduated from Stanford. She had hazel eyes, brown hair, and good features, and she chronicled the couple's daily life in voluminous journals. On 11 May, the night before the performance, Grace went to dinner at the Huxleys' apartment—saw Aldous so tall and youthful looking, his lean figure crowned by a mass of thick, brown hair; saw Maria so petite and angular and talkative—and there met Frieda and Angelo for the first time. Impressed, she found Frieda "an unbeaten Valkyrie, or like the women Tacitus wrote of who followed their fighting men through the ancient forests of Europe. She was sitting on the lounge, a broad-shouldered deep-chested shapeless bulk in a burgundy-red chiffon dress, and long strings of beads, and grey stockings. Her hair was a small wild mass of silky light-coloured stuff, like something out of a basket-maker's cache. Her blue eyes danced or looked straight through one, and she laughed a great deal, a wide mouth, a wide-curved upper and lower jaw. She is still handsome, her nose is aristocratic, long and straight."

Although Grace sat between Aldous and Ravagli at dinner, it was Frieda who fascinated her. The next evening Remsen Bird, president of Occidental College, arranged the seating at the college's open-air Greek theater, placing himself, Frieda, Aldous, Edwin, and Grace together. Grace thought the play *David* captivating—it was both ingenuous and innocent—and she overheard Frieda say, "How Lawrence would have liked it, the young people and the way they are doing the play. And his lines are strong, they come up from depths." More than anyone, Frieda knew how the play had arisen out of Lawrence's long illness in Oaxaca, how writing the play had helped him recover his strength in the spring of 1925. She was deeply moved by it.

## MORAL TURPITUDE

By the summer of 1938 Frieda and Angelo had installed themselves at what they now called the upper ranch. They were always busy. Their assorted animals, their work in the alfalfa fields, the two cabins, the many guests who dropped in to see Frieda or to offer homage to Lawrence—all took time. Always solicitous toward their friends, both were surprised by the suicide attempt of Una Jeffers, of Carmel, California, which occurred after Mabel's friend Hildegarde Nathan—estranged from her own husband— responded to Mabel's manipulations and flirted with Una's husband, Robin. But Frieda, writing to Robin in July, acknowledged that "[t]hese shocks are sometimes good in the long run—give one a deeper sense of life and happiness." In the short run, Ravagli was even busier than Frieda, experimenting with different kinds of clay, fine-tuning the firing process, and creating shapes and sizes of pots he liked. He was transforming himself into a genuine artist. By autumn Frieda could tell Jake Zeitlin that "Angelino . . . has made some handsome things." He hoped to sell some of them in Albuquerque. Frieda also thanked Jake for the payments—an estimated $175 a month—that Ed Hanley continued to make. Soon these payments would become her lifeline.

During the following winter, when they had closed both upper and lower ranches and gone west to Hollywood, they began to meet some famous people. Paying about seventy-five dollars a month for a furnished house at 1425 North Crescent Heights Boulevard, just one block from the Huxleys (who lived briefly at 1320), they met Charlie Chaplin (1889– 1977). Married to the beautiful, bubbly movie star Paulette Goddard, Chaplin often performed for his guests wicked imitations of Hollywood "names" or extraordinary bits from films like *Modern Times,* in which he and Goddard had acted together. They loved to entertain. In October 1938 Chaplin had begun filming *The Great Dictator,* which also featured him and Goddard. It was a powerful burlesque of Hitler.

A couple Frieda especially liked proved much less mercurial than the Chaplins. The Nicholses—Dudley (1895–1960) and his wife, Esther ("Esta")—offered her both friendship and sane advice. A distinguished screenwriter, Nichols had worked on the scripts of *Stagecoach, Men without Women,* and *The Informer;* he had become president of the Film Writers Guild; and he owned a farm in Connecticut. His love of pastoral retreats linked him to Frieda, who found him warm and intelligent—qualities she also admired in Ravagli. Nichols once thrilled her by taking her to see John Ford at work directing *The Long Voyage Home.* Frieda also hoped (though in vain) that Jake and Aldous would find time to fashion a filmscript of Lawrence's *St. Mawr.*

Frieda Lawrence, 1938 (Courtesy of Jenny Vincent)

By mid-April 1939, braving a blizzard, Frieda and Angelo returned to the upper ranch, Frieda so happy to be back that "I want to crow," she told her old friend Witter Bynner. After weeks of sustained work, she invited her son, Monty, now thirty-eight, to visit. Wanting a rest from his job at the Victoria and Albert Museum in London, he accepted his mother's gift of a trip to Taos. He stayed for two weeks. He radiated, she thought, *her* infectious vitality. After he left, she wrote him a letter praising his courtesy and tact with her neighbors: "Angelino was so impressed how you adjusted yourself straight from London to finding the right tone for Bill and Rachel

Hawk, when you found them making hay." The once-abrasive aspects of Frieda's character were dissolving into a gregarious warmth. She had only just begun to think of herself as old.

As soon as Monty had gone, Frieda and Angelo were struck cold. They found with horror that they were the subject of a federal investigation. Though extremely liberal, Taos was still a small town, and when Frieda and Angelo applied for their American citizenship, someone's complaint sparked a formal inquiry among the townspeople. Suddenly an agent of the Immigration and Naturalization Service appeared at their door and "asked us questions of our intimate life. We answered truthfully (beastly of course) and first me then Angie—To Angie he said [']you have a jewess in Taos, that you take to the nightclub and then sleep with her.' When Angie denied this, the man jeered and Angie got cross. Anyhow in 3 months Angie went 3 times to the nightclub with people who had been *here* first, was back at 1½ and talked to me—The official took both our passports and they have not come back. . . . But you can imagine how awful I feel for Angelino's sake, if I have messed up his life—He could'nt stand Italy and the tightness anymore after this." Mabel Luhan, now openly sympathetic, talked to Frances Perkins, who promised to help. Appointed secretary of labor in 1933, Perkins had become the first female member of Roosevelt's cabinet. Both Dudley Nichols and Aldous Huxley offered to go to Washington and offer testimony. As Frieda said to Jake, she supposed she and her paramour were guilty of "[m]oral turpitude" and so shrank from reclaiming their passports. She worried that Angelino faced deportation, but she also knew that he would have to curb his free and easy behavior with other women.

Frieda herself had become more circumspect. Gradually her letters become more solicitous and kind but more scattered in their subjects—and, like telegrams, more concise. Like Lawrence, she responds with simple joy to the life around her, but what she does *not* say speaks too. She rarely mentions housework or cooking or baking, the books she reads, the vehicles she buys, or (unlike Mabel) the gossip she hears. She projects a hearty, warm, matronly presence. A faithful friend, honest, generous with money and time, she often tries, in her unfocused way, to enhance Lawrence's reputation and influence. He was her one great love.

## HITLER INVADES EUROPE

For her sixtieth birthday—on 11 August 1939—Frieda and Bynner decided to invite all their friends to the upper ranch for an outdoor supper. They called it their "Coming of Age Party." The invitation, printed by Spud Johnson, drolly advised, "R.S.V.P.D.Q." While Angelo put up a flurry of lights, half an ox roasted at the outdoor fireplace. It was a grand celebration. The consummate writer Frank Waters brought them a bottle of fine whiskey. But the mood of elation soon shifted.

War broke out on 1 September 1939. After Germany invaded Poland, Britain and France both declared war on Germany, and within a month an estimated ten thousand Poles had been murdered. Frieda wrote to Monty: "So the horror has come! On the radio I hear everything! Out there the [horse] Azul and the cows are having their noses to the ground, and I told them there was war, but they did'nt listen! Peaceful and sunny and warm, you cant believe it! . . . It is paralysing!" She shared her feelings with Bynner—by now her most faithful friend—when she learned on the eighteenth that Germany and Russia would divide Poland: "a whole nation disappearing from the face of the earth." So incomprehensible an act impelled her to clarify her belief: "Only the individual matters really," she told him, "that is my belief. These mass and nation-things are just meaningless really—I will stick to my guns and keep calm and enjoy the things I always enjoy—friends and chickens and trees and being alive the unsensational way!" Politics rarely interested her except when it curtailed her personal freedom, still the central article of her faith.

Moving to the lower ranch, she invited Bynner and his partner, Robert "Bob" Hunt, the son of an architect, to come for Christmas. Tall, lean, and splendidly handsome, Bob remained with Bynner from 1930 until 1964. Frieda liked his wry humor and refined manners, though not his bouts of drinking. She told the pair they could use Spud Johnson's small adobe house (Spud and Brett were going to New York City with Mabel). Frieda knew that, in her house, they would be uncomfortable without a bathroom (still too expensive to install) but urged them to spend their time with her. In 1939 she had used Hanley's checks for a new car. Later she recalled "what a good time we had, in spite of the arguments."

The coming of the war grieved her, made travel more difficult, and reduced her income. Money could not leave England except by special permit. Once again she would need to become a resourceful entrepreneur. She offered the *Virginia Quarterly Review* an unpublished Lawrence story, "Delilah and Mr. Bircumshaw," which someone had found in the desk of George Duckworth, once Lawrence's publisher; and she hoped the journal's editor might print two of Lawrence's early plays, which he did—*The Married Man* in 1940 and *The Merry-Go-Round* in 1941.

Undeterred, she and Ravagli went on to California. After a week in Laguna Beach, they moved in January 1940 to a comfortable house at 2136 Laurel Canyon Boulevard, in the Hollywood hills, about six blocks from where they had stayed the previous winter. At first they saw just the Nicholses, who lived on North Harper Avenue a few blocks away, and the Huxleys, who, almost rich now, lived farther away, in exclusive Pacific Palisades. But after a while they sought out others. On 20 March, Grace Hubble spent an evening with them (Edwin and Aldous having gone elsewhere) and left this fine account of dinner for eight:

Maria . . . and a Mrs. Barrett and I drove to Frieda's on a steep side of Laurel Canyon. Gerald [Heard], Angelino, Rosalind [Rajagopal?], Peggy Rodakiewicz [Kiskadden]. Frieda resplendent in gold lamé, a brocade jacket and a necklace of Chinese turquoise, pale grayish blue. Angelino had made delicious pasta and a sauce equally inspired, and baked a loaf of bread. For dessert fresh strawberries that had been soaked in cognac, and after the coffee Angelino opened a bottle of champagne that Maria had brought. Frieda said "We were once friends of Bertrand Russell, he and Lawrence were thinking of ways to change the world but Lawrence wrote Russell a letter and said he was nothing but a brain and his ideas were no good, and after that we didn't see him." Gerald talk[ed] like a singing bird. Growth of the divine right of kings, strange things in the Court of Louis XIV. . . . Dreadful story of Lord Hinchcliffe and the flayed cats. Incredible memory of Gerald. Maria and I rejoined Edwin and Aldous at 11.

Grace Hubble's account shows the social center consisting of Frieda and an intelligent man. Gerald Heard—thin, intense, erudite, and British—has replaced Lawrence. Ravagli, not described, cooks and serves the food. At age sixty Frieda, in Hollywood as in Taos, still attracted cultured people. For her, friendship was a form of incomparable expression. She felt she had a genius for it.

Frieda and Angelo spent many evenings with their friends, but on many winter days Frieda was also busy trying to market Lawrence. At this time Hollywood, which exported many films to Europe, cultivated British themes: hence Aldous Huxley and Dudley Nichols gave Frieda easy entrée to established writers and directors such as William Dieterle, Zoë Akins, William Goetz, and Melchior Lengyel. Dieterle, a German director who had come to Hollywood in 1930, had just completed *The Hunchback of Notre Dame*. Frieda, full of excitement, persuaded him to consider filming *The Plumed Serpent* in Mexico from a "treatment" she had made with a minor MGM writer named John Beckett. Moreover, she boldly asked Zoë Akins to turn *The Virgin and the Gipsy* into a play, but Akins, well established as a writer, was busy crafting the screenplay for MGM's *Pride and Prejudice* (it was later wholly rewritten by Aldous Huxley).

Once, however, Frieda maneuvered a kind of success. To William Goetz, who had married Louis B. Mayer's daughter and produced *Cardinal Richelieu* for Twentieth Century–Fox, she sold the film rights to *Lady Chatterley's Lover*, which Melchior Lengyel and Aldous Huxley, working together, had hoped first to mold into a top-tier play. A Hungarian immigrant who was Frieda's age, Lengyel had come to Hollywood in 1937 and written the filmscripts of *To Be or Not to Be* and (for Greta Garbo) *Ninotchka*. Although Frieda liked him, she was not impressed with his stage adaptation of Lawrence's last novel. When Aldous read it, he told Frieda on 14 August

1940 that the play, as shaped by Lengyel, had lost Lawrence's descriptive poetry, needed to be elevated more tastefully, confessed now his own lack of time to undertake the job, and recommended handsome young Christopher Isherwood as Lengyel's replacement. But Isherwood was shackled by his studio work, and John van Druten, whom Aldous approached, also declined, judging the task of reconstruction "enormous."

Later, William Goetz urged Zoë Akins to adapt *Lady Chatterley*. Nothing, however, seems to have come of these efforts. Frieda had immense enthusiasm for Lawrence's work but neither the artistic vocabulary nor the necessary persistence that her on-site presence might have furnished. Confronted by the industry's rapid technological changes, she probably lacked the expertise to be an effective advocate for Lawrence's work.

When Isherwood visited Taos in April 1940, Frieda tried to lasso him into helping her, but he was too wily even for her:

I had expected to find Frieda intense and domineering. Actually, she is already an old woman, with a croaking, witchlike laugh. She is very lively, interested in everybody and everything. Her figure is a lump. Her grizzled blonde hair is cropped very short. She and Angelino are a charming couple—living, apparently, in a state of continual unmalicious bickering, like children. She wanted me to help her with an outline of *The Plumed Serpent* which Dieterle has requested for a possible film. Obviously, the material is hopelessly undramatic, in its present form. Frieda wandered through the story, stopping at intervals to squabble with Angelino, who kept throwing cold water on the whole scheme. Finally, I suggested that Berthold [Viertel, the Viennese film director] was just the man to help them, and thus slipped gracefully out of the noose.

Frieda's loyalty to Lawrence and her personal courage in the teeth of such discouragement compel admiration. She never complained and never blamed others. She simply went on trying.

Her failure to market Lawrence's work must have been doubly discouraging when she learned that money from England had been curbed by wartime restrictions. Not only had she bought a new car, she had also spent two thousand dollars on legal fees to help speed the process by which she and Ravagli could become U.S. citizens. They felt poor. Yet she also relished "being thrifty," she wrote in July. At the upper ranch they spent little, having their own milk and eggs—and a pig to butcher in the autumn. But they felt the pinch, and a year later Frieda wrote Dudley Nichols a letter that gauges their plight: "Dudley, you remember some time ago you asked me if I would sell you the Lady Chatterley Mss for 5000 [dollars]? I was afraid you did it out of friendship and now you may have spent so much money on your farm that you would not like to spend such a sum—But the money from England is not coming through as you know and soon I may not have any left—over here. But, please, say no, if you dont really want the Mss, and I can manage some way." Nichols apparently declined, and a quarter of a century later the University of Texas bought the manuscripts for ten times Frieda's price. To make matters worse, Jake Zeitlin's business had collapsed. Knud Merrild—whose integrity was unblemished—rescued the Lawrence manuscripts from Jake's creditors and put them in a bank, then shipped them back to Frieda in 1942. Acting alone, she may have sold an occasional manuscript to the rich collector Ed Hanley, but in these lean war years, she was especially grateful to have both ranches free of debt.

With the summer spent and their move to the lower ranch complete, they had to make a decision about wintering in Hollywood. Angelo, his pig now butchered, was eager to go west: "[I]t does me good for a change," he had written to the Merrilds. Frieda too loved Hollywood—it is "so odd and varied and amusing," she said, as billboards jostled with filling stations, Mexican immigrants with tycoons like William Randolph Hearst, and days of bright sunshine turned even the hills to toast.

But nothing was so amusing as to make them forget the war. Dreading each radio bulletin, they worried about how the war would affect their relatives in Europe. In November 1940 alone, German bombs had killed nearly five thousand British civilians. A few weeks later, on the Libyan frontier, the Italian fortress of Bardia fell, yielding over thirty-five thousand Italian prisoners. As Brett wrote to Una Jeffers on 5 January 1941, "[C]an you imagine what poor Angelino is feeling? The whole Italian army prisoners or dead, it's just frightful." Brett, who had lunch every Sunday at Frieda's house, knew well what they were thinking and feeling. After a while, when letters to Italy were blocked, Angelo was wholly cut off from his family.

Despite the expense, they went on to Hollywood and a house at 8591 Crescent Drive in the Hollywood hills, not far from Laurel Canyon Drive. It would be their last extended stay in Hollywood for more than a decade. In the canyon below the house, eucalyptus and mimosa trees rose like decorative sentries, and for Frieda the warm air and pervasive sunshine proved as refreshing as, years earlier, the balmy weather around the Mediterranean.

This time, knowing their way around, they sought out interesting people. One February evening Edward James—thin, elegantly dressed, heir to a large fortune—took them to the Beachcomber. Through him they met Salvador Dalí and his Russian wife, Gala, whom Frieda disliked as "the wrong sort"—merely salivating after success. George Biddle, having been introduced to Frieda, painted her portrait—now at the Philadelphia Museum of Art—and made her, she said, look old but interesting. They invited Gerald Heard to lunch. Heard's vehemence reminded Frieda of Lawrence's, he wrote widely on science and religion (eventually publishing thirty-five books), and he seemed to her lovable and genuine. Walter Arensberg and his wife came to tea: they were friends of Witter Bynner's and avidly collected modern art. And seeing Walt Disney's *Fantasia*, a brave Hollywood experiment, thrilled her. While Angelo took chemistry lessons to improve his glazes, Frieda had hoped to write more of her memoirs, but she accomplished little: "I get too interested in people and things," she told Brett on 21 March 1941, ten days before they packed their car and returned to Taos. Frieda was like Virginia Woolf's heroine Clarissa Dalloway: "What she liked was simply life."

## Sick of War

The next three years passed beneath the darkening shadow of war, which slowly escalated so that even Frieda, listening intently to the radio, became "so very sick of war." In September 1941 more than ten thousand bombs fell on London, the metropolis where her children lived; earlier a bomb had hit Monty Weekley's Chiswick house. Worse would follow. The United States, though long maintaining its neutrality, was finally provoked into declaring war on the Axis nations—Germany, Italy, and Japan. On 7 December, without warning, Japan attacked Pearl Harbor as it lay peacefully under the clear skies of Hawaii. Now Angelo Ravagli was an enemy alien, his status (Bynner warned) potentially "lead[ing] you both into difficulties." While American forces slowly retreated in the Pacific, the Germans advanced into Egypt and Russia, and in 1942 German submarines sank Allied ships by the hundreds. Early in 1942 Frieda—worried about Ravagli's status—wrote to the Merrilds, "Well, I am thankful to say I had a very nice letter from Francis Biddle, he is the attorney general and so I feel safe about Angie, inspite of his being an enemy alien." George Biddle, his brother, had intervened.

By 1943, however, armed forces led by Britain's General Montgomery and Russia's Stalin helped repel the enemy, and the Allied invasion of Italy forced that country to surrender on 8 September. "I try not to think about the war," Ravagli wrote to the Merrilds a month later. Coordinated by General Eisenhower, the Allied landing in Normandy succeeded—by October 1944—in clearing German forces from France and Belgium; by 25 April 1945, when Allied and Russian forces converged in Saxony (some three hundred miles from Frieda's birthplace, Metz), Germany had all but collapsed. Five days later Hitler killed himself.

Frieda was astonished by America's generosity. The atrocities of the war seemed incalculable, yet she and Angelo had been spared humiliation: "There is Angie, who was in the italian army and I of the german aristocracy, we could'nt be *worse* and yet nobody cares and nobody bothers us," she wrote, amazed, to Dudley Nichols. But in the Pacific, Japan stubbornly resisted surrender until the United States dropped atomic bombs on Hiroshima and Nagasaki. Surrender was swift, coming on 14 August 1945.

But as these devastating atrocities stirred a deep sense of dread, Frieda and Angelo warily went forward, preserving their routines, alternating upper and lower ranches, holding fast to their friends—and spending far less money than before. They adapted as best they could and welcomed all visitors. In June 1941, six months before America entered the war, Richard Aldington came with his wife, Netta, and their daughter, Catherine, to live briefly at the upper ranch. At Port Cros, Aldington had spent several weeks with the Lawrences in 1928, had eventually left Arabella Yorke and Brigit Patmore—both of them intimates who had joined him there—and in 1938 had married Brigit's former daughter-in-law. An astute judge of others, he wrote on 14 June to A. S. Frere-Reeves, who had published Lawrence and Frieda in England, conveying verbal photographs of the upper ranch and its tenants:

Frieda and Angie have built a large and comfortable house of logs and adobe . . . and immediately behind it is the original Lawrence ranch. It is virtually one long room, with an L containing kitchen and bathroom—the latter added (I'm glad to say) because Maria Huxley refused to live without a bath. The chimney and hearth Lawrence built are there and so is the little fireside seat with a rope mat where he sat every evening. . . . Beyond that is a little English orchard of cherry and quince and apple and vegetable garden, then two alfalfa fields, then two or three rough pasture fields, all surrounded by forest of pines, some superbly tall, and beyond that the Taos plateau, and about 30 miles off the Sangre d[e] Cristo mountains. . . .

Frieda, I am glad to say, is still amazingly her old self, and though well over 60 as full of zest and energy as ever. . . . Angie is a little man, a bit like Pino [Orioli], but without Pino's wit or vices—a bit dull, but very conscientious and industrious. He is always at work on the place.

This is a view as Lawrence would have registered it—with one difference: it has none of Lawrence's incisive apprehension of landscape or personality. That comes later in the letter when Aldington quotes Frieda: "This morning I said to Frieda: 'There's something wrong with that pig of yours, Frieda. He . . . looks melancholy.' 'Yes,' she said, 'I don't understand it. We've always had such *gay* pigs.'" Frieda was always good company. But she also confided how poor they were. On the twelve thousand pounds she had invested in British securities, no dividends now reached her, and she painfully acknowledged that she would probably have to sell the ranch and live down at Los Pinos. But in September her luck turned: "Now, thank goodness," she told Bynner, "I got some money to go on with, canadian shares."

Not long afterward, when Dan Wells, who now operated a private school in nearby San Cristobal, decided to go to California, Frieda discovered that she could go along and make a surprise appearance. They left Taos on 25 March 1942. After spending a day or two with Helen Bauer, who lived at Ojai, fifty miles from Los Angeles, Frieda went to see the Merrilds on South Robertson Boulevard. They gave her a fine party. After she returned home, Ravagli—in wartime having felt safer in Taos—sent the Merrilds his appreciation for a visit Frieda had obviously enjoyed: "[T]hank you for all the fiesta you make for Frieda, and [Elsa] I bet was pleased, for once, *to [h]andle Frieda in the way she want.*" It is clear that Frieda liked the adulation; those who came to celebrate her return probably included Gerald Heard, the Huxleys, the Nicholses, the Zeitlins, and the Biddles. Nor was Ravagli idle in her absence. At Los Pinos two workmen helped him install electricity, hot and cold water, and a bathroom to make the house more comfortable.

Although gas rationing had by now restricted travel all over the country, Ravagli discovered in January 1943 that he too could go to California—in the company of their neighbor Spud Johnson. Angelo wanted to sell hundreds of ceramic buttons he had made. In due course he visited the Huxleys. Writing to Grace Hubble a year later, on 9 January 1944, Maria described his uneasy status as a gigolo who, though always tolerated, struck Frieda's friends as halfway between "hired help" and "husband." Maria's kindness is therefore all the more remarkable:

He came to see us last year very low and discouraged. Obviously his situation of a Gigolo was becoming more and more difficult and Frieda none easier to live with.— But the later letters seem satisfied and contented.—They will of course not come here until the war is over and are in the lower ranch at Taos itself.—His pottery business is so good that if he had efficient help he could make much money; the orders pour in but he cannot pour them out.—And the specimens he sends me so constantly are getting better and better.— He is a kind, honest man whom I have always been fond of in spite of his very trying surface which I could understand well having lived in Italy many years.—The putting on airs had so many reasons.— He heard from his family immediately after the Italian occupation.—Nothing since.—They were all still alive.—He accumulates things for them which is so touching.—A little money of course and the clothes I send him which are too small for Matthew and which he could wear but keeps.

Coming from Maria, the word "Gigolo" is surprising, but it is clear that Ravagli accepted his situation while recognizing its risks. In Maria's account he maintains his two lives uneasily—balancing his servile status with Frieda against his strong need to assist his family in war-torn Italy. He was a father agonizingly separated from his children, yet to Frieda he was a husband without any moral authority. Hence he apparently "put on airs" to try to leverage respect. A kept man, he still desired dignity and purpose. Maria, though she might have patronized him, does not. Her worldly tact, which enabled her to arrange occasional dalliances for Aldous, was impeccable. Frieda thought her a perfect friend.

In these dark war years, Frieda's efforts on behalf of Lawrence's work had no issue until 1943. Then she met a man who helped focus her energies. Willard Hougland (1906–58) worked at the Laboratory of Anthropology in Santa Fe. He had ambition and liked Lawrence's work, but made only a slight impression on others. Miranda Masocco Levy (b. 1919), Frieda's good friend from 1939 on, remembered Hougland as a connoisseur of art and his wife, Georgine, as an amusing woman who "played the piano at Witter Bynner's parties."

On Frieda's behalf Hougland approached Houghton Mifflin in Boston and proposed a uniform edition of all of Lawrence's work. It never materialized. Nor did the Viking Press reach out to Frieda; in Carmel she had heard that Viking's Marshall Best, the firm's general manager, thought her a very domineering woman. What did materialize however was a decision by the Dial Press in New York to issue the first *Lady Chatterley's Lover* with an introduction by Frieda. Published in April 1944, the volume roused a flurry of publicity when John S. Sumner, of the New York Society for the Suppression of Vice, found ninety-two "spots" that (he thought) made it unfit for distribution. Armed with a search warrant, Sumner marched to the Dial Press on 27 April and seized 398 copies of the book. One month later, Magistrate Charles G. Keutgen agreed that the novel "is clearly obscene." But two judges in a special sessions court disagreed, dismissing the case on 2 November. Because of the publicity, Dial's original print run of 17,500 copies soon sold out. Reviewers praised the book's narrative economy, its psychological understanding, and its cultural insight.

## A Texas Border Town

As Frieda grew older, she came to dislike the cold winters of Taos, even when she stayed at the lower ranch. The war had forced her to remain sequestered there from March 1942 until December 1944—close to three years. Now she craved a change. Johnie Griffin (1896–1962), a wealthy Texas friend, generously arranged for Frieda and Ravagli to stay for several months in a house that she had rented six miles from Brownsville. Years before, Johnie had responded to an ad in a Philadelphia newspaper, placed by Herbert S. Griffin, a cattle rancher who owned ten thousand acres in Texas. They married but later Herbert was murdered by a tenant farmer, and Johnie (along with their son, Ephraim) inherited the ranch. The discovery of oil on their land made them immensely rich.

Frieda was glad to try a new part of the country—southern Texas—while minimizing her expenses. She also welcomed some distance from Dorothy Horgan (1908–2001), a well-heeled New Yorker who in July 1943 began to spend time in Taos and soon caught Ravagli's roving eye. His longstanding dalliance with Mrs. Horgan may initially have disturbed Frieda. Janet Byrne assumes that in 1945 Frieda "keenly felt the loss" of his sexual attentions. But Miranda Levy believes that Frieda not only tol-

Angelo Ravagli, Frieda Lawrence, and Johnie Griffin, c. 1951 (Courtesy of Arthur J. Bachrach)

erated but may even have encouraged his liaisons, so long as they were discreet. Dorothy Horgan's daughter Barbara (b. 1932) believes that her mother, who sometimes lived apart from her father, always preferred to keep the affair with Ravagli simple and uncomplicated. "For some years she and Angie loved each other," Barbara Horgan surmised, "but for her I don't think it was ever a passion." Later, Frieda carefully measured the distance she needed when she wrote to Dorothy: "I hope you understand my reasons for not knowing you more intimately." Accepting without envy Dorothy's "charming relationship with Angelino," Frieda openly respected his freedom. He counted on her generosity.

Regardless, Frieda and Angelo went on to Brownsville, Texas, just across the meandering Rio Grande River from the parched Mexican town of Matamoros. In 1945 Brownsville, bordering the Gulf of Mexico, was a small place of thirty thousand people near the edge of long, swampy flats where mosquitoes bred. The winter tourists who flocked to South Padre Island nearby, the huge oil refineries, and the pawn shops at the border would come later. At her house outside of town, Frieda loved the sight of sweet peas, colorful flowers, and globes of grapefruit hanging on the trees. The orange, lemon, and lime trees, ready to burst with intoxicating scent, would have reminded her of Taormina, whose winters were as mild. Angelo, though badly bitten by mosquitoes, went fishing and came in "breathless when he gets a fish!" Frieda laughed. After a time, he spent most of his hours fishing—the Port Brownsville channel was only three miles from their house. Occasionally Frieda went with him, saw the banana and pineapple boats, watched the noisy oil tankers flanked by raucous gulls, and caught her own big fish. Their neighbors brought them quail and wild duck, which Frieda cooked with parsley, oranges, and sherry. After some initial loneliness, she was delighted that she had "lots of lovely time to myself." They swam in the Gulf of Mexico, Angie (as he was often called now) painted some pictures while Frieda tried to write, and of course they entertained. Judge James D. Hamlin, a colorful, cigar-smoking raconteur, paid them a visit, and the Texas writer Frank Dobie came with his wife. On Saturdays Frieda listened to the Metropolitan Opera on the radio. Although she found the local people dull, Brownsville gave her peace in the midst of the war, an inexpensive winter haven, and an appealing way to retire. She was already sixty-five.

The memory of good fishing in Brownsville lay quietly, like a lure, in their imaginations. When they returned to the lower ranch in April 1945, they had the usual cleaning and repairing to do. The upper ranch—the "Lawrence" ranch—also demanded attention. Aided by Brett and Brett's close friend Joe Vanderbilt, Frieda spent many days renovating it: "We did the walls and the woodwork," she told Dudley Nichols, "and worked hard and it looks elegant—It was so peaceful with the pinetrees and there was no 'world'—except the cloud and pinetree world." Once the isolated ranch had been spruced up, Frieda gave a big party for ninety people on Sunday, 14 October, when the leaves of the cottonwoods had turned yellow and the woods smelled of autumn. Angelo roasted two big lambs.

But when the first snow fell in late October, Frieda began to pine for a warm climate. She wrote to the Merrilds, offering to pay up to $120 a month for a small house in Hollywood. When Merrild could find nothing, she wrote to novelist Henry Miller (1891–1980), whom she had probably met through Merrild, to ask him to secure them a house in Big Sur, where he lived. Tall, balding, with a long, sad face, Miller was a rugged individualist whose love of Lawrence had led him to write *Tropic of Cancer* and *Tropic of Capricorn,* erotic novels published in Paris in the thirties. Big Sur clung to rough, rocky cliffs overlooking the Pacific Ocean; not far from Monterey, it was some three hundred miles north of Los Angeles. For seventy-five dollars a month Miller found them the oceanfront home of a doctor. But sometime after Frieda and Angelo had begun their journey from El Prado in mid-December, the rental fell through; they opted instead for two cabins in a tourist camp near the ocean. They went for lunch to the home of their old friends Robin and Una Jeffers, and they spent Christmas with Henry Miller, his wife, Lepska, and their newborn baby. Frieda found Miller "a strange free bird." Settling into the River Inn, she and Ravagli looked in vain for accommodations. Una Jeffers even tried to get them John Steinbeck's house in Monterey. Finally, Frieda told Willard Hougland, "We have done something a bit wild—On the 15th we move into a *mansion* [in nearby Carmel] with private beach, a ballroom, a library etc 4 elegant bathrooms, it is a dream place, but there is *hardly* any furniture—We share it with 2 young couples."

Their experiment in communal living was a success. They pooled their money, bought food in turns, and cooked and cleaned in shifts. The couples included Cecil Smith and John Ney, with their respective companions. At first they spent most of their time on the beach below the house. The rocky coastline around Point Lobos was dotted with coves, and, away from the crashing surf, dark seals sunned themselves. Angelo fished for crabs. But whenever it rained or turned cold, Frieda and the two young men began to fashion a filmscript of *Lady Chatterley's Lover.* It too was an adventure. Everyone wondered if Frieda could sell it. In 1981 Smith remembered Frieda's exuberant earthiness—her big-fingered hands, her stance (feet planted far apart), her chain smoking, and her big pots of savory soup. "Frieda was our cook."

Before returning to Taos for the summer, she and Angelo drove down to Hollywood and spent time with the Huxleys and a few days with the Nicholses in their palatial house. Then Nichols put Frieda in touch with his friend Allan Simpson, a young film agent who soon interested a Hollywood producer named Wolfgang Reinhardt in Frieda's new filmscript of *Lady Chatterley's Lover*. In 1934 Reinhardt had come to the United States with his famous father Max; later he made two German films about the von Trapp family, which eventually led to *The Sound of Music*. Nothing, though, came of Simpson's efforts.

In Taos the summer months brought them lively company. Henry Miller's close friend Jean Varda, a painter of collages, came twice from Monterey. From Hollywood came actress Janet Gaynor—much praised for her role in *A Star Is Born* (1937)—with her husband, Gilbert Adrian, who designed glamorous clothes for movie stars like Greta Garbo. They were a talented, appealing, invigorating couple. In June came a playwright who would later become a towering figure. He was Tennessee Williams (1911–83). Short and chain smoking, he had a smile as broad as Frieda's— and a rampaging sexual energy. In August 1939 he had first met Frieda when he stopped in Taos to pay homage to Lawrence, whose fusion of sex, nature, and power had strongly influenced his own writing. Now he brought with him his partner, Pancho Rodriguez y Gonzalez, an adoring young man who preferred stability to sensuality. Like Frieda, Williams gave his lover a stipend—two hundred dollars a month. In Taos for a vacation, both men came to Frieda's door and were warmly greeted: "I am going up with Tennessee Williams to the ranch with a friend of his. . . . I like him very much," she wrote to Una Jeffers on 21 May 1946. For his part Williams liked strong, maternal women, and for her part his sexual preference never mattered. But his restlessness surprised her. Later he captured her essence when he said that her eyes were "lit with lightning."

These summer visitors, having rejuvenated Frieda, left all too soon. A long winter lay ahead. The difficulties of finding a winter home in postwar California prompted Frieda to think about a less expensive option. Johnie Griffin, who owned a house in nearby Ranchos de Taos, no doubt urged her again to explore southern Texas, where, near the Gulf of Mexico, costs were low and the fishing a lot better than in California. Frieda's lack of success in marketing her Lawrence titles had tarnished Hollywood's appeal. Not one of her established filmwriting friends—Aldous Huxley, Dudley Nichols, or Sonya Levien—had gladly tackled *Lady Chatterley's Lover*, Frieda's most valuable property. Not one of them had, by currying favor with their studio czars, managed to get it made into a film. She had had to be content with second-string writers. But Frieda's royalties from *The First Lady Chatterley* and the release—at last—of her accumulated British royalties made her think of fresh options. Where could she find a small, inexpensive house that lay secluded on an unspoiled beach? Where could she enjoy her retirement in a place that gave her anonymity and time to herself? These were now her concerns.

Departing for Brownsville, Texas, in January 1947, Frieda and Angelo left knowing they would prefer a place of their own. They soon found a tiny waterfront settlement near Port Isabel that delighted them. It was called Laguna Vista. Frieda, who had reinvented herself so many times, must have felt that she had come full circle—from living with Lawrence at the edge of the Lago di Garda in Italy back in 1912, without her family, to living now at the edge of a sleepy lagoon, with boats drifting by, fish jumping, and another hard-working partner at her side. The patterns of the past had become strong driving forces. Never one to look back with regret, Frieda was nonetheless completing the long journey she had begun when she left Nottingham in 1912. Lawrence's money had given her the freedom she had always sought. Still in good health, she could—as she chose— write, entertain, cook, or read the classics. By husbanding the quarterly income that came to her like a boon and by not marrying Ravagli, she could remain "Mrs. Lawrence." It was the only crown she wanted.

# 24

# Port Isabel, Peace, and Marriage

## 1947–56

It is a mistake to regard Frieda in her last years as a woman who lost her zest—who faded and disappeared like a pale sunset. That image, which readers might expect, is false. She maintained her friendships, rescued her sister Johanna from poverty, went once more to Hollywood, traveled to London on her own, married Angelo Ravagli, and accumulated enough money to be generous. But her unexpected sense of fulfillment obscured a deeper need. Committed unconditionally to her friends, Frieda needed to recreate a family in America to replace the family she had sacrificed forty years earlier. That family she had lost forever, despite the ties she urgently claimed. No one visited her as she had visited her own mother—faithfully and often—for thirty years. So she acted for herself. In her seventies she sought increasingly to make a surrogate family of the close friends (most of them without children, many of them unmarried) who now surrounded her. To gather them into a tight, intimate clan was the central achievement of Frieda's last years.

In January 1947 James and Ellen Nabers sold Frieda a seaside lot with a small house. It was located in Laguna Vista, Texas, a hamlet five miles from Port Isabel and thirteen miles from the mouth of the Rio Grande River. Brownsville lay twenty miles southwest. Port Isabel (Frieda told the Merrilds) seemed "like a European fishing village"—much like those she and Lawrence had long found congenial, with their simple people and easy rhythms. For the next decade it was Frieda's winter home. She liked its mild climate (January temperatures averaged sixty-four degrees), its peaceful vistas of channel and boats, its busy gulls and pelicans and wild ducks, the blinking lighthouse at Padre Island—and the paucity of people. "Such heavenly peace here," she wrote to Witter Bynner on 17 February, "not a house in sight, only the lights of the fishermen's boats at night." In the early mornings the fishermen brought fresh oysters and flounder.

To make the small house livable required diligence. While Frieda made curtains, Ravagli got the lights, appliances, and windows to work; together they planted roses, shrubs, and palm trees. He even had time to paint pictures of fish. A short distance away, General Leonard Pierce and his wife, Kate, began building a house. Pierce (1895–1959) had served in both world wars and in 1943 had become a brigadier general. Until his stroke in 1952, he and his wife remained Frieda's close friends, providing conversation and, later, a new experience—television in the evening.

The waterfront property fixed to their liking, Frieda and Angelo departed for Taos on 20 April 1947 to cast out, once again, their social net. Just as Mabel Luhan had created her famous "Mabeltown," which her friends both coveted and mocked, so now did Frieda begin to parcel out her El Prado acreage into "Friedaland." She gave Dorothy Brett two acres, across the road, for a house; next to Brett's land she gave two young friends, William "Bill" Goyen (1915–83) and Walter Berns (b. 1919), two acres on which to build their own little adobe house. Comrades rather than lovers, these tall, lanky men had served together in the navy, waited tables at the Sagebrush Inn outside Taos, and yearned now to become writers. Goyen, brooding and passionate, found Taos "beautiful and remote, like a Himalayan village"; he lived in Frieda's shadow. In 1948 Berns left to pursue a doctorate in political science; he was replaced four years later by Joe Glasco (1925–96), a gifted painter with a sweet face, green eyes, and gentle manners. Goyen and Glasco were often nearby. To Spud Johnson's hopeful inquiry in 1947, Frieda responded at once: "Yes, Spud, have a piece of the land! It's there!" She began to embrace those she liked into a surrogate family. She enjoyed people. Miranda Levy remembered that "Frieda was a welcoming person. They were extremely well liked, very friendly and engaging." They often had company—people just dropped in, even tourists.

## A ROOM FOR NUSCH

The dry Taos summer, punctuated by dramatic thunderstorms, passed quickly, and the first frost came like an ambush. By now Frieda dreaded cold weather. When she and Ravagli reached Texas to spend the winter of 1948–49 in Port Isabel, he wrote Mabel a nice paean: "Here we have an ideal life—Frieda is happy at home—washing, reading, writing, walking in the sun in her nighty, and go[ing] to Bocachica swiming together—I am happy going hunting and fishing—when Frieda doesent need anything at home." Thus ensconced by the sea, Frieda had followed her bent for fifty years: she read the classics or her friends' books, she always *talked* about writing, she spotted boats crawling along the channel, and she sometimes walked, swam, boated, or fished. She liked life simple. But Ravagli's words "when Frieda doesent need anything" convey his ambiguous status. He long displayed touches of half-insolent deference typical of an employee allowed special liberties.

Around Christmas Frieda was jubilant to discover that she might be reunited with her younger sister, Johanna, whom she called "Nusch," and whose Austrian villa had been confiscated as German property. Now penniless, her husband Emil von Krug having died five years earlier, Nusch yearned to taste—at last—America's bounty. Arriving from Vienna in January 1949, she still possessed "the grand manner" and was vibrant and full of fun. Angie, aided by a carpenter, had already added a room for Nusch with huge windows and oak floors. Frieda told the Merrilds, "I am so grateful to the Lord and Lawrence, that I can afford to look after her!" In fact, Nusch was able to spend the next one and one-half years with Frieda and Angelo. The Lawrence estate, under Laurence Pollinger's skillful management, continued to supply Frieda with plenty of money. On Pollinger, Frieda lavished unending praise.

Good news flowed from all directions. A Lawrence revival had burst like a dam amid postwar prosperity. When Harry Truman became president after FDR's death in 1945, the American economy began to expand. As returning veterans poured into colleges, aided by the GI Bill, the demand for books rose rapidly. And in Britain, where access to higher education had always been far more limited than in America, the slow turn toward socialism also enfranchised the working classes. An English publisher named Allen Lane (not a university graduate himself) had shrewdly observed that good books could not be bought at modest prices. He took a risk. Choosing novels like *A Farewell to Arms, South Wind,* and *A Passage to India,* which had sold well in hard cover, he reprinted them as Penguin Books. Later, he too responded to postwar demand. In 1950 he simultaneously published ten of Lawrence's novels in huge editions. For all their cheapness, they were impeccably designed and printed, and were a great success. Lawrence, Frieda said, "would have liked the cheapness" of the new Penguins.

A further boost came in 1950 with Richard Aldington's biography of Lawrence, *Portrait of a Genius But . . . ,* which Frieda had long awaited. Highly readable but derisive in tone, Aldington's book provided a clear-eyed, even-handed assessment of Lawrence and his work. Yet, apart from Aldington's close personal observation of Lawrence (he noticed with alarm that Lawrence chose *red* wine to go with his bouillabaisse), his book offers a familiar story. Frieda found reading it "a strange experience." She found her marriage to Lawrence quickly slipping into legend—into what *Time*'s reviewer of the book glibly called "one of the strangest, most strenuous marriages imaginable. . . . When [Lawrence] raged at her, she merely picked up a dish and heaved it at his head." The word "merely" shows how easy simplification came. This legend-soaked marriage would become the staple of Lawrence biographers from Emily Hahn to Brenda Maddox.

But two Frenchmen had a different idea. Gaston Bonheur and Philippe de Rothschild accomplished what Hollywood had failed to do. They turned *Lady Chatterley's Lover* into a play. Reading it in French, Frieda found it "delicate and alive." She invited Rothschild to Taos. *El Crepusculo*, the weekly Taos paper, reported in May 1950 that Frieda gave a dinner party at La Doña Luz restaurant "in honor of Princess Gabriele Liechtenstein of Kesselstate, Germany, and Baron Philippe de Rothschild of Paris." Much later, in 1959, this delicate play served as the basis for the first film of *Lady Chatterley's Lover,* done in French, with Danielle Darrieux playing Connie Chatterley and Erno Crisa playing Oliver Mellors. Though moving and competent, the film took few erotic risks.

And the Lawrence revival kept flowing. In 1950 in England—long more hospitable to Lawrence than America had been—Anthony Pelissier cleverly adapted Lawrence's story "The Rocking Horse Winner" for film, focusing on the panic felt by the young Paul, played by John Howard Davies. By riding his toy horse, he tries desperately to satisfy his mother's insatiable craving for money. The film itself rides back and forth, in a complex rhythm, between the realistic world of privileged greed and the fantasy world of Lawrence's fable.

As the Lawrence tide washed in, two more books surfaced, both in 1951, illustrating the two kinds of books that Lawrence, even today, tends to attract. Harry T. Moore's *Life and Works* illustrates the plodding but comprehensive academic study, with fresh material on Lawrence's youth, whereas Witter Bynner's *Journey with Genius,* written twenty-five years after his encounters with Lawrence, is lively, highly personal, often scintillating, but drenched in malice. It celebrates Frieda's brave patience (she loved Bynner and his memoir). She cared less for Moore's book. "Harry Moore's Lawrence is not my Lawrence," she complained to Louis Gibbons. Even those who praised Moore's book complained of "a style without flavor or distinction." For years to come, Lawrence would inspire books by those who passionately resisted him (such as Kate Millett) and those who avidly interpreted him.

But despite all this attention, Frieda, now past seventy, endured her share of disappointments. To her dismay she learned that she owed eleven thousand dollars in back income taxes. At Christmas 1949, she told Mabel, "I feel very poor and have to be stingy!" A good income had its penalties. Moreover, now that Nusch could stand in as Frieda's companion, Ravagli wanted a holiday by himself. A month later, in January 1950, he boarded a train in Brownsville and, two days later, stepped off in New York City. He had gone to see Dorothy Horgan at 1088 Park Avenue. He stayed for more than three weeks. With delicious courtesy Dorothy sent Frieda a perfume bottle. Frieda, surely remembering her own erotic excursions in the last years of Lawrence's life, chided Ravagli before he returned home for imagining that she minded his dalliance: "Why should I begrudge you a holiday? Life is so short! You need'nt be so surprised!" Jealous feelings bored Frieda. She wanted the peace that comes from amicable relationships and simple well-being.

But her health, always extraordinarily good, at last began to fail. She developed symptoms of diabetes. "I have been so very well all my life that it is a nuisance having to fuss about myself," she told Ravagli while he was gone. She had had to alter her diet (no sugar, few starches), then later to have shots of insulin, which—luckily—a friendly neighbor named Bunny Goldtrap could teach her to inject. Later, she said to Mabel, who was spending the winter in Cuernavaca, Mexico, "My diabetis was really a blessing in disguise, because I look after my health now, I never did before." Still, her diabetes was a warning.

There were others. At Christmastime a year later, a circus came to Port Isabel. One of the hawkers enticed Ravagli to bet thirty-five cents on the outcome of a game. Soon he had lost one hundred dollars. To try to win back his loss, he persuaded Frieda to cash a check for two hundred dollars. He lost that too. "We felt so small and sad, all that money at Xmastime!" she lamented to Brett. To a careful, frugal, practical man like Ravagli, the loss was stunning. He had pitted his pride and skill against a rigged game: "For the first time in my life, I felt very low and miserable," he told Dudley Nichols. Frieda accepted the loss as a joint misfortune. Her good nature tolerated error as the simple outcome of human frailty. She never worried about perfection.

But she did worry about a more serious matter. She had been a widow for twenty years. The charisma that she had proudly worn as Lawrence's widow had long been fading; old age, delivering its threat of infirmity, was fast approaching; and she believed that Ravagli's faithful service should have a tangible outcome. Sensitive to these concerns, Frieda pondered matrimony once more. Accompanied by a friend named Robert "Bob" Davidson (1925–98)—later a successful New York attorney—Ravagli went to Las Vegas, secured a divorce from Serafina that was valid in the United States (though not in Italy), and finally, after twenty years as a couple, he and Frieda were married in Taos on 31 October 1950. Because Frieda announced the news without fanfare, some biographers have assumed that the marriage simply ratified a business arrangement. But Frieda recognized that Ravagli was as much her mate as Lawrence had been, though in a very different way. As a couple she and Ravagli were so well matched that marriage was a satisfying outcome. Whereas Lawrence had been demanding and disciplined, Ravagli was accommodating and pleasure seeking. He had always returned to Frieda, whether from Italy or from New York City (where he had gone twice). She loved him because he complemented her. He was active and driven—a savvy hunter; she was contemplative and social—and relished peace. He offered her companionship and affection; she provided his financial security. If his deepest allegiances were split among several women, Frieda's remained largely with Lawrence. She knew that a woman "can only have *one* husband in a lifetime!"

## WORLD TRAVELERS: THE LAST PHASE

Frieda also knew that some of her California friends were seriously ill. Maria Huxley was suffering from a mysterious fatigue, Aldous's right eye had succumbed to iritis and his vision had worsened, Esta Nichols and Louise Arensberg had developed medical problems, and in 1950 Knud Merrild suffered a debilitating stroke. Her love of old friends made her yearn to go to Hollywood one last time. Long before leaving for the West Coast, Ravagli had begun to study America's Constitution, history, and government. Although Frieda decided she was too old to bother, he wanted his American citizenship so that, when he returned to Italy to see his family, he could be sure to come back safely to Frieda. But when he finally gained his citizenship in December 1951, he lost his Italian military pension: "and we must pay the wife another 50 dollars a month," Frieda confided to Brett. Frieda's "another 50" suggests they were already supplementing Serafina's income from high school teaching.

In Hollywood, still a mecca of cinema glitter, the Huxleys provided a social center from which Frieda and Angelo could reconnect with old friends. Maria helped them find an apartment at 1270 North Havenhurst Drive, eight blocks from North King's Road, where she and Aldous lived. Seeing the Huxleys every day and hearing Aldous describe a proposed screenplay of Gandhi's life, Frieda felt relaxed and peaceful. She splurged on an Elizabeth Arden hairdo, went for drives through the sumptuous Palos Verdes estates, and soon found an active social life with Peggy Kiskadden and her surgeon-husband Bill, the Walter Arensbergs, the Igor Stravinskys, writer Sonya Levien, Frenchy and Edith Hutton (they were Germans who owned La Doña Luz restaurant in Taos, which Frieda liked), and Nicolai Fechin, a talented Russian painter whose wife, Tinka, had driven him away from Taos. When Maria went into the hospital to have a malignant cyst removed from her breast, Frieda fixed Aldous's meals. He stimulated her mind, she told Brett, but with his unfailing tact he never "makes one aware of one's ignorance." Whenever Aldous needed to go to the hospital, the film studio, or the UCLA library, Ravagli drove him.

Old friends gave way to new. "Best of all," Frieda said, "I liked Edwin Hubble the astronomer of Mount Wilson, a truly noble fellow" whom she had met much earlier—and who would be dead in a year. She also made friends with Richard Tregaskis (1916–73), a writer, war correspondent, and director, age thirty-six, who lived in the apartment directly above her and who had written *Guadalcanal Diary* (1943), a raw, day-by-day account of the American invasion of Guadalcanal Island in 1942. A Harvard man (like Bynner and Dan Wells before him), he had been more fortunate than Frieda: Twentieth Century–Fox had successfully filmed his book. Tregaskis, like Hubble, helped satisfy her need for intellectual companionship.

In time, Ravagli came to feel that he had earned a trip to Italy. His father was old, and in Genoa he wanted to meet his daughter Magda's ambitious husband, Dr. Gambetta, and their son, Rodolfo (b. 1947). He soon secured a passport and on the *Vulcania* booked a cabin from New York to Genoa, departing 5 April 1952, arriving five days later. He would stay four months. As he and Frieda contemplated their final farewell to Hollywood, he wrote to Mabel: "We had a wanderfull busy time—but we did not accomplish anything. I did no painting and Frieda did not write a line for her book—but the funny part was to be busy all the time in doing nothing." For Ravagli, social engagements were "nothing." Whenever Frieda sought social pleasure, he bent his desires to hers.

Just before he left for Italy, he was extra nice, she told Dudley Nichols, but she worried that his return to Italy would be sad: his brothers and sisters in Tredozio, all with large families, were very poor. In his absence Frieda managed well, paying the bills on time; and, inspired perhaps by Miranda Masocco's transatlantic travels, she decided to fly to London to see her children, her grandchildren, and her children's old German nanny, Ida Wilhelmy. Terrified to go by herself, she departed on 6 June with Miranda Masocco (Levy), a fashionable young friend, age thirty-three, who was on her way to France. Interviewed in 1999, Miranda remembered an amusing story about Frieda: "We stayed in New York several days because Carl Van Vechten gave a little dinner for her. And she insisted on going shopping, so we went to Gristede's, a very famous chain in New York, a specialty food shop that had absolutely everything. She wanted to buy [her family] a ham—she thought that it would take care of them for a meal— so we got a ham and other things like crackers that she picked out. She was wearing a Mexican blouse, a full Mexican skirt, ballet slippers, and a little Mexican beanie (she always dressed this way). Anyway, we got to London, and she had this huge ham over her shoulder—I thought I would die. But she never let go of the ham; she wouldn't put it in the luggage compartment—she carried it!" Frieda was secure enough to be entirely herself; propriety held no luster for her.

Arriving in London on 14 June, she stayed two weeks. Her first-class round-trip ticket on TWA cost $711—a tiny fortune in 1952, when per capita personal income in the United States averaged $1,639. She stayed with Monty and his wife, Vera, in London; tender and solicitous, they "treat me like a raw egg," she told Brett on 17 June, even serving her breakfast in bed. When Allen Lane came to tea, her grandson Ian Weekley remembered her "presiding majestically at the garden table under an old cherry tree, her raucous laughter disturbing pigeons in the plane trees and sunlight flashing on the various pieces of turquoise rings, brooches, and bracelets with which she seemed to be covered." Near the end of her visit, she migrated to her old hotel, the Kingsley, where she could more easily see Laurence Pollinger, A. S. Frere-Reeves, Middleton Murry, and Martin Secker, now seventy. Three of these men, she proudly remembered, had known Lawrence.

⳥

Reunited in El Prado, Frieda and Angelo resumed their life together on the Taos plateau, attending to their chores, visiting and being visited, lulled into a desert Cranford, while Brett served up the spicy local gossip—about wealthy Millicent Rogers and her Navajo lover, Benito; about Tinka Fechin fighting foreclosure on her fine Taos home; about Johnie Griffin's son becoming unbalanced; about Mabel entrusting her manuscripts and letters to Yale. Brett added bits about their neighbors the Montoyas—Joe, Juanita, and their children—who sometimes worked for Frieda. Interviewed in 1998, Juanita (b. 1904) and her son Ernesto remembered Frieda's lively interest, her warmth, and her generosity. They were cooler toward "Angelino." One time, during a severe drought in 1951, the Montoyas' cattle—their livelihood—were dying. Their wells had run dry. Ernesto ran across the field to Frieda's to ask for help: "Angelino brought out a gallon bucket with a gallon of water. I said to him, 'I wanted to see if I could get water from your well to fill a big tub so the cattle could drink.' (We had about twenty head of cows and calves.) And he said, 'No, that's all I can give you.'" Ravagli may honestly have worried about their supply of water, because a year later Frieda had to drill a new well.

But another time, after Juanita had finished cleaning the El Prado house, Frieda opened her purse and pulled out seven dollars. "What?" cried her husband. "You pay too much money. Why? She doesn't do that much." Frieda shot back: "Don't say anything. It's *my* money!" This little squabble probably typified many like it—Frieda giving generously, Ravagli boisterously pulling on the financial reins, aware of the privations his extended family suffered back in Italy. He may have felt that Frieda's money was his nemesis, her generosity a constant reminder of his dependency. Occasionally, Frieda may have mentioned the extra fifty dollars siphoned regularly to his first wife. In a sense he earned back the alimony payments by being frugal, but sometimes he seemed cheap. Ernesto Montoya, when just a boy, often helped Ravagli with his pottery, "but he never gave me anything."

## THE LAST AMIGOS

During her last years, Frieda liked making new friends among young people. She liked their vitality and their good looks, found them amusing, and regarded them almost as loyal children; her own children by now (her daughter Barby recalled) had "grown completely apart from her."

In 1953 she met a strikingly beautiful woman named Amalia de Schulthess, not quite thirty, who was a superb sculptress and a friend and client of Jake Zeitlin's. Amalia and a friend had come to Taos for a visit, driven up toward the Lawrence ranch, and on the narrow, bumpy, rutted road met Frieda. They became good friends. Youthful and blond, Amalia soon perceived that the triumvirate of Mabel, Frieda, and Brett were like three splendid vultures "looking for an heir to take over and keep on attracting people, getting people to come to Taos. And for a moment they thought, 'Oh boy, she has arrived.'" But Amalia, fiercely committed to her art, could not fulfill their hope.

When she brought her husband, Hans, to Taos the following year, Frieda was delighted: "Frieda *liked* good-looking men; she liked the adulation—being something of a star." The scion of an aristocratic family of Swiss bankers, Hans de Schulthess (1918–62) had left Europe earlier, in 1941. Jake Zeitlin remembered his flamboyant *machismo:* "He liked doing spectacular things." Eventually, from under her bed, Frieda pulled out the box of Lawrence's manuscripts that she had held on to. Although some manuscripts had been sold—and even more given away to friends—Frieda prized most highly the three handwritten manuscripts of *Lady Chatterley's Lover.* Looking at them thrilled her, brought her again close to Lawrence, gave her access to his creative life. After Hans saw them, he wanted them for his wife. He was determined to have them. Never skilled at setting prices, Frieda asked Jake to come and appraise them in October 1954. He did—and valued them at $10,000, an exorbitant price but no barrier to Hans, who bought them. But his star was already falling. In 1962, speeding to pass another car in Austria, he died in a terrible crash. Three years later Amalia reluctantly sold the manuscripts to Jake for $30,000, and he in turn (with another dealer) sold them to the University of Texas for $50,000. The market for Lawrence was, to say the least, buoyant.

The privileged de Schulthesses were not the only young friends who warmed to Frieda. From a more humble background came Louis Gibbons (b. 1922) and Johnny Morgan (1926–61). They were typical of those who saw Frieda, in her later years, as a shrine. A poet, a TV producer in Dallas, square shouldered and crew cut, Louis Gibbons was good looking and adoring—and he was hard at work on a very personal book about Lawrence. Louis and Johnny, who regarded themselves as a pair of Texas country boys, drove all night to reach Taos, and on 21 August 1953 they met Frieda in El Prado. Wearing a yellow dress and a red apron, she boomed: "I love Texans! They're so full of life!" Pulling a Pall Mall from her pack, she began to smoke—one after the other—then showed them inside to the bedroom, where she pulled out her Lawrence manuscripts and spontaneously gave Johnny twenty pages titled "My mother made a failure of her life" (an early version of *The Lost Girl* worth about three hundred dollars). She was generous to a fault.

Hungering for an epiphany in Frieda's presence, Louis went to Port Isabel, where the Ravaglis had gone for the winter. There he and a fair-haired, blue-eyed cotton broker named Tom Young (1915–84) were invited to lunch on 1 December 1954. Frieda insisted that lunch be her own. While she worked in the kitchen, Ravagli described, with dismay, their visit to the University of Texas at Austin.

Back in April 1954 two university officials, Harry Ransom (1908–76) and Warren Roberts (1916–98), had approached Frieda with a proposal to buy her entire Lawrence collection, build a beautiful library to house it, and take over the Lawrence ranch. Because she would be relieved of so much responsibility, Frieda was excited. But when she and her husband stopped in Austin for a grand reception, Ravagli grew angry that the university, awash in oil money, would not buy Frieda's collection outright. Harry Ransom, offering them only a vague verbal promise, thereby lost the chance to acquire Frieda's complete collection. The Austin encounter "was a fiasco!" she told Louis, a little hurt; for she was stung to see the university ostentatiously displaying such finery as Persian carpets.

But lunch was waiting. Louis's account captures incomparably Frieda's mature charm:

> "I think I have a surprise for you," she said: "chopped deer!". . . The four of us sat at a modern counter-like table in the kitchen. There was a thin, clear soup; followed by a delicious salad, with an oil-and-vinegar dressing; and then came the main course—the chopped deer, which was undoubtedly the wildest-tasting meat I have ever bitten into. Immediately, Angie, aware that it was too wild for me, got up and cut me some smoked sausage, which was a great deal better. I felt terrible, for Tom ate the wild meat with relish and called for more! The clear wine was delicious and so were the ice cream and frozen strawberries that Frieda served afterwards. When lunch was over, Angie suggested that we have our coffee and ciga-

Louis Gibbons and Betty Cottam at the Kiowa Ranch, 1953 (Courtesy of Louis Gibbons)

rettes on the front porch that faced the sea. . . . So, taking up our cups, we filed out to the porch, settled ourselves in rustic chairs, and watched the flat gray waves heaving eternally forward, breaking in foamy whiteness on the silver beach, and making a lulling music in our ears—perfect background for a casual discussion of Catholicism and Protestantism.

Louis's account records the easy companionship of the Ravaglis; their wild meat spiced their unconventional appeal.

Spontaneously, Frieda suggested a drive to Padre Island, a long tongue of sand accessed by a newly constructed causeway. Even at age seventy-five, she relished adventure.

She reappeared shortly, resplendent in a snowy white blouse; a full, bright-red skirt; and a pair of brown suede moccasins, with little bells attached. To complete this gay and colorful costume, she carried a great, square purse made of bright green cloth and a small, white handkerchief edged with white lace—one of the six we had sent her. . . .

"Bring your manuscript!" she said. . . .

As we drove across the Port Isabel Causeway . . . the fragrance of the heaving, silver-crested sea rose up to meet us. How refreshing it was! Suddenly, we found ourselves driving along the sand-packed beach of Padre Island, Angie at the wheel, with Tom at his side, and Frieda and myself in the back seat. Our ears were so full of the lulling sounds of the sea and the petulant cries of the sea gulls that we could hardly converse. . . .

When Angie brought the car to a stop, Frieda jumped out, kicked off her brown suede moccasins, and ran wading into the sea. She was as happy as a child on a holiday.

"Isn't it lovely?" she laughed. Then she beckoned us to join her. Tom and I took off our shoes and socks, rolled up our trousers, and followed her. It was . . . ironic that a sophisticated woman of the world would take so much delight in such a simple pleasure. . . . Meanwhile, Angie got out his rod and reel, cast a line into the water, and waited patiently for a bite.

"Now," Frieda said, "you must read to me what you have written about Lawrence."

Settled in the car again, Frieda reclined in the back seat on some pillows and listened eagerly as Louis expounded Lawrence's view of sex:

At times she became so excited, so deeply moved, that she spontaneously punctuated my statements with her ever-reassuring "Ja!" At other times, however, she corrected me. . . .

"What a pity you couldn't have written about Lawrence during his lifetime!" she said sadly. "No one has quite written about him as you have.". . . I seemed to feel a breath of immortality in my face, the coolness of eternity at my finger tips.

Frieda often inspired this kind of reverence in young men. Her strong, husky voice; her maternal compassion; her conviction and approval; her deep connection to the earth—these attributes energized young men in the

Frieda's winter home, near Port Isabel, Texas, 1954 (Courtesy of Louis Gibbons)

same way that Lawrence, too, had once been energized by her profound belief in his potential. She never lost the capacity to inspire.

Frieda was coming full circle. In her last year she invited Ida, her children's old nurse, to spend three months with her in Port Isabel. Ida arrived from Bremen on a banana boat, Frieda paying a mere $430 for her round-trip passage. Thrilled to be in America, Ida kept the house spotless. A fisherman-chauffeur drove them where they wanted to go. During this time Angie was free to visit his sister for six weeks in Buenos Aires (he had not seen her since 1934); he returned on 31 March. Although Frieda had missed his efficient support, death had intruded too. Koteliansky, never Frieda's champion, died in London. Then Maria Huxley succumbed to cancer. "I still feel the blow of Maria's death in my bones," she wrote to the Nicholses. Strongly protective, Maria had proved to be Frieda's most loyal female friend, a woman who had never uttered a harsh word against her. She especially admired the noble way that Aldous had helped Maria to die: "I would urge her," he wrote, ". . . to go deeper and deeper into the light, ever deeper and deeper. . . . I told her to let go, to forget the body, to leave it lying here like a bundle of old clothes, and to allow herself to be carried, as a child is carried, into the heart of the rosy light of love." When Aldous visited Port Isabel with Maria's sister Rose in April 1955, Frieda dreaded seeing him without Maria, but instead, she told Brett, she found him "lovely and natural and unconceited."

## THE FLIGHT OF THE HUMMINGBIRD

After Millicent Rogers died in 1950, and after Mabel and Tony began drinking heavily, Frieda and Brett were the lights of Taos, luring visitors with their fragrant memories of a bygone Europe. They were like Gertrude Stein in Paris or the Sitwells in England—a shrine to which young friends such as Miranda Masocco brought talented young people like Scottish writer Ludovic Kennedy and ballerina Moira Shearer. "I spent half my life driving [from Santa Fe] to Taos," Miranda wryly recalled.

But as the Ravaglis were returning from Port Isabel in April, Frieda succumbed briefly to an illness—"A virus jumped on me like a lion out of the blue!" she told Rebecca James, an artist whose parties Frieda had always liked. Released from the Santa Fe hospital after two weeks, Frieda slowly regained her strength and began to see her friends again—lunches with Helene Wurlitzer and Earl Stroh, dinners with Mabel and Dorothy Benrimo, and of course Brett came or called every day.

In May 1956 Frieda's daughter Barby came to El Prado while Ravagli went to Italy for his holiday. Unlike Louis Gibbons, Barby observed her mother not as a source of inspiration but as a person whose earlier defiance had now shaded into quiet wisdom. Strong differences in temperament and style, though they had separated mother and daughter in the thirties, had at last given way to tolerant affection: "Frieda would get up as soon as it was light and water all the plants with a hose, make coffee in the kitchen, and then go back to bed again to smoke 'Luckies' and read Dickens's books. . . . She would come into the kitchen much later, while I was having breakfast, and tell me how much Dickens's morality infuriated her: 'I *loathe* that Little Dorrit!'" Barby records not even a hint of illness but, instead, Frieda's pull toward the elements, her absorbed contemplation of natural phenomena, resembling what Lawrence had enjoyed many years earlier, when Brewster Ghiselin came upon him staring raptly at the Mediterranean: "In the evenings she sat outside looking across the great stretch of sage brush to watch the sun setting behind the mountains. . . . Her hair had turned a white-gold, with green shadows, and her turquoise eyes were still young looking. Sitting by herself each evening, watching the sunset so absorbedly, she seemed to understand the elemental world." This quiet image of Frieda entranced by the soft summer sunlight is like the last frame in a film.

Resembling other summer days, 8 August dawned hot and dry. But to Frieda the sun may have seemed like a pitiless vulture overhead. At 11 P.M. she suffered a severe stroke. The doctor came, administered a sedative, but did not admit her to the hospital. Her whole right side was paralyzed; she could not speak, except to say "thank you," and her breathing was erratic. Her neighbors Bill Goyen and Joe Glasco arrived at once to find Angie distraught. "I almost faint[ed] to see in such condition my good Frieda," Angie wrote to the Nicholses.

She had been expected in Santa Fe, where Miranda and Winfield Townley Scott were hosting a joint birthday party for her and Witter Bynner. Three days later, on her seventy-seventh birthday, she died. But she died as she would have wished—at home, in the company of friends. In this, as in so much else, she followed Lawrence's footsteps.

Simplicity marked Frieda's end. On 13 August, at the Hanlon Funeral Home, people came all day to see her. At 4 P.M. the funeral cortège followed the hearse to the ranch; the six pallbearers carried the casket upward to the Lawrence shrine; and there, just outside the little chapel, Frieda was buried. Trembling, Bill Goyen said a few words, read Lawrence's "Song of a Man Who Has Come Through," and recited Psalm 121, which begins "I will lift up mine eyes unto the hills, from whence cometh my help." Louis Gibbons, standing among the mourners, remembered a poignant detail: "As the crowd began to disperse, an exquisite hummingbird flew toward Frieda's flowers." Although it is tempting to think that the bird sought Frieda's spirit, and fled upward and away, yet contradictions abound, for Louis also remembered Frieda's confident assertion two years earlier: "I wonder where we go when we die?" someone asked. "I know," said Frieda.

"Back to the elements." She was not a mystic but a great force of affirmation, rooted in cycles like those Lawrence sought, at the end of his own life, when he proposed "living in ritual adjustment to the cosmos in its revolutions, in eternal submission to the greater laws."

๛

In her long life Frieda had found what she wanted. Her youthful rebellion was a clue to her lifelong flouting of convention—from her adventure with the charismatic Otto Gross, to her defiant departure from Ernest Weekley and their children; from her escape with Lawrence in 1912, to her occasionally fierce chafing against his efforts to dominate her. A woman of great resilience and buoyancy, she ignored the rigid behavioral codes of both Bismarck and Queen Victoria. Like other radicals of her time, she elevated love above responsibility, sex above sanctity. Although her options were partly defined by the domestic ideals of her age (sewing, visiting, reading, writing letters), she also repudiated those ideals by choosing her own company and going where she pleased. She was neither a paragon of domestic virtue nor a gentle exponent of family values. At times she could be opinionated, lazy, and unfocused. But she was seldom unkind, rarely spiteful, and never ungenerous. Above all, her hearty laughter and her vital interest in others defined her appeal. Looking back, Brigit Patmore realized that Frieda "sailed over small matters like a ship gliding over weeds. . . . I never saw her fussing about anything."

It took years for Frieda to strike the right balance between assertive behavior and calm acceptance. When she came to America in 1933, to live at the ranch with Ravagli, she came full of insecurity and anger at those who, she felt, had insulted her—first, Lawrence's family; afterward, in 1935, those who would defile his ashes. Even after she won the bulk of Lawrence's estate, she spent years fighting to gain respect for Lawrence—and for herself. But once her insecurity about her intelligence gave way to confidence in her own character, she learned to control the assertiveness that, to some observers, had made her seem truculent rather than powerful.

The men she admired did most to shape the woman she became. Although her mother curbed Frieda's natural masculine preferences, she learned from her father to be proud, brave, and strong. If Otto Gross freed her from the Christian precepts of chastity and duty, Lawrence taught her to express her feelings directly, to honor her impulses, and to approach their life together not as a series of obligations to others but as an unfolding adventure. Ravagli gave her a new respect for practical efficiency. If Lawrence had both earned and managed their money, after 1931 it was all hers. Money gave her a different kind of power—power over her own destiny. When she wanted to be lavish, she could; when she wanted the El

422

Prado ranch or a new car, she bought it; when she wanted a new room or a new house, Ravagli built it. Although he was a dilettante and a womanizer, he was also an affectionate companion who yielded to her wishes. In short, he too liked to cultivate pleasure without fretting about its consequences. Always a social asset to Frieda, always gallant and courteous, he had great charm as a man.

In her quest for a life lived on her own terms, at the edge of propriety, her optimism sustained her to the end. Once she had reconciled herself to the loss of her children, she was rarely depressed, rarely defeated, rarely bitter. She channeled unhappiness into a ready embrace of her immediate surroundings. She was a flower, waiting each morning for the new day to pour out its joy.

## RAVAGLI LEAVES TAOS

After Frieda's death, Angelo Ravagli was never the same. Financially, of course, he was well set. Frieda's will provided one hundred dollars a month to Nusch, then gave half of the rest to Ravagli; the other half she split among her three children. He soon disposed of Frieda's possessions. A few months before her death, Frieda had given the Lawrence ranch to the University of New Mexico as a retreat for writers. Just after her death, Ravagli gave Joe Glasco's reverential portrait of Frieda to Amalia de Schulthess. In 1957 he sold Frieda's books to the Taos Bookshop; in 1959 he sold the El Prado ranch; and to his good friend Saki Karavas he sold the Lawrence paintings that had hung in Frieda's house for more than thirty years. Warren Roberts trekked from the University of Texas to Taos and purchased what remained of Lawrence's and Frieda's papers for five thousand dollars.

Adrift, Ravagli took a small apartment near the Taos post office, but without Frieda his American world shattered, his friendships hung like husks on Frieda's memory, his amatory conquests were no longer sustainable. He was sixty-seven. After disposing of the Port Isabel property in 1960 for $3,750, he packed his possessions, said his farewells, and went back to Spotorno, Italy—back to the Villa Bernarda where he had first met Lawrence and Frieda walking up the steep road to their destiny. There, at the Bernarda, he hoped to pick up the thin threads of a life, once enmeshed in his family, which he had discarded almost thirty years before.

In 1961, having retrieved his Italian citizenship, Ravagli traveled to Buenos Aires to see his sister, and in 1962 Dorothy Horgan visited him in Spotorno. Their bittersweet reunion lasted only a few days instead of the week they had planned. As the years passed, Ravagli walked along the beach, wrote numerous letters, took a course on drawing and painting, and spent long holidays with his three children.

In 1965 his health declined, but in ways he had not anticipated. To

Dorothy he wrote: "The Dr. found my arteries almost poisoned by *nicotine*—the blood more thick—the liver in a mess." On 10 June 1965 he was nearly killed. Having gone to Chianciano for a liver cure, he was—without warning—hit by a motorcycle. His left leg was smashed, three ribs broken, his shoulder damaged. For six months he remained at the Santa Corona Hospital in Pietra Ligure. In July came a worse tragedy. His younger son, Federico, age thirty-five, drowned in a diving accident. "It brake my heart to think of it," he told Dorothy. Four years later he lost his first wife, Serafina. Of the nine children in his family he was, by 1969, the only one left. By 1971—now eighty years old—he often felt empty and forlorn.

In Spotorno, a journalist named Ruth Hall visited him in 1973, long after Frieda's death. She found him amusing and wily, his appetite for women now waning: "Frieda?" He paused and thought. "She wasn't an intellectual. Always gay, always laughing. Like a child." Then he added, "Give me a kiss before you go." Ravagli remembered Frieda not with reverence but with mild appreciation, and he found in her the simplicity that had always marked his own character. White haired and paunchy, living alone in a small annex to the Bernarda, he spent his days playing bocce ball with his friends. It was the harvest of his years with Frieda. He died on 8 February 1976; he was eighty-four. Today his surviving son, Stefano, and his daughter, Magda, rich from the royalties that still come their way, remember his legacy of ambition and adventure; they remember his active concern for his family; they remember his pottery and his painting; and above all they remember a man whose amorous drive and practical skills allowed him to supplant the affection of a great novelist.

ᖇᖚ

As this biography of Lawrence and Frieda ends, readers will see that it signals not the end of two important lives but the beginning of their potent influence and meaning. One may well ask, Were their lives unique? In truth, the oppositions that united the Lawrences in their lifetimes make them a metaphor for their age—and for ours as well. They joined oppositions that are seldom joined so forcefully. They were both religious and pagan, both visionary and pedestrian, both puritanical and hedonistic, both quarrelsome and quiescent. These tensions, so characteristic of postmodern life, capture the fiercely contested space between rebellion and submission. As our new millennium dawns, the Lawrences resonate in our collective imagination because they courageously insisted on living at the edge of a mystery. It was the mystery of how to join their deepest impulses, sent from the unconscious, with the seductions of a material life. Frieda explored the mystery socially—made relationships central, valued vital human contact.

Lawrence perceived it artistically. Across his life he sought the angle which allowed him to explore his personal anguish, with increasing complexity, in novels, stories, and poems that have remained enormously appealing. Frieda once said of him, "He ran through the whole scale of human emotions." In the past ten years, almost two hundred books, worldwide, have been written about him and his work. They continue to rediscover the nuances of feeling and thought that are still being teased out of his art. Most of his major novels have been made into films; Cambridge University Press has published scholarly editions of all his works; and in 1998 a poll showed three of his novels among the top one hundred written in English in the twentieth century. His power lingers because his works capture the essence of his life—and the essence of our own.

Acknowledgments
Notes
Works Cited
Index

# Acknowledgments

Books, like marriages, benefit from the goodwill and cooperation of others. In the six years that we spent researching and writing this book, many individuals helped.

Lawrence scholars who read the manuscript at various stages gave us invaluable suggestions. Jack Stewart offered us the benefit of his wide knowledge of Lawrence and his milieu. Dennis Jackson read the manuscript with his customary sensitivity and wisdom. With a keen eye on the literary marketplace, John Hale offered us a valuable critique. Ray Caffrey shrewdly responded to one chapter. For the University of Wisconsin Press, James C. Cowan and Howard Harper wrote exceptionally helpful reports that allowed us to refine our approach. Keith Cushman, drawing on his encyclopedic knowledge of Lawrence's circle, commented incisively on every manuscript page, saving us from infelicity and error. We are grateful to all of them for their intelligence and generosity.

Because the book was written for a wide audience, we asked some of our students to respond to our reading of the Lawrences. We appreciate their candid judgments and good sense, and especially thank Jason Wienke, Keith Lockwood, Sara E. Marks, David Boylan, Amy Brittain, and Tiffany Trent. Erica Pedersen and Michael Germana provided excellent research support.

Our close friend Paul Sorrentino, as he worked on his own biography of Stephen Crane, shared with us his insights and practical experience. We thank him—and his wife, Peg—for their affection and support. Linda Elliott Ambrose has given thirty years of devoted friendship, and from the outset Anne Cheney, Christopher Byrne, and Gerald Pollinger offered their strong encouragement.

We especially value those who remember Lawrence and Frieda and allowed us to interview them. We thank Jake Zeitlin (now deceased), Lawrence Clark Powell, Jennie Wells Vincent (on whose remarkable memories we often relied), Miranda Masocco Levy, and Walton Hawk (who grew up two miles from the Lawrence Ranch in New Mexico). Juanita and Ernesto

Montoya, Earl Stroh, Eya Fechin, Lucille Pond, and Chilton Anderson made Frieda Lawrence and the Taos Valley come vividly alive. Margaret Needham, Lawrence's niece, helped us understand her family. Pat Davidson and Barbara Horgan contributed much to our understanding of Frieda and Angelo Ravagli and sent us unpublished letters. In Italy, Stefania Michelucci visited Stefano Ravagli on our behalf and skillfully coaxed from him recollections of his father and mother. Our warmest thanks to all of them.

Louis Gibbons not only submitted to interviews but lent us his Frieda letters, his photographs, and his unpublished memoir about Lawrence and Frieda. His great kindness was a reward for writing the book.

Still others provided valuable information, showed us their letters or photographs, granted us permission, or answered our questions. We are glad to acknowledge the assistance of Arthur J. Bachrach, Tom Bettendorf, James T. Boulton, Hilbert H. Campbell, Helen Croom, Amalia de Schulthess, Paul Eggert, David Ellis, William M. Harrison, Rosemary Howard, Russel E. Kacher, Joan King, Mark Kinkead-Weekes, Brenda Maddox, Stephen O'Connor, Carla Perna, Charles Rossman, Keith Sagar, Geoffrey Seaman, Robert and Jane Siegle, Roy Spencer, George Tyson, and Louise E. Wright. Alessandro Mirenda and Rodolfo Nanni gave us a fine tour of the Villa Mirenda. Dr. Craig F. Talbot answered our medical queries. Jay A. Gertzman assisted us often and welcomed us into his home. Janet Byrne gave us many useful leads, lent us scarce items, and shared with us the Frieda Lawrence letters she had collected. John Worthen helped us initiate the task of organizing and editing Frieda's letters and gladly shared his extraordinary knowledge of Lawrence and his epoch.

We needed help translating Frieda's letters to her mother, which she wrote in *Suetterlinschrift,* an old-fashioned German script. We are grateful to David West and especially Gertrud Rath-Montgomery.

Librarians became our resourceful allies, making letters available, assisting with permissions, and locating critical information we might have overlooked. With pleasure we acknowledge the assistance of Anita Malebranche Haney and Marilyn Norstedt at Virginia Tech, Rebecca Heller and Pat Scott at Roanoke College, Dorothy Johnston and Linda Shaw at the University of Nottingham, Cathy Henderson at the University of Texas at Austin, Ronald Vanderhye at the James S. Copley Library, in La Jolla, California, Bruce Cammack at Texas Tech University, Betty Bustos at the Panhandle–Plains Historical Museum in Canyon, Texas, Mary Kearby at the Wichita County (Texas) Historical Archives, Leigh Hays at the Western Australia Public Library, Jennifer Lee at Columbia University, Lori Matthews at Penguin Putnam, Patricia C. Willis at Yale University, Anthony Bliss at the University of California at Berkeley, Anne Caiger at UCLA, and Kari Schleher and Beth Silbergleit at the University of New Mexico.

## Acknowledgments

We would like to thank Gerald Pollinger and Laurence Pollinger Limited for permission to quote from the unpublished works of D.H. and Frieda Lawrence and Angelo Ravagli. We offer acknowledgment and thanks to the following libraries and institutions for access to and permission to quote from unpublished materials: Ellen Clarke Bertrand Library, Bucknell University; Bancroft Library, University of California at Berkeley; Steven Schwartz, Executive Director, Witter Bynner Foundation; Department of Special Collections, Charles E. Young Research Library, University of California at Los Angeles; James S. Copley Library, La Jolla, California; Houghton Library, Harvard University; Huntington Library, San Marino, California; Dorris Halsey, agent for the Aldous Huxley Estate; Library of Congress, Washington, D.C.; T. M. Pearce Papers, Center for Southwest Research, General Library, University of New Mexico; Berg Collection of English and American Literature, New York Public Library, Astor, Lenox and Tilden Foundations; Poetry/Rare Books Collection, University Libraries, State University of New York at Buffalo; Principal Archivist, Nottinghamshire Archives; Carl Zigrosser Papers, Rare Book and Manuscript Library, University of Pennsylvania; Special Collections, Morris Library, Southern Illinois University; Society of Authors, Literary Representative of the Estate of Norman Douglas; Harry Ransom Humanities Research Center, University of Texas at Austin; A.P. Watt Ltd. on behalf of the Executor of the Estate of David Garnett; Yale Collection of American Literature, Beinecke Rare Book and Manuscript Library, Yale University. Every effort has been made to locate copyright holders for materials used in this book; the authors would be pleased to hear from anyone overlooked.

At all stages of our work, Roanoke College and Virginia Tech provided generous financial and technical support, and at the University of Wisconsin Press we were assisted with exemplary courtesy by Raphael Kadushin, Sheila McMahon, Adam Mehring, Carla Aspelmeier, and Sheila Leary. Diana Cook edited the manuscript with astonishing care.

Finally we acknowledge the sustaining love and support of those closest to us. Our mothers, to whom we dedicate the book, and our fathers, Fay C. Squires (1905–1991) and Gerald B. Talbot (1912–2000), gave us moral encouragement, confidence, and direction. Our son, Andrew, joined our Lawrence expeditions, even to Oaxaca and Lake Chapala, cheerfully helped us find our way, and rarely complained. The book became part of his daily life. We appreciate his patience and enthusiasm.

# Notes

Notes to the text are keyed, by page number, to the last several words of a quotation or passage. Most works are cited by their author's last name and (if needed) a short title. Full references to books and essays appear in Works Cited. Lawrence's letters, published in eight volumes by Cambridge University Press, are cited by the abbreviation *L* and volume and page number. Hence, *L*, 2:200 refers to volume 2, page 200, of Lawrence's letters. Conjectural dates are placed inside square brackets. Unless otherwise noted, all interviews were conducted by the authors.

The following abbreviations identify sources that are frequently used:

| | |
|---|---|
| *AR* | *Aaron's Rod*, by D. H. Lawrence |
| AvR | Baroness Anna von Richthofen |
| Berkeley | Bancroft Library, University of California at Berkeley |
| DB | Dorothy Brett |
| FL | Frieda Lawrence |
| Harvard | Houghton Library, Harvard University |
| HRC | Harry Ransom Humanities Research Center, University of Texas at Austin |
| *K* | *Kangaroo*, by D. H. Lawrence |
| *L* | *The Letters of D. H. Lawrence*, by D. H. Lawrence, in eight volumes |
| *LCL* | *Lady Chatterley's Lover*, by D. H. Lawrence |
| *M&C* | *Frieda Lawrence: The Memoirs and Correspondence*, ed. E. W. Tedlock, Jr. |
| MDL | Mabel Dodge Luhan |
| Nehls | *A Composite Biography of D. H. Lawrence*, ed. Edward Nehls, in three volumes |
| *NIBTW* | *Not I, But the Wind*, by Frieda Lawrence |
| *Phoenix* | *Phoenix: The Posthumous Papers of D. H. Lawrence*, ed. Edward D. McDonald |
| *PS* | *The Plumed Serpent*, by D. H. Lawrence |
| *R* | *The Rainbow*, by D. H. Lawrence |
| *SLC* | *The Second "Lady Chatterley,"* in *The First and Second "Lady Chatterley" Novels*, by D. H. Lawrence |
| *WL* | *Women in Love*, by D. H. Lawrence |
| Yale | Beinecke Library, Yale University |

PREFACE

xiv  "know yourself": *M&C*, 120
xiv  she once said: *L*, 2:290
xiv  "was so deep": Moore and Montague, 91
xv  "that is significant": Strachey, vii
xv  "glory they are grinding": FL to DB, 15 February 1932, HRC
xv  "overvulnerable, but alive": *L*, 2:426

CHAPTER 1. LAWRENCE IN THE ENGLISH MIDLANDS

4  "an unspoken threat": Hilton, 13
4  "fathomless ugliness": D. H. Lawrence, "Autobiographical Fragment," *Phoenix*, 817
4  a first-rate workman: Worthen, *The Early Years*, 12
4  Lawrence remembered: *L*, 4:209
5  niece Margaret recalled: Margaret Needham, letter to authors, 8 October 1998
5  "to replace it": FL to Laurence Pollinger, c. 23 April 1932, HRC
5  "Lawrence's *unusualness*": Spencer, 22
7  from birth: Nehls, 1:17
7  "with other boys": Nehls, 1:23
7  "out of them": *L*, 6:61
7  "Flag of England": quoted in Griffin and Griffin, 158
7  "to *love* them": *L*, 2:589
8  "sense of responsibility": *M&C*, 438
8  "her own rightness": Chambers, 36
8  "inconquerable fugitive": D. H. Lawrence, *England, My England*, 201–8
8  "would have said": FL to Louis Gibbons, 27 September 1954, privately held
8  "violent in reaction": *M&C*, 438
9  "to the rule": Lawrence, "Autobiographical Fragment," *Phoenix*, 817
9  "rising into them": Worthen, *The Early Years*, 84
9  mathematics prize: Spencer, 27
10  "enough to eat": Brett, 279
10  "in me there": *L*, 4:618
11  toward rhapsody: D. H. Lawrence, *Sons and Lovers*, 174
11  "whipped into colour": Chambers, 40–41
11  "all of us": Corke, *D. H. Lawrence's "Princess,"* 45
12  shocked and disgusted: Nehls, 3:543 n. 40
12  "strange, wild creatures" . . . "lawless": Lawrence, *England, My England*, 40, 43
12  "and determination": Chambers, 36

CHAPTER 2. THE APPRENTICE SCHOOLTEACHER

13  4.7 million children: Mitchell and Jones, 212–13
14  school full time: see Ringer, table 5.1 (p. 221) and table 5.3 (p. 229)
14  "uncontrollable about him": Nehls, 1:48
14  quick tempered: Nehls, 1:42
14  "admit it": Nehls, 1:52
14  "love his wife": Chambers, 66
15  "efficient teacher": quoted in Worthen, *The Early Years*, 118
15  "on his studies": Chambers, 75

15   "do not use": quoted in Brewster and Brewster, *Reminiscences and Correspondence*, 255
15   "very fond of": *L*, 1:68
15   "superfluous details": *L*, 1:29–30
17   "you see": *L*, 1:45
17   "to the head": Nehls, 3:605
17   "College" . . . "in position": *L*, 1:49
17   "a joke?": *L*, 1:79
17   "great darkness": quoted in Sagar, *A Calendar of His Works*, 9
17   unemployed man: *L*, 1:76
19   "in Croydon": *L*, 1:79
19   "a part" . . . "more satisfactory": *L*, 1:66
19   "sex sympathy": *L*, 1:67
19   "I regret it": *L*, 1:208
20   "very flabby": *L*, 1:93
20   "his class work": Nehls, 1:86
20   "me teaching": *L*, 1:85
20   "one's teacher": quoted in Brett, 277
20   "zest of Life": *L*, 1:107
20   "can make better": *L*, 1:103
21   Davidson Road in 1907: In *Neutral Ground* (1933) Corke wrote a fictionalized account of her relationship with Lawrence.
21   in 1912: See *M&C* (247) for Dax's claim, though Frieda later said that she "[did]n't believe the story" (ibid., 461). In 1915, referring to Alice Dax, Lawrence wrote enigmatically: "I . . . always shall feel her an integral part of my life; but that is in the past" (*L*, 2:391).
21   "mostly so": *L*, 1:103
21   "lusty Atalantan strength" . . . "a good Bacchante": *L*, 1:113–14
21   "to be cultivated": *L*, 1:122
21   "this frankness": *L*, 1:292
23   "he must marry": Chambers, 154
23   "editor's attention": ibid., 157
23   "to show Mother": ibid., 159
23   "quite unvoiced": quoted in Nehls, 1:109
23   treated him kindly: Nehls, 1:121
23   "sufficient material": *L*, 1:275
24   "published for me": *L*, 1:144–45
24   "state yesterday": *L*, 1:135
24   "mother says": *L*, 1:147
24   "do not count": *L*, 1:174
24   "a father": Chambers, 88
25   "in his grief": ibid., 183
25   "sick inside": *L*, 1:182
25   "horrid tortoises": *L*, 8:113
25   "offensive morsels" . . . "the most docile" . . . "scented soap": *L*, 1:158
25   "sorrel cresset": D. H. Lawrence, *The White Peacock*, 221
25   "in the wind!": ibid., 208
25   "complex modern life": ibid., 319
26   "three months": Corke, "The Writing of *The Trespasser*," 233
26   "horribly poetic": *L*, 1:167

26 "enduring the rest": D. H. Lawrence, *The Trespasser,* 14
27 "all his life": ibid., 180
27 "course to follow": Corke, *In Our Infancy,* 180
27 "She will" . . . "I cannot": *L,* 1:160
27 "towards him": Corke, *In Our Infancy,* 191
27 "the sexual part": *L,* 1:164
27 "in action": Corke, *In Our Infancy,* 221
28 "very good ages": *L,* 1:197
28 "on his quest": D. H. Lawrence, *The Complete Poems,* 128
28 "dark and handsome": *L,* 1;190
28 "hieroglyph of woe": *L,* 1:195
28 "abnormal": *L,* 1:190
28 "like an atmosphere": *L,* 1:191
28 "not held": *L,* 1:285
28 "as the sun": *L,* 1:195
29 "off your mouth": *Guardian* (London), 9 November 1990
30 "impersonal novel": *L,* 1:184
30 "bright and strong": *L,* 1:212
30 "in these days": *L,* 1:219
30 "matter so much": *L,* 1:220
30 "ironic and bitter": quoted in Nehls, 1:142
30 "shall we?" . . . "to Eastwood": *L,* 1:229
30 "for Louie": *L,* 1:231
30 "stupid decree?": *L,* 1:240
31 "form of abnormality": *L,* 1:251
31 "still be alone": *L,* 1:285
31 "return to school": *L,* 1:297
31 "to death": *L,* 1:298
31 "my income": *L,* 1:303
31 "as mathematics": *L,* 1:247
32 "her own way": D. H. Lawrence, *The Prussian Officer,* 59
32 "mathematical working out": ibid., 50
32 "not [yet] a man": ibid., 68
32 "in perfect taste": *L,* 1:314
32 "in my writing": *L,* 1:315
32 "terribly busy": *L,* 1:316
33 "and last time": *L,* 1:321
33 "to be said": ibid.
33 "leave school, really": *L,* 1:323

### CHAPTER 3. FRIEDA FINDS HER DESTINY

34 "natural lords": quoted in Kirchhoff, 167
35 "very kind": *L,* 1:409
35 the following year: Byrne, 17–20
35 "splendid soldier": diary, 1870–71, trans. Frieda Lawrence, HRC
35 "his heart never": Lucas, 8
35 the area's land: FL, Unpublished fragment, n.d., Bucknell University
36 "fierce old aristocrat": *L,* 1:409
36 "doing things, impatient": *M&C,* 55
36 "cameo face": *M&C,* 54

36    "belief in life": *M&C*, 79
36    "outside Metz": *NIBTW*, 37
36    "straw-coloured hair": *M&C*, 44
36    "like a tadpole": *M&C*, 54
36    "bullet had torn": *L*, 2:215
37    "carefully away": *M&C*, 143
37    "for years": *NIBTW*, 37
37    "interest I wanted": ibid.
37    "had built": *NIBTW*, 38
37    "begin anew": ibid.
37    "She was" . . . "trusting love": *M&C*, 63, 68
37    "like butterfly wings": *M&C*, 68
38    "not so perfect": *M&C*, 55
38    "faith in himself": *M&C*, 55
38    "he was a father": ibid.
38    conceived in 1897: Byrne, 150, 422 n. 40
39    "those gentle nuns": *NIBTW*, 37
39    "of the family": quoted in Kirchhoff, 24
39    "mother and housewife": ibid., 257
39    "are overburdened": cited in Bernstein and Bernstein, "Curriculum," 295 n. 66
39    singing, needlework: see Bernstein and Bernstein, "Attitudes"
39    "never included": Jacobi-Dittrich, 211
40    "no bluestocking": *M&C*, 296
40    "no fun" . . . "with genuine living": *M&C*, 75
41    "firm ground": *M&C*, 80
41    "to anyone before": quoted in Byrne, 41
43    "far away" . . . "stiff and unbending": *M&C*, 83
43    "Go to bed" . . . "more than horrible": *M&C*, 84
43    "beginning with Ern[e]st": *L*, 1:404
43    "code of morals": *M&C*, 85
43    "'married to an earthquake'": *M&C*, 375
44    "could not express": *M&C*, 91
44    "one is married!": *M&C*, 151
45    "like Ernest" . . . "only livelier": *M&C*, 148, 151
45    "looking at us": *M&C*, 87
45    "love me so much": Turner, "The Otto Gross–Frieda Weekley Correspondence," 195
45    "wonderful, magical": R. Jackson, 53
45    "fun of them": *M&C*, 387
45    "felt alive again": *M&C*, 93
45    "little significance to her": Lucas, 33
45    "old prejudices and taboos": *M&C*, 55
46    "a grateful audience": *M&C*, 94
46    "unusual mind": McGuire, 155–56
46    "toxic cocaine paranoia": ibid., 141
46    "no mystery": *M&C*, 94–95
46    "overrate me so much": Turner, "The Otto Gross–Frieda Weekley Correspondence," 195
46    "set ideas": *M&C*, 378. For a dissenting view of Weekley, see Worthen, "'Cold Hearts and Coronets,'" 1–21.
46    "light and refreshment": Turner, "The Otto Gross–Frieda Weekley Correspondence," 197

48   "gloomy millennia?": ibid., 165
48   "for your ideals": ibid., 194–95
48   "shame into the world": Green, 44–45
48   "abnormal" . . . "merely convenient": McGuire, 69, 90
48   "your own life": Turner, "The Otto Gross–Frieda Weekley Correspondence," 172 (authors' translation)
48   "an unknown world": *M&C*, 98
48   "her own soul": *M&C*, 102
49   "have something": *M&C*, 161
49   "a real destiny": *M&C*, 21
49   "you know I think": *M&C*, 166

## CHAPTER 4. THEIR ADVENTURE BEGINS

50   "world's conventions": *L*, 1:362
50   "legs for my life": *L*, 338
50   "lady's watch": *L*, 1:341
50   "forlorn lost lamb": *L*, 1:346
51   "the air suits me": *L*, 1:347
51   "sensitive self": *L*, 1:353
51   "fault is all mine": *L*, 1:361
52   "idea of school": *L*, 1:367
52   "Croydon crew violently": *L*, 1:368
52   "flippant": *L*, 1:361
52   "wits against her": *L*, 1:343
52   "best thing I've done": *L*, 1:381
52   "had liked me": *L*, 2:154
52   "conventional set life": *NIBTW*, 3
53   "light, sure movements": *NIBTW*, 4
53   "attempts at knowing women": ibid.
53   "no notice of him": ibid.
53   "lots of guts": *M&C*, 453
53   "hard bright shell": *NIBTW*, 5
54   "but to submit": *NIBTW*, 5–6
54   "only my Englishness": *L*, 1:391
54   "own intrinsic self": *NIBTW*, 3
55   "to Metz": *L*, 1:385
55   "to your house?": *L*, 1:386
55   "I've ever met": *L*, 1:384
55   "monogamistic fashion": *L*, 1:388
55   "you tell me": *L*, 1:389
55   "anything to anybody": *L*, 1:390
55   "and ourselves": *NIBTW*, 7
55   "insane" . . . "shipwreck": *M&C*, 163
55   "It is her nature": *L*, 1:392
56   "All compromises" . . . "agree to a divorce": *M&C*, 162
56   "all this mean?": *M&C*, 166
56   "cast off like this": *M&C*, 167
56   "I love you so much": *L*, 1:394
56   "all richness": *L*, 1:398
56   "more than I can bear": D. H. Lawrence, *The Complete Poems*, 215

56    "*never* with each other": *L*, 1:400
56    "I am an English officer": *L*, 1:394–95
56    "with my German": *L*, 1:399
57    "love you all my life": *L*, 1:401–3
57    "dose of morphia": *L*, 1:404
57    "before he was a husband": Maddox, 132
57    "ill than I am, now": *L*, 1:404
57    "I'll never teach again": *L*, 1:407
57    "and life hurts": *L*, 1:410
58    "on our love": Lawrence, *The Complete Poems*, 204
58    "to see how they looked": *L*, 1:413
58    "*much* more than sex": *L*, 1:415
58    "and every night": *L*, 1:418
58    "could'nt get on" . . . "went through anyhow!": *M&C*, 321 (manuscript punctuation restored)
59    "and the agony of it": *L*, 1:421
59    "not so strongly" . . . "I pass in Bavaria": *L*, 1:417
59    "in the book": *L*, 1:421
59    "God help me": *L*, 1:422
59    a rotten Jew: *L*, 1:424
60    "I maintain it" . . . "I must live": *L*, 1;423
60    "I was so undisciplined": quoted in Davidson, 8
60    "I want to wander": *L*, 1:425
60    "be tied down": *L*, 1:427
60    "pale green water": *L*, 1:425
60    "dancing with gaiety": D. Garnett, *The Golden Echo*, 241–42
61    "fetch the tools": ibid.
61    "had been lying": ibid., 243
61    "at once worshipped them": ibid.
61    "' his neighbours will think!'": D. Garnett, *Great Friends*, 78
61    "a perfect agony": *L*, 1:438
61    "very unforgiving": quoted in R. Jackson, 23
61    "to unknown parts": *NIBTW*, 48
61    "mountains draped" . . . "bright as glass": *L*, 1;433
62    "I am afraid": *L*, 1:439
62    "things and people": ibid.
62    "must be two-sided": *L*, 1:440–41
62    "*when it doesn't show*": *L*, 1:439 (emphasis added)
62    "breathing-space between us": ibid.
62    "not to interrupt him": D. Garnett, *The Golden Echo*, 245
62    "ripping": *L*, 1:443
62    "masculine charm": D. Garnett, *The Golden Echo*, 246
63    "as best they knew how": ibid., 247
63    "we had gone": D. Garnett, *Great Friends*, 80
63    "no gentleman": ibid., 81
63    "massive . . . egoism": R. Garnett, *Constance Garnett*, 274
63    "fearfully": *L*, 1:444
63    "quarrelled like nuts": *L*, 1:450
63    end of August: The quasi-autobiographical *Mr Noon*, although helpful to biographers, must be used with caution since the narrator's taunting irony about narrative conventions may extend to his recording of actual events. The work's fictional distance is dif-

ficult to gauge. John Worthen sees *Mr Noon* as "a remarkable [biographical] guide" yet also a fictional work (*The Early Years*, 382).

63     "perfectly Italian": *L*, 1:447

64     "I love it": *L*, 1:448

64     "clean as a flower": *L*, 1:453

64     "further in love": *L*, 1:458

64     "nothing is" . . . "simple and real": *L*, 1:449

64     "come into being": *NIBTW*, 35

64     "dare'nt think of him": FL to Hopkin, 25 December 1912, University of Nottingham

64     "What shall I do?" . . . "never grumbling": *NIBTW*, 55

64     "horror": *L*, 1:466

66     "at my novel": *L*, 1:451

66     "'felt like then?'": *NIBTW*, 56

66     "but can't save herself": *L*, 1:462

66     "an anarchist": *L*, 1;476

66     "a great book": *L*, 1:477

66     "constructed that novel": *L*, 1:478. It is worth knowing that in December 1910 producer William Archer had rejected Edward Garnett's play *The Trial of Jeanne d'Arc* because, he said, "your play is unconstructed," episodes following each other "like beads on a string" (quoted in Jefferson, 125).

66     "[A]ny new thing" . . . "a real artist": *L*, 1:479

66     "I sit in sadness" . . . "I daren't say anything": *L*, 1:481

67     "publish to live": *L*, 1:485

67     "in your debt": *L*, 1:496

67     "what you think necessary": *L*, 1;481

67     "*she quivered*": D. H. Lawrence, *Sons and Lovers: A Facsimile*, 473–74

67     "powerful . . . novel": Templeton, 243

67     "an ultimatum": D. H. Lawrence, *Sons and Lovers*, xlvii (Unless otherwise noted all references to *Sons and Lovers* are from the Cambridge edition edited by Baron and Baron.)

67     "take to teaching again": *L*, 1:492

67     "spurious": *Sons and Lovers*, xlviii

67     "jolly well" . . . "prolix" . . . "barber": *L*, 1:517

68     "more than he could afford": *L*, 1:486

68     "wouldn't have let me go": *NIBTW*, 56

69     "and holds them": *L*, 1:476–77

69     "all his blood fell back": *Sons and Lovers*, 333

70     "builders' specifications": Pound, 267

70     "tradition of the novel": Hough, 53

70     "in English fiction": O'Connor, 272

## CHAPTER 5. EXPLORING THE UNKNOWN

71     "quite madly personal": D. H. Lawrence, *Study of Thomas Hardy*, 20

71     "and stimulation": Meyers, *D. H. Lawrence*, 86

71     "two tails left": *L*, 1:521

71     "communication with the unknown": *L*, 1:503

72     "vast movement": D. H. Lawrence, *The Trespasser*, 78

72     "life wild" . . . "tremendous heave": D. H. Lawrence, *Sons and Lovers*, 398

72     "pure forgetfulness" . . . "from consciousness": ibid., 670 (textual apparatus 454:28)

72     "that is" . . . "turns up": *L*, 1:514

72 the whole of England and Wales: Rowntree and Carrier, 201
73 "bury her alive": *L*, 1:502
73 "so good": *L*, 1:507
73 "curse unto myself": *L*, 1:526
73 "in a novel": ibid.
73 "Gothic cathedrals": *L*, 1:533
73 "you will be surprised": *M&C*, 182 (conjecturally dated April 1913)
73 "We shall go first" . . . "coming to England": *L*, 1:530
73 "and such a grand one": *L*, 1:532
74 "where I was last year": *L*, 1:541
74 "blighting in England": *L*, 1:548
74 "slow with nasty": *L*, 1:550
74 "it did me good" . . . "portrait": ibid.
74 "between two parents": *L*, 1:551
75 "*won't* stand it!": *M&C*, 178 (undated letter)
75 "youthful period": *L*, 1:551
75 "a fearful treachery": Corke, *D. H. Lawrence's "Princess,"* 33
75 "ignore him entirely": ibid., 34
75 "brutality of *Sons and Lovers*": *L*, 1:550
75 "for two days": *L*, 1:551
75 "sense of guilt aside": Feinstein, 95
76 "nor is Frieda": *L*, 2:19
76 "Wolfratshausen alone": *L*, 2:20–21
76 "mild and good!": *L*, 2:23
76 abusive husband: Doody, 6
76 "hardly for hours": *L*, 2:23
76 "I have ever done": *L*, 2:21
77 "ran in his blood": D. H. Lawrence, *The Prussian Officer*, 4
78 "arduously as ever": *L*, 2:30
78 "rage again soon": *L*, 2:37
78 "trying to be respectable": R. Garnett, *Sylvia and David*, 49
78 "thinning the carrots": R. Garnett, *Constance Garnett*, 276
78 "I don't like Mrs G": *L*, 2:54
79 "delicate skin, and brown eyes": *NIBTW*, 67–68
79 "Oh, I could" . . . "I would be satisfied": O'Sullivan and Scott, 61
80 "a mania for confession": quoted in Meyers, *D. H. Lawrence*, 139
80 "fearfully nice": *L*, 2:55
80 "sexual anarchy": Tomalin, 118
80 "made for one another": Nehls, 1:198
80 "at Lerici in Italy": Nehls, 1:200
81 "very happy together": Nehls, 1:199
81 "son of the Prime Minister": *L*, 2:48
81 "entirely his own": Nehls 1:205
81 "generosity of nature": Nehls, 1:209
81 "when friends were rare": *NIBTW*, 68
81 "I do miss Frieda": *L*, 2:55
81 "whirling around": *L*, 2:56
82 "pulled it together": *L*, 2:58
82 "nothing satisfying": D. H. Lawrence, *Plays*, 92
82 "my autumn burst of work": *L*, 2:68
83 "on the hills all round": *L*, 2:78

83  "The cottage at Fiascherino" . . . "drown like one, anyhow": *NIBTW,* 69–70
83  "and was happy": *R,* 473
83  "reputation for laziness": FL to Garnett, 7 November 1913, New York Public Library
84  "cross with you" . . . "I've only ruined myself": *L,* 2:75
84  "pedestal again": ibid.
84  seven printed pages survive: The surviving pages are printed in *R,* 473–79
84  "our passions are uncharted": V. Woolf, *Jacob's Room,* 94
84  "wonder what it is like": *L,* 2:82
85  "endeavouring to acquire one": Middleton, 129
85  "her sonnets": ibid., 131
85  "The one intellectual" . . . "is a fool": ibid., 150–51
85  "that was equal to him": *L,* 2:97
85  "that killed him": *L,* 2:96
86  "throws him away": *L,* 2:94
86  "deny life unto us": *L,* 2:95
86  "a wholly indecent reticence": Middleton, 143
86  "of her body in torture": *R,* 475
86  "lot out of . . . *Art and Ritual*": *L,* 2:114
86  "the personal and the universal": Harrison, 167
87  "trust intuition once again": ibid., 223
87  "rhythm hitherto unattempted": ibid., 233
87  "I love living by the sea": *L,* 2:123
87  "and the food so jolly": FL to McLeod, n.d., HRC
87  "lost to the world": *L,* 2:86
87  "I don't want to be a fraud" . . . "a mistake, a sin": *NIBTW,* 71
87  "I shall laugh": *L,* 2:133
88  "Frieda blooms like a rose": R. Garnett, *Constance Garnett,* 278
88  "breaking new ground": *NIBTW,* 71
88  "is very industrious": R. Garnett, *Constance Garnett,* 281
88  "another language almost": *L,* 2:132
88  "widened and deepened": *L,* 2:134
88  "I begin to feel it in myself": *L,* 2:138

## CHAPTER 6. THE DAWN OF *THE RAINBOW*

89  "under the sea": *L,* 2:145
89  eight pounds a month: *M&C,* 187
89  "I knew" . . . "begun it again": *L,* 2:144
89  "getting it out clean": *L,* 2:146
90  "almost puritanical": R. Garnett, *Constance Garnett,* 37
90  "very promising": quoted in ibid., 281
90  solicited by Mitchell Kennerley: The report appears in *R,* 483–84.
90  "ones soul is worse": *L,* 2:153–54
90  "my own sweet will": *L,* 2:153
91  "I have to write differently": *L,* 2:142
91  "I am going through" . . . "everything vague": *L,* 2:143
91  "I have been" . . . "You see I dont" . . . "a good thing too!": *L,* 2:150–51
92  "branch of medical science": *L,* 2:218
92  "really very deeply happy": *L,* 2:161
92  "it is beautiful, I think": ibid.
92  "I am not after all" . . . "in your own eyes": *L,* 2:165–66

93  "hurt anybody": *L,* 2:167
93  "my heart aches after": *L,* 2:174
93  "for my novels, to live": *L,* 2:166
93  "when there is also Frieda": *L,* 2:174
94  "grey-haired sphinx": quoted in Meyers, *Joseph Conrad,* 204
94  "a mere legal contract": *L,* 2:179
94  "red and blue and cream with stripes": *L,* 2:172
94  "watering them every night": ibid.
94  his faultfinding: Nehls, 1:218
94  "it is a good title": *L,* 2:173
95  "all the burden put on her": *L,* 2:171
95  "too discursive, formless, unrestrained": Jefferson, 190
95  "sand takes lines unknown": *L,* 2:184
95  "under the great flood": *R,* 295
95  "balancing all in its revelation": *R,* 296
96  "carried their bodies in tune": *R,* 114
96  her protagonist, Rachel: V. Woolf, *The Voyage Out,* 283–84
96  "I gave my old one" . . . "respectable married people": *NIBTW,* 77
97  "I suppose I am one": *L,* 2:196
97  "scenes with indignant aunts": *L,* 2:198
97  "the maggoty Weekley household": *L,* 2:199
97  "Their passions are volcanic": quoted in Draper, 81
98  "opinions in the margin": *L,* 2:188
98  "rapid but never restless movement": Carswell, 15
98  "keen emotion presented objectively": Aldington, "Modern Poetry," 202–3
98  "passionate intensity and integrity": quoted in Zytaruk, xv
99  "I ever knew": quoted in Peters, 394
100  "I had been walking" . . . "all sorrows and hopes": *L,* 2:268
100  "this machinery piercing and tearing?": "With the Guns" is reprinted in D. H. Lawrence, *Twilight in Italy,* 84.
100  "nothing for 3 months": R. Garnett, *Constance Garnett,* 287
100  "like the rest of us": *L,* 2:213
100  "flagrant love-passages": *L,* 2:270
100  "always the final writing": quoted in Duffy, 50
101  "We can't stay here much longer": *L,* 2:206–7
101  "tiny, but jolly": *L,* 2:208
101  "allow such a thing": Nehls, 1:248–51
102  "enjoys it like hot punch": *L,* 2:244
102  "the 'baby killers' of Scarborough": Gilbert, *The First World War,* 110
102  "let him give them you": *L,* 2:199
102  "colossal idiocy" . . . "anything *but* Thomas Hardy": *L,* 2:212 (emphasis added)
103  "it was just the same": Carswell, 17–18
103  "the underlying stream of life": ibid., 18
103  "without mental knowledge or acquiescence": D. H. Lawrence, *Study of Thomas Hardy,* 20
103  "has taken us all captives": *R,* 324
103  " slovenly laboratory for the factory": *R,* 403
103  "diastole of the human heart": Sagar, *Life into Art,* 121
104  "Come here": *R,* 89
104  "He . . . touched her delicately": *R,* 155
104  construct a novel like *The Rainbow:* Squires, "Scenic Construction"

104    "We are not sad" . . . "hoar-frost world": *L*, 2:235
104    "I've been miserable this autumn": *L*, 2:224

### CHAPTER 7. CRISIS

105    "hideous stupidity of war": *L*, 2:218
105    "such a rage": *L*, 2:232
105    "my tirades": *L*, 2:228
105    "my tirades of Sunday": *L*, 2:233
105    cheated him: On 12 January 1917 Lawrence wrote to Pinker that Kennerley "has swindled me unscrupulously," having paid only ten pounds for "everything of mine he has ever done" (*L*, 3:74).
105    "rage with *me*": *L*, 2:245
106    "quarrelsome—nothing decided": *L*, 2:241
106    "interfere with the children": *L*, 2:244
106    "enjoying myself willy-nilly": *L*, 2:245
107    "we were really gay": *NIBTW*, 82
107    "rewriting my novel": *L*, 2:239
107    "the war, the winter": *L*, 2:241
107    "full feather at last": *L*, 2:255
107    "unwieldy [in one]": *L*, 2:256
107    "house and shop together": *L*, 2:272
107    "form the nucleus" . . . "eternal good part in us": *L*, 2:271
108    "treble to baritone": quoted in Heilbrun, 7
108    "highly sexed": L. Woolf, *Downhill All the Way*, 102
108    "*really* nice": *L*, 2:274
108    "in her debt": Seymour, 6
110    "no class holds it": *L*, 2:265
110    "I love it": *L*, 2:261
110    "so beautiful and white": *L*, 2:264
110    "corpse in its grave clothes": *L*, 2:276
110    "germination and quickening": *L*, 2:276
111    "end of this month": *L*, 2:270
111    "pots of gold at its feet": *L*, 2:299
111    "all your life": *NIBTW*, 82
111    "decidedly object to": *L*, 2:299
111    led Lawrence to delete them: *R*, lii
111    "paragraphs or pages": *L*, 2:327
111    "scratch the door today": *L*, 2:293
112    "real and deep": *R*, 377
112    "source of the mystery": *R*, 404
113    "soft brown hair": *R*, 278
113    soft as butterfly wings: *R*, 278; *M&C*, 68
113    "disease within her": *R*, 309
113    "no life of its own": *R*, 319
113    "wilderness of phallicism": Draper, 92
113    "from the unknown": *L*, 2:102
113    "moon, consummation": *R*, 296
113    "submit to be swept away": *L*, 2:218
114    "lurking on the edge": *R*, 405–6
114    "feeling of apprehension": *L*, 2:122

115   "great ideas of himself": *R*, 50
115   "beast ate in silence": *R*, 75
115   "spanned round with the rainbow": *R*, 187
116   "do not think much of women": *L*, 2:290
116   "very nice": *L*, 2:280
116   "ignored his own homosexual side": quoted in Furbank, 2:12
116   "I think is rather nice": *L*, 2:282
116   "telling him about himself": *L*, 2:293
116   "I regret I cannot know him": quoted in Maddox, 200
117   "a sort of logic machine": quoted in Moorehead, 157 (letter from Bertrand Russell to Ottoline Morrell)
117   "unliving, impervious shell": *L*, 2:286
117   "perhaps it is passionate": *L*, 2:295
117   "foolish and over-insistent": *L*, 2:294
117   "I am rather afraid": *L*, 2:300
117   "in politics as in work": Moorehead, 234
118   "real, in the darkness": *L*, 2:307
118   "[that] I can't escape": ibid.
118   "must die": *L*, 2:309
118   "'sterilizing' effect of homosexuality": Skidelsky, 302
118   "so plainly in Keynes at Cambridge": *L*, 2:311
118   "[while] . . . professing love": ibid.
118   " subterranean love for him": *L*, 2:314
119   "even by men": quoted in Cohen, 174
119   "I have had a great struggle" . . . "secret and rotten": *L*, 2:315
119   "sensual lust": quoted in *L*, 2:331 n. 2
119   "a matter of life and death": *L*, 2:319
119   "death of self to homosexuality": Maddox, 203
120   "that their love" . . . "inexcusable": Forster, *Maurice*, 151
120   "sublimation, and rationalizaton": Coleman, 33
120   "not strength to open": *R*, 378
120   "She could see him . . . bestial": *R*, 234
120   "colouring": *R*, 286
120    "power": *R*, 294
120   "dressed": *R*, 308
120   "grossness of him": *R*, 322
120   "marshy, bitter-sweet": *R*, 326
120   "the brittle, marshy foulness" . . . "houses and factories": *R*, 459
121   "might be homosexual": Maddox, 202
121   "I have learnt" . . . "strength and direct it": *L*, 2:322
121   "a rabbit hole" . . . "make me cross": *M&C*, 197
121   he hated Frieda: Hankin, *Letters between Katherine Mansfield and John Middleton Murry*, 52
121   "could become an animal": *M&C*, 197
121   outdoors working with plants: *L*, 2:344
121   "from which I can't wake": *L*, 2:339
121   "hate for the 'Huns'": *M&C*, 192
121   "to destroy each other": D. H. Lawrence, *England, My England*, 220 (all references to "England, My England" are to the 1915 *English Review* version, which is reprinted in *England, My England*)
122   "leave me alone": *L*, 2:343

122    "hopelessly unsatisfied": *L*, 2:345
122    "deep rage": *L*, 2:344
122    "corrosive darkness": *L*, 2:352

## CHAPTER 8. DISAPPOINTMENT

123    "elevated form of knowledge": quoted in Miller, 77
123    "more terrified than I have ever been": *L*, 2:346
123    "bites off [one's] nose": *L*, 2:362
124    "stars and moon blown away": *L*, 2:390
125    "on top not always": *L*, 2:303
125    "Whore of Babylon": Hankin, *Letters between Katherine Mansfield and John Middleton Murry*, 51
125    "intimate part of his soul": ibid., 54
125    "point of leaving her": ibid., 55
125    "can't understand by myself": *L*, 2:302
125    "personal affection": Murry, *Between Two Worlds*, 332
125    "his arguments and principles": ibid., 333
125    "a warm atmosphere of love": ibid., 337
125    "union in an *idea*": *L*, 2:380
126    "action or achievement": quoted in Skidelsky, 141
126    "something very good": *L*, 2:402
126    "sympathy with him": *L*, 2:472
126    "not purely personal": *L*, 2:472–73
126    "he is not a man yet": *L*, 2:481
126    "may be true": Hankin, *Letters between Katherine Mansfield and John Middleton Murry*, 71
127    "You must [go]" . . . "terribly hurt": Gathorne-Hardy, 267
128    "high temper to London": ibid., 36
128    "Frieda, his 'dark abode'": ibid., 36–37
128    "unreasonable hostility": Seymour, 215
128    "no relation at all with her": *L*, 2:398
129    "so great, so magnificent": *L*, 2:432
129    "see it any more": *L*, 2:435
129    please her: Eventually the manuscript, after it was returned to Lawrence, came to Frieda and was sold to a Lawrence collector named T. E. "Ed" Hanley for thirty-five hundred dollars (Squires, *D. H. Lawrence's Manuscripts*, 276).
129    "mere denunciations do no good": Gathorne-Hardy, 40
129    "They say I cannot think": *L*, 2:380
129    "She has not found" . . . "not to have created": *L*, 2:437
130    "But one's soul rebels": *L*, 2:465
130    "That annoys the Ottoline": *L*, 2:466
130    "madly jealous": Gathorne-Hardy, 77
130    "traitor to her": *L*, 2:462
130    "which is creative life": *L*, 2:468–69
130    "unseen loving forces of life": *L*, 2:443
131    "*change* people's thoughts": quoted in Moorehead, 242 (letter of 10 February 1916)
131    "regards all my attempts" . . . "mad exaggeration": Gathorne-Hardy, 58
131    "Why don't you own it": *L*, 2:392
132    "struggling away from in myself": *L*, 2:442
132    "a spiritual coward": *L*, 2:635

132   "entering into destruction": Lawrence, *England, My England*, 225
132   "He ought [therefore] to die": *L*, 2:360
133   "smile came on his face": Lawrence, *England, My England*, 223
133   "curiously flawed": Harris, 117
133   "beauty of language": Nehls, 2:329
134   "all are more or less drunk": Brett, 19
134   "I shall die": *L*, 2:429
134   "I only curse them all" . . . "change my public": ibid.
134   "arrange to be legally represented": Carter, 216
134   " Peccavi! Peccavi! [he] wept": Nehls, 2:328
134   the lesbian chapter: Duffy, 58
135   fewer fiction titles: ibid., 61
135   "defend the book": Nehls, 2:335
135   "for the sake of beating them": *L*, 2:462
135   "rather far gone with consumption": Nehls, 2:329
135   "could not take any useful action": *L*, 2:469 n. 3
135   "dark and hideous": *L*, 2:461
135   "We were saturated with war": *NIBTW*, 83
135   "a house on my head": *L*, 2:478
135   "ceased to fret about them": ibid.
136   "living in Leicester Square": Hankin, *Letters of John Middleton Murry to Katherine Mansfield*, 73
136   "very much impressed": Gathorne-Hardy, 80
136   "irretrievably gone by": *L*, 2:487
136   "look forward into the unknown": *L*, 2:482
136   "for my health": *L*, 2:483
136   the figure Murry reported: Hankin, *Letters of John Middleton Murry to Katherine Mansfield*, 83
137   "strength to go to America": *L*, 2:612
137   "it is splendid": *L*, 2:491
137   "one is free": *L*, 2:493
137   "We *love* being here": *L*, 2:495

### CHAPTER 9. THE DISCOVERY OF CORNWALL

138   "like solid darkness": *L*, 2:519
138   "Celtic civilisation": *L*, 2:499
138   "such peace": *L*, 2:491
139   "hear the sound of it": *L*, 2:493
139   "right out to sea!": FL to Morrell, [1 January 1916], HRC
139   "no connection": *L*, 2:499
139   "doesn't trouble": *L*, 2:527
139   "just *how* to do it": *L*, 2:496
139   "doesn't know what to do": *L*, 2:500
139   "old strength coming back": *L*, 2:526
140   As early as 1840 . . . introduced in 1918: Meachen, 24–28
140   "milk casein stuff is *very* good": *L*, 2:522 (text of complete letter in *L*, 8:17)
140   "remained alert" . . . "contributed to genius": Shryock, 39
140   "They are very miserable": *L*, 2:520
141   "nice living with him": *L*, 2:523
141   "not very happy": *L*, 8:17

141 "I'm . . . existing on charity" . . . "support me improperly": *L*, 2:498
141 "subserv[ing] the senses": D. H. Lawrence, *Twilight in Italy*, 116–17
141 "destruction of natural life": ibid., 132
142 "light falls on my face": ibid., 128
142 "from 20 to 26": *L*, 2:521
142 "Out of darkness" . . . "the shadow we see": D. H. Lawrence, *Amores*, 112–13
142 "beastly health": *L*, 2:560
143 "a lovely place" . . . "come to pass there": *L*, 2:554
143 "prowling poverty": *L*, 2:572
143 "exasperate one past bearing": *L*, 2:559
143 "we are *very poor*": *L*, 2:579
145 "a wild little flourish": *L*, 2:573
145 "nice with each other!": *L*, 2:578
145 "a great and attractive personality": quoted in B. Smith, 85
145 "let the whole relation" . . . "a Kouyoumdjian sketch": *L*, 2:598
145 "rather pathetic": B. Smith, 92
146 "all mad reactions": *L*, 2:557
146 "inability to grow up": B. Smith, 73
146 "calculated to do so": quoted in B. Smith, 92
146 "coming down the lane to Tregerthen": *NIBTW*, 84
146 "which is life": *L*, 2:557
146 "now the fine weather has come": *L*, 2:591
146 "all the treasures we had bought": *NIBTW*, 85
147 "I don't belong to anybody here": O'Sullivan and Scott, 263
147 "tall in the small window seat": *NIBTW*, 85
147 "full of light and beauty": *L*, 2:613
147 "I am quite happy here": *L*, 2:599
147 "I love it": *L*, 2:611
147 "It *was* thrilling": *L*, 2:606
147 "I don't know what": *L*, 2:607
147 "distrusted the very idea" . . . "pretending": Nehls, 1:373
147 "inventor of false versions": Tomalin, 57
147 "[S]he's a liar out and out": *L*, 3:663
148 "sex in everything": O'Sullivan and Scott, 261
148 "I almost die of horror": *L*, 2:641
148 "an outlaw" . . . "noiseless bullets": *L*, 2:540–42
148 "I hate the 'public'": *L*, 2:593
149 "forget rest of life": *L*, 2:539
149 "original self": *L*, 2:538
149 "more and more a oneness": *L*, 2:539
149 "laughed kindly and affectionately": *L*, 2:535
149 "alone in the world": *L*, 2:612
149 "I am full of black revenge!!": *M&C*, 200–201
149 "she is unhappy about it": quoted in B. Smith, 87
150 "you tried to interfere": FL to Morrell, [May 1916], HRC
150 "in my genuine friendship": ibid.
150 "cheapness and vulgarity": *L*, 2:606
150 "robust and virile" . . . "succumb": Gathorne-Hardy, 94
150 "[T]he stark truth is all that matters": *L*, 2:657
151 "observed among his friends and enemies": Burgess, 115–16

151    "*three months* to type my novel": *L*, 2:632

151    "fourth and final draft": *L*, 2:637

152    "The things are growing splendidly": *L*, 2:621

152    "goodly roots he had grown": Nehls, 1:390

152    "spinach and endive": quoted in Stevens, 56

152    "not so hot as the time before": *L*, 2:641

152    "some beautiful days": *M&C*, 202

152    "just enough to scratch along with": *L*, 2:668

152    transportation to Penzance for excursion: Frieda probably paid for her train fare to London (£2/10) out of money she apparently received from Germany, by way of Switzerland (see Stevens, 56).

153    "an occasional chicken or rabbit": quoted in Stevens, 57

153    "weary me, truly": *L*, 2:647

153    "when you were here": *L*, 3:127

153    "it is very horrible and agonising": *L*, 2:662

153    "only real friends in the world": *L*, 2:533

153    "when she knows better herself": *L*, 2:667

154    "how he *admired* her!": Carswell, 69

154    "he being an artist wanted *many* things": FL to Carswell, [October 1916], Yale

154    the friction between his parents: Feinstein, 141

156    "he is very plucky" . . . "give him wings": *L*, 2:643

156    "It is true" . . . "burden": *L*, 2:647

156    "one can smell the northern oceans": *L*, 2:654

156    "November and December will be worse": *L*, 2:664

157    "the sky is all grey and moving": *L*, 2:665

157    "as the winter comes on": *L*, 3:29

157    "everybody will hate, save me": *L*, 2:659

### CHAPTER 10. *WOMEN IN LOVE*: THE MASTERPIECE

158    "to go back to the past": *L*, 3:19

158    "he never expected me to do it": *NIBTW*, 86

159    "the final draft in pencil": *L*, 2:637

159    "rather wonderful and terrible": *L*, 3:22

159    "were anarchic and rebellious": Gathorne-Hardy, 143

159    "to bring that solid equilibrium" . . . "the third thing . . . art": *L*, 2:638

159    "something new and creative": *L*, 2:636

159    "a man's woman," "friction": *WL*, 16

159    "inevitable next step": *WL*, 9

160    "the most remarkable woman in the midlands": *WL*, 15

160    "temper of her blood": *WL*, 22

160    "Lawrence himself": Millett, 347

160    repeats Millett's identical words: Burgess, 118

160    "Birkin is certainly his mouthpiece": MacLeod, 38

160    two hundred pounds a year of his own: This is the figure given in the typescripts; in 1921 Lawrence changed it to "four hundred a year" (*WL*, 132).

160    needs in order to be secure: *L*, 2:620

161    "I could crush anyone": Gathorne-Hardy, 99

161    "I wouldn't give a straw" . . . "let yourself go": *WL*, 250–51

161    "always shouting": *WL*, 290

161   "want[ing] to *dictate*": *WL*, 326
161   "dreadful reaction": *WL*, 296
161   "feel for the other sex": *WL*, 501 (Lawrence's prologue appears in this edition of *WL*)
161   "additional to marriage": *WL*, 352
162   "she enjoys everything": Feinstein, 152
162   "She wanted to have no past": *WL*, 409
162   " Gilbert [Cannan] made me": *L*, 3:52
162   "ineffable darkness and ineffable riches": *WL*, 314
163   "no dark shameful things were denied her": *WL*, 413
163   "might plunge with gratification": *WL*, 68
163   in order to satisfy him: Maddox, 147–48
163   "their vile underneath way": *L*, 3:49
163   Germans had lost many more: Gilbert, *The First World War*, 299–300
163   "gone out of my imagination": *L*, 2:526
163   "consumption": *L*, 2:623
163   "endless process of death": *L*, 3:27
163   "not with us": *WL*, 184
163   "in the deepest sense": *WL*, 26
164   "to us": *WL*, 438
164   "beautiful and soldierly": *WL*, 58
164   "full of male strength": *WL*, 64
164   "cried Ursula": *WL*, 111
164   "the living body of the horse": *WL*, 113
165   "passed into nothingness for Gudrun": *WL*, 112
165   "Lawrence's [fictional] account" . . . "essential Katherine": Tomalin, 151–53
165   "precise model for Gudrun": Meyers, *D. H. Lawrence*, 152
165   "like Katharine Mansfield": *L*, 3:41 (Lawrence always spelled "Katherine" with a second *a*)
165   "she's always on the defensive": *WL*, 95
165   "she challenged the whole world": *WL*, 239
165   "contrariness" . . . "goes by contraries": *WL*, 94
165   "a certain amount of money": *WL*, 211
165   "an act of death": *L*, 2:636
165   "new schemes for going away": *WL*, 211
165   "but also from Murry": *L*, 2:628
165   "depends which way the wind blows": *WL*, 470
165   "to produce something": *WL*, 56
165   "will ever make my life": *WL*, 58
166   "not *love*": *WL*, 275
166   "terrible hopelessness of fate": *WL*, 181
166   "And I shall strike the last [blow]": *WL*, 171
166   "beyond, the obscene beyond": *WL*, 242
166   "to swear to love each other": *WL*, 206
166   "till I understand it better": *WL*, 207
166   "one of life's outcasts": *WL*, 376
167   "having said [that you love me]": *WL*, 443
167   "and the setting the Burrows": *M&C*, 327
167   "*that* happened": *M&C*, 348
167   "practically true": *M&C*, 343
168   "I like him": *L*, 1:388
168   "tired to death": *M&C*, 86

168    "was sorry for" . . . "loved her with intensity": *WL*, 215
168    "*fearfully* in love with F[rieda]": *L*, 1:420
168    "she has gone wrong, perhaps": *WL*, 208
168    "like Ernest in temperament": *M&C*, 148
168    "a vision of power": *WL*, 222
168    "a girl of thirteen or fourteen": *WL*, 27
168    "instinctive critical faculty" . . . "dark hair and quiet bearing": *WL*, 219–20
168    "avoided her mother": *WL*, 220
168    "if we saw our mother": Nehls, 1:320
168    "a little older than Winifred": *WL*, 27
168    "just in her teens": *WL*, 30
168    "a fretting, negated thing": *WL*, 185
169    as others have noted: Emile Delavenay says, "Lawrence must have created his charac-
       ter [Loerke] by combining at the last moment certain traits of Gertler's personality and
       work with a model originally inspired by *Crime and Punishment*" (*The Man and His
       Work*, 391). Keith Sagar says only that "Loerke acquires aspects of Mark Gertler"
       (*Life into Art*, 149).
169    "who put these 'ideas' into her head": *L*, 1:424
169    "thin hair" . . . "rather shapeless mouth": *WL*, 426
169    "like a child": *WL*, 405
169    "wouldn't work for anybody": *WL*, 425
169    "hostility to his father": McGuire, 158
169    "abnormal affective life": ibid., 69
169    "specifically homosexual nature": ibid., 151
169    young male lover named Leitner: Leitner's name is an anagram (with two reversed let-
       ter-pairs) of Heseltine's: *Le*/*it*/*ne*/*r* = (Hes)el/ti/ne/-. Like Halliday, who is a "heavy, fair
       young man" (*WL*, 67), Leitner is a "large, fair young man" (*WL*, 405). Both Halliday
       and Leitner are described as "soft" (*WL*, 68, 411), and both are mocked—Halliday by
       Pussum, Leitner by Loerke.
169    The two men . . . now despised each other: In an epilogue that Lawrence canceled, Gu-
       drun wrote to Ursula that she had "lived for some months with Loerke, *as a friend*"
       (D. H. Lawrence, *The First "Women in Love,"* xxxiii; emphasis added).
169    "the last degree of intimacy": WL, 422
169    "You are an extraordinary woman": *WL*, 457
169    "accord with him": *WL*, 426
169    "Come to Dresden": *WL*, 458
169    "come to me": Turner, "The Otto Gross–Frieda Weekley Correspondence," 191
169    "*if* you were to come to Holland": ibid., 193
169    "would only want her to be herself" . . . "almost like a criminal": *WL*, 427
169    psychopath and then confined: Green, 66
170    "free individual[s]": *WL*, 563
170    "to a girl-friend she had there": *WL*, 568
170    "I can hardly bear it": *M&C*, 343 (undated letter to Edward Gilbert)
170    "death and corruption": *L*, 3:21
170    "[and] with Lady Ottoline": *L*, 3:23
170    "a place in the far west" . . . "new" unknown: *L*, 3:25
171    "to interview the leading authors": *L*, 3:27
171    "[and] more innocent than children": *L*, 3:25
171    "infinitely welcome just at the moment": Healey and Cushman, 130
171    "the kindness is given": *L*, 3:29
171    "like the snakes and the dormice": *L*, 3:40

171   "most probably not": *L*, 3:47
171   "only suggested by her": *L*, 3:44
171   "Hermione was a very fine woman": Gathorne-Hardy, 128–29
172   "insulted by petty dogs as that [book] was": *L*, 3:55
172   "a masterpiece": *L*, 3:37, 61, 67
172   "and [become] fine steel": *Times*, 20 December 1916, p. 10
172   "mechanically does what Germany does": *L*, 3:57
172   "down altogether": *L*, 3:64
172   "I am only at war with them": *L*, 3:63

## CHAPTER 11. SUSPICION

174   "destructive philosophy" . . . "forms of English civilisation": *WL*, xxxiv
174   "there is no peace of being": *L*, 3:80–81
174   "the maximum of evil": *L*, 3:88
174   "refuses to go [by] English boat": *L*, 3:85
175   "foul inward poison": *L*, 3:92
175   "whom I like": *L*, 3:89
175   "life will never be destroyed": *L*, 3:97
175   "pinched for food": *L*, 3:102
175   "incessant stirring of the soil" . . . "with white sauce": Sutton and Sons, 30
175   "conclusion of the old life in me" . . . "intimate and vital": *L*, 3:87
175   "that we yield up" . . . "new and vivid": *Phoenix*, 671–72
176   "life and death and are fulfilled": ibid., 686–87
176   "[t]he herd will destroy everything": *L*, 3:143
176   "the last respectability": *L*, 3:109
176   "living only in her emotions" . . . "when he is with you": Nehls, 1:416
177   "I hate the Midlands": *L*, 3:114
177   "a very sick man": Nehls, 1:454
177   "on the face of the earth": *L*, 3:118
177   "when nothing else would": FL to Witter Bynner, [15 October 1943], Harvard
177   "and some that I didn't know": Nehls, 1:366
178   civilians in London: Gilbert, *The First World War*, 340
178   "I hate[d] it so much": *L*, 2:618
178   "I have a bad feeling about Bodmin": *L*, 3:132
178   "much good out of the doctors": *L*, 3:134
178   "drive Lawrence to utter despair": *NIBTW*, 87
178   "on the verge of utter collapse": B. Smith, 113
179   "they were visiting me": Gray, 126
179   Gray's priggish conceit: "I am [unflatteringly] portrayed in *Aaron's Rod* under the guise of a musician called Cyril Scott," Gray wrote (Gray, 136). Of Lawrence he said confidently: "His physical personality was puny and insignificant, his vitality low, and his sexual potentialities exclusively cerebral. There can be no possible doubt about that" (ibid., 138).
179   "a process of refinement" . . . "volume should be modified": *L*, 3:148 n.
180   "hands full of her breasts": quoted in *NIBTW*, 45
180   "infantile solipsism": Maddox, 139
180   "transcendence takes place": *Phoenix*, 693
180   "what he could [to help]": quoted in Stevens, 77
181   "Mrs. Lawrence was a lady": ibid., 82
181   "could talk by the hour" . . . "quarrel with me": *NIBTW*, 87–88

181 "sex is the clue to marriage": D. H. Lawrence, "A Propos of *Lady Chatterley's Lover*," 318

181 "softly-strong limbs": *WL*, 505

181 "Keynes at Cambridge": *L*, 2:311

181 slinking "rat": *WL*, 428

181 "strong man opposite": *WL*, 505

181 "no matter *what* the desire": *L*, 3:141

182 "my own long 'war' experience": *L*, 4:320

182 "as they waited for a wain": *K*, 236

182 "her touch of derision": *K*, 237

182 Jeffrey Meyers: Meyers, *D. H. Lawrence*, 214

182 Brenda Maddox: Maddox, 239, 269

182 "above all, fear of death": *K*, 237–38

182 "It always slides into death": D. H. Lawrence, *Studies in Classic American Literature*, 251

183 "talk to him about it a lot": quoted in Stevens, 32–33

183 destroyed the letters Lawrence sent him: In 1955 Frieda Lawrence wrote: "But William Henry was not a faithful friend to L[awrence]. When we were turned out of Cornwall he was scared and wrote no more to L[awrence]" (*M&C*, 388).

183 "innocent native son": Meyers, *D. H. Lawrence*, 224

183 "the homosexuality" . . . "that we consist of": *M&C*, 360

183 "formed such [a] friendship": *L*, 3:302

183 "I *have* gone to bed with her (twice)": quoted in King, 365

184 "a beauty that is not in the eyes": *L*, 3:163

184 "[Y]ou have a camera in there": *NIBTW*, 88

184 "'signalling to the enemy!'": *NIBTW*, 86

184 "it is dated 9th": *L*, 3:147

184 "through a friend in Switzerland": *L*, 3:175

184 "German submarine crews": *NIBTW*, 89

185 "I was full of foreboding": *NIBTW*, 90

185 "Be quiet," said Lawrence: ibid.

185 "I don't know what we shall do": *L*, 3:168

185 "something changed in Lawrence for ever": *NIBTW*, 90

185 "One grasps for support": *L*, 3:170

## CHAPTER 12. WARTIME CASTAWAYS

186 "torture . . . to live with him": *NIBTW*, 91

186 "seems one big curse": FL to Willie Hopkin, n.d. [1918–1919], University of Nottingham

187 "it seems to occupy my heart": *L*, 3:175

187 "*something* to look forward to": *L*, 3:214 (emphasis added)

187 "railway fares so high": FL to Mary Hutchinson, 8 February 1918, HRC (composed by D. H. Lawrence)

187 "exactly six pounds". . . arriving in Italy: *L*, 3:207

187 "you would help us again!": Healey and Cushman, 131

187 "if I'd got any": *L*, 3:211

188 "villages that will sleep forever": *L*, 3:223

188 "never have a neighbour": *L*, 3:224

188 printing 120 copies . . . Anne Estelle Rice: Beaumont, 92

189 "wrong road goes": D. H. Lawrence, *Bay*, 22–23

189   "quite pleasantly and simply": *L*, 3:232
189   with Beecham conducting: According to the *Times*, the last performance of *The Marriage of Figaro*, with Sir Thomas Beecham conducting, was on Saturday, 6 April 1918.
190   "'now that we have got ten shillings'": Barr, "Step-daughter to Lawrence," 28
190   full military honors: For details about Manfred von Richthofen, see Franks, Giblin, and McCrery.
190   "a fine fighting man": *Times*, 23 April 1918, p. 6
190   "what it can be I don't know": *L*, 3:240
190   "a walking phenomenon of suspended fury": *L*, 3:239
191   "She brought forth to him his imaginations": *Sons and Lovers*, 241
191   "[W]e became very fond of her": *L*, 3:257
191   "I remember one night" . . . "we would all start to sing again": Hilton, 31–32
192   "usually I am so glad to be alone": *L*, 3:258
192   "even with myself, these days": *L*, 3:252
192   "only just endure the days": *L*, 3:257
192   "this first essay at once?": *L*, 3:270
192   "direct the life-mystery": D. H. Lawrence, "The Spirit of Place," 327
193   "crucial study of American literature": Poirier, 37
193   "unconscious or subconscious soul": Lawrence, "The Spirit of Place," 322
193   "profound emotional disorder": Vivas, 269
193   "deep, philosophic reverence": *L*, 3:269
193   "the broken pots" . . . "thread" of significance: *L*, 3:322
193   "venerable aspect of age": Gibbon, 920
193   "a few bristles here and there": D. H. Lawrence, *Movements*, 66–67
194   "You, my dear Kot" . . . "since open enmity is avowed": *L*, 3:277
194   "very seedy": *L*, 3:274
194   "worth a lot, really": *L*, 3:278
194   "But having been badgered" . . . "and gasping": *L*, 3:281
194   "prove a shroud if I don't": *L*, 3:282–83
194   "do what I can": *L*, 3:285
194   "I want a job" . . . "London next week": *L*, 3:287–88
195   "if you hear of anything": *L*, 3:289
195   "because I am so hard up": *L*, 3:291
195   "a book than a supplement": *L*, 3:323
195   "if there's peace": *L*, 3:292
195   "did not live to see the break-up": quoted in Byrne, 224–25
195   "where we become all 'vagabonds'": Nehls, 1:477
195   "marvellous Peace report on Thursday night": *L*, 3:297
196   David Garnett . . . looking ill: About the dialogue attributed to Lawrence on this occasion, Garnett wrote: "I do not suppose that a single phrase reproduces his actual words" (Nehls, 1:479). However, both Robert Lucas (156–57) and Janet Byrne (223) quote the improvised dialogue as if it were a transcript.
196   "very dark" . . . "very lonely": *L*, 3:300
196   "a little reassuring of some sort": *L*, 3:305
196   "cross the threshhold of the human psyche": *L*, 3:302
196   "thin and worn" . . . "not lovers, friends": D. H. Lawrence, *England, My England*, 55–58
196   "the rainy dusk". . . now seems disoriented: ibid., 46–48
197   "trembling in every fibre" . . . "hot, poignant love": ibid., 63
197   "human relationships": *L*, 3:303
197   "She was spell-bound" . . . "possessed by him": D. H. Lawrence, *The Fox*, 10–11

197    "[the fox] any more": ibid., 18
197    "she wanted to touch him" . . . "across her face": ibid., 20
197    "cat's paw": ibid., 272 (manuscript ending, p. 18)
197    she feels a "swoon": ibid., 15
197    "Trust the tale": Lawrence, *Studies in Classic American Literature*, 3
198    "and roared—Lord above": *L*, 3:312–13
198    "putrid disease" influenza: *L*, 3:330
198    "I feel two hundred years old" . . . "must have plenty of sugar": *M&C*, 215
198    "at the end of everything here": *L*, 3:332
199    "into the world, to wander": *L*, 3:333
199    "I am reduced to vituperation": *L*, 3:335
199    "lesson to her, it has to me": *L*, 3:337
199    "till we can get away": *L*, 3:345
199    "taking shaky walks": *L*, 3:343
200    "then I hope" . . . "There is a sum for you!": *L*, 3:347
200    "as if" . . . "no future to wonder over": *L*, 3:348
200    "I promise you" . . . "short stories will come": *L*, 3:355
200    "walk a long way home": Nehls, 1:488
200    "With all he had to do" . . . "with her lessons": Nehls, 1:488–89
200    "like a bolt from the blue": *L*, 3:366
200    "glum and unresponsive": Nehls, 1:486
201    "large and striking": Nehls, 1:487
201    "lazy and useless" . . . "every insult she could conjure up": Nehls, 1:504
201    "But I like not to have a home": *L*, 3:389
201    "in some log hut out west": *L*, 3:368
201    "one's sense of adventure": *L*, 3:368
201    "setting out for new adventures": *M&C*, 214
201    "generated in a test-tube" . . . "answered them": Thomas, 100
203    "Frieda busy about the house": *L*, 3:377
203    "filthy [financial] terms": *L*, 3:397
203    "shrill, penetrating, unforgettable": Nehls, 1:407
203    "down a stone staircase": Nehls, 1:499
203    "the passport would come all right": *L*, 3:397
204    "so soon after the war": *NIBTW*, 97
204    "Another quandary": *L*, 3:395
204    "too much married": Nehls, 1:503
204    "more space and independence": Kinkead-Weekes, 517
204    "the best of my books": *L*, 3:390
204    "five years of persistent work": *L*, 3:400
204    "an effort for my own rights": *L*, 3:403
204    "a different book": *L*, 3:385
204    "so near the quick": D. H. Lawrence, *New Poems*, vi
204    "no one in the world has seen": *L*, 3:400
205    "to preserve its own integrity": Lawrence, *Studies in Classic American Literature*, 262
205    "a risky venture": *L*, 3:405
205    "Pinker never submitted [the typescript]": *L*, 3:409 n. 1
205    "She says food *very* scarce there": *L*, 3:412
205    "sad, different Germany": *NIBTW*, 98
205    "*utterly* gone": *L*, 3:571
205    "Compton Mackenzie on Capri": *L*, 3:405
207    "alone against the world": Aldington, *Life for Life's Sake*, 233

207    "*slow slow—slow*": *L,* 3:415
207    "seemed not to care" . . . "a river to run to the sea": *Life for Life's Sake,* 233
209    "cast away into the new beginning": *Phoenix,* 6

## CHAPTER 13. THE SUN RISES AGAIN

213    "further and further south": *L,* 3:416
213    "the impotent old wolf" . . . "parvenu": *L,* 3: 417
213    "shockingly wearisome tirades": quoted in Douglas, 285
214    "not so gay any more": *L,* 3:416
214    "the blazing blazing sun": *L,* 3:417
214    "am not quite alone": *L,* 3:418
215    "such a lovely colour!": D. H. Lawrence, *Memoir,* 38
215    "all the big towns of Europe": ibid., 31
215    "full of life and plenty": *L,* 3:421
215    "not that pressure": *L,* 3:425
215    "One loafs one's life away in Italy": *L,* 3:420
215    "to see what it is like": *L,* 3:423
215    "very well in health": *L,* 3:427
216    "delicate and flowery": *NIBTW,* 98
216    "secret rejoicing in wickedness": *NIBTW,* 98
216    "deeply disturbed by Magnus": *NIBTW,* 99
216    "touched or frightened": *L,* 3:463
216    "staggeringly primitive" . . . "to Naples or Capri": *L,* 3:431–32
218    "and only just": *L,* 3:444
218    "with boisterous laughter". . . a phenomenon, or a freak: Mackenzie, 165
219    "a disappointed creature": *L,* 3:534
219    "danced the Tarantella": *M&C,* 216
219    "a beautiful scarf" . . . "when we are out": *L,* 3:454
219    "and so life passes": *L,* 3:449
219    "go down red into the sea": *L,* 3:461
219    "precise and explicit": *L,* 3:458
219    "on Freudian Unconscious": *L,* 3:466
220    "in Bavaria since early 1914": *L,* 3:459
220    "semi-literary cats" . . . "to Sicily, I think": *L,* 3:469
220    "a dirty little worm": *L,* 3:467
220    "stewing" in her own deathly consumption: *L,* 3:470
220    "have [his] day": *L,* 3:477
220    "more green and succulent herbage": *L,* 3:481
221    "Frieda loves the house" . . . "very grand": *L,* 3:480
221    "really lovely": *L,* 3:483
221    "like coming to life again": *NIBTW,* 100
221    "Let us go ahead": *L,* 3:484
221    "leave out a chapter of *The Rainbow*": *L,* 3:490
221    "I'll take them": *L,* 3:490
221    "all my rights over the books": *L,* 3:491
222    "*never* speak to each other again": *L,* 3:502
223    "*nothing* left [of Cannan's friendship]": Mackenzie, 177 (text corrected from Frieda's holograph letter, HRC)
223    "I felt it so strongly": Lawrence, *Memoir,* 39
223    "with a tender" . . . "ecstasies in my ear": ibid., 42

223 "isn't quite sure of her lover": ibid., 46
223 "straight to you": ibid., 62
224 "He is looking" . . . "Never speaks of it": quoted in Maddox, 269
224 "to the coast of Greece": *L*, 3:539
224 "I like it so much": *L*, 3:503
224 "all set across a distance": *L*, 3:549
224 "heroines in similar circumstances": D. H. Lawrence, *The Lost Girl*, 32
224 "withering towards old-maiddom": ibid., 81
225 "beyond her usual self, impersonal": ibid., 140
225 "lost her soul": ibid., 175
225 "darling" landlord: *L*, 3:515
225 "do anything you want": Lawrence, *Memoir*, 87
225 "before I get myself free": *L*, 3:522
225 "inhospitable to foreigners": *L*, 3:573
226 "gnat of economy": *L*, 3:568
226 "We should have to be economical": *L*, 3:569
226 "not to know people closely": *L*, 3:554
226 "in the dining room": *NIBTW*, 113–14
227 "what he had written": *NIBTW*, 115
227 "I might drift off anywhere": *L*, 3:585
227 "picnic à trois": *L*, 3:591
227 "great fun, even alone": *L*, 3:592
228 "to deny life": "Cypresses," in D. H. Lawrence, *Birds, Beasts and Flowers*, 31
228 "fissure" . . . "within the crack": ibid., 2
228 "put[ting] your mouth" . . . "bursten figs won't keep?": ibid., 5–9
228 "linger with you": *L*, 3:585
228 "the time, the place, the beloved": Thornycroft, 79
228 "rottenness" . . . "distilled in separation": "Medlars and Sorb Apples," in *Birds, Beasts and Flowers*, 11–12
229 "the obscene beyond": *WL*, 242
229 "radiated a wonderful sympathy" . . . "to the world": quoted in Thornycroft, 32
230 "long before she married him": quoted in ibid., 61
230 "the sand hills, and bathe": *L*, 3:609
230 "bad feeling between French and German": *L*, 3:594
230 "tired of wandering about": *L*, 3:606
230 "glad to be together again": *L*, 3:615
230 "What a dash we had!" . . . "So they are all right anyhow": FL to Hansard, [30 October 1920], HRC
231 "connected with him": Lawrence, *Memoir*, 92

## CHAPTER 14. FAREWELL TO FONTANA VECCHIA

232 "in a worse state than ever": FL to Réné Hansard, [30 October 1920,], HRC
232 "inevitably revolute": *L*, 3:612
232 "revolutionary socialists": *L*, 3:649
233 "in a temper over the exchange": *L*, 3:640
233 "house for another year": *L*, 3:637
233 "first new carrots": FL to Hopkin, 10 December 1920, University of Nottingham
233 "friends for life": *L*, 3:635
233 "two or three excisions": *L*, 3:647 n.
233 "the same bedroom": *WL*, note on 422

233  "copies already sold": B. Smith, 192
234  "since you wish it": *L*, 4:94
234  "he is a simple shit": *L*, 4:116
234  "a fascinating trip": *L*, 3:667
234  "an interfering female": D. H. Lawrence, *Sea and Sardinia*, 96
234  "sends my blood black": ibid., 41–42
235  "to have a boat": *L*, 3:698
235  "nothing to anchor for": Lawrence, *Sea and Sardinia*, 46
235  "making casual acquaintances": *L*, 3:655
235  "I am not": *L*, 4:49
235  "I must come to America": *L*, 3:659
235  "her mother is very ill": *L*, 3:678
236  "very empty": *L*, 3:685
236  "the old life and Europe": *L*, 3:693
236  "cold and depressing": FL to Violet Monk, 28 March 1921, Southern Illinois University
236  "It is very cheap": *L*, 3:683
236  "It was a typical day" . . . "to your solar plexus": Brewster and Brewster, *Reminiscences and Correspondence*, 18
238  "with a light tactful touch": ibid., 14
238  "devil of a journey": *L*, 3:706
238  "completely gone": *L*, 3:725
238  "great blank": *L*, 4:33
238  "inwardly tired and very sad": *L*, 3:732
238  "the impudent Pinker": *L*, 4:28
238  "Keep him in his place" . . . "an inch to these people": *L*, 3:710
239  "spit in the eye of love" . . . "who tries to insult me": *L*, 3:734
239  "spasms of fulfillment": *L*, 3:567
239  "in a delirium of icy fury": *AR*, 25
240  "in bits only": *L*, 4:48
240  "eternally inseparable": *AR*, 104
240  "like brothers" . . . "the same class": *AR*, 106
240  "without betraying one another": *AR*, 101
240  "younger sister": *AR*, 261
240  "blasted": *AR*, 262
241  "a violation": *AR*, 266
241  "stunned, withered": *AR*, 275
241  "a thread of destiny": *AR*, 288
241  At the close . . . prophetic role: For this reason Jeffrey Meyers mistakenly calls Lilly "Lawrence's female self longing for a male" (*D. H. Lawrence*, 258). Indeed, Aaron Sisson—Mark Kinkead-Weekes reminds us—"is only part of Lawrence" (650). Novels, writes biographer Victoria Glendinning, "can tell you a great deal about an author . . . but they can only be used very warily as biographical evidence" (57).
241  "a new mode": *AR*, 291
241  "a homosexual novel": Meyers, *D. H. Lawrence*, 259
241  "a town of men": *AR*, 212
242  "peppery" . . . "wicked joy": *L*, 3:645–46
242  "bit of a spoon?": D. H. Lawrence, *Mr Noon*, 25
243  "Says it will be unpopular": *L*, 4:57
243  "Much cooler here": *L*, 4:54
243  "I will write you a Tyrol story": *L*, 4:58

243 "I want to go away": *L*, 4:64
243 "awfully depressed": *L*, 4:189
243 "I have been so happy" . . . "I want to go south again": *L*, 4:71
244 "the shadows together": "Bat," in D. H. Lawrence, *Birds, Beasts and Flowers*, 92
244 "[W]e are so thankful" . . . "worn to ribbons": *L*, 4:92
244 "the body of mankind": *L*, 4:95
245 "very good friends": D. H. Lawrence, *The Fox*, 93
245 "glad she was dead": ibid., 68
245 "in the midst of the Alps": ibid., 118
245 "tiresome word Love": ibid., 115
245 "the rampant, insatiable water" . . . "silent hostility": ibid., 129–30
245 "physical feelings": ibid., 150
246 "the marriage service," [she responded tartly]: ibid., 152–53
247 "I want to go" . . . "glamour and magic for me": *L*, 4:125
247 "I'm sure we want to go": quoted in Luhan, 7 (n.d.; text corrected from holograph letter at Yale)
247 "I shall be glad to go": *L*, 4:142
248 "Dio Mio": *L*, 4:171
248 "frustration and struggling through": *L*, 4:154
248 "I think one must" . . . "when one is quiet and sure": *L*, 4:175
248 "Isn't it thrilling?": *L*, 4:189

## CHAPTER 15. THE VOYAGE OUT

250 "some queer dream": *L*, 4:216
251 "entrancingly beautiful": L. Woolf, *Growing*, 150
251 "so terribly alive!": *NIBTW*, 117
251 "what we feel": *L*, 4:216
251 "footband or waistband": FL to AvR (in German), [April 1922], HRC
252 that characterizes her artwork: The Brewsters' paintings are reproduced in their exhibition catalog *The Divinity That Stirs within Us*. Achsah's *Homage to Buddha* is Plate 72. Earl's celestial *Buddha Meditating*, painted about 1918, is Plate 83.
252 "her [subjects'] solid flesh": quoted in Luhan, 22
252 "physical and psychic environment": Brewster and Brewster, *Reminiscences and Correspondence*, 47
252 he had contracted malaria: *L*, 5:211
252 "than to talk together": Brewster and Brewster, *Reminiscences and Correspondence*, 49
252 "Can't stand Ceylon": *L*, 4:222
252 "So there's the programme": *L*, 4:228
253 "the nights fresh and cool": FL to AvR (in German), 10 May 1922, HRC
253 "like a dream" . . . "taken a breath from it": *L*, 4:238
253 "round the world": *L*, 4:238
253 "discovering how I hate them": *L*, 4:239
254 "we'll get out": *NIBTW*, 119
254 "Winter T[er]ms": Davis, 32
254 "torn canvases removed [from the porches]": *NIBTW*, 119
254 "are very comfortable": *L*, 4:249
254 "rolled gently on to the sand": *NIBTW*, 120
254 "if democracy is to endure": *Sydney Bulletin*, p. 6
255 "it is so raw—so crude": *L*, 4:249
255 "I just shrink away from it": *L*, 4:253

255 "a kind of dream": *L*, 4:264
255 "like Paradise before the Fall!": FL to AvR (in German), 22 June 1922, HRC
255 "extraordinarily good company": *L*, 4:266
255 "nobody in the whole country": *L*, 4:262
255 "we get on each other's nerves": *L*, 4:269
256 "the only man as well as the only woman": *K*, 70
256 "by August": *K*, 20
256 "its secret": *K*, 8
257 "A new intoxication of loneliness": "Medlars and Sorb-Apples," in D. H. Lawrence, *Birds, Beasts and Flowers*, 11
257 "involuntarily" . . . "carry him into action": *K*, 143
257 "without foundation": *K*, xxviii. See the Cambridge edition of *Kangaroo*, ed. Bruce Steele, xxiii–xxxv, for a refutation of the theory that Lawrence used real-life models for his Australian characters; see also Joseph Davis, *D. H. Lawrence at Thirroul*. Brenda Maddox (300–305) intelligently weighs the evidence.
257 "the whole Darroch thesis": Davis, 225
257 "well-educated people here": FL to AvR (in German), 9 August 1922, HRC. In German her sentence reads: "Wir haben gar keine gebildeten Leute gekannt hier."
258 "handsome, well-built" . . . "quiet finesse": *K*, 58–59
258 "a sort of embrace": *K*, 92
258 "queen bee to a hive": *K*, 95
258 "a power behind the throne": *K*, 161
258 "intense knowledge of his 'dark god'": *K*, 155
258 "out of the unseen": *K*, 138
258 "apprehended intuitively": MacLeod, 69
258 "qualities that make a man noble": *K*, 385–86
259 "so long in the outer dark": *K*, 265
259 "His great relief was the shore": *K*, 328
260 "staggering over the sea": *L*, 4:284
260 "on the ocean one plays" . . . "It is a very delightful ship!": FL to AvR (in German), 1 September 1922 and 25 August 1922, HRC
260 "you are my guests": *L*, 4:289
260 "She has eyes one can trust": *NIBTW*, 135
260 "insist that she was there": Bynner, 4

## CHAPTER 16. THE LURE OF THE INDIANS

261 "new life": *NIBTW*, 135
262 "old darkness, new terror": D. H. Lawrence, "Indians and an Englishman," *Phoenix*, 95
262 "I have ordered a fourth printing": Gertzman and Squires, 73
262 "the *deepest* of my novels": *L*, 8:57
262 "and my little Zegua": *L*, 4:515
262 "Frieda too": *L*, 4:304
263 "under the wing of the 'padrona'": *L*, 4:305
263 "fascinating and rather terrible": DB to Carl Zigrosser, 7 May 1930, University of Pennsylvania
264 "I'll leave as soon as I can'": *NIBTW*, 136–37
264 "don't come too close to me": *NIBTW*, 137
264 "to develop this impulse" . . . "with anyone else": MDL to Stein, 29 December [1922], Yale
264 "I believe that" . . . "antagonistic": *L*, 4:337

264 "the mountains at your back": *L*, 4:334

264 "and simplify everything": *L*, 4:343

265 "during the winter": FL to AvR (in German), 10 January 1923, HRC

265 "the parting was friendly": *L*, 4:348

265 "but Lawrence and she hated each other": *L*, 4:450 (letter of 30 May 1923, State University of New York at Buffalo; Lawrence crossed out the last seven words, which are omitted from the Cambridge edition of his letters)

265 "very beautiful wild country": *L*, 4:349

266 "because I feel he tried": *L*, 4:374

266 "No half measures will do": Gertzman and Squires, 59

267 "all my business personally": *L*, 4:376

267 "I put my trust in you": *L*, 4:410

267 "Mexico City via El Paso": *L*, 4:378

267 "gone out of our lives": *L*, 4:375

267 "It grieved us both deeply": Lacy, 64

267 "Lift up her face" . . . "slim yellow mountain lion!": D. H. Lawrence, *Birds, Beasts and Flowers*, 158–60

268 "*Orizaba, Oaxaca, Cuauhtla,* [and] *Cuernavaca*": Terry, xxvi. Lawrence may have noted Terry's admonition that a "room in which the purifying rays of the sun do not enter for at least one hour during the day is not healthy—particularly for weak lungs" (xxiv).

269 "and Johnson a young one": *L*, 4:434

269 "the Bynners": *L*, 4:412

269 "unadulterated spectacle": Terry, 244*k*

269 "Vile and degraded the whole thing": Lacy, 87–88

272 "still call themselves revolutionaries": *L*, 4:430

272 "live there a while": *L*, 4:435

272 "moonlit nights are very beautiful": Terry, 158

272 "meet you in Guadalajara": *L*, 4:435

272 the one-story house had six rooms: The house has since been greatly altered and turned into an opulent bed-and-breakfast on a one-acre lot. "When we bought the place in 1980, it needed a lot of renovation," said the current owner, Barbi Henderson, who renamed it Quinta Quetzalcoatl, or QQ (interview, 19 June 1997).

273 *César o nada*: For an assessment of the links between Lawrence and Baroja, see Talbot.

274 "here on this lake": *L*, 8:81

274 "nothing else, believe me": *L*, 4:463

274 "any other novel of mine": *L*, 4:457

274 "the most splendid thing he ever did": *L*, 4:455

275 before he could humiliate her: Bynner, 61–63

275 "pure pastoral patriarchal land": D. H. Lawrence, *Quetzalcoatl*, 67

275 "new, young, beautiful people": *L*, 4:454

275 "he felt whole again": Lawrence, *Quetzalcoatl*, 126

275 "made her shudder" . . . "fine sensuality against her": ibid., 95–96

276 "You are a woman of will": ibid., 287

276 "near enough to leave": *L*, 4:462

276 "go back to Mexico": *L*, 4:470

278 "poor little night light": *M&C*, 220

278 "God knows why": *L*, 4:477

278 "pack with a donkey in the mountains": *L*, 4:485

278 "mute towards almost everybody": *L*, 4:488

279 "Where we meet again, I don't know": *M&C*, 220–21

279 "I have had enough": Lacy, 106

## CHAPTER 17. RECONCILIATION

280 "turned to iron inside her": D. H. Lawrence, *Quetzalcoatl*, 310

280 "when I think of England or Germany": *L*, 4:488

281 reveal his chagrin: *L*, 8:85–86

281 "broken, lost, hopeless" . . . "brink of existence": *L*, 4:507

281 "unbearably hot, day and night": Merrild, 337

281 " I went to Chapala" . . . "it was alien to me": *L*, 4:519

281 "nothing for it but to go": *L*, 4:526

282 "I find it very hard": *L*, 4:541

282 "what a vague creature she is": *L*, 4:483

282 "god knows what else": quoted in Hignett, 138

282 he yielded: The evidence of Lawrence's art suggests that the affair was consummated. However, Murry later denied that he yielded to Frieda (Lea, 117–18), and some previous biographers of Lawrence have at least questioned Murry's denial. Keith Sagar (*The Life of D. H. Lawrence*, 165), Janet Byrne (293), and David Ellis (124–25) more or less believe him; Jeffrey Meyers (*D. H. Lawrence*, 306) disbelieves him; Elaine Feinstein judges the evidence "inconclusive" (195); and Brenda Maddox suggests that although Murry refused "cohabitation" with Frieda, he welcomed a brief, uncomplicated affair (339). Whatever happened, Murry soon married Violet le Maistre, a young assistant at the *Adelphi*.

283 "genuine feeling faithfully followed": *K*, 143

283 "*vilely*": *M&C*, 222

283 "had had *enough*": FL to Martin Secker, 8 October 1923, HRC

283 4.2 trillion marks: Bookbinder, 168

283 "they were living their own lives": *NIBTW*, 141

283 "alienated from her children": Meyers, *D. H. Lawrence*, 305

283 "and take my 'glad rags'!": Lacy, 121

284 "Murry is responsible for the 'drinks'": Lacy, 124

284 "aloof and scornful": Carswell, 212

285 "ceased to live together": D. H. Lawrence, "The Border-Line," 79

285 "subtle, cunning homage": ibid., 81

286 "in the dimness of her own contentment": ibid., 86

286 "he will be glad to see me?": *M&C*, 223

286 "too proud and unforgiving": Lawrence, "The Border-Line," 79

286 "gone wrong with him or his business": *L*, 4:553

287 "the moment D.H.L. has stopped speaking": D. Garnett, *Carrington*, 283–84

287 "bad influence": *L*, 5:16

287 "a very bad time last year": *L*, 5:22

287 "much nicer really": *L*, 5:46

288 "right away from the world": *L*, 5:38

288 "trees hissing, Richard scuttling": *L*, 5:40

288 "[Else] told me she had!": Lacy, 134

290 "I'm being very economical": *L*, 5:45

290 "where I must work on my novel": *L*, 5:46

291 "commands the invisible influences, and is obeyed": D. H. Lawrence, "The Dance of the Sprouting Corn," 457

291 "most people naturally dislike me": *L*, 5:84

291 "masterwork of misogyny": Maddox, 349

292 "barbaric" tale: Feinstein, 188

292 "mysterious, marvellous Indians": D. H. Lawrence, *The Woman Who Rode Away*, 42

292 "with spaces of dark between": ibid., 62
293 "his supple hindquarters": D. H. Lawrence, *St. Mawr*, 96
293 "it holds me up": ibid., 155
294 "googoo eyes" . . . "impertinence": Brett, 125
294 "as I have no more": ibid., 141
294 "some camphorated oil": FL to MDL, [3 August 1924], Yale
294 "hurts like billy-o! this evening": *L*, 5:90
294 "weird rather than beautiful": *L*, 5:100
296 "daisies and wild sunflowers": *L*, 5:112
296 "It is better to be gone" . . . "makes a strange break": *L*, 5:124
296 "the Zapotecs live": *L*, 5:139

## CHAPTER 18. THE MYSTERIES OF OAXACA

297 "and a nice little easy town": *L*, 5:176
298 "before we are artists": Brett, 163
298 "as if in constant meditation": Nehls, 2:368
298 "journey in a steep gorge": *L*, 5:162
298 "glinting eyes watch us unceasingly": Brett, 167–68
299 a wing of his rambling house: Today the house, renumbered 600 Avenida Pino Suarez, is owned by Señor José Alvarez Padilla. About 1960 his family divided and reconstructed the big house into three smaller units. "But above the kitchen closet you can still see the original pine beam, which went all the way across the old house," he explained (interview, in Spanish, 19 May 1995).
299 "quite fantastic in its wild politics": *L*, 5:190
299 "hemmed in, and shut down": *L*, 5:191
300 "But we must stand apart": *L*, 5:192
300 "I will go and tell Frieda": Brett, 205
300 "But Frieda" . . . "the correct behavior in a triangle?": ibid.
301 "from last year": *L*, 5:193
301 "not have it published": *L*, 5:207
301 "cross[ing] a dividing line": *PS*, 49
301 "black and empty": *PS*, 51
301 "leave me alone": *PS*, 211
301 "beyond her depth": *PS*, 67
302 "ruined his health": *PS*, 71
302 "her soft repose": *PS*, 81
302 "magnetic power": *PS*, 82
302 "great strength": *PS*, 89
302 "powerful will": *PS*, 167
302 "wild strength": *PS*, 139
302 "magic back into her life": *PS*, 103
302 "so utterly without desire": *PS*, 306
303 "not her own life": *PS*, 30
303 "Ramón had lighted it": *PS*, 30
303 "supreme passivity": *PS*, 311
303 "just a woman": *PS*, 325
303 "urgent softness from the volcanic deeps": *PS*, 422
304 "so intensely with one's characters": *L*, 5:293
304 "as if shot in the intestines": *L*, 5:230
304 "nothing at all": *NIBTW*, 149

304 "bewitched by his Mexico": FL to AvR (in German), 19 February 1925, HRC
304 "crawl through the days": *L,* 5:220
304 "I get thinner and thinner": *L,* 5:215
304 "'Lots of people have that'": *NIBTW,* 151
304 "that is the place for him": Squires, *D. H. Lawrence's Manuscripts,* 173
304 "I *must* stay in the sun": *L,* 5:221
305 "the responsibility [of Lawrence's recovery]": *L,* 5:222–23
305 "nearly killed me a second time": *L,* 5:230
305 "[s]heer degrading insult!": *L,* 7:144
305 "the wings of life": D. H. Lawrence, *David,* 11
305 "wrote himself back to health": Squires, *D. H. Lawrence's Manuscripts,* 174
305 "happy to feel better again": ibid., 173–74
305 "cool river along our meadows": FL to AvR (in German), 28 April 1925, HRC
306 "any other work of mine": *L,* 5:264
306 "the squabble forgotten": Brett, 229
308 "drawn to the Mediterranean again": *L,* 5:277
308 "Why don't you go to Capri?": Brett, 236
308 "pay our debts and die": *L,* 5:306
308 "material that is rotten": Lacy, 275
309 "rosy shadow on her face": McDonald, 64
309 "nothing between us": *L,* 5:332
309 "[Murry] exhibited hardly a trace": Lea, 139

CHAPTER 19. WHAT LAWRENCE DISCOVERED

311 "the love of God": *L,* 5:375
311 "incorrigible worm": *L,* 5:380
311 "I feel at home beside [the water]": *L,* 5:376
312 "as nice as the feathers!": *L,* 5:350
312 "he loved women": Stefano Ravagli, interview by Stefania Michelucci, Milan, 9 November 1998
312 "doing housework": Nehls, 3:17
313 "nose in the air, smelling, sniffing": *L,* 5:354
313 "had become impotent": quoted by Moore in *Richard Aldington,* 85
313 "she shouldn't house here": *L,* 5:347
313 "blind old woman" . . . "shown to our mother": Barr, "Step-daughter to Lawrence," 31
313 "spiteful about everyone": Nehls, 3:26
313 "get something out of life": *L,* 5:349
314 "fanatically afraid of the unconventional": D. H. Lawrence, *The Virgin and the Gipsy,* 89
314 "her own female power": ibid., 7
314 "like [that] at the ranch, only worse": *L,* 5:390
314 "I hate you" . . . "Now I don't care": *NIBTW,* 180
314 "'That's what you have to do with me!'": *M&C,* 225
315 "or I shall give up the ghost": *L,* 5:394–95
315 "having a good time": *L,* 5:399
315 "such a dear good boy, Bertie": Nehls, 3:44
315 "turned actually into a stone": D. H. Lawrence, *The Woman Who Rode Away,* 242–43
316 "to have their own way": Brett, 278
316 "the responsive male" . . . "looking at me": Brett, 284–86
316 "then too cold": *L,* 5:403
317 "a hopeless horrible failure": Manchester, epilogue in Brett, III

317 "certainly a fantasy": Meyers, *D. H. Lawrence,* 315
317 "*better* friends, instead of worse": *L,* 5:408
317 "and sloppy emotion": ibid.
318 "much more tolerant": *L,* 5:412
318 "just a cheap nothing": R. Jackson, 51. In 1931 Frieda told Mabel Dodge Luhan that Lawrence had intuited the liaison—"He just got it out of the air!" she said (FL to MDL, 2 July [1931], Berkeley).
318 "I dont a bit!": Irvine and Kiley, 69
318 "*and the rest of things*": *L,* 5:435 (emphasis added)
318 "which shouldn't be broken": *L,* 5;439
318 "old-maidish place": *L,* 5:434
319 "so perfectly placed": *NIBTW,* 186
319 "We both like the spot *immensely*": *L,* 5:444
319 "life seems rich and easy": *L,* 5:467
319 "bee orchids and purple orchids": *NIBTW,* 190
319 "lied freely": Byrne, 316
321 "rich in caring for people": Irvine and Kiley, 69
321 "typing German and making revisions": *L,* 5:474
321 "to the verge of disaster": *Times,* 3 May 1926
321 "the end of the world": *L,* 5:448
321 "potatoes—nothing more": *L,* 5:536
321 "such an odd couple": *L,* 5:476
321 "so we might run over": *L,* 5:476
322 "read the old novels": *L,* 5:492
322 "bracing and tonicky": *L,* 5:518
322 "glad to be at home in England": *L,* 5:521
323 "'you can go now if you like'": Turner, "D. H. Lawrence in the Wilkinson Diaries" (Wilkinson's punctuation has been regularized)
323 "I am working at a story": *L,* 5:563
323 "thinking about the strike": *L,* 5:565
326 "like Ottoline's Cinderella daughter": *L,* 5:586
000 "a short novel also very reprehensible!": FL to McDonald, [postmark 7 December 1926], HRC
326 "like a revelation": D. H. Lawrence, *The First and Second "Lady Chatterley,"* 16
326 "bottomless pools": *L,* 5:605
326 "dreary, dismal, priggish": *SLC,* 238
326 "should not go dead": *SLC,* 283
327 "and been restored to life": *SLC,* 263
327 "avoid his fellow-men" . . . "*rather than pounce* on them": Squires, *The Creation of "Lady Chatterley's Lover,"* 66
327 "almost correct": *SLC,* 428
327 "almost a sort of marriage": *SLC,* 317
327 "And I am ashamed": *Sons and Lovers,* 325
328 "that he should have to come" . . . "be tender to me!": Squires, *The Creation of "Lady Chatterley's Lover,"* 77–78
328 "terribly humiliating to him": *SLC,* 529
328 "gift of life": ibid.
328 "one's proper sex life": *L,* 5:648
328 "life which has been denied in us": ibid.
328 "*if you need it*": *SLC,* 532 (emphasis added)
328 "[i]f you need it": *SLC,* 244

329    "for the time being": *L,* 5:647
329    "very improper": *L,* 5:623
329    "awfully well this winter": *L,* 5:598

CHAPTER 20. *LADY CHATTERLEY'S LOVER:* THE LAST NOVEL

330    "connection with everything": *L,* 6:37
331    "he was not a man": D. H. Lawrence, "The Lovely Lady," 361
331    "clean-shaven face": ibid., 358
331    "squirming inside her shell": ibid., 372
331    "an abundance of life": D. H. Lawrence, *Sketches of Etruscan Places,* 12
332    "I liked [them] immensely": *L,* 6:31
332    "in the psyche": *L,* 6:58
332    "[W]e hardly see anybody" . . . "she doesn't want them": *L,* 6:76
332    "never been right": *L,* 6:59
332    "slow bitter revocation": *L,* 6:80
332    "see the last of them": *L,* 6:79
332    "I am risen!": D. H. Lawrence, *The Escaped Cock,* 57
333    "as popular as I can make it": *L,* 6:93
333    "sour by midday": *NIBTW,* 194–95
333    "were probably worthless": Caldwell, e-mail to authors, 25 March 1998
333    "I really get depressed": *L,* 6:98
333    "chagrin that goes deep in": *L,* 6:103
334    "touchingly gentle": G. Smith, 288
334    "to be cool again": *L,* 6:116
334    "among the mountains again": *L,* 6:120
334    "I am a good deal better": *L,* 6:144
334    "catarrh [is] clearer" . . . "and nothing else": *L,* 6:177
334    "write another book": *L,* 6:182
335    "like not getting well" . . . "put its eye out": *L,* 6:220
335    "aren't much, nowadays": *L,* 6:178
335    "this [whole] year?": FL to Secker, 17 December 1927, HRC
335    close to £75: We estimate £18 for rail fares, £37 for hotels and meals, and £20 for doctors, entertainment, gifts, and so on. By comparison, in 1929 Mildred Harrigan—who set out to see Switzerland, France, and northern Italy "at extremely moderate cost"—spent $390 [£80] on a two-month trip (Harrigan, ix).
335    "under lock and key": *L,* 6:196
335    "a windfall for me": *L,* 6:222
336    "to write intimately": *L,* 6:180
336    "died of chagrin": *LCL,* 12
336    "getting thinner": *LCL,* 71
336    "really amusing" tonic: *L,* 6:204
336    "almost before he had begun": *LCL,* 54
336    "keep anything up": *LCL,* 31
336    paralyzed his lower body: Although Lawrence's friend Rosalind Baynes served as a model for Connie—both are demure and soft spoken, both commit adultery and conceive another man's child—her husband's link to Clifford is as tantalizing. Godwin Baynes, like Clifford, was injured in France during the war, "bruised by a German shell . . . on the Somme" (reported his father), then in September 1916 "sent back to England on a month's sick leave" before being "sent back [again] to France" (Thornycroft, 57). Sim-

ilarly, Clifford came "home for a month on leave," then "went back to Flanders" before he was injured (*LCL*, 5).

336    "If Lawrence is doing well" . . . "very exhausted": FL to AvR (in German), 26 December 1927, HRC

337    "when he could not sleep": *LCL*, 140

337    "an appeal to its vices": *LCL*, 101

337    what Lawrence himself wrote: *L*, 6:248

337    "both Clifford and Mellors": *M&C*, 389

337    "That pneumonia" . . . "the lungs not so elastic": *LCL*, 191–96

337    "grown heavy": *LCL*, 263

338    "a woman" . . . "eternally in the universe": *LCL*, 329–30

338    "in the flood": *LCL*, 174

338    "Lawrence's inferior works": Maddox, 423

339    "utterly unknowing" . . . "unfathomable": *LCL*, 175

339    "this episode is necessary": MacLeod, 222

339    "the woman in me": *LCL*, 276

339    "between sun and earth": *LCL*, 301

340    "near the brink of the abyss": *L*, 6:247

340    "nobody": *L*, 6:249

340    "uncastrated": *L*, 6:253

341    "facts but not truths": J. Huxley, 118

341    "expurgated version of a man": ibid., 121

342    "all it was about": ibid., 122

342    "penis" . . . "lady's paramour": expurgated typescript of *Lady Chatterley's Lover*, pp. 302, 304, 399, 390, HRC

342    "a word of English": *L*, 6:322

342    "It's a phallic novel": *L*, 6:325

342    "I feel very bold": *L*, 6:322

342    "I'll sell the thing all right": *L*, 6:346

342    "like a Bach fugue": *L*, 6:353

343    "a few beautiful days": *L*, 6:375

343    "a right to its own secrets": Nehls, 3:189

343    "you can pay for me": FL to AvR (in German), 26 December 1927, HRC

343    "vulnerable like an orphan": J. Huxley, 125

343    "immensely proud": Nehls, 3:205

344    "hurry up": *L*, 6:391

344    "longing to have your show": *L*, 6:435 n. 3

344    "I felt very mad": *L*, 6:428

345    "[b]efore I know where I am" . . . "on my own stem": D. H. Lawrence, *Phoenix II*, 532–33

345    "soul of patience": *L*, 6:419

345    "never any peace": *L*, 6:485

345    "the air is really good" . . . "in another world": *L*, 6:451–54

345    "gasp going uphill": *L*, 6:456

345    "my tormenting cough": *L*, 6:457

346    "let them go unsigned": *L*, 6:463

347    "damn and damn them": *L*, 6:532

347    "emotionally, in Italy": *L*, 7:109

347    "get me back to Italy": *L*, 7:152

348    "only ourselves": *L*, 6:594

348 "those about to die": Nehls, 3:253
348 "found me not there": Gates, 93
348 "I don't write to him": *L,* 7:558
348 "a literary cesspool" . . . "a poisoned genius": Nehls, 3:262–63
348 "never bothered about them again": Nehls, 3:260

CHAPTER 21. THE END AND THE BEGINNING

350 "do him most good": *NIBTW,* 200
351 "miserable dwelling": Davies, *The Withered Root,* 288
351 "divined Davies's homosexuality" . . . "flirtation": Maddox, 449–50
351 "his mother": quoted in Nehls, 3:276
352 "her fine lioness quality": Nehls, 3:280
352 "other flesh to my own": D. H. Lawrence, "Man Reaches a Point," 98
352 "Only mid-ocean": D. H. Lawrence, "Desire Goes Down into the Sea," 45
352 "this dirty hypocrisy!": *L,* 7:147
352 "a comprehensive hatred": Draper, 310
353 "all-round chauvinist": Munro, 15
353 "a hole in the bourgeois world": *L,* 7:79
353 "ever I did before": *L,* 7:91 n. 2
353 "the back of presented appearance": D. H. Lawrence, "Introduction to These Paintings," 579
353 She looks like Frieda: On 17 October 1960 Richard Aldington wrote to H.D. about Frieda: "In October 1928 Arabella, Brigit, Frieda and I all bathed *naked* daily together on one of the plages of Port-Cros, and then lay in the sun. So warm it was. They were charming—Frieda of course a Rubens, Brigit a Titian, and Arabella a Giorgione—that is, putting them in the highest class of their type. Even then Frieda naked wasn't really *fat*—just opulent like the other Rubens ladies!" (Zilboorg, 251).
354 "every scene and event": Nehls, 3:293
354 "miracles happen if one lets them!": FL to Morrell, [25 January 1929], HRC
354 "tortures of angry depression": *L,* 7:183
354 "and suffered, I tell you": *L,* 7:186
354 "body that doesn't cough": *L,* 7:207
354 "resort in winter and spring": Baedeker, 263
355 "what I think of them": *L,* 7:234
355 "unspeaking but triumphant": Davies, *Print of a Hare's Foot,* 157
355 semblance of health: G. Smith, *Letters of Aldous Huxley,* 313 (13 July 1929). Huxley blamed Frieda for not honoring doctors: "We've told her that she's a fool and a criminal; but it has no more effect than telling an elephant" (ibid., 314). Yet Lawrence found evidence for his skepticism. When Frieda sprained her ankle in June, a London specialist could not fix her limp and charged her twelve guineas; a village bone setter in Germany set the bone in a minute. "Doctors should all be put at once in prison," Lawrence told the Brewsters with unusual venom (*L,* 7:464 [5 September 1929]).
355 "best items in food shops": Davies, *Print of a Hare's Foot,* 159–60
355 "my real will to live": *L,* 7:235
356 "last sort of cocktail excitement": *L,* 7:600–601
356 "shiny and glamorous here!": FL to Davies, [30 May 1929], HRC
356 "about the best in Europe": *L,* 7:284
356 "Spanish thing I've done": *L,* 7:260
356 "very successfully lazy": *L,* 7:291
357 "a house of my own now": *L,* 7:309

357  "a proper place to live in": *L,* 7:292

357  "very nice indeed": *L,* 7:337

357  "wild and overwhelming": *NIBTW,* 199

357  "recoil with horror" . . . "gross and obscene": Nehls, 3:338–39

357  "not a single erection": quoted in Holroyd, 641 (letter to Roger Senhouse, 15 July 1929)

359  "an important person": *L,* 7:373 n. 3

359  "under any circumstances": *L,* 7:369

359  "not of any sort": quoted in Luhan, 343 (letter of 5 [May] 1929)

359  "Do you see" . . . "ate the peaches": *NIBTW,* 199

359  "[N]ine people—very nice": *L,* 7:418

360  "afraid of the next step": *L,* 7:421

360  "I just leave her alone": *L,* 7:420

360  "[I] can't fight any more": *L,* 7:410

360  "a new diet and a new man": *L,* 7:466

360  Gerson Diet . . . buttress his health: Dr. Max Gerson (1881–1959) developed the no-salt, no-fat diet to treat his own migraine headaches but soon discovered that it cured skin TB. In 1929 his discovery that 446 of 450 TB patients who followed the diet achieved lasting cures was published in leading scientific journals. Five years later he published *Diet Therapy of Lung Tuberculosis,* which included Mrs. Albert Schweitzer as case 45.

360  "forgetful effect on [me]": *L,* 7:497

360  "I suppose for him too": FL to Ottoline Morrell, 29 September 1929, HRC

361  "Into pure oblivion": Sagar, "Which 'Ship of Death,'" 182 (We cite the final typescript version of the poem.)

361  "I am in bed again" . . . "unless I pick up very soon": *L,* 7:530

361  "Everything flourishes" . . . "I wish I could": *NIBTW,* 289

362  "Now don't be spiteful, Lorenzo": ibid.

362  "It's so bitter for him": FL to Edward Titus, [5 February 1930], Southern Illinois University at Carbondale

362  "I see very little hope for him": Rauh to MDL, 23 February 1930, Yale

362  "repellent to her": *NIBTW,* 293

362  "don't seem to know any more": *NIBTW,* 289

362  "yet I could not help him": *NIBTW,* 293

363  "I am delirious": *NIBTW,* 295

363  "over there on the table!": Nehls, 3:436

363  "I must have morphia": ibid., 3:435

363  "Hold me, hold me" . . . "I don't know where I am": *NIBTW,* 295

363  "who loved him deeply": FL to Ada Clarke and Emily King, 4 March 1930, Joan King

363  reported in major newspapers: For excellent commentary on the press coverage of Lawrence's death, see Dennis Jackson. The subsequent citations are drawn from his essay.

363  "as well as you did": Low to FL, 4 March 1930, Berkeley

364  "you'll give it them": FL to Ada Clarke and Emily King, 4 March 1930, Joan King

364  "I will make them pay now": FL to Emily King, [30 April 1930], Joan King

364  "you and Ada some of it": FL to Emily King, [8 March 1930], Joan King

364  "her child is dead": FL to Francis Hackett, [21 September 1930], HRC

364  "do my share for him yet": FL to Emily King, [21 March 1930], Joan King

364  "How it upset me!": FL to DB, 3 July 1930, Yale

364  "you don't put in your book": FL to MDL, 3 July 1930, Yale

365  "I will live for it": Irvine and Kiley, 102

365  "high up beyond the spring": FL to DB, [6 March 1930], Yale

365 "ought to be killed": FL to Philip Morrell, [7 March 1931], HRC

365 "wanted me to have everything": quoted in Christie's sale catalog, 16 October 1985

365 "how to behave legally": FL to Morrell, 19 February 1931, HRC

365 John Middleton Murry's testimony: As Frieda wrote to Brett about 13 April 1930, "Murry remembered that there *was* a will [made in Cornwall]" (Yale).

365 "I have *none* left": FL to Laurence Pollinger, [October 1932], HRC

365 "never to write to me again": Moore and Montague, 63–64

365 "[Frieda] as 'My Lady'": Margaret Needham, letter to authors, 8 October 1998

366 twenty-five thousand pounds: Moore and Montague, 11

366 "very little demand": Douglas to FL, 29 March 1930, University of California at Los Angeles

366 two thousand pounds for the rights: A. S. Frere-Reeves to FL, 17 January 1931, James S. Copley Library

366 "frightened" to be alone: FL to DB, 30 July 1930, Yale

366 "the most hopeless way": quoted in Bedford, 263

366 "a nymphomaniac": quoted in Gates, 120

367 "genuine warmth for me": Moore and Montague, 43

367 "see a new part of the world": Stefano Ravagli, interview by Stefania Michelucci, Spotorno, 5 September 1998

367 "I am thrilled at coming": FL to MDL, [April 1931], Yale

### CHAPTER 22. A NEW LIFE FOR FRIEDA

368 "I cant take his money": FL to Edward Titus, 18 July 1931, Southern Illinois University at Carbondale

368 "my feelings are in coming": FL to MDL, [23 May 1931], Yale

369 "and another at Las Cruces": DB to Stieglitz, 7 September 1931, Yale

369 "VERY JOLLY" . . . "FASCINATING": telegram, MDL to Jeffers, 2 June 1931, Berkeley

369 "gives me a pain": DB to Stieglitz, [2 June 1931], Yale

370 "she is now": ibid.

371 "how wonderful it really was!": FL to MDL, [6 August 1932], Yale

371 "much happier": DB to Stieglitz, 18 October 1931, Yale

371 "the muscle and brawn" . . . "exposés of their love": MDL to Una Jeffers, 3 June 1931, Berkeley

372 "'That is the danger!'": MDL to Jeffers, 2 July 1931, Berkeley (spelling regularized)

372 "do what they wanted": Lucille Pond, interview, 17 July 1998

372 "a sort of mecca": Eya Fechin, interview, 18 July 1998

372 getting Lawrence's books away from Thomas Seltzer's nephews: Frieda paid Albert and Charles Boni two thousand dollars "for remainders of books about *20* and *plates*" (FL to MDL, 30 August 1932, Yale).

372 "enough money to get him out": ibid.

373 "As for Lorenzo" . . . "'attend to your jobs'": FL to DB, 14 May 1932, HRC

373 stock certificates, transferred to Frieda in August: See letters from Otto C. Wierum, a New York attorney, to FL, 9 July 1934 and 4 September 1934, James S. Copley Library.

373 "and I never had a purse?": FL to MDL, [27 November 1932], Yale

373 "It was a real triumph": FL to Clayton, 7 November 1932, Nottingham Public Libraries

373 "sick of Europe": FL to DB, 16 November 1932, Yale

375 "New House in Kiowa Ranch": Squires, *D. H. Lawrence's Manuscripts,* 3

375 only five hundred pounds . . . the new house: FL to Pollinger, 2 August 1932, HRC

375 "fixing up [her] hacienda": Snyder to FL, 6 August 1934, James S. Copley Library

375   "but rather terrible": FL to MDL, [2 November 1932], Yale
375   "it comes, as it comes": FL to MDL, [December 1933], Yale
376   "her [own] story": Stevenson, 316
376   "That seemed unforgivable": FL to Collins, 2 August 1946, HRC
376   "not a human being": *M&C*, 71
376   "confidence trick": *M&C*, 32
377   "away from the cold?": *M&C*, 35
377   "suits my very soul": *M&C*, 126
377   "like my life with Lawrence was": FL to Pollinger, [25 June 1934], HRC
378   Over the years . . . in Santa Fe: For these sometimes-contradictory accounts, see Lucas (268–70), Green (255), Moore (*The Priest of Love*, 511–12), Maddox (500–501), and Byrne (366). In 1984 Emile Delavenay ("A Shrine without Relics?") interviewed a seventy-seven-year-old friend of Ravagli's who alleged that Ravagli threw Lawrence's ashes overboard at Marseille (fearing he might be charged with illegal transportation of a corpse) and that later, in New York, to placate Frieda, he placed common cinders into an urn and brought them to her.
378   "when I am dead": FL to MDL, [July 1935], Yale
379   "quota" of legal immigrants: U.S. immigration policy was strict. In 1921 legislation set a quota system based on national origins. By 1929 the yearly total of immigrant visas had been reduced to 150,000, which were assigned on the basis of ethnic ancestry as defined by the 1920 population census. This policy favored immigrants from the United Kingdom, Germany, and Ireland, which got 107,000 of the 150,000 visas granted, whereas Italian immigrants declined by 85 percent in the 1930s (Tucker, Keely, and Wrigley, chapter 4). Since the new legislation required immigrants to receive visas from a U.S. consul, Ravagli had gone to Juarez to await his. Mabel Luhan speculated that he had trouble getting his visa because Barby had sent an inflammatory letter to Washington, D.C. (MDL to Jeffers, 28 October [1935], Berkeley).
379   "its everlasting sunlight": quoted in Mariani, 300
379   "movie people lead a dog's life": FL to William Hopkin, 21 February 1936, Nottingham
379   "always be Hollywood to me": *M&C*, 478
379   "and trusted everybody": Squires, *D. H. Lawrence's Manuscripts*, 4
380   "the most out of them": ibid.
381   "'The Rainbow' . . . for $7,500": That price, though high, was not unreasonable. Three years earlier Walpole had sold MGM the rights to his *Vanessa* for $12,500 (Feather, 198).
381   "I will get credit, and cash too": Powell, journal, 1 April 1936, privately held
381   "too much of the goat in him": ibid.
381   "companion and handyman": Squires, *D. H. Lawrence's Manuscripts*, 14
382   "thrilled": ibid., 69
382   "our younger friends": Vincent, interview, 18 July 1998
382   "She was full of a clean". . . only $96.50: Fisher, 13–18
384   "for God's sake": Squires, *D. H. Lawrence's Manuscripts*, 9
386   "more to look after for Angelino": FL to Bynner, [13 October 1937], Harvard
386   "*como uno fungo*": MDL to Jeffers, 18 September [1933], Berkeley
386   "being kept by you": *LCL*, 225

## CHAPTER 23. FRIEDA AND ANGELO AT LOS PINOS

388   "and how it is!": *M&C*, 259
388   "glad you love the children": FL to Ravagli, 9 February 1938, HRC
388   "I feel you will not come back": *M&C*, 264

389  "except when you think of Italy": *M&C*, 255
389  "how he loved me!": *M&C*, 262
389  "Come soon": *M&C*, 361–62
389  untimely death in 1939: Diego Arellano died at the age of twenty-nine. When Frieda could no longer afford to employ him, he went to Wyoming to herd sheep, contracted Rocky Mountain spotted fever, and came home to die (information from Jenny Wells Vincent and Walton Hawk).
390  "nothing is real here but the salaries": quoted in Morley, 125
390  "aristocratic, long and straight": Grace Hubble, journal, 12 May 1938, Huntington Library
390  "they come up from depths": ibid.
391  "of life and happiness": FL to Robinson Jeffers, [5 July 1938], Berkeley
391  "some handsome things": Squires, *D. H. Lawrence's Manuscripts*, 181
392  "I want to crow": FL to Bynner, 22 April 1939, Harvard
393  "when you found them making hay": FL to Montague Weekley, 22 August 1939, Geoffrey Seaman
393  "the tightness anymore after this": FL to Dudley and Esta Nichols, [early July 1939], Yale
393  "[m]oral turpitude": Squires, *D. H. Lawrence's Manuscripts*, 18
394  writer Frank Waters: Waters's memoir, *Of Time and Change*, offers a balanced, accessible account of some Taos personalities who flourished in these years.
394  "It is paralysing!": FL to Weekley, 3 September 1939, Geoffrey Seaman
394  "from the face of the earth": FL to Bynner, [18 September 1939], Harvard
394  "being alive the unsensational way!": ibid.
394  "in spite of the arguments": FL to Bynner, 19 January 1940, Harvard
395  "Edwin and Aldous at 11": Hubble, journal, 20 March 1940, Huntington Library
396  "enormous": Grover Smith, 458
396  "slipped gracefully out of the noose": Bucknell, 95
396  "being thrifty": FL to Knud and Else Merrild, 23 July 1940, HRC
396  "I can manage some way": FL to Nichols, 17 May 1941, Yale
397  "good for a change": Ravagli to Knud and Else Merrild, 28 October 1940, HRC
397  "varied and amusing": FL to George and Helene Biddle, 15 April 1941, Library of Congress
397  thirty-five thousand Italian prisoners: Gilbert, *The Second World War*, 142–48
397  "it's just frightful": DB to Jeffers, 5 January 1941, Berkeley
397  "the wrong sort": FL to MDL, [February 1941], Yale
398  "people and things": FL to DB, 21 March 1941, Yale
398  "What she liked was simply life": V. Woolf, *Mrs. Dalloway*, 121
398  "so very sick of war": Moore and Montague, 80
398  "both into difficulties": Bynner to FL, 17 December 1941, Harvard
398  "an enemy alien": FL to Knud and Else Merrild, 14 January 1942, HRC
398  "think about the war": Ravagli to Knud and Else Merrild, 27 October 1943, HRC
398  "nobody bothers us": FL to Nichols, [September 1944], Yale
399  "Frieda and Angie have built" . . . "such *gay* pigs": Gates, 179–80
399  "canadian shares": FL to Bynner, 25 September 1941, Harvard
400  "*[h]andle Freida in the way she want*": Ravagli to Knud and Else Merrild, 13 April 1942, HRC
400  "but keeps": Huxley to Hubble, 9 January 1944, Huntington Library
401  "Witter Bynner's parties": Miranda Levy, telephone interview, 7 May 1999
401  "is clearly obscene": *New York Times*, 30 May 1944
401  "keenly felt the loss": Byrne, 390

403 "I don't think it was ever a passion": Barbara Horgan, telephone interview, 5 June 2403

403 "I hope you understand" . . . "relationship with Angelino": FL to Horgan, 9 September 1950, HRC

403 "breathless when he gets a fish!": FL to Willard Hougland, 21 January 1945, University of California at Los Angeles

403 "time to myself": FL to DB, 25 January 1945, Yale

404 "the cloud and pinetree world": FL to Nichols, 26 July 1945, Yale

404 "a strange free bird": FL to Spud Johnson, 7 January 1946, HRC

404 "We share it with 2 young couples": Squires, *D. H. Lawrence's Manuscripts,* 199

404 "Frieda was our cook": Cecil Smith, 3

405 two hundred dollars a month: Spoto, 130

405 "I like him very much": Squires, *D. H. Lawrence's Manuscripts,* 201

405 "lit with lightning": Williams and Mead, 114

CHAPTER 24. PORT ISABEL, PEACE, AND MARRIAGE

407 "like a European fishing village": FL to Knud and Elsa Merrild, 21 March 1947, HRC

408 "fishermen's boats at night": FL to Bynner, 17 February 1947, Harvard

408 "like a Himalayan village": quoted in Phillips, 66

408 "It's there!": FL to Johnson, 18 February 1947, HRC

408 "very friendly and engaging": Levy, telephone interview, 7 May 1999

409 "anything at home": Ravagli to MDL, 4 December 1948, Yale

409 "afford to look after her!": FL to Knud and Else Merrild, 12 March 1949, HRC

409 "liked the cheapness": FL to Bynner, 6 December 1949, Harvard

410 "a strange experience": FL to Richard Aldington, 30 April 1950, Southern Illinois University at Carbondale

410 "heaved it at his head": *Time,* 29 May 1950, 96

410 "delicate and alive": Moore and Montague, 98

410 "Baron Philippe de Rothschild of Paris": *El Crepusculo,* 18 May 1950, 2

410 "not my Lawrence": FL to Gibbons, 3 March 1953, privately held

410 "without flavor or distinction": William York Tindall, *Saturday Review,* 17 March 1951

411 "have to be stingy!": FL to MDL, 18 December 1949, Yale

411 "You need'nt be so surprised!": FL to Ravagli, 8 February 1950, HRC

411 "fuss about myself": ibid.

411 "I never did before": FL to MDL, 1 February 1953, Yale

411 "all that money at Xmastime!": FL to DB, 3 January [1951], Yale

411 "very low and miserable": Ravagli to Dudley Nichols, 11 January [1951], Yale

412 "*one* husband in a lifetime!": FL to Rolf Gardiner, 20 July 1956, Keith Sagar

412 "50 dollars a month": FL to DB, 12 January 1954, Yale

413 "aware of one's ignorance": FL to DB, 16 January 1952, HRC

413 "a truly noble fellow": FL to DB, 13 February 1952, HRC

413 "all the time in doing nothing": Ravagli to MDL, 6 March 1952, Yale

414 "she carried it!": Miranda Levy, telephone interview, 28 July 1999

414 "treat me like a raw egg": FL to DB, 17 June 1952, HRC

414 "she seemed to be covered": Weekley, 3–4

414 "'that's all I can give you'": Ernesto Montoya, interview, 17 July 1998

414 "It's *my* money!": Juanita Montoya, interview, 17 July 1998

415 "he never gave me anything": Ernesto Montoya, interview

415 "grown completely apart from her": quoted in Rosie Jackson, 50

415 "'Oh boy, she has arrived'": Amalia de Schulthess, telephone interview, 9 July 1989
415 "being something of a star": quoted in Squires, *D. H. Lawrence's Manuscripts,* 22
415 "doing spectacular things": ibid., 21
416 "They're so full of life!": Gibbons, 142
417 "a fiasco!" . . . "Catholicism and Protestantism": ibid., 191–93
418 "'written about Lawrence'": ibid., 195–96
418 "eternity at my finger tips": ibid., 198–200
420 "Maria's death in my bones": FL to Dudley and Esta Nichols, 15 February 1955, Yale
420 "the heart of the rosy light of love": quoted in Dunaway, 319
420 "natural and unconceited": FL to DB, 29 April 1955, HRC
420 "[from Santa Fe] to Taos": Levy, interview
420 "like a lion out of the blue!": FL to Rebecca S. James, 11 May 1956, Yale
421 "'I *loathe* that Little Dorrit!'": Barr, "I Look Back," 258
421 "understand the elemental world": ibid., 260
421 "my good Frieda": Ravagli to Dudley and Esta Nichols, 23 August 1956, Yale
421 "toward Frieda's flowers": Gibbons, 244
421 "I wonder" . . . "Back to the elements": ibid., 202
422 "eternal submission to the greater laws": D. H. Lawrence, "A Propos of *Lady Chatterley's Lover,*" 328
422 "fussing about anything": Patmore, 140
423 the Lawrence paintings: Frieda's young friend Earl Stroh (b. 1924), a longtime Taos painter, has explained his role in the survival of the paintings: "Frieda once said to me, 'I've got all those paintings of Lawrence's, and they're beginning to fall apart. Do you think you could save them?' I said, 'Well, I could do my best.' And I'm afraid I did. Do you know what they're painted on? Old-fashioned window shades that you pull down. They were cheesecloth impregnated with God knows what! That's what they were painted on, and they were painted with little cans of cheap enamel out of a five-and-ten-cents store. . . . Being on that self-destructing, highly acidic stuff, they were getting brittle. So I mounted them on . . . Masonite!" (telephone interview, 2 August 1999).
424 "the liver in a mess": Ravagli to Dorothy Horgan, 11 February 1965, Barbara Horgan
424 "to think of it": Ravagli to Horgan, 20 July 1965, Barbara Horgan
424 "Frieda?" . . . "kiss before you go": Hall, 25–27
425 "whole scale of human emotions": FL to T. M. Pearce, 1 March 1938, University of New Mexico
425 among the top one hundred: "Panel votes 'Ulysses' as century's best novel," *New York Times,* 20 July 1998, E1

# Works Cited

WORKS BY D. H. LAWRENCE

*Aaron's Rod.* Ed. Mara Kalnins. Cambridge: Cambridge University Press, 1988.

*Amores.* London: Duckworth, 1916; New York: B. W. Huebsch, 1916.

"A Propos of *Lady Chatterley's Lover.*" In *Lady Chatterley's Lover,* 303–35.

*Bay: A Book of Poems.* London: Beaumont Press, 1919.

*Birds, Beasts and Flowers.* New York: Thomas Seltzer, 1923.

"The Blind Man." In *England, My England and Other Stories,* 46–63.

"The Border-Line." In *The Woman Who Rode Away and Other Stories,* 77–98.

*The Complete Poems of D. H. Lawrence.* Ed. Vivian de Sola Pinto and Warren Roberts. New York: Viking, 1964.

"The Dance of the Sprouting Corn." *Theatre Arts Monthly* 8 (July 1924): 447–57.

"Daughters of the Vicar." In *The Prussian Officer and Other Stories,* 40–87.

*David, A Play.* New York: Alfred A. Knopf, 1926.

"Death-Paean of a Mother." *Guardian* (London), 9 November 1990.

"Desire Goes Down into the Sea." In *Pansies,* 45.

*England, My England and Other Stories.* Ed. Bruce Steele. Cambridge: Cambridge University Press, 1990.

*The Escaped Cock.* Ed. Gerald Lacy. Los Angeles: Black Sparrow Press, 1973.

*The First and Second "Lady Chatterley" Novels.* Ed. Dieter Mehl and Christa Jansohn. Cambridge: Cambridge University Press, 1999.

*The First "Women in Love."* Ed. John Worthen and Lindeth Vasey. Cambridge: Cambridge University Press, 1998.

*The Fox, The Captain's Doll, The Ladybird.* Ed. Dieter Mehl. Cambridge: Cambridge University Press, 1992.

"The Horse-Dealer's Daughter." In *England, My England and Other Stories,* 137–52.

"Indians and an Englishman." In *Phoenix,* 92–99.

"Insouciance." In *Phoenix II,* 532–34.

"Introduction to These Paintings." In *Phoenix,* 551–84.

*Kangaroo.* Ed. Bruce Steele. Cambridge: Cambridge University Press, 1994.

*Lady Chatterley's Lover* and *A Propos of "Lady Chatterley's Lover."* Ed. Michael Squires. Cambridge: Cambridge University Press, 1993.

*The Letters of D. H. Lawrence.* Vol. 1, *September 1901–May 1913.* Ed. James T. Boulton. Cambridge: Cambridge University Press, 1979.

*The Letters of D. H. Lawrence.* Vol. 2, *June 1913–October 1916.* Ed. George J. Zytaruk and James T. Boulton. Cambridge: Cambridge University Press, 1981.

# Works Cited

*The Letters of D. H. Lawrence.* Vol. 3, *October 1916–June 1921.* Ed. James T. Boulton and Andrew Robertson. Cambridge: Cambridge University Press, 1984.

*The Letters of D. H. Lawrence.* Vol. 4, *June 1921–March 1924.* Ed. Warren Roberts, James T. Boulton, and Elizabeth Mansfield. Cambridge: Cambridge University Press, 1987.

*The Letters of D. H. Lawrence.* Vol. 5, *March 1924–March 1927.* Ed. James T. Boulton and Lindeth Vasey. Cambridge: Cambridge University Press, 1989.

*The Letters of D. H. Lawrence.* Vol. 6, *March 1927–November 1928.* Ed. James T. Boulton and Margaret H. Boulton, with Gerald Lacy. Cambridge: Cambridge University Press, 1991.

*The Letters of D. H. Lawrence.* Vol. 7, *November 1928–February 1930.* Ed. Keith Sagar and James T. Boulton. Cambridge: Cambridge University Press, 1993.

*The Letters of D. H. Lawrence.* Vol. 8, *Previously Uncollected Letters and General Index.* Ed. James T. Boulton. Cambridge: Cambridge University Press, 2000.

*Look! We Have Come Through!* New York: B. W. Huebsch, 1918.

*The Lost Girl.* Ed. John Worthen. Cambridge: Cambridge University Press, 1981.

"The Lovely Lady: *The Black Cap* Version." In *The Woman Who Rode Away and Other Stories,* 355–73.

"Man Reaches a Point." In *Pansies,* 98.

*Memoir of Maurice Magnus.* Ed. Keith Cushman. Santa Rosa, Calif.: Black Sparrow Press, 1987.

*Movements in European History.* Ed. Philip Crumpton. Cambridge: Cambridge University Press, 1989.

*Mr Noon.* Ed. Lindeth Vasey. Cambridge: Cambridge University Press, 1984.

*New Poems.* New York: B. W. Huebsch, 1920.

*Paintings of D. H. Lawrence.* London: Mandrake Press, 1929.

*Pansies.* London: Martin Secker, 1929; New York: Knopf, 1929.

*Phoenix: The Posthumous Papers of D. H. Lawrence.* Ed. Edward D. McDonald. New York: Viking, 1936.

*Phoenix II: Uncollected, Unpublished, and Other Prose Works by D. H. Lawrence.* Ed. Warren Roberts and Harry T. Moore. New York: Viking, 1959.

*The Plays of D. H. Lawrence.* Ed. Hans-Wilhelm Schwartze and John Worthen. Cambridge: Cambridge University Press, 1999.

*The Plumed Serpent.* Ed. L. D. Clark. Cambridge: Cambridge University Press, 1987.

*The Prussian Officer and Other Stories.* Ed. John Worthen. Cambridge: Cambridge University Press, 1983.

*Quetzalcoatl: The Early Version of "The Plumed Serpent."* Ed. Louis L. Martz. Redding Ridge, Conn.: Black Swan Books, 1995.

*The Rainbow.* Ed. Mark Kinkead-Weekes. Cambridge: Cambridge University Press, 1989.

"The Rocking Horse Winner." In *The Woman Who Rode Away and Other Stories,* 230–43.

*Sea and Sardinia.* Ed. Mara Kalnins. Cambridge: Cambridge University Press, 1997.

"The Ship of Death" (Final Typescript Version). In Sagar, Keith. "Which 'Ship of Death'?"

*Sketches of Etruscan Places and Other Italian Essays.* Ed. Simonetta de Filippis. Cambridge: Cambridge University Press, 1992.

*Sons and Lovers.* Ed. Helen Baron and Carl Baron. Cambridge: Cambridge University Press, 1992.

*Sons and Lovers: A Facsimile of the Manuscript.* Ed. Mark Schorer. Berkeley: University of California Press, 1977.

"The Spirit of Place." *English Review* 27 (1918): 319–31. Revised for *Studies in Classic American Literature,* 1–12.

*St. Mawr and Other Stories.* Ed. Brian Finney. Cambridge: Cambridge University Press, 1983.

*Studies in Classic American Literature.* New York: Seltzer, 1923.

*Study of Thomas Hardy and Other Essays.* Ed. Bruce Steele. Cambridge: Cambridge University Press, 1985.

*The Trespasser.* Ed. Elizabeth Mansfield. Cambridge: Cambridge University Press, 1981.

*Twilight in Italy and Other Essays.* Ed. Paul Eggert. Cambridge: Cambridge University Press, 1994.

*The Virgin and the Gipsy.* 1930. Reprint, New York: Bantam, 1968.

"The Whistling of Birds." In *Phoenix,* 3–6.

*The White Peacock.* Ed. Andrew Robertson. Cambridge: Cambridge University Press, 1983.

"Whitman." In *Studies in Classic American Literature,* 241–64.

*The Woman Who Rode Away and Other Stories.* Ed. Dieter Mehl and Christa Jansohn. Cambridge: Cambridge University Press, 1995.

*Women in Love.* Ed. David Farmer, Lindeth Vasey, and John Worthen. Cambridge: Cambridge University Press, 1987.

*The Boy in the Bush.* With M. L. Skinner. Ed. Paul Eggert. Cambridge: Cambridge University Press, 1990.


## SECONDARY WORKS

Aldington, Richard. *Richard Aldington: An Autobiography in Letters. See* Gates, Norman T., ed.

Aldington, Richard. *Richard Aldington and H.D.: The Later Years in Letters. See* Zilboorg, Caroline, ed.

Aldington, Richard. *Life for Life's Sake: A Book of Reminiscences.* New York: Viking, 1941.

Aldington, Richard. *Portrait of a Genius But . . . : The Life of D. H. Lawrence, 1885–1930.* London: Heinemann, 1950.

Aldington, Richard. "Modern Poetry and the Imagists." *The Egoist* 1 (1914): 201–3.

Baedeker, Karl. *Spanien und Portugal: Handbuch für Reisende.* Leipzig: Karl Baedeker, 1929.

Barr, Barbara. "I Look Back: About Frieda Lawrence." *Twentieth Century* 165 (1959): 254–61.

Barr, Barbara. "Step-daughter to Lawrence." Parts 1 and 2. *London Magazine,* August/September 1993, 23–33; October/November 1993, 12–23.

Baynes, Rosalind. *See* Thornycroft, Rosalind.

Beaumont, Cyril W. *The First Score.* London: Beaumont Press, 1927.

Bedford, Sybille. *Aldous Huxley: A Biography.* London: Chatto & Windus, 1973; New York: Knopf, 1974.

Bernstein, George, and Lottelore Bernstein. "Attitudes toward Women's Education in Germany, 1870–1914." *International Journal of Women's Studies* 2 (1979): 473–88.

Bernstein, George, and Lottelore Bernstein. "The Curriculum for German Girls' Schools, 1870–1914." *Paedagogica Historica: International Journal of the History of Education* 18 (1978): 227–95.

Bookbinder, Paul. *Weimar Germany.* Manchester: Manchester University Press, 1996.

Brett, Dorothy. *Lawrence and Brett, A Friendship.* 1933. Reprint, with an introduction, prologue, and epilogue by John Manchester. Santa Fe, N.M.: Sunstone Press, 1974.

Brewster, Earl, and Achsah Brewster. *D. H. Lawrence: Reminiscences and Correspondence.* London: Martin Secker, 1934.

Brewster, Earl, and Achsah Brewster. *The Divinity That Stirs within Us. Catalog of the Exhibition of the Paintings of Achsah Barlow Brewster (1878–1945) and Earl Henry Brewster (1878–1957).* New York: Borghi, 1992.

Bucknell, Katherine, ed. *Christopher Isherwood: Diaries.* Vol. 1, *1939–1960.* New York: HarperCollins, 1997.

Burgess, Anthony. *Flame into Being: The Life and Work of D. H. Lawrence*. London: Heinemann, 1985; New York: Arbor House, 1985.

Bynner, Witter. *Journey with Genius: Recollections and Reflections Concerning the D. H. Lawrences*. New York: John Day, 1951; London: Peter Nevill, 1953.

Byrne, Janet. *A Genius for Living: The Life of Frieda Lawrence*. New York: HarperCollins, 1995.

Carrington, Dora. *Carrington: Letters and Extracts from Her Diaries. See* Garnett, David, ed.

Carswell, Catherine. *The Savage Pilgrimage: A Narrative of D. H. Lawrence*. 1932. Reprint, Cambridge: Cambridge University Press, 1981.

Carter, John. "*The Rainbow* Prosecution." *Times Literary Supplement*, 27 February 1969, 216.

Cavitch, David. *D. H. Lawrence and the New World*. New York: Oxford University Press, 1979.

Chambers, Jessie. *D. H. Lawrence: A Personal Record by E.T.* London: Jonathan Cape, 1936; New York: Knight Publications, 1936.

Cohen, Ed. *Talk on the Wilde Side: Toward a Genealogy of a Discourse on Male Sexualities*. London and New York: Routledge, 1993.

Coleman, Eli. "Developmental Stages of the Coming Out Process." *Journal of Homosexuality* 7 (1981–82): 31–43.

Corke, Helen. *D. H. Lawrence's "Princess": A Memory of Jessie Chambers*. Thames Ditton, Surrey: Merle Press, 1951.

Corke, Helen. *In Our Infancy: An Autobiography, 1882–1912*. Cambridge: Cambridge University Press, 1975.

Corke, Helen. *Neutral Ground*. London: A. Barker, 1934.

Corke, Helen. "The Writing of *The Trespasser*." *D. H. Lawrence Review* 7 (1974): 227–39.

Darroch, Robert. *Lawrence and Australia*. South Melbourne: Macmillan of Australia, 1981.

Davidson, Robert. "The Tranquillity of Frieda Lawrence." *The South Carolina Review* 24 (1991): 5–19.

Davies, Rhys. *Print of a Hare's Foot: An Autobiographical Beginning*. London: Heinemann, 1969.

Davies, Rhys. *The Withered Root*. London: R. Holden, 1927; New York: Henry Holt, 1928.

Davis, Joseph. *D. H. Lawrence at Thirroul*. Sydney: Collins, 1989.

Delavenay, Emile. *D. H. Lawrence, The Man and His Work: The Formative Years, 1885–1919*. London: Heinemann, 1972; Carbondale: Southern Illinois University Press, 1972.

Delavenay, Emile. "A Shrine without Relics?" *D. H. Lawrence Review* 16 (1983): 111–31.

Doody, Margaret Anne. "Sex in the Head: Lawrence's Struggle for Power over Frieda." *Times Literary Supplement*, 4 November 1994, 4–6.

Douglas, Norman. *Looking Back: An Autobiographical Excursion*. New York: Harcourt, Brace, 1933.

Draper, R. P., ed. *D. H. Lawrence: The Critical Heritage*. London: Routledge & Kegan Paul, 1970; New York: Barnes & Noble, 1970.

Duffy, Maureen. *A Thousand Capricious Chances: A History of the Methuen List, 1889–1989*. London: Methuen, 1989.

Dunaway, David King. *Aldous Huxley Recollected: An Oral History*. New York: Carroll & Graf, 1995.

Ellis, David. *D. H. Lawrence: Dying Game, 1922–1930*. Cambridge: Cambridge University Press, 1998.

Feather, John. *A History of British Publishing*. London: Croom Helm, 1988.

Feinstein, Elaine. *Lawrence and the Women: The Intimate Life of D. H. Lawrence*. London and New York: HarperCollins, 1993.

Fisher, Frederic A., Jr. "I Call on Frieda." In *Two Tributes*, ed. Fred B. Millett, 13–18. Whitman, Mass.: Washington Street Press, 1970.

478

Forster, E. M. *Maurice.* London: Edward Arnold, 1971; New York: New American Library, 1971.

Franks, Norman, Hal Giblin, and Nigel McCrery. *Under the Guns of the Red Baron.* London: Grub Street, 1995.

Freud, Sigmund. *The Freud-Jung Letters: The Correspondence between Sigmund Freud and C. G. Jung. See* McGuire, William, ed.

Furbank, Philip. *E. M. Forster: A Life.* New York: Harcourt Brace Jovanovich, 1978.

Garnett, Constance. *Constance Garnett: A Heroic Life. See* Garnett, Richard.

Garnett, David. *The Golden Echo.* New York: Harcourt, Brace, 1954.

Garnett, David. *Great Friends: Portraits of Seventeen Writers.* London: Macmillan, 1979; New York: Atheneum, 1980.

Garnett, David, ed. *Carrington: Letters and Extracts from Her Diaries.* London: Jonathan Cape, 1970.

Garnett, Richard. *Constance Garnett: A Heroic Life.* London: Sinclair-Stevenson, 1991.

Garnett, Richard, ed. *Sylvia and David: The Townsend Warner/Garnett Letters.* London: Sinclair-Stevenson, 1994.

Gates, Norman T., ed. *Richard Aldington: An Autobiography in Letters.* University Park: Penn State University Press, 1992.

Gathorne-Hardy, Robert, ed. *Ottoline at Garsington: Memoirs of Lady Ottoline Morrell, 1915–1918.* London: Faber & Faber, 1974.

Gerson, Max. *Diet Therapy of Lung Tuberculosis.* Vienna: Franz Deuticke, 1934.

Gertzman, Jay A., and Michael Squires. "New Letters from Thomas Seltzer and Robert Mountsier to D. H. Lawrence." *D. H. Lawrence Review* 28 (1999): 53–77.

Gibbon, Edward. *History of the Decline and Fall of the Roman Empire.* 1776–88. Reprint, New York: Modern Library, 1900.

Gibbons, Louis. "The D. H. Lawrences: What They Mean to Me." Unpublished memoir. Privately held.

Gilbert, Martin. *The First World War: A Complete History.* New York: Henry Holt, 1994.

Gilbert, Martin. *The Second World War: A Complete History.* New York: Henry Holt, 1989.

Glendinning, Victoria. "Lies and Silences." In *The Troubled Face of Biography,* ed. Eric Homberger and John Charmley, 49–62. New York: St. Martin's Press, 1988.

Goyen, William. "Interview with William Goyen." By Robert Phillips. *Paris Review* 68 (1976): 58–100.

Gray, Cecil. *Musical Chairs.* London: Home & Van Thal, 1948.

Green, Martin. *The von Richthofen Sisters: The Triumphant and the Tragic Modes of Love.* London: Weidenfeld & Nicolson, 1974; New York: Basic Books, 1974.

Griffin, A. R., and C. P. Griffin. "A Social and Economic History of Eastwood and the Nottinghamshire Mining Country." In *A D. H. Lawrence Handbook,* ed. Keith Sagar, 127–63. Manchester: Manchester University Press, 1982; Totowa, N. J.: Barnes & Noble, 1982.

Hahn, Emily. *Lorenzo: D. H. Lawrence and the Women Who Loved Him.* Philadelphia: Lippincott, 1975.

Hall, Ruth. "Angelino." *Observer* (London), 13 December 1970, Colour Supplement, 18–27.

Hankin, C. A., ed. *The Letters of John Middleton Murry to Katherine Mansfield.* London: Constable, 1983; New York: Franklin Watts, 1983.

Hankin, Cherry A., ed. *Letters between Katherine Mansfield and John Middleton Murry.* New York: New Amsterdam, 1991.

Harrigan, Mildred. *Travelling Light.* New York: Brentano's, 1930.

Harris, Janice. *The Short Fiction of D. H. Lawrence.* New Brunswick, N.J.: Rutgers University Press, 1984.

Harrison, Jane Ellen. *Ancient Art and Ritual.* London: Williams & Norgate, 1913; New York: Henry Holt, 1913.

Healey, E. Claire, and Keith Cushman, eds. *The Letters of D. H. Lawrence and Amy Lowell, 1914–1925.* Santa Barbara, Calif.: Black Sparrow Press, 1985.

Heilbrun, Carolyn G., ed. *Lady Ottoline's Album: Snapshots and Portraits.* With an introduction by Lord David Cecil. New York: Knopf, 1976.

Hignett, Sean. *Brett—From Bloomsbury to New Mexico: A Biography.* London: Hodder & Stoughton, 1984; New York: Franklin Watts, 1985.

Hilton, Enid Hopkin. *More Than One Life: A Nottinghamshire Childhood with D. H. Lawrence.* Dover, N.H.: Alan Sutton, 1993.

Holroyd, Michael. *Lytton Strachey: The New Biography.* London: Chatto & Windus, 1994; New York: Farrar, Straus & Giroux, 1995.

Hopkin, Enid. *See* Hilton, Enid Hopkin.

Hough, Graham. *The Dark Sun: A Study of D. H. Lawrence.* London: Duckworth, 1956; New York: Macmillan, 1957.

Huxley, Aldous. *Letters of Aldous Huxley. See* Smith, Grover, ed.

Huxley, Juliette. *Leaves of the Tulip Tree.* London: J. Murray, 1986; Topsfield, Mass.: Salem House, 1986.

Irvine, Peter L., and Anne Kiley, eds. "D. H. Lawrence and Frieda Lawrence: Letters to Dorothy Brett." *D. H. Lawrence Review* 9 (1976): 1–116.

Isherwood, Christopher. *Christopher Isherwood: Diaries.* Vol. 1, *1939–1960. See* Bucknell, Katherine, ed.

Jackson, Dennis. "'The Stormy Petrel of Literature is Dead': The World Press Reports Lawrence's Death." *D. H. Lawrence Review* 14 (1981): 33–72.

Jackson, Rosie. *Frieda Lawrence: Including "Not I, But the Wind" and Other Autobiographical Writings.* London: Pandora, 1994.

Jacobi-Dittrich, Juliane. "Growing Up Female in the Nineteenth Century." In *German Women in the Nineteenth Century: A Social History,* ed. John C. Fout, 197–217. New York: Holmes & Meier, 1984.

Jefferson, George. *Edward Garnett: A Life in Literature.* London: Jonathan Cape, 1982.

Jung, Carl. *The Freud-Jung Letters: The Correspondence between Sigmund Freud and C. G. Jung. See* McGuire, William, ed.

King, James. *Virginia Woolf.* London: Hamish Hamilton, 1994; New York: Norton, 1995.

Kinkead-Weekes, Mark. *D. H. Lawrence: Triumph to Exile, 1912–1922.* Cambridge: Cambridge University Press, 1996.

Kirchhoff, Arthur. *Die akademische Frau. Gutachten hervorragender Universitatsprofessoren, Frauenlehrer und Schriftsteller uber die Befahigung der Frau zum wissenschaftlichen Studium und Berufe.* Berlin: Hugo Steinitz Verlag, 1897.

Koteliansky, S. S. *The Quest for Rananim: D. H. Lawrence's Letters to S. S. Koteliansky, 1914 to 1930. See* Zytaruk, George, ed.

Lacy, Gerald M., ed. *D. H. Lawrence: Letters to Thomas and Adele Seltzer.* Santa Barbara, Calif.: Black Sparrow Press, 1976.

Lawrence, Frieda. *The Memoirs and Correspondence.* Ed. E. W. Tedlock, Jr. New York: Knopf, 1964.

Lawrence, Frieda. *Not I, But the Wind.* London: Heinemann, 1934; Santa Fe, N.M.: Rydal Press, 1934; New York: Viking, 1934.

Lawrence, Frieda. "D. H. Lawrence and Frieda Lawrence: Letters to Dorothy Brett." *See* Irvine, Peter L., and Anne Kiley, eds.

Lawrence, Frieda. *D. H. Lawrence's Manuscripts: The Correspondence of Frieda Lawrence, Jake Zeitlin, and Others. See* Squires, Michael, ed.

Lawrence, Frieda. *Frieda Lawrence and Her Circle: Letters from, to, and about Frieda Lawrence. See* Moore, Harry T., and Dale B. Montague.

Lawrence, Frieda. "The Otto Gross–Frieda Weekley Correspondence: Transcribed, Translated, and Annotated." *See* Turner, John, with Cornelia Rumpf-Worthen and Ruth Jenkins.

Lawrence, Frieda. Untitled, unpublished fragment, n.d., Bucknell University.

Lea, F. A. *The Life of John Middleton Murry.* London: Methuen, 1959; New York: Oxford University Press, 1959.

Lloyd George, David. "Mr. Lloyd George's Speech." *Times* (London), 20 December 1916, 10, 12.

Lowell, Amy. *The Letters of D. H. Lawrence and Amy Lowell, 1914–1925. See* Healey, E. Claire, and Keith Cushman, eds.

Lucas, Robert. *Frieda Lawrence: The Story of Frieda von Richthofen and D. H. Lawrence.* New York: Viking, 1973.

Luhan, Mabel Dodge. *Lorenzo in Taos.* New York: Knopf, 1932.

Mackenzie, Compton. *My Life and Times: Octave Five.* London: Chatto & Windus, 1966.

MacLeod, Sheila. *Lawrence's Men and Women.* London: Heinemann, 1985; San Diego, Calif.: Harcourt Brace Jovanovich, 1985.

Maddox, Brenda. *D. H. Lawrence: The Story of a Marriage.* New York: Simon & Schuster, 1994.

Mansfield, Katherine. *The Collected Letters of Katherine Mansfield. See* O'Sullivan, Vincent, and Margaret Scott, eds.

Mansfield, Katherine. *Letters between Katherine Mansfield and John Middleton Murry. See* Hankin, Cherry A., ed.

Mansfield, Katherine. *The Letters of John Middleton Murry to Katherine Mansfield. See* Hankin, C. A., ed.

Mariani, Paul. *The Broken Tower: The Life of Hart Crane.* New York: Norton, 1999.

McDonald, Marguerite. "An Evening with the Lawrences." *D. H. Lawrence Review* 5 (1972): 63–66.

McGuire, William, ed. *The Freud-Jung Letters: The Correspondence between Sigmund Freud and C. G. Jung.* Trans. Ralph Manheim and R. F. C. Hull. Princeton: Princeton University Press, 1974.

Meachen, G. Norman. *A Short History of Tuberculosis.* 1936. Reprint, New York: AMS Press, 1978.

Merrild, Knud. *With D. H. Lawrence in New Mexico: A Memoir of D. H. Lawrence.* 1938. Reprint, London: Routledge & Kegan Paul, 1964.

Meyers, Jeffrey. *D. H. Lawrence: A Biography.* New York: Knopf, 1990.

Meyers, Jeffrey. *Joseph Conrad: A Biography.* London: Murray, 1991; New York: Charles Scribner's Sons, 1991.

Middleton, Richard. *Monologues.* London: T. F. Unwin, 1913; New York: Mitchell Kennerley, 1914.

Miller, James. *The Passion of Michel Foucault.* New York: Simon & Schuster, 1993.

Millett, Kate. *Sexual Politics.* New York: Doubleday, 1969.

Mitchell, B. R., and H. G. Jones. *Second Abstract of British Historical Statistics.* Cambridge: Cambridge University Press, 1979.

Moore, Harry T. *D. H. Lawrence: His Life and Works.* New York: Twayne, 1951.

Moore, Harry T. *The Priest of Love: A Life of D. H. Lawrence.* 1974. Reprint, Carbondale: Southern Illinois University Press, 1977.

Moore, Harry T. Untitled essay. In *Richard Aldington: An Intimate Portrait,* ed. Alister Kershaw and Frédéric-Jacques Temple, 80–105. Carbondale: Southern Illinois University Press, 1965.

Moore, Harry T., and Dale B. Montague. *Frieda Lawrence and Her Circle: Letters from, to, and about Frieda Lawrence.* London: Macmillan, 1981; Hamden, Conn.: Archon Books, 1981.

# Works Cited

Moorehead, Caroline. *Bertrand Russell, A Life*. London: Sinclair-Stevenson, 1992; New York: Viking, 1993.

Morley, Sheridan. *Tales from the Hollywood Raj: The British, the Movies, and Tinseltown*. New York: Viking, 1984.

Morrell, Ottoline. *Ottoline at Garsington: Memoirs of Lady Ottoline Morrell, 1915–1918*. *See* Gathorne-Hardy, Robert, ed.

Morrell, Ottoline. *Lady Ottoline's Album: Snapshots and Portraits*. *See* Heilbrun, Carolyn G., ed.

Munro, Craig. *Wild Man of Letters: The Story of P. R. Stephensen*. Melbourne: Melbourne University Press, 1984.

Murry, John Middleton. *Between Two Worlds: The Autobiography of John Middleton Murry*. London: Jonathan Cape, 1935; New York: Julian Messner, 1936.

Murry, John Middleton. *Letters between Katherine Mansfield and John Middleton Murry*. *See* Hankin, Cherry A., ed.

Murry, John Middleton. *The Letters of John Middleton Murry to Katherine Mansfield*. *See* Hankin, C. A., ed.

Nehls, Edward, comp. *D. H. Lawrence: A Composite Biography*. 3 volumes. Madison: University of Wisconsin Press, 1957–59.

Nixon, Cornelia. *Lawrence's Leadership Politics and the Turn against Women*. Berkeley: University of California Press, 1986.

O'Connor, Frank. *The Mirror in the Roadway: A Study of the Modern Novel*. New York: Knopf, 1956.

O'Sullivan, Vincent, and Margaret Scott, eds. *The Collected Letters of Katherine Mansfield*. Vol. 1, *1903–1917*. Oxford: Clarendon, 1984.

Patmore, Brigit. "A Memoir of Frieda Lawrence." In *A D. H. Lawrence Miscellany*, ed. Harry T. Moore, 137–40. Carbondale: Southern Illinois University Press, 1959.

Peters, Margot. *May Sarton: A Biography*. New York: Knopf, 1997.

Phillips, Robert, ed. *William Goyen: Selected Letters from a Writer's Life*. Austin: University of Texas Press, 1995.

Poirier, Richard. *A World Elsewhere: The Place of Style in American Literature*. New York: Oxford University Press, 1966.

Pound, Ezra. "'Dubliners' and Mr James Joyce." *The Egoist* 1 (1914): 267.

Ringer, Fritz K. *Education and Society in Modern Europe*. Bloomington: Indiana University Press, 1979.

Rowntree, Griselda, and Norman H. Carrier. "The Resort to Divorce in England and Wales, 1858–1957." *Population Studies* 11 (1958): 188–233.

Sagar, Keith. *D. H. Lawrence: A Calendar of His Works*. Manchester: Manchester University Press, 1979; Austin: University of Texas Press, 1979.

Sagar, Keith. *D. H. Lawrence: Life into Art*. Harmondsworth: Penguin, 1985; Athens: University of Georgia Press, 1985.

Sagar, Keith. *The Life of D. H. Lawrence*. New York: Pantheon, 1980.

Sagar, Keith. "Which 'Ship of Death'?" *D. H. Lawrence Review* 19 (1987): 181–84.

Sagar, Keith, ed. *A D. H. Lawrence Handbook*. Manchester: Manchester University Press, 1982; Totowa, N. J.: Barnes & Noble, 1982.

Seymour, Miranda. *Ottoline Morrell: Life on the Grand Scale*. London: Hodder & Stoughton, 1992; New York: Farrar, Straus & Giroux, 1993.

Shryock, Richard Harrison. *National Tuberculosis Association, 1904–1954: A Study of the Voluntary Health Movement in the United States*. New York: Arno Press, 1977.

Skidelsky, Robert. *John Maynard Keynes*. Vol. 1, *Hopes Betrayed, 1883–1920*. London: Macmillan, 1983; New York: Viking, 1986.

Smith, Barry. *Peter Warlock: The Life of Philip Heseltine*. Oxford and New York: Oxford University Press, 1994.

Smith, Cecil. "Frieda Lawrence—A Personal Memoir." *Los Angeles Times,* 8 November 1981, Calendar, 3.

Smith, Grover, ed. *Letters of Aldous Huxley.* London: Chatto & Windus, 1969; New York: Harper & Row, 1969.

Spencer, Roy. *D. H. Lawrence Country: A Portrait of His Early Life.* London: Cecil Woolf, 1979.

Spoto, Donald. *The Kindness of Strangers: The Life of Tennessee Williams.* London: Bodley Head, 1985; Boston: Little, Brown, 1985.

Squires, Michael. *The Creation of "Lady Chatterley's Lover."* Baltimore: Johns Hopkins University Press, 1983.

Squires, Michael. "Scenic Construction and Rhetorical Signals in Hardy and Lawrence." *D. H. Lawrence Review* 8 (1975): 125–46.

Squires, Michael, ed. *D. H. Lawrence's Manuscripts: The Correspondence of Frieda Lawrence, Jake Zeitlin and Others.* Basingstoke: Macmillan, 1991; New York: St. Martin's Press, 1991.

Stevens, C. J. *Lawrence at Tregerthen.* Troy, N.Y.: Whitston, 1988.

Stevenson, Philip. "Postscript." *New Republic,* 24 October 1934, 316.

Strachey, Lytton. *Eminent Victorians.* New York: G. P. Putnam's Sons, 1918.

Sutton and Sons. *The Culture of Profitable Vegetables in Small Gardens.* London: Simpkin, Marshall, Hamilton, Kent, 1917.

Talbot, Lynn K. "Did Baroja Influence Lawrence? A Reading of *César o nada* and *The Plumed Serpent.*" *D. H. Lawrence Review* 22 (1990): 39–51.

Templeton, Wayne. "The *Sons and Lovers* Manuscript." *Studies in Bibliography* 37 (1984): 234–43.

Terry, T. Philip. *Terry's Guide to Mexico.* Revised edition. Boston: Houghton Mifflin, 1923.

Thomas, Helen. *Time and Again: Memoirs and Letters.* Manchester: Carcanet New Press, 1978.

Thornycroft, Rosalind. *Time Which Spaces Us Apart.* Batcombe, Somerset: privately printed, 1991.

Tomalin, Claire. *Katherine Mansfield: A Secret Life.* New York: Knopf, 1988.

Townsend Warner, Sylvia. *Sylvia and David: The Townsend Warner/Garnett Letters. See* Garnett, Richard, ed.

Tucker, Robert, Charles B. Keely, and Linda Wrigley, eds. *Immigration and U.S. Foreign Policy.* Boulder, Colo.: Westview Press, 1990.

Turner, John, ed. "D. H. Lawrence in the Wilkinson Diaries." *D. H. Lawrence Review,* forthcoming.

Turner, John, with Cornelia Rumpf-Worthen and Ruth Jenkins, eds. "The Otto Gross–Frieda Weekley Correspondence: Transcribed, Translated, and Annotated." *D. H. Lawrence Review* 22 (1990): 137–227.

Vivas, Eliseo. *D. H. Lawrence: The Failure and the Triumph of Art.* London: Allen & Unwin, 1960; Bloomington: Indiana University Press, 1960.

von Richthofen, Friedrich. "Diary of the Franco-Prussian War, 1870–71." Translated by Frieda Lawrence. Unpublished manuscript, n.d., Harry Ransom Humanities Research Center, University of Texas at Austin.

Waters, Frank. *Of Time and Change: A Memoir.* Denver: MacMurray & Beck, 1998.

Weekley, Ian. *Frieda Lawrence: A Memoir.* N.p.: Dunstable College of Further Education, 1962.

Williams, Dakin, and Shepherd Mead. *Tennessee Williams: An Intimate Biography.* New York: Arbor House, 1983.

Woolf, Leonard. *Downhill All the Way: An Autobiography of the Years 1919–1939.* London: Hogarth Press, 1967; New York: Harcourt Brace Jovanovich, 1967.

# Works Cited

Woolf, Leonard. *Growing: An Autobiography of the Years 1904–1911.* London: Hogarth Press, 1961; New York: Harcourt, Brace, 1961.

Woolf, Virginia. *Jacob's Room.* 1922. Reprint, San Diego: Harcourt Brace, n.d.

Woolf, Virginia. *Mrs. Dalloway.* 1925. Reprint, San Diego: Harcourt Brace, n.d.

Woolf, Virginia. *The Voyage Out.* 1915. Reprint, San Diego: Harcourt Brace, n.d.

Worthen, John. "'Cold Hearts and Coronets': Lawrence, the Weekleys, and the von Richthofens. Or, The Right and Romantic Versus the Wrong and Repulsive." Nottingham: D. H. Lawrence Centre, University of Nottingham, 1995.

Worthen, John. *D. H. Lawrence: The Early Years, 1885–1912.* Cambridge: Cambridge University Press, 1991.

Zilboorg, Caroline, ed. *Richard Aldington and H.D.: The Later Years in Letters.* Manchester: Manchester University Press, 1995; New York: St. Martin's Press, 1995.

Zytaruk, George, ed. *The Quest for Rananim: D. H. Lawrence's Letters to S. S. Koteliansky, 1914 to 1930.* Montreal: McGill-Queen's University Press, 1970.

# Index